THE
CORPORATION

**AN EPIC STORY OF
THE CUBAN AMERICAN
UNDERWORLD**

T. J. ENGLISH

Also by T. J. English

WHERE THE BODIES WERE BURIED

WHITEY'S PAYBACK

THE SAVAGE CITY

HAVANA NOCTURNE

PADDY WHACKED

BORN TO KILL

THE WESTIES

WILLIAM MORROW
An Imprint of HarperCollinsPublishers

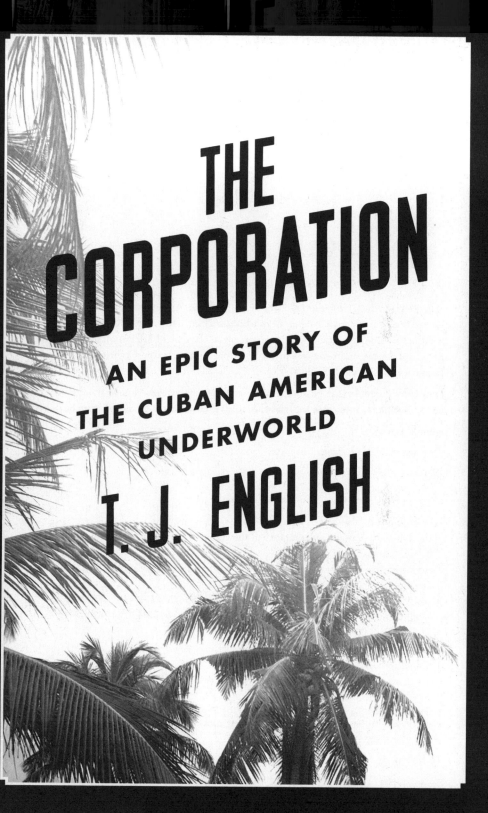

THE
CORPORATION

AN EPIC STORY OF
THE CUBAN AMERICAN
UNDERWORLD

T. J. ENGLISH

HarperCollins books may be purchased for educational, business, or sales promotional use. For information, please email the Special Markets Department at SPsales@harpercollins.com.

FIRST EDITION

Designed by William Ruoto

Appendix chart © U.S. Attorney, Southern District of Florida

Library of Congress Cataloging-in-Publication Data
Names: English, T. J., 1957– author.
Title: The Corporation : an epic story of the Cuban American underworld /
    T. J. English.
Description: First edition. | New York, NY : William Morrow, [2018] |
    Includes bibliographical references and index. |
Identifiers: LCCN 2017039510 (print) | LCCN 2017047577 (ebook) | ISBN
    9780062568977 (ebook) | ISBN 0062568973 (ebook) | ISBN 9780062568960
    (hardcover) | ISBN 0062568965 (hardcover)
Subjects: LCSH: Mafia—Cuba. | Organized crime—United States. |
    Cubans—United States.
Classification: LCC HV6446 (ebook) | LCC HV6446 .E539 2018 (print) | DDC
    364.106089/687291073—dc23
LC record available at https://lccn.loc.gov/2017039510

ISBN 978-0-06-256896-0

18 19 20 21 22 RS/LSC 10 9 8 7 6 5 4 3 2 1

*In memory of those who lost their lives April 17–19, 1961,
at the Bay of Pigs, Matanzas, Cuba*

Aquellos que van a retozar con los gatos deben esperar a ser rayado.
Those who'll cavort with cats must expect to be scratched.

—Miguel de Cervantes
Don Quixote

CONTENTS

INTRODUCTION

IN THE UNITED STATES OF AMERICA, THE TRUE MELTING POT HAS BEEN ORGANIZED crime. The process of becoming American is rooted in gangsterism. If you start with the supposition that the country is by its very nature a criminal enterprise—colonized and taken by force from the indigenous population, then facilitated by an economic system of human enslavement that was eventually determined to be illegal—you get the picture. The seed was planted long ago. The Mob is merely the flowering of that seed, watered with the blood of the many thousands of gangland slaying victims from over the last century.

Traditional organized crime—Irish, Italian, Jewish, and more—has its roots in the early decades of the twentieth century. The Prohibition era gave rise to a criminal system by which gangsterism and politics would be inexorably linked, and the American underworld was institutionalized. Aspects of this history have been memorialized in movies, novels, and popular culture. For many citizens, the very idea of gangsterism is rooted in this historical narrative of getting ahead in the social universe, what we sometimes refer to as the pursuit of the American dream.

For Cuban Americans, this storyline is of a more recent vintage. Whereas the traditional Mob arose in the early decades of the previous century, the Cuban underworld in the United States was spawned by a revolution back home in La Patria, the Homeland, which took place in the 1950s.

The tumultuous legacy of the Cuban Revolution, as led by Fidel Castro, Ernesto "Che" Guevara, and many others, has been chronicled in innumerable books, documentaries, paintings, plays, movies, and personal histories. Like other historical events of great consequence, it has been interpreted and reconstituted through the prism of political ideology, iconography, legend, and fantasy so that the lessons to be learned are fungible, depending on your point of view. Castro is a hero; Castro is the devil. The revolution was for the people, or it was done to centralize the power of the government, so that Castro could never be challenged.

One indisputable and rarely discussed point is that many men and women who contributed to the revolution, including some who fought alongside Castro and his 26th of July Movement, did not know—nor would it have been their intention had they known—that they were taking part in a communist takeover. Castro was scrupulous in not declaring the political movement of which he was a part to be a Marxist-Leninist enterprise. When he traveled to the United States in 1955–56 and gave speeches designed to raise money for his cause, he kept his cards close to his chest. It was only after the revolution was successful that Castro and Guevara made their designs clear.

Some prominent members of the revolution, including rebel fighters who had distinguished themselves on the battlefield, and also some leading minds of the underground resistance, expressed their dismay with the direction of the new revolutionary government. When it became clear that the Castro regime was to be a communist dictatorship, with no legitimate elections, people began to flee. Supporters of the deposed dictator, El Presidente Fulgencio Batista, were, for obvious reasons, among the first to abandon ship. Those who didn't escape were rounded up; some were put up against a wall and executed by firing squad. (*¡Paredón!*—To the wall!) The next to flee were the upper classes, which had seen their property and businesses seized by government decree. And then came the tens of thousands of others, common folk—teachers, professionals, artists, and the dispossessed— who fled the island any way they could, by plane and by boat, and, in later years, by raft, inflated inner tubes, and other flimsy, jerry-rigged vessels, some of which succumbed to the stormy realities of an unforgiving sea, resulting in death.

For those who fled, especially those who had originally been supportive of the revolution, the dominant mood was one of resentment along with a deep sense of betrayal. Where there are feelings of betrayal, there is often a need for revenge. This was a concept that flowed like ectoplasm through the veins of a newly vanquished people

They settled mostly in South Florida, primarily the city of Miami, which was 228 miles across the Florida Strait from Havana, a short forty-five-minute flight for those with the means and rarefied diplomatic status to make the journey. A number of Cubans continued north and settled in Hudson County, New Jersey, mostly in the town of Union City, which by the late 1960s would have the largest population of Cuban émigrés outside of Miami. There, they found work in the garment factories that had served as the area's main source of employment since the post–World War II years, when the town was populated mostly by citizens of Italian, Irish, and Jewish extraction.

Both in New Jersey and in South Florida—in fact, anywhere that Cubans settled—they brought their cultural traditions. Brilliant Afro-Cuban music; vibrant dance clubs; a devotion to Catholicism and also, in some cases, the pagan religion of Santería; cigars nonpareil; occasional cockfighting; the preeminence of family life; a diet heavy on chicken, *léchon* (suckling pig), plantains, and rice and beans; a taste for rum from the islands; and, for some, an affinity for games of chance, most notably a simple game known to all Latinos as *la bolita*.

Literally, the word *bolita* means "little ball." The designation stems from a time when the national lottery in Cuba was determined by small numbered balls being thrown into a bag, mixed up, and then randomly withdrawn to determine the daily number. Bolita, the illegal underground numbers game, was known as the poor man's lottery. The winning number was based on the Cuban national lottery; it was cheaper, so you could play for less and win more money. From the 1920s onward, it became something of a national passion in Cuba, as common as sugarcane fields, royal palms, and the distant, ever-present drumbeat of revolution.

Given the ubiquitous presence of bolita among Cubans of all classes and genders, it was perhaps inevitable that the game would thrive in the Cuban exile communities of Miami and Union City. And so it was. The man whose name would come to be associated with this illegal activity in the United States had not been a seasoned *bolitero,* or bolita boss, back in Cuba. He had been a cop in the city of Havana during the reign of the Batista dictatorship. His name was José Miguel Battle y Vargas.[1]

HAVANA IN THE 1950S WAS A ROLLICKING CITY OF CORRUPTION AND GOOD TIMES. Some would remember it as one of the most glorious localities for sensuality and vice in the entire twentieth century. Partly this had to do with the Caribbean's historical precedent as a crossroads for black market commerce and profiteering since the days of spice traders, international mercenaries, pirates, and buccaneers. Havana would eventually become a city unlike any other in the region—a sophisticated Latin American center of culture and grand architecture—but the city would forever maintain its sultry, sexually oriented underbelly as a draw for tourists and celebrities from around the globe.

Meyer Lansky, Charles "Lucky" Luciano, and Santo Trafficante Jr. were among the prominent mafiosi in the United States who had always recognized Cuba as the ideal location for an offshore base of operations. It also had great value as a moneymaking proposition by itself. Lansky was the first to establish a relationship with Fulgencio Batista, who in 1952 appointed the mobster as Cuba's director of gambling reform. Lansky cleaned up the island's bad reputation for rigged casino gambling. This would lead to an expansion in the gaming and entertainment industry in Cuba unlike anything seen before.

It all started with the casinos, which were mostly located inside the best hotels in town. The Hotel Nacional had the most elegant casino, and the swankiest was inside Lansky's own Hotel Riviera, which opened in 1957. Designed by internationally renowned architect Igor Boris Polevitzky, the room was oval, with luxurious wall-to-wall carpeting, gold leaf walls, and velvet banquettes, and from the ceiling hung seven custom-designed gold and crystal chandeliers. In the room's center were the gaming tables—roulette, craps, blackjack, chemin de fer (baccarat),

---

[1] Battle's birth name in Cuba was Batlle, pronounced "Bat-yey." Upon arrival in the United States, he changed both the spelling and pronunciation. The U.S. version, which became his official name in U.S. records and newspaper reports, and was the preferred usage by Battle and his family, is used throughout this book.

with a row of slot machines lining the curved perimeter wall. The sunken Doble o Nada (Double or Nothing) bar off the casino floor was one of the hotel's three venues for live entertainment.

From the outside, the casino's egg-shaped roof, adjacent to the hotel itself, was modernistic. The entire place was a work of art.

The casinos in Havana set the tone and generated a flow of cash that spilled into other areas. Every hotel had a nightclub that became the center of a fabulous entertainment scene, with hot Latin jazz orchestras, luscious showgirls, elaborate floor shows, and many top singers and entertainers from the United States. Outside these official worlds of casino gambling and live entertainment was a vibrant netherworld of bordellos, sex shows, private high-stakes card games, and access to narcotics.

José Miguel Battle worked this terrain from the highest levels to the lowest. He was a vice cop in 1950s Havana, which was something like being a centurion in the age of Caligula. Other branches of the police dealt with political dissent and underground political activity. The notorious Servicio de Inteligencia Militar (SIM), Batista's secret police, rounded up students and others who were believed to be involved in antigovernment activities and took them to warehouses and back rooms to be tortured and sometimes killed. Battle was not involved in this kind of policing. He was a member of the national police, not military intelligence. As a vice cop, he made the rounds at whorehouses, gambling parlors, nightclubs, cockfighting dens, and the hotels, where you could smoke a cigar in the lobby. He came to know the city's inhabitants, from the lowliest street pimps to people high up in politics and the entertainment worlds.

One of those people was Martín Fox, the proprietor of the most legendary nightclub in town, the Tropicana. Before he became a nightclub impresario, Fox had been one of the city's preeminent boliteros. He started as a lowly *listero,* one who takes bets and records the transactions on paper. By the late 1940s, after moving from his home province of Matanzas, he became one of the wealthiest *banqueros,* or bolita bankers, in Havana. He was the one who covered for all other boliteros if a particular number that had been bet on by multitudes—say, the number eight on September 8, the date of the Feast of the Virgin of Charity, Cuba's patron saint—was the number that day. Fox had enough "bank" to cover those losses, with the knowledge that over time his percentage of the winnings from all of the boliteros combined would greatly outstrip the losses. Eventually, he parlayed his winnings into establishing an underground gambling scene in Havana that, though illegal, was made possible through payoffs to the police.

José Miguel Battle came to Havana as a cop in June 1951. By then Martín Fox had risen from bolitero and underground gambling boss to being the owner of the Tropicana. Between Battle and Fox there was a natural affinity. They even looked alike. Both were heavyset men, salt-of-the-earth types, equal parts friendly and gruff. They resembled the movie actor Anthony Quinn. Both were *guajiros,* country bumpkins who had come to Havana with a dream of making something of themselves in the big city. Though the younger Battle was as dazzled as anyone by the Tropicana, when he met with Fox he was more curious about Fox's time as a bolitero and how he had used that to achieve high social status.

In time, they formed something of a business relationship. Fox made monthly payments of five thousand pesos to José Salas Cañizares, the chief of police. Sometimes the man who delivered that payment for Fox was José Miguel Battle. Later, Battle's role as a bagman in Havana would be upgraded considerably, when he began delivering much larger sums of cash from high-ranking U.S. mobsters to the presidential palace of Fulgencio Batista.

THE TOWN OF ALTO SONGO, IN THE PROVINCE OF ORIENTE, IS LOCATED NEAR THE eastern end of the island, far from Havana. In modern Havana, they have a joke about those from Oriente living in the capital city. They are referred to as *Palestinos* (Palestinians), because in Havana they are a people without land. Alto Songo, the birthplace of José Miguel Battle, was at the time of his birth nearly preindustrial, without modern plumbing and limited access to running water or electricity.

Battle was born at ten o'clock on the morning of September 14, 1929. He was the oldest child of José Maria Batlle Bestard and Angela Vargas Yzaguirre, who had been born and raised in Alto Songo. Eventually, José Miguel was joined by five brothers (Gustavo, Pedro, Sergio, Hiram, and Aldo) and a sister (Dolores). As a youth, he attended the Instituto Santiago de Cuba, the main school in the city of the same name. He graduated in 1947.

Just two years later, at the age of nineteen, Battle joined the Cuban national police in Santiago. A year and a half later he was transferred to Havana, which was a big step up for the young *guajiro*. Not only would he no longer have to wear the uniform of a cadet or patrol officer, but he was assigned to the vice squad, which meant he came to work in street clothes. Technically, he was a "delegate," or investigator, with the Bureau of Investigations, a division of the national police based out of a police station in the Rio Almendares area. Battle's unit dealt primarily with illegal gambling and robberies.

At the same time that José Miguel was inaugurating his career as a policeman in Havana, he began a family. In 1952, he married Maria Josefa Rodriguez y Vega, and within a year they had a son, José Miguel Battle Jr. They lived in the Luyano district, near the Port of Havana.

Most anyone who knew Battle during these years remembered him as someone who moved easily between the police and criminal worlds— when it came to gambling, there was little difference between the two. Gambling bosses paid the police for protection, and the money was spread throughout the chain of command. In Havana, as in many cities with an active underworld, criminals were not necessarily people you put in jail. For a detective, sometimes it was better to have crooks out on the street working for you. Battle always seemed to be looking to make alliances.

One street criminal who got to know Battle in Havana was a man we'll call "Jesús."[2] A year younger than Battle, Jesús was a black market gun merchant in the city at a time when weapons were in high demand, both with street criminals and with political rebels plotting against the government. Jesús was part of a crew that stole guns, sometimes from the police, and sold them to whoever was interested. Occasionally he served as a middleman receiving stolen guns from others and selling them to a third party. "Sometimes," he said, "we sold guns back to the same people they were stolen from."

---

[2] Jesús agreed to be interviewed for this account with the stipulation that his real name would not be used.

One day, a friend of Jesús's came to him and said, "There's a cop who wants to talk to you. His name is José Miguel Battle."

Jesús had never heard of the guy. "What's he want to know?"

"He knows you've been bartering stolen guns on the black market, guns that were stolen from the police." Jesús's friend knew Battle and vouched for him as someone who was "honorable," meaning someone who knew the rules of the underworld and would not use the meeting as an opportunity to arrest him.

Jesús agreed to meet the cop. They met in the restaurant at the Hotel Sevilla Biltmore, an establishment owned by Amleto Battisti y Lora, who was a key player in the Havana Mob. Battisti, an Italian national, was, among other things, a cocaine and marijuana peddler who made regular payoffs to the police. If this cop, Battle, was willing to meet him there, Jesús knew he had nothing to worry about.

Battle showed up at the Sevilla Biltmore with Vincente Juvenciente, his partner. Jesús was there with a friend.

Said Battle to Jesús, "Did you recently buy some revolvers from a black guy in El Centro [Havana's Central district]?"

"That depends," said Jesús.

"Well, we arrested *un negro*. He tells us he sold some guns to you. Those guns were stolen from the police."

Jesús thought about it for a few seconds and then said, "*Oye,* listen, I can't tell you where anything is or who anyone is, so just let me know what else you need from me."

Battle took full stock of him and said, "You are a real man. You don't snitch on your partners. That is a good quality."

From then on, Jesús and Battle became friendly. The street hustler and the cop occasionally traded information when it was mutually beneficial.

Many years later, far from Havana, Jesús would go to work for Battle's criminal organization in the United States. He is said to have performed many functions, including serving as a hit man.

Alliances are what Havana in the 1950s was all about. Another underworld figure Battle came to know, who in the pecking order of crime was in a universe far above that of Jesús, was Santo Trafficante Jr.

Battle was introduced to Trafficante by Martín Fox. Though the Tropicana nightclub was known as the only club in town that was not owned or co-owned by the Havana Mob, the gambling concession there was controlled by Trafficante. Fox and Trafficante had a decent working relationship, and for the club owner to introduce the young vice cop to one of the premier mobsters in town was the kind of thing that made their world go round.

The Trafficante family was legendary in Cuba. Back in the 1930s, Trafficante's Sicilian-born father was among the first mafiosi to establish a beachhead in Cuba. Santo Trafficante Sr. had been a founding father of the Mafia in Tampa, Florida, a city with a vibrant Cuban American population going back to the days of the Spanish-American War. Trafficante Sr. did criminal business with Cubans in Tampa. He learned to speak fluent Spanish, which had similarities to his native Sicilian. He came to know and appreciate Cuban culture: cigars, Spanish food, and a strong patriarchy with the women at home raising the family and the men out in the street taking care of business.

From early on, bolita was a primary aspect of the Mob's operations in Tampa. And then there was heroin. In the 1930s, Trafficante Sr. established Cuba as a major transshipment point for heroin coming from the city of Marseille, on the French Riviera.

By the 1950s, Trafficante Sr. was old and in his last days (he died in 1954). Heroin was no longer a major aspect of the Mob's business in Cuba. Meyer Lansky had taken over, and he made it clear that the narcotics business was out. There was no need to jeopardize the casino gambling empire they were creating on the island by bringing down the wrath of the Federal Bureau of Narcotics (FBN). Already in 1947 the FBN had brought about the deportation of Charles "Lucky" Luciano, a prominent heroin smuggler, from Cuba. From then on, the Havana Mob mostly stayed clear of the dope business.

Santo Jr. had a prickly partnership with Lansky, but he understood. With his wire-framed glasses and mostly placid demeanor, he had the look of a banker, not a gangster. He considered himself to be a businessman—granted, one who ordered hits on rivals and associates and spent his entire day scheming to commit crimes. But he was part of a proud tradition. And in Havana, that tradition had coalesced around the tried-and-true business of casino gambling, which wasn't even illegal in Cuba.

It didn't take long for Trafficante and Battle to form a partnership. Trafficante had other ongoing criminal rackets in Cuba, including the importation of bootleg cigarettes. Battle kept the mafioso abreast of gossip both in the law enforcement world and on the street.

Eventually, José Miguel was entrusted with an important job. Each week, he met with emissaries of Trafficante's and picked up a suitcase or suitcases filled with cash. It was his responsibility to see that these were delivered to the presidential palace, where they eventually made their way to the president. These payments came from the "skim" at the casinos, the money that was pilfered from the counting rooms and delivered into the hands of the Mob. In Havana, there was no gaming commission. In effect, the Mob was the gaming commission.

Batista's estimated weekly payment was $1.5 million.

Everyone benefited. The mobsters got rich. President Batista got rich. And José Miguel Battle played a small but pivotal role in a criminal alliance that would go down in history.

WHEN IT ALL CAME CRASHING DOWN, ON NEW YEAR'S DAY 1959, BATTLE AND MANY others did not initially see any reason to panic, even though the signs were not good. Batista fled the city by plane under cover of darkness. Trucks filled with guerrillas flooded into the city. One of the first actions of the people, after taking to the streets in celebration, was to trash the casinos. Slot machines and gambling tables were dragged out into the street, smashed, and set on fire. To those who were pro-Castro, the casinos had become a prime symbol of corruption and imperialist oppression.

Even so, there was reason to believe that the gaming industry might be preserved under the Castro regime. The profits generated by the casinos were too potentially remunerative for them to be shut down. As for Battle, he still had a job as a police officer, even though to have been a cop during the Batista dictatorship, with all the graft and corruption, would not put him in good standing with the new revolutionary government.

Battle stayed in Havana, but things quickly turned sour. After a period of negotiation, Castro shut down all the casinos. Battle was demoted from the vice squad to the transportation bureau. He was now a traffic

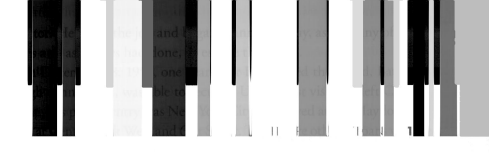

inspector. He hated the job and began planning a way, as so many of his friends and associates had done, to escape the island.

On December 28, 1959, one year after Batista fled the island, Battle, through connections, was able to secure a U.S. tourist visa. He left Cuba by boat. His port of entry was New York City. He stayed at the Mayflower Hotel, at Central Park West and 61st Street. There were other Cubans who had settled in Manhattan; mostly they lived in uptown tenement apartments in the area of St. Nicholas Avenue and Fort Washington Avenue. A key point of connection for many were the roving poker games that popped up in the backs of Latin restaurants and in people's apartments. There Battle met a number of Cuban émigrés who would become important players in his future as a gambling boss.

Occasionally, Battle made the short trip across the river to Union City, New Jersey, which was also becoming a popular locality for Cubans to settle. He bought into a bar in Union City called Johnny's Go Go Club, located on the corner of 48th Street and Palisade Avenue. The bar had female go-go dancers. Battle's investment was minimal, but it served its purpose as a beachhead in the new world.

The idea was for Battle to get settled and then somehow get his wife and young son out of Cuba. It was a struggle then being undertaken by thousands of exiles, part of a diaspora from an island that was being torn asunder by the consequences of revolution.

One person who met Battle during this period was Abraham Rydz, a Polish Jew who moved to Cuba with his parents at the age of two and grew up in Havana. The two men knew each other from gambling days back in Havana during the Batista era. They first met at a card game in the bustling district of Vedado. Now, a few years later, here they were as displaced refugees in New York and Union City, where they met once again over cards.

Rydz heard that Battle had a bar and was looking to establish roots in the area. Eventually they would become partners in a gambling enterprise that would make them both rich, but that was many years away. "At the time," said Rydz, "he had nothing. None of us did. We were struggling to survive."

In April 1960, Battle overstayed his visa—for a good reason. On the exile grapevine, he had been hearing some exciting news that the U.S.

government was recruiting people for a secret invasion of Cuba. This was almost too good to be true. Many Cubans who had left the island dreamed of overthrowing Fidel and taking back their country. With the power of the U.S. military behind them, and the support of a secret organization most had never heard of called the Central Intelligence Agency, how could they lose?

Battle traveled to Miami and booked a room at the South American Hotel, on 2nd Street and Second Avenue. With more than a thousand fellow Cuban refugees, he assembled in a hangar in the adjacent city of Hialeah. It was explained to the men by representatives of the CIA that the U.S. government was committed to overthrowing Castro and helping to establish a democratic government in Cuba.

Battle was down for the cause. Within days, he shipped out, along with hundreds of other Cuban exiles, first to a secret camp in the Homestead area of South Florida, and than on to a training facility hidden in the hills of Guatemala. It was the beginning of a new adventure that Battle and the others believed would lead them all back to their homeland, where they could live as proud Cubans in the country they loved.

THE STORY OF CUBAN ORGANIZED CRIME IN AMERICA HAS ITS ROOTS IN WHAT WOULD become known as the Bay of Pigs invasion. The overwhelming majority of men who signed on for this covert operation, which was initially put in motion by the administration of Dwight D. Eisenhower and the CIA, had no criminal inclinations. On the contrary, the men who were chosen were carefully vetted to make sure they did not have criminal records or reputations that would in any way damage the image of the operation. By and large these men were driven by patriotism and ideology. Their goal was to take back Cuba. The goal of the U.S. government, on the other hand, had more to do with the Cold War, a battle against the encroachment of communism in the Western Hemisphere, with Cuba as merely a piece on a chessboard.

Either way, all concerned were embarking on a course from which there was no return. Men like José Miguel Battle, forced out of their country by what they considered to be an undemocratic and vindictive process, gave their lives over to the cause with a dedication bordering on zealotry.

The Bay of Pigs invasion would become one of the most notorious military failures in U.S. history. The men who undertook the venture were put through a further process of humiliation that had a tremendous impact on their lives, and on the fortunes of both Cuba and the United States. Along with the political and historical consequences, the failed invasion would indirectly become the seed for a criminal underworld in America known as the Corporation.

This criminal enterprise was based on bolita, the numbers racket. Under the stewardship of Battle and others, it would become a multibillion-dollar operation. But the venture never shook its roots as an undertaking based in the politics of revolution and exile. The failure of the Bay of Pigs invasion would spawn further attempts to kill Castro and overthrow the Cuban government. These secret plots were undertaken by an alliance between the CIA and militant Cuban exiles, many of whom were veterans of the invasion. This narrative thread would run through American Cold War history like a tripwire, a bomb ready to explode. The Watergate burglary, political assassinations in the United States and overseas, the Iran-Contra scandal—these were just a few of the events that grew out of the anti-Castro movement, which became a catchphrase to describe many anticommunist efforts of the CIA throughout the second half of the twentieth century.

The story of the Corporation takes place in the shadow of this larger political narrative. The anti-Castro legacy is the context for the story of Cuban American organized crime, which rivaled the Mafia in its scope and body count.

José Miguel Battle Sr. rose from being a vice cop in Havana to being the Godfather—El Padrino—in America, but the story of the Corporation involves much more than one charismatic Mob boss. More than just a criminal operation, the Corporation was a way of life for those who became involved in it. There were the boliteros and gangsters, and the many lawmen who, over the years, became part of the effort to bring them down. There were also wives, girlfriends, sons, daughters, cousins, crime victims, snitches for the police, undercover agents—an entire generation of people who became caught up in an outrageous criminal history that lasted for nearly forty years.

Initially, cops in the United States trod lightly when it came to the

Cuban Mob. Along the way, Battle and other individuals were prosecuted, but not for being part of a criminal conspiracy. In some cases cops were bought off, and in others it was because the Corporation had a certain mystique. Links to the CIA and the underground anti-Castro movement through organization such as Alpha 66 and Omega 7, groups that carried out political assassinations in the United States and South America, made it seem as though the Corporation was untouchable. Over time, law enforcement zeroed in. In courtrooms in New York and Miami, the Corporation was bled dry and dismantled through indictments and convictions.

This book chronicles the rise and fall of Battle's organization from the Bay of Pigs invasion to the present day. Along the way, Cuban gangsters forged a partnership with the Mafia and then went to war with the Italians over control of lucrative numbers parlors in New York. This war was bloody, with much collateral damage. Eventually, mayhem and murder became a way of life, with revenge plots that spanned many years and wild shootouts on the streets of Miami's Little Havana and all around New York City and New Jersey. Though the main character of the story is El Padrino, this saga unfolds through a kaleidoscope of characters, male and female, and from many points of view. The canvas is large, because the story of the Corporation is the story not only of a criminal enterprise but also of a generation and a culture defining itself through a brutal version of the American experience.

The story of Cuban organized crime in America has never been fully told. For some, its parameters might seem exotic—murder plots are hatched at cockfights in Key Largo and carried out at Latin nightclubs in Harlem or Little Havana, all of it set to an Afro-Cuban beat. But the truth is that the narrative at play in the story of the Corporation adheres to a cherished American archetype. Irish, Italian, and Jewish gangsters have blazed this trail before, and newer versions of ethnic underworlds—African American, Asian, Mexican—have added their own unique flavors. The Horatio Alger myth—the self-aggrandizing trajectory of rags to riches, topped off with a dash of rosy optimism and American exceptionalism—may be the preferable myth to some. But stories of organized crime and the underworld are just as deeply rooted. And so room must finally be made on the shelf for this Cuban version of the classic American story.

IDALIA FERNANDEZ DIDN'T LIKE TO BE INTERRUPTED WHILE WATCHING *GENERAL Hospital*. Every afternoon at 3 P.M., she turned on the popular, long-running soap opera. While watching the show, she didn't answer the phone, and sometimes she wouldn't answer the door either. Lately she hadn't been answering the door anyway, because Idalia and her hit man boyfriend were on the run and hiding out in the Miami suburb of Opa-Locka. They were hiding from Cuban gangsters who were trying to kill them.

Even so, while on the lam, Idalia rarely missed an episode of *General Hospital*.

On the afternoon of June 16, 1976, she was watching the program when suddenly she heard a deafening cacophony of shattering glass and splitting wood.

Terrified, Idalia looked up and saw three men crashing through the apartment's jalousie door, glass flying, and rushing into the room. One of the men was Julio Acuna, whom she knew as Chino, a gangster from New York City. He was holding a big gun with a silencer on it, and he was coming straight at her with a demented expression on his face.

For more than a year, Idalia and her boyfriend, Ernesto Torres, had been fleeing on trains and in cars, bouncing between cheap motel rooms and apartments, hoping to outrun the devil. It was all Ernestico's fault. Idalia knew when she first met him in Union City, New Jersey, that he was a gangster who made his money from bolita, as the Cuban numbers racket was known. Idalia was Puerto Rican, but she knew all about bolita. It was hugely popular among Latinos of every nationality, many of whom placed a daily wager on a number or series of numbers. It was just like the lottery, now a state-run, legal form of betting. But back then it was an illegal enterprise controlled by organized crime. In New Jersey and all along the East Coast, the crime entity that controlled bolita among Latinos was sometimes called the Cuban Mafia. It was an organization that some in U.S. law enforcement said was more dangerous than La Cosa Nostra.

La mafia cubana was overseen by José Miguel Battle Sr., El Padrino, the Godfather. One of his most feared henchmen was Chino Acuna.

Idalia knew all this because not long ago, in Union City, her boyfriend Ernestico had worked for Battle and was friendly with Chino. But Ernestico had a falling-out with the organization when he kidnapped and shot one of its most valued bankers. This was an unfathomable act of betrayal against the organization, and so Ernestico was marked for death. One afternoon outside his and Idalia's apartment in Cliffside, New Jersey, a car bomb went off that destroyed Ernestico's car. He narrowly missed being blown up. A few days later, he was shot in the side outside a flower shop in upper Manhattan. Ernestico didn't even wait for his wounds to heal. He and Idalia wrapped up the bullet wound in his side and fled by train to Miami. They arrived on New Year's Day 1976.

Ever since, they had been slinking around like rodents, living off the land. No one was supposed to know where they were hiding out. But three weeks earlier, in the city of Hialeah, Ernestico had been targeted for death once again. He was standing on the sidewalk in front of the building where they were living when two men driving by in a car opened fire, hitting him in the forearm, shattering his radius bone. This had necessitated Idalia and Ernestico's moving for the fourth time in the six months they'd been hiding out in Miami. At the current location in Opa-Locka, the only people who knew they were there were the lady who rented them the apartment and a kid from whom they ordered groceries to be delivered from Los Hispanos Market.

That morning, Idalia had awakened Ernestico and helped him shower. He had a cast on his forearm from the recent shooting. She cooked him something to eat. In the afternoon, Ernestico lay back down to take a nap. Idalia turned on *General Hospital*. And then glass from the jalousie door came shattering into the room.

Idalia saw the two men behind Chino flash by, making for the bedroom. Chino pointed his gun at Idalia and pulled the trigger. A bullet hit her in the chest, and she went down. Then Chino stood over her and fired a shot into the back of her head. He rolled her over and with the butt of his pistol bashed her in the face and mouth. Idalia descended into unconsciousness.

She should have been dead. But she wasn't. The shot to the chest had not hit any vital organs, and the shot to her head—incredibly—entered her skull, circled around her cranium without penetrating the brain, and exited. There was so much blood and apparent damage that her attackers were sure she was dead.

When she regained awareness and opened her eyes, Idalia was covered in blood and surrounded by cops. "Who did this?" asked a detective. "Did you see who shot you?" Idalia was barely conscious. She said nothing. They loaded her on a gurney and rushed her to the nearest hospital, where she was ushered into emergency surgery.

Afterward, Idalia was visited in the hospital by more detectives. They informed her that her boyfriend Ernestico had been murdered. Hearing the killers enter the apartment, Ernestico had retrieved his gun and engaged in a shootout, but he was outgunned. He retreated deep into the bedroom. The cops found his dead body, riddled with bullet wounds, slumped in the bedroom closet. Whoever killed Ernestico had delivered a coup de grâce with the muzzle of the gun pressed against Ernestico's flesh, a single blast between the eyes.

Hearing this news, Idalia wept. Her head was shaved and her face was a mess: two black eyes, contusions, her front teeth broken. "They killed my husband," she said, struggling to formulate the words. "We tried. We did everything possible so they wouldn't do it . . . But we knew that someday we were going to lose, because he made a lot of money."

Said one of the detectives, "You don't have to be scared anymore . . . You're going to have to confide in us and help us out."

"*Estoy bien mareada* (I'm really dizzy)," said Idalia. She knew what the cops wanted to know. "I've been thinking. I can't remember if I see a movie. I think I saw El Chino coming inside the house, you know?"

One of the detectives talked, and another scribbled down notes. "You say you saw Chino come inside your house?"

"I didn't see El Chino. I said I've been thinking. It's like I saw Chino . . . I've got to be . . ." Idalia began moaning.

"What's the matter, what's the matter?" the detective asked.

"A pain."

"Where?"

"All over my head."

The detectives told Idalia to relax; they had lots of time. A nurse brought her a thimble of water.

"So, what do you think? Do you think it was Chino?"

"I think it was Chino . . . It must have been Chino. Because to me he looked so familiar. To me he was Chino."

"You know Chino?"

"I know Chino."

The other detective wrote it all down. The men paused in acknowledgment of the big moment: the victim identifying her assailant.

The detectives asked if she got a look at the other killers. Idalia said that she had been shot and passed out, so she had no way of knowing their identities.

She was lying. Idalia had clearly seen one of the other gunmen come in the door with Chino. The man she saw was the Godfather himself, José Miguel Battle Sr.

Idalia looked at the cops. "Regardless of what you may think, I'm a decent woman, you know. And I'm the mother of my daughter, and I love my daughter dearly. And my mother. I don't want anything to happen to them."

Idalia knew that identifying Chino would lead to a hunt to find him. Probably he would be apprehended and there would be a trial of some sort. Idalia would be called to testify, and perhaps some form of "justice" would be achieved. She knew this was true because she had seen it on TV and in the movies. But she also knew that in the real world there were certain truths that lay beyond the scales of justice, and if you expected to survive, as she had just done—miraculously—there were certain things you did not do. One of those things, if you hoped to live a long life, was that under no circumstances did you finger El Padrino, even if he was trying to have you murdered.

"That's it," said the woman to the detectives. "I don't have anything else. Now please, please, go away."

Part I
Traición/Betrayal

BRIGADE 2506

JOSÉ MIGUEL BATTLE SR. SAT WITH HIS MEN. THEY WERE SPREAD OUT AROUND THE hull of a boat, some staring out to sea and others looking up at the night sky. There were few clouds to obscure the deep blue canvas above, which revealed a dazzling amalgam of celestial asterisms and constellations— the Big and Little Dippers, Corona Borealis, Orion, the Milky Way. The moon provided the only light; it glistened off the surface of the ocean, illuminating a path that led due north.

Aboard Battle's vessel were nearly two hundred men with rifles. They hardly spoke. Quietly pondering the nature of the cosmos seemed an appropriate state of being for the undertaking at hand. Battle knew the drill: he and the other soldiers had been training for this mission for months. Now, sailing under a canopy of stars and planets, they consigned their fate to the gods.

They were on their way to Cuba to reclaim La Patria, which they felt had been unjustly seized from them by a silver-tongued despot with a scraggly beard and a prodigious cigar.

Battle's boat was one of six vessels, each filled with hundreds of men who comprised an invading army known as the 2506 Brigade. The ships had set sail from Puerto Cabeza, on the coast of Nicaragua, at 2 A.M. the previous day. The various boats traversed the Caribbean Sea through slightly different routes, so they would not be easily detected. They sailed through the dark, watched the sun rise, continued throughout the following day, saw the sun set, and then all boats converged under cover of darkness forty miles off the coast of Cuba.

At thirty-one, Battle was older than many of the men in the brigade, a motley army of soldiers who ranged in age from sixteen to sixty-one. Though José Miguel was stout, bordering on overweight, he was a born leader. His reputation as a tough vice cop in Havana preceded him, and while training for the invasion he had distinguished himself enough to be given the rank of second lieutenant and designated the leader of a platoon. His unit would be among the first to go ashore once the flotilla reached Cuba.

The date was April 16, 1961. The brigade was scheduled to land at an area of the island known as the Bay of Pigs, Bahía de Cochinos, on the southern coast in the province of Matanzas. The landing site had been changed at the last minute. In fact, though the men had trained hard and were more than ready to fight, the battle plan for the invasion had been sucked into a political vortex of compromise and indecision.

Plans for the attack had begun years earlier under the administration of President Dwight D. Eisenhower. It was a covert operation of the Central Intelligence Agency. In 1961, upon assuming office as the newly elected president, John F. Kennedy inherited the plan. It was controversial, to say the least. The U.S. government could not be seen as sanctioning the invasion in any way. As an undeclared act of war, it would be in violation of international law.

Within the Oval Office of the White House, Kennedy voiced doubts about the plan, but he had boxed himself into a corner. During the 1960 presidential campaign, Kennedy had taunted his opponent, Vice President Richard M. Nixon. He declared that the Eisenhower administration, in allowing Fidel Castro to gain a toehold in Cuba, was soft on communism. Now Kennedy could not squelch the invasion without appearing hypocritical and cowardly. Instead, what he did was systematically chip away at aspects of the plan, all in the interest of minimizing the appearance of U.S. military involvement in the operation.

There were many questionable decisions along the way, including the order to call off preinvasion bombings of Castro's air force. The original plan had been to take out Cuba's warplanes before the brigade landed. But after only one bombing raid, in which only a small number of planes were disabled, President Kennedy, fearing that the United States would be implicated, ordered a halt.

The men of the 2506 Brigade had no idea that President Kennedy was in the midst of a Hamlet-like internal struggle over the invasion's propriety and prospects for success. What mattered most to these men was their own morale, which was high. Many had left behind wives, children, and decent lives when they volunteered for the mission, and they did so with single-minded dedication. The overriding motive was vengeance, the desire to get revenge against Castro and reclaim Cuba.

How could they lose? They had been trained and were being guided by officers of the U.S. military, the most powerful fighting force on the planet. Many, upon joining the brigade, had never heard of the Central Intelligence Agency, but that hardly mattered. Their desire for victory and their blind faith were an emotional balm, a sedative that inoculated them from the reality that as they sailed the Caribbean Sea toward their homeland, their mission was shifting below them.

On board the command ship *Blagar*—Lieutenant Battle's boat—some of the men played cards to bide their time. Battle loved to gamble, and poker was his game. He played cards with members of his platoon. None of these men had been told that the plan to wipe out Castro's air force had been scrapped. It was supposed to be a surprise attack; these men were expecting to meet little or no resistance. They had no idea that the invasion had been compromised before they landed. They were sailing toward their doom.

FROM THE LONG VIEW OF HISTORY, A COMMON MISCONCEPTION ABOUT THE MEN OF THE 2506 Brigade is that they came from the upper classes in Cuba and from those in partnership with the dictatorship of Fulgencio Batista. The idea that the invasion was undertaken by people who were philosophically opposed to the revolution is not entirely true. Many *brigadistas* were men who had at one time been tolerant if not supportive of various dissident groups that emerged in 1950s Cuba. Some had even fought in the Sierra Maestra with Castro's 26th of July Movement and had risked their lives on behalf of the revolution.

The organizers of the invasion—both supervising agents with the CIA and members of the anti-Castro leadership in the United States—had made a deliberate point of not including known Batista sympathizers in the brigade. They did not want the invasion to be interpreted as an attempt by the dictator to reclaim power. Along with recruiting and training an invading force of soldiers, the organizers put together a "kitchen cabinet" of political figures who would assume power once the invasion was successful and Castro was overthrown. None of these men had ties to the Batista government.

Like José Miguel Battle, some in the brigade had an axe to grind. They had lost jobs and property. Some had been forced off the island in the most humiliating manner possible; they had been stripped of their belongings, their assets seized by the government. Many were shocked to hear of the political executions ordered and carried out by a revolutionary council led by Che Guevara. Others had gone through a sustained process of disillusionment. As the Castro government undertook a series of steps that revealed the new regime to be communist, they felt betrayed. They had been hoodwinked into believing the revolution represented positive social change, not just a case of trading one dictatorship for another. Personal aggrievement, political and philosophical outrage—these were potent motivators. The men of the brigade were driven by a powerful sense of *venganza*.

Soon after the counterrevolutionary force had been assembled, training began at a secret camp high in the hills of Guatemala. A force of approximately fifteen hundred men was secretly transported to Base Trax, the primary camp, where they lived and trained for six months. In a sweltering tropical jungle, they were bedeviled by snakes, spiders, and exotic insects. During drills and training exercises, some men succumbed to heat exhaustion and collapsed. They were isolated from the outside world; there were no newspapers, television, or radio. The men absorbed their training with the devotion of a scholastic Jesuit studying for the priesthood.

Boot camp was overseen by the CIA and officers of the U.S. Army and Air Force. The trainees lived at the encampment and went through physical and military training every day. Physically and psychologically, the routine was rigorous. Not everyone who had signed up for the brigade was able to pass the physical training.

Each man who passed was given a number. One of those men died during training; in honor of his sacrifice, the entire force was bestowed with his number—2506—and thus the men were officially christened the 2506 Brigade.

Among the members of the brigade were the Fuentes brothers, Fidel and Ramon. Like many who wound up in the platoon led by José Miguel Battle, they knew the former cop from their days in Havana. Fidel Fuentes met Battle at a meeting of the Freemasons. Both men were members of the secret Protestant organization that had existed in Cuba since 1763, when British and Irish settlers first came to the island. Over time, the organization developed a certain prestige among some noteworthy figures in Cuba. The revered patriot and poet José Martí had been a Mason, as was, allegedly, Fidel Castro, who is believed to have taken refuge at a Freemason lodge during violent student uprisings at the University of Havana in the late 1940s.

At a Masonic lodge in the 1950s, Fidel Fuentes and José Miguel Battle first stood in a circle and locked arms in the traditional ritual of the Masons. It was a bond that would come into play years later, when Fuentes found himself aboard the *Blagar,* along with his brother, sailing toward Cuba as a member of Battle's platoon. Of his platoon commander, years later Fidel Fuentes would remember, "He was a strong leader. There was no boss or chief as simpatico as Battle."

Just four months earlier, the Fuentes brothers had left their lives in Cuba to join the fight against Castro. Their father, who had been in the Cuban military, arranged for a twenty-six-foot sailboat—a mother ship—to be moored far out at sea. On the night of December 27, 1960, Fidel, age twenty-three, Ramon, age twenty-one, their father, age forty-eight, and sixteen others made their way to the mother ship via rowboats that carried four or five people at a time. In small installments, the human cargo was less likely to be detected by authorities. After each rowboat reached the sailboat, its passengers boarded the mother ship and the rowboat was sunk.

Of the nineteen people who boarded the vessel, eight were members of the Fuentes family. The engine-powered sailboat navigated the rough Florida Strait and arrived at a secret location near Key West. Within days of touching down on U.S. soil, Fidel, Ramon, and their father headed toward Guatemala to join the fight against the dictator.

The 2506 Brigade was comprised of four battalions, each with approximately 255 men. Each battalion was comprised of four platoons.

Battle was the leader of a platoon that was part of the Fourth Battalion, the initial battalion to come ashore at Playa Girón in the Bay of Pigs. Fidel Fuentes and his brother remembered it well.

"It was ten minutes to midnight when we disembarked," said Fidel. "The first thing we noticed was that we'd been dumped into water that was up to our necks and in some cases over our heads."

They heard the voice of Battle: "Don't let the machine guns get wet!"

The Fuentes brothers and the other soldiers held their rifles and machine guns high over their heads and tried to navigate their way to the beach. That was made difficult by the large rocks and jagged coral reef that lined the shore of Playa Girón, cutting their feet through their boots as they stumbled on the reef, arriving at the beach exhausted and soaking wet.

Everything about the brigade's arrival on Cuban soil was unexpected and disorienting. For one thing, Castro knew they were coming. The Cuban government had numerous spies and informants in the exile community in the United States who had relayed rumors and information about the assault. And if that weren't enough, just three days before the invasion there had been a front page article in the *New York Times* noting that rumors of an invasion were rife and that it was only a question of when and precisely where the force would attack.

Members of the brigade were not aware that they were expected; if they had been, perhaps they would not have been startled to find that when they landed at Playa Girón, they were met with klieg lights and incoming fire. The Cuban army was waiting for them.

Said Fuentes, "Anyone who was there will tell you, it was a bad situation from the moment we came ashore."

Even so, the soldiers of the brigade were there to fight. They traded gunfire with the enemy from the moment they arrived. Trucks, tanks, and artillery of the brigade disgorged from a separate boat; more were scheduled to arrive later by air.

The plan had been for the various battalions to assemble at Playa Girón and Playa Larga, thirty miles to the north. The landing zones were designated as Blue Beach and Red Beach. Astride both of these beaches was Ciénaga de Zapata, a massive swampland that stretched sixty-five miles from east to west and twenty miles north to south. The

Zapata swamp was comprised of dense hardwood trees and mangroves growing out of porous marshland.

The Fourth Battalion, which included Battle's platoon, were supposed to set up a command post at the village of San Blas, ten miles inland. Their primary mission was to secure the small airport near San Blas as a means for supplies—food, communications equipment, additional artillery, and other supplies—to be offloaded by plane. Their secondary mission was to secure the hospital at the nearby town of Yaguaramas.

It would take the battalion a full day and night to reach San Blas. Along the way, they encountered fire, including heavy artillery and bombing from the air. The brigade soldiers were stunned. "As far as we knew," remembered Fuentes, "Castro's air force had been wiped out. We were not expecting to encounter such ferocious resistance from the land and by air."

Before the brigade had even gotten its bearings, something occurred that the men would remember for the rest of their lives. As they made their way through the darkness toward San Blas, amid the sounds of rocket fire, airplanes, and the occasional bomb, there came from the shoreline an explosion so loud and powerful that it shook the earth below their feet. The men turned and saw a massive mushroom cloud rising into the sky.

"*Coño* (damn)," said a member of the platoon. "Does Castro have an atom bomb?"

Later, the men would learn that one of their primary supply ships, the *Río Escondido,* loaded with fuel tanks and artillery, had been hit from the air and ignited in a thunderous ball of flames. But at the time it shocked the men; they didn't know what it was, leading them to surmise that whatever they were up against was more massive and destructive than anything they had imagined.

The road to San Blas was littered with vehicles and artillery abandoned by the Cuban military. There were swamps on both sides of the road. They approached a sugar mill near the village of Covadonga. It had been nearly twenty-four hours since the platoon first came ashore; the men were hungry and exhausted. Suddenly, out of the darkness, they saw a group of cattle crossing the road. Someone exclaimed, "There's our dinner! We can kill them and eat them."

As they approached the cattle, the platoon came under attack. Out in the middle of the road, exposed to enemy fire, Battle's men had no choice but to use the cattle as cover to hinder the incoming rounds. The animals were shot to pieces. The men would have preferred to eat the beasts; instead, they sacrificed the animals to save their lives and were then forced to scurry into the swamp to hide.

Eventually, the Fourth Battalion achieved its primary goals: the men established a command post at San Blas and took over the hospital at Yaguaramas. There were many casualties along the way. The brigade may have been greatly outnumbered, but their training was superior. At least initially, most of the casualties were among their adversaries in the Cuban militia.

By day three of the attack, Lieutenant Battle's platoon was hunkered down at San Blas. Then an incident occurred that shaped the lives of numerous men involved—including the Fuentes brothers and José Miguel Battle. In later years, when the fog of war gave way to the harsh realities of civilian life, this incident would be used by defenders of Battle to suggest that, whatever else he was, he was a war hero. It would become the foundation of his legend, a facilitator and explanation for all that was to come in his life.

RAUL MARTINEZ URIOSTE HAD NEVER HEARD OF JOSÉ MIGUEL BATTLE WHEN, ON APRIL 17—D-Day—he departed from Puerto Cabeza in a C-46 cargo plane as part of the 2506 Brigade's paratroop unit, known as Company C. The company was comprised of four dozen paratroopers. They had trained separately from the other soldiers in an area of Guatemala known as La Suisa. As they approached the Bay of Pigs, their pilot flew in low at approximately six hundred feet. Gunfire struck the belly of the airplane.

Remembered Martinez, "We looked at each other: *Hey, we're being shot at. This is real.*"

At the time, Martinez was a young man, having left Cuba in the wake of the revolution at the age of nineteen. He'd grown up watching World War II movies starring John Wayne at the local cinema and on television. He'd turned twenty in the training camp at La Suisa. Earlier that morning, as the paratroopers boarded their plane, he was excited but also startled by something he had seen. The number on the side of his plane was 8-6-4. For Cubans who are superstitious, numbers have a significance or meaning. Eight-six-four translated roughly as "death under the moon for the soldier," or, as Martinez interpreted it, *muerte con muerte grande,* the big death.

"When I first saw that," he said, "I didn't want to get on that plane."

His training as a soldier overruled his superstitions, and he got on the plane.

The first squad of paratroopers jumped out over San Blas. Martinez was part of a second squad of nineteen men who were dropped over what had been designated Combat Outpost #2, a dirt road leading to the village of Covadonga. As he drifted down over Cuban soil, the first thing Martinez heard was what he thought was a police siren. *Wait a minute!* he thought. *We're soldiers, this is a war. And somebody called the cops!?* He was offended. But as soon as his platoon touched ground, they knew they were indeed in a war.

The siren, as it turned out, was from an ambulance, which was exactly what Martinez's squad needed. Upon landing, one of the men had accidentally shot himself in the thigh. The paratroopers commandeered the ambulance and headed toward San Blas. There they were reunited with the rest of Company C.

The command post at San Blas was bustling with activity. Over shortwave radio, the men heard reports from the front. Clearly, the battle was not going as planned, but at this point there was no sense that all was lost. The most disturbing reality was that even as they encountered Cuban armed forces that had advance knowledge of the invasion and were buttressed with an infantry and air force far greater in number than they expected, the brigade anticipated that they would receive backup from the United States. So far, that backup was nowhere in sight.

At San Blas, Martinez's squad was given an assignment by battalion commander Alejandro Del Valle. They were to return to Combat Outpost #2 and set up a roadblock to stop or delay the advance of enemy troops toward San Blas. Their unit of nineteen paratroopers would be augmented by nine men from the Fourth Battalion, including men from Battle's platoon.

It was at San Blas that Martinez first laid eyes on José Miguel Battle.

Their introduction was so brief that he might not have remembered it at all except that Battle, like him, was a man who clearly liked to eat. "He was fat like me," remembered Martinez, who had no idea that he and this man would soon cross paths in a way that would alter the trajectory of his life.

The paratroopers and the men from Battle's battalion headed back toward the front. They traveled with a tank, an ambulance, and a truck they had commandeered from the enemy. For artillery, they were outfitted with weapons from the heavy weapons battalion, which had landed by sea the night before. This included a .50-caliber machine gun and a 75mm recoilless rifle. Martinez was the unit's forward observer, outfitted with a PRC10 radio, binoculars, and an M-1 carbine.

Southwest of the Covadonga sugar mill, in the village of Jocuma— which was nothing more than a few houses on the side of the road—the unit spent the day without any disturbances. That night at 10:30 P.M., Martinez spotted an enemy jeep two kilometers south of the village, headed in their direction. "Hey," he said to his men manning the artillery, "I got a target for you."

The men were excited. They advanced forward to the side of the road, out in the open. As the jeep approached, they aimed the .50-caliber machine gun and fired.

They must have hit a gas tank, because the jeep exploded in a ball of flames. Martinez watched through his binoculars. "The driver of the jeep was trapped between his seat and the steering wheel. He was burned to a crisp and died a horrible death."

The brigadistas did not have time to celebrate. Twenty feet behind the incinerated jeep was a lumbering tank, a Soviet-made T-34 from World War II. With all that fire, the area had been illuminated. They could see that in the turret of the tank was a Cuban soldier with a heavy-caliber machine gun. The machine gunner spotted Martinez and his men and opened fire.

Martinez and his men were completely exposed; they had nowhere to turn. Incoming fire sprayed all around them like a violent hailstorm.

The man next to Martinez was hit and killed. The soldier to his right was hit in the back. "He made the mistake of screaming out and rising up. He was hit a second time and killed. The guy manning the

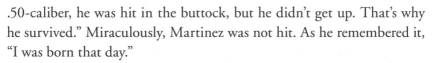

.50-caliber, he was hit in the buttock, but he didn't get up. That's why he survived." Miraculously, Martinez was not hit. As he remembered it, "I was born that day."

More enemy vehicles were approaching—another tank and infantry on both sides of the road. The squad was in danger of being surrounded and obliterated.

"I had no desire to play hero, but I didn't have any choice. The shooter of our machine gun was hurt, so I took over the machine gun. My principle was, whatever moves, shoot it. I had a good time with the machine gun shooting tracer rounds. The leader of the post came over from the other side of the road and told me, 'Hey, don't waste so many bullets.'"

One of their men fired a bazooka and hit the enemy tank, disabling the caterpillar treads so that the vehicle was dead in its tracks. Suddenly the occupants of the tank appeared through the turret; they were attempting to flee. In the darkness, Martinez opened fire. The enemy scattered for cover in the swamp.

The dust settled. There was no way of knowing if Martinez had hit any of the men. It was eerily quite until one of the enemy soldiers cried out, "*Teniente Julio, estoy herido* (Lieutenant Julio, I'm wounded)." Apparently, Lieutenant Julio, the soldier's boss, had vanished. He called out again, "*Teniente Julio, estoy herido.*"

Remembered Martinez, "We remained quiet. Then the guy made a big mistake, he called out, '*Teniente Julio, dónde estás?* (Lieutenant Julio, where are you?).' One of our men answered by calling out, '*Está templando con tu madre, maricón* (He's out fucking your mother, faggot.)'"

The guy tried to change his position; Martinez and his men saw him in the moonlight walking on the road, with his rifle raised, ready to shoot. "We took him out with the .50-caliber machine gun." Martinez advanced to make sure the enemy soldier was dead. "He was cut into two pieces, honest to goodness. It was terrible, but that's war. It was him or us."

It was a temporary victory, because more enemy vehicles were approaching. Martinez scurried back down into the swamp. It appeared hopeless.

And this was where José Miguel Battle came into play.

Apparently a man from Martinez's squad had escaped on foot and run all the way back to San Blas. He told commander Del Valle, "It's a slaughter up there. They are under attack from a tank column and infantry. The entire unit has probably been wiped out."

Del Valle suggested that they wait for tank support, which was expected to arrive shortly, but Battle spoke up. "What are we waiting for?" he said. "I'm going to get my guys."

"Battle," said Del Valle, "you only have one truck. It's a suicide mission. You'll be driving into enemy fire, and they're probably already dead."

"Well, then I'll bring back their bodies." Battle turned to his men and asked, "Who is with me?"

The Fuentes brothers, Fidel and Ramon, said, "Let's go."

The three men loaded the M-35 cargo truck with a .50-caliber machine gun and whatever hand weapons they had. That was it. They headed toward the front.

It was after 2 A.M. The dirt road was barely able to handle the truck. The men sat mostly in silence, shrouded in near-total darkness except for the truck's headlights, which illuminated the rocky, pockmarked surface of the road and the surrounding jungle of dense trees and mangroves. Watching the road was like looking through a keyhole: a sliver of light that stretched twenty feet and then a dark abyss. Battle and his men knew that there were enemy patrols likely all around them in the darkness. It was a journey into the unknown that could have ended at any moment in a hail of machine-gun fire or, even worse, a blast of artillery that would have blown them to pieces.

Down the road, also in darkness, were Raul Martinez and his platoon, hidden in a ditch where they had been taking cover for at least the last two hours. They had suffered only three casualties, which was amazing considering the intensity of the attack against them. But they were trapped and figured that as soon as the sun rose they would be wiped out. Some of the men said their prayers.

"We heard a truck coming," said Martinez. "Then we looked and there it was, one of ours. They even had their lights on. I'm telling you, those guys had balls."

Martinez called out to the truck. Battle and the two Fuentes brothers saw the men and pulled over.

Fidel Fuentes was the one manning the .50-caliber machine gun. "That was my baby," he said. As soon as incoming fire hit their truck, Fuentes blasted away in the direction where the Cuban militia was hiding out. Meanwhile, Martinez and his group loaded their 75mm recoilless rifle and .50-caliber machine gun onto the truck. All together, eleven remaining men from Company C and nine men from Battle's platoon loaded onto the truck. Martinez carried the M-1 rifle that belonged to one of the men who had been killed, thinking he could one day present the gun to the man's wife. He grabbed onto the front grille of the truck and rode in that manner all the way back to San Blas.

IT HAD BEEN A HEROIC ACT THAT SAVED MANY LIVES, BUT BACK AT COMMAND POST #2 there was no time for celebration. It was clear that in the last twelve hours much of the brigade had simply been overrun by Cuban forces. What was most shocking to the soldiers was that as the battle turned from bad to worse, the U.S. Air Force was doing nothing to back them up. Day and night, they waited for air support that never came.

On the afternoon of the third day, around 3 P.M., Martinez, Battle, and the others saw three U.S. Air Force planes fly low over San Blas. The men let out a cheer. Finally, they assumed, they were getting some support. But the planes abruptly circled around and disappeared over the horizon, never to return.

San Blas came under heavy attack from cannon fire. At the same time, over the airwaves the men could hear dispatches from Pepe San Román, a leader of the brigade, who was reporting from the front at Playa Girón to a communications center on the *Blagar*. These messages were relayed to military headquarters at Puerto Cabeza and by Teletype to Washington, D.C.

At 5:00 A.M.: "Do you people realize how desperate the situation is? Do you back us or quit? All we want is low jet air cover. Enemy has this support. I need it badly or cannot survive . . ."

At 6:13 A.M.: "Blue Beach under attack by B-26. Where is promised air cover?"

At 6:45 A.M.: "C-54 dropped supplies on Blue Beach. All went into the sea. Send more."

At 9:14 A.M.: "Blue Beach under attack by two T-33 and artillery. Where the hell is jet cover?"

At 9:25 A.M.: "Two thousand militia attacking Blue Beach from east and west. Need close air support immediately."

These and other desperate pleas for support went unheeded.

What the men of the brigade did not know was that back in Washington, D.C., President Kennedy, after consulting with CIA supervisors who had devised the invasion, ordered that no matter what the circumstances, U.S. jets would not and could not be involved in the fight. The soldiers would have to fend for themselves.

By April 19, it was clear that the mission was doomed. The various units of the brigade had begun to disintegrate. Rumors of an attempted evacuation circulated among the men. Everyone started to retreat back toward Playa Girón. "The trucks and tanks looked like a routa treinta on a Sunday morning," said Martinez. Routa treinta was the bus route in Havana that took people to the beach, and on weekends you would see the buses packed with people hanging off the sides and riding on bumpers.

Martinez jumped onto the tank and rode back toward the beach. At a junction in the road from Cayo Romano, the tank commander said, "Hey, hombres, this is the best I can do for you." Martinez got off the tank and followed on foot, part of a large cortege of defeated soldiers in retreat.

"When I got to Girón, I didn't like what I saw. The morale was down. The people from Battalion Number Two who had fought valiantly, they were there, some wounded. After waiting there for a while, I decided it was time to go. I started to walk on the road back toward San Blas. From the tank I had seen a couple of trails that led from the highway. My hope was that I could get to the border between Matanzas and Las Villas. I was trying to get to my father's farm that had been confiscated [by the revolutionary government]. I was trying to get to an area that I was familiar with."

Martinez slept in the woods during the day and walked at night, his face covered with charcoal from the coal deposits that were common in the area. The landscape changed from swampland to sugarcane fields to the occasional flamboyant tree, with its spectacular bright red blossoms that struck a discordant note of beauty amid the death and carnage of the war.

After three days, Martinez came upon an older brigade member, also on the run, who had a small transistor radio. They listened to local propaganda reports about how the war was over and the Cuban militia had won, but they chose not to believe this news. At one point they heard vehicles coming, so they hid in a ditch on the side of the road. Three trucks full of Cuban soldiers drove by with their guns raised in triumph; they were shouting, "*Vencimos!* We've won!" Martinez thought, *Oh my God, it's true. They won.*

Later that night, as they walked on the road, Martinez and his companion were suddenly approached from behind by a militia patrol of seven men. The militia soldiers opened fire, and Martinez returned fire with his M-3. But he was greatly outnumbered. His companion surrendered to the enemy and said, "Don't shoot him, he's just a boy."

A militia soldier with an M-1 rifle with a telescopic sight pointed his weapon at Martinez and said, "*Que 'ta haciendo?* (What are you doing?)" Martinez dropped his M-3 and said, "*Nada.*"

"I'm thankful that he did not shoot me," said Martinez of his captor. "I owe my life to this guy."

He was held with a group of other captured soldiers. While they were waiting to be taken away, up drove the head of the Cuban Communist Party in a big gray Buick. On the side of the car, painted in red, were the words *Muerte a los invasores!* (Death to the invaders!).

MEANWHILE, BATTLE AND HIS MEN WERE ENGAGED IN A SIMILAR STRUGGLE FOR SURvival, as was the rest of the brigade, which had been scattered into the Zapata swampland.

Battle had his truck—the same one that had been used to rescue his men. On the truck were eleven members of his platoon, including the Fuentes brothers. Six of the men were injured. The truck soon became stuck in the swamp, and the men were forced to abandon the vehicle and flee on foot. Their progress was hindered by their having to aid their wounded brethren.

For three days they struggled to survive. Because there was no water, they drank their own urine. They ate leaves from the trees. Turkey vultures circled in the sky above. Already the carnivorous vultures had been feasting on the carcasses of the dead. Battle and his men threw stones at the birds, trying to scare them away so that they would not alert the enemy of their whereabouts.

On the fourth day, as they came out of the swamps and into the woods, they discovered a well that contained fresh water and some small crabs. The men cracked opened the crabs and ate the raw flesh. It tasted good, but soon the men were overcome with fever and diarrhea.

Their enemy knew they were out there. Patrols drove by on the roads and military helicopters zoomed overhead. Castro's militia knew that the "mercenaries," as they called them, were starving, and so the helicopters sometimes dropped chocolate candy into open areas and hovered overhead. Remembered Fidel Fuentes, "If one of our men went for the chocolate, he would be shot dead."

Battle, the Fuentes brothers, and the others hunkered down in an area near the well, but they knew that by doing so they were risking capture. They constructed an igloo out of rocks so that they could hide inside and not be detected from the air. Under cover of darkness, they made periodic runs for water from the well.

On one of those water runs, a soldier from their own camp betrayed them. He crossed over to the other side and told Castro's forces where the men were hiding.

"We know you're in there," shouted the leader of a large platoon of *milicianos*. "Come out. We'll give you food, condensed milk, water."

"Be quiet," Battle told his men. "Don't say a word."

Castro's soldiers moved in and flushed out what remained of Battle's platoon, who were weak and starving.

As the men were rounded up, Battle saw a Castro soldier whom he recognized. It was his cousin. The two men's eyes met—a look of recognition and acknowledgment—but there were no smiles. The cousin sneered at Battle. Loudly, so that the other soldiers could hear him, he said, "If I'd known it was you, I'd have shot you in the head."

THE INVASION WAS AN INTERNAL FAMILY STRUGGLE, CUBAN VERSUS CUBAN. IT WAS not unusual to have family members on opposite sides, brothers fighting brothers, cousins fighting cousins. Battle had once been a powerful man in Cuba, an officer of the law. But now he was a captured prisoner of war, or, as the Castro government preferred to call the fallen brigadistas, traitors, mercenaries, or *gusanos* (worms).

Their capture and imprisonment would be another sorry chapter in the humiliation of Battle and his men. Castro and his armed forces had achieved victory on the battlefield, and now they had a major propaganda coup in their hands. The first order of business was to make sure the men of the brigade were fully aware that they had lost, to put the boot on their esophagus and press down with all the weight of Cuban history.

The prisoners were gathered together at Playa Girón, the site of their initial landing. They were to be loaded onto trucks, buses, and *rastras* (trailer trucks) and transported to Havana. In the first *rastra,* an inordinate number of men were forced into the back of the truck, a tightly sealed, unventilated cargo space. Osmany Cienfuegos, Cuba's minister of public works, oversaw the loading of the truck. At one point, one of his underlings said to him, "Sir, we can't put any more in there; they will die."

Loudly, so that everyone could hear, the minister said, "Let them die. It will save us having to shoot them." He called for "forty more *gusanos*" to be loaded on the truck.

One hundred forty-nine captured men were transported on an eighthour drive that one of the survivors later described as "like Dante's inferno." Packed so tight that they were unable to move or breathe, some of the men called out, "I have no air! I'm going to die!" The men banged and clawed at the aluminum walls of the truck. The heat was so intense that the condensation of moisture caused the walls and ceiling of the truck's interior to sweat, so that the men marinated in their own bodily juices. Later, one of the men said, "When you are going to die, the first is a very deep sleep. If you sleep, you die." If the men saw one of their brothers doze off or pass out, they jostled him back to life. Some sank into unconsciousness and could not be revived.

By the time the truck reached Havana, the men were too numb and depleted even to cry out for their lives. When the door was opened, they fell out like rag dolls, lifeless and drenched in sweat. Nine men had been asphyxiated to death on the drive. Another died shortly thereafter. It was a higher casualty total than many of the battles that had taken place during combat.

Eventually, 1,019 captured brigadistas were herded into the Palacio de los Deportes, Havana's Sports Palace, an arena normally used for such events as boxing and basketball. For the next twenty days, the men were held at the facility under primitive conditions. They were not allowed to bathe, shave, or change clothes; the stench of battle and days of survival in the swamps led to skin diseases and body odors that made them gag. Their names were called out one by one, and they were separated according to battalion. The men did not yet know who among them had survived. At one point, they were given food, but it was laced with jalap, a powerful purgative that made them violently sick, causing them to defecate uncontrollably. Firehoses were brought in to wash away the feces. The men were allowed only three hours of sleep a day upon soiled mattresses that were laid out in the center of the arena under bright klieg lights.

After a few days at the Sports Palace, Fidel Castro himself appeared. A master of psychological manipulation, Castro spoke to the men in the paternalistic tones of a schoolmaster. He told them that they had been used by the U.S. president, Kennedy, and that they had fought valiantly in an ignoble cause. He said that he had every right to shoot them as traitors, but that the revolution would be fair with them. He would spare their lives.

Over the next few days, the prisoners were paraded before television cameras from around the world as symbols of defeat. After that, they were transferred to the Castillo del Príncipe, an eighteenth-century stone Spanish castle that had been converted into a prison, located on the eastern edge of Havana, on a plateau across the harbor from Habana Vieja (Old Havana). From there the prisoners could occasionally see the great city that so many of them had left behind years ago when they first left their homeland.

In late March 1962, in an open courtyard at Príncipe, the show trials began. Each day the men were made to sit in their yellow prison fatigues and watch a tribunal take place, at which they were condemned for their actions and found guilty of the charge of treason. A five-man commission of Cuban government ministers imposed a fine—what they called reparations—ranging from $25,000 per man up to $500,000, depending on the person's role in the invasion. After everyone had been individually convicted, they were separated, with 114 of the prisoners transferred to the notorious prison on the Isle of Pines off the southern coast of Cuba.

Among those transferred to the Isle of Pines was José Miguel Battle, who at trial had been fined $100,000. As a former member of Batista's notoriously corrupt police force, and a second lieutenant in command of a platoon during the invasion, he held a special place as a *gusano* of distinction. He was placed in a section of the prison called the Squares, the punishment cells, where he was incarcerated with, among others, his fellow platoonmates Fidel and Ramon Fuentes.

At the Isle of Pines prison, Battle was also reunited with paratrooper Raul Martinez, whom he had rescued along with his men on the road to San Blas.

It was an emotional moment for Martinez. He told Battle, "Thank you for saving my life. You showed tremendous courage that night."

Battle said, "*Gracias*," but he did not brag or boast about his actions. "He seemed like a humble type of guy. If he was admired—and he certainly was—it was because of his actions, not his words, because he did not try to make himself out to be a hero."

It was at the Isle of Pines prison that members of 2506 Brigade began to develop a bond for which they would eventually became famous among Cuban Americans. Back at Base Trax, before the invasion, they had been trained separately as battalions; during the invasion they had been deployed as specialized units and were often unaware of how things had been going for other units; during capture and imprisonment, they were kept in separate cells. It was only now in their incarceration that they were reunited with fellow platoon members and allowed to circulate together as one large group.

For Martinez, who was to turn twenty-one during his time at the prison, it was a revelation. He got to know Battle, who was ten years his senior. They sat in the prison and talked about life. "We talked about whorehouses in Havana. He was an expert on that. We talked about our sexual initiations and the initiation of all our buddies in Havana. He said, 'Yeah, we had a lot of fun.' Everyone knew that the police under Batista had been corrupt; he didn't have to tell me that. I hadn't yet learned that he had been a bagman for [Santo] Trafficante or anything like that, but that wouldn't have surprised me. He was that type of guy. I'm sure that amongst underworld figures, he was very trusted."

What made Martinez sense that Battle could or might have been a power broker among all types was the ease with which he assumed control at the Isle of Pines prison. Battle took over the role, or had been acceded the responsibility, of the man who controlled access to the prison patio. It was a prestigious position. The patio was the only location where the men were able to take in the fabulous Caribbean sunshine. The space was limited and therefore access needed to be regulated. The prison guards allowed the inmates to police themselves in this regard, and Battle was the man in charge.

At the lieutenant's side during his time as guardian of the patio, Martinez noted, was Angel Mujica, who Martinez learned had been a member of Battle's vice squad in Havana and during the invasion had been a part of his platoon. Battle was fat, and Mujica was thin. To Martinez, they reminded him of the famous Hollywood movie duo El Flaco y El Gordo (Laurel and Hardy). At the Isle of Pines prison, they were inseparable.

THERE WAS NO GLASS IN THE PRISON'S BARRED WINDOWS; CARVED OUT OF THE STONE walls, they were open to the air. The prison was surrounded by hills comprised largely of iron ore. During torrential tropical storms, the iron deposits attracted lightning; the noise from the thunder and lightning was so loud that men covered their ears with their hands for fear of damage to their eardrums.

As with any extended period of incarceration, the days were mundane and filled with boredom. The men sought to use their time productively by holding classes on Cuban history and aspects of Cuban culture. They held English classes. Among the imprisoned brigade members were a number of Catholic priests who held mass on Sundays. During the week, the prisoners recited poems and sang songs together.

No visitors or letters were allowed in the punishment cells at the Isle of Pines prison. The prisoners held in them communicated with the others through Morse code, a skill they had all learned during their training at Base Trax. By spelling out words and phrases by waving a cloth, and receiving responses in similar fashion, the prisoners in the punishment cells gained information. In October 1962, via the code, they received news of an extraordinary event that was descending upon their narrow, cloistered little world like an ominous tropical storm.

To the outside world it became known as the Cuban Missile Crisis and was viewed as an extension of the Cold War. Earlier that month, U.S surveillance planes had discovered that Russian missiles were being stockpiled in Cuba, which the Kennedy administration viewed as a hostile act. Castro had covertly authorized the placement of the Soviet missiles in the wake of the Bay of Pigs invasion. Tense negotiations followed between JFK and Soviet premier Nikita Khrushchev. For a time it seemed that the fate of both countries and perhaps the world hung in the balance.

Since there were no newspapers or radios or television at the Isle of Pines prison, the inmates only knew what they were able to glean from visitors. Information spread through the prison as gossip and speculation. During the period of negotiation between the U.S. and Soviet governments, Cuban B-52s and MIG fighter jets flew low over the prison, which the brigade survivors took as a show of force to warn them that if the U.S. were to invade the island, it was going to be all-out war.

An incident during the crisis caught the attention of many prisoners. One afternoon, the commander of the Isle of Pines garrison—not the head of the prison, but rather the general of the Cuban troops stationed on the isle—came to the patio. The general was a good friend of one of the brigadistas, Albert Fowler, who came from a wealthy family that had owned sugar mills in Cuba. Back in the 1950s, the general and Albert Fowler had been in the Sierra Maestra together fighting against Batista.

The other prisoners were aware that the general and Fowler had once been fellow revolutionaries, and they made room for the two to sit together and talk. Many inmates nearby attempted to eavesdrop on the conversation. The general seemed to sense as much; he spoke loudly so that others could hear.

"Albert," he announced to his old friend, "I want to tell you something. You are my brother from the Sierra Maestra. We became brothers fighting against the dictator Batista. But, unfortunately, I have an order from the commander in chief to shoot all of you the minute an American lands here. You understand? If an American paratrooper happens to land on this isle, I personally am going to come here and kill all of you."

There was a long silence, and then Fowler said to his old friend, "General, don't be a *lambe culo* (ass kisser). If the Americans land, come with us. We'll protect you. Because they are our friends and will do as we say."

Many of the men laughed, in a display of gallows humor.

Within days, the crisis was over. Premier Khrushchev agreed to remove the missiles from Cuba. An international disaster was averted.

What the prisoners did not know at the time was that President Kennedy, as part of the bargain with Khrushchev—and by extension, Fidel Castro—had guaranteed that there would be no more invasions or acts of military aggression by the United States against the Castro government. Later, when this detail became known to veterans of the 2506 Brigade, some saw it as yet another example of JFK's selling them out behind their backs.

WITHIN WEEKS OF THE SOVIET MISSILES BEING REMOVED FROM CUBA, THE PRISONERS began to hear an astounding rumor. In letters from loved ones in the United States, they learned that Castro and the Kennedy administration were in negotiations that could bring about their release. This rumor was confirmed by Berta Barreto, the mother of a prisoner who had become the liaison with an organization in Washington, D.C., called the Cuban Families Committee and who was allowed into the prison on a semi-regular basis to give the prisoners updates on negotiations.

The United States would not pay cash to the Cuban government in exchange for the prisoners; this would have been viewed as paying ransom. Instead, they were offering to meet Castro's demand of $62 million by furnishing the equivalent amount in tractors and farming equipment, medical supplies, and other "necessities" that were in short supply on the island. There had already been ups and downs in the negotiations, with the mercurial Castro making unrealistic demands, and the U.S. negotiators sometimes making promises they were not able to keep.

"I want to caution you," Berta Barreto informed the prisoners. "The process has been slow and difficult, but we will continue until every prisoner is set free."

The men were hopeful. Recalled Raul Martinez, "All of the men wanted to gain access to the patio so they could get a suntan, in the event that we were released."

The weeks passed, and the rumors persisted. By December, the word was that they would be released in time for Christmas, which seemed too good to be true.

On December 22, a Saturday, the men were taken out, shaved, and given haircuts, shoes, and fresh uniforms. They were offered a lavish meal with fresh meat. The men devoured the food. Throughout the months of incarceration, their prison diet had been so poor, so devoid of nutritional value and taste, that their stomachs had shrunk. Now, as they gorged themselves, some became sick. That night, in expectation that freedom was near, few of them slept.

The following morning, the men were awakened early. They were taken from the prison and flown to San Antonio de los Baños Airfield in Havana province. There, they were met by the other prisoners from Príncipe Castle. The men were given new clothes and allowed to rest on brand-new cots.

Even though by now it appeared they were being released, some of the men could not believe it. Said Raul Martinez, "It wasn't until we were transported to the airport that I really believed what was happening. We saw the plane with the Pan Am logo, and then we knew: we were returning to the United States."

The men were flown to the Air Force base at Homestead in South Florida. They disembarked at 6:45 P.M. and were met by a throng of media people and by immigration officials and volunteers from the Red Cross. Two more flights filled with prisoners arrived that night.

The entire brigade was taken to Dinner Key Auditorium in downtown Miami, where they were reunited with their families and treated to another banquet-style meal.

The sudden return to civilization was jarring. Some of the men found it difficult to be in the company of their families, preferring to huddle with fellow members of the brigade. Though family members were understandably thrilled to see their loved ones, it was mostly a solemn gathering, with many of the newly freed men struggling to take it all in.

They had shared a singular experience; now there were mixed feelings of shame, pride, loss, and defiance. These men had been dragged through a process of defeat that was designed to crush their spirit. Though they were surrounded by family members and others in the community who had suffered along with them and had tirelessly advocated for their release, they knew that no one could possibly comprehend what they had been through except their fellow brigadistas. They had survived by banding together. Now they would be united by their shared legacy of what had taken place on the battlefield and as prisoners of war. It was a legacy that would, for better or for worse, shape their lives and the lives of those around them for generations to come.

2

BIRDS OF A FEATHER

A FEW DAYS AFTER 1,113 SURVIVING MEMBERS OF THE 2506 BRIGADE WERE RELEASED from prison (six men had died from war injuries or other causes while incarcerated), President John F. Kennedy announced that he and his wife would be attending a ceremony at the Orange Bowl in Miami to welcome the men home and thank them for their service. There was a strong difference of opinion among brigade survivors about whether or not this was a good thing. Some of the men made it known that they would boycott the event. Emotions ran deep. Pepe San Román, one of three commanders in chief of the brigade, years later expressed his feelings in an interview:

> I hated the United States and felt that I had been betrayed. Every day it became worse and then I was getting madder and madder and I wanted to get a rifle and come and fight against the U.S. Sometimes the feeling came very strong to me that they had thrown us there knowing they were not going to help us. Many times I had the feeling that we were thrown there to see what happened, because they were sure that Fidel was going to capture us and put all of us in front of a firing squad and we would be killed and there would be a great scandal in the whole world. Sometimes I felt like that. And sometimes I felt they had changed their minds at the last moment, and they didn't have time to give us the order to come back. But anyhow I felt that if they had organized us and taken us through a whole year of that training, even if the world was going to fall to pieces, they should not have forgotten us.

Even so, San Román believed that Kennedy's visit was a good thing. Not only would he attend, but he would do so as part of a ranking committee that would present to the president the flag of the 2506 Brigade that for three days of fighting had flown over the command post at Playa Girón.

José Miguel Battle would also be in attendance at the Orange Bowl. In later years, Battle would sometimes express the presentment common to many former brigadistas that the United States had betrayed the brigade and that the main person responsible was Kennedy. But in the days and weeks following his release from prison, he, like many anti-Castro activists, had not yet given up the fight. And whether the Cuban militants liked it or not, the United States was still their best hope for removing Castro and establishing an alternative government on the island.

It was an overcast day on December 29, 1962, when President Kennedy and his wife, Jacqueline, were driven into the stadium in a white convertible. The cavernous Orange Bowl was filled nearly to capacity with forty thousand people—brigade survivors and their families, community members, Kennedy supporters, and a huge phalanx of media personnel in place to cover this extraordinary event.

A platform had been set up at the fifty-yard line, with a podium adorned with the presidential seal of the United States. Before stepping to the podium, Kennedy greeted a line of brigade members, some of whom were missing limbs and others on crutches.

The first to speak was Pepe San Román. Into a microphone, he said to the large crowd, "We know how precious liberty is and we know that Cuba has no liberty. The 2506 Brigade, we offer ourselves to God and to the free world as warriors in the battle against communism . . . We don't know how or in what form the opportunity will come for us to fight in the cause of Cuba. Whenever, however, wherever, in whatever honorable form it may come, we will do what we can to be better prepared to meet and complete our mission."

San Román turned to the president. "Mr. President, the men of the 2506 Brigade give you their banner. We temporarily deposit it with you for your safekeeping."

To thunderous applause, the flag, which had been neatly folded, was handed to the young president. Kennedy unfurled the flag—to even louder applause—then stepped to the microphone. The first thing he said was, "I want to express my great appreciation to the brigade for making the United States the custodian of this flag." And then, his voice rising with emotion, he declared, "I can assure you that this flag will be returned to this brigade in a free Havana."

The entire audience rose to its feet, cheering wildly, with shouts of "*Guerra! Guerra!*" and "*Libertad! Libertad!*" Some of the brigade members had tears in their eyes.

The president then gave a formal speech, which he addressed directly to the men of the brigade. "Your small brigade is a tangible reaffirmation that the human desire for freedom and independence is essentially unconquerable. Your conduct and valor are proof that although Castro and his fellow dictators may rule nations, they do not rule people; that they may imprison bodies, but they do not imprison spirits; that they may destroy the exercise of liberty, but they cannot eliminate the determination to be free." He urged the Cubans in exile to uphold the mythology of the brigade. "Keep alive the spirit of the brigade . . . The brigade is the point of the spear, the arrow's head."

After the president finished his short speech, the First Lady stepped to the microphone. In Spanish, she said to the brigade survivors, "It is an honor for me to be today with a group of the bravest men in the world, and to share in the joy that is felt by their families who for so long lived hoping, praying, and waiting. I feel proud that my son has met the officers. He is still too young to realize what has happened here, but I will make it my business to tell him the story of your courage as he grows up. It is my wish and my hope that someday he may be a man at least half as brave as the members of the 2506 Brigade. Good luck."

By appealing to the men's virility, Jackie Kennedy had charmed the crowd. Raul Martinez, the paratrooper whose life was saved by José Miguel Battle, spoke for many when he said, "Most of my attention that day was spent looking at the First Lady. She spoke in a very sexy Spanish."

The arena was filled with emotion. In the opinion of some, Kennedy had declared that *la lucha*—the struggle—was not over. It was a reaffir-mation of his commitment to unseat Castro. Others viewed the president's words with deep cynicism. Said one brigadista, "Kennedy stopped by and shook my hand. I shook his hand and all that, but under my breath I muttered, 'son of a bitch.'"

Another who was not in attendance stated, "I did not go to the ceremony. I repudiated the act . . . I thought it was demagoguery for Kennedy to [say that he would] give the flag back to the Cubans after he had betrayed us."

Grayston Lynch, a CIA agent who had been a key organizer of the invasion, said of the event, "It was the first time it ever snowed in the Orange Bowl: Kennedy gave them a snow job."

The feelings toward the president were complicated, to say the least. Certainly the overwhelming majority of the men of the brigade felt deep in their hearts that they had been betrayed by the U.S. govern-ment. The initial response was that this betrayal must have started at the top. Subsequent dissections of the invasion, in detailed media accounts, book-length investigations, and oral histories, shifted some blame to the CIA. In particular, Deputy Director Richard Bissell, who ran the operation for the CIA, had been asked by the president, "If I call off air cover for these men, can they still win?" Bissell said, "Yes." The fate of the brigade was sealed. Attempts by Kennedy supporters to shift blame to the CIA, and thus rewrite history, were resented by the CIA and its acolytes. But on the day of Kennedy's appearance at the Orange Bowl, there was a softening of the animosity toward him as an individual, a sense that the betrayal experienced by the brigade went beyond Kennedy and was somehow attributable to the vicissitudes of fate, or the gods, who for some reason had left them stranded on the beach.

One thing seemed clear: the guilt that Kennedy felt for whatever role he may have played in the failure of the mission was genuine. And guilt could be a powerful motivator. For some in the still flourishing anti-Castro movement, Kennedy's guilt was seen as a factor to be harnessed and manipulated.

The president sought to make amends through an unprecedented offer: since the men of the brigade had been trained by the U.S. military,

he announced that any and all members of 2506 Brigade could enter any
branch of the U.S. military, and in doing so, would be given status as
citizens of the United States. All they had to do was apply.

Many former brigadistas jumped at the chance; nearly half of the
brigade, including men who had been seriously wounded, enlisted in

he announced that any and all members of 2506 Brigade could enter any
branch of the U.S. military, and in doing so, would be given status as
citizens of the United States. All they had to do was apply.

Many former brigadistas jumped at the chance: nearly half of the
brigade, including men who had been seriously wounded, enlisted in
the U.S. armed forces just two months after their liberation. One of
those men was José Miguel Battle.

For Battle, it was an obvious choice. Arriving in Miami after his
release, like most of the prisoners, he had no job or profession to speak
of. He was a former Havana cop, perhaps tainted by associations with
the notoriously corrupt regime of Fulgencio Batista. He could return to
Union City, where he still had partial ownership in a bar, but what was
being offered by the president was a higher calling. Not only that, if he
joined the armed forces and became a legal citizen, his wife and son in
Cuba would be able to secure U.S. visas and finally join him in the land
of milk and honey.

On March 17, 1963, two and a half months after being released from
the Isle of Pines prison, Battle enlisted in the U.S. Army. He was allowed
to join at the same grade, or rank, he had had while in the brigade—
second lieutenant. It was noted on his enlistment form that he had been
an infantry unit commander. He was stationed at Fort Benning, Georgia,
where he was able to forgo basic training, which he had already received
at Base Trax in Guatemala. He was enlisted as a fully commissioned
officer, and would be receiving advanced military training at the U.S.
Army Infantry School.

Just as important to Battle, he was able to get his wife and son out
of Cuba. They traveled to Georgia and were able to live on the base, in
a complex of homes specifically designed for soldiers and their families.

At Fort Benning, Battle was stationed with other Cuban exiles, many
of whom had served with the brigade. Included in this group was Angel
Mujica, Battle's prison mate from the Isle of Pines.

The CIA had a strong presence at the base and had already begun
a vigorous recruitment campaign of Cuban exiles to serve in a newly
christened covert scheme to kill Castro. The plan to take back Cuba
was an anticommunist operation. It was made clear that by enlisting
in the clandestine war against Castro, the exiles would become soldiers

in the Cold War, which would involve proxy undertakings in other countries—especially in Latin America—that were in danger of falling under the thrall of Castroism.

Over the next twelve months, Fort Benning would serve as a nexus and incubation chamber for this "holy war." CIA agents and operatives, along with Cuban exiles in training, came together in a spirit of purpose and camaraderie. The overall mission may have been philosophical and global, defined by the parameters of communism versus capitalism, but the number one bullet point on the agenda remained the need to kill Castro and reclaim Cuba.

THE U.S. GOVERNMENT'S EFFORTS TO ASSASSINATE FIDEL CASTRO HAD RUN PARAL-lel with the Bay of Pigs invasion. Cuban exiles were always a central element in the assassination plots, though the overall plan had grown out of an alliance between the CIA and a group of American mobsters that the Agency designated in its internal communications as "the gambling syndicate." These were men who had been deeply invested in the casinos and nightclubs in Havana during the Batista era of the 1950s. Ever since Castro marched into the capital city, they had harbored dreams of exacting revenge and restoring Havana to its former "glory."

The key man was Santo Trafficante, José Miguel Battle's Mafia contact back in his days as a cop in Havana. Since leaving Havana, Trafficante had been absorbed in efforts to overthrow Castro. He had cofinanced and partnered with co-conspirators in assassination schemes devised by Cuban exiles, fellow mobsters, counterrevolutionaries, and at least two Cuban ex-presidents, Fulgencio Batista and Carlos Prío Socarrás.

By the time Trafficante met with a representative of the CIA, at the Fontainebleau Hotel in Miami Beach in October 1960, training of the 2506 Brigade was under way. The CIA plot to overthrow Castro was a two-track operation. Track one was the invasion. Track two was the assassination of Castro, which would pave the way for a new president and government council chosen by the CIA to be put into place. A cadre of high-ranking CIA officials had been selected by director John Foster Dulles to oversee what was initially referred to as "the Cuba Project."

Secretly, the U.S. government had allied itself with gangsters at various times as deemed necessary. During World War II, U.S. Naval Intelligence had enlisted the aid of the Mob in ferreting out German spies and saboteurs in various ports along the eastern seaboard. Meyer Lansky had been a primary liaison between the Navy and the Mob, most notably by making it clear that Charles "Lucky" Luciano, who was in prison on prostitution charges, was the only person powerful enough to authorize the Mob's cooperation. Out of what they called "patriotism," Lansky and Luciano agreed to aid the war effort. They also manipulated the relationship to bring about the commutation of Luciano's prison sentence.

So the U.S. government was not above partnering with professional hoodlums. But in initiating a program that included the use of the Mafia to carry out a political assassination, the CIA was entering new territory. It was the beginning of an expedient alliance between the CIA, the Mob, and Cuban exiles that would last for half a century and change the course of U.S. history.

At the Fontainebleau, Trafficante was present along with fellow mafiosi Johnny Roselli and Sam Giancana. The CIA representative in attendance was a man named Robert Mahue. Technically, Mahue was a retired agent working as the chief executive of Nevada operations for the billionaire industrialist Howard Hughes. He also had his own investigative agency, which he would many years later admit was a CIA front so that he could undertake "cut-out" assignments—jobs in which the Agency could not be officially involved.

Mahue's initial contact had been with Roselli, a West Coast–based mafioso, but Roselli had quickly brought Trafficante into the loop. Santo was the one with contacts in the militant Cuban exile community who could be used to facilitate any assassination plot.

Various exile groups were already deeply involved in efforts to kill Castro. One of these was Rescate, a counterrevolutionary group that had begun in Havana and was still active on the island. Trafficante had contacts in this group that, he surmised, had spies inside the Castro government who could get close to Fidel.

Mahue, speaking on behalf of the Agency, told the mobsters they would be paid $150,000 to get the job done. But Trafficante, Roselli, and Giancana made it clear that they did not expect or want to be paid. They were willing to undertake the assignment out of a sense of "patriotic duty."

The timing was propitious for the mobsters, and almost too good to be true. The Kennedy Justice Department, led by Attorney General Robert Kennedy, had been hammering the Mafia ever since the Kennedys came into office. During the first six months of 1961, 171 Mafia-related defendants around the United States were given prison sentences, compared to just four in 1960. If Trafficante, Roselli, and Giancana could somehow blunt the Justice Department's Mafia obsession by helping out another branch of federal law enforcement—the CIA—then it was well worth the effort.

Over the next few months there would be many assassination schemes facilitated by the CIA's Technical Services Division (TSD). Many of the most outlandish ideas never got past the planning stage. There was the scheme to plant an exploding seashell near where Castro went snorkeling. The idea was that he would be drawn to the exotic seashell, would bend down to pick it up, and it would blow up in his face. There was the plot to dust Castro's shoes with thallium salts, a strong depilatory that would cause his beard to fall out, bringing about public humiliation for the dictator. There was the plot to infiltrate Havana's preeminent broadcasting studio, where Fidel regularly gave speeches over the radio, and spray it with a chemical similar to LSD, causing the dictator to talk gibberish and go mad. There were the exploding cigars, or the cigars contaminated with a botulin toxin so potent that a person would die after putting one in his mouth. There was a plot to insert a syringe containing deadly poison inside a ballpoint pen; if an infiltrator could get close enough to Fidel, they could plunge the syringe into his neck and kill him instantly.

Some of these plots were actually put into action, including one involving Trafficante and Roselli.

The CIA's technical lab had created some poison pills that could be dropped into a glass of liquid; they would dissolve and be virtually undetectable. In March 1961, shortly before the Bay of Pigs invasion, the pills were passed along to the mobsters, who informed Robert Mahue that, through their contacts in the Rescate group, they could find someone close enough to Castro to plant the pills in his drink.

The man who provided the mobsters with this information was Manuel Antonio de Varona, better known as Tony Varona, one of the cofounders of Rescate. An active anticommunist in the United States, Varona had been friendly with Santo Trafficante back in Havana. Since leaving Cuba after the revolution, Varona and others had established a camp outside of New Orleans, aided by the CIA, that was currently training counterrevolutionaries for covert ops and clandestine acts of sabotage, industrial and otherwise. In addition, Varona, along with Manuel Artime, one of the three commanders in chief of the 2506 Brigade, had founded a group in the United States called Movement for the Recovery of the Revolution (MRR). Varona also maintained active contacts among the many underground groups in Cuba.

Through Varona and his contacts in Havana, the mobsters learned that Castro was known to frequent a Chinese restaurant called Pekín. The idea was to deliver the pills to a worker at the restaurant who could do the deed. Varona informed Trafficante and the others that they would need to pay $1,000 for communications equipment to carry out the plot, and $50,000 to pay the operatives in Havana who would pull it off.

The money and pills were delivered at a meeting between Mahue, Trafficante, Roselli, and Tony Varona at a room in the Fontainebleau Hotel. Many years later, at the hearings of a U.S. congressional committee in Washington, D.C., Johnny Roselli recalled that Mahue "opened his briefcase and dumped a whole lot of money" out onto the bed. Mahue "also came up with the capsules and he explained how they were going to be used. As far as I remember, they couldn't be used in boiling soups and things like that, but they could be used in water or otherwise, but they couldn't last forever . . . It had to be done quickly as possible."

The pills were delivered to Cuba and the plot became active, but then the Bay of Pigs invasion occurred. Given the results of that fiasco, this particular plot was aborted.

While captured soldiers of the 2506 Brigade languished in prison, the assassination plots continued. One involved the use of James B. Donovan, the Washington, D.C., lawyer who was acting as the Kennedy administration's primary negotiator with Fidel Castro to gain the release of prisoners. It was learned that throughout the often tense negotiations, Donovan and Castro had developed a friendly bond. The Agency saw this as an opportunity. A plan was devised to have Donovan present Castro with the gift of a skin diving suit contaminated with an invisible fungus that would produce a disabling and chronic skin disease and infect the breathing apparatus with a lethal tubercle bacillus. The plan advanced to the stage where a suit was created and prepared for delivery, but then it was learned that Donovan had already given Castro a wetsuit.

There is no record that Donovan, or, for that matter, President Kennedy, who were involved in delicate negotiations with Castro based on trust and honesty, were ever informed of this ill-fated scheme.

After the prisoners were released, the plots to get Castro did not end. In fact, they ascended to a new level of development.

In a room at the Mayflower Hotel in Washington, D.C., Attorney General Robert Kennedy personally met with former brigade commander Manuel Artime and a handful of exiles who constituted a ruling body in a renewed effort to take back Cuba. RFK apologized on behalf of the U.S. government, telling the men, "My brother was wrong. We made some tactical mistakes. We accept responsibility for what you went through and we want to make it right. This will be an all-out effort. We want your men to proceed in their activities and use any means necessary to take out Castro."

Present at that meeting was Francisco "Pepe" Hernandez. Back in the 1950s in Havana, Hernandez had been a member of Rescate with Tony Varona. Later, as a member of the 2506 Brigade's Second Battalion, Hernandez landed at Playa Larga, at the northern end of the Bay of Pigs. There, as with the entire invasion, events turned ugly almost from the inception. Hernandez's platoon was overrun, and for two weeks he sought to stay alive in the Zapata swamps with no food or water. Eventually, famished to the point of being delusional, he saw what he thought was an orange tree, though he would forever after be unsure whether the tree was real or a hallucination. In any event, he and three other men tried to get to that succulent fruit and in so doing were captured by Cuban militia. Coincidentally, one of the men captured with Hernandez was José Miguel Battle's brother-in-law.

Hernandez was thrown into the Castillo del Príncipe prison and held there until James Donovan negotiated the prisoners' release. Like many others, Hernandez took advantage of President Kennedy's offer to gain U.S. citizenship by joining the military, in his case, the Marine Corps.

So now, in early 1963, Hernandez was standing in a hotel room with Robert Kennedy, the attorney general. "I got the impression," said Hernandez, "that the Kennedy brothers were of a type that they were not going to take what had happened with the invasion lying down. It was not their nature to accept defeat." The president's brother reiterated that the commitment to overthrow Castro was stronger than ever. The president had described the brigade as "the point of the spear, the arrow's head" for a reason. Said Pepe Hernandez, "The phrase I remember from Bobby Kennedy most vividly was that we were to use 'any means necessary' in the pursuit of our goals."

The main headquarters would be in Miami, where the CIA opened a newly reinvigorated station code-named JM/WAVE. It would be the largest CIA station in the world. The new initiative was code-named Operation Mongoose. The operatives in this battle were spreading far and wide: there were double agents active in Cuba, operatives training in places like Louisiana and in South America, and CIA operatives active in the U.S. military. And in the summer of 1963, the place where many of these people crossed paths, interfaced, and traded intelligence was the U.S. military training base at Fort Benning, Georgia.

TO JOSÉ MIGUEL BATTLE, PLAYING POKER WAS A HIGHLY SOCIAL ACTIVITY, LIKE HANGing out at the corner bar or going to church on Sunday. It was through gambling that he met with old friends, made new ones, and established alliances. Those who knew him said he was never so relaxed as when he was playing cards, even when he lost money, as he often did. To Battle, playing poker wasn't about the money; it was about the camaraderie. Around a card table was where he held court.

At Fort Benning, José Miguel became known for presiding over card games that lasted for hours. The games took place inside the barracks where the 212 Cuban exiles were stationed separately from the other U.S. Army trainees.

There was nothing on the official record of Battle or of the other Cubans that would show that there was anything special about their activities. And yet in fact they were training covertly under the auspices of the CIA. In the spring and summer of 1963, some of the most ambitious and notorious figures in the anti-Castro movement would receive training at Fort Benning.

One of those men was Luis Posada Carriles, who many years later would say to a *New York Times* reporter of his time at Fort Benning, "The CIA taught us everything . . . They taught us explosives, how to kill, bomb, trained us in acts of sabotage."

Posada met Battle for the first time in a card game. Battle, who was sometimes referred to by the nickname "El Gordo," because he had put back on much of the weight he lost while in prison, was with his sidekick, Angel Mujica, his fellow cop from Havana, platoon mate, and fellow doorman to the patio at Isle of Pines prison.

The game was for small stakes, four to six guys sitting around a table. The Cubans, recently out of prison, did not have a lot of money to throw around. The poker games were mostly a way for the men to get to know one another, and in any case, gambling for money was prohibited on the base. When a player was not sitting in on a game, he acted as a lookout, though the sergeants and other officers seemed to be tolerant of the Cubans' card playing.

To Posada, Battle had presence. His skin was dark; he was friendly and had an earthy sense of humor. "I liked him," remembered Posada, "and I could see that he was not a man to be taken lightly." Unlike Posada, who had attended university, Battle did not have much formal education, but he had street smarts. Posada had good feelings about him even though he recognized something about the man almost immediately: he cheated at cards. Posada caught Battle stacking the deck, but they both laughed about it, since the games were not serious.

The stories of Battle's heroism during the invasion were part of his reputation. As a fellow operative in the invasion, Posada was impressed. Posada himself had not been part of the invading brigade. Rather, he had played a different role as part of what were known as "infiltration teams," an aspect of the invasion that some viewed as even more important than the military incursion.

Born in Cienfuegos in 1928, Posada had attended the University of Havana in the late 1940s, where he studied medicine and chemistry.

There, he made the acquaintance of Fidel Castro, a student at the university who was known to be politically active.

Posada was not overtly political at the time. Like many young Cubans, he was intrigued by the possibilities of the revolution but quickly turned against Fidel. In 1958 and 1959, he was employed by Firestone Tire and Rubber Company in Havana while secretly serving in the underground resistance. He was briefly jailed, and in 1961 he fled to Mexico, where he sought political asylum in the Argentine embassy. He made his way to the United States and, thanks to his previous connections, landed a job with Firestone at their plant in Akron, Ohio. Once again, his job with Firestone was something of a cover for his clandestine activities. He was officially listed as a Firestone employee in Akron while he was off in Guatemala training at Base Trax.

Even before the invasion, Posada was committed to the cause; he was part of a CIA initiative code-named Operation 40, a counterintelligence group that in 1960 had been authorized by President Dwight Eisenhower and overseen by Vice President Richard Nixon, the State Department, and the National Security Administration.

Operation 40 was composed of men who would go on to be among the most active Cuban exiles in the anti-Castro movement, including, among others, Orlando Bosch, Felix Rodriguez, and future Watergate burglars Bernard Barker and Frank Sturgis.

Sturgis in particular had a notorious personal history. He had been involved in the Cuban Revolution with Castro and later served as the revolutionary government's liaison with the gaming industry (that is, Lansky, Trafficante, and others). But then he switched sides and become a double agent. Sturgis personified the American soldier of fortune. Born Frank Angelo Fiorini in Norfolk, Virginia, he had been at varying times a member of the U.S. Marine Corps, the Navy, and the Army. He'd also been a Norfolk cop. Eventually, he became a gun-toting mercenary and a CIA bottom feeder involved in various Cold War covert ops.

In the late 1970s, in an interview with a journalist, Sturgis described the purpose of Operation 40. The mandate, he explained, was to incite civil war in Cuba through various sabotage operations. The group also had an even darker purpose as a political assassination squad. "This assassination group," he said, "would, upon orders, naturally, assassinate either members of the military or the political parties of the foreign country that you were going to infiltrate, and if necessary some of your own members who were suspected of being foreign agents . . . We were concentrating strictly on Cuba at that particular time."

Luis Posada, like Sturgis, was down for the cause, though even his family members were not supposed to know. José Miguel Battle might not have been aware of the details of a clandestine initiative such as Operation 40, but he knew enough to believe that Luis Posada and others like him were avenging angels in a holy crusade. At Fort Benning, he treated Posada with deference and respect. Said Posada, "He made it clear to me that we had a huge common ground in our fight against Castro. Anytime we met, the topic of conversation was the same—the need to kill Castro by any means necessary. He was a patriot. He said many times that whether he was directly involved or not, we could always count on him as a supporter of our activities."

Another thing the two men had in common was that they both liked guns. At Fort Benning, Battle presented Posada with a gift—a black snub-nosed Smith & Wesson .38-caliber handgun. It was not an expensive or fancy weapon; the gun probably sold for around $40. But Posada was touched by the gesture.

Through the summer of 1963 and into the fall, Posada and his cohorts dreamed about and actively planned for the overthrow of Castro. Operation Mongoose was gathering steam. According to declassified CIA documents, between June and September 1963, President Kennedy approved more than twenty acts of sabotage against Cuba. For those looking to deplete and disorient Castro's government through a relentless campaign of counterrevolutionary activities, it looked promising. That is, until an event occurred that not only drastically altered their operations, but also changed the course of history. On November 22, in Dallas, Texas, JFK was murdered.

THE KENNEDY ASSASSINATION IS THE RUBIK'S CUBE OF AMERICAN HISTORY: THE subject can be held up to the light and viewed in many different configurations. Over many decades, there have been the Warren Commission Report (first released to the public in September 1964); multiple congressional hearings in the late 1970s; investigative studies by nearly all branches of U.S. law enforcement; an infinite number of documentaries; and a large library of published material, both investigative and speculative. And still no one has solved the puzzle.

In the early days following the shooting, after the gunman Lee Harvey Oswald was apprehended, the emphasis in U.S. media accounts was on the Cuba connection. Oswald was described as a leftist sympathizer and a member of a pro-Castro organization called Fair Play for Cuba. Much was made of a trip he made to the Cuban consulate in Mexico City two months before the assassination to secure a visa to travel to Cuba. An incident was cited from just seven days before the assassination, in which Oswald was in New Orleans passing out pro-Cuba literature on the street and got into a shoving match with three Cuban exiles.

The most provocative piece of evidence of Cuban involvement in the assassination was a quote by Fidel Castro, a comment he had made on September 8, 1963, at the Brazilian embassy in Havana. "The U.S. leaders must realize that if they assist in the terrorist plans to eliminate Cuban leaders, they themselves will be in danger . . . Kennedy is the Batista of our time, and the most opportunistic president of all time . . . The United States is fighting a battle against us that they cannot win."

Eventually, the rush to blame Castro fizzled out. The Warren Commission Report made little mention of a Cuban government connection. A countertheory took shape. In this conspiracy, Oswald had been manipulated by Cuban exiles to carry out the assassination, the theory being that certain exiled militants, in conjunction with Mafia figures such as Santo Trafficante and others, wanted Kennedy dead. These exiles blamed Kennedy for the Bay of Pigs failure and for delivering Cuba into the hands of the Soviet Union; the Mafia despised the Kennedys because of Attorney General Robert Kennedy's vendetta against certain Mafia figures. A marriage of convenience that began with various plots to kill Castro had boomeranged and turned into a conspiracy to murder JFK.

The home base for this conspiracy was New Orleans, where Trafficante met with local Mafia boss Carlos Marcello, who more than any other mobster despised the Kennedys. In April 1961, two weeks before the Bay of Pigs invasion, RFK had humiliated Marcello by having him apprehended by immigration officials and deported by force from the United States. The Sicilian-born Marcello sneaked back into the country and was waging war in federal court with the Immigration and Naturalization Service over his legal status. It was alleged by one of the participants in a 1962 conversation with Trafficante that while discussing a possible assassination of Robert Kennedy, Marcello said, "If you want to kill a dog, you don't cut off the tail, you cut off the head."

Trafficante is alleged to have made it happen, using his contacts in the Cuban exile community. According to a prominent exile activist, José Aleman, when President Kennedy's name came up in a conversation he had with Trafficante, the Mafia boss said, "Don't worry about him. He's going to be hit." According to this version of the conspiracy, Oswald was lured into the plot by New Orleans Mafia co-conspirators and anti-Castro Cuban exiles.

The theory may have seemed far-fetched, but it received considerable support years later in the congressional testimony of Marita Lorenz, a woman known as "Castro's mistress."

In 1959, while visiting Havana as a nineteen-year-old German tourist, Lorenz became romantically involved with Fidel Castro. She became pregnant by him and had an abortion, a fact Castro confirmed to be true. Later that year, after the abortion, she left the island thinking she would never return—that was until she met Frank Sturgis, whom she knew as Frank Fiorini.

Sturgis became Marita's CIA overseer. He convinced her to take part in another assassination attempt on Castro in 1960. Armed with poison pills provided by the CIA, she traveled to Havana and met with Castro, intending to poison his food, but she was forced to abandon the plot when she discovered that the pills had dissolved in a jar of cold cream, where she had hidden them. According to Lorenz, this plot had been devised and carried out under the auspices of Operation 40.

Back in the United States, she continued to circulate in the orbit of Frank Sturgis and the anti-Castro exiles. Before the U.S. House Assassinations Committee in 1977, she testified that, in October 1963, she was present at a meeting in a Miami safe house that included Sturgis, various Cuban exiles affiliated with Operation 40, and Lee Harvey Oswald, whom she knew on that occasion by the nickname "Ozzie."

The group was discussing a trip to Dallas, a map of which was spread out on a table. Marita testified that a few weeks later, just days before the Kennedy assassination, she drove from Miami to Dallas with Sturgis and the same men she had seen at the Little Havana safe house in Miami. They drove in two cars containing eight men, including Orlando Bosch, a man she knew by name, and two brothers whose names she didn't know at the time. They turned out to be Guillermo and Ignacio Novo. All of the men, Sturgis told her, were members of Operation 40.

The group arrived in Dallas with numerous rifles and handguns in the trunks of their cars. The Cubans didn't like that there was a woman present for "the operation," so Lorenz flew back home the following day. She was on a flight to New York City when she learned that JFK had been assassinated in Dallas.

Marita Lorenz was generally dismissed as an unreliable source, but some of the details she mentioned were corroborated by other sources. One name that came up in many of the accounts was Luis Posada. As a member of Operation 40, he carried out operations with many of the men Lorenz claimed to have seen together in Miami and Dallas. Most notably, Posada was part of an Operation 40 group stationed in New Orleans. They had a safe house outside the city from which they based operations, which included a scheme, partially financed by Mob boss Carlos Marcello, to smuggle military equipment to Cuba to carry out counterrevolutionary activities on the island.

In this hornet's nest of co-conspirators, alliances were formed, paths crossed, and assumptions made that led to a tantalizing classification: guilt by association. These names and alliances may or may not hold the key to understanding the killing of President Kennedy. Over time, they have come to comprise a historical sinkhole of personages that has spread a patina of suspicion over many, including, at least peripherally, José Miguel Battle Sr.

In 1977, the House Committee on Assassinations, as part of its investigation into the Kennedy assassination, asked the Cuban Department of State Security if they would undertake a joint investigation into the killing of Kennedy. Through a thorough examination of declassified files of the U.S. intelligence community and the Cuban Security Agency, it was felt that a more complete account of the conspiracy could be formulated. The man in charge of this investigation on the Cuban side, Fabián Escalante, published a number of books based on the joint investigation in a series subtitled *The Secret War*. In a section of the book where the author speculates on the many co-conspirators, including those who may have been among the alleged backup shooters on "the grassy knoll," at least two were described by an underworld source as "Cuban exile friends of Trafficante." Writes Escalante, "It was rumored that one of the Cubans was a former police agent from the Havana vice squad who had gone on to become a gangster."

There is no verifiable evidence, or even credible rumors, that Battle was among the men who assassinated JFK. In fact, the evidence that Cuban exiles were involved in the assassination is intriguing but hardly conclusive.

Certainly there were people within the militant core of the exile underground who hated Kennedy enough to want him dead, and some of those people had the skills to plan and attempt such a plot. But the exiles had nothing to gain by killing President Kennedy. The Kennedy brothers had been steadfast benefactors of Operation Mongoose.

As for Battle, like some other veterans of the 2506 Brigade, it was said that following Kennedy's appearance at the Orange Bowl he had developed some degree of affection for the young president. Particularly, the appearance of wife Jackie Kennedy was fondly remembered. Now to see on television the famous "Zapruder film," eight-millimeter footage from November 22 of JFK's head being blown open by gunfire, the First Lady sprayed with brain matter and then hysterically attempting to climb out of the convertible limousine, was poignant bordering on heartbreaking. Some brigade members may have felt that given how they had been betrayed, Kennedy got what he deserved. But others were horrified.

FOR WEEKS, MONTHS, AND DECADES TO COME, THE KENNEDY ASSASSINATION REVERberated like an atom bomb, with a centrifugal force that threatened to expose the nation's darkest secrets. The immediate effect was that it shut down all official U.S. government efforts to kill Castro. Operation Mongoose was terminated. If indeed the assassination was somehow related to Cuba and the multilayered efforts to destabilize Castro's government and eliminate the Bearded One, the prospect of unprecedented blowback sent shock waves throughout the intelligence community. The mandate now was to cover up the previous years of intensive clandestine activity, little of which had been authorized by Congress or the American people. It was to be buried away under a cloak of secrecy, and would stay that way for more than a decade.

At Fort Benning, activity didn't exactly halt, but there was a cessation of CIA training for clandestine purposes.

José Miguel Battle still had four months left on his tour of duty, but they were not especially distinguished. In January 1964, he accidentally ran a tank over an Army truck during training. He was reprimanded, and it was noted that he had "failed" his training in the area of "automotive." On the other hand, in arms training he was rated "exceptional."

In March, Battle had come to the end of his one-year military commitment with a less than sterling overall record. In the areas of training that might have been useful to an ambitious covert operator—"counterinsurgency" and "survival, escape, and evasion," for example—he hardly showed up. When it came time for his evaluation for promotion from second-grade to first-grade lieutenant, he had not accrued the necessary points for advancement. His promotion was denied.

At the age of thirty-five, Battle was older than many of the men with whom he'd been training. His military record listed his weight at 234 pounds, hefty for someone who stood five feet nine inches tall. Crawling in ditches and submitting to extensive physical training may have lost their appeal to him. By mutual consent, after serving one full year in the armed service, he received an honorable discharge from active duty. He would remain in the Army Reserves for three more years.

With his wife and son in tow, Battle was first discharged to an address in New York City, at 137 West 83rd Street, on the Upper West Side of Manhattan. There he was reunited with Angel Mujica, who had left the Army a few months before and settled in New York. Recently, Mujica had started a gambling operation that was based in the Bronx, near Yankee Stadium. It was a small-time operation—late-night poker games, sports betting, and, most notably, the numbers racket, what the police call "policy" and what Cubans and other Latinos refer to as bolita.

Mujica suggested that he and Battle could become partners. Not having Battle's social or leadership capabilities, or his reputation as a Bay of Pigs hero, Mujica saw the advantage of letting Battle build on what he had already started. And for Battle, having spent the last four years of his life in some form of military service, combat, or prison, it was time to create a life in America with his wife and kid—at least until his militant exile compadres succeeded in killing Castro and they could all move back to Cuba.

In the meantime, he set his sights on the modest bedroom community of Union City, just across the Hudson River from Manhattan. Five years earlier, when Battle first fled Cuba, he'd spent some time there. Though there was nothing physically attractive about Union City, Cuban émigrés were settling there in large numbers. The town of some forty thousand people was known as "the Embroidery Capital of the World," and there were many garment-related factories and jobs. In an earlier era, Union City had also been a significant stop on the vaudeville circuit, and it still held many large theaters—now defunct—along Bergenline Avenue, the town's main commercial thoroughfare.

Coincidentally, the town's overlords—its politicians and police force—had a reputation for corruption. They could be bought—which is what you wanted if you had the idea of setting up a system of money-making based on an illegal venture such as the numbers racket.

Battle and his family had no furniture and little in the way of belongings. Through Cuban contacts in New Jersey, they were able to find an apartment near Union City's central commercial area. With little in the way of money, the former Bay of Pigs hero was able to put down roots, but when it came to establishing a gambling business, he had a problem.

One characteristic of a bolita operation was that people who liked to bet the number—whether it was with dimes or dollars—preferred to do so with people they knew. For one thing, if you happened to hit on a given day, you had to know that you would be paid without delay. It was a relationship based on trust. Partly, this was an extension of how the system operated back in Cuba. It was a grassroots business, deeply entwined with the community. Nearly everybody liked to bet the number: little old ladies, priests, cops, teachers, nurses, and those with a more serious gambling habit. You could bet a nickel, or you could bet a hundred dollars, and if the system was set up properly—if it was expertly designed and user-friendly—when people won, they immediately funneled their winnings back into betting on a new set of numbers. Because doing so was irresistible.

With his reputation as a Bay of Pigs legend, Battle had the stature and the know-how to build an effective operation. What he didn't have was money. A numbers operation needed to have a banker, or a series of them, to guarantee payment and cover potential daily losses. Cash money ebbed and flowed on a regular basis; it was the lifeblood of a whimsical game of chance. An organization was only as successful as its ability to absorb sudden and drastic swings in financial fortune.

Mujica's bolita operation was low-end, operating on a shoestring, but it had great potential. Battle recognized the possibilities. He'd seen the way bolita was supposed to be run back in Havana. He'd been friendly with Martín Fox, owner of the Tropicana nightclub and the most successful bolitero in Cuba. Fox made it happen by using as his benefactors some of the most respected—and feared—gangsters in Havana at the time. Battle knew what every cop knows, that people are attracted to power. A bolita operation was like other businesses: to be successful, you needed to have a reputation that was above reproach. You needed to have an operation where no one could challenge you, because they knew it would be against their best interests to do so.

It was time for José Miguel to cash in some chits, to utilize the contacts he'd made and the reputation he'd established over the previous five or six tumultuous years. It was time for him to rekindle his relationship with the man who had helped make it possible for Fox back in Havana, a man who knew his way around the Cuban exile community and would know a stellar business opportunity when he saw one.

From his new base in Union City, Battle knew that it was time to reach out to his old friend Santo Trafficante.

3

SANTO

IN THE YEARS SINCE SANTO TRAFFICANTE HAD BEEN KICKED OUT OF CUBA, HE HAD been a busy man. There were the revenge plots against Castro with Johnny Roselli, Sam Giancana, and the CIA. They had not borne fruit, but they were fun, gangsters and spooks putting their heads together out of a mutual lust for revenge. In retrospect, it might have been more of a fantasy than anything, but for the mafiosi, it had the added benefit of maybe helping to mollify AG Robert Kennedy. How could RFK persist in persecuting Trafficante and his friends if they were out on a limb, doing their patriotic duty, with another branch of the same tree? That was the thinking, anyway. Things hadn't worked out that way. Even as the mobsters were plotting with the CIA to kill Castro, they were being arrested, tried, and convicted at an alarming rate. This, perhaps, had necessitated a change in strategy, a shifting of targets. You don't cut off the tail, you cut off the head.

In the wake of the Kennedy assassination, Trafficante had been interviewed by the FBI at his home in Tampa. Unsurprisingly, he had an ironclad alibi for that day. He was nowhere near Dallas on the date in question. If and when the boys from the Bureau learned that Trafficante had been in bed with the Agency is not known. What the G-men did know was that Santo was deeply embedded with the Cuban exile junta, and that he was fleshing out the ranks of his own criminal operations with Cuban exiles, a group the FBI was beginning to see as a potential new criminal threat.

Meanwhile, José Miguel Battle sought and was given a conference with Trafficante. He surmised that it would be a good idea to bring along his brother Gustavo. In recent months, while José Miguel had been awaking to reveille and playing cards at Fort Benning, Gustavo had been spotted by FBI surveillance teams meeting on a semiregular basis with Trafficante at various restaurants in Dade County. It may have been José Miguel, the older brother, who first established a partnership with Trafficante back in Havana, but it was Gustavo who up until now had kept things cozy in the Sunshine State.

In the absence of any one person with the stature or power to call himself "the Cuban Godfather," Trafficante was it (even though he wasn't Cuban). Partly this had to do with the reputation of his father, Santo Trafficante Sr., who had been working with Cuban racketeers going back to the days of Prohibition. During those years, the Sicilian-born Trafficante Sr. had established political connections in Cuba that made it possible for him to use the island as a transshipment point for narcotics coming primarily from the Mediterranean port city of Marseille. Back at his home base in Tampa, Trafficante Sr. used heroin smuggling proceeds to establish himself as the preeminent bolita banker on the Gulf Coast.

Bolita was big in Tampa. Long before Miami established itself as a haven for post-Castro Cuban refugees, Tampa, nicknamed "Cigar City," had been on the receiving end of Cuban immigration since at least the Cuban War of Independence in 1898. The immigrants settled primarily in an area known as Ybor City, which was originally its own municipality but eventually became part of Tampa.

In Ybor City, cigar-making factories and Cuban *cafecitos* and restaurants were one manifestation of the influx; another was bolita. In 1950, the city's bolita empire was dissected during the Kefauver hearings, an unprecedented congressional investigation of organized crime chaired by Tennessee senator Estes Kefauver. Trafficante Sr. had somehow managed to avoid being subpoenaed by the committee, but many notable Tampa crime figures were called to testify, setting off a chain reaction that led to many local gangland slayings. Public exposure of the city's bolita racket was a primary cause of the upheaval.

In the early 1950s, even before Santo Sr. died after a protracted illness, the son already had been assuming control of the business. Santo Jr. was respected by the Cubans, and he had underworld connections at the highest levels throughout Tampa, South Florida, and all the way to New York. As someone who had attended all of the major Mob conferences over the years, including the infamous gathering at the Hotel Nacional in Havana in 1946, he had the ability to open doors and smooth the waters in various criminal jurisdictions well beyond his home city.

Battle revered Trafficante; he expressed as much to friends and associates. He had watched the Tampa Mob boss, along with Meyer Lansky and a few others, glide through 1950s Havana like royalty. In the Cuban realm, there was no mobster more exalted than Trafficante. His pedigree as a businessman/gangster was beyond reproach.

Though there is no record of the two men having met since their days together in Havana, Trafficante would have been well aware of the burgeoning Battle legend. He likely had heard the stories of his former police bagman's heroic exploits at the Bay of Pigs. He had heard the stories from many of his Cuban friends about the prisons in Cuba, at the Isle of Pines and elsewhere.

For his part, Battle may or may not have known the full extent of the Mafia kingpin's collaboration with the CIA to kill Fidel, but it hardly mattered. These men constituted a mutual admiration society that had been tenderized during the abomination of a communist revolution and similarly flavored with bitter doses of betrayal and a sometimes psychotic compulsion for revenge.

Trafficante welcomed the men into his house. Likely, Cuban coffee was served.

José Miguel laid it all out. "I'm here to talk about bolita," said Battle to the Man.

Santo adjusted his wire-rimmed spectacles, sipped his coffee, and said, "I'm listening."

José Miguel was not the most verbally dexterous of men, but he was on solid turf, talking about a subject he knew and loved.

So, okay, here's the deal . . .

Tampa already had a solid bolita structure in place—numbers runners who reached out to *el pueblo;* a system of corruption among politicians and police that helped facilitate the operation; bankers, auditors, and counting rooms to take in money and maintain the books; and a solid financial structure to deal with the occasional crisis, like when a specific date or occurrence led every Tomás, Ricardo, and Harry to bet the same number and then that number came in, meaning the bank had to be solvent or the entire racket would collapse under a crimson cascade of stabbings, beatings, and shootings, topped off by an ugly trail of raids and prosecutions.

Miami also had its bolita structure in place. Things were changing down there; the influx of Cubans fleeing Castro's revolutionary paradise was transforming the city. The Battle brothers—Gustavo, Pedro, Aldo, Sergio, and Hiram—were making inroads in Miami. Maybe there was room for expansion there. But that's not what José Miguel was there to talk about. He wanted to talk about the granddaddy of all bolita possibilities, the Big Show, where the density of the population and number of daily bettors made it a gold mine just waiting to be buggered: New York.

What made the Big Apple especially attractive, noted José Miguel, was Union City, across the river, close, but in a different state. In Union City, you could stand in Memorial Park, high on a bluff looking straight across the Hudson River at the majestic skyline of Manhattan. It was one of the most breathtaking views of the city in the entire metropolitan area. Almost literally, Union City was in the shadow of the greatest city on earth. For Battle, it was an empire to be conquered.

Furthermore, using Union City as a base of operations, the Cubans believed, would insulate the business from prosecution. Cops in New Jersey would not have jurisdiction to arrest them in New York, and vice versa.

Battle was basing this theory on the knowledge that investigations and prosecutions of policy rackets had heretofore been undertaken primarily by local law enforcement. In many ways, policy was considered to be small potatoes. Even after the public Kefauver hearings, federal prosecutions for this kind of gambling were few and far between. And local prosecutions were easy to manage—cops, judges, and politicians could be bought off. Battle was confident that through political connections and graft, he could make himself virtually untouchable in Union City.

It didn't take much convincing for Trafficante to see the value in what Battle was proposing. Along with everything else, there was a historical precedent to putting a Cuban in charge of the Mob's numbers ventures.

Back during Prohibition and into the 1930s, one of the preeminent numbers bankers in New York City was Alejandro "Alex" Pompez, a

Cuban American born in Key West and raised in Ybor City. As a young man, Pompez moved to New York and became a key operator in the numbers racket of Arthur Flegenheimer, better known as Dutch Shultz, one of the most powerful gangsters of his day. Having made a fortune off of bootlegging, a business that was regulated through extortion, violence, and murder, Shultz in 1931 parlayed his financial fortune into becoming perhaps the biggest numbers banker in America.

The center of betting activity was Harlem. Wagering coins or small bills on a series of numbers was largely a poor person's activity, easily accessible to people of limited means—especially those with dreams of a better and more prosperous world beyond the horizon. The man who became the face of Shultz's policy empire in Harlem was Alex Pompez, an elegant Afro-Cuban operator with a pleasant manner and organizational skills who also spoke fluent Spanish.

To the various Sicilian, Italian, and Irish Mob bosses in New York, Pompez was recognized as a valuable asset. Money was the common denominator, not racial enlightenment. A 1929 article in *New York Age,* a local newspaper, was headlined "The Spanish Menace in Harlem." The article decried the arrival of Spanish-speaking immigrants from the Caribbean and cited gambling as a threat to the stability of the community. Pompez countered the negative publicity by becoming a legitimately successful businessman in other areas, particularly as the owner of the New York Cubans, a baseball team in the Negro League whose home stadium was in the nearby Manhattan neighborhood of Washington Heights.

The numbers operation financed by Pompez, which in turn was financed by one of the most prominent Mob bosses in the city, set a precedent for Cuban American racketeering in the United States.

José Miguel Battle would be following in the footsteps of Pompez, but still he would need the proper introductions. If Battle was going to operate in New Jersey, not to mention the highly competitive boroughs of New York City, he would be doing so in territory that was already spoken for by various factions within the Five Families. He could not go anywhere near the New York City area without first having someone of Trafficante's stature make it happen.

"I could open some doors for you," said Trafficante to Battle.

"You would do that for me?" replied José Miguel.

Trafficante set up some important meetings for Battle, and José Miguel headed north, where he had already established a home with his wife and kid in Union City.

The first meeting was with Sam DeCavalcante, known as "Sam the Plumber," the powerful Mob boss who controlled gambling, loan-sharking, and racketeering in northern New Jersey. DeCavalcante claimed to have descended from an Italian royal family in Naples; he liked to have underlings refer to him as "the Count." If Battle were to set up shop in Jersey, DeCavalcante would get a piece. Their meeting took place in Newark, the mobster's home base.

Another important meeting took place in upper Manhattan, in the neighborhood of Spanish Harlem. This was the territory of Anthony "Fat Tony" Salerno, acting boss of the Genovese crime family. Fat Tony always had a cigar in his mouth, and he spoke the language of the streets, motherfucker this and cocksucker that (some of it captured in later years on FBI wiretaps). The meeting was at Patsy's Restaurant on First Avenue and 117th Street. Trafficante also attended this meeting, traveling from Tampa, as he was a personal friend of Salerno's. Another meeting was held with representatives of the Bonanno family in Brooklyn.

In all of these meetings, José Miguel was introduced as "Mike." He was paraded around like a beauty pageant contestant who didn't need to do much but sit there and look pretty. The mafiosi knew what bolita was all about, and they knew that, if properly organized, it was a license to print money. *Hey, paisano, meet Mike Battle, the Cuban from New Jersey, the guy who's gonna make us all rich by breathing new life into the Spanish lottery.*

The Italians all liked Mike Battle. He was a tough guy who was conversant with the practices of the underworld. He spoke their language—that is, the language of black market capitalism. From now on, he would be *un nostro amico,* a friend of the family.

IT WAS GOING TO TAKE A LOT OF PEOPLE TO RUN A SUCCESSFUL BOLITA OPERATION IN the greater metropolitan area of New York and New Jersey. At the street level would be dozens of runners, people out there taking bets, writing them down, and bringing them back to various "offices" or calling them in over the phone. The offices were mostly cheap apartments turned into work areas, with a few tables, chairs, and a half dozen phones. Recording equipment was used to record each and every call, in case of disputes over transactions.

Then there were the accountants, those with a head for math, who maintained the all-important ledgers. The organization paid out a percentage of the money flow to hundreds of people. The various Mafia factions received their cut. The bankers—some of whom were mafiosi in the area and some Cubans back in Miami—also received a cut. Then there were payouts to various members of the organization, the street runners, bookkeepers, underbosses, and bosses, all the way up to Battle himself.

Money was constantly in motion, flowing in and out of the barely furnished apartments that served as counting rooms, and so there were those whose job it was to safeguard and transport the cash. In 1966, less than two years after Battle took over and expanded upon the business started by Angel Mujica, the organization was taking in between $30,000 and $60,000 a day. That money was often gathered in the smallest of denominations. Money was gathered in one of three main counting rooms, one in the Bronx and two in Manhattan. At the end of the day, the cash was placed in suitcases, and the suitcases were brought out to a caravan of cars, which were driven and protected by an assortment of armed men. The middle car was the money car, with the front and back cars serving as protection. The three vehicles drove through the Midtown Tunnel or over the George Washington Bridge into New Jersey, destined for Union City. The cortege was never disturbed, because the Battle organization had paid off cops in upper Manhattan and throughout Hudson County, New Jersey, the kind of payments that were designed to reach into the upper structures of law enforcement.

It was a vibrant, multilayered operation, based on a simple principle. There were a number of ways a person could wager, but the payout was the same—six hundred to one. Those odds were better than anything seen before in the area; the payout before had been four hundred or five hundred to one. Battle's operation offered the best return. People flocked to his runners to place their bets.

The winning number was based on the total mutual handle from the racetrack, published each day in the morning newspapers on the sports page. This was the way it had always been. In the metropolitan area, there was the Brooklyn number and the New York number, based on daily results in those jurisdictions, with a person's winning number determined by where they placed their bet. In order to make rapid payoffs, Battle's organization did something different—they had spotters at the racetrack monitoring results as they came in. Thus they had that day's track totals at the close of the day. If you bet with Battle's organization, you didn't have to wait around till the next day to find out the winning number when newspapers hit the newsstands. And, most important, if you hit the number, you got paid immediately, unlike with the Italians, where the payout was always on their terms and could take days.

Battle liked to reward hard workers. If you were a low-level runner who hustled, bringing in a lot of bets and money on a daily basis, you would be promoted to a midlevel banker. This way you had your own bank, which was cofinanced by a higher bank within the organization. You were now midlevel management; you had your own runners, your own little area of operation, and you were a big shot in your domain.

Word went out on the Cuban immigrant pipeline—the Battle organization was hiring. *La bola en la calle* (street gossip) spread from New Jersey all the way to Miami and even Havana. If you were someone the Battle brothers already knew, you were in a good position to secure a role in the operation. If you were a veteran of the 2506 Brigade, like José Miguel and Mujica and others, you were royalty, likely to come into the business as a high-level banker. If you were blood, you were also in a privileged position. Most of the Battle brothers were involved, and eventually the man who married the Battle brothers' only sister—Nene Marquez—became a high-level banker, as did Marquez's father (Battle's father-in-law), who became what was known as a superbanker, with the privilege of sitting back and stockpiling their proceeds while out on the streets the minions hustled for a living.

In the mid- to late 1960s, Battle's organization was usually referred to as "the Cuban Mafia." This was partly in recognition of the group's alliance with the Italians—the traditional Mob—and all the muscle that implied. Clearly, Battle's operation was protected. It operated mostly out in the open. And, given that the Cuban Mafia was connected at the highest levels, there were few problems with robberies of money couriers or attempts to muscle in on Battle's turf. The word was out—you mess with the Cubans, you were taking on the entire Five Family structure.

Still, José Miguel knew that his entire business was based in large part on the reputation of the man at the top. He assumed the role of the Padrino, the Godfather, from the very beginning. Only in his late thirties at the time, he projected the image of a more mature man who conveyed leadership through his demeanor and gravitas rather than inspiring rhetoric or brilliant business strategies. It was a role he seemed destined to play and had been rehearsing ever since he'd first witnessed the likes of Santo and Meyer lording over the casinos and nightclubs in Havana. Partly that role required that the boss project an image of magnanimity and fairness; partly it had to do with his being tough.

Battle had a temper. Those who knew him well had seen that temper in action. Though he was generally friendly and calm, his anger could emerge suddenly, with ugly consequences.

One person who witnessed this was Jesús, the black market gun merchant who had first encountered José Miguel as a cop back in Havana. Battle had been impressed that Jesús did not rat on his partners, and it formed the basis of a mutual respect that proved to be long-lasting.

Like so many Cubans whose lives had been scattered far and wide by the upheaval of the revolution and what came after, Jesús and José Miguel had parted ways and then were reunited years later in the United States. In 1962, Jesús fled the Castro regime and became a small-time criminal in Miami. *La bola* in the city was that things were hopping up in New York and New Jersey. Though Jesús had never been to New York, he headed north and settled with his brother in an apartment on 135th Street and Broadway. Soon he hooked up with the Battle organization, working mostly in Manhattan, but he routinely hitched a ride or took a bus across the Hudson River to Union City.

One afternoon in December 1968, Jesús was in Tony's Barbershop, located at 137 48th Street, half a block from Johnny's Go Go Club. The barbershop was owned by Nene Carrero and had become something of a social club for members of Battle's bolita organization. Wagers were made there, payments dropped off, and information passed back and forth.

That day, a local Cuban was sitting in a chair getting a haircut and a shave from the barber. Jesús was looking over a newspaper, checking out the previous day's racing results. Along with the barber and his customer, three or four others were in the shop waiting for a haircut or just hanging out.

José Miguel Battle came into the shop. Jesús said *hola* to the boss. The others nodded a greeting.

The customer in the barber chair saw Battle and, incredibly, started "talking shit" about Battle's wife. Battle had opened a jewelry store on Bergenline Avenue in the adjacent New Jersey town of West New York. The customer had done some business in the jewelry store and wasn't happy about something.

"If you know what's good for you," said Battle to the hombre, "you'll shut your fucking mouth right now."

Apparently oblivious, the guy kept talking—loudly, so everyone in the place could hear him.

Jesús couldn't believe what he was hearing. He looked at Battle, knowing that the guy in the barber chair was treading on thin ice.

Battle wasn't even looking at the guy, but Jesús could see that his boss was steaming. The guy in the chair kept yakking.

Suddenly, Battle pulled out a snub-nosed .38-caliber handgun. He rushed over to the guy in the chair, stuck the gun under his chin, and pulled the trigger. *Boom!* The sound of the shot reverberated through the barbershop.

Fortunately for the guy, he jerked his head back at the moment the shot was fired, so the bullet did not go through his head. It entered at an angle, piercing his neck. There was blood everywhere.

Jesús, acting as an underling should, helped rush his boss out of the location before the police arrived.

In the days that followed, Battle realized that he'd created a problem for himself. The shooting victim told the cops exactly what happened, and on December 12, 1968, Battle was charged with aggravated assault with a firearm. It would be the first of many criminal charges filed against him over the following decades.

It was Jesús who helped resolve the problem. Many years later, he remembered how it occurred. "I went to the guy with ten thousand dollars in cash. The shot caused the guy to be paralyzed in one arm. I told him that El Gordo regretted what had happened. He wanted to make a payment—an offering—to make the charges go away. The guy wanted more money. I told him, no, it was ten thousand or nothing. He took the money. When the date for his court appearance came up, the guy didn't show up. The case was dismissed."

For Battle, it was a close call. Much like the hombre he shot, he had dodged a bullet. Some might say it had been a mistake, a stain on his reputation, but like so many things in the criminal world where violence was involved, it also had a reverse effect. The moral of the story was clear: Don't mess with José Miguel Battle. He will not send others to do the dirty work for him. He will take matters into his own hands and shoot you in the face.

MEANWHILE, BACK IN MIAMI, SOME OF THE BATTLE BROTHERS WERE STAKING THEIR claim. Not so much with bolita, which in Miami was already under the control of a consortium of Cubans associated with Santo Trafficante, but through another racket on the rise: the importation and selling of cocaine.

Publicly, José Miguel Battle's position was that he was against narcotics as a business. It was a dirty way to make money, with a high body count. He told his underlings that he didn't want anyone dealing drugs—heroin, cocaine, or marijuana. How serious he was with this edict against narcotics is hard to determine, but what is known is that his brothers Gustavo and Pedro were active players in the Miami cocaine business.

Their benefactor was none other than the Man, Santo Trafficante, and their direct boss was Evaristo Garcia Sr., Santo's primary underboss in Florida's growing Cuban underworld. Garcia had been the Mafia don's number two man back in Havana. He'd co-owned a hotel with Trafficante and had been one of the key people to help line up women and entertainment for visiting "dignitaries," including in 1957 a young senator from Massachusetts named John F. Kennedy.

In the late 1960s, cocaine trafficking in Miami was not yet the mega-business it would become, but it was substantial enough that there were turf wars and territorial disputes. Unlike bolita, where it was felt that there was enough activity to go around, cocaine at the time was in the hands of only a few operators, and the competition was fierce.

It was this competition that would engulf the Battle brothers in Miami and nearly bring about their immediate demise.

One local player in the city's nascent cocaine underworld was a man named Hector Duarte Hernandez. His slight, almost gaunt physique was in contrast to his reputation, which was fearsome. Back in the 1950s, Duarte had been politically active in Cuba. He was a member of a revolutionary student federation aligned with the Auténtico Party, led by Carlos Prío Socarrás.

On the afternoon of March 13, 1957, Duarte had taken part in one of the most extraordinary events in the Cuban Revolution. He was one of a large group of student insurgents who attacked the presidential palace and made a kamikaze attempt to assassinate President Fulgencio Batista. With pistols, machine guns, and hand grenades they stormed the majestic palace, its broad cascade of steps making the approach to the building akin to climbing the steps of an ancient temple.

Batista's people had been hearing rumors of an attack, so military personnel and police were nearby to repel the onslaught. But the fighting was fierce. There were over fifty student attackers and nearly one hundred soldiers. A palace guard opened fire on the students with a machine gun, mowing down more than a dozen. In the shootout, numerous guards and soldiers were also killed.

A group of student gunmen actually penetrated the perimeter and made their way into the building. There, in the massive interior lobby, another shootout took place, with more men on both sides being killed. President Batista, whose office was on the second floor, heard the commotion and escaped out a back exit into a stairwell. Some of the attackers made it all the way to the president's office before being shot dead.

Forty student rebels were killed that day, as well as ten soldiers and policemen. The steps of the palace were littered with dead bodies and splattered with blood. Though the primary purpose of the attack, to assassinate the president, had been unsuccessful, the number of students involved and the level of carnage that ensued shocked the country and would forever after be remembered as a seminal event in the Cuban Revolution.

Hector Duarte was one of only a handful of rebels who survived and escaped. For weeks and months afterward, Batista's military police went on a rampage attempting to hunt down Duarte and the other survivors. People were tortured for information by the notorious SIM, Batista's repressive secret police. Duarte hid out, protected by the urban underground. And he fought back. Duarte was believed to have been involved in the killing of at least two Havana cops in his years on the run.

Duarte was a revolutionary, but he was not a communist. The student underground had been in alliance with Castro's 26th of July Movement, but when Castro came into power and revealed himself to be a communist, Duarte, like many others, felt betrayed. He fled Cuba and settled in Miami.

For those in Cuba who had been actively caught up in the revolution, living a life of guns, clandestine activities, and guerrilla warfare, adjusting to life afterward was not always easy. Duarte may have become involved in criminal activity because he had the skills to do so; he may also have needed to find a way to make a living. Either way, upon his arrival in Miami, he became a gangster and a narco peddler. A classified CIA dispatch from the chief of station in Miami described him as "a dangerous hoodlum."

In the middle of 1960, the Cuban government tried to have Duarte extradited back to their country. The United States had not yet severed diplomatic and economic ties with Cuba (the embargo against it would be imposed by President Kennedy on October 19). Duarte was brought before federal judge George Whitehurst. His attorney argued that sending him back to Cuba would be the equivalent of sentencing him to death. Judge Whitehurst denied the plea for extradition and instead levied a $300 fine for illegal entry.

In America, cocaine may have been the substance that brought the former revolutionary into conflict with the Battle brothers, but no doubt the ghosts of the past also had something to do with it. Back in Havana, Duarte and the Battle brothers had been on opposite sides of the political divide. Likely, Duarte was aware of José Miguel's reputation as a

vice cop in Havana back in the day. The Battles certainly knew Duarte's
history. It was a conflict waiting to happen.

On the day after Christmas, December 26, 1969, Gustavo Battle
was in a car dealership located at NW 27th Avenue and 30th Street. It
was late in the day, around 4:30 P.M. He had just treated himself to an
extravagant after-Christmas gift, a new four-door Buick sedan, which

vice cop in Havana back in the day. The Battles certainly knew Duarte's
history. It was a conflict waiting to happen.

On the day after Christmas, December 26, 1969, Gustavo Battle
was in a car dealership located at NW 27th Avenue and 30th Street. It
was late in the day, around 4:30 P.M. He had just treated himself to an
extravagant after-Christmas gift, a new four-door Buick sedan, which
he paid for in cash. Apparently his cocaine business was doing well.
As he completed his purchase and prepared to leave the dealership, he
noticed three cars filled with men parked outside. They seemed to be
waiting for something. Gustavo could see that in one of the cars was
Hector Duarte.

"Could I use your phone?" Gustavo asked the car dealer.

"Sure," said the dealer.

Gustavo called his brother Pedro and said, "I think we got a problem." He explained that Duarte and a few carloads of gunmen had surrounded the dealership. "I need you to get over here pronto," he said.
"And come well armed."

Gustavo was thought to be a bit of a wild man. Though he was
loyal to his older brother, José Miguel, he sometimes resented being
told what to do. His dealing narcotics against his brother's wishes was
one example. Leaner and more rough around the edges than José Miguel, Gustavo seemed often to be looking for ways to demonstrate his
independence.

Pedro, on the other hand, seemed to worship José Miguel, but he was
also close to Gustavo. With thick black hair and bedroom eyes, six feet
tall and trim, Pedro was considered the most handsome of the brothers.
But as a force on the street, he did not have the fearsome reputation of
either José Miguel or Gustavo.

Upon ending the phone call with his brother, Pedro hopped into
his late-model Plymouth Valiant and drove to the Buick dealership. It
took twenty minutes. He parked as close to the entrance as he could and
entered the building, where he met Gustavo. Through the plate-glass
windows of the dealership's show floor, they could see Duarte and the
others waiting for them. They got their weaponry together: Gustavo and
Pedro each had a pair of .45-caliber pistols. Said Gustavo, "We're gonna
make a run for it. I'll go first in the Buick. You follow."

The Battles headed toward their cars, jumped in, started their engines, and pulled out of the parking lot, with Gustavo in the lead and Pedro following in his Valiant. They were immediately chased by the other cars—a Mustang, a Chevy sedan, and, in the lead, a VW Beetle. In each car were two men; Duarte was in the VW.

In was nearing rush hour and traffic was substantial, but that didn't matter to the hunters and the hunted. The chase was on. A wild pursuit ensued through the streets of Little Havana, with shots fired from all vehicles. The high-speed shootout continued for nearly half an hour, with much squealing rubber, reckless navigation, and the rat-a-tat-tat of gunfire echoing through the streets.

Eventually, Gustavo's Buick and Duarte's Beetle arrived on Flagler Street, heading west. The Mustang and Chevy had apparently gotten lost during the chase.

Pedro Battle, who had been trailing behind, arrived on Flagler just as the VW crashed into his brother's brand-new Buick. The driver of the VW, Manuel Chacon, stumbled out of the VW first; he was brandishing a 9mm handgun. Then came Duarte with a .30-caliber military carbine, which had been modified to shoot automatically and handle a thirty-round banana clip.

Gustavo ducked behind his Buick and opened fire. An insane shootout followed, with Duarte standing in the middle of the street blasting away with the machine gun. Gustavo was hit, but he still returned fire. Bleeding heavily, he took aim at Duarte. The former student rebel, who had survived the attack on the presidential palace of Batista a decade earlier, took three .45-caliber bullets in the chest and died instantly.

It wasn't over yet. Duarte's accomplice, Chacon, was still firing from over the hood of the VW. He and the Battle brothers traded gunfire, and then Chacon ran off on foot, northward on Red Road. Gustavo, badly wounded, stumbled back into his now damaged Buick. With metal scraping the pavement and the engine smoking, he floored it and took off after Chacon.

Running down the street, Chacon fired shots over his shoulder at Gustavo's vehicle. Gustavo sped up and ran over him. Then his Buick veered out of control and crashed into another car.

Pedro, following the pursuit in his car, saw his brother's car slam into the other vehicle. He wasn't sure what to do. Police and emergency sirens were sounding from all directions. Believing that his brother was dead, he fled the scene. It was an act he would regret the rest of his life.

Gustavo was rushed to Jackson Memorial Hospital. After police sorted out all the mayhem, it was determined that there was one man dead: Duarte. Chacon, who had survived being run over by Gustavo's Buick, was charged with aggravated assault. But Gustavo refused to co-operate with police, so the charge was dropped.

The shootout on the streets of Little Havana lit up the Miami underworld. Everyone was talking about it. To some, the incident would become a historical signpost, an opening salvo in the city's co-caine wars, a notorious era that would become even more crazed and homicidal in the decades ahead.

LIKE MANY GANGLAND EVENTS, THE BATTLE-DUARTE SHOOTOUT HAD A RESIDUAL effect for those involved. Gustavo's reputation as a badass in Miami may have been enhanced, and the name Battle, if it was not known before, was now uttered with reverence among some in the underworld. But there were also negative consequences: Gustavo Battle would spend a month in the hospital recovering from his gunshots wounds, and he also had legal issues to deal with that would change the direction of his criminal career.

With all the attention garnered by the shootout, local prosecutors were inclined to charge Gustavo with something. For law enforcement, it was bad business to have a wild shootout take place in broad daylight during rush hour and not have somebody be held accountable. Conse-quently, on February 5, 1970, a Miami coroner's inquest was held in the courtroom of Judge John V. Ferguson.

José Miguel Battle flew down to Miami for the occasion. Though he himself would not testify at the inquest, El Padrino had arranged for a number of Bay of Pigs veterans to speak at the hearing. These men were iconic figures in the community, and to have them testify on Gustavo's behalf was powerful.

Hector Duarte's checkered career as a rebel was explained to the judge. Along with his political and criminal activities, it was noted that

Duarte had recently been recruited by Castro's Cuban Intelligence Service as an operative in the United States. It was surmised by Gustavo's Bay of Pigs defenders that Duarte was on a professional assassination mission to kill the Battle brothers. The attempted murder of Gustavo, they explained, was a kind of political hit.

Given the climate of the times, it was not a difficult case to make. Ever since the release of prisoners from the Bay of Pigs invasion, the Cuban exile underground had been swarming with spies and counterspies, with acts of espionage and murder that few were aware of outside the corridors of the CIA, or the *cafecitos* and bars along Calle Ocho in Miami and Bergenline Avenue in Union City.

Judge Ferguson had no trouble grasping the implications. He concluded that the assailants had fired first and that Gustavo Battle acted in self-defense. The case was ruled a justifiable homicide.

Gustavo had avoided a homicide or manslaughter charge, but the victory was short-lived. The forces of the law had set their sights on Gustavo Battle, with a high degree of prosecutorial scrutiny. The Drug Enforcement Agency quickly threw together a case against Gustavo. In July, just five months after having been cleared in the Duarte shooting, he was arrested for the sale and possession of cocaine.

The case against him was strong enough that he admitted guilt and took a plea deal. He was sentenced to six to eight years in prison. He would be the first of the Battle brothers to do time in America.

José Miguel was beside himself. Gustavo was going off to prison; that was bad enough. But also, the Godfather had been telling his men not to deal narcotics. It was wrong, and it was too risky. Given his own brother's violation of that proclamation, he had good reason to be upset, and he was not above telling anyone who would listen: *I told you so.*

FOR THE CUBAN MAFIA, THE TEMPORARY LOSS OF GUSTAVO WAS UNFORTUNATE, BUT as a new decade dawned, José Miguel had other problems to deal with.

Since the mid-1960s, the FBI had been tracking the militant Cuban exile community in the United States. Partly this was a result of the Bureau's JFK Task Force, which sometimes overlapped with the Cuban Task Force.

The American public had been spoon-fed a theory of the Kennedy assassination as presented by the 888-page Warren Commission Report. That report concluded that the murder was the act of a lone gunman, with no conspirators. Many in the intelligence community suspected otherwise. The CIA–Cuban exile militant alliance was a source of rumor and confidential investigation within the FBI, and would remain so for decades.

In May 1966, an internal memo was sent from the Miami office of the FBI to the regional office in Newark. Special agents in Miami had been tracking a number of Cuban exiles, including a suspect named Bernardo de Torres. Through an informant, Miami agents had garnered a piece of information they felt would be of interest to the Newark office:

> C.I. (confidential informant) advised SA FRANCIS J. DUFFIN on 4/28/66 that JOSE MIGUEL BATTLE is rumored to be a very big bolita banker in New Jersey. He is reputed to be very rich. BERNARDO DE TORRES, the brother of CARLOS DE TORRES, was in La Brigada during the Bay of Pigs invasion in Cuba. BERNARDO is a very good friend of Battle.

The Miami agents further noted that they had been investigating Battle "in connection with possible espionage and security activity." As a result, they contacted the Immigration and Naturalization Service (INS) to follow up on details regarding Battle's status, and they were informed by an INS investigator that their office "would not be conducting an active investigation with regard to the subject since it is their belief that the subject is anti-Castro and anti-communist in his beliefs."

The Cuban Task Force in Miami was not closing the books on Battle, but they thought it important to pass along what they were hearing about his bolita activities.

Normally, FBI agents do not get too excited about gambling or policy cases. These investigations and prosecutions are usually left to local law enforcement. But what they were hearing from Miami coincided with what they were hearing in New Jersey—that in a few short years the Battle organization had become substantial, and that the so-called

Cuban Mafia was conducting their business with the full cooperation of the Italian Mafia.

Starting in June 1966, the Newark office of the FBI began sending out surveillance teams to follow José Miguel Battle and others. The idea was to accumulate working knowledge about the structure of the organization and determine where they did business.

One of the more startling discoveries of the FBI investigators was that Battle was seen meeting with Peter Kelly, a man in his sixties, an old-time policymaker, or bookie, going back three decades in northern New Jersey. In the towns of Union City and West New York, Kelly and his brothers—Peter, James, Thomas, and Joseph—were well known to many in the police departments and political clubhouses of Hudson County. Back when the area was largely Irish and Italian, before the Cubans arrived, the Kelly brothers, an Irish American clan, were major conduits between the bookmakers and the cops. In 1936, they had been arrested together in a major policy raid, which only enhanced their reputations. Peter was the last remaining Kelly with ties to the old structure of gambling bosses making payoffs to people in the police and political precincts so that their operations would not be busted.

Battle's meeting with Kelly was like a passing of the baton, from the Irish to the Cubans. Battle may not have needed an old-timer like Kelly to rustle up customers; they were everywhere among the area's growing Latino population. But if he hoped to control the cops, it was wise to reach out to an old-school gambling kingpin like Pete Kelly.

It didn't take long for the agents to figure out what the Battle-Kelly relationship was all about. On June 23, 1966, an FBI agent who had Battle's apartment building under physical surveillance filed the following report:

> 9:50 A.M., Jose Battle walked down the steps of 405 New York Ave. and entered a 1966 Buick Wildcat. Battle was carrying a brown paper bag. Battle drove north on New York Ave. . . .

> At 9:55 A.M. Battle parked across from the side entrance of the Union City, N.J. Police Department and entered the basement carrying the brown paper bag.

At 9:59 A.M. Battle left the Police Department carrying the brown paper bag. He entered his car and drove north on Hudson Ave.

It was a eureka moment for the investigators. Battle was either making payoffs to the Union City police, or taking betting action, or probably a

At 9:59 A.M. Battle left the Police Department carrying the brown paper bag. He entered his car and drove north on Hudson Ave.

It was a eureka moment for the investigators. Battle was either making payoffs to the Union City police, or taking betting action, or probably a combination of both.

The agents followed Battle. He drove to a Tony's Barbershop on 48th Street. He parked and entered the barbershop, then almost immediately reappeared.

At 10:05 A.M. Battle came out of the barbershop and walked east on 48th. He was carrying the above brown paper bag which appeared half full as he was swinging it as he walked.

They followed Battle as he entered a nearby bank, approached a teller, and completed a transaction. Then he returned to the barbershop.

The agents had captured Battle on his usual morning routine, collecting and dispensing cash among cops and other customers in his town.

Eventually, the FBI surveillance expanded well beyond Battle. Slowly and methodically over the next fifteen months, the agents began to formulate a set of target subjects who they felt comprised an inner circle of what was shaping up to be a large-scale gambling operation.

Angel Mujica emerged as a prime suspect, as did Battle's two younger brothers, Aldo and Hiram, who had only recently arrived from Miami.

The agents monitored these men and a dozen others as they met in places like the Cuban Coffee Shop on 22nd Street in Union City, at Mujica's home in West New York, at Battle's home, and at other locations. They documented the transfer of cash, mostly in brown paper bags and manila envelopes, and betting slips. More important, they followed the various suspects as they traveled over the bridges and through the tunnels to Manhattan.

In terms of the FBI's investigation, this was the most significant activity. By traveling from New Jersey into New York, the boliteros were engaging in a conspiracy involving interstate commerce in furtherance of an unlawful activity. That alone was enough to put Battle and his people away for five years or more.

It was something of an irony: the reason that Battle believed Union City was such a good location for starting a bolita business in New York City was because the two locales were in different states. He felt that that would make it harder for competing prosecutors to make a case against him. Apparently he was not aware of laws pertaining to interstate commerce. The very thing he thought would protect him from being prosecuted was exactly the thing federal investigators were using to build a case against him.

To document the existence of a conspiracy with multiple co-conspirators, it would take the FBI agents many months of observing and recording activity—trips back and forth by Battle and his minions between the two states. But they were definitely on the trail.

Battle was unaware of it, but his newly prosperous gambling operation was being monitored by the feds on a near daily basis.

4

THE RAIN IN SPAIN

JOSÉ MIGUEL BATTLE HAD A WAY WITH PEOPLE. EVEN THOUGH HE COULD BE CRUDE, and he was obviously someone you did not want to cross, on a personal level he was charismatic and appealing. He projected a mix of ego and humility at the same time. He was down-to-earth, and he made friends easily.

There were close associates who had once been cops with him in Havana, like Joaquin Deleon Sr., now a bolita banker; there were associates who had been with him at the Bay of Pigs, like Angel Mujica and others; and there were friends and associates that he made around the poker table.

One such friend was Carlos Rodriguez, whom Battle met during a poker game in 1970. Rodriguez was known by the nickname "Trio de Trés." A trio of threes is not a great hand in poker. Carlos had a habit of losing at cards; his nickname was a reference to his bad luck.

Rodriguez knew very little about Battle when they sat down with three or four other Cubans to play poker at a flophouse casino in Union City. One of the first things he noticed was that Battle was cheating. He had surreptitiously retrieved a card that had been discarded from his hand. Rather than make a commotion about it, Rodriguez said to Battle, "*Que buen caballo que lo montan dos jinetes en la misma carrera* (What a good horse that two jockeys can ride him in the same race)." It was his way of letting Battle know that he knew he was cheating without making an issue of it.

Battle looked at Trio de Trés, assessing this slick hombre he had just met. The Godfather's lips tightened into a slight smile. Rodriquez nodded in acknowledgment. And a great friendship was born.

After the card game, Battle gave Rodriguez a business card and said, "I like your style. If you ever need anything, call me at the number on my card. I will help you out."

Rodriguez left the poker game that day with no idea that he would ever need to call Battle. He asked around about the guy and was told that he was the bolita king of New York and New Jersey. He learned of Battle's reputation as a hero at the Bay of Pigs invasion and of the time he spent in Castro's hellhole of a prison on the Isle of Pines. Some friends told him that if he were to have José Miguel Battle as a friend, he would have a friend for life. That's the kind of guy he is, they told him.

Rodriguez shrugged and wondered if that was true. Clearly, Battle couldn't be trusted in a card game. Rodriguez was not the first, nor would he be the last, to catch José Miguel cheating at cards. But it had seemed so obvious and lighthearted, as if Battle didn't care if someone saw him stacking a deck or hiding a discarded card. It was all part of the camaraderie of playing the game.

Trio de Trés tucked José Miguel Battle's business card into his wallet without thinking much about it.

Though he liked to play cards, and he did occasionally bet the number, Rodriguez was not a habitual bolitero. Born in Matanzas, Cuba, on August 30, 1934, he left the island in 1962 and arrived in Union City with his wife in the mid-1960s. He earned a living by working in a garment factory. The garment business was the primary industry in Union City; it was the main reason most Cubans had come there in the first place. The work was sporadic. Rodriguez did not have a full-time job. He worked when he could find it, and when he wasn't working he hung out at neighborhood poker games or at one of the many Cuban bars and *cafecitos* in Union City or West New York.

One night Rodriguez was at a bar called El Brinque in Union City, shooting pool with a couple of strangers who had walked into the bar. He took turns playing eight-ball with the two shady-looking characters. They were playing for money. As Rodriguez racked up one victory after another, taking bill after bill from the losers, he began to get the sense that these hombres were not about to let him leave the bar with their money. Quite possibly his life was in danger.

Rodriguez noticed that he still had Battle's business card in his wallet.

He handed the card to someone he knew at the bar and said quietly, "Find a pay phone. Call this man. Tell him Trio de Trés is in trouble at El Brinque."

"What if he asks who is calling?"

"Just do it."

His friend called Battle. Within ten minutes, there he was, El Gordo, in a suit and tie, with two bodyguards. The men with whom Rodriguez had been playing billiards seemed to recognize Battle, and they backed off. Battle said, "Hey, *chico,* what are you doing here? I told you to go pick up that thing."

Rodriguez recognized this as his cue to skedaddle, and so he did.

The next time Rodriguez saw Battle, he told him, "You may have saved my life."

"I'm glad I could help," said Battle. Then he asked Rodriguez if he'd like to work for his organization.

Carlos Rodriguez quit working in the garment business and became Battle's confidant and errand runner for the next thirty years. On various FBI surveillances, he became a new face on the radar. He was seen driving around with Battle and others in his organization.

One day, Rodriguez was at his home in Union City. There was a knock at the door. His wife answered. He heard her talking to some men—in English, which was unusual.

Then his wife came to him and said, "The men with three letters are at the door."

Rodriguez thought, *F-B-I. Coño (damn).*

He let the two agents into his home. They said, "We're going to record everything that's said here."

Rodriguez didn't know if that was legal, but he didn't want it to appear that he was hiding anything.

They showed him a photo of José Miguel Battle. "Do you know this man?" they asked.

Rodriguez was pretty sure they must have been following him around. Why else would they be here?

"Yes," he said.

"Is he a friend of yours?"

"Yes, he is."

The men became very serious. One of them asked, "Why is he a friend of yours?"

Without hesitation, Rodriguez said, "Because he's a war hero."

They asked him if he knew what Battle did for a living. Carlos said, "He owns a jewelry store on Bergenline Avenue."

Then they asked Rodriguez if he knew three other people. One was Celin Valdivia, a politico–law enforcement liaison in Union City. The second they identified only as Rafaelito. And the third was Captain Frank Scarafile, a powerful figure in the Union City Police Department.

Said Rodriguez, "I know one and two, but not the captain."

The FBI agents wanted to know if Battle was making payoffs to Captain Scarafile.

"I know nothing about that," Carlos told them.

The agents finally left the house.

Rodriguez waited till later that night. He left the house and made various evasive maneuvers to ensure that he was not being followed. He met Battle at La Gran Via Restaurant on Bergenline Avenue and told him about the visit from the FBI agents.

Battle did not seem surprised, nor did he seem too worried. He told Carlos, "*Gracias* for bringing this information to me." Then they ordered some food. Battle had what he usually had for breakfast, lunch, or dinner—*harina* and *picadillo* (cornmeal and ground beef). Years later, Trio de Trés would remember, "That man, he sure did like to eat."

ON JULY 22, 1970, NEWARK U.S. ATTORNEY FREDERICK B. LACEY ANNOUNCED THE indictments of fourteen people, including Battle, Mujica, and José Miguel's brothers Aldo and Hiram. Bench warrants were issued for all of the defendants.

José Miguel turned himself in at the police station in Union City and was taken to the federal courthouse in Newark to be arraigned. His friend Trio de Trés, Carlos Rodriguez, was there in a show of solidarity. Said Rodriguez, "I remember we were in the hallway, and there was a woman crying. She had been fined five hundred dollars for some matter, and she didn't have the money. Battle reached into his wallet and took out five hundred. He gave her the money. The woman was stunned. So was I. Here was this man facing serious legal problems of his own, and still he stops to help this woman. He was very generous."

Battle's attorney was Maurice M. Krivit, a Jersey City criminal lawyer. Krivit cautioned Battle to keep his mouth shut. They stood before the judge, who read the charges: "The defendants herein did knowingly, willfully, and unlawfully combine, conspire, confederate, and agree together and with each other, and with diverse other persons whose names are to the Grand Jury unknown, to commit an offense against the laws of the United States . . . It was a part of said conspiracy that said defendants and co-conspirators would travel and cause others to travel in interstate commerce between Hudson County in the state and district of New Jersey and New York City in the state of New York, with intent to promote, manage, establish, carry on, and facilitate the promotion, management, establishment and carrying on of an illegal activity, said unlawful activity being a business enterprise involving gambling offenses."

Various counts were read as they related to each individual defendant. It took some time. Eventually, bail was set for the lead defendant, Battle, at $50,000. José Miguel posted a surety bond for that amount and was released from custody.

The charges were substantial, but it could have been worse. Three months later, federal courts would enact the Racketeer Influenced and Corrupt Organizations Act (RICO), a law aimed at criminal conspiracies that allowed for much steeper sentencing. Under RICO, Battle might have been facing thirty years; under the current laws his sentence would be more like three to six.

Even so, he had no intention of going to prison. He expected his lawyer to negotiate a deal that would involve perhaps a fine but no jail time.

Battle was out on bail and free to circulate in his world, but his business suffered because of the government's case. FBI surveillances were still ongoing, and it had been revealed in court that the case would be based in part on informant testimony. That meant Battle's Cuban Mafia had a *rata*—a rat—in their midst. Who was the rat?

Battle's attorney filed a motion in court arguing that the government should be forced to reveal the name of their informant so defense lawyers could adequately prepare for trial. Prosecutors claimed that if they provided this person's name, his life might be in danger. The judge sided with the government and dismissed the motion.

Meanwhile, Battle's gambling operations suffered. *El jefe,* the boss, may have been feeling pressure, but he had a way of keeping it bottled up until it exploded, usually in an act of violence.

Just such an event occurred in September 1970 in Jersey City. And it had to do with Battle's son, with whom José Miguel had a difficult relationship.

José Miguel Battle Jr., whom everyone knew as Miguelito, had come to the United States at the age of nine. His first home was at Fort Benning, where he lived with his father and mother. They had then moved to Union City.

Miguelito was quiet as a child. As a teenager, he showed little interest in his father's business—bolita—and seemed determined to go his own way. His primary interest was music; he became part of a band that played rock music like the Beatles with a Cuban flavor, what would later be identified by musicologists as "the Latin tinge." He and his bandmates came up with the idea of holding block parties around Hudson County, mostly for teenagers like themselves. There would be food, non-alcoholic beverages, and live music. The events were popular and helped to give Miguelito a sense of identity and accomplishment, something he did with little or no involvement on the part of his father.

One afternoon, at a block party in Jersey City, Miguelito got into a fistfight with another kid. An acquaintance of Miguelito's named Alejandro Lagos stepped in to break up the fight. At that moment, José Miguel Sr. arrived on the scene. He saw Alejandro with his arms around Miguelito and assumed he was the person Miguelito was fighting. Battle snapped. He pulled out a gun and began pistol-whipping Lagos, putting him in the hospital. Later that day, Senior was arrested by officers from the North Bergen Police Department, charged with aggravated assault, and released on his own recognizance.

It was a situation similar to when Battle had shot the guy at the barbershop a few years earlier. He had acted impulsively, created a problem for himself, and now he needed to find a way to make the problem disappear.

The day after the incident, Lagos was visited in his hospital room by four men who said they were there representing José Miguel Battle Sr. One of them was Rene Avila, a well-known figure in the community. Avila owned a Spanish-language newspaper called *Avance* and was active in community events and local political campaigns. Lagos was told by

The day after the incident, Lagos was visited in his hospital room by four men who said they were there representing José Miguel Battle Sr. One of them was Rene Avila, a well-known figure in the community. Avila owned a Spanish-language newspaper called *Avance* and was active in community events and local political campaigns. Lagos was told by the visitors, "Listen, the man that hit you is El Padrino. He feels bad about what he did. He wants to make the charges go away."

Lagos was told that he would be paid $3,000 and given a job in the organization if he dropped the charges. Lagos had some inquiries made on his behalf; he learned whom he was dealing with. He dropped the charges and, once he recovered from his injuries, went to work as a pickup man for the Battle organization.

El Padrino was fortunate. Since he was out on bail on federal gambling charges, an assault charge would certainly have muddied the waters. As it was, the gambling case was not going well. The judge overruled every pretrial motion put forth by defense lawyers. It appeared to Battle that he was being railroaded and would likely be sent to prison. He did not want to go to prison. Memories of the Isle of Pines were still fresh in his head. He would do almost anything to avoid that.

In February 1971, seven months after he had been indicted, Battle disappeared. He packed up with his wife and son, boarded a plane, and headed for Spain.

On February 16, FBI special agent Anthony Vaccarino, who had worked the Battle case from the beginning, notified the judge that Battle had not appeared for his latest court date. He had apparently skipped bail and left the country. A charge of unlawful flight to avoid arrest was levied against him, and a warrant was issued for his arrest.

THE LIGHT IN MADRID IS OFTEN SPECTACULAR. SINCE THE CITY WAS FIRST LAID OUT in the Middle Ages, the morning sun comes from the east and brightens its darkest corners. This was sometimes seen as a problem, as the city was designed as a series of fortresses, making it a place of refuge for some, but also a haven for scoundrels. It was in this ancient capital of Europe that José Miguel Battle would hunker down and try to figure out his future.

As it turned out, Battle and his family were not the only Cuban exiles in Spain. Angel Mujica had also skipped bail and fled to Madrid. The two men who had guarded the patio together at the Isle of Pines prison seemed to be inseparable.

Pedro Battle also wound up going to Madrid as an act of solidarity with his brother even though he wasn't facing charges. In Spain's capital, José Miguel would meet many other Cubans in flight from Castro's Cuba, which every day was evolving more and more into the full-fledged communist disaster they had predicted.

Battle had a nice apartment in Madrid, at Calle Jaime Conquistador No. 48, in a residential area on the outskirts of the city. Since Spain did not have an extradition treaty with the United States, El Padrino was in no danger. He circulated openly in business and political circles and was seen on occasion socializing at the Venezuelan embassy.

Among his many Cuban friends who were in Madrid was Joaquin Deleon Sr., who had moved there only recently. Battle knew Deleon from Havana, where they had been cops together in the same police station. They had even been born on the same day, September 14.

Short and lean, like a long-distance runner, Deleon had come to New York and became a key banker in Battle's bolita operation. He was based in upper Manhattan, in the neighborhood of Washington Heights, a key barrio where the brain trust of the Cuban Mafia often met in restaurants and bars to talk business.

Deleon was in Spain with his wife, whose uncle had been a colonel in the Cuban police, and his son Joaquin Jr., or Joaquinito, who was thirteen years old. Joaquinito was a godson of José Miguel, having been christened back in Havana, where he was born in 1957.

The younger Deleon was the quiet type, always observing and saying little. He was especially fascinated by his godfather, whom he felt had a charisma that made him a natural leader. Of Battle, Joaquinito remembered, "He could be loud, but he could also be quiet and intense. He had a way of looking at you and slightly tilting his head, assessing you . . . He would say to me, 'You're not going to say anything, right?' And my dad would say, 'Joaquinito never talks.' 'That's what I like about this kid,' Battle would say. We had a special connection because he was my godfather."

Joaquin Jr. also got to know Battle's son, Miguelito, who was a few years older. "He wasn't like his father. He didn't seem to have any interest in his father's business, unlike me. I was into it. I watched everything and listened." Miguelito was spoiled. He drove a red Grand Prix in Madrid and was known by all the doormen at the nightclubs.

Also present as part of Battle's circle of friends and associates in Madrid was Humberto Dávila, an esteemed bolitero going back to Cuba in the 1940s and 1950s. Dávila was from a family of boliteros. When he arrived in New York in the early 1960s, he established a base of operation, mostly in Brooklyn, at the same time Battle was forging his alliance with the Italians.

Dávila and Battle could have seen themselves as competitors. Dávila had more knowledge of the bolita business than Battle, who was a Johnny-come-lately to the numbers world. Dávila made the business work at the retail level. He knew all of his customers and runners by name. He was not by nature a gangster, and preferred to run his business free of violence.

Dávila's nickname was "Isleño," which meant "the Islander." He was built like a small island, five feet nine inches tall, and stout. Though he had dropped out of school after the sixth grade and was functionally illiterate, he was a genius with numbers and had recently pioneered a method of operation that would transform the bolita business. Rather than have numbers runners circulating in the community taking bets and collecting money, why not have a set location for people to place their bets and do business? Isleño saw the value in purchasing or renting commercial space and setting it up as a "numbers hole," a location where people would come to do bolita business. There could be no narcotics or guns at the numbers hole; people had to know it was a safe location to place a bet.

Isleño knew that most gamblers were creatures of habit. Many bet the same number every day. And the idea of a set location to place a wager was part of creating a routine for gamblers that was as important to their compulsion as winning.

Unlike Battle and other bolita bankers in the New York area who invested their gambling proceeds in businesses such as bars, clubs—or, in Battle's case, a jewelry store; a car wash in Washington Heights; and a *botánica* on 48th Street in Union City that sold candles, religious figurines, beads, and incense—Isleño was old school. For years he had been smuggling cash out of the United States and depositing it in banks in Spain. Earlier that year, on a flight to the Dominican Republic, he had been stopped at a New York airport carrying $408,000 in cash (equivalent to over $3 million today). Because he had not declared the cash at customs, the money was seized. Isleño wrote off the loss and continued on to Santo Domingo, where he secured a false passport and boarded a flight to Madrid, where he was now hiding out for a while.

Isleño Dávila was bolita royalty, but in Spain, Battle also established relationships with much shadier characters.

Ernesto "Ernestico" Torres had been born in Cuba and come directly to Spain in the late 1960s. In Madrid, he became friendly with Pedro Battle. It was Pedro who introduced Ernestico to his brother. At the time, Ernesto's hair was neatly trimmed and schoolboyish, though he eventually let it grow long and maintained a wispy beard, earning him the nickname "Rasputin." He had a feral intensity that José Miguel in his days as a vice cop would have recognized as the demeanor of a killer.

As it turned out, Battle knew Ernestico's father, who had been a gangster and drug dealer in Havana. The father was also named Ernesto Torres, and by the time José Miguel Battle met him in the early 1950s, he was already something of a legendary figure. Born in Galicia, Spain, he had migrated with his mother and sister to Cuba in the 1920s. In his early teen years, he became a professional criminal. Before long, he was in trouble with the law and fled to the United States. He was imprisoned for a time in New York, where, he claimed, he trimmed the hair of Mafia boss Charles Luciano (Torres was a barber by trade).

During World War II, like many prison inmates in the United States, Torres was offered a deal in which he could join the military and in exchange would be given an early pardon. He joined the U.S. Army to get out of prison. When his division arrived on a U.S. warship in the Caribbean, he went AWOL and returned to Cuba. It was there that Ernesto Jr. was born in 1952.

In mid-1967, Ernesto Sr. decided to return to the country of his birth. He more or less kidnapped his son from his mother and took him to Madrid, where he intended to groom Ernestico as a young hoodlum.

By the time the Battles arrived in Madrid, Ernesto Sr. had once again gotten into trouble with the law and been imprisoned in Spain. Ernestico, only nineteen years old, was basically living as an orphan.

Both José Miguel and Pedro Battle formed an immediate bond with Ernestico. The relationship with José Miguel was more of a patriarchic connection, with the elder man serving as a replacement for Ernestico's own absent father. With Pedro (who in Madrid went by the name of Raymond) the bond was more of a brotherly relationship.

As a Cuban street urchin in Madrid, Ernestico was a seductive character. He was a teenage con man and hustler who could take care of himself in the criminal world, but he was also sickly and vulnerable. He was thin to the point of being gaunt, and he suffered from rheumatoid arthritis, which caused him great pain.

Antonia Izquierdo was a young woman who met Ernestico during this time. He became infatuated with her. One year later, she became the mother of his first and only child, an occurrence that also brought the young hoodlum even deeper into the realm of the Battle family.

When Antonia met Ernestico, she was working as a domestic servant for a general in the army of Francisco Franco. It was a full-time job. She lived in the general's home but had been given time off to sit in on flamenco guitar classes two days a week. At her very first class, Ernesto Torres walked in. He was friendly with Antonia's friend and asked to meet her. He said to Antonia, "I want to get to know you better. If I have a party and invite you, will you come?"

Antonia said that she would. But when Ernestico had his party, she didn't show up. At the next guitar class, Ernestico confronted her. "Do you have something against me?"

She said no but that she had a job that kept her busy much of the time. Ernestico asked if on her day off he could take her dancing, and she agreed.

They went to a small club. Now that they were alone together in an intimate setting, Antonia felt the chemistry. A song by a Spanish pop group called Los Angeles came on the jukebox. The song was "Monica," a lush love ballad with swelling strings and sentimental lyrics. Ernesto said, "Forever after, this song will remind me of you. In fact, from now on I'm going to call you 'Monica.'"

A week later, Ernestico told her, "I want to be your man, and I want you to be with me. I don't want you working for that general anymore."

"Are you going to take care of me?" she asked.

"Yes," he answered.

They moved together into an apartment in the center of Madrid. Antonia quickly understood that her new boyfriend was a hustler who conned people out of money, but somehow that only made the situation more romantic. After a few months living with Ernestico, she became pregnant.

At the same time this was happening, Ernestico had become tight with the Battles and other Cubans from New Jersey who had formed their small community on the lam in Spain. Not everyone was enamored with Ernestico. Isleño Dávila, for one, believed that the young hoodlum was a hopeless case. One night, when the Cubans were all gathered together at a party, Isleño saw Antonia with Ernestico, and he said to her, "You're too good to be hanging out with this guy." Ernestico heard that and went crazy. He pulled out a knife that he always carried and threatened to kill Isleño. Others who were there separated the two men before it escalated into a physical altercation.

By mid-1971, Ernesto and Pedro Battle had become so close that when Antonia gave birth to their child, the father asked Pedro if he would be the godfather. Said Pedro, "Of course, Ernestico. I would be honored. You're like a brother to me."

The child was baptized in a majestic Catholic cathedral in Madrid. Pedro was there to serve as godfather, along with a female friend of Antonia who served as godmother. Having a rebel spirit, Ernestico did not want to give his son the traditional name of Ernesto Torres. He wanted to name the kid Ringo, after Ringo Starr of the Beatles. However, this being Spain under Franco, a Catholic traditionalist, the church would not let him baptize his child as Ringo, and so the child was christened, inevitably, as Ernesto Torres.

Fatherhood did little to tame Ernestico. He remained impulsive, with a self-destructive streak that defied logic.

One day, José Miguel Battle was explaining to the young Cuban that a man was coming to see him. The man owed him $10,000 but was coming to explain that he did not have the money. It was Battle's intention to terrify the man so that he would realize that he could not trifle with José Miguel Battle, the Cuban Godfather from America.

Ernestico listened carefully and took it all in. Later that day, the guy arrived in a Madrid taxi, black with a red stripe along the side.

Battle was inside the apartment on Calle Jaime Conquistador. He heard *Pop! Pop!* He went outside, and there was the guy in the back of the cab, shot twice in the head, Ernesto standing by with a gun. "You'll have no more problems with this guy," said Ernesto.

Battle was astonished. "What do you mean? Are you crazy?"

"Let this be a message to your enemies."

"You just cost me a lot of money. You are crazy. Get this body out of here."

Battle pulled out some cash and handed it to the driver. "Go. Disappear. We'll take care of it."

The driver took the money and split.

Battle looked at Ernestico, both stupefied and somewhat impressed. It says a lot about Battle that he looked at the dead body, and at Ernesto, knowing that this was an outrageous act, but also perhaps the thought entering his consciousness that he could use this kid.

Aside from Ernestico's impulsive acts of violence, Battle and the other Cubans in Spain had a wonderful time. They traveled together to the ruggedly beautiful area of Costa Brava, on the north Mediterranean coast, and all stayed at the same hotel. Spain was the motherland, the maternal womb for all Latinos, and together they could squint their eyes and almost believe they were back in the fatherland, La Patria, Cuba. They were able to speak in their native tongue every day. The weather was similar to La Isla, hot and humid. And the cuisine was close enough to remind Battle of his home province of Oriente. It was a time of fantasy in vacationland, a place where the men with three letters—FBI—could not bother them. For a while, it seemed like paradise.

However, by September 1972, Battle had been in Spain for nineteen months. His fellow bolita banker, Isleño Dávila, had a saying: "*El circo está cerado, pero los leones siguen comiendo* (The circus is closed, but the lions are still eating)." There were mouths to feed back in New York. By then, Dávila and Joaquin Deleon Sr., who were not facing criminal charges, and his brother Pedro, had returned to the United States. Ernestico, for whom Battle saw so much potential, had also departed to the States. José Miguel was mostly alone with his wife and Miguelito. He was getting restless. You could only neglect the bolita business for so long before it fell apart, or into the hands of someone else.

In early September, Battle sent his wife and son ahead on a flight to Newark. On the twenty-fifth of that month, Battle himself boarded a plane in Madrid under a false passport. The flight was destined for Costa Rica and then Miami.

Apparently someone tipped off authorities in the United States, because when Battle landed at Miami International Airport, he was immediately arrested by federal agents.

While stewing in custody, El Padrino pondered his predicament. He was facing two substantial charges, the gambling case in New Jersey, and now the charge of unlawful flight to avoid prosecution.

He was soon transferred to a federal facility in New Jersey. There, he huddled with his lawyers, who decided that it was best for him to avoid trial. In exchange for his pleading guilty to both charges, the lawyers would attempt to work out the best deal they could.

It was a sweet deal. By pleading guilty, Battle received a sentence of just eighteen months. At the Isle of Pines, eighteen months had seemed like an eternity, but for Battle, who had been expecting a longer sentence and would be serving his time at the federal prison in Danbury, Connecticut, this eighteen months would be a piece of cake.

BATTLE ARRIVED AT DANBURY CORRECTIONAL FACILITY WITH A BOUNCE IN HIS STEP. Once he got settled in, he was a minor celebrity among the mafiosi, who had heard he was a "friend of the family." To the Cuban American inmates, he was a major celebrity, El Padrino, a war hero from the Bay of Pigs.

Whatever notoriety Battle might have had, however, was overshadowed by the arrival of some new celebrity inmates—the Watergate burglars, otherwise known as "the Plumbers."

The infamous Watergate burglary had occurred while Battle was in Spain; the arrest of the burglars had riveted Battle's attention, as it did many Cuban émigrés in the United States. Most Americans followed the evolving scandal as it related to the administration of President Richard Nixon—whether or not the break-in at Democratic Party National Headquarters in the Watergate hotel and office complex in Washington, D.C., had been authorized by Nixon's people, and was being covered up by Nixon himself. Most Cuban Americans saw the story as a home movie. A number of the burglars were Cuban exiles, and four were former members of the 2506 Brigade. Also involved were retired CIA agent E. Howard Hunt, who had been a crucial organizer of the Bay of Pigs invasion, and Frank Sturgis, a recurring character in recent counterrevolutionary history whom Castro's mistress claimed to have seen in Dallas, in the company of Lee Harvey Oswald, days before the JFK assassination.

Battle knew most of these men, and he was excited to have them in his presence. Five of the seven Watergate burglars had come into Danbury prison at the same time the Senate Watergate hearings were playing out on national television. Unlike Howard Hunt and some of the others, the Cubans in the group had refused to cooperate with the Senate committee and had been sentenced to thirteen months in prison. They saw themselves as prisoners of *la lucha,* or prisoners of war.

Battle's interpretation of the Watergate scandal was, as with most Cuban exiles, different from that of the average American citizen. The exiles saw the Watergate caper as a continuation of the struggle against Castro. And for them it was deeply rooted in the Bay of Pigs invasion.

The burglars had been recruited by Hunt, who was putting together a team of political saboteurs to work on behalf of the Committee to Re-Elect the President (CREEP). Hunt had met with Eugenio Rolando Martínez, Virgilio González, Bernard Barker, and Felipe de Diego at the Bay of Pigs monument on SW 8th Street, Calle Ocho, in Little Havana. His pitch was simple. Hunt explained that Nixon was reigniting the U.S. government's secret war against Castro. Becoming involved with the Plumbers, a unit dedicated to committing subversive acts against communist sympathizers and other political enemies, was the first step in this renewed effort. "Do the Watergate caper, and then we go after Fidel," was how it was presented to the Cubans.

Rolando Martínez, Gonzalez, and Barker had all worked as part-time agents for the CIA. Martinez in particular had in the early 1960s taken part in numerous maritime sabotage activities against the Castro government, all sponsored by the CIA. According to Agency records, he was placed on a retainer of $100 a month and not taken off the books until the day he was arrested for the break-in.

Battle, like everyone else in America, was learning about the details of the Watergate story as it evolved in the public arena, first in the *Washington Post* and then through the dramatic, televised public hearings of the Senate Watergate Committee. But he knew more than the average citizen about the bona fides of the burglars.

At Danbury, Battle greeted Martinez and the others as patriots and war heroes. Just as he had once presented Luis Posada Carriles with the gift of a gun, in honor of his efforts on behalf of La Causa, the Cause, Battle presented a brand-new expensive watch to Rolando Martínez. He was able to get the gift into the facility by paying off some guards.

"This is for your integrity, your principles, and your track record in combating Castro," Battle told Martínez.

The ex-CIA operative knew Battle from when he was a cop in Havana, though they were not close friends. Upon receiving the watch, Martínez said, "Battle, thank you for the watch, but, *coño,* we can't use this in here. *Estamos jodidos* (We're screwed)." They both laughed at their mutual predicament.

Doing time with the Watergate burglars was something Battle would never forget. It somehow ennobled his criminal efforts, and added meaning to his time in prison. These men were fellow brigadistas, fellow anti-Castro warriors, and the fact that their drama was playing out on such a grandiose national level was awe-inspiring.

As the saga unfolded, the legacy of the Bay of Pigs invasion seemed to lurk in the shadows. During the hearings, it was dramatically revealed that Nixon had secretly taped many of his conversations in his office in the White House. Eventually, those tapes were transcribed and released to the public, and it was made clear that Nixon, who as vice president had been an early enthusiast of the invasion, saw the legacy of that disaster as a means to an end. In attempting to blackmail the CIA director into dropping the Watergate investigation, he warned that it would dredge up "the whole Bay of Pigs thing." Nixon was using the Bay of Pigs as a metaphor to reference Operation Mongoose; perhaps the JFK assassination; and other secrets that sprang out of covert efforts to kill Castro. Nixon was using the dark legacy of the Bay of Pigs invasion as a club to intimidate whomever he could.

On August 9, 1974, Nixon was forced to resign as president of the United States, a monumental event in U.S. history.

It was also personally monumental for Battle and his friends watching the news unfold on television at Danbury prison. The legacy of the invasion—the brigadistas' own personal history—and the ongoing efforts to undermine Castro and reclaim Cuba were now in the bloodstream of the body politic. The personal history of the exiles had become a living history of the United States, and it made Battle and those who were caught up in this history feel as if, on some profound and near-cosmic level, they were part of an ongoing political narrative that was still being written.

At Danbury prison, as Battle's release date approached, he might have been asked, "Padrino, when you get out of here, what are you gonna do?"

The answer was predictable, burned as it was into the man's DNA: "We're gonna go get that bastard, Castro, and take back La Patria."

IN THE DECADE OR SO THAT BATTLE HAD BEEN GROWING HIS BOLITA BUSINESS, THE months on the run in Spain, and, later, while he was serving time at Danbury—through it all *la lucha,* the struggle, lived on, and the dream never died. With the assassination of JFK bringing about the discontinuation of Operation Mongoose, the anti-Castro movement had broken open like a piñata, spewing forth a generation's worth of CIA-trained spies, killers, and covert operators. The Mafia was no longer involved, but the relationship between the militant exiles and the CIA had become, if anything, even more entangled.

A primary player in this alliance remained Luis Posada Carriles, Battle's poker buddy and friend from the army base at Fort Benning. Like the Watergate burglars, Posada was a dedicated combatant in the secret war against Castro. But unlike Rolando Martínez and the others, he remained on the front lines as a CIA operative, active in South Florida and in various anticommunist efforts throughout Latin America. In Miami, Posada was one of the cofounders of a paramilitary organization called Alpha 66, which was created to carry out anti-Castro terrorist bombings, political assassinations, and other counterrevolutionary acts.

In 1965, Posada took part in what became known as "the Alejos conspiracy." In an elaborate plot to stage a coup d'état in Guatemala, the CIA devised a plan to infiltrate operatives and a huge cache of weapons into that country. Posada was one of numerous Cuban exile conspirators who were apprehended in the United States and forced to turn over guns, ammunition, and explosives to U.S. Customs. At the same time, Posada was active in Mexico, where he became part of an anti-Castro cell that intended to blow up some Russian ships in the port town of Veracruz.

Posada's partner and primary financier on the Mexico operation was a 2506 Brigade veteran named Jorge Mas Canosa. At the time, Mas was active in the anti-Castro underground; in later years, he would become a prominent figure aboveground as the president of the Cuban American National Foundation, the most influential Cuban American political lobbying group in the United States.

Posada, for his part, remained firmly underground. Since leaving the Firestone Tire and Rubber Company and preparing for the Bay of Pigs invasion, he had opted for the life of a covert operator. The failure of the invasion, and the fact that so many of his compadres had spent time in Castro's prison, had instilled in him a sense of mission that would keep him occupied for many decades to come.

As Posada engaged in various clandestine operations and began to leave a paper trail within classified files of the CIA, his internal evaluations were laudatory. One report noted:

His performance in all assigned tasks has been excellent . . . It is [my] observation that although A/15 [Posada] is dedicated to the overthrow of Castro, he is acutely aware of the international implications of ill planned or overly enthusiastic activities against Cuba.

Another report noted:

Subject is strongly anti-communist. In addition he sincerely believes in a Democratic/Reform government for his homeland . . . He is strongly pro-American, and believes that when [Castro] is overthrown, the only hope for his country is through U.S. government indirect participation in [Cuban] affairs.

Posada's file noted that he traveled undercover as a professional jewelry salesman, and that the CIA was paying him $300 a month. Under the section titled SUBJECT'S PERSONAL HABITS, it read, "Subject does not gamble."

Apparently, playing poker for money, as he had at Fort Benning, did not qualify. But the point was well taken. Compared to his friend José Miguel Battle, he was an amateur.

In 1971, Posada ran into his old friend once again. By then, Posada was heavily active in the war against communism in Venezuela. Castro had sent armed intelligence operatives into that country in an attempt to influence its direction, and Posada was part of an armed Cuban exile unit that resisted. There had been actual combat, and Posada had been shot. Later, the exiled activist was appointed head of Venezuela's secret intelligence unit, which apprehended and tortured communist sympathizers believed to be enemies of the state. Posada was now on the vanguard of the war to seek out and fight Castroism wherever it reared its head.

On a visit to Miami for recruitment purposes, Posada ran into Battle at a cockfight. Though illegal in the United States, cockfighting was a strong cultural tradition among Cuban men, and there were often illegal cockfights set up in makeshift arenas around South Florida and in the Keys.

Posada and Battle embraced. They had not seen each other since their days together at Fort Benning. Through the Cuban exile grapevine, Battle would have known of Posada's activities in the war against Castro and communism—maybe not the details, but enough to know that his old friend was on the front lines. Posada knew that José Miguel was the bolita kingpin of New York and New Jersey. He knew that Battle had recently been indicted on federal gambling charges. Though the two men were on different career paths, they still shared the common goal of wanting to see Fidel Castro dead. They both believed this was going to happen one day—hopefully soon—and they would all return to their beloved Cuba.

At the cockfight in Miami, Battle did something that Posada would remember for the rest of his days. He placed a wager of $1 million. "Had I not seen it with my own eyes, I wouldn't have believed it," said Posada years later. In 1971, $1 million was the equivalent of $6 million today.

Battle lost the bet.

Posada was astounded by the sum involved. Immediately, Battle rose higher on the list of people he would lean on for financing of anti-Castro operations.

What Posada did not know at the time was that José Miguel was about to flee the United States for Spain. This bet may have been a last grand gesture before he became an international fugitive from the law.

LA LUCHA WAS A VAST WEB, AND IT WAS ALIVE ON MANY FRONTS, INCLUDING NEW Jersey, where Battle was king. Two notorious militants who lived in Union City, in the shadow of Battle's bolita operation, were the Novo brothers, Guillermo and Ignacio. These were the men that Castro's mistress, Marita Lorenz, claimed to have seen with Frank Sturgis and Oswald in Dallas.

Their hypothetical involvement in the JFK assassination, if true, was below the surface, known only within the inner sanctums of the Agency, and presumably among the participants. But the Novo brothers had made themselves famous for another event that was undertaken out in the open for all to see.

Back in 1964, while Che Guevara was giving a speech at the United Nations, the Novo brothers positioned themselves at a location in Queens, across the East River from the U.N. building. From a home-made bazooka they had constructed out of parts purchased at a local hardware store, they fired a missile at the location in the building where Guevara was giving his speech. The missile did not have the range to hit the building; it came up short and fell into the river. The Novo brothers were arrested but did no time for the attempted assassination. They be-came heroes among anti-Castro Cuban exiles everywhere, but especially in New Jersey. In Union City, they cofounded Omega 7, a clandestine terrorist group that was viewed as New Jersey's equivalent to Alpha 66 in Miami.

The Novo brothers and José Miguel Battle knew each other, but because they were all engaged to one degree or another in a clandestine field, they knew better than to be seen together in public.

in New Jersey. In Union City, they cofounded Omega 7, a clandestine terrorist group that was viewed as New Jersey's equivalent to Alpha 66 in Miami.

The Novo brothers and José Miguel Battle knew each other, but because they were all engaged to one degree or another in a clandestine war against Fidel, they knew better than to be seen together in public. The FBI was watching. And yet they somehow managed to interact and perhaps commit crimes together as soldiers in the war against Cuba.

In April 1974, while Battle was still in prison, there occurred in Miami a notorious political murder. The victim was José Elías de la Torriente, a vocal anti-Castro activist who had been raising money for something he called "Work Plan for Liberation." On April 25, Good Friday, Torriente, age sixty-nine, was shot dead by a sniper while watching television with his wife in his Coral Gables home. Outside his front door, a message was found, a piece of paper with a large zero and a line drawn through it.

In recent months, the exile activist had made enemies within his own community by continuing to raise money for a plan that some suspected he had no intention of carrying out. To these people, Torriente was seen as a profiteer, a scam artist, who was using anti-Castro rhetoric to cheat Cuban exiles in Miami and New Jersey out of money.

The day after Torriente's murder, a lengthy communiqué, typewritten in Spanish, was delivered to various media outlets in Miami and in Hudson County, New Jersey. It was addressed to "public opinion" and signed by an entity that called itself "Zero Group." Labeling Torriente "a traitor to La Patria," the statement spelled out the group's intention to eliminate any and all exile leaders who "block this process of liberating their homeland by working only to advance their own bastard ambitions." Within days, another letter went out in which Zero Group listed ten names of prominent exile activists marked with a zero. The letter read, "Each in his own time and in a cool and dispassionate way will start getting his zero. An infinite zero that will adorn their soon to be forgotten tomb . . . Cemeteries are very big and we have more than enough time to fill them."

The messages set an ominous tone: many believed that Castro government functionaries were behind it somehow. To others, it was an example of how factionalized the anti-Castro movement had become, with various groups turning against one another. Militant activists weren't just targeting people and political entities that were believed to be sympathetic to Castro, they were killing each other.

Like many events within the anti-Castro movement, the Torriente murder remained a mystery for some time, until an FBI special agent in New York City reached out to a well-placed confidential informant in New Jersey. Special Agent Larry Wack filed an intelligence report that read, in part:

> This investigator contacted Source #1 in New York City in regards to an ongoing investigation of Omega 7, a Cuban terrorist organization based in the United States. Source #1 stated that Guillermo Novo is a close associate of Jose Miguel Battle, a known organized crime figure from the New Jersey area and a Bay of Pigs veteran (2506 Brigade). Source #1 said that in the early 1970s, Jose M. Battle contracted Guillermo Novo to subcontract assassination hits on several individuals in the New Jersey, New York and Miami areas.

> One of the assassination hits was of Jose Elias De La Torriente, a Cuban activist that was assassinated at his residence. According to street rumors, a day before the homicide of subject De La Torriente, Guillermo Nova's brother, Ignacio Novo, was caught in the backyard of the residence of subject De La Torriente; subject Ignacio Novo was stripped [*sic*] searched at gunpoint by subject De La Torriente.

The FBI was never able to make a case against Battle, the Novo brothers, or anybody else for the murder of José Elías de la Torriente. To this day, the murder remains an open case.

The fact that Battle was in prison at the time of the murder ultimately proved to be good cover for the Mob boss. To say that Battle was involved would have been a rebuke to security measures at the facility, an indictment of the system itself. Could this murder have been hatched from behind the walls of Danbury prison? Prison authorities might have scoffed at the idea. But there is little doubt that José Miguel Battle had the means, and the motive, to assemble a plan to carry out such an execution.

Among those in the know, it was a killing that seemed to suggest that there was taking shape within the womb of the exile community a sinister intermingling—a potential dark alliance—between the anti-Castro movement and the Cuban American gangster underworld.

PEDRO BATTLE WAS THE YOUNGEST AND MOST WELL LIKED OF THE BATTLE BROTHERS. He was not physically intimidating, like José Miguel, nor sometimes surly, like Gustavo. He had a friendly disposition, which some may have interpreted as a sign of weakness.

Since the infamous shootout between the Battle brothers and Hector Duarte in the streets of Little Havana, Pedro had moved north to New York City. With brother Gustavo having been convicted and imprisoned on cocaine charges, José Miguel, El Padrino, reiterated his ban on narcotics as a source of revenue for his organization. But by early 1974, he was away in prison. Pedro, who had originally transplanted himself to New York to oversee the Cuban Mafia's bolita operations in the Bronx, had begun selling cocaine on the street. A key partner of Pedro's in this enterprise was Ernestico Torres, his friend from Madrid. Pedro had served as godfather to Ernestico's son, and after leaving Spain and returning to the United States, they had remained close.

Knowing that José Miguel had prohibited the selling of drugs, Pedro and Ernestico were aware that they were treading on thin ice. It was important that news of what they were doing did not travel on the underworld grapevine to El Padrino in prison, or they were going to be in trouble. In the year or so since they had returned from Spain, things had gone well. They were making money by peddling coke, mostly in the South Bronx, and there were few problems. That all changed with the emergence of an ambitious Cuban gangster named José "Palulu" Enriquez.

Palulu was an old rival of Pedro's from Miami. Back in the 1960s, while selling coke in the Magic City, the two had territorial disputes that on at least one occasion led to gunfire. By the early 1970s, Palulu had moved north. The New York–New Jersey area was where the money was, and like many enterprising Cuban exiles from South Florida, he came looking for a piece of the action. In Miami, Palulu had mostly been a bolitero. He knew that in New York the Battle organization had that sewn up. And so he focused on the cocaine business, which appeared to be wide open. His primary area of operation was the Bronx. He established a modest system, with cocaine being brought into the country mostly by drug "mules"—body smugglers—across the Mexican border into California. When the product arrived in the New York metropolitan area, Palulu purchased in bulk, warehoused his product in the Bronx, and sold it on the street through a network of dealers.

It was a solid operation, until suddenly Pedro Battle and his crazy sidekick Ernestico Torres started moving in on his territory. Now here he was in the Bronx, years after his territorial dispute with Pedro down in Miami, having to deal with the Battles once again. To Palulu, the Battles were like the plague; left unattended, they spread like a disease.

The situation in the Bronx quickly came to a head. A heated dispute developed over one street corner in particular where both organizations were selling their product. Pedro Battle believed that this corner belonged to him. One night, when he received word that Palulu's people were selling product at the location, he sent out a crew headed by Ernestico. There was a shootout. Ernestico shot and killed one of Palulu's dealers, a Puerto Rican known as "El Raton," the Mouse. Not only did Ernestico kill the man, but he and the rest of his crew then absconded with $20,000 worth of Palulu's cocaine, claiming that it was a legitimate street tax for the rival dealer's having violated their territory.

When Palulu heard what had happened, he was deranged with anger and vowed revenge. He was known to be relentless. Born in Cuba, he had—as with nearly everyone else among his generation of exiles, clandestine operators, and gangsters—tried to make a go of it under Castro's revolutionary regime but soon found out that communism was not conducive to the kind of street-level entrepreneurship he most admired. He fled the island and became a professional criminal.

He had always harbored resentment, or perhaps jealousy, toward the Battles. José Miguel was El Padrino, and the others rode his coattails. Pedro in particular he saw as a fraud. Back in Miami and also in New York, Palulu had enthusiastically circulated his opinion that Pedro Battle was a coward. In the shootout with Hector Duarte in Little Havana, Pedro had fled the scene, leaving his brother Gustavo bleeding in the street. Palulu's jealousy toward the Battles was crystallized in his disdain for Pedro.

Right around the time of the El Raton murder, something happened that altered the landscape somewhat. After having served sixteen months of an eighteen-month sentence, José Miguel Battle was released from prison.

As always when a boss returns after a stint away in the joint, the news created a buzz throughout the Cuban American underworld. The boss was back. For some, the prospect of once again making big money was the primary stimulator. For others, there were old scores that needed to be settled. In family squabbles, one sibling might say to another, "You just wait until Daddy gets home." The criminal underworld, especially with racketeering operations that revolved around blood relations and "family," had a similar dynamic. The return of El Padrino held the promise of old accounts being settled and dormant operations being put into motion.

It is not clear at exactly what point Battle learned about Pedro's cocaine business, and Ernestico's involvement in that business, but when he did, he was livid. Their own brother Gustavo was in prison on drug charges. It was too damn risky. And then there was the killing of El Raton, which created a blood feud with Palulu that Battle suspected would put everyone on edge and become a major distraction. Clearly, what he needed to do was tend to his bolita business. Between his time on the lam and time in prison, he'd been away for three years. The best use of his time was to make a full accounting of his criminal operations and make adjustments, if necessary. Having to deal with a street war that had been generated by an aspect of the black market—narcotics— that he'd forbidden was a headache he did not need.

Battle was concerned about consequences. He could not have known that those consequences would become apparent almost immediately, just two months after his release from prison.

The neighborhood of Washington Heights had become a primary locale for the Cuban Mafia in the area. It was an easy drive from Hudson County, New Jersey, where many of them lived. You crossed the majestic

George Washington Bridge and you were in the heart of Washington Heights. It was also a short drive from the Bronx. The neighborhood was New York's version of Miami's Little Havana, without the palm trees, homegrown cigars, and persistent sunshine. The Colonial restaurant, on 181st Street and St. Nicholas Avenue, was a place where the boliteros— Battle, Mujica, Isleño Davila, Joaquin Deleon Sr., and others—met to discuss business, especially the bankers. But Washington Heights was also a place where the Cubans socialized, in clubs and after-hours locations where music blared and the revelry sometimes spilled out into the street.

In the early morning hours of December 23, two days before Christmas, the Guanabo Bar and Grill at 1487 St. Nicholas Avenue, between 184th and 185th streets in Washington Heights, was overflowing. Pedro Battle was there with his wife, Elda. Wearing a maroon jacket, a red tie, and a pink shirt, clearly Pedro was not concerned about being noticed in a crowd.

Palulu Enriquez entered the bar with an entourage of four other men. Palulu had a distinctive look: he was a dark-skinned, Afro Cuban, with a Fu Manchu mustache that made him resemble the famous major league baseball pitcher, Luis Tiant, who was also Cuban. As Palulu often did, he was wearing a hat. Even though it was after 3 A.M., the place was so filled with customers that Palulu was there for a while before he spotted his nemesis in the maroon jacket, Pedro Battle, seated with his wife in a booth near the entrance to the ladies' room. Palulu felt the .45-caliber handgun tucked in his waist. He walked over to Pedro and said, "Well, look who's here, the *maricón* who had one of my men killed. Didn't even have the cojones to do it himself, ordered that scumbag Ernestico Torres to do the hit."

Pedro tightened; he also was packing heat, a .45 inside his jacket. He was ready for a moment just like this. "Palulu," he proclaimed, "you been a *lambe culo* ever since Miami. Get out of my face before I have to teach you a lesson."

Raising his voice a couple decibels, loud enough so that he could be heard over the jukebox, Palulu responded, "You gonna teach me a lesson? The guy who deserted his own brother? Left him to bleed in the street while he ran away? You gonna teach me? You and what army, you fucking coward."

Being publicly called out for having deserted his brother hit Pedro where it hurt. For years he had harbored guilt and shame about having fled the scene after the shootout on Flagler Street. Now that shame was being summoned by a person he despised more than any other.

Pedro reached for his gun, and Palulu reached for his; the two men started blazing away.

Customers in the bar stampeded for the exits. It was not uncommon in a bar in Washington Heights for someone to whip out a gun and start talking trash, but this was the real deal. *Boom! Boom!* Bullets were flying. The two gunmen traded shots across the bow. Palulu was grazed in the shoulder, but he kept blasting.

Pedro was hit three times, twice in the left arm and once in the face. He crashed to the floor and did not move.

Elda cried out. She turned over the body of her husband and saw that he was dead. She stumbled out of the club and said to a gypsy cab driver in front of the place, "My husband is dead, they killed my husband." The cabdriver quickly drove to the nearby 34th Precinct station house and informed the officer at the front desk about the shooting. The desk officer immediately put out a radio call that included the location of the bar.

By the time cops arrived at the Guanabo Bar and Grill, the place was mostly cleared out except for the manager of the bar, a few staff, and Elda Battle, who was on her knees crying over the body of her dead husband.

After a quick look at the body, the cops could see that Battle, lying in a pool of his own blood, was dead. Detective Thomas E. Henry, standing over the body with a pad and pen, made note of Battle's colorful attire, his expensive Lucien Piccard watch, his black patent leather loafer-style shoes, and the gold wedding band on his left hand.

Other detectives questioned the handful of workers at the bar. The employees described the mayhem that had taken place, but none of them knew or had seen the shooter—at least that's what they said.

The wife was still wailing over the dead body. Uniformed cops had to peel her off and lead her away, so that emergency personnel and a forensics team could address the crime scene.

It was now 4 A.M. Outside the Guanaba bar, squad car lights flashed and the area was marked off. At that hour, you wouldn't expect there to be many people on the street, but there they were mingling in the winter cold, some talking under their breath, others shocked and startled. After hours could be brutal in *el barrio*.

Those who knew anything about the assailant and the victim—patrons who had perhaps fled the bar and were now on the sidewalk or in the street pretending to be anonymous onlookers—had intimations of what lay ahead. Pedro, the youngest of the Battle brothers, had been murdered in a very public way. This was a dagger aimed squarely at the heart of the Battle organization, an act that would resonate throughout the Cuban American underworld.

Palulu had declared war on El Padrino, and now there would be hell to pay.

5

BRING ME THE HEAD OF PALULU

CARLOS RODRIGUEZ, OTHERWISE KNOWN AS TRIO DE TRÉS, WAS HOME ASLEEP WHEN his phone rang. It was early in the morning, around 6 a.m., not an hour when he was usually at his best. But when he answered the phone and heard the voice of Chino Barquin, an assistant of José Miguel Battle's, he shook himself awake. "Get dressed," he was told by Barquin. "We're coming by to pick you up in twenty minutes."

Rodriguez rolled out of bed. He went to the bathroom and splashed some water on his face. He put on some clothes, quickly brewed some coffee, and had had only a few sips before he saw outside the window Battle's red Cadillac pull up in front of his building.

Rodriguez headed outside. As he approached the Caddy, he saw Barquin in the driver's seat, and in the front passenger seat, José Miguel. Rodriguez got in the backseat and pulled the door closed. He sat there for a beat or two, didn't say anything. Then Battle turned around, and Rodriguez saw something he had never seen before: El Padrino was crying.

"They killed Pedro, my little brother," said Battle. His face was contorted with grief.

Rodriguez was stunned. His heart sank for his friend. He said, "Oh my God," because there were no other words to express the sadness he was feeling.

Without looking back, Barquin said, "We gotta drive into the city and go identify the body."

"Okay," said Rodriguez.

The Cadillac drove through Union City, onto the New Jersey Turnpike, and into the Holland Tunnel, which would take them into lower Manhattan, where the city morgue was located. On the drive, José

Miguel related what he knew of the shooting so far, what the cops had told him, and what he was able to learn through contacts of his own. There was no question who had pulled the trigger. It was Palulu Enriquez.

At such an early hour, finding parking was not difficult. They entered the morgue and explained why they were there. An official from the Medical Examiner's Office led them downstairs to the morgue.

The room was like a crypt, with smells that were strangely antiseptic and clinical. The men were led to a gurney, where a body lay covered with a white sheet, except for the feet, which peeked out from the sheet. The assistant medical examiner looked at a tag on the toe of the left foot.

"Okay," he said, "which one of you is a relation of the deceased?"

José Miguel nodded and stepped forward. The medical examiner pulled back the sheet.

From where Rodriguez was standing, he could not see behind the sheet. And so he watched José Miguel's face. He saw the sadness and the grief, the tears again coming to his friend's eyes. Whimpering like a wounded animal, Battle nodded that, yes, this was his brother, Pedro Battle.

The assistant medical examiner pulled the sheet back over the body. He asked the men to wait there as he wheeled the body away.

Rodriguez put a hand on his friend's shoulder, which seemed to snap Battle out of his grief. His crying stopped, and Rodriguez saw something take hold of his friend. It was anger. "*Hijo de puta* (son of a bitch)," said Battle, to no one in particular. And then the anger transformed itself into an even deeper subset of emotion—rage. Battle's face reddened, his breathing became labored. "We gonna get that motherfucker," he said to Rodriguez. "We gonna make him pay for what he did."

El Padrino was like a volcano, ready to blow.

Over the days that followed, that rage never did subside.

The funeral service for Pedro Battle was held in Union City on December 27, 1974. Throughout the day and into the evening, well-wishers stopped by to offer condolences, deliver floral arrangements, and, in some cases, breathe in the pungent aroma of revenge that hung over the funeral parlor like a tropical depression.

IT IS NOT KNOWN EXACTLY WHEN JOSÉ MIGUEL BATTLE SAW THE MOVIE *THE GODFATHER* for the first time. The movie debuted in New York City, Los Angeles, and other major U.S. cities on March 24, 1972, while Battle was on the lam in Spain. It opened in Madrid later that year, in October, but by then, Battle had already returned to the United States, where he was immediately arrested and held in detention for the next sixteen months. Determining when he first saw the movie may be elusive, but for those who knew him, there is no question that he did indeed see the film, and that it had a profound impact on the boss of the Cuban Mafia.

Battle talked incessantly about the movie and seemed to view the story of Mafia boss Don Vito Corleone, as played on-screen by Marlon Brando, as a kind of metaphor for his life. The movie's storyline was a bloody and dramatic explication of the American dream, with the God-father, Vito Corleone, attempting to retain aspects of his Old World Sicilian culture while adapting to the realities of the New World. At the center of Corleone's universe was the concept of family, something that Battle held dear, or at least paid lip service to on many occasions. Don Corleone had his sons, and José Miguel had his brothers. There was also the fanciful aspect of the plot in which Corleone, as boss of the family's criminal enterprise, is against the selling of narcotics. In the real world, many Mafia bosses, including, most notably, Santo Trafficante Sr., had peddled dope since at least the 1930s, but in the movie, the Godfather's resistance to narcotics is presented as an example of Old World nobility, with the boss choosing morality over profit.

Mostly what captured the imagination of Battle was Marlon Brando's performance as the Don. Battle bore a resemblance to Brando as Corleone—the jowls, the raspy voice, and also the air of noblesse oblige, as if the responsibilities of the world weighed heavily on his shoulders. After Battle had viewed the movie more than once, many in his circle of friends and associates got the impression that José Miguel would sub-consciously slip into an impersonation of the Godfather, and no one thought of this as an affectation. Many felt that indeed there was some kind of connection between the El Padrino they knew and the iconic screen character. Somehow, Battle as Corleone made perfect sense.

The movie was a huge critical and box-office success, and in 1973 it won multiple Academy Awards. Battle saw in the culture's embracing of the movie a reaffirmation of his own life choices, and yet the benefits were ephemeral. *The Godfather* was a movie. What had arrived on Battle's doorstep were the harsh vicissitudes of real life.

José Miguel's personification of Brando's Godfather was very much on display at the funeral parlor on the night of his murdered brother's memorial service. While friends and family members paid their respects at the closed coffin of the deceased, Battle was in a room nearby receiving condolences and speaking to his underlings. Already he had made it clear to his people that he wanted Palulu Enriquez dead or alive— preferably alive, so he could torture him to death himself. He offered a bounty of $20,000 for anyone who killed Palulu, and $50,000 for anyone who captured him alive. He also declared that anyone who was with Palulu as part of his crew had until Pedro's burial to come to his organization and join their side, or they too were fair game.

At the funeral parlor, he eulogized his brother, saying that Pedro was "too kind and gentle." His emotions ebbed from sorrow and regret to fulminations of vengeance. Of Palulu, he proclaimed, "*¡Quiero la cabeza y los cojones de ese hijo de puta montadas en mi pared, mañana!* (I want the head and balls of this son of a bitch mounted on my wall, tomorrow!)"

At the funeral parlor that night, and in the days that followed, a few of Battle's most trusted hit men stepped forward to offer their services. One person who approached him was not a member of his organization—at least not yet. He was Julio "Chino" Acuna, a mocha-skinned mestizo who at the time was a gunman in Palulu's crew.

Chino was another of the thousands of Cubans fleeing the island of Cuba every year. In his case, the journey had been recent; he arrived by boat in Miami in 1971 and eventually requested asylum at the Newark office of the Immigration and Naturalization Service as a Cuban refugee. His mixed-blood features earned him the nickname "Chino" (Chinaman). He knew Palulu from Cuba and went to work as his bodyguard and enforcer. Standing five feet nine inches tall, and lean, he was not physically intimidating, but Chino Acuna was known to be a proficient killer.

Chino showed up under the guise of paying his respects to Battle on the occasion of his brother's memorial service, but his true motive was to tell El Padrino that he would switch sides and help him get his revenge against Palulu.

"I am here to help you," he whispered in Battle's ear.

They agreed to talk in more detail later.

Others came forward, including Ernestico Torres. In Spain, Ernestico had emerged as a crazed, up-and-coming gunman willing to kill on behalf of El Padrino at the drop of a hat. Since arriving in the United States, he had served as a mule by strapping loads of marijuana and cocaine to his body and crossing the border at Tijuana, Mexico. The drugs were delivered to a house in Los Angeles. Since arriving in New Jersey, he had been scuffling to get by, ripping off Colombian drug dealers—a highly dangerous proposition—and eventually going into the cocaine business with Pedro Battle. He had also contracted himself out as a professional hit man.

Ernestico approached José Miguel Battle with some trepidation. He had heard that Battle held him partly responsible for having stirred the hornet's nest that led to his brother's death—first by getting involved with Pedro in the coke business, and second by killing El Raton. Palulu had used the murder of El Raton and the stealing of his product as the motivation and excuse for going after Pedro.

At the funeral parlor, when Ernestico heard how much was being offered for the capture or murder of Palulu, his eyes lit up. He wanted a piece of that action. But he had to convince Battle that he was the man for the job.

José Miguel was in a room separate from the coffin viewing area, where mourners gathered to pay their respects. Ernestico was allowed into the room. With him was a sidekick and criminal partner named Carlos "Charley" Hernandez, a professional lock picker and thief with whom he'd recently been doing burglaries. Charley, whose nickname was "El Pincero" (the Lock Picker), stood at a distance as Ernestico spoke to Battle.

"Pedro was your blood," said Ernestico, "but he was like a brother to me, too. Remember, he was the godfather to my son, Ernesto Jr. I blame myself for what happened. I should have protected him from that cocksucker. It was my fault." Ernestico rubbed the wetness from his eyes.

For all his hardness, José Miguel could be a soft touch. He took in stray dogs and was known to give out money indiscriminately to people who were in need. Ernestico's tears worked.

"Listen," José Miguel said to Ernesto, "you need to show more discipline. You need to use your brain and not go off half cocked all the time."

"I know. Listen, I promise to you. I give you my word. No more *coca*. I'm done with that business."

Battle nodded his approval.

"Let me get Palulu. Give me the contract. I won't let you down."

Battle glanced toward Charley Hernandez with a trace of disdain. He said to Ernestico, "Tell your friend to wait in the other room. We talk privately."

Ernesto told Charley to wait outside. When he was gone, Battle said, "Listen, *niño*"—he often called Ernestico *niño* (child)—"I'll give you this contract, but I don't want this friend of yours involved. I've heard about this guy. He's a common thief, you know that, and he drinks too much and runs his mouth. He can't be trusted."

"Okay," said Ernestico, "whatever you want."

El Padrino had them hold hands and make a pledge that they would not rest until they had avenged Pedro's murder.

Charley Hernandez was waiting outside when Ernestico appeared. Years later, he remembered it well: "So Ernestico went out of the funeral parlor, and he was happy. I said, 'What went on?' He told me what went on: 'I'm working for José Miguel. Tomorrow I'm gonna start looking for this guy [Palulu].' And I say, 'Well, now you're in the money. These people are bankers. They got a lot of money, you know? Good for you.' He says, 'Don't worry, I'm gonna try to get you in with [Battle]. You my ace in the hole.'"

The hunt for Palulu started immediately. Teams of hit men in cars began roaming northern New Jersey, upper Manhattan, and the Bronx. Ironically, the first to encounter trouble from these efforts was not Ernestico or Chino Acuna; it was Battle himself.

IT WAS AROUND 2 A.M. ON THE MORNING OF DECEMBER 30, JUST TWO DAYS AFTER THE funeral service. José Miguel was at a bar called Club 61, in the town of West New York, just north of Union City. From a pay phone at the club, he called his wife at home. The level of paranoia in the Battle universe was high. Everyone was concerned about further shootings, and the Battle family in particular suspected they might still be a target of Palulu and his crew. José Miguel routinely called in to check on his family. He was told by his wife that just a few minutes before there had been some men in a car outside their apartment building, and that a man with a gun had confronted Aldo Battle, José Miguel's younger brother, in the garage. Battle immediately called his other brother Sergio, telling him and Aldo to meet at his home on 45th Street in Union City.

José Miguel grabbed an associate at the bar, Michael Depazo, who was currently under indictment on a murder charge. The two drove to a safe house apartment where the Battle organization kept an arsenal of weapons. They picked up some guns and headed on to meet the other Battles.

Aldo and Sergio were waiting in front of the building. Aldo told José Miguel the story of confronting a man with a gun in the garage. The man, it turned out, was an off-duty cop investigating a stolen car incident; the man showed his police identification. But now the paranoia of the Battles had been stoked. They loaded into Battle's four-door Buick, which was listed as belonging to Latin American Jewelers, his jewelry shop on Bergenline Avenue. They carried with them an assortment of weapons, including revolvers, automatic pistols, and a shotgun.

What these men didn't know was that the off-duty cop had called in a report of four Spanish-speaking men driving around in a car loaded with guns.

Depazo was driving, with José Miguel in the front passenger seat and the other Battle brothers in the back. They were on the hunt for whatever they might find, preferably someone from Palulu's crew, or Palulu himself, in which case they would blast him to smithereens.

On Palisades Avenue, they were suddenly surrounded by cop cars with lights flashing. Two cops from the patrol car in front were the first to get out and approach the Buick. One of the cops, Patrolman Diego Mella, a Cuban émigré, approached on the driver's side. His partner approached the vehicle on José Miguel's side and opened the door. The first thing he saw was a shotgun wrapped in a blanket between Battle's legs. "He's got a gun," he called immediately.

The two cops pulled out their weapons. "Out of the car with your hands in the air," shouted Officer Mella.

The Battles and Depazo piled out of the vehicle. They were all searched. In addition to the shotgun, José Miguel was carrying a .38-caliber Colt revolver and also a 9mm Luger automatic. Aldo Battle was carrying a .38-caliber revolver and extra shells for the shotgun. The driver, Depazo, was carrying a .38, fully loaded with five rounds. In the back of the Buick, on the floor, was a fully loaded .380 automatic pistol.

"What are you dong with all these weapons?" asked Officer Mella.

"I can explain," said Battle. "They're not ours. Somebody dropped them and we picked them up."

At this point, from the police vehicle in the rear, a sergeant approached. His name was John Messina, and he was the supervisor at the scene.

As soon as Battle saw the sergeant, he said, "Messina, it's me." And then, nodding toward the arresting officers, he asked, "What is this?"

Messina looked at José Miguel, then looked at the patrolmen and said, "I know this man."

Mella said to Messina, "We confiscated a small arsenal from these men."

Messina looked at the assortment of guns. He seemed to be thinking, assessing the situation. He said to Mella, "All right. Take them back to the station and we'll sort this out."

Battle and the others were cuffed. José Miguel was put in the back of Patrolman Mella's car. As they were driving to the police station house, Battle became chatty in the backseat. At first he spoke in English, but when he determined from Mella's accent that he was a Cuban, he switched to Spanish.

"Do you know who I am?" Battle asked Mella.

Mella studied the man through his rearview mirror. Given the way Sergeant Messina had reacted, and Battle's own privileged attitude, he was beginning to think maybe he should know him. But he was relatively new to the area and had never seen him before.

Battle explained to Mella, "You know, there's a contract out on my life. I know it's against the law for me to have those guns, but it was for my own personal defense. They murdered my brother."

Battle made small talk with Mella. The cop could tell he was an old-school Cuban. Eventually, Battle said, "If somebody could help make this whole thing go away, the gun charges, I would be very grateful. And I know how to show my gratitude to policemen. Just ask around."

"Are you offering me a bribe?" asked Mella.

"No, no, no," said Battle. "It's nothing of the sort. I'm just saying that I would be grateful." He sank into glum silence for the rest of the ride.

By the time they arrived at the station house, José Miguel seemed angry. As they entered, he saw Sergeant Messina and shouted, "Messina, I want to make a phone call."

Sergeant Messina tried to avoid him. Later, cops at the station referred to it as "the Messina Waltz," as Messina tried to sidestep Battle, and Battle sidestepped right along with him.

"I get to make one call," Battle reiterated. "Call Bolte. Call the chief. I want him here now."

Officer Mella's ears pricked up. Herman Bolte was the legendary chief of the department. This guy was claiming to know Chief Bolte. The entire incident had just been kicked up to a higher level.

It was Mella's intention to charge Battle and the others with possession of a dangerous weapon, but he was told by Sergeant Messina that they had received a call of two more suspicious characters in the area where they had arrested the Battles. "Take your partner and go search the area," he told the patrolman.

"But we've got prisoners to book," protested Mella.

"Don't worry about that. We'll take care of it."

Reluctantly, Mella and his partner left the station and drove back to the scene. It was 3 A.M.; there was no one there. They discussed how strange it was for them not to have been allowed to book their prisoners. It was against regular procedure. Said Mella, "It's not right. I'm going back there and insist we are on record as the arresting officers."

Back at the precinct, there had been a shift change. Mella explained to the new sergeant on duty what had happened. The sergeant said, "Okay. You're right. Go ahead and book them."

Mella headed downstairs to the holding area. What he saw was José Miguel Battle sitting with three or four other cops. They were laughing, smoking cigarettes, and telling stories to each other, like old friends at a barbecue.

Patrolman Mella was allowed to book the suspects. He and his partner took statements from the three Battles and Depazo. It dragged on
until after 4 A.M. And then the suspects were released. Nothing ever
happened. No state gun possession charges were lodged against Battle
or the others.

Patrolman Diego Mella later heard that it was the chief himself,
Herman Bolte, who had called the desk sergeant and told him to release
the suspects without bond.

BEING RELATIVELY NEW TO UNION CITY, MELLA DIDN'T KNOW THE HISTORY OF HOW
things operated in his town. The tradition of cops on the take, particularly as it related to illegal gambling, ran deep in Hudson County. For
those in the know, cops and gambling bosses were all part of the same
consortium. One hand washed the other.

Though it would never be proven in court, many believed that the
man who protected the gambling rackets was Chief Bolte. At the station
house in Union City, José Miguel Battle had called out that name for a
reason. Bolte was arguably the most powerful figure in Hudson County.
Mayors and county commissioners came and went, but the Bolte name
remained carved in stone.

Herman Bolte had joined the police department straight out of the
Army Air Corps in 1946. His father had been a captain in the department before him. Cops who came out of the service were sometimes
known as Lucky and Camels guys. They smoked cigarettes nonstop and
talked like tough guys out of a Jimmy Cagney gangster movie. Little
thought was given to sartorial style or overall physical appearance. There
was one detective in Union City who, while you were talking to him,
would pop out his false teeth and roll them around in his mouth.

Cops in this part of Jersey were physically intimidating, but mostly
they let it be known that they could be bought. "Cabbage" was the preferred term when talking about cash. When it came to maintaining
a gambling operation in North Hudson, cabbage made the world go
round.

Bolte received his chief's badge in 1972. The man who presented it to
him in a public ceremony, Union City commissioner Paul J. Lombardo,

months later was indicted for fraud. Rather than do time in prison, he became a federal witness and disappeared into the witness protection program.

Even before he became chief, Bolte had established a reputation as a daring cop. He had florid reddish-blond hair and the face of a cherub, and though he was of average height and somewhat portly, he had swagger.

The event that sealed Bolte's legend, especially in the increasingly Cuban enclaves of Union City and West New York, was a night in 1956 when he received a radio call of a fight in a local bar involving a bunch of Latin males. Bolte arrived on the scene and sorted it all out. The primary suspect was a young Cuban who spoke little or no English, named Fidel Castro.

At the time, Castro was touring the Unites States raising money for his revolution in Cuba. He spoke in cities where there was a significant Cuban population—Miami, Tampa, New York City, and Union City. After speaking to a large group at an old vaudeville theater on Bergenline Avenue, he retreated to a bar on 26th Street. The talk at the bar turned political, and a fight broke out between Castro's people and supporters of the Cuban dictator Fulgencio Batista.

Bolte and other cops separated the two opposing camps. Many of the agitators, including Castro, were taken to police headquarters and charged with disturbing the peace.

Forever after, Herman Bolte dined out on this legendary anecdote, noting that he was the only cop in America who had ever placed handcuffs on Fidel Castro. This would have put him in high standing with the likes of José Miguel Battle and others among his Cuban American constituency in Union City.

Bolte was the chief, but when it came to gambling, the man in charge was Frank Scarafile. There was a reason that when FBI agents came to the home of Trio de Trés, they asked him about Captain Scarafile. The captain was known to be the department's primary receiver of cabbage from gambling rackets and other syndicate activity. When federal agents conducting a surveillance on Battle saw him disappear into the Union City police headquarters, he was likely on his way to the captain's office. Behind closed doors, there were handshakes, hugs, and the transfer of cash.

Like Bolte, Scarafile was a tough-talking local boy who'd made good. Born in Union City on August 18, 1928, he went to Emerson High School, where he graduated in 1946 and went directly into the U.S. Army. He spent two years fighting the enemy in Korea before returning stateside, and in 1952 he joined the Union City Police Department. He quickly rose through the ranks, serving as a sergeant, lieutenant, and captain.

Scarafile wore plaid sports coats and striped ties. Twice a month, he made the two-hour-plus drive down the Jersey Turnpike to Atlantic City, where he played cards and bet the ponies. Eventually, he and his wife purchased a summer house on the shore at Seaside Park. On weekends during the summer, that's where he could be found.

In 1974, just as Battle was returning to New Jersey after serving time in federal prison, Scarafile received yet another promotion, this time to the position of deputy chief of police. That made him the second most powerful man in the department after Bolte, but Scarafile had an avenue of power that Bolte did not: he was the bagman for the city's mayor, William V. Musto.

Musto was not only the mayor, he was an elected New Jersey state senator. In the entire state, there were few politicians more popular than Billy Musto. He was part of the Democratic Party machine and was believed to be a progressive in the manner of Franklin Delano Roosevelt. He had been quick to open doors for the area's Cuban American population, advocating for bilingual education. He was rewarded by the new immigrants, who turned out the Cuban vote for him in election after election.

Like Bolte and Scarafile, Musto was a local product, born in a hospital in West Hoboken, which later became a part of Union City. He served in World War II as an artillery officer under General George Patton and was awarded a Gold Star.

Musto was not a tough guy in the mold of Bolte and Scarafile; he was personable and had a compassionate manner. He was admired by men for his military service but was even more popular among older Italian and Cuban immigrant women who found him charming. He was a strong advocate for his constituents.

Part of advocating for his voters meant that he was in favor of legalized gambling, which in the state of New Jersey brought with it legions of co-conspirators. Ever since the Prohibition era, when games of chance on the boardwalk at Atlantic City had established the state's bona fides as a gambling mecca, certain local political figures had been pushing to establish the state as the Las Vegas of the East. Musto saw gambling as a relatively harmless vice and a potential source of revenue for the state. Some believed that he was personally benefiting from gambling rackets in Union City.

In January 1975, within weeks of the Battle brothers having avoided gun charges, thanks to Chief Bolte, Musto became the subject of a secret federal grand jury inquiry into gambling and political corruption. Earlier in 1974, FBI agents had raided an illegal baccarat operation at 516 47th Street in Union City. Within a few months, that operation, with some of the same backers, had reemerged as a high-stakes baccarat parlor in a bar on Bergenline Avenue named Coll's Neck Tavern. This establishment was owned by the wife of the same corrupt county commissioner—Paul Lombardo—who had first presented Bolte with his badge as chief.

The person who sought police protection for the gambling operation at Coll's Neck was Celin Valdivia, a local Cuban facilitator. Valdivia had reached out to Deputy Chief Scarafile to secure police protection—at a price. Scarafile introduced the scheme to the mayor.

Allegedly, the mayor's role was to make phone calls "urging" a Union City municipal court judge to acquit several men who had been arrested during the first raid on 47th Street so that they could continue the operation at Coll's Neck Tavern. Musto also agreed to guarantee the gambling operation's ongoing protection, for a price, and Deputy Chief Scarafile made the same guarantee to Celin Valdivia—for a price. This was a tried-and-true method of graft in Hudson County going back to the earliest days of the area's founding.

It was certainly a familiar method to José Miguel Battle, who had been weaned on municipal corruption as a vice cop in Batista's Havana. Battle's bolita operation likely operated under a similar system of graft. You would see no photos of the men together out in public. At a benefit for the Patrolman's Benevolent Society or at a fund-raiser for some

Cuban American political organization, Battle and Scarafile and Musto might shake hands and offer one another words of praise and encouragement. But their true bond was surreptitious, based on a belief that in order to protect your people and build a strong organization, you did what you had to do. Being able to line your own pockets with cash wasn't so bad either.

THE EFFORT TO FIND AND KILL PALULU CONTINUED. IN JANUARY, AFTER PEDRO BATTLE was laid to rest, José Miguel teamed up Ernestico with Chino Acuna, who no longer sought to maintain the fiction that he was a loyal member of Palulu's crew. He was with Battle now, looking to score big by bringing Pedro's killer in alive or dead, whichever came first.

They made an odd couple. Chino, though usually dressed in blue jeans and a T-shirt, had the intensity of an African warrior. Ernesto had a slight resemblance to another Ernesto—Ernesto "Che" Guevara. He thought of himself as a ladies' man, and perhaps he was, but in the hunt for Palulu, he assumed a number of unflattering disguises. He grew a beard and mustache, and then shaved them off. He cut his hair short and then shaved his head altogether. He wore an assortment of cheap wigs that occasionally made him look foolish. Always when they went to do a hit, he donned leather race car driving gloves with a zipper at the wrist.

Ernestico was having fun, but the effort was no joke. Battle had told the two hit men they would be paid $4,000 to $5,000 for every member of Palulu's crew they killed. They would be paid $2,000 for every crew member they tortured that led to useful information. Regarding Palulu, Battle told them to "flush that *hijo de puta* out of his hole."

Chino and Ernesto were supplied with untraceable firearms and silencers. They were sent to the Amato Gas Station in nearby Jersey City to choose from a fleet of cars, trucks, and vans that Battle's organization used to conduct criminal business.

For the next three months, in the Cuban American underworld throughout the New York–New Jersey metropolitan area, there were screams in the night and the sounds of Palulu's people crying for mercy. Since Chino had once been part of Palulu's crew, he knew where they lived, worked, and hung out. Chino and Ernestico snatched people off the street at gunpoint and took them to flophouse apartments and abandoned warehouses, never using the same location twice. Palulu's crew members were hog-tied or bound to a chair and tortured for information. Others were stabbed in the street, shot at, or shot dead. Bodies were left in car trunks and back alleyways in Union City, Washington Heights, and the Bronx. The idea was to create a reign of terror, to turn Palulu's world upside down so that he would have to come out of hiding and expose himself to the justice they felt he so richly deserved.

There were eleven murders and at least three torture sessions attributable to the sixteen-week hunt for Palulu. One of those torture sessions, in March, led to a piece of information that was potentially a game changer. Bloodied and beaten, one of Palulu's dealers informed them that there was a location in Central Park in Manhattan where Pedro Battle's killer met regularly with his most trusted crew members. In the north end of the park, between 106th and 107th streets, close to one of the pedestrian entrances, was a grassy area covered by trees. That's where Palulu held semiregular meetings.

Ernestico and Chino began casing the area, and it wasn't long before they spotted their target. Palulu was sitting on a park bench talking to another man.

Said Ernestico to his partner Chino, "I got this fuck. You my wheel man." He opened the car door and tucked a MAC-10 submachine gun under his jacket. He started walking toward his target.

Palulu saw Ernestico coming before he even entered the park. He took off running. Ernestico started after him in pursuit. They ran deep into the park, into an area known as the North Woods. It was one of the most bucolic sections of the most renowned urban park in America.

Ernestico, the younger man, was gaining ground. Palulu said fuck it; he pulled out two .45-caliber pistols and started shooting at Ernestico. Ducking behind a tree, Ernestico readied his machine gun, reached around the tree, and returned fire.

It was a fine day. There were many people in the park: mothers pushing baby carriages, joggers, and the occasional cyclist. People were startled to see two men exchanging gunfire in the afternoon. A few people screamed, others ducked for cover behind garbage bins or whatever else they could find. Flocks of pigeons scattered at the jarring sound and movement of people.

Palulu continued running, turning occasionally to fire with his two guns at Ernestico, who answered with bursts of machine-gun fire.

At one point, Ernestico surmised that he might have hit Palulu in the leg, because Palulu began limping.

As long as they were in the park, Palulu had some degree of cover. But as they came to the northern edge of the park at 110th Street, he was exposed. He scampered across the two-way street, almost getting hit by a passing car. Ernestico steadied himself; he had a nice open shot. He emptied a clip on Palulu. He was certain that he had hit his target, but the bastard was still running, sort of. He was dragging his leg, obviously disabled, but he would not go down.

By this time, Chino Acuna, Ernestico's partner, had come screeching around the corner in the getaway car, barreling toward the scene. Ernestico motioned for Chino to pull over. He jumped in the front seat of the car and said, "He went that way," pointing north on Lenox Avenue. Chino drove in that direction.

Even before they found Palulu, Ernestico saw the trail of blood on the sidewalk, and judging from the reactions of pedestrians, he knew his target had come this way.

As they approached 112th Street near Lenox, Ernestico commanded Chino, "Stop!" There was his man, collapsed on the sidewalk. He was shot up pretty good. His left leg looked as though it had been through a mechanical shredder; it was sticking out at a strange angle. Palulu had also been hit in other parts of his body, with a lot of blood spreading beneath him on the pavement. He wasn't moving.

Ernestico thought about getting out, emptying the rest of his clip into the body of Palulu, just to make sure. But there were a lot of people beginning to gather. Cars had stopped to see what was going on. Ernestico figured there was no way this guy would survive, if he wasn't dead already. To Chino, he said, "This motherfucker is dead. *Vamonos.*"

Chino hit the gas and peeled away.

Cops arrived shortly thereafter. It was quite a scene: a man shredded with machine-gun fire on a pleasant late afternoon in Harlem. The sun had dipped low in the sky, with the light glimmering off the façades of the brownstones. Palulu was loaded into an ambulance and rushed to the hospital.

When news of the shooting went out over police frequencies, the name José "Palulu" Enriquez caught the attention of homicide detectives in the district of Manhattan North. In recent weeks, Palulu had emerged as the number one suspect in the murder of Pedro Battle. Elda, wife of the deceased, had finally given a detailed statement about her husband's murder, identifying Palulu as the killer. Employees of the Guanabo bar had also come forward and identified Palulu, whom they knew well; he was a regular at the bar. An arrest warrant had been issued for Palulu. He had been hiding from the police at the same time he was avoiding Battle's henchmen. Now he was in the emergency room at St. Luke's Hospital on Amsterdam Avenue and 114th Street, fighting for his life.

The prognosis was good. He would survive. But he was going to lose his leg. The damage was irreparable. The leg would have to be amputated.

The operation took place immediately, and it went well. Palulu's left leg was removed just below the hip. After the area healed completely, he would likely be able to use a prosthetic limb.

On April 5, Palulu had stabilized enough that he was transferred to the prisoner ward at Bellevue Hospital. There he was officially charged with the murder of Pedro Battle.

Detectives came to his room at Bellevue and did what investigators who are holding a strong hand are wont to do: they hinted to Palulu that if he gave them information on the shootout in Central Park, including the name of the shooter, that would greatly enhance his chances of negotiating a plea deal on the murder charge. Basically, Palulu told them, "*No me joda.*" Fuck off.

NEWS OF PALULU'S PREDICAMENT MADE ITS WAY TO UNION CITY. JOSÉ MIGUEL BATTLE was not happy. He didn't care that Palulu had been arrested for the murder of his brother. Battle wasn't looking for that kind of justice. He wanted street justice.

"The son of a bitch is still alive," he said to Ernestico and Chino

Acuna. El Padrino met with the two hit men at a restaurant on Bergen-line Avenue. "He's still alive, and that's not good."

Ernestico and Chino ate their carne asada. Not completing the hit was going to cost them money.

Said the boss, "We'll just have to get him on the inside." Battle was confident that wherever Palulu was being held, whatever hospital or prison facility, they could find someone to finish the job. He told his men, "I think I know maybe what the problem has been."

Ernestico and Chino looked at him. "Tell us."

Battle explained that a member of their organization, Ismael "Loco" Alvarez, ran a bolita counting house in Union City. Working a count-ing room was a highly trusted position. Suitcases filled with cash were brought from Manhattan, under armed guard, and stored and counted at a specified location, which led Chino to ask the obvious question: "Stealing?"

No, worse than that, said Battle. He'd learned that Loco Alvarez had been feeding information to Palulu's crew so that Palulu had been able to stay one step ahead of the hit squads. And if that wasn't bad enough, Battle heard from an informant of his in the police department that Loco was also a police snitch, supplying detectives with information about their group.

"Motherfucker," said Ernestico.

For Battle, there was a problem, a moral quandary. Loco Alvarez was his cousin by marriage. He was family. Even so, Battle had reached a conclusion: the cousin had to go.

"I want him taken out," he said. "Just him. Don't hurt nobody else in his family. And I want it done in a very public way."

Ernestico and Chino were pleased. They would be paid for the hit. And compared to the hunt for Palulu, this promised to be a piece of cake. Loco Alvarez was a visible figure in the neighborhood, and he would likely never suspect that his cousin, El Padrino, would send hit men to have him killed.

On the night of April 25, 1975, Ernestico and Chino made their move. They had done so many killings together in the last few months, they hardly needed to talk about it. It was all second nature. In a 1970 powder blue Cadillac, they staked out the home of Loco Alvarez at 400

17th Street. Chino was in the driver's seat, armed with a .357-caliber Smith & Wesson, and Ernestico, sitting in the backseat, had a 9mm Browning automatic.

Alvarez was at the Rancho Luna restaurant in Washington Heights that night. At around 11:15 P.M., he hopped in his car and drove across the George Washington Bridge into Union City. He parked near his building, and that's where Ernestico and Chino saw him come strolling down the street.

Alvarez, fifty-nine years old, was a bit of a dandy. He was dressed in a plaid sports coat, white dress shirt, white slacks, and white shoes. His hair was mostly gray, and he had long sideburns in the 1970s style.

The hit men cruised up in the Cadillac and opened fire.

Loco was caught off guard; he tried to run, but it was too late. He was hit seven times and fell to the pavement.

Ernestico and Chino sped away in the Cadillac. They didn't get very far. Powder blue Cadillacs are easy to remember. A witness at the scene had not seen the gunmen clearly, but did see the Caddy and gave a description to a couple patrolmen. A radio call went out over police frequencies, and within minutes of the shooting, cops in the area were on the lookout for a blue Cadillac.

Ernestico and Chino were pulled over on Route 3 in North Bergen. Two cops prepared their weapons and approached the vehicle. "Step out of the car with your hands in the air," one of the cops ordered. The cop saw Ernestico stuff his gun into the crease of the front seat before stepping out. Chino's gun was found on the floor of the car. Both men were cuffed and placed under arrest for possession of a dangerous weapon. The charge was later upgraded to attempted murder.

IDALIA FERNANDEZ WAS PUERTO RICAN, BUT SHE KNEW A THING OR TWO ABOUT Cubans. She had a habit of dating Cuban men, which was why when she first met Ernesto Torres at a bar in Union City, she liked what she saw. He was handsome, in a raffish street hoodlum kind of way, and he had that Cuban swagger. Clearly, he was a hustler, and he seemed like someone who could navigate the world of the streets and make money from various ventures, legal or otherwise. She had no illusions that he was anything but a criminal. She was hoping he was a smart criminal, as opposed to some others she had known.

Idalia had a child, ten years old, and another one on the way. Ernesto said that he also had a child, Ernesto Jr., who was being raised by his mother in Spain. Not long after they met and started up a romance, they moved into an apartment together in the neighborhood of Cliffside Park.

She met a friend of Ernestico's named Pedro Battle. Not long after that, Ernestico told her that Pedro had been murdered. Ernesto was upset, and she was pretty sure that he was caught up in efforts to avenge the murder. Mostly she tried to stay out of these things; the less she knew, the better.

On the morning of April 26, Idalia received a strange call from a Union City lawyer named Perkins. He told her, "Your friend Mr. Martinez has been arrested. But he will soon be bailed out. He wants you to meet him at the courthouse."

Idalia had to think about that. Who the hell was Mr. Perkins? (She later learned that "Mr. Perkins" was an attorney supplied by the Battle organization.) She remembered that Alejandro Martinez was a name that Ernestico used sometimes in his various criminal ventures.

She left her child with a neighbor and drove to the courthouse. Ernestico was there with his friend Chino, whom she had met before. Ernestico smiled, and before she even had a chance to open her mouth, he said, "Don't say anything until we get outside."

Outside the building waiting for them was a slightly older man dressed in a beautiful suit. Idalia was introduced for the first time to José Miguel Battle. She had heard about the man, whom Ernestico sometimes referred to as El Gordo. She knew he was the boss, and even if she hadn't known, she would have been able to tell just by looking at him.

Battle seemed pleased. He said to Ernestico and Chino, "He's in intensive care, on the critical list. God willing, he won't make it through the night."

Battle told his men, "I want you to go home and get dressed up. Put on your best suit. We're going out in Manhattan tonight. I want all the bankers to see us out on the town. We'll drink Dom Perignon and toast our enemies. That's the way it is with us."

Later that night, José Miguel came by Ernestico and Idalia's apartment. He was with another guy named José Herrera, who was introduced to Idalia as Monino. The men all sat around a table and talked bolita business. Idalia watched from afar. Seeing her man Ernesto talking privately with the boss, she had to admit, she was impressed. Maybe, for once in her life, she had picked the right guy.

THE SHOOTING OF LOCO ALVAREZ DID NOT GO AS BATTLE AND HIS MEN WANTED. AFTER weeks in the hospital, Alvarez recovered from his wounds and was released. Aware now that the organization of his cousin, El Padrino, was out to kill him, he made himself scarce. He knew the key players in the organization—especially hit men such as Ernesto and Chino—and he was vigilant to the point of being a ghost in his own neighborhood.

And so Battle went outside his bolita organization to a team of political assassins known by the nicknames Malagamba, Tati, and Monchi. Tati and Monchi were brothers. These three men were associated with Omega 7, the anti-Castro terror organization that claimed among its affiliate members the Novo brothers, Guillermo and Ignacio, who had once fired a homemade bazooka at Che Guevara while he was giving a speech at the United Nations. Omega 7 would later become notorious for a series of politically motivated bombings and assassinations in furtherance of what the FBI designated the Cuban Nationalist Movement (CNM). But, in the mid-1970s, their bombing campaign was in its nascent stage. The killing of Ismael "Loco" Alvarez may have been an early practice run.

On a cold winter morning in January 1976, Alvarez was backing into a parking space on Bergenline Avenue when suddenly his car exploded. Alvarez was killed instantly and the car was destroyed. An explosive device had been placed under the driver's seat. The inside of the car was blown out, and the force of the explosion was so great that it shattered windows in the surrounding area.

Ernestico Torres and Chino Acuna may have considered themselves professional assassins, but when it came to getting the job done, they had a lot to learn from Malagamba, Tati, and Monchi.

6

THE PRODIGAL SON

THE BOLITA BUSINESS WAS LIKE A BIG COFFEE-MAKING MACHINE: YOU SET THE AUTO-matic timer, and it started up in the morning and produced a pungent brew all on its own. You did not need to recruit people to play bolita. For those who bet the number, it was a daily ritual like eating breakfast, lunch, and dinner.

Structuring the business, however, did take foresight, and even genius. There were many ways a person could bet a number or series of numbers. The possibilities were nearly endless. In the Latin community, especially among the islanders, betting the number was a tradition that ran deep. Your grandmother did it, and so did your uncle. By playing bolita, you were participating in a cultural tradition as rich as the church and as ubiquitous as the *clave,* the five-beat rhythm pattern at the base of all Afro-Cuban music.

At the center of this culture was the dream book, pamphlets that promised that the secret to winning the lottery was to be found in your dreams. Since early in the twentieth century, dream books were sold at candy stores, pharmacies, and bodegas. Under titles such as *Aunt Dinah's Dream Book of Numbers, Dr. Pryor's Lucky Number Master Dream Book* (*El Libro de los Sueños*), or *El Libro de Astrología y Numerología de Zolar,* the books were designed to help you interpret your dreams and translate them into numbers.

The dream books were an extension of *la charada,* the system in Cuba since the nineteenth century of assigning numbers to certain animals or objects. A horse was the number 1; a rooster was 11; a pocketwatch was 21; opium smoking was number 17—and on and on, an infinite catego-rization of things, activities, and numbers. The idea was that as certain objects or events occurred in your dreams, if you knew the numbers associated with those objects or events, you were being given a secret formula to win the lottery.

It was a form of superstition, a kind of black magic, but many who bet the number swore by some form of numerology. The bolita king, then, wasn't just a racketeer, he was the man who made dreams come true.

In the New York metropolitan area, the man who made dreams come true and turned this phenomenon into a highly lucrative business was not José Miguel Battle, it was Isleño Dávila.

Isleño had concerns about Battle. They had spent time together in Spain with their wives and children but had known each other before that, since the mid-1960s, when Battle first arrived in the New York–New Jersey area. Isleño, Battle, Angel Mujica and all the early Cuban bolita bankers had been poker buddies together playing cards primarily at a bar called El Baturro in Washington Heights. It was there that they first divided up various territories in the metropolitan area. It was mostly an agreeable arrangement. Isleño's concerns about Battle had nothing to do with territorial disputes or the division of spoils. They were about his temperament, and his penchant for violent solutions, which Isleño suspected would one day cause them problems.

For someone like Isleño, whose roots in the bolita business went back to Cuba, violence was a sign of failure. Bolita was not supposed to be, nor had it been in Cuba, a violent business. Unlike smuggling guns or drugs, or established vices like prostitution or other forms of gambling, the numbers game was not meant to attract a sinister clientele. If it was a vice, it was meant to be a benign vice. And if people were dying over the racket, it meant that something else had taken over—something like greed or avarice or the lust for power and control.

To Isleño, Battle seemed to have many dubious characteristics. For one thing, he had an overweening compulsion for vengeance that may have had something to do with his personal history as a Bay of Pigs veteran. The mission of the 2506 Brigade had been to overthrow the Castro military and thus reclaim Cuba, but there was another motive: revenge. That desire had been thwarted in a most humiliating manner that included defeat and incarceration. This entire generation of men carried with it the burden of that legacy, part of which was an unsatisfied lust for revenge.

Isleño Dávila was not a psychoanalyst; he was a sixth-grade dropout with a love for bolita, a proud family tradition going back to his own parents. He had trepidations about Battle based on the man's personal history. Battle was a man who would use whatever power he had to settle old scores and to leverage his enemies—in other words, activities that had little to do with the business of making money.

In the first ten years or so that the Cuban consortium had been up and running in New York and New Jersey, Isleño had sat back and let matters take their own course. There were obvious advantages to having Battle as a partner. As a hero from the Bay of Pigs invasion, he had a stature in the community that Isleño lacked. And as a former vice cop from Havana in the 1950s, he had an advanced understanding of graft, how to economically compromise cops and politicians in ways that would mitigate the dangers of unwanted raids or investigations. El Padrino was master of the well-placed payoff.

It was only lately, since Battle had undertaken his aggressive campaign of terror to get revenge for his brother's murder, that Isleño had begun to realize he had the capacity to take them all down together.

Isleño lived with his wife and three children in Union City. Initially the base of his bolita operation was in Brooklyn and parts of the Bronx. He had started his operation on his own, through his own contacts, some of which were similar to Battle's. Back in Havana, Isleño had also known Santo Trafficante Jr. In the 1950s, Isleño did business with the powerful mobster, who in addition to his many other rackets was an importer of bootleg cigarettes into Cuba. Isleño bought cigarettes from Trafficante to sell at his cafeteria in Mariel Harbor. Tony's Cafeteria, named after Isleño's brother, was the epicenter of the Dávila family bolita business in the Havana area.

Isleño brought a lifetime's worth of knowledge into the business of bolita. In New York, he introduced the concept of a numbers hole. He introduced other innovations such as *pulito,* in which a customer could bet a single number, thus greatly enhancing his chances of winning. It was Isleño's hunch that bettors would immediately use those winnings to spread their bet, and eventually lose, which proved to be the case.

Isleño also knew that bolita was a grassroots kind of racket. You had to know your clientele, what day of the week they received their paycheck from work or their Social Security checks from the government. You knew better than to open a numbers hole at the top of an incline or hill, because people getting off the bus or subway after a long day at work would be too tired to climb that hill to place a bet.

In Spanish Harlem, at 117th Street and Park Avenue, Isleño sponsored street festivals with beer, rum, Cuban food, and music. It was known and appreciated by people from all over the city that the boliteros were throwing this party. It was all part of giving back to the community, and creating a community of loyal bolita customers that pretty much guaranteed that if cops came snooping around looking for info about a local operation, they would get nothing out of *la gente en el barrio.*

Isleño was allowed to run his own thing, even though Battle was considered to be El Padrino. The partnership was based on the fact that they were all bankers. There would come a time when one of the bankers had a bad day or week, when a particular number hit and that banker incurred big losses. He knew he was covered, because he could lay off part of his action with other bankers. Thus the Cuban bankers protected one another.

Isleño did better than most, and he accumulated a small fortune. In 1975, he purchased a second home in Fort Lauderdale, Florida. It was a sizable property on the water, a dream home for a Cuban émigré who had come to the United States with very little.

It is possible that José Miguel Battle was jealous of Isleño's financial success. In late-night drinking sessions with his young protégé, Ernestico (they usually drank champagne), he used to complain, "We are the true boliteros out on the street taking care of business. We don't spend our time down in Florida, living like fat cats. We fight for what is ours right here on the streets of New York."

The bolita bankers met every week to discuss business, usually at the Colonial restaurant on St. Nicholas Avenue in Washington Heights. They drove in from Union City or Brooklyn or the Bronx, put together some tables in the back of the restaurant, and laid out a big spread of Cuban food: *puerco asado, congrí,* roast chicken, *platanos,* and, in memory of their time together in Spain, a steaming paella. They ate and they talked, almost always in Spanish.

Isleño saw that José Miguel was restless. He knew that as long as his brother's killer, Palulu, remained alive, El Padrino would remain a volcano on the verge of eruption. His concern was that the mere anticipation of that day, much less when it did happen, might impede the most essential aspect of their business: the daily flow of cash from the streets of the city into the counting rooms, and eventually the pockets of the reigning boliteros.

JOSÉ MIGUEL HAD A NICKNAME FOR ERNESTICO. HE SOMETIMES REFERRED TO HIM AS "El Hijo Pródigo," the Prodigal Son. Battle had snatched the young Cuban off the streets of Madrid and was in the process of grooming him to be a bolitero. At least that's how Battle saw it. Most everyone else thought that El Padrino was grooming his young protégé to be a gangster.

The other bolita bankers couldn't figure it out. To them it seemed obvious that Ernesto Torres was a reprobate, a disaster waiting to happen. But Battle had some kind of strange loyalty toward the kid. One of the bankers compared Battle's affection for Ernestico to the way he was with stray dogs. He picked them up off the street, gave them homes, and tried to restore their confidence. He had a soft spot for the lost and downtrodden. But Isleño Dávila saw it differently. To him, the more accurate comparison was the way Battle was with his fighting roosters. Battle loved cockfighting. He lavished great attention on the birds themselves, seeing to it that they were trained with loving care. When one of his trainers noted that a rooster had injured its leg while training and would have to be put to death, Battle said, "Is that how you would treat your own child? If your son injured his leg, you would have him killed?" Battle coddled his cocks; he held them in his arms and cooed loving sounds in their ears. Then he put them in the *valla*, the cockfighting arena, and watched as they sliced each other to death.

In the spring of 1975, following the attempt by Ernesto and Chino Acuna to murder Loco Alvarez, the young hit man began to pester his boss about becoming a banker. There had been a long four-month period of torture sessions and killings, and Ernesto let it be known that he was tired of doing hits. He felt that he had earned the right to be elevated to a higher role in the organization.

At first, Battle kept him at bay, telling him he would consider giving him a promotion only after Palulu was found and eliminated. But that was proving to be problematic. Palulu had an upcoming trial date for the murder of Pedro Battle. It made more sense for José Miguel to sit back and allow the trial to happen, then take out Palulu.

Ernesto was insistent. And so on a night in May 1975, Battle brought Ernesto Torres along to the weekly meeting of bolita super-bankers at El Colonial restaurant on 181st Street in Washington Heights. They were all there: along with Battle and Isleño Dávila were Joaquin Deleon Sr.; Luis Morrero, who was related to Battle by marriage; a banker known as Mallin; Nene Marquez, who was married to Battle's sister; and Abraham Rydz, the Polish Jew whom Battle first met at card games back in Havana. These were men who had mostly started at the bottom of the bolita chain and worked their way up to the level of superbanker. Also present was the owner of El Colonial, Luis DeVilliers Sr., a valuable banker with the organization, as was DeVilliers's son, Luis Jr.

Battle announced to the assembly that he was elevating Ernesto to the level of banker, and that each person at the meeting would kick in $2,000 to help him set up a bank. Battle was also asking that they kick over some of their weekly action to Ernesto so that he could get his business rolling.

All of these men knew what Ernesto was all about—he was Battle's gunman. They knew that Ernestico was probably not up to the challenge of being a banker, which required patience and brains and organizational skills. But they also knew that José Miguel probably had his reasons. Dávila went along with Battle's proposition because he saw it as a way to get Ernestico off the street; maybe the killings and mayhem would now quiet down. Most of the others also went along with it, for various reasons. But there were two bankers who objected—Mallin and Luis Morrero.

The most vociferously against it was Morrero. Said Battle's uncle-in-law, "I work hard for my piece of the action. I don't give it up to nobody." At five feet five inches tall, Morrero was short, and he had a Napoleon complex. He made it clear that a banker of his stature should not have to subsidize a stray dog like Ernestico Torres.

Nonetheless, it was a good night for Ernesto. Most of the bankers had shown support, and he was now free to set up his own bolita bank.

In the early days and weeks, it went well. Ernesto set up an office in the apartment of his father, who had recently moved from Spain to New Jersey. Now that his son worked for the organization of Battle, the father was looking to take advantage of the situation. He had a part-time job working at an auto garage in Union City, but he also knew people with access to bettors and betting action throughout the metro area. He could help his son build up his business and also provide a physical space for him to organize his books.

Ernestico now often traveled with ledgers and shoeboxes filled with envelopes of betting slips. This was the detritus of a bolitero, or, in Ernestico's case, the manifestation of a street hoodlum trying to turn himself into a higher class of criminal.

For Idalia Fernandez, watching all this, it was as if her man had gone from punk to reputable boss. El Padrino himself sometimes came to the house, usually with Chino Acuna (who was always armed), and patiently explained to Ernesto how to best organize his business. The main thing, Battle explained, was that he couldn't do it all himself. Being a banker meant having a network of confederates whom he could trust.

Ernesto did not have a great feel for the business, and in the first month he was to learn a hard lesson. A number of his clients bet winning numbers over a series of days, and he was literally wiped out. This was something that happened often with bankers just starting out; when a number of bettors won, or even just one bettor hit it big, the neophyte banker had not yet built up enough in reserves to cover the bets. Ernesto had gone broke. He came to Battle, hat in hand, and borrowed $25,000. A couple of weeks later, much of that money was gone. Ernestico had hit a streak of bad luck, and he was getting frustrated.

At their apartment, Idalia watched; she wanted to help, but there was nothing she could do. She thought that El Padrino, in his efforts to help Ernesto, was patient. "Don't worry," he told Ernestico. "You're going through a bad streak. It happens. But it will all even out eventually. You will make a profit. Don't panic."

Battle had one warning for Ernesto—no sports betting. It was absolutely forbidden. For one thing, it was an entirely different racket. The Cubans had approval from the Mafia to conduct bolita, not sports betting.

If Ernesto or anybody else started taking bets on baseball games, they would be stepping on somebody's toes, stepping over the line, and there would be repercussions.

Also, there was the fact that sports betting was the crack cocaine of gambling. People bet huge amounts on something like baseball. A

If Ernesto or anybody else started taking bets on baseball games, they would be stepping on somebody's toes, stepping over the line, and there would be repercussions.

Also, there was the fact that sports betting was the crack cocaine of gambling. People bet huge amounts on something like baseball. A banker could win big one day, then lose big the next three. It was a crazy high-wire act that had nothing to do with bolita; any bolitero with half a brain knew that.

Battle had heard that Ernestico was working a sports book. He asked him flat out, "Are you taking baseball bets?"

"Hell, no," said Ernestico. "I wouldn't do that."

Later that night, José Miguel sat down with Idalia at the kitchen table. She was impressed that he was talking with her, showing respect. He had a message to deliver: "Listen to me, your man, Ernestico, has the heart of a lion. But sometimes he lacks confidence. I'm telling you, he cannot make sports book. It is against the rules. He will get us all killed. You understand? I'm telling you so that you know. And so that you will talk sense to him. If he takes baseball bets, or bets on baseball, he's going to get himself—and you—into a lot of trouble."

After that, Ernesto hit another bad streak. Soon he was another $20,000 in the hole. Battle was losing patience. He heard that Ernestico had not yet paid a $5,000 win to one of his customers. He also heard that Ernestico was not only taking baseball bets, but that he had placed a large wager himself on a game and lost big.

One night, Battle, with Julio Acuna at his side, came to the house. Idalia could see that he was mad. El Padrino shouted at Ernestico, "What's the matter with you? The money? I told you, don't play. That means don't bet on baseball. You lied to me."

Ernestico did not admit any wrongdoing. "Well, forget about it," he said. "I don't want to be a banker anyway. This is not for me. I'm not making any money at it."

"It's true you are no banker," said Battle. He told Ernesto that he was removing him from the position, demoting him back to being a hit man for the organization.

Later that night, at the kitchen table, Ernestico told Idalia, "Fuck El Gordo. I don't need him. I've got my own plans."

EL PINCERO WORSHIPPED ERNESTICO, THE PRODIGAL SON. ALL HIS LIFE, CHARLEY Hernandez had been small potatoes, a working-class hoodlum. He always carried around his small bag of lock-picking tools, because you never knew when a job might come your way. You had to be ready at all times.

Charley was always ready, but still he struggled to make ends meet. He had four children at home with a common-law wife, an Italian American whom he called "the Americana." Her name was Carol Negron. She could be tough on Charlie. Whenever he came home with a wad of cash, she took most of it for the household.

Charley's kids did not know exactly what their father did for a living, but they knew it was unconventional and possibly criminal. He was not around for days and weeks at a time, and sometimes when he did come home he had a bloody nose or a black eye and bruises. When they asked their father what he did for a living, he told them he was a tradesman. They lived in the projects, at 3901 Kennedy Boulevard in Union City. Where they lived was on the wrong side of the tracks, but that was hardly noticeable since Union City was a working-class town to begin with. The girls went to public schools, and their mother sometimes took them to mass on Sunday at St. Rocco's Catholic Church.

Charley was mostly an absentee father, but when he was home, he showered his daughters with love and affection. He sang songs to them in Spanish and told them stories of his Cuban homeland.

"When will we get to visit Cuba?" the daughters asked.

Charley was a sentimental man, and when he talked about Cuba, tears often came to his eyes. "We can't go there now," he would say. "There's a bad man in charge there. Fidel Castro. A monster. But hopefully that will change soon. It is my dream to be able to take my girls there one day."

Carol, the mother, had no such dreams about Cuba. She was Italian American, born in New Jersey, and she raised the girls to be Americans. They did not speak Spanish around the house, only English. And when she took them with her to shop at the markets on Bergenline Avenue, she made sure they spoke English, even with the Cubans.

When Charley first met the Prodigal Son at a bar on 48th Street in Union City, Ernesto had bragged about his relationship with José Miguel

Battle. Charley knew how powerful Battle was; the rumor was that he controlled the police and the politicians in Hudson and Bergen counties, and in New York City he also had powerful people in his pocket. Charley had doubted that Ernestico really knew José Miguel until the day of Pedro Battle's memorial service. Since then, Charley had been spending a lot of time with Ernesto and his hit man partner, Chino Acuna.

It was Charley's hope that he might become a numbers runner for the Battle organization. It was an entry-level position that paid $200 to $300 a week—steady cash, which was something Charley had never known in his life of crime.

Seeing how frustrated his friend Ernestico was in his attempts to be a bolita banker, Charley had tried to help. He took bets and called them in to the office, but he found it to be boring. He was relieved when he heard that his friend would no longer be a banker. Maybe now they could get back to making money through robberies and other scams.

Charley was not a killer. He had close to a dozen arrests on his rap sheet, but none were for crimes of violence. He was a softhearted guy, loyal to a fault, who in many ways was out of his league doing business with the likes of seasoned killers like Ernestico and Chino.

One night, Ernestico came to Charley and said, "We got a job. El Gordo wants us to kill El Morro."

Charley knew El Morro, whom he thought of as a harmless operator in the neighborhood. "What did he do?" asked Charley.

Ernestico explained how El Morro had been overheard in a bar talking trash, saying that Palulu was going to live to be one hundred years old, and that El Gordo was a *maricón* and a *puto* and that the Battle organization were a bunch of assholes.

"You do this hit with us," said Ernesto, "you can probably join the Battle organization if you want."

"How much is he paying?" asked Charley.

"Five thousand."

Charley thought the fee was an insult, but he needed the money.

"Well," said Ernesto, "the least you can do is help us find the guy."

Over the next few nights, Ernesto and Charley and Chino drove around looking for El Morro, who must have known he was on a hit list, because he was nowhere to be seen.

On the third night, Ernesto and Charley made arrangements to meet Chino at a White Castle on Bergenline Avenue. Chino never showed up. Ernestico was angry. Ever since his disastrous attempts to become a banker, he'd begun to feel that Chino had sided with Battle against him, and that he was secretly snitching on him to the boss behind his back. He didn't say anything to Chino, preferring to mask his feelings behind a façade of brotherly friendship, but to Charley he referred to Chino as "the nigger."

The next morning, Charley heard the news on the street: El Morro had been murdered. He immediately headed to Ernestico's house and told his friend.

"Chino," said Ernesto. "That nigger must have done the hit without us, to keep the money for himself."

Charley and Ernesto drove over to Chino's place and confronted him. "You hit El Morro," said Ernesto.

"No I didn't," answered Chino. "You two must have hit El Morro." The men all looked at one another.

The relationship between Ernesto and Chino quickly deteriorated after that, though they pretended they were still friends. Chino spent much of his time on the phone trying to stir up Ernestico. "This guy is talking about you," he would say.

"Who's talking about me?" asked Ernestico.

Chino knew that Ernesto was insecure. Ernesto had recently bought a new car, a fancy Lincoln Mark IV, no doubt, to counterbalance any perception that he was suffering financially because he'd been demoted by the boss. Chino knew that he was showing off by buying the car. "Listen, Paquito is saying he copied your Mark IV and that he just bought one and now he's Mr. Paquito." Paquito was a neophyte banker with the organization.

"Who?" asked Ernesto.

"Paquito."

"What did he say?"

"He bought a Mark IV. He said he's the one. 'The only one who can have a Mark IV here is me. I already took the Mark IV from this guy, and now I'm the only one that can have a Mark IV.'"

"Is that what's he's saying, that *maricón*?"

"I swear on my mother, it's true . . . He said that since you want to kill him, he'll play the cards to kill you too . . . He said he is Don Paquito, the banker." This was a direct poke at Ernesto's failed efforts as a banker.

"Listen, brother," said Ernesto, "the thing is, I don't like to talk. Let time go by and things will become obvious, you understand me?"

"I swear on my mother, it's true . . . He said that since you want to kill him, he'll play the cards to kill you too . . . He said he is Don Paquito, the banker." This was a direct poke at Ernesto's failed efforts as a banker.

"Listen, brother," said Ernesto, "the thing is, I don't like to talk. Let time go by and things will become obvious, you understand me?"

Then Chino got right to the point: "Paquito called El Gordo to tell him that you said that you were going to kill me and him."

"That's a lie, brother. You know that I know where you live. If I'm going to hit you, I don't have to say anything about what I'm going to do. Of course, that *maricón* is just trying to get us to fight."

"Of course. They say one thing first and then they say something else."

Ernesto could hear Chino breathing into the phone. "Those people can suck my prick," said Ernesto.

"Of course," said Chino. "I know you are a guerrilla fighter."

"You know."

"We know," said Chino.

"You and I know each other well."

Ernesto and Chino called each other "brother" on the phone, but really they had become like two roosters, spurs raised and ready, circling each other in the arena.

ONE MORNING IN JUNE, CHARLEY CAME TO ERNESTO AND IDALIA'S APARTMENT. IT WAS a humble place that Idalia had given a woman's touch; it was decorated with numerous religious artifacts—a framed picture of La Virgen de la Caridad del Cobre (Our Lady of Charity); an altar with beads and a candle to San Lazaro; a crucifix made of wood.

Charley noticed that his friend could hardly contain a sly smile.

"What's up?" Charley asked.

"You don't know it yet," said Ernestico, "but you are about to become a rich man."

Ernestico showed Charley a list he had made, ten names written out on a piece of a paper. "You know what this is?" he asked.

Charley looked at the list. He recognized nearly every name. "These are all big bankers in the Battle organization."

"That's right," said Ernestico. "And you know what we're gonna do? We're gonna abduct all these bankers who are millionaires, one by one, and if they don't give us the money when we ask for a ransom, we're going to start killing them. The ones that pay, they will not have any problems. The ones that don't pay, we'll kill them."

Charley could hardly believe what he was hearing: they were going to be like Robin Hood, stealing from the rich and giving it to themselves. It was dangerous, maybe even crazy, but also audacious in ways that crystallized why Charley admired Ernestico Torres as much as he did.

"It will be easy," explained Ernestico. "We'll walk up to a banker and ask him to borrow some money. If at this time he will not let us borrow the money, we kidnap him."

It sounded too good to be true, but in fact, in their first effort, they approached Mallin, the banker who had objected to giving money to Ernesto back when El Padrino first announced that Ernesto was becoming a banker. They cornered him on a street in Washington Heights. Ernesto showed Mallin that he had a gun and said, "I need to borrow five thousand from you."

Mallin looked at the young hoodlums. He said, "I don't have five thousand, but I'll give you two thousand." He handed over the cash.

Later, they hit another guy on Ernestico's list, someone that Charley didn't know. Again, the guy forked over a couple thousand.

That night, Charley and Ernestico partied, bouncing around to different bars in Washington Heights and Union City to show that they were men of means. Charley said to Ernestico, "Jesus Christ, I never seen people give up money so easily, just by asking. You really got it made with these people. I ask them for fifty dollars, they don't give it to me. You ask for five thousand and they give you two thousand. They afraid of you, they really afraid of you."

Ernestico beamed with pride.

A week later, Charley and Ernestico were ready to check off another name on the list; this time it was Luis Morrero. Charley was concerned, because he knew that Morrero was some kind of relative of José Miguel Battle. This would be much riskier. But Ernestico assured him, "Don't worry. I have Battle wrapped around my finger. I am the Prodigal Son.

Besides, Battle hates these people because when Pedro got killed, they did nothing to help."

Late one night in early August, Ernestico and Charley tracked down Morrero at a bar in Washington Heights. Ernestico told Charley, "Wait here. I'm gonna go in and talk to him." Charley waited in the car.

Ernestico entered the bar. He saw Morrero sitting there, a short guy with his Napoleon complex. Big black mustache. Ernestico walked up to him and said, "I need five thousand dollars."

Morrero looked at this kid, who he felt was nothing more than a thug. "You been asking me for money ever since I've known you. Who the hell are you? Why are you asking me for money? You never did shit for me." He returned to his drink.

Ernestico looked at the guy. He wanted to kill him right there. But he was older now. Wiser. He was a smart gangster.

Ernestico returned to the car and said to Charley, "This is the one we're going to hit. He's good for fifty grand, at least. He's probably got it in his house in New Jersey. Let's follow him home."

They waited till Morrero came out of the bar. The little fucker was drunk, probably shouldn't have been driving, but he was. "Let's snatch him right here," said Charley.

"No," said Ernestico. "Better we get him on the other side of the bridge."

They followed Morrero in his car. It was obvious he was inebriated, his vehicle drifting across lanes of traffic. As he crossed the George Washington Bridge and exited into Union City, he at one point side-swiped a parked car.

"Look at this motherfucker," said Charley. "Fucking *borracho* (drunk)."

Morrero stopped at a bodega and disappeared inside.

Charley and Ernesto agreed. Let's take him now. Charley had a police badge that he could hang on a chain around his neck, and a set of handcuffs. He looked like a Hudson County detective. When Morrero came out of the deli, they pulled up hard and Charley popped out of the front seat: "Stop right there. Police. You hit a car back there."

Charley cuffed one of Morrero's hands and was getting ready to cuff the other, but suddenly Ernestico jumped out and grabbed Morrero, forcing him into the backseat of their car. When Morrero saw Ernestico, he knew what this was all about.

Morrero fell to the floor of the backseat. Charley was still trying to cuff his hands together when he said defiantly, "You got to kill me here, you piece of shit. You got to kill me right here."

Ernestico said, "All right. I gonna kill you right here."

Charlie heard *Boom!* and blood splattered on his face. Then again— *Boom!*

He pulled himself out of the car. There was Ernesto running fast down Kennedy Avenue. He was running away.

Charley wiped blood from his face with the sleeve of his coat. And then—*what the fuck!*—Morrero popped out of the backseat, bleeding from his face and his arm, handcuff dangling from his wrist, and ran off into traffic.

Charley jumped into the driver's seat. The key was in the ignition, and the car was running. Charley floored it. He drove right by Morrero, drunk and bloody, running down the street. *Ain't this a fucking bitch!* He drove around looking for Ernestico, couldn't find him anywhere. So he drove over to Ernesto's apartment in Cliffside Park, which was only a few minutes away. He rang the doorbell and Idalia answered. Without saying anything, she stepped aside so Charley could enter.

Ernestico was sitting at the kitchen table, drinking a beer.

"Are you fucking crazy?" said Charley. "You shot this guy. He's out there bleeding all over the street."

"Don't worry about it," said Ernestico.

"The gun. What did you do with the gun?"

"I dumped it right on Kennedy."

"Oh my God. Fingerprints. They gonna find the gun. This guy Morrero gonna go straight to Battle. Battle's gonna find out. He gonna come after us. We're fucked!"

Ernestico was remarkably calm. "Charley, how many times I gotta tell you. Battle is on my side. He gonna be with me. I'm the Prodigal Son."

Idalia said, "Charley, have a beer. Calm down. Ernestico knows what he's doing."

Charley looked at the two of them, dumbfounded. "Listen," he said, "I can't go home. I got daughters at home, you understand? I don't want to put them at risk. Once I get settled somewhere else, I'll contact you."

Charley didn't run very far. He had a girlfriend named Lydia Ramirez who lived on 175th Street in Manhattan. He stayed there. The next couple of days he scoured the newspapers looking for anything about the shooting of Luis Morrero. There was nothing. Which meant the guy had not been killed. That meant that at least Charley wasn't facing a murder rap.

From friends in Union City, Charley learned that Morrero was out walking the streets, with a bandage on his face and his arm in a sling. Everywhere he went he had two bodyguards at his side. He was telling everybody exactly what happened and who did it—that fucking *maricón,* Ernesto Torres, and his sidekick Charley, El Pincero.

Hardly able to speak, and in great pain, Luis Morrero vowed to get revenge.

ERNESTICO TORRES CERTAINLY DID HAVE A KNACK FOR MAKING ENEMIES. SOMETIMES he could even turn a good situation into a bad one. Not long after the Morrero incident, Ernesto was approached by the wives of two very dangerous men, Tati and Monchi, who, along with Malagamba, comprised a hit squad associated with Omega 7. Tati and Monchi were in jail at the time, but before they were arrested, they had been involved in a $40,000 jewelry heist. Now that they were locked up, the wives were looking to fence the jewelry.

At an apartment in Washington Heights, Ernestico and a partner brought along $10,000 and a couple ounces of cocaine. They had a little party. Ernestico then had the two women engage in sex together, and then he joined in. He took photos of the orgy. When the women brought out the jewelry to be sold, Ernestico handcuffed them together, took the jewelry, and left with the $10,000.

Not only had Ernestico just ripped off the wives of two very bad hombres who were away in prison, but he had photos of the two women in compromising positions that he threatened to spread all over town if he wasn't paid by Tati and Monchi.

When Charley saw the photos, he shook his head. Tati and Monchi's partner, Malagamba, was still out on the street. It was not far-fetched to surmise that Tati and Monchi would be looking for revenge, and Malagamba was their man to do the job. It had become increasingly apparent to Charley that because of his friendship with Ernestico, the enemies of Ernestico were now his enemies. Anyone who wanted Ernestico dead likely wanted to kill him as well.

Charley was scared. He told Ernestico as much when they spoke on the phone. Ernestico was not oblivious; he knew they were in danger. But he didn't let it bother him.

A couple weeks after the Morrero incident, Charley for the first time felt secure enough to show his face in Union City. He was driving with Ernestico in the middle of the afternoon.

"Hey," said Ernestico, "look, there's El Gordo with his brother Richie" (as Sergio Ricardo Battle was sometimes known).

"Go the other way," said Charley.

"No, I'm gonna go talk to him. I haven't had a conversation with him since the thing with Morrero."

Ernesto pulled over and parked. They got out and approached the Battle brothers.

"Well, well," said José Miguel. "It's the Little Godfather and his counselor."

Ernesto asked, "So where do I stand with you?"

Said Battle, "Look, this thing with Morrero is serious. He's angry. He has a contract out on both of you. I'm in the middle, and I can't take sides."

Ernestico tried to explain why they had snatched Morrero, but Battle didn't want to hear it. "I'm just telling you," said El Gordo, "he gave the contract to Malagamba, Tati, and Monchi. They driving around looking for you"—Battle pointed at Charley—"and you."

Ernesto asked, "You know what they driving, what plate numbers?"

"I'll see if I can get those for you," answered Battle.

They parted ways. Charley was amazed that Battle had been so friendly. "Hey, I think we okay with this guy. Maybe he's not looking to have us killed."

Ernestico kept driving and said nothing. Truth was, he wasn't sure whom he could trust.

Ernestico maintained his relationship with the boss. Their connection was deep, like father and son, with all the psychological layers that implied.

One afternoon, Ernestico called Battle on the phone. He secretly tape-recorded the conversation. What he didn't know was that Battle had also begun taping certain friends and associates. The two men were taping each other.

"Hello, brother, how are you?" Ernestico asked.

Battle had just undergone a minor hernia operation. "They opened me up from the chest to the beginning near my prick. Two hernias."

"You must be skinny," said Ernestico.

"Yes, I lost some fat."

When talking about anything business-related on the phone, the two men used code. Battle was referred to as Butin, or El Butin, and Ernesto as Rasputin, and they spoke of themselves in the third person.

"Listen," said Battle, "I just learned, by means of some recent commentary, that Rasputin has another person who is putting up the apparatus on him." This was Battle's way of telling Ernesto/Rasputin that there was another contract on his life. "Rasputin must be super cautious. He must be cautious of everyone. Because everybody is after Rasputin."

Ernesto defended himself, saying that Rasputin hadn't done half the things he was being blamed for.

Said Battle, "Yeah, you know people are always talking and, you know, if you listen to them, you go crazy."

"You go crazy. That is true, brother."

When Battle mentioned that El Butin had an apparatus for Rasputin, Ernesto knew what that meant: a job. A hit for hire. Ernesto was excited; he needed the money.

"How is Rasputin feeling?" he asked. (How much do I get paid?)

"I believe the ink man set aside for him five lucas." (You get paid five thousand dollars).

They agreed to meet the next day to talk about the details.

The next day, Ernesto awoke to go meet Battle. He kissed Idalia goodbye and headed out to the parking garage, where his turquoise Mark IV, as always, was looking majestic.

As he opened the driver's side door, he heard a slight ping. A curious sound. A million thoughts whirled in his head, like the Wheel of Fortune, and then the needle stopped on one word: *Bomb.*

Ernesto started running. He was about thirty feet away when the car exploded. He was lifted off his feet and slammed against a concrete wall. His ears went numb.

Idalia was standing at the kitchen sink washing dishes when she heard an explosion. At first she wasn't sure what it was, but then it occurred to her that it might have something to do with Ernesto. She ran out of the apartment, down the hallway toward the elevator. The elevator door opened and Ernesto, looking scuffed up and shaken, hurried out of the elevator. "Let's go," he said. "They're trying to kill us."

They gathered up their things. Ernesto called Charley and said, "They blew up my car. Idalia and me need a place to hide. We gotta come over there."

"*Coño.* Motherfucker. Of course you can stay here."

On the way out, Idalia looked toward Ernesto's car. Not only was it destroyed, but the two cars on either side were also badly damaged.

Ernesto and Idalia crashed at the apartment of Lydia Ramirez, along with Charley. Times were tense. Was it El Padrino who was trying to kill them? Was it somebody Morrero had hired? Or was it Tati and Monchi getting revenge for Ernesto having had an orgy with their wives? It was hard to say.

Ernesto called Battle. He knew all about the car bombing; it had been in the local newspapers. Ernesto did not ask Battle if he did it, and Battle did not deny it, for to do so would have given credence to the supposition that he was ever a suspect to begin with. Instead, Battle said, "This is terrible, *niño.* We will find out who did this." Meanwhile, he let Ernestico know that he was still offering him the contract to do a hit.

"Of course," said Ernestico.

He received information about the hit later that day. It was a Cuban named José Morín Rodriguez, who had run afoul of Battle's organization for some reason Ernesto didn't care to know.

One thing about hiding out at the apartment in Washington Heights was that it put Ernesto a few steps closer to Morín, who owned a flower shop called Cuban Florists at 161st Street and Broadway.

On December 27, Ernestico went to do his hit.

Charley, having borrowed a friend's car, was acting as getaway driver. Double-parked across the street, he waited for Ernesto as he disappeared into the flower shop. Within a few minutes, Charley heard gunfire. He saw Ernestico come running out of the shop, shouting, "I'm hit! I'm hit!" Ernesto had shot and killed Morín, but it seemed as though they knew he was coming.

Ernesto jumped into the backseat of the car. Charley was packing heat; he said, "Let me go get them. I'll kill those motherfuckers."

"No," said Ernestico. "Can't you see I'm hit? Get the fuck out of here."

Ernestico was bleeding from his side. Charley put the car in gear and peeled away.

Back at Lydia's apartment, Idalia tried to make the bleeding stop. Ernesto was jabbering, "It was an ambush. They were waiting for me. They knew I was coming. Somebody set me up."

Ernesto did not want to go to the hospital. Lydia Ramirez knew a doctor who lived nearby. She called the man, who came over and gave Ernesto an injection of a powerful antibiotic so that his wound would not become infected.

It was Idalia who said, "Ernesto, we need to get out of New York. They're gonna kill us here. We can go to Miami. We have friends there."

Over the next couple days, they made arrangements for a place to stay in Miami with a friend of Ernestico's. The wound wasn't too bad. Ernestico was lucky; he had been shot in the side. The bullet had gone in the front and come out the back. It was mostly a flesh wound, but they had to wait for the bleeding to stop, clean it, and wrap it up. Ernestico was in pain, but he would live.

Late one night, Charley drove Ernestico and Idalia to the train station. They had everything they owned in a knapsack.

"Hope you gonna be okay, *compadrito*," said Ernesto.

"If things get too hot up here," answered Charley, "who knows, I may join you."

They were unable to embrace because of Ernesto's gunshot wound.

The train drove through the night, down the East Coast. Ernesto and Idalia watched as the climate changed from the frigid Northeast to the mild conditions of the Carolinas and on into Florida. When they arrived in Miami, the sun was shining, and it was warm.

It was New Year's Day 1976.

MIAMI IN THE MID-1970S WAS MOSTLY A SLEEPY TOWN. THE DOWNTOWN SKYLINE WAS unimpressive. The port was modest compared to other port cities in the Gulf and on the East Coast. Miami Beach was a haven for retired Jews, mostly from New York City, with few tourists or nightclubs. The city's Cuban population was expanding at a rapid pace, and so Little Havana was a lively neighborhood, but the peak crime years in the city were a decade away. Since the days of Henry Flagler, Miami's founding bene-factor and booster, the place had been promoted as the Magic City. But in the mid-1970s, few would have viewed Miami as one of the nation's glittering hot spots.

When David Shanks first became a police officer, the Miami police and the Dade County police, known as the Dade County Public Safety Department, were two separate entities. More and more, local police were handling cocaine cases, and occasionally violent crimes stemming from narcotics transactions gone bad. The annual homicide rate was climbing higher each year.

Shanks was a local boy, born and raised in Little Havana, within walking distance of the Orange Bowl football stadium where President Kennedy back in 1963 addressed surviving members of the 2506 Bri-gade. Shanks knew about Cuban culture; he grew up with the aroma of *lechón asado* wafting through the neighborhood. He had experienced the *botánicas,* where various accoutrements of the Santería religion are sold. He knew about bolita, how that was the community's true religion, with pretty much every little old lady or recent émigré betting the number daily.

Shanks joined the police force in 1974. At the time, it seemed like a fairly tranquil way to make a living. The city was not yet a hub of international narcotics activity. As in many American cities at the time, there were racial disturbances that to some extent began to turn the people against the police. But by and large a cop could go off to work in the morning and not have to worry about whether he would be returning home that night.

In 1976, around the same time that Ernesto Torres and Idalia Fernandez arrived in Miami, on the run from various assassins, police officer Dave Shanks had two experiences which signaled that his career as a cop

work in the morning and not have to worry about whether he would be returning home that night.

In 1976, around the same time that Ernesto Torres and Idalia Fernandez arrived in Miami, on the run from various assassins, police officer Dave Shanks had two experiences which signaled that his career as a cop might be changing with the times.

One of these occurrences was Shanks's first narcotics seizure. In the trunk of a car, he and his partner discovered a kilo of cocaine, carefully wrapped in plastic. To the two young cops it seemed like a major bust, though this type of seizure would soon be dwarfed by cocaine busts many times greater. Shanks didn't know it at the time, but it was a harbinger of things to come for law enforcement throughout Dade County and much of South Florida.

The other incident was one that Shanks did not experience firsthand, but that would deeply affect all cops in Miami at the time.

On the night of April 1, detectives Tommy Hodges and Clarke Curlette, members of the department's Auto Theft Squad, were following up on reports of a stolen Lincoln Continental Mark IV, then the vehicle of choice for gangsters and pimps. They had an address of someone they were told might be a suspect, a car thief who specialized in Mark IVs. He was living in Miami Beach at a seedy motel called Starkey's Beach Motel at 8601 Harding Avenue.

Hodges and Curlette arrived at the horseshoe-shaped dive and were led to room number 5. The detectives believed they were making a routine inquiry. They did not have their guns out, and in fact, their guard was down.

The man they were looking for was named Joe Born, a professional car thief who was wanted on two arrest warrants. Born was the type of criminal who had done time in prison and did not want to go back. Discovering that two detectives were at his door, he blasted them with a double-barreled shotgun—killing them both—and fled the room. In the parking lot, he had a shootout with a responding officer, Frank D'Azevedo, who was also shot dead with a shotgun blast. An hour later, hiding in the weeds on the beach side of Collins Avenue, Born blew his brains out with a snub-nosed .38.

It was a shocking night of carnage, one of the worst seen by Miami cops at that time.

Dave Shanks had been working the late shift that night, and he heard reports of the cops being killed as they came across department airwaves in real time. When he got home, he watched the reports on television and saw the dozens of responders from the Miami Beach police, Public Safety Department units, Florida State troopers, and the media. It was a horror show of large proportions.

The next day, the entire department was in mourning. And supervisory officers were angry. The cops had approached the motel room of Joe Born having overlooked the fact that he was a violent felon. They had felt they could handle it.

A lieutenant who had been at the hospital and seen the bloodied bodies of the officers told the cops that morning, "I wish I could have marched every cocky young cop in the department through that room. I'd have pulled back the sheet and said, 'Take a good look . . . This is what taking this job lightly will get you.'"

Shanks never forgot those words, and he never forgot that night. It was a tough lesson, but one that he would take to heart.

At the time, Shanks had never heard of José Miguel Battle Sr. Although there were cops in Miami who did know who Battle was—because of his reputation in the Cuban community, and also perhaps because of the infamous shootout on Flagler between Hector Duarte and the Battle brothers—Shanks was not privy to police intelligence on organized crime figures at the time. He was a lowly street cop.

What he did know was that diligence was what kept a cop alive and helped him make cases. Never get sloppy, never take the job lightly. Though he didn't know it at the time, it was a lesson that would serve him well in the years ahead, when his entire career as an officer of the law would be consumed by the desire to take down José Miguel Battle Sr., Godfather of the Cuban Mafia.

7

RASPUTIN IN MEXICO

AT TIMES IT SEEMED AS THOUGH JOSÉ MIGUEL BATTLE HAD ALL OF HUDSON COUNTY IN his back pocket. His influence in law enforcement was far-reaching, with Deputy Chief Scarafile on the payroll, and he had pull with Mayor William Musto of Union City, whose various political campaigns were believed to be partially financed by illegal gambling money. But Battle had other connections designed to lubricate the system and give him a standing in the community above and beyond that of a crime boss.

One such connection was Rene Avila, the publisher of *Avance,* who sometimes acted as Battle's liaison between the underworld and the upperworld. Avila had risen from being an ad salesman for a monthly Cuban magazine to a player in Hudson County political circles. He was friendly with Battle to the point of providing crucial services for the organization. For example, on April 24, 1975, when Ernestico Torres and Chino Acuna were arrested following the attempted murder of Loco Alvarez, it was Avila who showed up at the jail to pay their bail—$15,000—on behalf of the Cuban Mafia.

If you asked Avila if he was affiliated with any criminal organization, he would deny it, and if you stated it in print, he might have you sued for libel. Avila presented the veneer of an upstanding businessman. Upon arriving in New Jersey from Cuba in 1961, he had risen from nothing to become an independent publisher. With his newspaper, he had the influence to promote and support various county commissioners, some of whom were hand-selected by Battle, who for a brief period was even listed as an employee of Avila's newspaper.

In 1975, Avila bought a house on Manhattan Avenue in Union City for $69,000 (which would be nearly $300,000 today). He owned a 1972 Rolls-Royce as a second car, wore designer suits, and purchased fur coats for his wife. His declared annual income at the time was $10,000. Eventually he would be called to answer for these financial discrepancies via a grand jury corruption investigation in Hudson County. Investigators concluded that there was a "shadowy relationship" between Avila, Battle, and key political and police figures in Union City in which Avila was "the lynchpin." It was also implied that Avila was on the payroll of El Padrino, a charge he denied.

The role that Avila played in Hudson County cultural and political circles was a classic function of organized crime, as it had existed in the United States at least since the Prohibition era. The criminal underworld may have been a separate entity, comprised of hoodlums and hit men like Ernestico and Chino, but organized crime did not operate in a vacuum. Battle was a typical Mob boss in that he was constantly looking for ways to ingratiate himself in the upperworld. If an anti-Castro political group was holding a fund-raiser at a restaurant or former vaudeville hall on Bergenline Avenue, Battle would make a bulk purchase of seats or tables. The man who would broker that sale was Rene Avila, who seemed to know everyone in the community. If a county commissioner was being put forward for office, or running for reelection, Avila had tremendous influence, not only with his newspaper, but, more important, by making a phone call in support of a particular candidate. It was understood that Avila represented the interests of José Miguel Battle.

As influential as Avila may have been, he was part of a network that reached deep into law enforcement and politics in Hudson County. He was not operating alone. Another person with tremendous influence was Eusabio "Chi Chi" Rodriguez.

In 1976, Chi Chi was called to testify in front of an ongoing federal grand jury investigating gambling-related activities of, among others, Deputy Chief Scarafile and Mayor Musto. It was a potentially explosive investigation. Chi Chi Rodriguez was a well-known bolitero, part of Battle's organization, with many arrests, mostly for gambling offenses. He was also friendly with politicians and cops throughout Union City. In front of the grand jury, he refused to answer questions, an act of defiance—or loyalty, depending on where your bread was buttered— that would eventually cost him eighteen months in jail on the charge of contempt. Upon his release, Chi Chi's standing among crooked politicians, dirty cops, and local gangsters was greatly enhanced.

Chi Chi became a power broker of some renown. He was a frequent visitor to city hall and was able to secure an audience with any commissioner at will, but most especially Commissioner Manuel Diaz, who had gone to school with José Miguel Battle Jr. and was a close personal friend of the Battle family. Chi Chi's influence was so far-reaching that when Deputy Chief Scarafile, after a political shake-up at city hall, was looking to protect the teaching jobs of his son and daughter-in-law, he didn't contact the commissioners or members of the Union City Board of Education, all of whom he knew personally. He contacted Chi Chi Rodriguez to ask him to intercede on his behalf, because Chi Chi represented the Battle organization.

A grand jury report on corruption in Hudson County put it this way:

If you want a job, call Chi Chi. If you want to influence a commissioner, call Chi Chi. If you want the head of a national crime syndicate to influence a newspaper and affect an election, call Chi Chi. All of this is so, despite the fact that Chi Chi Rodriguez is not registered to vote.

This same report stated:

The conclusion which this panel must draw is that elements of organized crime have been knowingly and intentionally integrated into the general governmental structure in Union City and those organized crime elements are using their power and positions for their own advantage . . . Chi Chi Rodriguez could not have attained and maintained this position of importance in the community by himself. He had, and still has, the help of public officials and employees who have become far too cozy with individuals in organized crime . . . The picture is frightening.

The findings of this particular grand jury, based on wiretapped conversations between Rene Avila, Chi Chi Rodriguez, and others, were still a few years away. In the meantime, these men were at the peak of their powers helping to create a universe of influence that was conducive to the criminal objectives, and personal whims, of José Miguel Battle.

ERNESTICO AND IDALIA WERE ON THE RUN, AND THIS WAS CAUSING MUCH ANXIETY for Charley Hernandez. Charley was aware that there was a contract out on all their lives, for various transgressions, but mostly for the aborted kidnapping of Luis Morrero, Battle's uncle-in-law. Charley didn't want to die, so after slinking around New York for a while, hiding in the shadows, he headed down to Miami to stay with Ernestico and Idalia.

They stayed at the home of Tomás Lopez, a friend of Ernestico's who lived in Allapattah, a low-income neighborhood north of the civic center, near the courthouse and Dade County jail.

The main reason Charley was there was to help fulfill a dream that Ernestico had had for some time to kidnap Isleño Dávila, the richest of the bolita bankers. Isleño's Fort Lauderdale home was an hour's drive from where they were staying. Though Ernestico was in hiding, it did not mean he was in retirement. Kidnapping Isleño, they believed, would make them all rich.

Isleño lived on a luxurious estate on the intracoastal waterway in a big house with twenty acres of land. The estate was surrounded on three sides by water. Isleño kept three pumas in cages. The security system at the estate was designed so that if anyone breached the perimeter of the property, the cages would open automatically and the animals would be released.

Ernestico and Charley cased the joint, sitting in a car outside the home's front gate. They were like two medieval bandits trying to figure out how to get into a castle. Charley's bag of quaint lock-picking tools would do him no good here. They wondered which one of them would first get eaten by the pumas. They weren't even sure if Isleño was staying at the estate or if he was in New York City.

The idea of kidnapping Isleño was put in dry dock, but Ernestico remained a hustler; he always had something up his sleeve. They decided to burglarize a private home that Ernestico had been told about. They broke in and stole, among other things, a gun they found on the premises.

Afterward, they found out that the place they had broken into was the home of a former Los Angeles cop now living in Miami. A deal was worked out for them to return the gun, and in exchange, the former cop would not make their lives a living hell. Ernestico and Charley's knack for getting into trouble followed them from New Jersey to Miami.

Even while this was going on, Ernestico maintained contact by phone with El Padrino and also with Chino. With Battle, he pretended he was still in the New York–New Jersey area, lying low because various people were trying to kill him. To Chino, Ernestico confided all, believing that his former partner was still a friend. Chino reported everything he was told by Ernestico back to José Miguel, his boss and benefactor.

AROUND THE SAME TIME THAT ERNESTO AND IDALIA FIRST DISAPPEARED ON THE RUN, the bolita bankers called a special meeting at the Colonial restaurant in Washington Heights. Everyone was there, and quite a few of the bankers were upset with El Padrino. The one who was most upset was Luis Morrero, who spoke for the entire group when he said, "José Miguel, with all respect, you are responsible for this *cucaracha,* Ernesto Torres. You are the one who brought him into our group. You made us contribute to his becoming a banker, which was a disaster. You created this monster. He's your responsibility."

It had come to the attention of everyone that the kidnapping and shooting of Morrero had only been the beginning. Word on the street was that Ernestico had a list of bankers he intended to kidnap and hold for ransom. Everyone in that room was likely on that list. Said Morrero, "This guy has become a big problem for us. He has to go. You, José Miguel, have created this problem, and so you must take care of it. It's only fair. It's the right thing."

Battle did not argue with the other bankers. He knew they were right. He had allowed the Prodigal Son to run amok for too long.

The next afternoon, El Padrino met with Chino. The only matter on their agenda was to find and kill Ernestico, who had recently cut off phone contact with both Battle and Chino. Ernestico had gone deep underground. Battle and Chino knew he was in Miami, but they had no idea where he was hiding out.

"What about that friend of his, Charley Hernandez," said Battle. "Maybe he knows."

"El Pincero? I hear he's back in town."

"Find him," said Battle. "Find out what he knows. It's time we put the squeeze on that fool."

IN MARCH 1976, AFTER SIX WEEKS ON THE LAM IN MIAMI, CHARLEY WAS BACK IN UNION City. He'd been slinking around, only going out at night. Eventually, he got the impression that maybe the dangerous times had blown over. Then he visited a friend of his named Manuel Cuello, who was associated with the Battle organization.

"Charley, my friend, you're in a lot of trouble," said Cuello.

"What do you mean?" asked Charley.

Cuello explained that Chino Acuna and another hit man had been by his place that morning. They knew that Cuello and Charley were friends. Chino told him that they were looking for Charley because the boss, Señor Battle, had put out a $15,000 contract on his head.

"Why?" Cuello had asked Chino.

Chino explained that it was because of the botched Morrero kidnapping.

Hearing this, Charley was alarmed. "But that was all Ernesto's idea."

Said Cuello, "That's what I told them. I said, 'Ernesto Torres is the instigator. Charley is not the bad guy.' Chino said, 'Well, as it stands right now, Charley is marked for death. The only way he's gonna survive is if he helps us get rid of Ernestico.'"

"Oh my God, what do I do?" Charley asked Cuello.

"Call Chino," answered his friend. "See if you can make a deal. Otherwise they gonna hunt you down and take you out."

The next day, Charley called Chino. They arranged to meet on 60th Street in the town of West New York, near where Chino lived. When Charley arrived, Chino was already there. They were standing at a street corner right in front of—of all places—the West New York police station.

Chino explained to Charley that there was a contract out on both him and Ernestico. The contract had been initiated by Luis Morrero, but Battle had taken over responsibility for the killings.

Said Charley, "But I thought Ernesto was supposed to be like a son to El Gordo, that they were thicker than blood."

"Look," said Chino, "Ernesto has been out of control for a long time. He called up El Gordo and told him he was going to start kidnapping all his friends. He's crazy. And we know you were in on some of that. The one we really want is Ernesto. He betrayed El Gordo. He has betrayed the organization . . . If you don't help us, you're dead. If you do, El Gordo will forgive you."

Fuck. Charley wasn't sure what to make of all this. Maybe it was a trick. He said to Chino, "I'm gonna help you, but right now I'm completely broke. I need two hundred dollars. Can you arrange for two hundred to be dropped off at my wife's house? As a sign of good faith." It was a test on Charley's part, to see whether Chino could be trusted.

"Sure," said Chino, "I can do that."

Charley wasn't even staying at the house in Union City with his wife and kids. He'd been hiding out at the apartment of his girlfriend, Lydia, in Washington Heights. That night, he called his wife in Union City and asked, "Hey, did you receive two hundred dollars from a guy tonight?"

She said yes, a man had dropped off two hundred in cash earlier that evening.

Charley didn't tell his wife anything, except to say, "See, don't I always take care of you?" Then he called Chino and said, "Okay, we're good. My wife got the money. We can do business."

Chino said, "All right, tomorrow at noon we gonna meet at Battle's apartment. I see you there."

A bell went off in Charley's head. He knew Battle's building, a big new apartment complex on 45th Street in Union City. Luis Morrero lived in that same building.

"Wait a minute. Morrero lives in that building. That man wants me dead."

Said Acuna, "Listen, *chico,* if Morrero or Battle still wanted you dead, you would already be dead. I'm the hit man, remember? You are safe, as long as you do this thing for us. Come by El Gordo's home. He wants to talk with you face-to-face. We gonna figure this all out."

Charley hung up and thought, *What have I gotten myself into?* He'd never been to Battle's apartment before, never had a one-on-one conversation with the Godfather. He was way out on a limb now, all on his own, thanks to his good buddy Ernestico.

TO BATTLE'S WAY OF THINKING, THE LIVELIHOOD OF ANY BOLITA OPERATION WAS based primarily on two things: discipline and trust. There were other bankers—like Isleño Dávila, for example—who knew more about the ins and outs of bolita than he would ever know. But Battle knew about leadership, and he knew that leaders knew how to keep their men in order. What he was facing now, with Ernestico, was an insurrection. His entire reputation as a bolita boss rested on how he went about resolving this crisis.

Battle had his doubts about El Pincero. In fact, from what he knew, Charley Hernandez was a small-time *pendejo,* an asshole. But he was also the key to their entrapping Ernestico. There was no better way to handle this problem than to have Ernestico's closest friend do the deed. It was the kind of message Battle liked to send: You betray the organization, and you will never be safe. Anywhere, anytime, we will get you. And it may be your closest friend who betrays you, just like you betrayed us.

José Miguel was ready when Charley Hernandez came over to his apartment, 3H, in a building at 45-30 45th Street. The apartment was spacious but hardly luxurious. From his balcony, Battle looked out on a typical Union City street of double-decker homes and modest apartment buildings; he was only a couple blocks away from Johnny's Go Go Club, Tony's Barbershop, and other establishments on 48th Street, which was now the center of the Cuban bolitero universe.

Chino Acuna was at Battle's apartment that day, and so was José Miguel Battle Jr., then twenty-two years old.[1]

---

[1] The account of Charley's meeting with Battle Sr., Acuna, and Battle Jr. comes from Charley Hernandez, who was called upon to give this account on numerous occasions, including three lengthy debriefing sessions with detectives and federal prosecutors, twice in Grand Jury testimony, and once in trial testimony. During his debriefing interviews, Charley gave a detailed description of the interior of Battle's apartment, which involved drawing a map of the premises. Later, in preparation for trial, he submitted to a lie detector

Battle Jr.'s presence was unusual. The previous year, Miguelito, as he was known to most everyone, had graduated from St. Peter's College, a Catholic college run by the Order of Jesuits, located in Jersey City. Throughout his adolescence and young adulthood, Miguelito had kept his distance from the rackets. In a way, he also had become part of the *Godfather* syndrome. If Battle Sr. was Don Corleone, it seemed as though Miguelito had assumed the role of Michael Corleone, as played by Al Pacino. Miguelito had no interest in the family business; he was following the straight and narrow path to a respectable career. The story was that he was going to be completely legit.

Charley Hernandez, for one, was surprised to see Miguelito there. He looked like what he was: a nice college boy. Charley remembered a conversation he once had with Ernestico, who claimed that Battle Sr. once told him, "My son is going to be a prosecutor, maybe a U.S. attorney. And you will take over from me as Padrino, the Godfather of bolita. With the two of you at the top, our Cuban thing will be more powerful than anything the Italians ever dreamed of."

Charley found that ironic, because now here they all were setting out to plan Ernestico's murder.

"He betrayed everything we stand for," Battle Sr. told Charley. "I raised him like he was my own son. I made him a banker when everyone in my organization was against it. I stuck my neck out for this guy. What he did, I take it very personally. I do. So now we gonna deliver a message: I don't care who you are. You betray us, you pay the ultimate price. You understand?"

"I do, yes," said Charley. "Uh, but what about Morrero. He wants me dead."

Battle told Charley not to worry about that. He controlled Morrero.

---

test, which he passed. During his testimony, Charley submitted to rigorous cross-examination on the subject of this meeting and other subjects. He proved to be a credible witness, with his testimony leading to the conviction of Jose Miguel Battle Sr. on murder conspiracy charges. Nonetheless, Battle Jr. contests Charley's account of this meeting and a subsequent meeting he allegedly took part in. At his father's trial, on the witness stand, he admitted having met Charley Hernandez once, having been introduced to him by Ernestico Torres, but when asked if he was present at this meeting between his father, Charley, and Chino Acuna, Battle Jr. said, "That is not true. That is a lie."

"If anyone tries to bother you, you tell them to call me. Call Battle. If you are with me, I protect you."

Chino explained what they wanted Charley to do. He was to call Ernestico and lure him to New York. "What do you think would be the best way to do that?"

Charley thought about it for a few seconds, and then said, "He's been trying to kidnap Isleño Dávila. He tried to do it in Fort Lauderdale, but he couldn't find Dávila. I could tell him that I spotted Dávila here in New York, at the Colonial restaurant in Manhattan. That might get him up here right away." Charley told him that he would call Ernestico that night and tape the conversation, so that they could hear it.

"That's good," said Battle Sr. "Do you have a recorder?"

Charley did have a recorder, but he didn't want Battle to know that. He said no.

"Go with Chino," said Battle. "He'll buy one for you."

That afternoon, Charley drove around with Chino. They bought the tape recorder and a suction cup for recording phone calls at Sears. Then Chino took Charley along as he ran various errands for the organization. For Charley, it was something he had dreamed about. He was now being treated as if he were a partner with Chino and the boss, a member of the Cuban Mafia. For a lowly lock picker and thief, it was the ultimate promotion.

"You know," said Chino to Charley, "you shouldn't feel bad about this, because Ernestico was going to kill you anyway. He told me many times. 'I gonna use Charley on a big score, then I'm gonna make him disappear.' He said that."

Charley listened. He doubted that was true. Ernestico and him were best friends.

Chino made a stop in Manhattan. They were there to pick up some silencers. They met a man in his apartment. The man was introduced to Charlie as Manolo Lucier, and he seemed to be a trusted adviser of the Battle organization. Chino explained how Manolo was one of the men who kidnapped the famous Argentinean race car driver Juan Manuel Fangio. The kidnapping of Fangio, in 1958, was one of the most famous incidents of the Cuban Revolution. Just before the Gran Premio Formula One race in Havana that year, Fangio was kidnapped by rebels and held for ransom. When he was finally released, he spoke highly of his captors, making the incident a public relations coup for the rebels.

At that time, Manolo had been part of the revolution. Somewhere along the line, he became disenchanted with Castro and switched sides. Now he was a Cuban gangster in the United States, part of the Battle organization.

Charley was amazed. In the Cuban American underworld, you never knew who you were going to meet—a revolutionary, a counter-revolutionary, or a counter-counterrevolutionary.

THAT NIGHT, CHARLEY CALLED ERNESTICO IN MIAMI. "DAMN," HE SAID, "YOU REALLY got me into a mess here. What I'm dealing with is unbelievable." He explained everything to Ernestico, his meeting with Battle and Chino, and that they wanted Ernestico dead, and how he was being used as the bait. Not only that, they wanted him to do it. "They want me to kill you, brother."

Ernestico went quiet on the phone for a few seconds, and then said, "How much you think they would pay you for that?"

"I don't know," said Charley. "Maybe fifty thousand."

"Take the job," said Ernestico. "That's good money. Take the job. But tell them I wouldn't come to New York. Tell them that I want you to come to Miami. Say I told you I have a big robbery job down here, a big pile of money just waiting for us at a warehouse. We gonna rob that warehouse. You tell them you gonna kill me here in Miami."

"Wow," said Charley.

"Yeah. Take the job, get them to give you the money. Bring the money down here and we split it between us. Then we go on the run."

Charley agreed to the plan. "Okay," he said, "I'm gonna hang up now, then call you back. I'm gonna tape-record the conversation. You tell me how you have this job for me in Miami. I will play this tape to El Gordo and Chino."

Charley and Ernestico did just that. They carried on their fake conversation, like actors playing out a scene. Charley could feel his heart pumping. It was crazy, but it was also kind of exciting.

The next day, Charley again visited the apartment of El Padrino. The same people were there—Battle Sr., Chino Acuna, and Battle Jr.—with the addition of another person, Rene Avila, the newspaper publisher.[2] Charley knew who Avila was; he was a well-known person in the community. And Ernestico had once explained to him how, after the attempted hit on Loco Alvarez, it was Avila who paid his bail and got him out of jail. To Charley, it was an example of Battle's reach, how he had people in high places—cops, politicians, and community leaders—on his payroll.

Charley played for them the recorded phone conversation between him and Ernesto, with Ernesto telling him to come down to Miami right away. After the conversation came to end, he turned off the recorder and said, "That's it. I'll go down to Miami and I'll do the thing down there."

Battle Sr. and Chino seemed skeptical. Battle Jr., the son, was only partially involved in the conversation, and Avila was in and out of the room, not involved, though it was clear to all what the men were talking about; they did not hide it.

"How you gonna do this?" asked Chino, the experienced hit man.

"Well," said Charley, "you give me the money, and I fly down to Florida tonight. He will pick me up at the airport. When I get a chance, when he stops the car or he goes out with me to do the job he's talking about, I'll kill him."

Battle Sr. and Chino looked at one another, then Battle Sr. said, "You think you can do this, Charley? I mean, you're not a killer. As far as I know, you've never done this before. And now you're killing your good friend? Will you be able to go through with it?"

"Listen," said Charley, "don't worry about it. I can do it. This guy is no good. Anyway, Chino said Ernesto was gonna kill me after we make a big score. So now I gonna get him first. You don't have to worry. I'm gonna take care of him, believe me."

---

[2] As with the previous meeting between Battle et al and Charley, this account comes largely from the recollections and testimony of Charley Hernandez. Rene Avila, like Battle Jr., publically denied, during a legal deposition, that he was present at this meeting. He admitted having met Charley on previous occasions, and having been present at Battle's apartment numerous times. Avila was never charged with any wrongdoing for any role he might have played—as alleged by Charley in depositions and trial testimony—in this incident.

They talked for a bit about how exactly Charley might do the job and what was the best way to dispose of the body. Battle Sr. seemed to be having doubts. At one point, he turned to his son and said, "Miguelito, what do you think?"

Battle Jr. said, "I think what Charley is saying is the simplest way. He is the one who can gain Ernestico's confidence."

Battle Sr. said to Charley, "Maybe we should send Chino down there with you."

"No," said Charley. "Look, Ernestico is a paranoid guy. You send me down there with Chino it could get me killed. Better I do this my way."

"You have a gun?"

"Yes, I have a gun down there. A .38 Special. He holds it for me. The only thing I need is bullets. Because when he gives me the gun, it may be empty. Or it may have dummy bullets."

Battle Sr. pulled out his own gun and emptied the chamber. "Six bullets. Nice bullets. You don't have no problem with these." Battle Sr. then put the empty gun to Charley's forehead. "You make sure you put one in his head. And be sure his head is straight, understand? Not at an angle. So the bullet goes in the front and comes out the back."

"Don't worry, boss. I'm gonna do it."

Battle Sr. nodded. "You leave tonight. What name you want on the ticket?"

Charley shrugged. "My name. Carlos Hernandez."

Battle Sr. nodded to Rene Avila, who said, "I'll be back in an hour." Then Battle Sr. said to Chino, "You go with Rene, bring back the ticket." Avila and Chino both left the apartment.

The boss left the room and came back with a gym bag. He zipped it open. It was filled with neat stacks of cash. Battle Sr. said, "I'm gonna pay you fifteen thousand dollars to complete the job. It's your first job for us. But you do this right, you gonna make a lot of money with us." He pulled out some stacks of money wrapped with rubber bands and handed them to Charley.

One hour later Chino returned with Charley's ticket to Miami on Eastern Airlines, the flight leaving at 11 P.M. that night. Said Battle Sr. to Charley, "Go home. Get prepared. We're gonna pick you up at nine o'clock and drive you to Newark airport."

In his car driving to the projects on Kennedy Avenue, where he lived with his common-law wife and four kids, Charley looked at the neat stacks of cash on the seat. It wasn't the fifty grand he had imagined, but, *Damn,* he thought, *I'm doing all right.* Fifteen large, which he had finagled out of the Godfather himself. Amazing. Of course, he had no intention of killing Ernestico. It was all a scam. Which somehow made it even more exhilarating.

At home, Charley greeted two of his young daughters, Kelly and Carol. Lately, he hadn't seen the girls very often. Particularly after the botched Morrero kidnapping, he had deliberately stayed away from the wife and kids because he did not want to bring danger into their house. The girls smothered him with hugs and kisses, to the point where tears came to Charley's eyes. For the girls, this was no surprise. Their father cried easily. Years later, the older of the two, Kelly, would say, "He was a very sentimental man."

Charley gave his wife, "the Americana," $300 and told her that he had to go to Florida for a few days.

She said to him, "You know, that Ernestico Torres is going to take you down. You were a lock picker, and then you're a kidnapper, and now you are God knows what."

Charley said, "Don't worry. I got everything under control. This time I'm gonna make it. You'll see."

Charley didn't tell his wife about the fifteen thousand. At the last minute, he decided to take $1,000 with him down to Miami and stuff the rest of it under the mattress in his bedroom. He placed the neat stacks of cash in the middle of the mattress, so if someone lifted the edge the money would not be seen.

At 9 P.M., Battle Sr. and Chino drove up in Battle's blue-and-white Cadillac Eldorado. Charley kissed the girls goodbye, then went outside and got in the backseat with El Padrino, while Chino drove.

On the way to Newark airport, Battle Sr. said to Charley, "My friend, we have an expression. When someone is playing two sides against the middle, we call that 'playing two cards.' You ever hear that expression?"

Charley said, "Yes. I've heard that expression."

"Charley, are you playing two cards with me?"

"Señor Battle. I don't do that. Never. I am going to take care of this guy in Miami. You'll see."

Battle said, "I hear you have a nice family, a young boy that you love. That is important. I admire that in a man. But let me tell you something, if you run away with the money, or if you are playing two cards with me, I will kill your entire family. You understand me?"

Charley said, "Yes."

They arrived at Newark airport, the Eastern Airlines departure gate. Said Battle, "Okay, when the job is complete, you call Chino's house and say that you had supper already and I will know that Ernestico is dead and that everything is all right."

Said Charley, "All right. 'I had supper already,' you want me to say. 'I had supper already.' You will hear that from me very soon."

On the plane to Miami, Charley had time to think about what he was doing. The anxiety had begun to build, and he attempted to keep it at bay with little bottles of scotch whiskey. One of the flight attendants seemed to like Charley, and she kept slipping him bottles for free. As he became more inebriated, he thought about many things, like, for instance, *Maybe I should go through with this and kill Ernestico after all.* That way, he would get to keep all the money. But Charley knew he could not do that. He loved Ernestico like a brother.

JOSÉ MIGUEL BATTLE WAS AN ARDENT BASEBALL FAN. HE ESPECIALLY LOVED THE NEW York Yankees, whom he associated with preeminence. In 1976, he bought season tickets to Yankee Stadium. Box-seat tickets, row nine, behind home plate.

The Yankees were generating tremendous excitement that year, partly because the newly refurbished stadium had opened that year after two years of renovation. After playing the previous two seasons at Shea Stadium in Queens, the Yanks were back in their glimmering new home in the Bronx, and they had a good team to go with it.

Battle liked to use his box seats to reward friends and associates. But the person he took most often to the Yankee games was his son Miguelito. Their mutual love of baseball and the Yankees seemed to be one of the few things they had in common.

It was perhaps inevitable that Battle Sr. and his son would have a complicated relationship. When Battle left Cuba in late 1959, Miguelito, age six, was left behind in Havana with his mother. Growing up without a father was difficult enough, but Miguelito had the added pressure that his father went on to become a member of the 2506 Brigade, which was in Cuba a source of controversy, ridicule, and ostracism. Like all brigade members locked away in prison in Cuba, Battle's father was seen as a traitor to his country. Harassment from the Castro government was constant.

By the time Miguelito came to the United States to live at the Fort Benning Army base, he hardly knew his father at all. When the family moved to Union City, it was more or less mutually agreed that Miguelito was cut from a different cloth than his father. For one thing, the son was an excellent student. After graduating from college—the first in his family to do so—he made the decision to apply to law school; it was a decision that was wholeheartedly endorsed by his parents.

Arriving at Cleveland Law School, also known as Cleveland-Marshall College of Law at Cleveland State University in the Ohio city of the same name, Miguelito suffered something of a personal identity crisis. He was uncertain whether law school was really for him. After just two weeks, he dropped out and returned to New Jersey. He moved in with his parents at the apartment on 45th Street in Union City, which was an odd choice, given that Miguelito often felt smothered by his father's larger-than-life personality.

The father cut a powerful public figure, to be sure. There were other kids in the community of boliteros who worshipped Battle. Joaquin Deleon Jr., whose father had been a cop with Battle in Havana, was one of those people. In Madrid, as a teenager, he first fell under the spell of El Padrino. One of the factors that captured his imagination was the way Battle and other reigning boliteros, including his father, used to present themselves in public. "They had great style," he remembered many years later.

Partly this was the gangster style of mafiosi the world over, but there were certain aspects unique to the Cubans. "They used to have their wives iron their money so it was always smooth and crisp. They used wallets where the bills were always flat, never folded. Then they sprayed the money with perfume, so that when Battle slipped a few bills to a maître d', a doorman, or whoever, the fragrance of the money lingered long after he was gone."

They also mixed the cologne they wore with a little champagne, so that the cologne would stick to their skin. This way, its aroma would not dissipate so quickly.

Deleon Jr. also marveled at Battle's confidence and wit. He was once part of the Godfather's entourage at a Cuban diner in Union City. It was a time when Battle was constantly under surveillance by FBI agents and local police. At the diner, he spotted a local cop they all knew named Lieutenant Frank Mona, along with his partner, a Latino. In Spanish, the word *mono* means "monkey." Battle went up to Lieutenant Mona, slapped him on the back, and said to his Latino partner, *"Ese es el unico mono que es amigo mio* (This is the only monkey that is my friend)." The partner understood the play on Mona and *mono* and chuckled. Battle walked off, leaving it to the partner to explain the joke to the lieutenant.

Joaquin Deleon Jr. worshipped what he perceived to be Battle's swagger, but Miguelito was not so captivated. Miguelito had grown up a rock and roll kid. He loved his father, but he was also ambivalent, which had created a personal crisis about what role he would play in the family legacy. His dropping out of law school was a major disappointment to his parents. But this also was part of Miguelito's ambivalence, because his being a lawyer was more a dream of his parents than it had been for him.

In September 1976, as the Yankees were in a pennant drive for the first time in many years, Miguelito, for the first time in his life, was arrested. The charge was possession of an unlicensed gun. It was a relatively minor charge, and as a first time offender in the state of New Jersey, he was given the option, under the Hudson County Pretrial Intervention Project (PTI), of meeting with a counselor on a regular basis. If the counselor felt that the person charged understood the seriousness of the charges and showed remorse and atonement—if he or she wasn't revealed to be a hopeless delinquent—the charges would be dropped.

Miguelito seemed to enjoy the counseling sessions. A court liaison filed a report that read, in part:

Arriving promptly for his appointments with PTI, Mr. Battle Jr. was cooperative and spontaneous throughout, attempting to answer questions and supply information to the best of his ability. To what extent he selectively eliminated potentially damaging information is, of course, difficult to assess . . . While he is articulate and intelligent, his insight is relatively limited. His attitude and behavior during the interviews were appropriate, although a very limited range of emotion was displayed.

The counselor noted that the instability of Miguelito's early years may have contributed to his recent arrest:

To what extent the hostile environment affected Mr. Battle Jr. is difficult to say, but there is little doubt that the trauma left its mark. Mr. Battle Jr. feels he is stronger and able to tolerate more pain because of his experience. The lack of emotion with which he speaks at times is perhaps a manifestation of this.

And then there was the relationship with his father:

[Mr. Battle Jr.] speaks respectfully of his family, but particularly admires his father with whom he indicates he has very close emotional ties . . . When he dropped out of law school in 1976 after only a few weeks, his parents, particularly his mother, were very upset. Mr. Battle Jr. describes somewhat matter-of-factly a time in his life which must have been quite difficult. He feels that he strove all through college and when arriving at the goal of law school suddenly was not sure that this was what he wanted—a delayed identity crisis perhaps . . . The nature of his relationship with his father, with whom he feels one, demands further exploration. One final important point for evaluation is the effect that his exposure in his formative years to the violent environment in Cuba and subsequent military life [of his father] had on him.

Miguelito told the counselor that he was currently employed at the Latin American Jewelry store, "a family owned enterprise," and that he also worked part-time for the Spanish-language newspaper published by Rene Avila.

In some ways, Miguelito's evaluation by a criminal justice intervention counselor revealed a profile not unlike that of many young adult males. Battle Jr. was seeking to reconcile a messy upbringing with his strong desire to achieve success on his own terms and rise above his station. He professed love for his father, but there was perhaps buried underneath this love a degree of resentment and tension. This was not unusual for a young man, particularly the son of an immigrant who had fought hard to make his way in the new world.

Of course, the idea that Miguelito's situation fit the standard psychological profile was belied by the fact that, according to Charley Hernandez, his father, in his presence, had ordered the murder of an underling in his organization. And that Miguelito had been consulted, not on moral grounds, but as a strategic matter, whether using Charley to entrap and murder Ernestico was the best way to get it done. Miguelito had said, *Yes, go for it.*

For a man who had spent much of his early life and adolescence going against the grain of his father's image and style, it now seemed as though he was being groomed to be a successor to the throne.

IDALIA FERNANDEZ LOOKED AT HER BOYFRIEND, ERNESTICO, AND HIS BEST FRIEND, Charley, seated at the kitchen table deep in conversation, and she thought, *Damn, these two men are probably more emotionally bound together than I and Ernestico could ever be.* Okay, maybe she was the one who went to bed with Ernestico, she was the one who gave herself in a sexual way, but these two had some kind of weird connection that was stronger than blood.

Charley had arrived in Miami in the wee hours of the morning, ostensibly to murder Ernestico for money. It was Ernestico's father, now living in Miami, who met Charley at the airport and brought him to his apartment. Ernestico and Idalia then met Charley over at the father's place. As Ernestico explained it to Idalia, it wasn't that he didn't trust Charley. But it was possible that Charley was being followed, and he didn't want to risk revealing the location of their new apartment in Hialeah, near the famous Hialeah racetrack.

Ernesto Sr. had recently moved to Miami. As the father of the most wanted hombre in Union City, he was not safe there. He sneaked down to Miami, making sure he had not been followed. His son and the girlfriend visited him, but even he didn't exactly know where they were living.

In Senior's apartment, Ernestico and Charley sat at the kitchen table. Charley was in tears, explaining that there was no way he could ever kill Ernestico.

Idalia felt sorry for Charley. He seemed like a guy who was in over his head. Her boyfriend was a fuckup also, but at least Ernestico always seemed to be in control, even if he wasn't. He never lost his confidence. Charley, on the other hand, was a follower, and he always seemed on the verge of a nervous breakdown.

Ernestico and Idalia were disappointed that Charley had not brought the $15,000 for the hit. To them, that's what this was all about. They desperately needed the money.

Charley explained, "Look, there's only one way you will get that money. You have to return to Jersey with me. We will gather every gun we have and we'll sit across from Battle's building until he comes out the door. We kill El Gordo. It's the only way. Otherwise, this guy is gonna kill you and then he's probably gonna kill me. So we have to kill him first."

Ernestico laughed. He was the one who was supposed to be hotheaded and crazy. Charley Hernandez had never killed anyone, and now he was talking about taking out the Godfather of the Cuban underworld.

"My friend," said Ernestico, "what have you been drinking? You think we can just go kill El Gordo and then it's gonna be over? You kill Battle, and then you gotta shoot it out with his brother, and he's got many brothers. How many Battles you gonna kill, Charley? And there's no money in any of that. I'm gonna stay right here. I'm gonna kidnap Isleño Dávila and make a million dollars."

Charley believed the kidnapping of Isleño was a pipe dream; it would only make matters worse, like the Morrero kidnapping.

The argument went back and forth all day. Idalia listened with growing concern. Charley had not brought the money, and the men had no plan. They may have thought of themselves as blood brothers, but as criminal partners they were a disaster.

That night, alone in his motel room, Charley came up with a plan. He told it to Ernestico and Idalia the following morning. "Last night I saw on the TV news there was a million-dollar robbery. Three guys walk into a hotel, get the manager, and they break every safe box and make off with the loot. A witness described the robbers as three Hispanic males. I'm gonna tell Battle that was you. You cut me out of the robbery, made a million-dollar score, and you took off for Mexico."

"What about the money he paid you?" asked Ernestico.

"I'll give it back to him. Tell him I wasn't able to do the job. As long as you're alive, I don't think he's gonna kill me. Because he needs me to find you."

Said Ernestico, "If he believes that line of shit, then you're in. You're a member of his organization for life."

Charley was too spooked to take a plane back to Newark. Maybe he would be whacked by one of Battle's men. So Idalia and Ernestico drove him to the train station.

Idalia watched as the two men hugged. She heard her boyfriend say, "Brother, so far we win every war. They tried to get me with a bomb, and they didn't kill me. They tried to hit me in the flower shop, they couldn't kill me. They sent you down here to kill me—nothing. One day, you and me, we gonna do a big score, because we are the ones who are winning. It's our destiny."

Idalia was amazed. As long as she had known Ernestico and Charley, it had been one failed score after another. And yet they somehow remained naively optimistic. It seemed as though they were doomed by the very nature of their irrational brotherhood.

The two men agreed that after Charley delivered his story to El Gordo about Ernestico's hotel robbery, if Battle bought the yarn, Charley would send a telegram that read: *Rasputin in Mexico.* That would be the code that they were in the clear.

JOSÉ MIGUEL BATTLE LISTENED TO CHARLEY'S COCKAMAMIE STORY ABOUT ERNES-tico pulling off a million-dollar robbery in Miami and hightailing it to Mexico. *What does this guy take me for?* he thought. He let Charley talk.

"Maybe you catch him at the border," said Charley. "Tijuana. Maybe you catch him there trying to cross over."

They were in Battle's home, Charley, José Miguel, and Chino Acuna. Charley had brought visual aids to support his story, newspaper articles from Florida that reported of the hotel robbery in Miami. Three Hispanic males, said a witness. From what he'd been told, said Charley, the loot was mostly diamond watches and jewelry, not cash, and Ernestico's cut was not a million dollars, more like forty thousand. But it was good money, enough so that his friend could split town before he'd had the chance to blow his brains out.

Battle looked at the newspaper articles and said, "I don't know, Charley, there's something funny about this. I'm going to ask you what I asked before: are you playing two cards?"

"Boss, I know it's not how we wanted things to go, but that's how it is. I wouldn't lie to you. I'm not playing two cards."

Battle looked at Chino, who was sitting there showing no emotion. Chino just shrugged, as if to say, *What're you gonna do? You win some, you lose some.*

Charley gave Battle back his cash. "Here," he said. "Here's the money. Minus one thousand I used for the trip."

Battle didn't bother to count the money. He put it back in the gym bag. He spread open the bag to show Charley the contents, stack upon stack of cash held together by rubber bands. Charley guessed there might be fifty or sixty grand in there. "See this?" said Battle. "This is all for whoever gets Ernestico. The contract is still open."

"Well," said Charley, "he still thinks he's gonna kidnap Isleño one day. So he will contact me. I'm still his best friend." Charley wanted Battle to believe that he was still his best opportunity for tracking down Ernestico.

Battle and Chino let Charley go. They knew they had to act fast. Even if Charley's story was bullshit, as it most likely was, it meant that Ernestico would soon flee.

IT WAS A MORNING IN LATE MAY WHEN IDALIA AND HER BOYFRIEND WENT OVER TO HIS father's apartment and discovered that there was a telegram waiting for them. It read: *Rasputin in Mexico.* Both Idalia and Ernestico were relieved. This meant that Battle had accepted Charley's story. They were safe, at least for the time being.

A few days later, Idalia was in their apartment on 74th Street in Hialeah. Her boyfriend had stepped outside. Minutes later, she heard the sound of gunfire. She ran to the window and looked out and saw a blue-and-white car making a U-turn. On the passenger side was a man wearing a hat and white gloves. He was holding something that looked like a gun with a long silencer. The man fired a few more shots.

Idalia ran downstairs. By then, the blue-and-white car was speeding away. Ernestico was on the sidewalk, down on one knee. He had been hit in the left forearm. It looked as though his bone had been shattered, and he was bleeding profusely. Idalia got him back to the apartment and wrapped a towel around his arm.

Ernestico was in pain. He said, "I saw them. It was José Miguel's brother Gustavo. And Manolo Lucier. I know those men. Battle must have sent them to kill me."

Idalia said, "We have to go to the hospital. Now. Or you will bleed to death."

Ernestico objected. A hospital would be unsafe. But Idalia was able to convince him that they had no choice; this was an emergency. She raced her boyfriend to Palmetto General Hospital, where he spent the next forty-eight hours. He was discharged with a thick cast on his left arm from wrist to elbow.

They didn't even go back to the apartment in Hialeah. They hid out for a few days at their friend Tomás Lopez's apartment until they could find a new place.

It was Idalia who found the rental at 1125 Sharazad Boulevard in Opa-Locka through an ad in a magazine. It was an efficiency apartment, a dwelling common to South Florida, a single-room apartment with few frills except for a pool. Idalia and Ernesto would not be hanging out by the pool in the complex. They rented the place under the names Margie and Ricardo Villo. Nobody knew their true identities, except for a delivery boy who delivered groceries from Los Hispanos Market, which was located eight miles away in South Miami. It was the only place they trusted. The owner was a friend of Idalia's from New York.

After they had been there a week, a vacancy in the building allowed Idalia and Ernestico to move from the efficiency to a one-bedroom unit on the ground floor. Their new hideout was sparsely furnished. It was a typical 1950s layout, with terrazzo floors, an eat-in kitchen, and glass jalousie windows and doors that made it feel like a tropical bungalow.

WHEN JOSÉ MIGUEL BATTLE HEARD ABOUT THE FAILED ASSASSINATION ATTEMPT ON Ernestico, he was annoyed. Failed hits were a hazard of the life, but he did not want the contract on Ernestico to turn into another saga like the ongoing efforts to kill Palulu. Too many failed attempts could damage the reputation of a criminal organization. After a while, you become like the gang that couldn't shoot straight, the laughingstock of the underworld. With Palulu, Battle had been forced by circumstances to bide his time. But the Ernestico issue had already dragged on too long. To solve this dilemma, Battle would do what he always did in his life: he would take control of the situation.

It did not take long for them to identify the apartment complex where their targets were now living. Using a local contact who posed as a prospective tenant, they had been able to case out the Pinetree Gardens apartment complex on Sharazad Boulevard, checking out entryways and exits on the property.

Putting together a hit team, that was the tricky part. It would take three men to kill Ernestico and his girlfriend in their apartment. To assure that the hit would not be botched necessitated that they use men from deep within the inner circle of the organization. Chino Acuna, of course. And then José Miguel decided that he himself would take part in the hit. As for that third person, it would be once again his brother Gustavo, who had only recently been released from prison after serving six years on cocaine charges and was already back doing hits for the organization.

Battle called Gustavo, who was living in Miami. They made arrangements to meet in the Magic City the following day. Battle and Chino flew to Miami on separate flights.

At five minutes past three on the afternoon of June 16, the three men arrived at the apartment complex. They were all armed with various handguns. They sneaked up to the door of Ernestico and Idalia's apartment. They took out their guns, stopped, and listened for a few seconds. They heard the sound of a television. It was *General Hospital,* the TV soap opera, which Idalia never missed.

They busted in through the jalousie door, glass shattering everywhere. José Miguel and Gustavo let Chino take care of Idalia, who was watching TV in the front room. They rushed down a hallway toward the back bedroom.

Ernestico awakened from his nap. He heard the crashing door, heard Idalia scream, and knew his moment of reckoning had arrived. He grabbed two guns he kept next to him on the bed and started firing. The Battles returned fire, blowing holes in the plaster wall of the bedroom.

Ernestico slid off the bed and retreated toward the closet. He blasted away with both weapons, though his efforts were inhibited by the cast on his left arm. The Battles charged into the room. Gustavo was hit, not badly, but enough that he was bleeding. One of the attackers, either Battle or Gustavo, shot one of the guns out of Ernestico's hand. With the other gun, Ernestico continued firing as he scampered into the closet for cover. After sixty seconds or so, Ernestico fired no more; he wasn't moving.

Cautiously, the Battles moved forward. There was Ernestico, crumpled in an odd position. He'd been shot multiple times—twice in the torso, in the forearm, and in the hand.

Ernestico moved ever so slightly. He was still alive.

José Miguel, the Godfather, bent down and put his 9mm handgun to Ernestico's forehead, right in the middle, a half inch above the eyebrow line. He positioned Ernestico's head so the trajectory was straight and true. Then he pulled the trigger, shooting the Prodigal Son right between the eyes.

The two Battles hurried out of the room, Gustavo dripping blood as they met up with Chino in the hallway. They exited through a rear doorway in the kitchen.

Later, an eyewitness from across the street, not close enough to identity the assailants by face, did notice that there were three of them, and that two of the men helped the third along, as if he were injured.

The three men jumped into a Cadillac and sped away. It had been messy, but the deed was done.

AT THE AGE OF FORTY-SEVEN, BATTLE WAS ARGUABLY A BIT LONG IN THE TOOTH TO BE carrying out hits himself. Normally, Mob bosses in his position would have created a buffer between themselves and the actual killing, for legal reasons, if nothing else. But Battle wanted to let the other bolita bankers know that he was not like them.

On the night of the shooting, Battle called Oracio Altuve, a Cuban bolitero from New York who had recently moved to Miami. Altuve was from Battle's generation, in his late forties, living in an apartment in North Miami Beach. At the time Battle called, he happened to have a visitor in his home—Isleño Dávila, who lived nearby in Fort Lauderdale.

The two men were surprised to hear from Battle, who they did not know was in town. Said Battle to Altuve, "I need you to come over to the place where I'm staying." He gave his friend the address of a cheap motel in Little Havana.

"Isleño is here with me," said Altuve.

"Good," said Battle. "Bring him with you."

Altuve and Isleño drove to a location on SW 8th Street, Calle Ocho. Battle was in the parking lot waiting for them. He climbed into the backseat of the car. The first thing he said was, "He fought like a lion."

Altuve was behind the wheel, Isleño in the front passenger seat. They both turned around and looked at Battle, who explained, "Ernestico. He defended himself with great courage. Until he ran out of bullets. We shot him in the closet."

Battle asked them to drive him to the Fort Lauderdale airport. He had a plane to catch.

Back in New York a few days after the murder, Battle called for a meeting of the bolita bankers at the Colonial restaurant in upper Manhattan. Many prominent members of the organization were in attendance: Abraham Rydz, Luis Morrero, Nene Marquez, and Luis DeVilliers, owner of the Colonial, to name a few. Battle announced to the group, "You won't have problems with Ernesto Torres no more. It's been taken care of. I shot him myself."

For Battle, it was a matter of principle: if you wanted something done right, you had to do it yourself. By handling it the way he did, it was as if he were back on the beach at Playa Girón, at the Bay of Pigs, taking matters into his own hands.

Part II
Venganza/Revenge

8

COUNTERREVOLUTION

PALULU ENRIQUEZ WAS LUCKY TO BE ALIVE. HE HAD KILLED PEDRO BATTLE, BROTHER of El Padrino, and lived to tell about it. He had survived being machine-gunned in Central Park by Ernesto Torres and having lost his leg. If he could survive the street, surely he could handle a court of law.

In May 1976, Palulu went on trial for the murder of Pedro Battle at the Guanabo bar in Washington Heights. The Manhattan District Attorney's Office, led by Robert Morgenthau, had a case, but it wasn't a very good one. The owner and staff of the bar claimed that they could not identify the shooter. Pedro's widow, Elda, took the stand and testified that Palulu shot her husband in cold blood. But the defense countered with witnesses who claimed that Pedro fired first. In the back-and-forth of "he said, she said," the seeds of reasonable doubt found fertile soil. On June 3, 1976, the jury deliberated for a few hours and delivered a verdict of not guilty on the murder charge and guilty on one count of illegal possession of a firearm.

The judge sentenced Palulu to serve two to three years on the firearms charge. It was a relatively light sentence. With time off for good behavior, he could be out in less than a year.

Given that there was an open contract on his life that stood at $100,000, Palulu may have felt that his incarceration was propitious. On the surface, it would seem that the circumscribed routine of life in prison was a safer alternative than the wide-open streets of New York City. Out there, anyone could take a shot at you. Inside, ostensibly, only the guards were armed.

Palulu was shipped out to serve his time at the Clinton Correctional Facility, better known as Dannemora after the town in Clinton County, New York, where it is located. Built in 1844, the prison is a bleak maximum-security facility located in the northernmost reaches of the state, near the Canadian border. The walls are made of concrete, and the circular watchtowers, added to the grounds in the 1870s, give the building the look of a Gothic fortress. Chilly both inside and out, for a long time Dannemora was the home of the state's electric chair, before New York State did away with capital punishment in the 1960s.

Palulu did not expect to be there for long. He kept to himself and made few friends.

In mid-July, after he had been at the prison for six weeks—and less than a month after Ernesto Torres was murdered far away in Miami—Palulu was in the exercise yard one afternoon. From seemingly out of nowhere, an inmate walked up and plunged a homemade knife into his back. Palulu dropped to his knees. Blood gushed from his wound, forming an expanding stain on his prison jumpsuit. An alarm sounded, and guards rushed to the scene.

Palulu was taken to the prison's medical ward. He had lost a lot of blood, but the knife had not penetrated any vital organs. He would survive.

As with many prison assaults, no one talked, and the assailant was never identified.

During an investigation of the incident, prison authorities discovered a second plot to kill Palulu. It seemed that someone was determined to use his incarceration as an opportunity to go duck hunting, with Palulu as the sitting duck. The warden at Dannemora decided to segregate the inmate in an isolated wing for special prisoners, such as cops, celebrities, or convicts whose crimes were so notorious that they could not be left to the wolves in general population. Palulu was assigned there to serve out the balance of his sentence.

News of Palulu's survival would have reached José Miguel Battle like a fetid breeze blowing downriver from the city dump. Not what he wanted, but eventually the winds would change direction. He was going to get Palulu, whether it was inside or outside prison walls.

IN THE YEAR 1976, THE IDEA THAT FIDEL CASTRO WAS STILL ALIVE, FOR MANY CUBAN Americans, was like a horrible case of gastritis. The pain was surprisingly acute, and it would not go away. Every day, there it was, like a dagger in the intestines. What was needed was a thorough cleansing, the mother of all bowel movements, but it wasn't happening. The discomfort had backed up to the point where it was affecting other vital organs—the kidneys, the liver, the heart. There was no pharmaceutical remedy for what had become a nagging existential reality.

It had been sixteen years since the CIA and various components of the militant Cuban underground committed itself to eliminating Castro and taking back Cuba. With the murder of Kennedy, the CIA officially disengaged from assassination efforts, but it remained involved in other anti-Castro activities. To the Agency, this effort was a subset of the Cold War. Using Cuban exiles as covert proxy warriors in this ideological battle between communism and capitalism was to become part of history's connective tissue.

No one was supposed to know. When the Watergate scandal exploded, lawyers from the special prosecutor's office approached the CIA. An investigator had noticed that four of the Watergate burglars were veterans of the Bay of Pigs invasion. It dawned on the lawyers that perhaps the CIA-Cuban connection was a more important aspect of this strange covert op than anyone realized. The lawyers demanded to see the full file on Eugenio Rolando Martinez, who they learned had been a paid CIA operative for many years leading up to the burglary. The CIA refused and the file was kept buried for four decades.

In the mid- to late 1970s, the secret war against Castro heated up. The idea of actually killing Fidel—attempted and thwarted many times in the 1960s—now gave way to a conspiracy of terror against Castroism. In this war, any country, individual, or group of individuals that expressed support for the Castro government was a target.

One of the most notorious salvos in this war occurred on September 21, in the nation's capital.

Orlando Letelier, a former Chilean ambassador to the United States, Marxist economist, and political activist, had arrived in Washington, D.C., to speak at a gathering of the Institute for Policy Studies, a leftist think tank. Letelier had been imprisoned in Chile, and tortured, for speaking out against the dictatorship of General Augusto Pinochet. Since his release one year earlier, he had become popular among leftists. He had also recently made a trip to Cuba at the invitation of Fidel Castro.

Letelier was driving in a car that morning with Ronni Moffitt, an American associate, and Moffitt's husband of four months. They were on Embassy Row, in morning traffic, with Letelier driving, when a bomb affixed to the car's undercarriage exploded. Letelier and Ronni Moffitt were killed; Moffitt's husband was critically injured but survived.

Earlier that morning, Letelier's wife had been awakened by a phone call. A voice asked, "Are you the wife of Orlando Letelier?"

"Yes, I am," she sleepily answered.

"No. You are his widow."

The caller hung up, and the line went dead.

It was an audacious political assassination. In some ways, it seemed like the culmination of a recent bombing campaign by anti-Castro activists, both in Miami and the New York City area. Groups such as Alpha 66 and Omega 7 let it be known that both candidates in the upcoming presidential election of 1976—Jimmy Carter and Gerald Ford—were likely to sell out the movement, but the militants were not going to let up in their efforts to undermine the Castro regime.

The Letelier bombing was unprecedented, but it was exceeded just two and a half weeks later. On October 6, a Cuban airliner flying from Panama City, Panama, to Havana was blown out of the sky. All seventy-three people on board were killed, including the entire Cuban fencing team, which had been performing at an exhibition in Panama.

The FBI's Cuban Terrorism Task Force had been busy in recent years, and these two recent events seemed to be part of an escalating pattern. In recent months, five different anti-Castro militant groups had coalesced into a governing body called the Coalition of United Revolutionary Organizations (CORU). Among the ruling council of this group were some familiar names, including Orlando Bosch; the Novo brothers, Guillermo and Ignacio; and Luis Posada Carriles.

In the Letelier/Moffitt murder investigation, the FBI had an informant high up in Pinochet's notorious intelligence service (DINA) who helped them construct a case. The hit had been authorized by General Pinochet himself, who gave the order to his secret police. To carry out the hit, DINA agents turned to a growing network of anticommunist terrorists, among which CORU now played a major role.

An article in the *Washington Post* touched upon the conspiracy. Under the headline "Evidence Links Letelier Death to Anti-Castro Unit," a team of *Post* reporters wrote:

> Within the last two weeks . . . at least six members of a Miami-based anti-Castro Cuban veterans of the Bay of Pigs invasion, known as the 2506 Brigade, have been called as witnesses before a federal grand jury . . . Brigade 2506 has been reported to have taken part in the formation of a right-wing, anti-Castro umbrella organization known as CORU.

The FBI learned that the man who authorized both the Letelier murder and the bombing of the Cuban airliner was Luis Posada Carriles. Among the men who carried out the Letelier hit—planting the bomb under the former ambassador's car—were Guillermo and Ignacio Novo.

Arrest warrants were issued for all of these men. Posada remained out of the country and became an international fugitive from the law; he was later arrested and incarcerated in Venezuela. The Novo brothers were arrested in Union City and charged with murder. Their case became a cause célèbre in the exile community, with rallies and fund-raisers in support of their legal defense both in Miami and along the Union City–West New York–Weehawken corridor in New Jersey.

For some, these new tactics represented an untenable escalation. The bombing of the Cuban airplane, resulting in the death of innocent civilians, was a bridge too far. A heated debate began within the militant community and also the Cuban American population at large about the morality of these actions. Polls showed that most Cuban Americans favored an open dialogue with Cuba, but the extremists had a method for squelching such opinions: violence. For those who spoke out against the bombings and assassinations, there were repercussions.

In Miami, an influential news director at WQBA-AM radio, Emilio Milián, publicly condemned the "terrorism." In April 1976, he was on the receiving end of a car bomb that blew off both his legs. A former leader of the 2506 Brigade Veterans Foundation, Juan José Peruyero, spoke out in defense of Milián. Peruyero had been one of the earliest presidents of the foundation comprised of brigade veterans; he was revered by many in the community.

On the night of January 6, 1977, Peruyero called Emilio Milián at his home in Little Havana. He told Milián that he had some new information about who might have been behind the bombing of his car, which, though he had survived, left him in a wheelchair for the rest of his life. Milián was curious and asked Peruyero to come over right away to discuss it, but the former brigadista said it was late. He would come by Milián's home the following day.

Peruyero never made it to Milián's house. The next morning, he was assassinated in front of his house in a drive-by shooting that had all the earmarks of a professional hit.

There had been acts of violence against organizations and people believed to be sympathetic to an open dialogue with Castro, but the assassination of a popular brigadista who had devoted his life to *la lucha* was something new. Anti-Castro militancy had turned into an internecine battle among Cuban exiles.

Between 1975 and 1978, according to an internal analysis by the Organized Crime Bureau of the Dade County Public Safety Department, there were forty terrorist bombings in Dade County, all of them Cuban-related. The report also noted that in New York City and New Jersey, there had been forty-one Cuban-related "terrorist incidents." The report stated:

> Cuban exile terrorists have blown up ships in Miami harbor; they have placed bombs on Russian ships in Puerto Rico and in New Jersey; they have blown up an aircraft in the air, killing all seventy-three souls on board; they have placed a bomb on an airliner in Miami, this bomb being set to explode while the plane was in the air, full of passengers; they planted a bomb in a car owned by a former Cuban

senator and later the editor of a newspaper in Miami, killing him instantly; they have blown off both legs of the news director of the largest radio station in Florida . . . In one twenty-four hour period in December 1975, a Cuban exile terrorist placed eight bombs in the Miami area. Most of these bombs were placed in government buildings such as Post Offices, Social Security offices, the State Attorney's Office, and even the Miami FBI office.

Within the community, there was fear, and among academics and commentators there was much discussion about the concept of shame and what role it played in the stoking of violence. It was noted that the legacy of the Bay of Pigs invasion, both for some of the men who had participated and also for many in the community who felt obligated to defend the brigade no matter what, had created a psychological justification for violent action.

Whether or not José Miguel Battle was motivated by shame is not known; he never expressed as much to anyone who knew him. If he did feel shame, it likely had more to do with the fact that he had been unable to play a more active role in *la lucha*. The FBI suspected that he had undertaken some political assassinations, and he was certainly a supporter of the cause. But while others he knew were on the front lines of the anti-Castro campaign, Battle had become consumed by the daily operations of his bolita empire, which increasingly involved revenge plots and killings that were more personal than political.

AS A GANGSTER, BATTLE HAD SOME ISSUES TO DEAL WITH THAT THE MILITANTS DID not, most notably the Mafia.

Ever since the Cubans had begun to expand their bolita operations in the New York City area, the Mob boss they dealt with the most was Fat Tony Salerno.

Since the death of renowned mafioso Vito Genovese in 1969, Salerno had become the face of the Genovese crime family based in East Harlem, or Spanish Harlem, as it was sometimes called, especially after Aretha Franklin recorded her megahit of the same name in 1971. You could hear that song coming from phonographs or transistor radios along 115th Street near the Palma Boys Social Club, where Salerno and other underbosses sat in folding chairs in front of the club.

With his felt fedora, jowly cheeks, and ever-present cigar, Fat Tony was a mobster from the old school. He was not seen in high-class night-clubs like the Copacabana or the Stork Club, as were more famous mafiosi. Salerno was a proletarian gangster who gave the impression of being a man of the streets. Nonetheless, he was rich. He had a home in Miami Beach, a hundred-acre estate in Rhinebeck, New York—horse country—and an apartment in Manhattan near ritzy Gramercy Park. He made the most of his millions from the city's numbers racket.

You did not address him as "Fat Tony." "Big Tony," maybe. But "Mr. Salerno" was even better. In later years, Salerno was heard on a wiretap bemoaning a disrespectful young gangster who had called him Fat Tony to his face: "If it wasn't for me, there wouldn't be no Mob left," he complained. "I made all the guys."

In late 1976, Salerno was indicted on federal tax and gambling charges. Prosecutors noted that Fat Tony had been accepting at least $10 million annually in illegal policy wages but reporting only $40,000 on his income taxes. The Mob boss's lawyer, the infamous Roy M. Cohn—formerly co-counsel for Senator Joe McCarthy's House Un-American Activities Committee in the 1950s—described his client as a "sports gambler," but the Internal Revenue Service wasn't buying it.

All of the early Cuban bolita bankers—Angel Mujica, Isleño Dávila, Battle, and others—had made the pilgrimage to the Palma Boys Social Club, which looked like a storefront club from the Prohibition era. There, the Cubans received Salerno's blessing, with the understanding that the Mafia would receive a piece of the action.

Throughout 1976 and into 1977, Battle made semiregular stops at the social club, especially during the holidays. At Christmas, he came by with an envelope filled with $10,000 in cash, which he handed to Salerno, who remained out on bail. This was not the Mob's cut of bolita, but rather a holiday gift.

Everybody was happy to see Mike Battle. By having Battle serve as a numbers boss, they were carrying on a tradition that went back to Alejandro Pompez, the Mafia's Cuban numbers king back before the war.

Of course, the arrangement was based on the Cubans regularly greasing palms at the Palma Boys Social Club, and in light of Salerno's recent indictment, the price of doing business had gone up. A boss facing criminal charges meant costly legal expenses, a good excuse for increasing operating costs and taxes paid by various subsidiaries.

Battle never minded paying the money. He knew that you got what you paid for, and Salerno was the man in charge of the numbers racket in New York. It was money well spent. His concern was not Fat Tony, it was the other Cubans who had been cultivating the Mafia boss themselves.

Isleño Dávila, in particular, had formed an alliance with the Italians to establish a network of "bolita holes," or shops, in neighborhoods along the Brooklyn-Queens border. Isleño's contacts were mostly with the Lucchese crime family based in Brooklyn. But the Luccheses would have cleared everything with Fat Tony, the man who had been designated within the Five Families structure as the overseer of the numbers racket.

Isleño and Battle had coexisted peaceably for close to a decade. Battle was believed to have approximately one hundred bolita spots around New York, and many "runners" in Hudson County, New Jersey. Isleño probably had just as many shops in New York. They each employed hundreds of people. They each made multiple millions, which was used to finance their operations and also line their own pockets. This peaceful coexistence was based on their not stepping on each other's toes. Battle was concerned that with Isleño Dávila presenting himself to the Mafia as a Cuban bolita boss, he was sowing the seeds of confusion. In Battle's mind, he was the Cuban Godfather. There was no other.

So far, none of this was affecting business. Battle had not heard anything from Fat Tony Salerno about Isleño Dávila, or any other Cubans, intruding on his territory. But Battle was a strategist. As a leader, he liked to anticipate problems before they happened. He could see himself getting caught up in a war with Isleño. And not only that, but Isleño was in a position to complicate his relationship with Fat Tony and the Italians, which would become an existential threat to his organization. In all of this, Battle saw dark clouds forming on the horizon. And he was beginning to suspect he might need to take action.

BY THE CHRISTMAS SEASON OF 1976, CHARLEY HERNANDEZ WAS A WRECK. FOR SIX months—ever since first hearing about Ernestico's murder—he had been living in fear. When he first heard about it, he didn't believe it. At Tony's Barbershop, a friend, Luis Valdez, told him, "Hombre, did you hear? Your friend Ernesto Torres is dead."

Charley remained in denial, until the next day when he read an article about the murder in *El Diario,* a Spanish-language newspaper, with a picture of Ernestico and everything. Then Charley received a call from Chino Acuna: "We took care of your friend in Miami. He won't be making any more orphans. Keep your mouth shut or you will wind up just like him."

Later, Charley was put on the phone with El Padrino, who told him the same thing: "We took care of the kid." You talk, you die.

Charley went into hiding. He stayed with his girlfriend, Lydia Ramirez, in Washington Heights, and rarely left the apartment. On one occasion when he did try to visit Carol Negron and his kids in Union City, he was jumped in the courtyard outside the building and beaten to a pulp. His son and three young daughters were shocked when he arrived at the apartment bloodied and bruised, though it was not the first time they had seen him in this condition. Charley had become something of a punching bag for the Battle organization.

By winter, Charley had returned to the neighborhood; he watched his back and was always armed.

On the night of December 20, he thought he would hide away for a couple of hours in a movie theater. He was carrying his burglary tools in a knapsack, as he often did. And he was carrying a gun. He was spotted by a police detective he knew well—Lieutenant Frank Mona, who had arrested him a couple times over the years. Instinctively, Charley ran. Mona chased after him. Charley ditched his burglary tools in the bushes. He also got rid of his gun.

Mona saw all this. He caught up with Charley, cuffed him, and placed him under arrest, then he retrieved the illegal items. Charley was taken to the Union City police station. It was a place he knew well; he'd been pinched numerous times for possession of marijuana and possession of burglary tools. Just walking into the place gave him the creeps, because he believed that Battle owned the Union City Police Department.

It was late on a Friday night. The courts weren't open until Monday. As was often the case in these situations, Lieutenant Mona asked Charley—a known professional criminal—if he wanted to make a deal. Who did he know that he could provide information on? Charley said he had nothing to offer, and so he was left to stew in a rancid station-house cell.

Late that night, two uniformed police officers came into the station. One was white, Irish American, and the other Hispanic. The white one said, "Carlos Hernandez, we need to speak with you for a minute. Come with us."

Charley was suspicious. He said, "Do I need to bring my coat?"

The cop said, "No. Leave your coat there. It might get messed with blood." Then the two cops chuckled.

The hair stood up on Charley's neck; he went with the cops, feeling as though he might be walking into an ambush.

The cops sat him down in an interrogation room. The Hispanic one said, "Do you know who ordered the killing of a guy named El Morro?"

Charley knew that was one of Ernestico's hits, ordered by Battle. "No, I don't know who killed him," he said.

"Do you know who ordered the hit on Ismael Alvarez?"

Again, that was a killing ordered by Battle. "I only know what I read in the papers," said Charley.

The other cop asked, "Do you work for José Miguel Battle?"

"Are you kidding me? I'm a burglar, he's a banker. You think he's going to trust me with his money?"

"You mean to tell me you would rip off Battle's money? You have the heart to do that?"

"You better believe it. If I knew where the money was, I would take it."

The cops smiled. They took Charley back to his cell and left him there.

The entire weekend, Charley thought about those cops. It entered his body like a virus: *Those cops are with Battle. They were telling me that I'm going to be hit by the same man who killed El Morro and Alvarez. I'm going to be hit right here in this police station.*

First thing on Monday, Lieutenant Mona came to Charley's cell.

"Did you send some cops to talk to me?" asked Charley.

"No," said the lieutenant. "Why?"

Charley was quiet for a few seconds, and then he said, "I have information that will blow your mind. But I'm not talking to anybody here in this station house. I wanna see somebody from the FBI."

Mona made some pro forma remark about being able to guarantee Charley's safety.

Charley shouted loudly, his voice ringing throughout the precinct, "I don't even feel safe right now in this police station. Get me out of here!" He reiterated that he would not talk until they removed him from the precinct house.

Mona did not call the FBI, but he did call in an assistant U.S. attorney from Newark and the lead organized crime investigator for the Hudson County Prosecutor's Office. Also, once Charley hinted at what he was willing to talk about, the investigators contacted Detective Richard Kalafus from the NYPD.

Kalafus had worked the Pedro Battle murder case, the Palulu shootout in Central Park, and a number of other Cuban-related homicide cases. He was considered to be a local expert on the Cuban Mafia in and around New York City. Kalafus had already begun looking into the murder of Ernesto Torres. In July 1976, he flew down to Miami and took a statement from Idalia Fernandez, while she was still recovering from her wounds. Again, Idalia identified Chino Acuna as the assailant. She also told Kalafus all about Charley Hernandez. What she did not tell Kalafus was that José Miguel Battle had been one of the assailants that day.

For Kalafus, roping in Charley Hernandez was like ordering the daily special: you weren't sure what you were getting, but you hoped it was good.

The investigators moved their perp from the Union City police station to a hotel in Newark. The next day, he sat in a back room at the Renaissance Restaurant in Newark and spilled his guts.

There were a half dozen investigators, agents, and detectives in the room that day, but the lead questioner was Detective Kalafus. He was the most knowledgeable.

Kalafus was a bona fide character. In his early fifties, he presented himself as a cowboy, with leather boots, a western-style belt buckle, and a cowboy hat. He had a craggy face that made him resemble the actor Ben Johnson, who had won an Academy Award a few years earlier for his performance in the movie *The Last Picture Show*. He spoke with a slight Texas drawl, though the rumor among some in the NYPD was that he was from the Bronx (he was actually born in a small town outside of Amarillo, Texas). Kalafus may have been modeling himself on the TV series *McCloud*, about a marshal from New Mexico who is temporarily assigned to the NYPD. The show was immensely popular, and the character of Sam McCloud, played by actor Dennis Weaver, had reached iconic status in pop culture.

Kalafus took off his cowboy hat, sat back, and said to Charley, "I'm always interested in homicides. Especially homicides involving Ernestico. Are you a friend of Ernestico's?"

"I was a good friend of his, yes," said Charley.

A cassette recorder sat on the table in front of Charley, the tape whirring round and round, recording it all for posterity.

Said Kalafus, "You're a good friend of Ernestico, who was shot sixteen times."

"Sixteen times," repeated Charley. That was a big number: sixteen bullet holes.

"We know that Ernestico committed upwards of thirteen homicides. Is that about the right number?"

"It's probably the right number, yeah," answered Charley.

"And how many do you have knowledge of that Ernestico did?"

Charley told about his friend, who in death continued to cause him as much trouble as he had in life. Only now the lawmen seemed to want to know about Ernestico's murderous history so that they could clear many unsolved homicide cases. Charley would use his friend's criminal legacy to save his own neck. He guessed that Ernestico would not have minded.

He told the cops about how Ernesto had killed a guy named El Raton, the drug dealer who had been a competitor of Pedro Battle. He told them about the murder of Pedro by Palulu, how Ernestico had approached El Padrino at the funeral service for his brother and pleaded that he be given the contract to find and kill Palulu. Charley explained to the investigators how Ernestico was paired with Chino Acuna, and then the killing really began. "There was a lot of work for [Ernesto]," said Charley. "Every night he had a different car. He cut his hair and used a lot of wigs, and every night they were kidnapping somebody. Anybody who was a friend of Palulu's got it. They went into every bar, and I read the newspaper sometimes, and I see that so-and-so got killed, and I knew they were doing the killing. They were getting paid for it."

Charley went on and on. Occasionally, Kalafus or one of the other investigators asked a question, but mostly it was a monologue. Charley had a lot to get off his chest.

The grilling continued for two straight days. Charley slept at the hotel in Newark with an armed detective outside his door. During the day, he was brought to the back room at the restaurant. Each day there was a different configuration of agents, prosecutors, and cops, though Detective Kalafus was always there.

The more Charley talked, the more comfortable he became. He was a natural storyteller, relating episodes like the kidnapping and shooting of Luis Morrero as if it were a scene from a movie. The investigators were mesmerized. Eventually, Charley got down to a specified retelling of the events leading up to Ernestico's murder, his dealings with José Miguel Battle; his contract to murder his friend; the transfer of money; his traveling to Miami to meet with Ernestico; returning to New Jersey to tell Battle and Chino Acuna that he had not been able to complete the job.

As the days passed, it was as if Charley had fallen off the face of the earth. Christmas Eve and Christmas Day came and went, and his family wondered where he was. His children had become accustomed to their father's sudden unexplained absences, so they should have been used to it, but it was an especially empty Christmas at the Hernandez home that year.

On December 28, at 11:45 A.M., Charley was brought to the Hudson County Prosecutor's Office in Newark to give an official statement. Present were Deputy Chief Charles Rossiter; an investigator with the prosecutor's office named Lieutenant Steve McCabe; and two detectives from the Union City Police Department. Charley repeated what he had been going over ad nauseam throughout numerous interrogations with Detective Kalafus, only this time the chief deputy prosecutor narrowed in on criminal activities related solely to the murder of Ernesto Torres.

With the statement from Charley, investigators in New Jersey and New York were aware that, given what Miami detectives had already been learning from Idalia, a big piece of the puzzle had fallen into place. Idalia knew about the murder from the point of view of a victim, but Charley had been privy to the initial conspiracy. Together, they connected the sequence of events that led to the brutal killing of Ernestico.

Nonetheless, the New York–New Jersey people wanted to make sure they had squeezed every last bit of Cuban gangland intelligence out of Charley Hernandez before turning him over to the district attorney in Dade County, where any trial for the murder of Ernesto Torres would take place.

In the hierarchy of Cuban American organized crime, Charley may have been a small fish, but he had learned a lot from Ernesto, El Padrino's prodigal son. And he liked to talk. All in all, Charley had the potential to be a devastating witness for the prosecution.

JULIO OJEDA WAS A MIAMI DETECTIVE WITH AN IMPRESSIVE RÉSUMÉ. WHEN THE Ernesto Torres murder occurred, Ojeda had been on vacation. But as soon as he returned on June 29, 1976, he was assigned to the case. Before long he was bumped up to lead investigator. It was clear that the investigation needed a lead agent who spoke fluent Spanish. Ojeda was a solid detective, but even he would admit that perhaps the biggest advantage he had as a cop in Miami was that he was bilingual, especially back when he first came on the job, in 1969, when there were maybe three Julios in the entire Public Safety Department.

As soon as he looked over the case file—crime scene reports; preliminary eyewitness interviews; a bedside statement from Idalia Fernandez identifying the gunman—he knew the case against Chino Acuna was strong. Idalia knew Chino. She'd had him in her home in New Jersey, and she'd been present on many occasions when Chino and Ernesto were present together. They were partners in crime.

Once a first-degree murder warrant was issued for Chino Acuna, an all points bulletin went out for his arrest. Local law enforcement and the Florida Highway Patrol were notified, as were the Hudson County Prosecutor's Office, the NYPD, and the Union City Police Department. Also notified were the FBI, which issued an UFAP (unlawful flight to avoid prosecution). Wanted fliers were circulated, though after a thorough search by all of these agencies it was believed that Chino Acuna had likely already fled the country.

Even without their prime suspect in custody, Ojeda and the others continued to build their case. Already, some startling evidence had been uncovered. At Idalia and Ernestico's apartment in Opa-Locka, the investigators confiscated a trove of tape recordings that Ernesto had made before he was killed, phone conversations with various criminal associates, including Chino Acuna, José Miguel Battle, Charley Hernandez, and others. The detectives had not yet been able to identify all the voices on these taped phone calls, and the conversations were in code to a point where it wasn't always possible to understand what was being talked about, but there were some extraordinary exchanges.

One conversation was between Ernesto and his mother in Cuba. The cops sat in the office of the state's attorney Henry Adorno and listened to the voice of Ernestico.

"Listen, Mami, did you receive the telegram I sent you?" Ernestico asked his mother.

"Yes," said the mother, "and I waited for the phone call, and I went to call you on the nineteenth. I sent you a telegram yesterday. Didn't you receive it today?"

"No, no. But none of that matters. How you are feeling is what's important."

The mother knew from having spoken with Ernesto Sr. that Ernestico was being hunted by killers.

Ernestico explained, "You know, Mami, remember I spoke with you on the fourth of December? Thirteen days afterwards, on December seventeenth, they made an attempt on me . . . It's a phenomenon, you know. The seventeenth of December, Saint Lazaro Day. I was born that day, you know. But you don't have to worry. I'm just telling you so that you know, okay?"

"Yes. Imagine that, Ernestico."

"So pray for me. A lot. And play for me a lot of *buemba,* because they are playing a lot of *buembas* on me over here, you hear me?"

Buemba is a vernacular word for a spiritual ritual common in Santería referring to sainthood. In Santería, a saint can be either a positive spirit or one with bad intentions, depending on the *buemba.*

"I got a fucking war over here with some saints," said Ernesto to his mother.

"And the names," she asked, "don't you know them?"

After some prodding, Ernestico gave his mother some names that she could use in her *buemba.* He was telling her that should he be murdered, these were the people who had done it. He gave her the actual birth names of Tati and Monchi, the hit men associated with Omega 7. And then he said, "Here's another one, write this down. José Miguel Battle. Do you understand? José Miguel Battle."

"Battle?"

"Battle. B-A-T-T-L-E. José Miguel Battle. And now, listen, another one. Julio Acuna."

"Julio Acuna."

"Yes. My war is with these saints."

Ojeda, along with other detectives and the prosecutor, listened to this taped conversation and marveled. It was as if the victim were speaking from the dead to identify his killers.

Charley Hernandez was a name that had come up in their interviews with Idalia. Charley was on the tapes too, speaking in code about how he had been given a contract by Battle to kill Ernestico. Idalia filled in the blanks, telling them about Charley staying with them in Miami and then hatching a scheme to supposedly kill Ernestico for money. She told them how Charley cried at the prospect of killing his best friend, how the two men had said goodbye to one another at the train station and vowed to reconnect somewhere down the line.

So the Miami detectives knew that Charley Hernandez was a key person of interest. But they had no idea where he was. Until Detective Ojeda received a phone call from Detective Kalafus that changed the direction of their investigation.

Ojeda and a fellow detective flew to New York City. As Ojeda remembered it in a deposition years later, "On April 23rd, 1977, we left Miami and arrived at LaGuardia Airport. We were met at LaGuardia Airport by Detective Kalafus, who took us to a horrible hotel in New York City."

That night, at the office of Sam Mandarin in the Hudson County Prosecutor's Office in New Jersey, Ojeda and his partner met Charley Hernandez. Ojeda liked what he heard. Charley was a talker, and he directly linked Ernesto to Battle. Right away, the Miami detectives realized that with what Charley was giving them they could make a murder conspiracy case against the Godfather, whether Chino Acuna was ever found or not.

The detectives made arrangements for Charley Hernandez to be transported to Miami. It was a tricky negotiation, with one jurisdiction handing off a coveted witness to another, but it was believed that the case against Battle could only be made in Dade County, where the murder took place.

In Miami, Charley was set up in a motel near the airport. The investigators brought him food and supplies. Over the next week, he led them to many of the locations he had been telling them about: apartments in Allapattah and Hialeah where he had stayed with Ernestico and Idalia; the home of the retired cop that he and Ernestico had burglarized; the apartment complex where Ernestico Sr. had been living; the motel where Charley stayed when he was in town to "murder" Ernestico.

Concurrently, the detectives went about building their case. They tracked down and interviewed tenants at the apartment building where Ernesto and Idalia had lived in Opa-Locka. They sought to find the delivery boy who delivered groceries to the apartment, and discovered that he had only recently died in an automobile accident at the age of seventeen. The investigation was frequently interrupted by the fact that Ojeda and his partner were busy working other cases at the same time as this one.

One of Ojeda's open cases was the murder of Rolando Masferrer, a notorious gangster from the 1950s era in Cuba. Masferrer had been the leader of Los Tigres (the Tigers), a political assassination squad affiliated with the government of President Fulgencio Batista. After the revolution, Masferrer escaped from Cuba and became a political firebrand in

Miami's volatile anti-Castro universe. He published a newspaper titled *Libertad,* in which he called for the car bombing of his political enemies. On October 31, 1975, Masferrer was himself blown up by a bomb attached to his car.

Political assassinations in the anti-Castro underground were like Mob hits. Everyone had a theory about who did it, but the cases almost always went unsolved. Ojeda felt that Masferrer had likely been killed by Castro spies in the United States. FBI agents working the case believed it had been done by rivals within the anti-Castro sphere, most likely the Novo brothers out of Union City. With little hard evidence, the case remained open.

Another case that Ojeda became involved with was the murder of mafioso Johnny Roselli. On August 9, 1976, Roselli's decomposed body was found stuffed inside a fifty-five-gallon steel drum floating in Dumfoundling Bay in Miami. The murder of Roselli was no small matter. Having partnered with fellow mafioso Santo Trafficante and the CIA in efforts to assassinate Fidel Castro, the mobster had been an underworld operative at a very high level.

On June 24 and September 22, 1975, Roselli had been called to testify in front of the U.S. Select Committee on Investigations in Washington, D.C. Known as the Church Committee, because it was chaired by Senator Frank Church of Idaho, the committee had been unraveling, for the first time in public, Operation Mongoose and other anti-Castro efforts from the 1960s. Days before Roselli was scheduled to testify, one of his other partners in Operation Mongoose—mafioso Sam Giancana—was shot dead in the basement of his Illinois home. This murder had motivated Roselli to move from his homes in Los Angeles and Las Vegas and settle in Miami, where he felt he was safe.

It was a logical assumption, as traditionally Miami was a safe haven for mafiosi. Mob hits took place in New York, Chicago, Philadelphia, Boston, and other places. Miami was where mobsters like Meyer Lansky came to retire, and no one in the underworld bothered them. Apparently Roselli was a special case. His testimony before the Church Committee had been so riveting and explosive, with many juicy details about the CIA-Mafia efforts to kill Fidel, that the committee had called him back for a third appearance on April 23, 1976. The date came and went and Roselli was nowhere to be found, until he was discovered—to paraphrase the old Sicilian phrase—asleep with the fishes.

Like the Masferrer murder, the Roselli case was one about which there were many theories and little hard evidence to secure an indictment, much less a conviction.

Ojeda thought that one person who might know something about the murder was Santo Trafficante. How could he not know? Since he was the most powerful mafioso in the state, the murder could not have taken place without his approval. If someone had done that murder without his blessing, they would certainly wind up dead as a result.

Trafficante was based in Tampa, but he had a house in North Miami, and he was there often. Ojeda simply went to the house and knocked on the door. Trafficante's wife answered.

Said Ojeda, "How are you, ma'am? My name is detective Julio Ojeda with the Dade County Public Safety Department. I'd like to speak with your husband, if he's at home."

The wife invited Ojeda in, then she went and got her husband. Years later, Ojeda remembered, "Santo was very cordial. 'You want coffee?' I said, 'Of course.' He said, 'Cuban coffee?' He spoke in fluent Spanish. We talked about Roselli. He was very friendly. He said, 'You know, I really like you. But you need to talk to Henry.' Henry Gonzalez was his lawyer."

So Ojeda did talk to Henry Gonzalez. He said to Gonzalez, "Look, I'd like to take a statement from your client. Honestly, it's a smart thing for him to do. Everyone from the FBI to the CIA will be on him about the Roselli murder. If he gives a statement, he can say, 'That's it. I gave my statement. I have nothing more to say.' "

The lawyer agreed.

Trafficante was concerned that no one see him giving this statement, not even other people in law enforcement. So the mafioso was brought to the First Union Building, the southernmost building in downtown Miami. They set up a table and stenographer in the garage, with fold-out chairs for Trafficante and his lawyer.

Remembered Ojeda, "It was the first time anyone had taken a statement from Santo Trafficante. He was shrewd, extremely smart." Trafficante gave away nothing useful.

Ojeda came away from the incident believing that the Mafia boss was an impressive individual, even though it was almost certain that he had sanctioned the murder of his good friend and former partner in crime, Johnny Roselli.

THE ANTICS OF CHARLEY HERNANDEZ HAD WREAKED HAVOC WITH HIS FAMILY. HIS young children knew very little of what was going on with their father, except that it was causing major disruptions in their life.

Within weeks of Charley's moving to Miami, Carol Negron, his common-law wife, received a visit from two men in suits, one of whom was Sam Mandarin from the Hudson County Prosecutor's Office. They told Negron that for their own safety it was likely her family would need to be relocated to Florida, where Charley was being prepped for a big trial. The investigators were introduced to the children—three girls and son Carlos—as Tom and Sam, friends of their father, who would soon be reuniting them with their dad.

Carol and Kelly, the two oldest girls, were eight and nine. They didn't really pay much attention until a few days later when Tom and Sam showed up at their school and removed them from class. They were told they were being taken home for lunch. At home, they saw that all their things had been packed up. Kelly, the oldest and most inquisitive of the girls, said, "What is this?" Tom and Sam told her that they were going down to the Jersey Shore for the weekend. It was all very strange, and young Kelly wasn't buying it.

What neither Kelly nor any of the other girls knew was that that morning, someone in a car had tried to snatch their six-year-old brother, Carlos, off the street. Carlos had escaped. The investigators believed it was Battle's henchmen. Battle must have learned that Charlie was co-operating with authorities. The investigators told the children's mother, "Your family is in danger. There's no choice here. You cannot stay. You cannot run. Listen to us and we will protect you."

As the children readied to leave, they noticed that their aunt and grandmother were crying hysterically. They didn't understand it. The aunt grabbed Kelly by the hand and said to her, "Kelly, take care of your sister."

The elevator was loaded with suitcases, so Kelly and Carol took the stairwell. In the stairwell, Kelly took her sister by the hand and said, "Something is not right here. We need to run."

It was a pivotal moment; these two young girls were about to have their childhood snatched away from them. They could run and live as feral animals in the street, or they could submit to their fate.

Carol didn't understand what her sister was talking about. "You're scaring me," she said. They continued down to the car. There, they were crowded into a van, four young kids, the mother, and two investigators.

Once the van was under way, Kelly noticed that they were not going in the direction of the shore. "Where are we going?" she asked. Sam the investigator told her that there had been a fire at the Meadowlands blocking their route to the shore. They would have to take an airplane. Even to a nine-year-old, that sounded bogus. Then Kelly felt the gun of Tom the investigator poking into her side.

"Why do you have a gun?" she asked.

There was silence in the car. Tom said, "Well, in the United States of America you can have a gun. I choose to have a gun. It's not breaking the law."

They arrived at Newark airport and boarded a commercial flight. The girls still believed that they were going to the Jersey Shore, though it seemed strange that these two men in suits and patent leather shoes were coming with them.

As they were landing, an announcement was made: *Welcome to Miami.*

The children were startled. The mother said, "Surprise! We're going on vacation."

They still did not know they would be seeing their father, until they disembarked into the terminal and there was Charley Hernandez down on one knee, arms wide open and a big smile on his face. On each side of their father were two men who looked the same as Tom and Sam, lawmen dressed for work.

The three girls and the boy hugged their daddy, and thus began their life in Miami, which became more unusual with each passing day.

At first it seemed as though it might be fun. They lived in a nice hotel with a big pool, which was where they spent most of their time. Tom and Sam tried to help them learn new names; they made a game of it. "Think of a name you always wanted, your favorite name." Then the two agents trained them not to react if anyone called out their old names.

It was a weird fantasy life. They were kept out of school. Kelly never finished fourth grade, and she was kept out of fifth grade.

It was fun at the hotel, but one day Tom and Sam showed up and said, "Get out of the pool now. We have to go." They told Carol Negron to get all the kids together. They would bring their clothes and belongings later. They had to go. A grandparent of one of the girls' friends had called local authorities and said, "Something's not right. My granddaughter has these girlfriends, they never go to school."

The agents loaded Negron and her family into a van. Years later, daughter Kelly remembered, "They drove us around for hours, all day and all night. They didn't know where to put us. They took us to one of those two-story apartments you see in Florida, with a pool in the front. They put us on the first floor and said, 'You're going to stay here for the night.' Until they could figure out what to do with this family. No extra clothes, no anything. They kept us there for a while. They told us we were vacationing. It was a surprise. Our father came home sometimes, but not every day. He was always in the company of other men who would sit outside; they never came in the house."

After a few months, the kids adapted. They were unaware that in July 1977, authorities in Florida were ready to make their move on José Miguel Battle. A warrant for his arrest was issued, though it wasn't acted on immediately. Lawmen in New York and New Jersey followed him around for days, waiting for the opportunity to make the arrest.

JULY 13 WAS A SEASONABLY WARM AND HUMID DAY IN MANHATTAN. BATTLE HAD JUST come from one of his bolita operation's main offices on West 79th Street near Amsterdam Avenue. It was incumbent upon a bolita king to occasionally visit his minions at work—at least in the offices, where the money was kept. He rarely, if ever, visited the actual bolita holes where the bets were placed. It would be unwise for a banker or boss to be seen there; those places were sometimes under police surveillance. It would be like the CEO of a supermarket corporation visiting one of his retail outlets; it was unnecessary and would only diminish the CEO's stature as his company's great and powerful chief.

Battle arrived at a restaurant in Washington Heights, located at 163rd Street and Broadway, and settled in for a meal. The investigators had been tailing him most of that day. Their entire operation was based on his not detecting the surveillance. It wasn't until he was inside the restaurant that they alerted the other units.

Detective Kalafus was the lead officer; he was executing the warrant on behalf of the Dade County Prosecutor's Office. Detective Ojeda was on vacation and unable to attend the party, but there were police officers from Miami. One of them, a special guest, was Diego Mella.

Mella was the cop who as a member of the Union City Police Department had arrested Battle and two of his brothers on illegal gun possession charges back in 1974. Mella had been so shocked to discover the depths of Battle's influence with the police department and political structure in Hudson County that shortly thereafter he resigned as a cop. He moved to South Florida and joined the Dade County Public Safety Department.

Late in the Ernesto Torres murder investigation, when Detective Ojeda and the others learned of Mella's history in Union City, they arranged for him to be assigned to the investigation as part of the apprehension squad. Having Mella involved was a tip of the cap to the officer, and a middle finger to Battle.

The cops waited until the Godfather finished his meal and walked out of the restaurant. On the sidewalk, he was surrounded by dozens of New York City police officers and Miami detectives. Kalafus served the warrant, and Mella was there to place the handcuffs on Battle.

Said Kalafus, "José Miguel Battle, you are under arrest for conspiracy to commit murder and for the murder of Ernestico Torres."

Battle looked out over the sea of arresting officers and said nothing. Within the hour, he was on the phone with his esteemed criminal defense lawyer. He would not go down without a fight.

9

THE COUNSELOR

RAYMOND A. BROWN WAS NOT YOUR USUAL CRIMINAL DEFENSE ATTORNEY. IN THE state of New Jersey, his home base, he was, at the age of sixty-two, already a legend. There were numerous reasons for this, one being that he was African American, a rarity in the profession. In the early 1950s, when Brown was first admitted to the state bar and became licensed to practice, there were few black lawyers on either side of the aisle. There were, however, many black defendants. Among Brown's earliest litigations were civil rights cases in New Jersey and the Deep South.

The civil rights cases gave Brown credibility among the people, but his notoriety came later in a series of high-profile cases that established the lawyer as among the best in his profession.

By the time of José Miguel Battle's arrest for his involvement in the Ernesto Torres murder, he and Brown already had a working relationship. In 1974, Brown had been involved in helping Battle with his legal entanglements after he returned from Spain. It was Brown who, on behalf of Battle, negotiated a plea on federal gambling charges and also a charge of unlawful flight from prosecution. Battle had been facing a combined sentence of twelve years. Brown plea-bargained his case down to five years, of which El Padrino served two and half, an unusually light sentence.

Battle knew that Brown was worth his weight in gold. Not only was the lawyer a tall, elegant black man with tremendous acumen in the courtroom, but with his civil rights background it was implicit in most cases he undertook that not only was his client innocent, but also that he or she was a victim of a grave injustice. Brown was not afraid to take on the powers that be.

One of his first big trials, in 1964, had been the case of John W. Butenko, of Orange, New Jersey. Butenko, an unassuming employee of the International Telephone & Telegraph Corporation, had been charged with passing secrets of the U.S. Strategic Air Command to Soviet spies operating in the United States. It was a sensational case that garnered international headlines. Butenko was found guilty, but the trial established Raymond Brown as a defense lawyer willing to take on difficult and unpopular cases.

His fortitude as a lawyer was rooted in his upbringing. Brown was born in Fernandina Beach, Florida, the son of a railroad mechanic. When he was two years old, he moved with his parents to Jersey City. Later in life, he returned to Florida to attend Florida A&M University, which he paid for in part by working as a longshoreman. After college, he served in the U.S. Army, fought in World War II, and stayed in the military as a member of the National Guard. When President Harry Truman officially integrated the U.S. armed forces, Brown became one of the first black officers. He retired from the National Guard in 1970 at the full rank of colonel.

Having acquired a personal education that included physical labor, academic achievement, and national service, Brown had a sense of justice that was rooted in the real world. Later in life, he would say that what attracted him to the law was having experienced and seen the way people of color were mistreated in the military.

Under the G.I. Bill, Brown attended Fordham Law School. Upon being admitted to the state bar, he did something very few black lawyers of his era would have thought possible—he opened his own independent practice.

By the mid-1960s, Brown found himself on the cusp of a new era. Not only was the civil rights era transforming America, but many of the issues brought about by protest marches, sit-ins, and acts of civil disobedience were being played out in courtrooms, where lawyers like Raymond Brown, and many others, became the legal warriors for a generation.

In 1967, Brown represented boxer Rubin "Hurricane" Carter, who, along with a codefendant, was charged with having murdered three people outside a bar in Paterson, New Jersey. What might have been viewed by some as a simple murder case was in the hands of Brown a case of racial prejudice in the criminal justice system. The trial resulted in a conviction for Hurricane Carter, but the verdict was later overturned.

By the 1970s, Brown's legal practice found itself serving as virtually the legal wing of the Black Power movement in New Jersey. In 1970, the lawyer represented three members of the Black Panther Party who were accused of shooting up a Newark police station in a drive-by shooting. A few years later, Brown became involved in perhaps his most notorious case, involving Joanne Chesimard, a.k.a. Assata Shakur, who was accused of killing a New Jersey state trooper in a wild shootout involving numerous assailants and troopers on the New Jersey Turnpike.

With her prodigious Afro and magazine model beauty, Assata Shakur became a striking symbol for her generation. A member of a Black Panther splinter organization known as the Black Liberation Army, she was alleged to have gone on a crime spree in the early 1970s that involved bank robberies and shootings throughout the New York area. Already she had gone on trial in New York for various crimes before she arrived in New Jersey to be tried for murder. Shakur's legal odyssey led her through numerous convictions, reversals on appeal, more convictions, and more reversals until she eventually escaped from prison in New Jersey and secretly fled to Cuba.

Raymond Brown and other notable criminal defense attorneys such as William Kunstler represented Assata over the years, always pro bono, either because they believed in the politics of the case or because the notoriety that came from it was payment enough.

Kunstler was an avowed leftist, but Raymond Brown's political motives were not as clear. Certainly when it came to civil rights or race-related cases he was an antiestablishment figure. But he was also an ex-military man. He was motivated not so much by leftist or counter-culture politics as by the pursuit of freedom as the ultimate right under the U.S. Constitution.

In representing Battle, Brown, on the face of it, was going against the grain of leftist politics. The left in the U.S. revered Fidel Castro and his revolution. The anti-Castro movement, starting with the Bay of Pigs invasion and everything that came afterward, was viewed by the left as a fascist undertaking. The differences could not have been starker: Assata

Shakur found refuge in Cuba. She likely was viewed by Battle and his cohorts as a pro-Castro communist sympathizer.

Brown saw no contradiction in representing both points of view. He represented other anti-Castro Cuban Americans based in New Jersey, including Armando Santana, the president of the Cuban Nationalist Association (CNA). With their headquarters located in a small store-front office in Union City, the CNA was believed to be the political wing of Omega 7. In representing prominent anti-Castro militants, Brown was equating their struggle with that of the civil rights movement. He was defending the belief that by engaging in counterrevolutionary efforts, the anti-Castro militants were fighting for the freedom of the Cuban people.

With the Ernesto Torres murder case, Battle's lawyer did not seem to have a political dimension to defend. Battle was alleged to have conspired in Ernestico's death because the man had become a threat to his reputation as a Mob boss. To interpret his actions as in any way connected to the struggle for freedom in Cuba seemed like a monumental leap, to say the least.

Brown and his client had a more immediate problem: Brown was not licensed to practice in Florida. He could not try the case on his own, though he could serve as co-counsel with a lawyer who was licensed in the state.

Battle needed to find a local lawyer. As with so many things in his life, he did so through a Bay of Pigs connection.

Alfredo Duran was a local attorney of some renown. He had his own law firm, and eventually he would serve a stint as chairman of the state Democratic Party. He was also a veteran of the 2506 Brigade. He had taken part in the invasion and served time at Isle of Pines prison with Battle. As with so many who had shared that experience, he remained in touch with his fellow brigadistas. It was a brotherhood that endured, as many survivors of the invasion excelled in life or struggled to varying degrees. They knew they could count on one another.

Duran was a corporate, not a criminal defense, lawyer. But when asked by Battle if he could make a recommendation, he immediately thought of a counselor from his law firm named Jack Blumenfeld.

Blumenfeld was a former prosecutor, now a criminal defense lawyer, who knew the Florida state criminal justice system inside out. He and Ray Brown could hardly have been more different in style and appearance: where Brown was tall, lean, and erudite, Blumenfeld was burly, blunt, and balding. If Brown was a gazelle, Blumenfeld was a bulldog.

On August 11, 1977, Battle was transferred from Rikers Island prison in New York to Dade County jail, where Blumenfeld, accompanied by Raymond Brown, met his client for the first time.

Battle was calm, and he immediately struck the lawyer as someone who could take care of himself, even under such extreme conditions as county lockup, the most dangerous form of incarceration. Battle listened well, and he seemed to grasp the legal ramifications of what he was up against. One matter that needed to be dealt with was that the lead prosecutor, Hank Adorno, had offered Battle a plea deal of sorts. If Battle would agree to a six-person jury as opposed to the standard twelve-person jury in a capital case, the prosecutors would waive the death penalty.

It was generally believed that it was easier for prosecutors to convince six people of guilt than it would be to convince twelve. The smaller jury gave Adorno a tactical advantage. On the other hand, not facing the death penalty was often an attractive option to a defendant.

In the lawyer-client visiting area at Dade County jail, Brown and Blumenfeld asked Battle what he wanted to do.

"Let me think about it," he said.

Blumenfeld had been told that Battle was an occasional devotee of Santería. He surmised that Battle wanted to consult a *babalawo,* a spiritual guide, who would seek the input of a higher power. In the Yoruba language, *babalawo* meant "father of the mysteries." No doubt in the Dade County jail system there were Cubans, or people of Cuban descent, who were trained *babalawos.* Battle would meet with one. They would light candles, burn incense, and perhaps engage in other ceremonial efforts to seek divination, and answers, to Battle's dilemma.

Raymond Brown was incredulous. "What do you need to think about? This is your life we're talking about."

Battle said, "Listen, I'm not afraid of death. You're not gonna scare me with death. I faced death in Guatemala training for the invasion, faced death in Cuba with the invasion and in prison at Isle of Pines. I'm not afraid. I'll make that decision later."

Blumenfeld took stock of his new client. He'd heard this man had cojones. Clearly, that was the case.

A week later, Battle consented to the deal and accepted a six-person jury, not necessarily because he wanted to, but because his *babalawo* recommended it as being in his best interest.

SINCE RETURNING FROM VACATION, DETECTIVE JULIO OJEDA HAD RESUMED FULL CONtrol of the Ernestico Torres murder investigation. This involved gathering evidence and tracking down potential witnesses, as well as safeguarding the two most important witnesses so far, Idalia Fernandez and Charley Hernandez.

The trial was scheduled to begin jury selection in early November. Until then, Idalia and Charley were being kept at separate locations. Idalia was with her daughter in a motel. She had a twenty-four-hour guard. Charley was allowed to stay with his family some of the time, but he often spent his time with Ojeda and the other detectives.

For a while, the cops lent Charley to agents from the Drug Enforcement Agency. Charley was such a good talker that it was felt he might be adept at working as an undercover agent making drug buys on behalf of the DEA, but it was determined that this might be too dangerous. Instead, he worked for the narcotics agency as a Miami cabdriver whose job it was to cruise the streets looking for illegal activity. The agents told him this might be the beginning of a career in law enforcement, but he quickly discerned that they were not sincere, and so he stopped driving a cab.

Eventually, Detective Ojeda found another driving job for Charley, one that would bring the government's star witness in the Ernestico murder case into direct contact with one of the biggest narco gangsters in Miami.

The moral underpinnings of this arrangement were questionable. Ojeda and his detective partners were headed down a road that would eventually destroy their careers and bring about one of the biggest scandals in the history of the Dade County police department.

MARIO ESCANDAR WAS ONE OF MIAMI'S FIRST COCAINE KINGPINS. BACK IN THE 1950S, he had run a nightclub in Havana; since his arrival in Miami in 1960, he had been a hustler and a criminal. Though English was not his first language, he adapted quickly. Over six feet tall, with lank black hair, he was a talker who believed he could bullshit his way out of any situation.

Arrested on various criminal charges, he claimed to have met during his incarceration a who's who of the American underworld. In 1962, while at the federal penitentiary in Atlanta, he had served as an inmate kitchen boss in the prison mess hall. He had helped prepare a special birthday dinner for Mafia boss Vito Genovese. Later, Escandar was approached by someone looking to procure a kitchen knife for mobster Joe Valachi, who believed that Genovese was trying to have him killed. Escandar suggested that Valachi's emissary try the prison machine shop instead. Apparently, Valachi's emissary took Escander up on his suggestion. As Escandar remembered it years later, "So [Valachi] got a piece of pipe and a few days later a guy got killed and I was ten feet away from it." (The "guy" who got killed was a fellow inmate who Valachi believed had been sent to kill him.)

Joe Valachi went on to become one of the most notorious informants in history, testifying in 1963 in front of a nationally televised congressional committee on organized crime and the Mafia. Mario Escandar, on the other hand, burrowed deeper into the underworld. Upon his release from prison, he became an international dope dealer. In 1970, he was arrested as part of Operation Eagle, the largest heroin and cocaine bust in U.S. history at the time. He was named by Attorney General John Mitchell as one of five "principal subjects" in the raid, which resulted in 133 arrests in ten cities. Heroin and cocaine valued at $2.5 million was seized.

If convicted, Escandar was looking at a life sentence. It was then that he made the deal of a lifetime. He agreed to become a covert informant for the FBI. He was put back out on the street to continue his life of crime while supplying the feds with information about fellow criminals.

It was a good deal for Escandar, until in July 1977 he and two criminal partners were arrested by Miami detectives on felony kidnapping and armed robbery charges. The FBI refused to step in on his behalf.

Again, he was facing serious time. It was then that Detective Julio Ojeda entered the picture.

Around the same time that José Miguel Battle was arrested in New York for the murder of Ernesto Torres, Ojeda made a visit to Mario Escandar at the federal prison in Miami. Ojeda had been among the team of detectives who arrested the cagey criminal, and the two men seemed to have made a connection. Ojeda was there to talk with Escandar about two open homicide cases he thought Mario might know something about—the murders of Rolando Masferrer and Johnny Roselli. Escandar had nothing to offer on those crimes, but he was sure he could help the detective out if he were to secretly take him on as an informant.

The detective saw that having the legendary Mario Escandar on the street as his eyes and ears in the underworld could be a tremendous advantage.

Once Escandar was released on bail, he and Ojeda formed a relationship that would change Ojeda's life and that of the entire Dade County homicide squad. Escandar became an informant for Centac-26, a joint unit of Ojeda's homicide squad and the DEA. What Escandar did not tell cops and agents from this special unit was that he was still at the same time acting as a covert informant for the FBI.

Meanwhile, Ojeda and his partners Fabio Alonso, Robert Derringer, Pedro Izaguirre, Charles Zatrapalek, and George Pontigo became criminal partners of Mario Escandar. Starting in mid-1977 and over the next two years, some of them robbed cocaine dealers during illegal raids; kept money they found during murder investigations; stole and then resold marijuana; bribed other police officers to help them steal confiscated cash from the police property room; and used and became hooked on cocaine that was provided to them by Mario Escandar.

Escandar served as the group's gang boss, and the detectives became his goon squad. He had a palatial home in Miami Springs, off Okeechobee Road, where the cops regularly met. There they hatched schemes and partied on a regular basis. Escandar supplied the drugs and the women—high-caliber prostitutes whom he provided to the detectives at no charge. It was the Miami high life in spades circa the late 1970s—unlimited cocaine, beautiful women, high crimes and misdemeanors, all of it headquartered at the home of one of the most notorious narco kingpins in the city.

And all of this was taking place while the Dade district attorney, along with Detective Ojeda and the homicide squad, were preparing for the murder trial of José Miguel Battle.

Charley Hernandez could hardly believe what he had stumbled into. He'd been living in a motel under armed guard when he was approached by Detective Ojeda, who said, "We want to put you in the home of Mario Escandar. Are you willing? He is a gangster like you. You will get along with him. I know he won't give you up. You will be safe. We will put you to work as his chauffeur, his driver."

Charley agreed, not knowing what he was getting into. He became Escandar's driver, which mostly involved going on cocaine runs with his new boss. Years later, in a deposition, he recalled, "Mario couldn't live without cocaine, so he made sure that he had his fix."

Charley also became a middleman in drug transactions, delivering the product and picking up payments. Some of these deals were facilitated by Escandar's band of dirty detectives.

Charley served as Escandar's gofer. He answered the phone and the door if anybody came to the house. He kept the house clean. He took Escandar shopping at the mall. "He had a lot of enemies," said El Pincero. "I was like a bodyguard for him."

The detectives came by the house on a daily basis. Escandar was providing information to get a reduced sentence on his kidnapping charge. He was debriefed by Ojeda and the other detectives. On the weekends, they all partied.

"It was unbelievable," said Charley. "Those were some parties . . . The prettiest broads in Florida, the best whores, they went to that house . . . I had a lot of ass, no problem. It was beautiful. The swimming pool, the drugs."

Eventually, Idalia Fernandez was also moved into the Escandar house in Miami Springs. Ostensibly, Charley and Idalia were being held at a secret location while preparing to testify at the Battle trial. There was work to be done. Neither of them had ever testified at a trial. No doubt they would be grilled during cross-examination. Everything about their criminal histories would be brought out, and they would be presented as lowlifes and excoriated by some very skilled defense lawyers. It was important that they be prepared, but also apparently that they be relaxed. Idalia smoked marijuana most every day at the Escandar house.

Not only that, but she undertook an improper sexual relationship with the lead detective, Julio Ojeda. Three or four times a week, when Ojeda came to the house, he and Idalia disappeared into one of the many bedrooms. "Ojeda was getting laid by Idalia," said Charley. Everyone knew it, including Escandar, who noted later that the detective and witness were often "smooching."

No one seemed to find anything wrong in the unseemly arrangement. A lead investigator in a murder case having a sexual relationship with a witness? *¿Cómo no?* (Why not?) Cocaine, sex, cops operating as gangsters—it had become the norm, and would continue to be, in the weeks leading up to and during the murder trial of José Miguel Battle.

ON THE MORNING OF OCTOBER 18, JACK BLUMENFELD WAS IN HIS OFFICE IN MIAMI preparing for the trial, the commencement of which was two weeks away. Blumenfeld knew nothing of the two main witnesses in the case being lodged at the home of one of the city's preeminent criminals, and that the detectives had become crime partners of Mario Escandar. Not even the prosecutors knew about this arrangement. It was between Escandar and his dirty police partners. Later it would become public, with a sensational trial involving Escandar and the detectives, but at the time it was a well-hidden time bomb, a corrosive fault line buried deep below the surface of the Battle trial.

That morning—a Thursday—Blumenfeld received a call from the office of Raymond Brown in New Jersey. He assumed it was something having to do with trial preparation, so he was surprised to hear his fellow litigator say, "Jack, we've got an extra ticket to game six of the World Series tonight. Yankee Stadium. If you can get on a plane and get up here, the ticket is yours."

The tickets belonged to José Miguel Battle, row nine, behind home plate. Battle, of course, was indisposed.

Blumenfeld wasn't much of a baseball fan. He hadn't really been following the series, which had the Yankees up three games to two against the Los Angeles Dodgers. Some might have been attracted to the idea of going to Yankee Stadium for the first time. It had recently been refurbished to its historical glory; it was one of the most revered sporting facilities in the United States. But this all meant very little to Blumenfeld. On top of that, he had work to do. The idea of dropping what he was doing, getting on a plane, and being at the stadium in time for a seven o'clock start time seemed like more trouble than it was worth.

"That's a nice offer," said Blumenfeld. "But I'm swamped with work today. I think I'll pass."

Brown was incredulous. "Jack, are you fucking crazy? How many times in life will you have an opportunity to sit in a box seat at Yankee Stadium for a World Series game between the Yankees and the Dodgers? Besides, our client is offering you his box seats. He'll take this almost as an insult if you say no."

"Well," said Blumenfeld, "if you put it like that, let me see if I can get a flight."

There was an Eastern Air Lines flight leaving at midafternoon that would bring him in to Newark airport. The idea was to land, and quickly check into a hotel in East Orange, on the New Jersey side of the Hudson River. From there, Raymond Brown's son, Raymond Brown Jr., would pick Blumenfeld up and they would drive to the Bronx for the game.

It was a two-and-a-half-hour flight to Newark. Blumenfeld had just enough time to land, make a quick stop at the hotel to drop off his bag, and continue on to Yankee Stadium.

It was a spectacular fall night at the ballpark. The stadium was already packed to capacity with 54,113 fans by the time Blumenfeld arrived. An usher showed the Miami lawyer and Ray Brown Jr. to their seats. There they met Raymond Brown Sr. and also José Miguel Battle Jr., who was there with a couple friends.

In the third inning, the Yankees cleanup hitter, Reggie Jackson, came to the plate for the second time (he had walked in the first inning). Jackson hit a line-drive home run into the rightfield bleachers. The crowd went wild. In the next inning, with two men on base, Jackson hit another home run.

Blumenfeld could hardly believe what he was seeing. Though he was hardly a student of the game, he knew that one player hitting two home runs in a game was rare, even more so in the World Series. And Jackson had hit those two homers on two swings of the bat—no swings and misses, no foul balls. Two swings, two home runs.

In the eighth inning, Jackson came to the plate and did it once again—one swing of the bat, a towering 450-foot shot to the centerfield bleachers. Everyone went crazy. Nothing like it had ever been done in the history of baseball. The Yankees won the series in style.

After the game, Blumenfeld was driven back to his hotel in East Orange. He had not even wanted to go to the game—and almost didn't.

Already, representing José Miguel Battle Sr. had brought him a once-in-a-lifetime experience. Courtesy of his client, he had witnessed an event of historic proportions. It made him wonder what else might be in store for the future.

THE TRIAL OFFICIALLY GOT UNDER WAY IN MIAMI ON NOVEMBER 7, WITH AN OPENING statement by co-prosecutor Lance Stelzer. "The story you are about to hear will sound so bizarre that you would expect to see and hear it on television," Stelzer told the jury. "But it didn't happen on television. It happened in real life." The prosecutor knew that with Idalia, a victim, and Charley, an associate of both the victim and the assailant, the testimony he presented to the jury would be unusually intimate. His job as prosecutor was to present the dramatis personae and a narrative that was as compelling as anything the jurors might see in a movie theater. Of the case, he said, "It's a story which starts with love and ends in hate. It starts with peace and ends with war . . . Starts with birth, the commencement of one life, and ends in the death of another."

Stelzer outlined his story; it began with the murder of Pedro Battle, godfather to Ernestico's child born in Spain. Steltzer described the murder of Pedro Battle, and how Ernestico and Chino Acuna took on the responsibility of avenging that murder. He explained how Charley Hernandez, their primary witness, would in his testimony take them through the tangled set of circumstances that led José Miguel Battle to call for the death of his prodigal son.

Stelzer informed the jury that they would be hearing taped conversations between Ernesto Torres and the man who engineered his killing. At the time, few in the courtroom knew or even suspected that Battle himself had been one of the triggermen that day. Idalia had revealed it to no one.

After Stelzer finished his opening remarks, Jack Blumenfeld stood to offer an opening statement for the defense. Blumenfeld's style as a courtroom practitioner was workmanlike but thorough. If he had been a boxer (and he did look like one), he was the kind of fighter who would work in close, landing short, sharp punches to the body. He was no Muhammad Ali, like his fellow counselor Raymond Brown, who danced like a butterfly and stung like a bee, but he was effective. He said to the jury, "Ladies and gentlemen . . . the evidence upon which your verdict must be based comes from that witness stand." Blumenfeld pointed to the empty chair. "I say the evidence, or lack of evidence. And I am going to emphasize that point—lack of evidence—as I go through this opening statement. I say that because Mr. Stelzer has outlined for you during the past hour a story as he told it, which contained a good deal of quantity. I submit to you, ladies and gentlemen, that the evidence upon which a verdict must be based has to do with quality, not quantity."

The first week of the prosecution's case dealt mostly with the physical circumstances of the murder itself. Crime scene investigators, forensic examiners, and Dade County assistant medical examiner Dr. Ronald Wright took the stand. A startling detail from the medical examiner's testimony was that Ernesto Torres, after having been shot multiple times and likely already dead, was shot between the eyes, with the barrel of the gun pressed against his forehead. This coup de grâce was likely delivered as some sort of message to anyone who knew the deceased.

Idalia was certainly a compelling witness. She described the relationship between her late boyfriend and his boss. She detailed in personal terms how that relationship turned sour, and how Ernesto had come to believe that Battle, among others, was out to kill them. Idalia described being brutally attacked and left for dead by Chino Acuna. But as compelling as her testimony may have been, not much of what she had to say could be used against the defendant. If she was not going to identify Battle as one of the assailants, her testimony brought little hard evidence to bear on his participation in the murder of Ernestico.

Charley was another story. Since he had been a party to the conspiracy with Battle, his testimony was crucial; it would determine whether Battle walked free or not.

Charley's hair had been neatly trimmed, and he wore a white dress shirt. He looked more like a bank clerk than he did the notorious El Pincero, whom Blumenfeld had described in his opening statement as "a sneak thief." From the witness stand, Charley seemed to be well prepared. The late-night parties at Mario Escandar's house must have agreed with him, because he came into court relaxed, with little of the fear and anxiety that can overcome some witnesses, especially those with little formal education, or those speaking in a language that is not their native tongue. Charley did not seem intimidated, and as his time on the witness stand progressed over four full days, he sometimes even seemed to be enjoying himself.

Hank Adorno handled the presentation of Charley's direct testimony. Given that the witness had by now given many statements; been deposed under oath; taken a lie detector test (he passed); and been rigorously prepared by Adorno and others, his testimony was a recitation of what were to him well-worn facts. It wasn't until cross-examination by Raymond Brown that his feet were put to the fire.

The first question asked by Brown was, "Tell me, did you tell this jury that you have a wife and four children in New Jersey?"

"Yes."

"Is that the compete truth?"

"That's the truth."

"Do you not have six children?"

Charley squirmed in his seat. "Two from a previous marriage."

"And four from whom?"

"Four are mine."

"Is that a marriage that you have?"

"No. It's not a marriage. I have been living with her for ten years. I believe she is my wife."

Brown then quickly segued into Charley's history of stealing from people, sneaking into their homes, and how he sometimes impersonated a police officer, using a police badge he had stolen from a Union City police officer.

Charley had not been under cross-examination for ten minutes and already Raymond Brown had reduced him to a deceiver and a con man, in both his personal and professional lives.

The idea of a professional liar, or someone perceived to be one, taking the stand in a criminal trial was nothing new. At the core of criminal prosecutions in the United States was the concept of using a crook to catch a crook. In his opening statement, the prosecutor had repeated the old line, used in courtrooms all over America, about how he wished his witnesses could be upstanding citizens—"angels"—but given the nature of the co-conspirators in this case, you played the hand you were dealt. Normally, defense lawyers were in an easier position; they could use statements made by the witness in earlier settings against them in the courtroom. But Charley had been remarkably consistent since he first began talking to detectives at the Renaissance Hotel in Newark.

Brown was not having much luck making Charley out to be a degenerate liar. His next order of business was to perhaps turn the jury against the witness simply because they didn't like him. But Brown didn't have much success here either. On the stand, Charley Hernandez had a certain streetwise charm. He was unassuming and lighthearted. He always referred to the defense lawyer as "Mr. Brown." Though Brown tried, he could not get under Charley's skin. If the trial was to come down to whether or not the jury liked Charley Hernandez, Battle was in trouble.

There were a few more witnesses, including Detective Ojeda and Detective Kalafus, down from New York City. Kalafus sought to expand the parameters of the case by establishing Battle's reputation as a bolita boss. Another witness, Monino Herrera, was called in an attempt to take the case in a political direction. Herrera had served in the 2506 Brigade with Battle. He referred to "the cause," and how he and Battle had been dedicated to the struggle for freedom in Cuba for a long time. The prosecutors interrupted much of his testimony with objections on the grounds of relevance; most of their objections were sustained by the judge.

In the home stretch of the trial, with only a few days left, Jack Blumenfeld received a staggering piece of information from his secretary, Julie.

The secretary was an attractive woman in her early thirties. Battle, who was known to have an eye for young women, had taken a liking to her. He chatted with her often on breaks in the courtroom proceedings.

One afternoon, after chatting with Battle, Julie came to Jack Blumenfeld. She seemed to be shaken by something, which she explained to her boss.

According to Julie, Battle had admitted to her that he was one of the three gunmen who broke into Ernesto and Idalia's apartment. He told Julie that when he burst into the apartment, Idalia looked at him; she clearly recognized him. He put a finger to his lips, the universal sign meaning "keep quiet." Then he rushed toward the rear of the apartment, toward the bedroom, where Ernestico was hiding out.

Battle went on to describe the shootout, and how he was the one who shot Ernestico between the eyes.

It was startling information, to say the least. Blumenfeld told Julie, "Okay, thanks for telling me." Later, he met with Raymond Brown, his co-counsel, to discuss this unusual development.

The legal issues involved were clear-cut: Battle relaying his version of events to Julie, and Julie telling Blumenfeld, all came under the rubric of attorney-client privilege. Legally, the defense team was not obligated to report this development to anyone. On the issue of whether or not what Battle told Julie was true or not, there was no way to know without further investigation. This was a burden not shouldered by the defense; it was not their job, nor in their interest, to prove that their client had pulled the trigger.

Battle was facing a sentence of thirty years or more for conspiracy to commit murder, solicitation to commit murder, and first-degree murder. The lawyers had been hired to defend him on these charges. His conversation with Julie was interesting, but the lawyers concluded that it had little bearing on their case. Maybe what Battle had told Julie was true, or maybe he was boasting. The lawyers would never know. They chose to simply ignore their secretary's private conversation with Battle.

The trial continued. It was the goal of all parties involved to present the case to the jury in time for them to reach a verdict before the Thanksgiving holiday.

Hank Adorno delivered the closing argument for the prosecution, noting that "Mr. Brown and I agree on one thing, and that is that this case stands or it fails on the testimony of Charles Hernandez."

It was an unusual admission that required Adorno to spend nearly the entirety of his one-hour closing statement bolstering the testimony and character of El Pincero. Said the prosecutor, "Charlie knows he is a criminal, and Charlie knows that nobody is going to like him for that. He says, 'I'm going to tell you the truth. If you want to believe me, fine. If you don't, all right. But I'm not going to lie.'" The prosecutor spent the next forty minutes going through each and every statement by Charlie that linked Battle to the crime.

Near the end of his statement, Adorno became personal in his condemnations of Battle. Acknowledging that Charley was not "a priest or a nun or a businessman," he explained that "the state has to give you a barracuda, what Charlie is, to get to this animal"—he pointed at Battle—"and that is what he is."

"Objection," interjected Brown, saying to the judge, "Your Honor, I ask for a curative instruction."

The judge admonished the prosecutor: "Stick with the evidence. The jury will disregard that last statement."

Adorno ended his argument by saying to the jury, "I submit to you that once you look at the evidence in this case and discuss it among yourselves, and apply the law to it, you will reach but one conclusion, and that is to come out here and speak for the people of the State of Florida . . . Come out and say, 'José Battle, you cannot kill for money.' Because José Battle kills with this . . ." Adorno held up a twenty-dollar bill. "It is only twenty dollars, but this is what he kills with. This is how much a human life is worth to that man, and I submit that you cannot allow this man to get away with it, and I submit that the only true verdict that speaks the truth in this case is guilty as charged as to each and every one of the counts of this indictment."

After only five hours of deliberation, the jury came back with a verdict. Battle was convicted on two counts: conspiracy to commit murder and solicitation to commit murder. He was found not guilty on the third count, first-degree murder. It was a stunning defeat for him.

That night, there was a party at Mario Escandar's house. Ojeda and his fellow detectives were there, as were Charley and Idalia. There were also prostitutes, known drug dealers, and at least one ex-magistrate judge. Cases of Dom Pérignon were trucked in, and there was much white powder and marijuana. Escandar presented Ojeda with an imitation Cartier watch and a gold chain.

Three weeks later, Judge Fuller sentenced Battle to the maximum: thirty years in prison.

WITH THE VERDICT AND SENTENCING, IT SEEMED AS THOUGH THE CAREER OF JOSÉ Miguel Battle was over. A Mob boss can run his operations from prison in the short term. Knowing that the boss will be back on the street one day, or that he still has the juice to make and back up vital decisions, is sometimes enough to keep everyone in line. But when a boss is put away for what is essentially a life sentence, a shift in the organizational structure is likely. Often the result is a hostile maneuvering for power, with much underworld mayhem and many dead bodies.

Battle was not about to allow this to happen. For one thing, he was not going to take the verdict lying down. And for good reason. Even before the trial was over, his lawyers informed him that there were solid grounds for an appeal. The trial, they said, never should have been held in the state of Florida. Under both state and federal statutes, for someone to be tried on conspiracy charges they must be tried in the state where that conspiracy was hatched. The evidence put forth in *The People of the State of Florida v. José Miguel Battle* clearly showed that the conspiracy to murder Ernesto Torres had been initiated in New Jersey. Battle's lawyers believed that the grounds for an appeal were strong. They believed they could get the verdict overturned.

But it was going to take time. "You'll have to be patient," Blumenfeld told his client in the visiting room at the Florida State Prison in Raiford, in the northern part of the state, near Jacksonville. Battle had been transferred to Raiford nine days after the verdict. Said his lawyer, "The case law is strongly in our favor. Chances for an appeal are better than average, but this will take years to work its way through the courts. Stay positive, but you can put off buying season tickets to the Yankees for a couple seasons."

There was, however, an additional complication. On the day he was sentenced, Battle was hit with another indictment, this one stemming from his and his brothers' arrest for gun possession in New Jersey in 1974. Back then, Officer Diego Mella, in one of his last acts as a Union City cop, had called the local office of Alcohol, Tobacco and Firearms (ATF), a federal agency. Realizing that local law enforcement in Hudson County was corrupt and would never bring charges against Battle, he reached out to the feds. Would they be interested in bringing federal gun charges against the Godfather of the Cuban underworld? Mella met with federal agents, but even he did not know what they had done with the case, until just before the start of the Ernesto Torres murder trial. After consulting with Detectives Kalafus in New York and Ojeda in Miami, the feds agreed to hold off until the murder trial was over.

Being hit with the gun possession indictment on the same day as being sentenced for conspiracy to commit murder might have seemed like a double whammy, but Mssrs. Brown and Blumenfeld were not overly concerned. If they could get the murder charges thrown out, they felt there was a good chance they could negotiate a plea deal on the gun possession charge.

In March 1978, Battle was transferred from Raiford prison to the federal correctional facility in Manhattan, officially named the Manhattan House of Detention for Men (MHD) but more commonly known as the Tombs. To be charged with gun possession, Battle needed to be brought to the New York area on a writ of habeas corpus, an order to literally "produce the body." At the same time, his lawyers worked out an ingenious plea deal.

Battle would plead guilty to the gun possession charge, but only if the sentence was served concurrently with the Florida murder conviction. The feds agreed. Battle received a sentence of five years in prison. His lawyers surmised that if they could get the murder conviction overturned in a court of appeals, the concurrent sentence for gun possession would also be thrown out. By pleading guilty and folding the gun possession sentence into the murder sentence, they were pursuing a strategy that might possibly negate all charges.

Battle would eventually be transferred back to Raiford to await his appeal, but while incarcerated at the Tombs, he seized on the opportunity to address a couple of matters crucial to the continuation of his bolita enterprise.

From prison, Battle summoned Abraham Rydz, one of his organization's most crucial bankers. Heretofore, Battle had had a mixed relationship with Rydz. The two men had known each other since they both arrived in Union City way back in 1960, before the Bay of Pigs invasion. Battle admired Rydz's brains and financial acumen. All of the Cuban bankers thought of Rydz as their Meyer Lansky. He was a Polish Jew and financial wizard who had even had a couple years of college, where he studied business. But Battle had come to believe that Rydz was too close to Isleño Dávila. He may have respected him, but he never completely trusted him because of his ties to Isleño.

On the other hand, in recent years, Rydz had also become friendly with Miguelito Battle. Battle Jr. had also attended college and saw himself more as a businessman than a gangster. Now that José Miguel would be away in prison for at least a couple years, he intended to put Miguelito in charge of the bolita business. El Padrino was worried. Did Junior have the knowledge and experience to assume the role of boss? And would he have the protection on the street to maintain the business if someone attempted a hostile takeover?

Rydz was called to meet with Battle to address the first of these concerns. In the visiting room at the Tombs, Battle said to him, "I want to ask you a favor."

"Okay," said Rydz.

"I want you to look out for my boy, Miguelito. It's time for him to step up and take control of the business, but I'm worried. I'm not sure he has what it takes." Having to ask for a favor was not something that came easily to Battle. "You and him have always been close."

"He's a good kid. I like him."

Battle nodded. "Yes. Well, can you school him about the business, teach him what he needs to know? I need someone to look after him while I'm gone."

"Sure," said Rydz, "I'll talk to him. I don't want to impose myself, but I'll talk to him and offer my help in any way I can."

Battle said thanks. They talked about his legal situation and about the old days in Havana, and said their goodbyes.

The other matter that Battle needed to address involved Fat Tony Salerno. It just so happened that Salerno was being held at the Tombs. He had recently reached a plea deal on his tax evasion indictment and been given a sentence of eighteen months.

For Battle and Salerno, it was not that different from their semi-regular meetings at the Palma Boys Social Club. Battle arranged to have a face-to-face meeting with Salerno in his cell, at which he explained to the Mafia boss that while he was locked up, he was putting his son in charge of his bolita business. He wanted to make sure this was understood, and he was hoping that Salerno could put the word out on the street that Miguelito was the man until he, José Miguel, was able to resolve his legal entanglements and reenter the free world.

"Sure, no problem," said Salerno. "You know who you need to meet? Fish Cafaro. He handles the numbers racket for us. I'll have him come down here and we'll set up a sitdown."

Salerno made arrangements for Vincent "Fish" Cafaro, an up-and-comer with the Family, to visit him and Battle in the visiting room at the Tombs. Fat Tony did most of the talking. "Fish, this here is Mike Battle. He's with the Cubans. They been making a lot of money for us. Mike has been our guy for years, and now his son is taking over. Make sure you treat the kid right."

Battle and Fish said hello. El Padrino explained a little bit about the business. He was especially concerned that others might try to present themselves as the boss of bolita while he was gone.

"Don't worry about it," said Fish. "I take my orders from Mr. Tony. If he says your kid is our guy, that's all I need to hear."

As far as Battle was concerned, the meetings with Rydz and Fat Tony had gone well. His ducks were now aligned in order.

A week later, he was transferred back down to Raiford prison. Some men might have bided their time, laid low, in anticipation of some good news from their attorneys. Not Battle.

THE GHOST OF PALULU WAS STILL OUT THERE, HAUNTING EL PADRINO. THE MAN WHO had killed his brother had been released from prison around the same time that Battle had been arrested for the murder of Ernestico. The contract remained open, and there was no shortage of suitors who hoped to endear themselves to the Cuban Mob boss by exterminating the *cucaracha* that killed his brother.

Upon his release, Palulu found an apartment in the Bronx. He was now one-legged and broke, with few of the connections that had once made him a major cocaine dealer. Seeing that his nemesis, Battle, was in prison on what appeared to be a life sentence, he tentatively began running numbers. He knew it was dangerous; the Battle organization still controlled the bolita business in the New York area. But Palulu had bills to pay—lawyers' fees, medical bills, rent. He had to make a living the only way he knew how.

On the afternoon of August 4, Palulu and his bodyguard, Gerardo Juan, were walking on a South Bronx street when they were ambushed by a hit man with the street name of Matanzas, so named after the province in Cuba. Everyone was armed, and the men traded gunfire. Matanzas was wounded, but Palulu and his bodyguard received the worst of it. Palulu took a bullet in the chest. Gerardo Juan was hit multiple times; he was dead.

Matanzas stumbled away from the scene. Sirens sounded, as police and eventually an ambulance arrived to collect Palulu and rush him to the hospital. There, cops arrested him for illegal possession of an unregistered firearm.

The saga of Palulu had become like a broken phonograph record, or a short cartoon film running on a loop. Hospital, arrest, then, over his lawyer's objections, a repeat visit by Palulu to "gen pop," or general population at Dannemora prison. It was, as Yogi Berra once famously said, déjà vu all over again. In keeping with this theme, Palulu was even stabbed again in the yard by an inmate, just as he had been two years earlier. He survived the attack, and, after an extended stay in the prison medical ward, was housed in the prison's isolation wing, as he had been during his previous incarceration.

Hearing the details, Battle might have laughed, except that this was the man who killed Pedro. José Miguel would stop at nothing until this man was dead.

10

CORRUPTION

THE HELLHOUNDS OF JUSTICE, NIPPING AT THE HEELS OF FATE, FINALLY CAUGHT UP with Julio Ojeda and the other Miami detectives who were in cahoots with Mario Escandar. It had been fun while it lasted. There were parties with hookers and cocaine, and possibly Escandar had even occasionally delivered on his promise to provide information on others in the criminal underworld. But within this relationship between Centac-26 and the narco kingpin was a built-in flaw: Escandar was a professional snitch. When his legal situation with the U.S. government became complicated, he simplified matters for himself by agreeing to deliver the dirty cops on a silver platter.

In 1978, the FBI planted a bug in Escandar's home where the parties were going on. One year later, the feds had accumulated enough evidence to put the squeeze on two detectives who were targets of the investigation. The detectives became informants against their fellow officers.

A search warrant was executed at the home of Mario Escandar. The agents felt that even though Escandar was their informant, he probably was not telling them everything. That's the kind of guy he was. Sure enough, among the items found at his house was the case file for the Ernesto Torres murder investigation. It was the original file, not a copy. A Dade police spokesperson was quoted in the press saying that he was "concerned." Among other things, the file—found in the home of a notorious criminal—revealed the name of a cooperating witness. The police spokesperson cited the danger of "jeopardizing the department's credibility with other informants and witnesses." Apparently the spokesperson did not know that the cooperating witness—Idalia Fernandez—had been living at Escandar's home, smoking weed every day and sleeping with one of the detectives in the case.

As it turned out, the case of the missing file was a small matter. Detective Julio Ojeda and the others had bigger things to worry about.

In 1979, Ojeda and seven other Dade homicide detectives were named in a forty-one-count indictment that alleged a staggering array of crimes, including a conspiracy to violate the RICO Act. It was a dark day in the history of the Dade County Public Safety Department.

BY THE TIME THE POLICE CORRUPTION SCANDAL EXPLODED IN THE MEDIA, DAVID Shanks had been a Miami cop for five years. Like most clean cops on the force, he was disgusted by what he read in the press. He did not know Ojeda or any of the other indicted detectives, but he knew the type. By now the city was awash in cocaine and drug money, and it would lead to the downfall of certain cops who didn't have the integrity to resist temptation.

The issues or scandals that dominated the media were not what normally determined the daily realities of the job. Out on the street, fate bowed to no man or woman who put himself in the position of being an officer of the law. And unexpected events were sometimes just around the corner.

Take, for example, the afternoon of Wednesday, May 16, 1979. It was a typically warm day in Miami when Shanks received an urgent radio call of an officer shot on a corner in Liberty City, one of the city's toughest neighborhoods.

Shanks was nearby and raced to the scene. When he arrived, another cop, Detective Don Blocker, was also arriving in a separate vehicle. What they both saw was a gunman, later identified as twenty-one-year-old Lewis Randall Pearsall, an Army deserter, standing over an unconscious reserve officer named Scott Lincoln. Pearsall was about to fire a shot directly into Lincoln's face.

A few minutes earlier, Lincoln and his partner, Billy Cook, had arrived at the corner in response to a police radio call of an armed kidnapping in progress. Pearsall had abducted his estranged wife at gunpoint and forced her into a car. They hadn't driven more than three blocks before police vehicles arrived on the scene. Lincoln and Cook used their car to block

Pearsall from the front. Another officer, Keith DiGenova, blocked Pearsall from the rear.

The cops had Pearsall penned in. They got out of their cars and drew their guns. Positioning themselves at various locations around Pearsall and his wife, they aimed their weapons and told the gunman, "Drop your gun! Release the hostage! Now!"

Officer DiGenova crawled up to the car from the rear. It was his intention to free Pearsall's wife. He got to the side of the car, popped up, and tried to snatch Pearsall's weapon from his hands. What DiGenova did not know was that Pearsall's weapon was empty. Pearsall let DiGenova have his weapon and immediately grabbed for the cop's loaded gun. A struggle ensued.

Meanwhile, the other cops, seeing the tussle, ran up on the opposite side of the car in an attempt to rescue Pearsall's wife. But she had already bolted out of the car. A large woman weighing over two hundred pounds, she ran into officer Lincoln, knocking him off his feet. Lincoln's head hit the pavement, and he fell unconscious.

While this was going on, Pearsall wrested the gun from Officer DiGenova and shot him in the head. DiGenova fell to the ground.

From the rear of the car, Officer Cook took a shot at Pearsall. He saw blood spurt from Pearsall's forehead. Pearsall dropped. Assuming he had shot Pearsall, Cook immediately went to check on Officer DiGenova.

It turned out Cook had not hit Pearsall. The bullet had ricocheted off the frame of the car's open door, and a piece of metal from the door had splintered and hit Pearsall in the forehead. Stunned by the impact, he had dropped to the ground. But within seconds, he regained consciousness. He felt the blood from his forehead running down his face; he stood up, collected himself, and fired a wild shot at Officer Cook. The shot ricocheted off the same doorframe as before and hit Cook in the side. He collapsed to the ground.

By now, another officer had come on the scene. Bob Edgarton, a veteran cop, arrived as the exchange of gunfire was taking place. He saw Cook go down. He jumped from his car, pulled out his service revolver, and shot Pearsall twice in the back. Pearsall convulsed and fell face-first into the open front seat of the car.

Sure that Pearsall was dead, Edgarton rushed to check on Cook. "Billy, hold tight, an ambulance is on the way," he said. While tending to Cook, Edgarton sensed that something was not right. He looked up and saw a bloody hand with a gun sticking through the open window of the car door. The gun fired and hit Edgarton in the stomach. He fell to the ground.

Lewis Randall Pearsall emerged from inside the car, like something out of *Night of the Living Dead*. He'd been hit in the head by a metal projectile, shot twice in the torso, but he was alive. He had shot two of the cops; they were down and looked as though they were dead. But there was another cop—Scott Lincoln—who was lying on the ground, unconscious, though he had not been shot. Pearsall stumbled over to Lincoln, stood over him, and prepared to shoot the officer in the head.

This was when Shanks and Detective Blocker arrived on the scene. Both jumped out of their vehicles and unholstered their weapons.

Seeing the cops, Pearsall, who had been about to shoot Lincoln, quickly turned his gun and took a shot at Blocker. The detective ducked down behind his car; as he did so, he stuck his arm and gun over the hood of the car. Blindly, he squeezed off one shot. The shot miraculously hit Pearsall, severing his spine and killing him instantly. Pearsall collapsed and fell on top of Lincoln on the ground.

Lincoln regained consciousness around the same time Pearsall was being shot. He struggled to get the body off him.

Shanks ran over and helped extricate Lincoln from Pearsall's dead body. Then he ran over to Cook, who did not look good. Shanks had seen that look before; he knew that Cook was either dead or very close to being so.

By now, fire/rescue units and paramedics were arriving, sirens wailing. Shanks ran over and took care of traffic management, trying to get cars to pull over to the side of the road so the rescue trucks could get through.

It was a day of utter carnage that affected everyone involved. Shanks had at one time or another been platoon mates with all of the cops. He was especially close to Billy Cook, who died that day. Scott Lincoln, who had been knocked unconscious and survived, had been recruited and trained by Shanks. He was one of the men most emotionally scarred by the incident. He carried heavy survivor's guilt.

DiGenova, the cop who was shot in the head, went into emergency surgery. Shanks talked to the neurosurgeon, who told him DiGenova's prospects for survival were good. "The brain is an amazing organ," he told Shanks. "With gunshot wounds to the head, if a surgeon can get inside quickly and stop the flow of blood, undamaged parts of the brain will recuperate, and so will the person." The neurosurgeon told Shanks that if parts of the brain died or had to be excised, whatever memories they contained would be lost, but that other parts could be trained to take over. DiGenova would have to relearn how to walk, talk, read, and write, but after years of physical and occupational therapy he would be a new man.

Having known so many of the players in this tragedy, Shanks assumed the role of consoler in chief. One of the more difficult tasks was at the funeral of Billy Cook, where he escorted Cook's widow and mother. It was a huge event, with hundreds of police cars in a motorcade arriving at the cemetery. At the gravesite, there was the flag-draped coffin, a high mass, and a final salute. The widow and mother held up well, until they were presented with the flag; they both broke down crying and became inconsolable.

The aftereffects of the shooting became deeply ingrained in the psyches of the survivors. Shanks, for one, took it to heart. He thought about Ojeda and those dirty homicide detectives who were under indictment, their corrupt activities in the media every day, and he thought about the good cops he had known—Billy Cook, who was dead; Keith DiGenova and Scott Lincoln, who would never be the same. He could be depressed and immobilized by what had been lost, or he could carry on in the memory of those men. He could be the good cop who did his job even though there was corruption all around him.

It was this principle that Shanks would draw on in the years ahead when he became involved in the case against José Miguel Battle. Few utilized corruption to their advantage as well as Battle. His ability to compromise the system would become, to Shanks and anyone else who investigated the bolita methodology, one of the Godfather's distinguishing characteristics.

IN OCTOBER 1979, LESS THAN TWO YEARS AFTER HIS CONVICTION IN THE ERNESTICO murder trial, Battle received some extraordinary news. All this time, Jack Blumenfeld and Alan Silber, a lawyer from Raymond Brown's law firm who specialized in appeals, had been filing motions in appeals court. The first of these filings had been in the Third District Court of Appeal in Miami. A panel of judges had looked at the case and ruled that the original indictment had been "defective." Their ruling hinged on the repetitive use of the word "or" instead of "and" in the indictment, especially as it pertained to the conspiracy count against Battle. The indictment read, "The defendant conspired with Julio Acuna *or* Charley Hernandez *or* . . . other persons unknown." Had that phrase read, "Julio Acuna *and* Charley Hernandez *and* other person unknown," Battle's lawyer might have lost his appeal. The judicial panel felt that the wording made the indictment too "vague," and left the defense having "to guess as to the conspiracy." This unfairly hindered defense lawyers in their efforts to mount a defense. In the opinion of the Third District, Battle's conviction should be thrown out.

The State Attorney's Office disagreed and appealed the ruling to the Florida Supreme Court, the highest court in the state. It took months for the court to reach its decision. In a majority vote, it decided against hearing the case at all, and kicked it back to the Third District. This meant that the original decision still held sway. Battle's conviction was overturned. The only question was whether he would be put on trial again for the same charges.

Meanwhile, El Padrino was still being held in prison to serve out his gun possession conviction. Technically, he still had three years to serve on that charge.

The October decision was crucial. Since Battle's conviction, the original judge who sentenced him had retired and a new judge was assigned to make a decision regarding a retrial. Judge Alfonso Sepe now presided over Battle's case. It was one of those strokes of luck that sometimes happen; Jack Blumenfeld had been mentored by Sepe back when they were both prosecutors in the State Attorney's Office.

In response to a motion filed by Blumenfeld and Silber, Sepe ruled that Battle could only be retried on one count, conspiracy to commit murder.

The defense lawyers saw an opening. They immediately hunkered down with representatives of the State Attorney's Office and began negotiating a plea deal.

Oftentimes when negotiating a deal, defense lawyers have one slight advantage. The criminal justice system in the United States is so overloaded, primarily with minor narcotics cases, that the government is prone to accept any deal that will keep the system moving forward. Resolving cases is key, cleaning sludge from the clogged pipes. Retrying Battle on one simple count was not cost-effective. If Battle were willing to plead guilty to conspiracy to commit murder, allowing the State Attorney's Office to save face without having to go to trial, there was a deal to be made.

This meant that Battle's fate would truly be in the hands of the sentencing judge.

The appellant was to appear in circuit court in Miami. A date was set—December 17, eight days before Christmas. In the courtroom of Judge Sepe, Battle would plead guilty to the one count of conspiracy to commit murder. It would be up to the judge to decide if he would walk free that day, or if his incarceration would be prolonged by various other legal entanglements.

BETWEEN THE TIME OF THE OCTOBER RULING AND THE DECEMBER DATE TO DETERMINE Battle's fate, an event occurred that reminded everyone that the anti-Castro movement in the United States was alive and well.

On November 25, in Union City, Eulalio José Negrin, age thirty-eight, was getting into a car with his twelve-year-old son, Richard. Negrin was a political activist, which in the vengeance-driven world of the anti-Castro underground was a potentially perilous endeavor.

Already Negrin had incurred the wrath of Omega 7 by forming an organization called Committee of 75, which had been negotiating with the Castro government for the release of thirty-six hundred political prisoners in Cuba. Many of these prisoners had relatives in the Union City area. Negrin and others with the Committee of 75 viewed their effort as a humanitarian gesture, but the hard-line militants could not countenance any kind of negotiation with the Castro government, even if the intentions were benign. To negotiate with Castro was to legitimize his government, which Omega 7 saw as a treasonous act punishable by death.

In the previous four years, the militant anti-Castro group had been especially active. They blew a hole in the Venezuelan consulate in Manhattan; attacked a Soviet freighter in Port Elizabeth, New Jersey; blew up a sporting goods store near Madison Square Garden in Manhattan. They planted a bomb in the doorway of Avery Fisher Hall at Lincoln Center, where the acclaimed Cuban ensemble Orquesta Oregón was scheduled to perform. The bomb blew out glass three stories up in the famous concert hall and caused the orchestra to cancel its remaining Manhattan performances. That same night, they detonated another bomb at the Cuban mission to the United Nations. Later, an operative of Omega 7 checked a suitcase bomb onto a TWA flight from JFK to Los Angeles. Omega 7 wanted the airline to cease commercial flights to Havana. Only a premature explosion in a baggage cart on the tarmac saved the passengers on board the flight.

In the case of Eulalio José Negrin, there were ominous warning signs. A year earlier, a prominent member of Negrin's organization was murdered in Puerto Rico. A Catholic priest in Union City, Reverend Andre Reyes, had been moved out of Holy Family Roman Catholic Church to a parish in Newark because of death threats. In March, the storefront of the New Jersey Cuban Association in Weehawken, which Negrin headed, was bombed. Omega 7 claimed responsibility for that bombing and also the attempted bombing of the TWA flight at JFK Airport, which occurred the same day.

Just one week earlier, Negrin had called a reporter from the *Hudson Dispatch,* a local newspaper, to say he feared for his life. He told the reporter that he'd received more death threats recently, including a letter from Omega 7 that said he had only two months to live.

November 25 was a Sunday. The streets of Union City were mostly quiet as Negrin and his son approached their car outside 711 10th Street. It was 9:50 A.M. Because of the recent threats, Negrin was wearing a bulletproof vest underneath his shirt and coat.

Negrin put his son in the backseat on the passenger side and was walking around the front of the car to the driver's side when a Ford

Granada with a red roof came speeding down the road. A man wearing a black ski mask leaned out of the car with a MAC-10 submachine gun and opened fire on him.

The bulletproof vest did Negrin no good. Whoever was doing the shooting seemed to know he was wearing one; he was shot five times in the face, neck, and arm.

Young Richard Negrin, from the backseat of the car, watched in horror as his father was assassinated in the street.

The hit men sped away.

Negrin was still alive when police reached the scene, though he was unable to respond to questions. He was rushed to Riverside General Hospital in Secaucus, where he was pronounced dead on arrival.

Negrin had been carrying $7,400 in a briefcase when he was killed. The assassins had no interest in the money. "It was a hit," a cop on the scene told a reporter with the *Dispatch*.

Reverend Reyes was quoted saying, "I think the whole community is aware of what is being done. These men are armed and that is [causing terror] in the community."

Police chief Herman Bolte warned that Union City cops couldn't protect the enemies of Omega 7 and other militant groups. "I just don't think any Committee of 75 member would be safe walking the streets of Union City at night. The feelings of the Cuban people here just run too deep concerning Castro."

Late on the night of the shooting, the Associated Press office in New York received a telephone call from a man who said he was a member of Omega 7. The man claimed responsibility for the shooting, and, in what the AP described as a Spanish accent, he said, "We will continue with these executions until we have eliminated all of the traitors living in this country."

The FBI in recent years had stepped up their investigations of Omega 7. In the wake of recent bombings, the Bureau's Cuban Terrorism Task Force had nearly doubled in size. Led by Special Agent Lawrence Wack, the task force had been accumulating intelligence and gathering forensic evidence at various bombing sites. Through a network of informants on the street, they had been able to construct a hierarchy of Omega 7's internal leadership.

Guillermo Novo was currently in prison serving a life sentence for the car bomb assassination of former Chilean ambassador Orlando Letelier (that conviction would later be overturned in appeals court and Novo set free). The leader of the organization was now Eduardo Arocena, one of the original founders. The FBI believed that Arocena was the mastermind of most of the recent bombings for which Omega 7 had claimed credit.

The political assassinations seemed to emanate from a separate cell within the organization. Sometimes these hits were contracted out to gangland killers. An inside source in Miami told task force agents that the Negrin hit had been put in motion by Omega 7 but that the killers were professional gunmen supplied by the organization of José Miguel Battle.

For years the FBI had been attempting to establish such a link. Back in 1974, a source told them that Battle had contracted Omega 7 to murder José Elías de la Torriente in Miami. What they were hearing about the Negrin hit was the reverse: Omega 7 contracting out the hit to Battle.

Street chatter was sometimes reliable, and sometimes not. But more and more it was beginning to appear to the FBI's Cuban Terrorism Task Force that the anti-Castro militant underground and the Cuban Mafia underworld led by Cuban gangster José Miguel Battle were one and the same.

At the time, none of this had any bearing on Battle, who was in Raiford prison in Florida awaiting his sentencing date in December. If Battle had in any way facilitated the political assassination of Eulalio José Negrin, he had done so from within the prison walls, which was entirely possible. For a professional racketeer like Battle, behind prison walls or out on the street was all part of the same universe.

ON DECEMBER 17, BATTLE WAS BROUGHT BEFORE JUDGE ALFONSO SEPE IN MIAMI DIStrict court. As instructed by the state supreme court, the prosecutors had reconfigured the indictment so that it now stood at one count of conspiracy to commit murder. As a result, a plea deal had already been arranged.

"How do you plead?" asked the judge.

"Guilty, Your Honor," said Battle.

The judge was ready to impose a sentence. He sentenced Battle to "credit time served" for the two years and nine months he had already spent in jail since his arrest for murder. As for the remainder of his sentence—also two years and nine months—the judge gave him probation. He was free to walk out of court.

The prosecutors were stunned. They had not been expecting the judge to give Battle probation and immediately set him free.

For Battle and his attorneys, it was a big victory. The appeal had worked. José Miguel would be home in time for Christmas.

Forever after, Battle would occasionally refer to Judge Sepe's sentencing as one of his great sleights of hand. "That judge and his wife had a nice vacation in Vegas thanks to me," he said to Joaquin Deleon Jr., a bolitero who would follow Battle wherever he led. Deleon had no doubt what he meant. "Ben Franklin got Battle that light sentence," he later said, meaning that El Padrino had made an under-the-table cash payment to the judge.

There would be no proof of such a payment, except that several years after the sentencing, Judge Sepe was caught in a major sting operation known as Operation Court Broom, one of the largest federal and state investigations ever into judicial corruption. A bug was planted in Sepe's chambers. Eventually, the judge pleaded guilty to accepting $150,000 in bribes to fix cases and was removed from the bench. He had been taking money for years. The possibility that he had accepted a bribe from Battle was in keeping with his general modus operandi, one that would bring his illustrious career to a sudden and ignominious end.

WHILE EL PADRINO WAS AWAY, THERE HAD BEEN SOME SIGNIFICANT CHANGES IN THE New York–New Jersey bolita universe. For one thing, Miguelito Battle and Abraham Rydz had taken over the running of the enterprise. It was their intention to structure the operation almost as a legitimate business. Battle Jr. insulated himself from the enforcers and other street-level aspects of the business. He and Rydz committed fully to the concept of bolita holes. There would be no more numbers runners: the bolita holes were more profitable, and they made it possible to streamline personnel.

More important, Battle Jr. and Rydz initiated the process of creating shell companies based in South Florida as a way to launder the operation's huge cash profits in New York.

Given the refurbished organizational structure, and the new emphasis on reinvesting profits, the two men began referring to their version of the Cuban Mafia by an entirely different name. They called it the Corporation.

The name had been around for a while. The first to use it was Angel Mujica, who had returned to New York from Spain around the time Battle was arrested for murder. Mujica had opened up a number of bolita holes, mainly in his old stomping grounds of the Bronx. He called his business the Corporation, which was grandiose considering its modest size. In 1979, he let Abraham Rydz know that he was looking to cash out. He was willing to sell his bolita business to Rydz and Battle Jr. for $300,000. Rydz and Battle took him up on the offer. They took over his network of bolita holes, and they kept the name.

With the Battle organization having taken it over, the name caught on. Calling themselves a corporation seemed to fit the image the bolita bankers had of themselves. Ever since these men left Cuba, their identities had been formed in counterbalance to what was happening back in their homeland, under the reign of a man they considered a communist *diablo*. Economically speaking, Cuba had became a Marxist backwater, with more and more refugees fleeing the island every year. Meanwhile, the Bay of Pigs generation, cured in a toxic brew of humiliation and exile, exalted their identity as capitalists. What was more capitalist than the concept of the corporation, a financial conglomerate that was endowed with the rights of the individual? A corporation was everything a Marxist despised; to the capitalist, it was the ultimate expression of Adam Smith's dictum that "All money is a matter of belief." Believe in the corporation, and you shall be rich.

And what was the point of having a powerful name if you did not advertise? In bolita holes around the city, a sign was sometimes posted on the wall. Occasionally it was artistically drawn, while in other places it might be written in a scrawl. Sometimes it was written in Spanish, sometimes in English. And sometimes it was translated into both languages: *Este es un lugar de la Corporación/This is a Corporation spot.*

The Corporation rose from the womb of the Cuban Mafia to become an entity in the underworld as notorious as the Italian Mafia.

One person who was in a position to capitalize on the newly invigorated reputation of the Cuban boliteros, reborn as the Corporation, was Isleño Dávila. Battle's sometimes partner and sometimes competitor was especially active during El Padrino's incarceration. For a time, it had looked as though Battle might never be returning to the free world. Isleño began to expand rapidly. From 1978 to the early 1980s, the number of bolita holes operating in Brooklyn, Queens, and the Bronx under his umbrella expanded from one hundred to two hundred. And he even took a chance by opening a dozen bolita spots in central Harlem.

Harlem was the crown jewel of the numbers racket. Since the time of Prohibition, the famous African American neighborhood in upper Manhattan had been the most lucrative domain for numbers in all of the United States. Part of it was the density of the population, thousands of people packed on top of one another in tenements, wooden shacks, and brownstones. And most everyone was looking for a miracle, so they put down nickels, dimes, and dollars on a game of chance that required no real skill or education, just luck.

Harlem's numbers racket was under the control of the Mafia, specifically the Lucchese family based in Brooklyn. The Luccheses made sure that Fat Tony Salerno, Fish Cafaro, and the Genovese family got their cut, but mostly the Luccheses were left alone to run Harlem as they saw fit.

In the spring of 1978, *soldatos* (soldiers) of the Lucchese family noticed that Cuban bolita spots were opening up around the neighborhood, in all the prime locations. Isleño did not try to hide what he was doing. As an experienced bolitero, he knew that you wanted bolita spots in well-traveled areas—near a supermarket, or a fish market, or around the corner from a bus stop. You needed to know if there was a dope spot nearby, because you did not want to locate your bolita hole anywhere near it.

One of the first gangsters to take note of the Cuban's sudden bolita expansion in Harlem was neither a Cuban nor an Italian, but rather an Irish American mobster named Robert Hopkins, who was affiliated with the Lucchese family.

Traditionally, the Luccheses were more open than some families to doing business with non-Italian associates. Irish, Cuban, black American—it didn't really matter. If you could be trusted—if you were a goodfella—and you had the connections to pull off a score or conduct criminal business, you were partnership material. In Queens, the Lucchese family had recently partnered with a multiethnic crew of hoods, including, notably, the Irish American gangster Jimmy Burke and half-Irish Henry Hill, to pull off the Lufthansa heist, at the time the largest airport cargo robbery in history. Neither Burke nor Hill could be "made men," given that they were not of pure Sicilian ancestry. But both had been actively affiliated with the Lucchese family since the beginnings of their criminal careers.

Robert Hopkins was cut from the same mold as Burke and Hill. He was not a tough guy but was believed to have brains. In the mid-1970s he was assigned to the numbers racket, a business that required organizational skills and a head for figures.

Hopkins was told about the Cuban bolita spots that had recently opened in Harlem. He checked them out and saw that they were being professionally run by someone who knew what he was doing. Technically, the Cubans were not authorized to do business in central Harlem. Spanish Harlem, yes, but not central Harlem. Hopkins could have immediately sought to deliver a message, to force the Cubans out of Harlem. But that's not what he did. First, he checked in with a prominent Cuban bolitero he knew named Omar Broche. In Latino bolita circles, Broche was well known.

"Who's behind these new bolita stores?" Hopkins asked Broche.

"Humberto Dávila," said Broche. "They call him Isleño. Biggest banker in New York and New Jersey. That guy knows what he's doing."

Hopkins asked Broche if he could set up a meeting. Of course, said Broche, but it would take a while. Isleño spent most of his time in Fort Lauderdale. Every month, he came to New York for a week or so.

Within a couple weeks, at a restaurant in Manhattan, Isleño and Omar Broche sat down with Hopkins, along with a couple of his people. Hopkins said to the Cuban, "I see you know what you're doing. From what I hear, you know more about numbers than I do. The people I work for, they feel they have the right to run you out, but maybe there's a better way."

"Okay," said Isleño. "What are you suggesting?"

Said the Irishman, "Harlem is a big pie. There's enough for everybody. Why don't we find a way to work together, reach an agreement that makes us all happy?"

"Fifty-fifty," said Isleño. It was asking a lot, going fifty-fifty with the Mafia, but Isleño knew he was playing a strong hand.

"I gotta clear that with my friends," said Hopkins. "But I don't see any problem."

They shook hands.

So Isleño was now partners with the Lucchese family. And Hopkins became an intermediary between the Cubans and the Italians, successfully keeping the peace—for a while.

BOB HOPKINS WAS BORN AND RAISED IN QUEENS, IN A MIDDLE-CLASS NEIGHBORHOOD far from the denizens of organized crime. He was a good kid, destined for college, until he fell in with a group of friends from the wrong side of the subway tracks. One of Hopkins's best friends as a young man was Peter "Petey Beck" DiPalermo, the son of a Lucchese family capo. DiPalermo and two of his brothers formed an up-and-coming crew of aspiring mafiosi based on Prince Street in the heart of Little Italy. The mafiosi liked Hopkins, the Irish kid with a big mop of auburn hair, rosy cheeks, and an inclination toward the criminal life. Hopkins did not promote himself as a tough guy, though he could handle himself in the streets. His true value was as a hustler and breadwinner who could be trusted.

Along with his prospects as a budding goodfella, Hopkins liked to sing. He entertained the wiseguys with his renditions of songs made famous by the likes of Neil Diamond, Dion and the Belmonts, and others.

In 1976, Hopkins was taken under the wing of a Lucchese family soldier named Willie Monk. It was Monk who taught him the ins and outs of being an illegal lottery operator.

On the face of it, the business seemed simple. People bet money on a combination of numbers. They hit the number, or they did not. Monk warned Hopkins that the game itself may have been simple, but the business was not. With proper accounting, policy could be one of the underworld's most lucrative endeavors. If poorly organized, it could descend into a free-for-all of reckless profiteering and infighting.

The key, said Willie Monk, was that there had to be rules. And those rules had to be followed.

Even before Hopkins met Isleño Dávila, he'd met a number of the Latino boliteros. Along with Omar Broche, he met Raul Rodriguez, a powerful independent bolita banker. He met "Spanish" Raymond Márquez, a legendary Puerto Rican bolitero who had been doing business with the Mafia since the 1960s. He also did business with Luis DeVilliers, owner of the Colonial restaurant and veteran bolita banker, and the team of Manny Alvarez Sr. and Jr., based in Brooklyn.

Many of these men were independent bolita bankers who financed operations that paid a percentage to the Mafia, in order to operate free of territorial disputes. It had always been a nice arrangement for the Italians, who received proceeds from the Cubans without having to do any of the work.

As Isleño and Hopkins forged their partnership, many of these superbankers began to coalesce around Isleño. When word spread that Battle had a good shot at receiving a favorable ruling on his appeal, being set free, and returning to the business, Isleño sensed there might be a problem. He knew that if he continued to operate under the auspices of what was now known as the Corporation, it was probable that Battle would want to take over the Harlem bolita business. Isleño did not want to give that up; it was a landmark merger that he had negotiated with Hopkins. He felt it was all his. So Isleño did something risky. He formed his own bolita consortium and called it La Compañía, the Company.

If Battle wanted to view La Compañía as a subsidiary of the Corporation, that was okay with Isleño, as long as he understood that it was an independent operation, with an independent revenue stream. Battle would still get his percentage, but auditing and personnel decisions would be made by Isleño.

On phone calls from Fort Lauderdale, Isleño warned Hopkins, his new partner, about El Padrino. "When he gets out, we may have problems. He makes his own decisions. He's bullheaded. And he usually gets what he wants."

"I'm not too worried," said Hopkins. "I try to get along with everybody. And, really, how bad can this guy be?"

SINCE HIS RELEASE FROM PRISON, BATTLE HAD BEEN SETTLING OLD SCORES. FOR A Mob boss, time in the joint sometimes presents an opportunity for underlings to become bold. When the cat is away, the mice will play. Over the years, the Corporation had become a multileveled enterprise, from street operators, to midlevel managers, all the way up to super-bankers like Battle, Isleño, and others. There was much room for pilfering or insubordination or outright betrayal.

In the years since Battle Jr. and Abraham Rydz had taken over the daily running of the organization, they had shown little inclination toward internal discipline or acts of retribution against enemies. Violence was not their style. Battle, on the other hand, seemed to feel as though the reputation of the organization needed to be established with an iron hand.

Chino Acuna was no longer around to act as Battle's enforcer. Consequently, the boss needed to find a new man, which he did, in the person of Conrad "Lalo" Pons.

Pons had started out in the organization as a numbers writer, a person who sits in a policy hole and writes down wagers as they are placed by people in the neighborhood. He quickly rose to the level of manager of the numbers location. Pons was responsible for hiring and supervising personnel, and also, twice a day, picking up money from the spot and delivering it to the "bank" or office where the money was stored.

A scrappy Cuban émigré, just five feet six inches tall and 130 pounds, Pons was what cops refer to as a "stone-cold killer." According to NYPD intelligence files, he had been a professional criminal back in Cuba, and in the United States he seized upon the Corporation as a suitable vehicle for his criminal ambitions. Like many boliteros, he used Union City as his home but commuted into New York for work. His base of operations was Brooklyn, where he maintained a bolita spot on Tompkins Avenue that served as his headquarters.

It was Battle's brother-in-law, Manuel "Nene" Marquez, who recommended Pons to the Godfather. Marquez was in charge of Brooklyn, and he liked the way Pons conducted business.

A meeting was held at which it was explained to Pons that the Corporation was looking to establish what Battle referred to as his SS squad. This squad would be comprised of "men of action," killers, people willing to do the dirty work on behalf of the organization. The squad would be financed via a special fund, in which each of the organization's superbankers would make a monthly contribution of $10,000. The fund was sardonically known as the "UNESCO fund," so named after the international relief organization associated with the United Nations. Money from the UNESCO fund would be used to finance hits, for emergency legal fees, and for taking care of the families of boliteros who, for one reason or another, wound up behind bars.

Pons was offered the job of being in charge of the SS squad.

"It would be my honor," he told Battle.

Firstly, there was the issue of the Corporation having gone soft in Battle's absence. There had been a rash of robberies of Cuban bolita holes, and something needed to be done about it. There were myriad other disciplinary issues that Battle felt needed to be addressed.

Between 1980 and 1983, there were more than a dozen gangland murders related to bolita. Most of these were contract hits arranged by Lalo Pons in his role as chief of Battle's new SS squad. Local cops, even those with some knowledge of the Cuban underworld, were caught off guard by the unprecedented spasm of violence. Detectives from the NYPD's Cuban Task Force, led by Detective Kalafus, reached out to their C.I.s (confidential informants), and the intelligence reports piled up. These files read like a catalogue of intrigue, treachery, and a commitment to the concept of revenge as a primary operating principle. Some samples:

- *10/17/81: Informant stated that at the time of the homicide he was employed as a collector for Jose Miguel Battle, as was the deceased. Informant knew the deceased as VIEJO, and would only see him in the meetings with Battle and the other collectors . . . Informant stated that on the night of this homicide there was a meeting of the collectors at an after hours club on W. 172 Street off St. Nicholas Ave. Battle stated that he had put $25,000 on the street for infor-*

mation on who had killed VIEJO and that an additional $25,000 had been paid out to DIABLO to locate and kill the person or persons involved in this killing and other stickups of his collectors and spots . . . Informant stated that a few days after the contract was given out Battle received information that it was DIABLO who had killed VIEJO and had been sticking up his collectors and policy spots. A male Cuban named Victor was given the contract to kill DIABLO.

- 10/7/82: C.I. stated that FRANCISCO "FRANK" IRRIZARY was shot by one [name redacted] on order from the Corporation, the reason was that IRRIZARY was suspected of being involved with his cousin [name redacted] in the stick-up of several policy locations operated by the Corporation . . . A contract was put out on the cousin by Battle. Both the cousin and IRRIZARY answer to the name "Venezuela." And both resemble each other. Allegedly, DOMINGO thought he was shooting the cousin when he shot IRRIZARY.

- 8/17/83: C.I. states that [name recacted] killed two (2) male blacks, possibly Jamaican, on Eastern Pky and New York Ave, approx one year ago during the daytime hours. Reasons for shooting, Male blacks attempted to rob Cuban policy locations on New York Ave and Eastern Pky, 71 Pct.

- 8/23/83: Subject deceased, MARIO CABALLERO, male Hispanic, was found on January 7, 1982 on Cambridge Place and Fulton Street, dead of gunshot wounds. C.I. states that deceased is known to him as ITALIANO and that he worked for the Battle policy operation as a bodyguard for a pickup man. Further he stated that the reason CABALLERO was killed was because he was seeing Battle's girlfriend.

Intelligence files were like the gossip pages of a newspaper, filled with rumor and, occasionally, disinformation planted by wily gangsters. It was incumbent upon detectives to follow up on the information, check out the details, and see what turned out to be true. In the case of the Cuban underworld, most of the information checked out. Fear was a powerful motivator: it could scare low-level operators into silence, or it could make them feel desperate, with nowhere to turn except the law.

The irony was that as Battle reasserted his tendency toward brutality as a solution to most problems—thus creating something approaching a reign of terror in the Cuban underworld—he was rarely seen in New York or New Jersey anymore.

In prison, Battle had made the decision that it was time to move his personal base of operations to Miami. Way in the back of his mind, it had always been the plan. For Cuban Americans living in the frozen tundra of the Northeast, whether the concrete jungle of New York City or the gritty back alleyways of Union City, the dream of South Florida was ever present. There was sunshine every day and fellow Cubans at every level of the social strata.

In South Florida, Battle could re-create certain aspects of the homeland—not the homeland of Havana in the 1950s, with its bustling streets and torrid nightclubs, but that of his youth in Oriente. Wide-open spaces, the sound of the rooster in the morning, soil to till, and the sight of mamey trees blossoming in the afternoon sun. This was the Cuba that existed in Battle's memory and in his heart. If he could re-create this sense memory in Florida, it would signify that he had achieved something valuable with his life. Perhaps he could find peace and retire from the bolita business.

He and his wife, Maria, found a place in Redland, a rural area southwest of Miami, not far from the Everglades. The house was on 4.8 acres. It was nice, but hardly a mansion. There was a pool. And important for Battle, there was an area for raising roosters for cockfighting. Most appealing of all was that the house was surrounded by a number of large vacant lots. It was Battle's intention to buy up the property around the house so he could plant a large grove of mamey trees and begin harvesting the fruit for commercial purposes. It would be a smart way to launder his bolita money, but more important, it would connect him with his Cuban roots.

The entire setting could not have been more different than Union City and the beastly metropolis of New York. The idea was for Battle to remove himself from the maelstrom of the criminal underworld, to free himself from the stress and the constant need to prove himself. That was the idea, anyway.

ROBERT HOPKINS KNEW THAT AT SOME POINT HE WOULD HAVE TO MEET JOSÉ MIGUEL Battle. For more than a year, the young Mafia liaison had been putting it off. Isleño had warned him about Battle. He was a war hero, Isleño had said. Some people worshipped him as a Cuban patriot. And he had some good qualities. He was generous. He was a strong leader. If you were to go into battle with Battle, you would want him at your side, or, more accurately, out front leading your platoon. But he also had another side. He cheated at cards. And if he felt you had done him wrong in some way, he was psychotic. He would turn over the entire mamey cart to get at one piece of fruit.

In the months since Battle had returned to the bolita business, Hopkins sat back while the Cuban underworld was roiled with shootings and killings. Hopkins had seen this before. Back in the early 1970s, the Lucchese family had gone through growing pains. The *capo di tutti capi* was incarcerated, and there was much vying for who would take over as boss. Anthony "Tony Ducks" Corallo took over leadership of the family, but not until many soldiers and underbosses had wound up dead in the trunks of cars, stuffed into cast-iron barrels, or dumped in one of the city's many waterways.

With the Cubans, it was Hopkins's intention to stay out of the way. In a sense, it only mattered to the extent that the violence affected his bolita business. The mayhem so far had not caused the police to crack down on the bolita spots. Traditionally, the Public Morals department was kept at bay through judicious payoffs to whoever in the department had the power to keep raids from happening. It had worked that way for decades. But if the killings became too outrageous, and it became obvious they were related to the policy business, pressure from the media and public officials would lead to a police crackdown.

The bottom line was that a climate of ongoing violence was never good for business—especially with bolita, which was supposed to be nonviolent. Little old ladies and priests bet the number, and if they were made to feel as though they were taking part in something that was violent or overtly connected to organized crime, they would stop participating, and the business would dry up.

Hopkins's deal with La Compañía, Isleño's group, was going well.

With Isleño's know-how and Hopkins's connections, business was booming. La Compañía had opened well over one hundred bolita holes in central Harlem alone. With the volume of betting that took place, one numbers hole in Harlem was worth four in Brooklyn. For a spot in Brooklyn, a decent take was $6,000 to $8,000 a week in bets. In Harlem, you didn't see spots that took in less than $20,000 to $25,000 a week. Everyone was getting rich. If things continued to run smoothly, the deal that Hopkins and Isleño had put together would become the most profitable numbers consortium that ever existed.

And then it happened: in the summer of 1982 a series of events in Brooklyn threatened the whole arrangement.

The cause of the crisis was an aspect of the arrangement between the Cubans and the Italians that went back decades. From the beginning, the two factions had established what they called "the two-block rule." This unwritten law stated that no organization, Cuban or Italian, could open a bolita hole closer than two blocks to a preexisting one run by the other camp. The rule, which had been agreed to by Fat Tony, Battle, Isleño, and everyone else who did bolita business in New York, had held strong since the late 1960s, when it was first instituted. But there was a loophole in the rule that would lead to a dispute.

In Brooklyn, a prominent bolita hole belonging to La Compañía—located at 50 Albany Avenue in the neighborhood of Bedford-Stuyvesant—was shut down in a police raid. This alone was enough to cause Hopkins and Isleño consternation, but more to the point, it exposed a flaw in the two-block rule. What happened when a spot was shut down through no fault of its own? If a bolita spot were burned down, for instance, did that mean a competitor could move in and open a spot? And if there were disputes, how would they be settled?

Nene Marquez, who was now leader of the Corporation's operations in Brooklyn, did not wait around for answers. Within a week of La Compañía's spot being closed down by the police, Marquez—acting on behalf of José Miguel Battle and the Corporation—opened a new spot at 75 Albany Avenue, across the street and half a block away from where La Compañía's spot had been located.

A few weeks after the original police raid, La Compañía's spot reopened. Now the Corporation and La Compañía had competing bolita holes across the street from one another. This was no way to run a business. The Corporation responded by assigning Lalo Pons and his SS squad to firebomb La Compañía's bolita location and burn it to the ground. Before the embers had even been fully extinguished, there was talk of revenge.

Robert Hopkins found himself caught in between. The boss of the Lucchese family, for one, was angry. Since the Luccheses were in a partnership with La Compañía, they saw the burning down of the Brooklyn bolita hole as a potential act of war against them. Hopkins was told, "You better settle this fucking dispute among those Cubans or we got a war on our hands."

Hopkins called up Isleño in Fort Lauderdale and said, "Look, my friend, I need you to set up a sitdown with Battle. We need to resolve this matter before it gets out of hand." The meeting was set to take place at Isleño's home on the intracoastal waterway in Fort Lauderdale.

Hopkins flew down to Florida and met the two Cubans. He was struck by how similar in appearance were Battle and Isleño. Both men were somewhere around 270 pounds, corpulent, with hefty appetites and gregarious personalities. They seemed to respect each other, but clearly their partnership, which had straddled the line between partners and competitors for years, had reached an impasse.

Said Hopkins, "I'm here to see if we can't settle this thing before it causes any more problems."

The setting was magnificent. Isleño's home, surrounded on three sides by water, reeked of South Florida nouveau riche. There were the pumas in their cages outside on the property, and inside, cockatoos and parrots that occasionally squawked. Large leisure boats passed by outside the windows. These men were a long way from the soot and cramped spaces of Harlem and Brooklyn, where they had turned a grimy little game of nickels and dimes into a financial empire.

Battle was adamant. "*Mira* (look), there are people opening up spots less than two blocks away from our spots, and you know it. And another thing, you have people paying seven hundred dollars even though the sign says six hundred to one. We know that they are paying eighty on the bolita, not sixty-four. You know this has to stop or it's going to be a problem."

"Wait a minute," Isleño said to Battle, "I been a bolitero since I was a kid in Guanajai, since before you were even a cop in La Habana. You can't tell me how to run my business."

The discussion went back and forth; it was not going well. Hopkins felt as though he was trapped between two stubborn Cubans, and that passion, not common sense, was likely to rule the day.

At one point, Isleño went into the kitchen to get a drink. His wife and kids were hanging out there. He said to his wife, "It's going to get ugly in New York and the grenades are going to fly." Then he said to the wife and kids, "Go upstairs for now. Until this is settled."

Eventually the men hashed out an agreement. Hopkins proposed that Battle be allowed to keep his bolita location at 75 Albany Avenue in Brooklyn, but that he would pay $50,000 as compensation to Isleño. Everyone agreed, but neither Battle nor Isleño seemed particularly happy about the resolution.

Later that night, Hopkins boarded a flight back to New York. A crisis had been averted, but the Irishman felt uneasy. He had been hoping that the long partnership that had existed between these two men would hold up, and that cooler heads would prevail. His Mafia bosses were expecting him to keep the peace. Right now, even though this particular dispute had been resolved, Hopkins felt that the entire arrangement was like an incendiary device that could explode unexpectedly at any moment.

11

SMOKE AND FIRE

PALULU.

All you had to do was say the name and Battle would tighten up; he would breathe in deeply, his ears would turn red, and his blood pressure would rise to levels that were clinically unhealthy for a man of his girth. Palulu was the stone in his shoe, the thorn in his side. If one of Battle's men mentioned the name of Palulu in his presence, he would find himself on the receiving end of a stare so chilling, so filled with bad intent that his gonads would inadvertently shrivel up in his scrotum.

It had been eight years since El Padrino first called for Palulu's head. Now the mere fact of Palulu's existence was, in Battle's mind, a rebuke to his manhood. If someone had put Fidel Castro and Palulu in front of him and said to kill whomever you must, Battle would first have to kill Palulu and then go after Fidel. Palulu had killed his brother in a very public way. Palulu had pissed on his family's name. Palulu, who by now had already survived half a dozen attempts on his life, just by the fact that he breathed the same air as José Miguel was an abomination. Palulu was making José Miguel Battle and the Corporation look foolish. This was a problem that had to be dealt with—pronto. Or Battle might as well retire to his finca in South Miami and spend the rest of his days stroking his rooster.

On April 30, 1982, Palulu Enriquez walked out of Dannemora prison after having served two years and five months for illegal possession of a weapon. From the moment he hit the streets, he must have felt like violating the terms of his release by doing the very thing that got him incarcerated. A gun was certainly what he needed. He knew there was a bounty on his head.

And yet, like a creature of habit, he returned to the streets of New York.

Throughout his legal troubles, Palulu maintained ownership of a condominium at 3240 Riverdale Avenue, in an upper-middle-class section of the Bronx. Riverdale was a pleasant neighborhood, mostly Jewish, with tree-lined streets. Over the years, Palulu had rented out the condo and lived off the proceeds. Ever since he had fallen afoul of the Battles, he had resided mostly in small one-room studios spread out around the boroughs of New York.

In December, eight months after his release from Dannemora, Palulu was limping along a street in Brooklyn, where he now lived. For a man who had lost a leg, suffered multiple gunshot wounds, and been stabbed on two occasions, he still got around.

The weather was unseasonably warm. December 2 had set a record of seventy-two degrees Fahrenheit, and the mild temperatures continued throughout the month.

Palulu was overdressed, wearing a heavy overcoat, which is what you expected to wear in New York in the winter. He was accompanied by his new bodyguard, Argelio Cuesta, who was a recent refugee from Cuba, part of a wave known as the Mariel boatlift.

The "Marielitos" were refugees whose exodus had been negotiated by President Jimmy Carter. At the time, Cuba was experiencing one of its periodic refugee crises. In Castro's Cuba, securing a travel visa to leave the country was a near impossibility. It was one of the more pernicious aspects of modern Cuba that the island had become like a penal colony. If you wanted to leave for any reason, it became necessary to create some kind of homemade vessel—a raft or inner tube or makeshift boat—and attempt to cross the ocean at nightfall. Already, thousands of Cubans had died attempting to make this journey, and in the decades ahead thousands more would perish.

In April 1980, President Carter announced that the United States would take in refugees from Cuba if Castro would allow them to leave. A week later, Fidel announced that anyone who wanted to could leave. They would be allowed to embark from Mariel Harbor.

Over the next six months, from April through September, Cuba would experience an exodus unlike anything that had been seen before.

Packed onto boats and other sailing vessels, a total of 125,000 asylum seekers flooded into the United States. They were processed primarily at immigration camps in Miami and elsewhere in South Florida. The majority were granted political asylum. Some journeyed beyond Miami to other localities with sizable Cuban populations, such as Hudson County in New Jersey, and New York City.

The Marielitos came from extreme economic deprivation. Some were criminals and mental defectives, whom, unbeknownst at the time to the United States, Castro had taken the opportunity to release as part of the exodus.

In the Cuban American underworld, the Marielitos represented an influx of desperate men, some of whom were willing to do anything for a price. They were recruited as gangland hit men, criminal errand boys, or, in the case of Argelio Cuesta, as bodyguards for someone with a longtime bounty on his head—a job not many people would want to undertake.

In Brooklyn, Cuesta and his boss, Palulu, were enjoying the mild December air when a team of hit men drove up and opened fire. Both men returned fire. Palulu was hit, but the wound was not fatal. Having Cuesta as his bodyguard probably saved his life. Palulu was rushed to the hospital.

Gunshot wounds; hospital emergency room; a visit from the cops; and once again charged with possession of a weapon—a routine so familiar to Palulu. But at least he was alive; he had survived another hit attempt.

Upon learning of this latest failure, Battle was angry enough to cause the earth to rumble. In a way, he blamed himself. It had been a half-assed attempt, one that was beneath the dignity of a true Mob boss. Partly it was because he had put out an open contract on the street. The attempts to kill Palulu had become like a turkey shoot, where anyone with a gun had an opportunity to collect the $100,000 fee.

Battle needed to step up his game. And so he turned to Lalo Pons, the head of his SS squad, who had distinguished himself as an organizer of hits and other acts of mayhem on behalf of the Corporation. Pons was given the assignment to exterminate Palulu.

By April 1983, Palulu had been released from the hospital and was out on bond awaiting yet another trial for possession of an illegal weapon. He had done something he did not want to do: he had moved into his condo in Riverdale. The condo was Palulu's symbol of achievement that he had not wanted to tarnish by dragging into his life of crime and violence. But he had no choice. The condo was the closest thing he had to a sanctuary. Far removed from the teeming Cuban enclaves of Union City, Brooklyn, or the South Bronx, it created for him the illusion of safety.

On a blustery evening, Palulu returned to the condo with Cuesta, his trusty Marielito. He entered the building, using his key, and pushed the button for the elevator.

Neither Palulu nor Cuesta noticed that there was a man hiding in a mass of artificial shrubbery that decorated the lobby. The man crept out from behind the shrubbery and rushed up on the two men from the rear.

Clearly this attempt had been designed so that the gunman could get as close to his target as possible. This would not be a drive-by shooting, or someone taking potshots from a distance. This would be up close and personal.

The gunman put the gun to the back of Palulu's head and pulled the trigger. Blood sprayed on impact, and Palulu fell to the marble floor. The shooter then quickly fired two shots at Cuesta, hitting him twice in the back. The bodyguard also collapsed onto the floor. The gunman ran out of the building.

A first-floor neighbor heard the gunshots and came into the lobby, where the two men were lying in pools of blood. Fire/rescue units arrived, and Palulu and Cuesta were rushed to Columbia Presbyterian Hospital, across the Harlem River at the upper tip of Manhattan.

There, in the emergency room, it would be determined that the bullet that entered Palulu's head had miraculously skirted around his skull and never penetrated his brain. He was alive. In fact, it wasn't even that bad an injury. The bodyguard, Cuesta, had also survived.

From his hacienda south of Miami, Battle received the news of yet another failed attempt on Palulu. Each time that his nemesis survived, Battle felt as if it took years off his own life.

Rumors circulated that Palulu was somehow protected by the orishas, the Santería spirits. He was protected by a *bembe*. This necessitated that Battle visit a *babalawo* and do his own *bembe* to overpower Palulu's *bembe*.

The effort to kill the one-legged gangster was now not just a matter for mortal men; it was a war between the spirits, competing *babalawos,* who conjured the power of various deities to manipulate the course of events in their favor.

Even after a full Santería ceremony with lots of candles, a sacrificial chicken, chicken's blood, some rum, and lots of cigar smoke, Battle left nothing to chance. He got on a plane and flew to New York.

This time, the hit would be painstakingly plotted out. Lalo Pons recruited a hit team of two Cuban American brothers, Gabriel and Ariel Pinalaver. The brothers were considered to be fearless killers who could get the job done. They would be backed up by a second team of hit men.

The hit would take place in a section of the Bronx known as Belmont, a working-class Italian neighborhood. Palulu had recently opened a lottery office on East 180th Street, from which he ran a modest bolita operation. After Palulu was followed for weeks to establish his routine, it was determined that he arrived at his lottery office late at night. The hit men would stake out the location, wait for Palulu, and shoot him outside his office.

Battle wanted to be there, near enough to the location so that he could respond immediately when the shooting occurred and verify for himself that Palulu was dead.

On the night of September 28, an hour before midnight, Palulu arrived in Belmont in his car. He drove around the block a few times looking for a parking space and eventually wound up having to park a couple blocks away from the building where his office was located, near the corner of 180th Street and Arthur Avenue. He got out of his car, locked the car door, and began limping along 180th Street. When he got near the intersection with Arthur Avenue, suddenly two cars approached, coming from different directions. One car pulled up in front of Palulu, blocking his way; Palulu turned to flee, but the other car screeched to a halt from behind, blocking that direction. Out of the car popped the Pinalaver brothers, armed to the gills with assorted weapons. They opened fire on Palulu, riddling him with eleven bullets.

Palulu twisted in the street and fell face-first onto the pavement.

He was pretty sure he was dead. Or maybe not. He could hear the sound of voices, feet walking on the pavement. He heard someone walk over to him, sensed the presence of someone looking down at him, felt someone put a foot underneath his torso and flip kick his body over onto his back. He could feel the blood oozing from his body, blood gurgling from his mouth. Barely able to open his eyes, in a haze, he looked up and saw someone hunched over looking down at him. He squinted, tried to focus. Looked like . . . could it be? It was. El Padrino. José Miguel Battle. The boss was standing over Palulu. And he was laughing. This was the last thing Palulu saw before his whole world descended into darkness, and he fell unconscious.

Was this the end for Palulu?

A fire/rescue unit arrived and rushed Palulu to the hospital. One miscalculation made by Lalo Pons and his hit team was that there was a hospital just three blocks away. Palulu arrived at St. Barnabas Hospital already on life support. A trauma team began immediate heart surgery. They were able to restart his heart, but he soon lapsed into a coma and stayed that way, in grave condition, for the next few days.

Battle stayed in the New York area, at his condominium apartment in Union City, which he maintained even though he had now fully relocated to Miami. He intended to remain in New York until he received word that Palulu was dead.

On October 2, five days after the shooting, Battle received word from a contact in the Bronx. The prognosis was not good. Not only had Palulu come out of his coma, but that afternoon Detective Kalafus of the NYPD had made a visit to his room. The *pendejo* was alive, and he was talking. Word was that he was in critical condition, but he had survived the shooting and given a statement to the New York detective who dressed like he was a cowboy from out west.

Battle and his people were stupefied, El Padrino most of all. He had seen Palulu for himself, riddled with bullets, bleeding to death in the street. He saw what he thought was Palulu expiring, savoring that moment as if it were a sweet kiss from the Angel of Death, the taste of revenge lingering in his gullet like fine Santiago rum. But now, it seemed, it was as if his eyes had played tricks on him. It was like many of his underlings had said: *Padrino, he can't be killed. He's El Diablo. I shot him in the head. I know he was dead. But he's alive. Incredible. I don't even think he's human.*

Among other things, Palulu's continued existence was causing great consternation for the Corporation, most notably the two men who were currently handing the day-to-day operations of the organization. Abraham Rydz and Miguel Battle Jr. had also recently moved to Miami. The move was motivated by Rydz's needing to be near his dying mother, who lived in Miami Beach. Rydz and Miguelito purchased plots of land within a half block of one another in Key Biscayne, where they planned to build their dream homes. In Miami, the two men established a company called Union Financial Research. Ostensibly it was a mortgage lending company, but it was also a front for the bolita business in New York. Proceeds from bolita were being funneled into the company, which was based out of an office in Miami, with real employees, including secretaries, an accountant, and Rydz and Battle as CEOs.

Battle Sr. was no longer involved in the day-to-day operations of the bolita business, though he still collected his cut and took care of various matters of strategy, development, and, most of all, discipline and retribution.

The Palulu matter had been an issue for many years. Now, as far as Rydz and Junior were concerned, it had become a major distraction. El Padrino hardly talked about anything else. It was in everyone's interest that the Palulu matter be resolved so that they could get on with their lives.

For the first time, Abraham Rydz, along with Battle Sr., Lalo Pons, and others among the ruling council of the Corporation, became involved in the planning of the hit. Everyone felt they needed to act fast. The idea was to kill Palulu while he was still in the hospital. The hit was planned quietly, so as few people as possible would know about it. The plan was devised by Rydz, among others, and Lalo recruited the gunman, a Cuban named Domingues.

On the night of October 7, two nurses were working the late-night shift at St. Barnabas Hospital, where Palulu was an inpatient on Wing Seven South, in room 711. Deloris Edwards and Romana Bautista were at the front desk. It was late—around 3:35 A.M.—a time when the hospital was at its most quiet.

Suddenly, from down the hallway came a sound—*Pop! Pop!*

"Did you hear that?" one nurse said to the other.

They agreed that it was likely the sound of an oxygen line popping off its wall fixture, which was a chronic problem on their wing. Nurse Edwards headed off to check the rooms, while Nurse Bautista stayed at the nurses' station working on paperwork.

At that moment, there appeared in the hallway a male nurse—or at least someone who the nurses assumed was a male nurse. He was wearing a hospital smock, like the other male nurses. But it was not anyone the nurses had seen before. He was Hispanic, with a caramel complexion, curly black hair, and a thin mustache. He had not checked in at the nurses' station, as all nurses are required to do at the beginning of their shift.

"Hey there, hold up a minute," Nurse Bautista called to the man.

The man did not respond; he quickly disappeared into a stairwell.

Meanwhile, that popping sound earlier had awakened Leroy Middleton, a patient in room 711, which he shared with Palulu. Middleton roused himself from a medication-induced slumber, got up, and headed to the toilet to urinate. As he walked past Palulu's bed in the semidarkness, he saw what he thought could be blood, but he wasn't sure what he was seeing. He went into the bathroom, peed, then walked back out to the room. By now, his eyes having adjusted to the darkness, he walked over and looked at Palulu, whose face was covered in blood. Leroy pushed the emergency call button.

The nurses rushed into the room and flipped on the light. What they saw was a ghastly sight: Palulu Enriquez had been shot multiple times at close range.

The hit was diabolical but effective. Domingues, disguised as a male nurse, had sneaked into Palulu's room and done the deed. No doubt there were people in security at St. Barnabas who had been bought off to facilitate his entering the hospital and making his way to Palulu's room without being stopped or questioned.

Palulu was finally dead.

It had been part of the plan that none of the originators of the hit—Battle Sr., Rydz, or Lalo Pons—would be in the New York area when the killing occurred. In the interest of plausible deniability, they were to be as far away as possible. Both Battle and Rydz had returned to Miami days before the hit was scheduled to occur.

On the afternoon of October 7, Battle, Rydz, and a handful of others were engaged in a card game at El Zapotal, Battle's home in South Miami. It had become one of the ironies of the Corporation that the brain trust of the organization was now almost completely based in Miami, while the business—and most of the events that shaped its fortunes—still emanated from the New York metropolitan area. And yet the universe of the Corporation was clearly defined and circumscribed; it had become a mind-set not necessarily defined by geography but by mutual interests. The Corporation had become an entity that defied time and space.

At the card game, Battle received a phone call. He left to take the call and then returned, grinning from ear to ear.

"It's done," he announced to the handful of men at the table. "Palulu is dead."

Abraham Rydz breathed a big sigh of relief. He immediately got on the phone with Nene Marquez, the Brooklyn boss of the Corporation, and authorized the release of $100,000 from the UNESCO fund to be paid to Domingues and a couple of others who had helped with the logistics involved in carrying out the hit.

Battle had stored on ice a dozen bottles of Dom Pérignon. He cracked open a few of them and poured champagne for everyone in the room. The men extended their glasses, and El Padrino proclaimed, "Let's drink champagne and raise a toast to our enemies. Drink up."

It was an auspicious occasion. After all these years, José Miguel had finally avenged the murder of his little brother.

The partying did not stop there. For the next week, Battle celebrated the death of Palulu. There were impromptu parties at a couple of favored restaurants in Miami, and parties at El Zapotal. Guests at the house noted that as they arrived, there was a new wrinkle, something they had never seen before. Upon entering the front door, each guest was individually presented with a small pouch. *What is this?* they asked. When they opened the pouch, they found out: cocaine. Each pouch was filled with cocaine.

Let the festivities begin!

THE DEATH OF PALULU WAS IN ONE SENSE MONUMENTAL. IT WAS AS IF A PRESSURE valve had been released, and everyone associated with the Corporation could breathe again. On the other hand, it had little effect on the daily running of the bolita business, which continued to grow throughout the early 1980s.

As partners and joint overseers of the organization, Abraham Rydz and Battle Jr. solidified a personal relationship that had been developing over the years. Rydz was more than a mentor; he had become a surrogate father to Junior, whom he referred to as Migue.

When Battle Sr. had first asked Rydz to "look out for my son" while he was away in prison, he had to have known that he was effectively switching his son's loyalties to El Polaco. His own relationship with Junior had been distant, though he often professed love for his son, and his loyalty was sacrosanct. But Battle knew that he would never have the closeness that Rydz and Junior had—a closeness based on an innate reserve and cautiousness they shared, as opposed to his own impulsiveness and blunt leadership style.

When Rydz first approached Junior, he had been characteristically shrewd. He did not tell Migue, "Your father wants me to take care of you." Instead, he said, "Migue, I need a favor. I'm going to say in the street that we have become partners so that I get protection by using the Battle name." Using the name was like life insurance. As Rydz said years later, "People were really afraid of José Miguel Sr.; they wouldn't fool around with Mr. Battle . . . I needed the name Battle for the protection . . . the respect."

Junior understood. He said to his friend, "Okay, do that, and maybe someday we will really become partners." The partnership became a real thing shortly thereafter.

By the early 1980s, Rydz's previous partner, Luis "Tinta" Rey, had left the business. Rydz and Migue spent nearly every day together. A year after they both moved to Miami, construction began on their dual homes located so close together they could share a cup of sugar. Rydz had a new wife and, from a previous marriage, an adult daughter who lived separately. Junior had two young sons. Their families shared personal time together as well as the time the two men spent reconfiguring the financial structure of the Corporation.

One of the first orders of business was to establish a number of offshore companies into which they would deposit cash overflow from the bolita business. There was a company called Lindseed, and another called Stenara, based in the Dutch Antilles. There was Voltaire and Darmont, based in Panama City. There was a company called Aztec, also based in Panama, and half a dozen others around the globe. The names of neither Rydz nor Battle were associated with these shell companies; the names listed as owners or CEOs were merely front men for the Corporation. And the companies themselves were designed solely as fraudulent financial entities that lent money to real companies in the United States owned by Rydz and Miguel Battle. In this way, tens of millions of dollars were laundered on an annual basis.

In addition to Union Financial Research, Rydz and Battle started a company in Miami called YMR, a clothing manufacturing company. This was a legitimate company; YMR had a factory in the Dominican Republic that manufactured women's apparel. Other companies owned by Rydz and Migue included Arnold Stores, a popular chain of stores throughout South Florida that sold women's clothing at affordable prices. They also bought into a company called Trends, and a subsidiary called Yes U.S., both of which manufactured clothing and sold their products to large retail stores like Target and Wal-Mart.

What Rydz and Migue created in a short number of years constituted a massive financial structure. "To operate these companies," Rydz would later say, "you need to have hundreds of millions of dollars. You have money tied up in inventory, money tied to the factories, and money tied up in the manufacture and distribution of merchandise." To sustain these operations, in addition to the money coming in from bolita, YMR took out a loan of $8 million from the Republic Bank of Philadelphia.

In Miami, both Rydz and Migue received a salary from YMR. Both were officially taking in around half a million dollars as owners and operators of the business. José Miguel Sr. was not a party to these endeavors. In time, the success of Rydz and Migue's financial empire would cause resentment between Battle Sr. and his two underlings, but in the 1980s there was so much money flowing down to Miami from New York that no one had any complaints.

Even with Isleño Dávila's organization, La Compañía, expanding into Harlem and forming a partnership with the Lucchese family, the Corporation suffered no loss of business in New York. If anything, the existence of La Compañía alongside the Corporation created a bolita frenzy in the city. As more and more Latinos from Cuba, Puerto Rico, and the Dominican Republic, as well as other Caribbean immigrants from Jamaica and Haiti, flooded into New York—alongside native New Yorkers, black and white, who had been playing the number for much of their lives—the volume of players was likely the highest it had ever been in history. This was truly the era of bolita in New York. There was no way to officially calculate the volume of business; every three months or so, records from the various offices were shredded and destroyed. Though it was a business that generated huge cash flow in the underground economy, there was no way to accurately quantify the numbers. Even so, it was likely that bolita was generating billions of dollars annually.

This created a problem: what to do with all that money? Bank accounts were opened in Switzerland and various other overseas locations. Rydz and Battle were careful to make sure that, given the criminal notoriety of José Miguel Battle, the Battle name was not linked to any of the accounts. Instead, they used Maurilio Marquez, the brother of Nene Marquez, as a front man. Maurilio was a Venezuelan citizen, a foreigner, and therefore could legally make investments to Union Financial Research and YMR from the various shell companies without triggering an audit by the Internal Revenue Service.

The enterprise created by Rydz and Miguelito was airtight. It had been brilliantly conceived, designed to make them and their offspring rich for generations to come.

Prerequisites of this fraudulent financial empire were caution and secrecy. Rydz and Battle Jr. never discussed business on the phone or in the car. To talk with each other, or with business associates, they only used public pay phones. Miguelito was especially paranoid. Anything to do with the financial structure of the bolita business was communicated mostly in person, with almost nothing written down on paper. Members of the Corporation would fly from Miami to New York and back simply to talk about business. Battle Jr. told everyone, "Act as if we are already under investigation, as if your phone is bugged, your car is bugged. Take every precaution. You can never be too careful."

The Swiss bank account was in Maurilio Marquez's name. Rydz and Battle flew to Nassau, in the Bahamas, or to Caracas, Venezuela, just to get on the phone to talk to the bankers in Switzerland. No calls to Switzerland were ever made from the United States.

The organization also had an accountant, Orestas Vidan, a Cuban who was partial to guayabera shirts. Vidan was known as "El Cocinero," the Cook, because it was his job to "cook the books."

At the root of this fulsome tree, with its many branches extending into multiple areas of high finance, was a nutrient as old as the republic: little green pieces of paper. Cash was the elixir that fed the beast. Stacks and stacks of bills came into the counting rooms of the bolita operation, and they needed to by moved out of New York to Miami and other destinations far beyond.

It all started at the street level in the money rooms where proceeds were stored. It was an unwritten rule in the business that the money was always kept at a separate location from the betting holes or even the offices where the record keeping took place. Usually the Corporation would have rented out a series of unfurnished apartments in a building; one might be set up as an office, and elsewhere in the building would be a money storage apartment. The storage apartments, or "banks," were heavily protected by armed soldiers of the organization. Typically the only people allowed in those rooms were the organization's "counters," people who used counting machines to count the cash and store it in envelopes, bags, and suitcases. The counters were often family members or relatives of people in the organization, the theory being that they could be trusted.

One person who counted money for La Compañía—Dávila's organization—was Jorge "George" Dávila, Isleño Dávila's nephew. George was the son of Jorge "Tony" Dávila, Isleño's brother, who was also a seasoned bolitero. As a teenager, George had become fascinated by the business, and, as only a young person can, he soaked up knowledge and information about bolita as if he were learning a new language. One of the things that caught his attention was the money.

"We had a saying about this era; we called it *La época de los sobres*, the season of the envelopes," remembered George Dávila. "There was so much money that by the time you had picked it up from the stores, traditionally in envelopes, you needed a large brown paper bag or even a satchel to carry the envelopes . . . I remember walking as a kid, my dad would take me on his routes to the best stores, or to a new store that had recently opened. He would go to the numbers offices and look at the ledgers, see what's going on. Then we would go to the money . . . The money office was usually a one-bedroom apartment where the living room or bedroom was the counting area, and the money was stored in the other room. I mean, the whole apartment smelled like money. Imagine that smell you get when you put a stack of bills to your nose. The whole room was like that. Especially for a teenager, a kid, it was an amazing experience."

From there, the cash was divided up and distributed, usually in hundred-dollar bills. Many people received a cut. With the Corporation, much of the cash was destined for Miami. José Miguel Battle received a monthly take of 17 percent. Battle Jr. received the same, as did Rydz. In total, the Miami brain trust received approximately 50 percent of the weekly take, which could be anywhere from $100,000 to $1 million. The other half was divided between people like Nene Marquez, Lalo Pons, the Mafia, and thirty or forty other entities that worked for or facilitated the organization, including dirty cops, lawyers, and judges.

Transporting the cash outside the city was often tricky. There was really no other way to do it than by human courier. Cash was constantly being transported by trains, planes, and automobiles to Miami and points beyond. Usually, underlings in the organization were assigned the task of transporting packages, briefcases, or suitcases, often not knowing what they were carrying. Sometimes, in emergencies, the bosses themselves were forced to serve as couriers.

One day in June 1983, Rydz and Miguelito made a run to New York to pick up half a million dollars in cash. It was nothing unusual. The two were so often in each other's company that even though there was an age difference of twenty years between them, they were referred to by family and friends as "the twins." On this occasion, the plan was to catch a flight in the morning to John F. Kennedy Airport, pick up the money from Nene Marquez, and then return on a flight later that evening.

It was not illegal to transport large amounts of cash from state to state. Sometimes the airlines even assigned an armed guard to a customer to take the cash to and from the terminal. On this occasion, however, Rydz and Battle were unaware that they were on an international flight that was leaving from Kennedy Airport, stopping in Miami, and then continuing on to Colombia. Different laws applied to international flights; the money needed to be declared.

The men were carrying the money in two shopping bags. Stacks of hundred-dollar bills had been wrapped in festive paper to give the impression that they were carrying birthday gifts. Rydz and Battle hadn't even noticed that the bills were wrapped in Christmas paper, which was oddly out of season.

"What is this?" said the female security person. "Christmas presents in the middle of June? Can I take a look at this?"

Battle Jr. was in front of Rydz. He froze and said nothing.

Seeing what was going on, Rydz stepped in front of Battle Jr. and said to the woman, "That's mine. It's money, that's all. We're taking money to Miami."

The woman peeled open one of the packages, then another. The realization that the dozens of brightly wrapped packets were filled with cash caused the other security personnel to gather around. This was definitely something out of the ordinary.

One of the male security people said, "How much money is here?"

"I don't know," said Rydz. "Maybe five hundred thousand dollars."

By now, the female guard had called a supervisor on a walkie-talkie, and more security people were arriving.

The male guard said to Rydz, "You can't just carry this on a plane. This money has to be declared."

"I do it all the time," said Rydz. "It's not illegal. We're going to Miami." Rydz held up his ticket, which showed that he was flying from New York to Miami.

"You may be stopping in Miami, but this is an international flight," said the guard. "This money has to be declared through customs and reported to the IRS."

While everyone was talking, Battle Jr. slipped away from the group. One of the things he was most worried about was that before he and Rydz parted ways with Nene Marquez, their junior partner had given him a ledger sheet, or invoice, with numbers for the bolita business that month. He had that sheet of paper in his pocket. It would have been indecipherable to anyone who didn't know what it was, but it occurred to him that if he and Rydz were searched, the security people would find that paper and start asking questions.

With no one looking, Battle Jr. tore the paper up into little pieces. As he sauntered over to a waste bin and threw away the pieces, one of the guards said, "Hey, you, what is that?"

"What?" said Battle Jr., acting oblivious.

The guard came over and moved Battle Jr. aside. He began digging in the garbage to retrieve the bits of paper. Not much was thought of this at the time, but they would be safeguarded, pieced together, and eventually decoded. One day far in the future, they would be used as evidence to take down the Corporation.

The various guards and supervisors were now somewhat alarmed; these guys were acting like they had something to hide. The airport police were called, and the money was confiscated. Rydz and Battle Jr. were not arrested—nobody knew of any crime they could be charged with—but they were detained. The cops brought them downstairs to a police office, where they were held for the next six hours.

At one point, an airport cop counted the money, while other cops stood nearby. After counting out $460,000 in hundred-dollar bills, the cop looked at Rydz and Battle Jr. and said, "For this amount of money, I would kill my mother."

A security lady came to the two men with a form to sign. She said, "The IRS will hold this money until you are ready to make a claim for it. Do you understand?"

Rydz and Battle nodded yes. They were allowed to go. They boarded a later flight back to Miami—without the money.

They were told by a lawyer, "If you try to reclaim the money, the IRS is going to come after you. If I were you, I would say, 'The money is not mine.'"

When contacted by a representative of the government, Rydz and Battle Jr. had their lawyer say, "My clients don't want the money."

"What do you want us to do with it?" asked the representative.

"Do whatever you want. Give it to the Cancer League. Give it to charity. That money does not belong to my clients."

In the end, Rydz and Battle Jr. simply wrote off the money. It was the price of doing business. To the Corporation, half a million dollars was chump change.

FOR MONTHS, ROBERT HOPKINS HAD BEEN TRYING TO SMOOTH THE WATERS. HE HAD brokered the deal between Isleño and Battle Sr. at Isleño's estate in Fort Lauderdale. Battle Sr. had proven to be a man of his word, delivering to Hopkins, in person, $50,000 in cash, which the Irishman passed on to Isleño. This should have been the end of it, but it wasn't.

Recently there had been at least two firebombings of bolita spots, one belonging to the Corporation and one to La Compañía, which the Lucchese family viewed as an act against them. The torchings were done late at night, so no one was hurt. No group claimed responsibility. But it was clear that someone was attempting to deliver a message. To Hopkins, it was as if they were one matchstick away from all-out war.

In the fall of 1983, Hopkins successfully arranged a high-powered meeting between himself, a partner of his named Kevin Quinn, Isleño Dávila, Abraham Rydz, and José Miguel Battle Jr. Having flown up from Miami, Rydz and Battle were there representing the Corporation. Hopkins said that he was speaking on behalf of his partners in the Lucchese crime family when he said, "The two-block rule must be honored."

Battle Jr. noted that in Brooklyn, a bolita spot had opened up a half block away from a Corporation spot. "Well," said Hopkins, "that spot was opened by La Compañía. That's a Cuban spot. You need to work that out between the two of you. I can guarantee that my people will not violate the two-block rule."

Rydz and Battle Jr. were suspicious. After the meeting, they spoke separately with Isleño, who told them, "Look, that spot a half block away from your spot, we did not open it. The Italians opened that spot. If you want to burn out that spot, you will get no objection from me."

After Isleño departed, Rydz and Jr. stood on a busy street corner in midtown Manhattan. "Isleño," said Miguelito, shaking his head. "He's sneaky. He wants us to take out that spot so he can take advantage of it. Whatever we do, make sure we leave that spot alone."

It may have been strategic thinking or paranoia on Jr.'s part, but it was a reflection of how duplicitous the bolita terrain had become.

Rydz noticed that at a movie theater across the street, emblazoned on the marquee was the title of the movie currently playing: *Gandhi*. Rydz thought, *Gandhi, wasn't he all about peace and nonviolence?* That was a philosophy far removed from where the boliteros seemed to be headed.

In an attempt to resolve the conflict, there were other meetings, including one at the Palma Boys Social Club in Spanish Harlem with Fat Tony Salerno and Fish Cafaro. Battle Sr. flew in from Miami for that meeting. Rydz and Battle Jr. also attended. Salerno, chomping on his ubiquitous stogie, warned the Cubans to keep the peace.

Battle said, "Tony, I'm never the one to throw the first stone. You know that. But if somebody crosses me, they're gonna be in trouble."

Salerno promised his Cuban associates that the Italians would honor the two-block rule.

There was one final meeting, in late 1983, a major summit of Cuban and Italian mobsters with controlling interests in the numbers racket. The meeting took place at a restaurant on the Upper East Side of Manhattan, at Third Avenue and 72nd Street, and it was attended by the reigning bolita elite at the time. Among those present were Isleño Dávila, Omar Broche, Spanish Raymond Marquez, and Pedro Acosta, all representing La Compañía. Bob Hopkins and his partners were present, as were representatives of the Five Families.

The Italians had a complaint, or "beef." It was alleged that the Cubans were deliberately tipping off the police about their spots, so that they would be raided and shut down. Then the Cubans would open their own spot at a nearby location. It was, the Italians complained, a sneaky way to get around the two-block rule.

The Cubans denied they had been doing this.

As everyone spilled out of this dinner meeting, it was clear that nothing had been resolved. The two sides were refusing to back down. As the group of Cubans stood on the sidewalk in front of the restaurant, a car drove by and someone in the car opened fire with an automatic weapon. Everyone ducked for cover. The car peeled away from the scene.

One of the Cubans, Pedro Acosta, was hit. He was rushed to the hospital, where he died in the emergency room.

Hopkins had been standing with the Cubans at the time the shooting began. He had taken cover like everyone else. Later, when he heard that Acosta had died, he knew his attempts to be a peacemaker were over. He had failed. The war was on.

EVEN THOUGH NEITHER JOSÉ MIGUEL BATTLE SR. NOR ANY OTHER REPRESENTATIVE OF the Corporation had been at the meeting, El Padrino took the killing of Acosta as a personal affront. A Cuban bolitero had been brazenly murdered by the Italians. Battle told Lalo Pons, the leader of his SS squad, "We are at war with the Mafia."

Over the next nineteen months, what became known to police as "the arson wars" exploded like a long-dormant volcano that had rumbled to life. In a city that was already experiencing a spiraling homicide rate due to the scourge of crack cocaine, the arson wars were an unwelcome addition to a hyperviolent era.

At first the arsons hardly made the newspapers. The city had famously weathered a previous era of arson, in the 1970s, when the torching of buildings, especially in the Bronx, became a common insurance scam. From the press box at Yankee Stadium, sportscaster Howard Cosell had witnessed the phenomenon and announced to a nationwide audience, "The Bronx is burning." It became a phrase that seemed to define the era.

So arsons were not particularly new or notable in New York. But it soon became apparent that these were not insurance fraud burnings. Something different was happening here. This became especially apparent when innocent people began to die.

From September 1983 to June 1985, there would be sixty fires set at dozens of locations in Manhattan, Brooklyn, and the Bronx. In these fires, eight people would be burned to death, including a four-year-old girl and her teenage babysitter. By the time it was over, the city would be repulsed, and the reputation of the Corporation would be dragged into the gutter.

Lalo Pons organized the team of arsonists who carried out the attacks. One of his key operatives was a hulking, nearly 350-pound lifelong street criminal named Willie Diaz.

A Brooklyn native, Diaz was Puerto Rican. When he was a baby, his parents moved from Puerto Rico to the neighborhood of Bushwick, where Willie was raised in a housing project. By the time he was fifteen, he was a member of a gang called the Champions. After graduating from Thomas Jefferson High School, he embarked on a life of petty crime. At the age of seventeen, he stole two hundred pigeons from a neighbor's coop and sold them to a pet store. Later that year, he got arrested for hitting his girlfriend in public. He was also caught stealing Social Security checks. By the age of nineteen, he had advanced to dealing drugs, mugging people, and robbing liquor stores to support himself.

At six foot one, with dark, sunken eyes, Willie had the sort of menacing look that helped him land a job as a nightclub bouncer. Not long after that, he became a pimp and even lived in an apartment with three prostitutes who worked for him.

Money was hard to come by. Willie was a low-level hustler, a punk. Left to his own devices, he was destined for prison, which is why when his Cuban girlfriend's mother, Grace, suggested he come work for her at a local bolita spot, Willie jumped at the chance. The place, an anonymous storefront designed to look like an OTB (off-track betting) outlet, was located on Greene Avenue. At first, Willie wasn't even paid. He was there as Grace's understudy. She taught him all about the business; eventually he was working at the bettor's window taking bets and reporting to a bolita manager named Manuel "Manny" Guzman.

Willie knew little about the organization he was now working for, and he didn't ask too many questions. In June 1981, he was to get an education when the bolita hole where he worked was raided by cops and he was arrested on a policy violation. He was cuffed and taken to arraignment court, where, out of the blue, a lawyer showed up and told him he was there to take care of everything. "The boys sent me," explained the lawyer. Willie pleaded guilty to a misdemeanor charge; the $250 fee was paid for by the Corporation. Willie was free to walk out of court.

Manny Guzman explained it: "Our organization is like a Mafia family of Cubans." He told Willie that he now owed the Corporation, and that they would call upon him someday to do "something special."

That opportunity presented itself in September 1983, when Lalo Pons put out the word within the organization that he was looking to assemble an "enforcement crew" whose first order of business would be to burn down rival bolita spots. Manny Guzman recommended Willie to Lalo Pons.

When Willie met Pons, the physical disparity between the two was comical: Willie was huge and fat, and Pons was short and wiry. Not only was the little man the boss, but he was fond of referring to himself as "Napoleon," a nickname he encouraged others to use.

Pons told Willie to put together a crew. They would be paid $1,000 for the first arson and $2,500 for each job after that. Though ostensibly the arson campaign began as a war against the Italians, eventually Pons was ordering hits on locations belonging to La Compañía as well. Willie would later admit to having undertaken upward of thirty arson contracts on spots in Brooklyn, the Bronx, and Manhattan. Among the most notorious of these crimes were:

99 Schenectady Avenue, Brooklyn

According to Willie, "I used a friend named Hector Aviles, because he needed the money. This was Hector's first arson for me, but we had run together growing up, and I knew Hector was bold." On September 29, 1983, as he always did, Willie first scouted out the location by going inside the bolita hole and placing a bet, always betting the same number—5-7-6. He placed his bet with Evelyn Herrara, the bolita writer behind the counter. Willie looked around the store to see who was present, where the entrances and exits were located, and how best to torch the place. "I saw the back door and figured the girl [working there] would have a way to get out. So I went back to the car and sent Hector in with the gas."

The technique was basic: Hector carried a pail of gas into the place, splashed it around, and lit it on fire.

Outside, half a block away, Willie had the hood of his car up to make it look as though he had stopped the car because he had engine trouble. He saw Hector come running out of the store with flames already visible behind him. "I slammed the hood down and we drove away. As we left we saw a guy go into the place, like to try to rescue the girl. We drove back to the old neighborhood slowly . . . I found a pay phone and paged

Lalo with a 'ten-four,' the signal that the fire was done. It was the signal I always used."

Later that day, Grace called Willie and told him that a woman had died in the fire. The official cause of death, according to the medical examiner's office, was asphyxiation due to carbon monoxide inhalation, as well as burn trauma to her body.

"Lalo was pissed," remembered Willie. He thought the death of the girl would cause them problems with the police. But then it was reported in the newspaper that the man who Willie and Hector had seen running into the store was Evelyn Herrara's fiancé. It was reported that the fiancé earlier on the day of the attack had had a loud public argument with Evelyn. The cops believed that he was the primary suspect.

Sure enough, a few days later, the fiancé was wrongfully arrested and charged with second-degree murder in the death of Herrara. Willie noted that Lalo, his boss, was "happy about that. Real happy."

291 Evergreen Avenue, Brooklyn

By March 25, 1984, Willie had assembled a more professional crew of arsonists. Among his people were two African Americans, Anthony "Red" Morgan and Calvin Coleman, who preferred to be known by the nickname "Truth and Understanding." Coleman was a spiritualist who sometimes spouted quotes from the Old Testament.

Willie owned an old yellow cab that was no longer operational as a taxi. The three men loaded into the car and drove to the location identified by Lalo as the place they were supposed to torch. It was a bolita spot disguised to look like a bodega. Willie went in first to scout out the location; he placed a bet on 5-7-6 and checked the place out. There were three people in there at the time, two boliteros—Carlos Rivera and Angel Castro—who were behind bulletproof glass, and a customer, Prudencio Crespo, who was there to place a bet.

Crespo became suspicious when he saw the two black guys enter carrying a pail of some kind of liquid. He saw one of them dump the contents of the pail. Crespo smelled gas and saw a liquid spreading across the floor.

"Let's go!" yelled Red Morgan to Calvin Coleman. They ignited the gas and bolted toward the door.

Crespo saw the eruption of the flames and ran. He was right behind the two arsonists, dashing through the fire.

Outside, Willie Diaz was standing by the taxi getaway car, watching the front of the store. As he later remembered it, "I heard a loud explosion . . . I saw [Coleman] fly right out the front door and land right on the street, the concrete . . . He got up. His feet were on fire. So he pounded them out and ran straight toward where I was at . . . He was running so fast he almost ran right past the car. I had the door open for him. He jumped in the car." Morgan, the other arsonist, also got in the car. Said Diaz, "The place was engulfed in fire. There was a lot of fire coming out of the place."

Prudencio Crespo was lucky to have escaped. The two boliteros inside were not so fortunate. Carlos Rivera and Angel Castro choked to death on the thick black smoke, and their bodies were incinerated in the fire.

1625 Westchester Avenue, the Bronx

It had been a sweltering summer in the city when, on August 23, Edna Rodriguez entered the bolita spot on a busy stretch of Westchester Avenue to place a bet. The location was a legitimate bodega with the policy operation in a rear room. Edna visited the place a couple times every day. Inside, she saw many familiar faces, including Trinidad "Trini" Rodriguez (no relation to Edna), who was taking the bets, and another woman, seventy-four-year-old Blossom Layton.

Down the street, Willie Diaz and Red Morgan exited the subway. Morgan was carrying a pail lined with a plastic bag that was filled with gas. Given the density of traffic on Westchester Avenue, the two arsonists decided it would be better to do this burning on foot, using the subway as their getaway vehicle.

Inside the bodega, Edna Rodriguez noticed a black male enter, carrying what she thought was a plastic bag. He set down the bag and bent over as if he were tying his shoe. Nothing seemed strange to Edna, until she saw the man leave the location and break into a run. The next thing she knew, the store was engulfed by smoke and flames.

Edna was able to help a customer out of the store, but the fire was too intense to help the others. Trinidad Rodriguez and Blossom Layton were trapped inside. Fire department units arrived and battled the blaze, but there was little they could do to rescue anyone. The charred bodies of Rodriquez and Layton were removed from the scene. A third woman, Marlene Francis, had fled to a bathroom to escape the flames. She survived for a week in the hospital burn unit, but the poisoning from the carbon monoxide and the infection from the first-degree burns on her body destroyed her immune system. She died a slow and painful death.

410 West 56th Street, Manhattan

A shoe repair shop in Hell's Kitchen, on West 56th Street between 9th and 10th avenues, served as a popular Mafia-controlled numbers spot. Victor Hernandez, who ran the place, had previously received a threatening phone call that he needed to stop taking bets or there would be trouble. Knowing that there were tensions between the Cubans and the Italians, and that there had been a rash of arsons at bolita spots around the city, Hernandez took the call seriously. It was his intention to shut down bolita operations in the back of the shoe repair store within the next couple days.

Willie Diaz was given the assignment to hit this spot by his boss, Lalo Pons. Willie put together a team that included himself, Red Morgan, Hector Aviles, and Nelson Guzman.

On the afternoon of October 27, following the usual routine, Willie went into the bolita location to place a bet and check it out. Then he departed and retrieved his car to serve as the getaway driver. The plan was for Aviles and Guzman to block the front door to the shop so no one could enter, while Red Morgan lit the fire in the rear of the shop.

Just before the arsonists arrived, Victor Hernandez received a visit at the shoe store from his girlfriend, nineteen-year-old Laura Sirgo. She had brought along a little girl she was babysitting that day, Jannin Toribio, who happened to be celebrating her fourth birthday.

The Bay of Pigs invasion, April 17, 1961, was a hellish ordeal for the men of Brigade 2506. The battle raged for three days until the invading soldiers were either killed or forced to surrender.

Many members of the brigade were held as prisoners by the government of Fidel Castro. It was a bitter defeat that would shape the lives of everyone involved.

After members of the brigade were captured, they were brought before Fidel Castro (far right), who smoked a cigar and reveled in the humiliation of his captives.

(© AP PHOTOS)

After the release of prisoners, President John F. Kennedy met surviving members of the brigade at the Orange Bowl in Miami. He was presented with the brigade's official flag. Eleven months later Kennedy was assassinated.

José Miguel Battle and Angel Mujica knew each other since Havana. They were both members of Brigade 2506, served time in the infamous Cuban prison on the Isle of Pines, and, on the same day, they both joined the U.S. Army.

Santo Trafficante Jr. (wearing glasses) proved to be an important contact for Battle as he forged a relationship with the Mafia in the United States. Here Trafficante is detained in Havana, where he was incarcerated for a time in 1959 before being released and deported back to the States.

Anthony "Fat Tony" Salerno, titular boss of the Genovese crime family, controlled the numbers racket for all Five Families in NYC. Salerno created a power sharing arrangement with Battle and the Cuban boliteros that lasted for more than a decade.

(© GETTY IMAGES)

Union City Mayor William Musto and Deputy Police Chief Frank Scarafile at their arraignment on gambling charges.

(© *JERSEY JOURNAL*)

Humberto "Isleño" Dávila, the most successful of the bolita bankers, seen here at a social function in mid-1975 with his wife, his mother, his brother Tony and Tony's wife.

(© DÁVILA FAMILY)

Ernesto Torres, who José Miguel Battle sometimes referred to as El Hijo Pródigo, the Prodigal Son.

(© ERNESTO TORRES IZQUIERDO)

Pedro Battle (left), stands with Ernesto Torres at the baptism of Ernesto's son. Pedro Battle served as godfather, with the woman holding the child serving as godmother.

(© ERNESTO TORRES IZQUIERDO)

Carlos "Charley" Hernandez, seen here with his mother.

(© KELLY NOGUEROL/CAROL DALEY)

Ernesto Torres, shot dead in the closet of
an apartment in Opa-Locka, Florida.
(© U.S. ATTORNEY, SOUTHERN DISTRICT
OF FLORIDA)

The coup de grâce, a bullet between the
eyes, was administered by El Padrino.
(© U.S. ATTORNEY, SOUTHERN DISTRICT
OF FLORIDA)

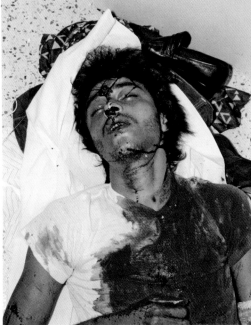

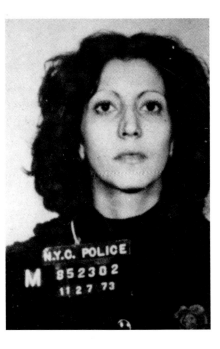

Idalia Fernandez in a 1973 police mug shot photo.
(© NEW YORK CITY POLICE DEPARTMENT)

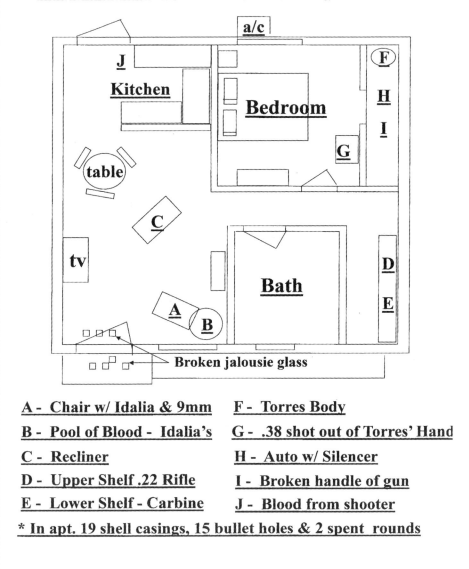

1125 Sharazad Blvd., Apt #28, OpaLocka, FL

a/c

J

Kitchen

Bedroom

F

H

I

G

table

C

tv

Bath

D

E

A

B

Broken jalousie glass

A - Chair w/ Idalia & 9mm

F - Torres Body

B - Pool of Blood - Idalia's

G - .38 shot out of Torres' Hand

C - Recliner

H - Auto w/ Silencer

D - Upper Shelf .22 Rifle

I - Broken handle of gun

E - Lower Shelf - Carbine

J - Blood from shooter

* In apt. 19 shell casings, 15 bullet holes & 2 spent rounds

The murder of Ernesto Torres and assault on Idalia Fernandez: this schematic of the crime scene was created by prosecutors for the trial of Battle on the charge of Conspiracy to Commit Murder. At the time, prosecutors did not know that Battle was actually one of the assailants.

José "Palulu" Enriquez

Gustavo Battle

Julio "Chino" Acuna

Robert Hopkins

Conrado "Lalo" Pons

Effugenia Reyes

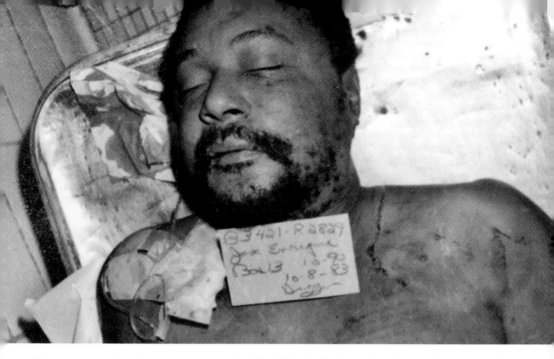

There were nearly a dozen attempts on the life of Palulu Enriquez, in prison and out, over the course of a decade, before the deed was finally done. Palulu was shot while convalescing in a hospital by a gunman disguised as a male nurse.

(© NEW YORK CITY POLICE DEPARTMENT)

Roberto Parsons, former CIA covert operator turned hit man for the Corporation.

(© U.S. ATTORNEY, SOUTHERN DISTRICT OF FLORIDA)

Miami police officer Dave Shanks (far right) with fellow detectives, including Sgt. Jimmy Boyd in white shirt.

BELOW: Shanks receives a special citation from Miami-Dade Police Director Fred Taylor

(© DAVID SHANKS)

Shanks making a street arrest. In 1984, he was temporarily demoted from the Organized Crime Squad to uniform street patrol.

(© DAVID SHANKS)

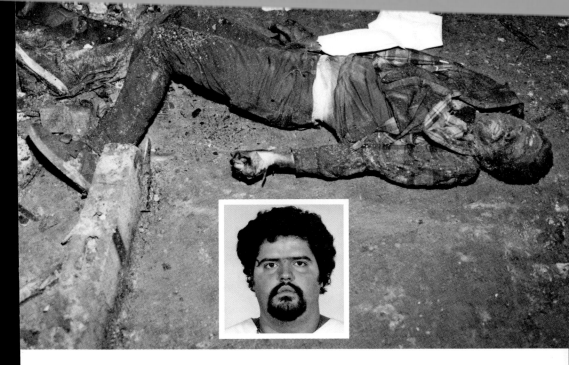

The bolita arson wars of the mid-1980s resulted in many gruesome homicides, including these victims, above and below, who were incinerated to death in a fire on Evergreen Avenue in Brooklyn that was undertaken by Willie Diaz (inset).

(© NEW YORK CITY POLICE DEPARTMENT)

José Miguel Battle being arrested in Miami for attending and betting on cockfights, surrounded by Miami-Dade police officers.

Battle was a financial and political supporter of the Contras, a rebel insurgency attempting to overthrow the leftist Sandinista government in Nicaragua. The Contras trained at camps in South Florida and were supported by anti-Castro Cuban exiles.

By the early-1990s, Battle had achieved considerable notoriety in the media, partly as a result of the Presidential Commission hearings on organized crime and gambling held in New York City. As a result, law enforcement and the press came after Battle, which partly motivated his move to Lima, Peru.

(© *NEW YORK DAILY NEWS*)

El Zapotal, Battle's estate in South Miami, as seen from the air, with the house, pool, and field hands' quarters surrounded by mamey groves.

(© U.S. ATTORNEY, SOUTHERN DISTRICT OF FLORIDA)

Miguelito Battle (left, with mustache), and Abraham "Polaco" Rydz (with glasses), seen here with their wives and the daughter of a business associate celebrating her bat mitzvah.

(COURTESY OF U.S. ATTORNEY, SOUTHERN DISTRICT OF FLORIDA)

bottom two floors of the Hotel Crillón, one of the most venerable hotels in the city of Lima. At left is a luggage tag from the hotel circa the early-1990s.

(© T. J. ENGLISH)

Abraham Rydz with his daughter Susan.

(COURTESY OF SUSAN RYDZ)

Dear Susan:

I am sorry I am ending this way, but I am tired of living like this that you for being my Daddy and giving me all the Pleasures that you did for me and my Wife.

that to may family for all the support they Gave me (have a Healthy and happy live) (Papá)

The suicide note that Rydz left for his daughter.

(COURTESY OF SUSAN RYDZ)

In later years, Battle suffered from poor health until his death in 2007. Here he is in better times, circa 1985, with his pet monkey.

The monument in honor of those who died at the Bay of Pigs invasion, located on Calle Ocho in Miami's Little Havana.

Victor was so pleased to see Laura and the little birthday girl that he hardly noticed a guy with a gas can slip by him toward the back of the store.

Suddenly, there was a loud explosion that knocked Victor off his feet. By the time he stood up, smoke and flames had engulfed the store. Victor found Laura and Janin and tried to lead them out of the store. Somehow the flames had circled in front of them and were blocking the exit. Victor and the two females were separated. His eyes singed in the fire, Victor was able to crawl out of the store, but the girls did not make it.

Little Jannin Toribio died from smoke inhalation. Laura Sirgo lived for twelve days at St. Clare's Hospital, in a coma, until she also succumbed to her injuries as a result of the fire.

ALL IN ALL, IT WAS AN UNPRECEDENTED CAMPAIGN OF TERROR AND DEATH, CULMINATing in this unfathomable tragedy, the killing of an innocent four-year-old child.

Lalo Pons was concerned. This latest atrocity received extensive coverage in the city's tabloid newspapers, the *Daily News* and the *Post,* and on the television news.

By this point, the Corporation's crews had committed more than fifty arsons, and Willie Diaz's team had done at least half of them. The Italians had retaliated and burned down nearly forty of the Corporation's spots. Twenty-five people had died on both sides, forty more had been injured, many seriously, and one man had been wrongfully convicted for the murder of his fiancée. Among themselves, many of the boliteros expressed revulsion. These were family men, with wives and children. The deaths of innocent women and children was sickening. And yet through it all, no one called for it to be stopped. No one demanded that the arsons be immediately discontinued.

The war between the Corporation and the Mafia had become a scourge of biblical proportions, an uncontrollable conflagration of smoke and flames tearing through the House of Bolita.

12

A PRAYER FOR IDALIA

IN SOUTH MIAMI, JOSÉ MIGUEL BATTLE HAD CREATED HIS OWN TROPICAL PARADISE. IT was located far from the fetid streets and crowded housing projects of places like Union City and New York, where the burning embers of the arson wars had yet to be extinguished. At El Zapotal, his hacienda in Redland, Battle could till the soil and feed the roosters, as if the troubles of the big city were a galaxy away. At El Zapotal, Battle was not a gangster; he was a gentleman farmer.

By late 1983, Battle had successfully purchased the five parcels of land that surrounded his home at 17249 SW 192nd Street, four blocks east of Krome Avenue. Altogether, Battle's property, purchased in the early 1980s at a cost of $1.5 million, now covered twenty-two and a half acres. There were two homes on the property, the one where Battle and his wife lived—a modest ranch-style, three-bedroom house with a pool—and a house for the men and women who worked there, located approximately two hundred yards to the rear of the main house.

To the west of both houses, Battle and his farmhands had cultivated the soil, planted seedlings, and in some cases grafted offspring from previously grown mamey trees. It was something that he had dreamed of since his youth in Oriente, where mamey trees grew wild and strong.

The mamey sapote was like Battle himself, a robust organism with a thick central trunk and large limbs. The fruit of the mamey is the size of a cantaloupe, shaped somewhat like a football, varying in length from six to nine inches. Its skin is thick, with a rough russet brown surface. The Cuban version of the fruit is known as mamey colorado, because its pulp is salmon pink to red, soft and smooth in texture. The flavor is sweet, almond-like, with a unique aftertaste.

Among Cuban Americans in South Florida, mamey has a nostalgic popularity, its presence in the kitchen a reminder of the island. As well as being eaten raw, it is used to make milkshakes, ice cream, jams, and jellies.

By the time it was up and running, Battle's ten-acre grove of more than one hundred mamey sapote was a thing of beauty. The fruit was harvested in the spring and sold throughout South Florida under the name of Battle's company, El Zapotal, Inc. El Padrino employed a dozen workers to oversee his grove, some of whom lived on the property. Growing and selling the fruit was more than just an act of nostalgia for Battle. It served as a front for his bolita business, the profits of which could be laundered by way of the blessed fruit of his youth.

Along with his new farming enterprise, Battle had on his property at any given time more than two hundred fighting roosters. He built a *valla,* or arena, for staging cockfights, but it was used mostly for training the birds, not staging actual fights. Cockfights were illegal and usually staged at clandestine locations.

Battle loved his birds and treated them with great care. Each bird had its own individual pen and was tended to by the half dozen trainers that Battle employed.

Cockfighting was deeply rooted in the culture of Latin America. Battle had seen his first cockfight as a child in Oriente, and in Havana, when he was a vice cop, the cockfights were important meeting places for cops and criminals. They were also hugely popular gambling events, where a man could make a name for himself either through the size of his bets or the quality of his cocks.

The day started early at El Zapotal. Imagine the sound of hundreds of roosters crowing and cackling at the crack of dawn. Battle loved it. The only thing he enjoyed more than the sound of the roosters in the morning was their sound at night, when they were fighting in an arena, squawking, strutting, and flapping their wings as they clawed each other with their sharp spurs, and the losing birds sometimes bled out while wads of cash were passed back and forth among the spectators.

Another feature of El Zapotal were the dozens of stray dogs that Battle picked up off the street and brought to his property for safekeeping. Many of his underlings could attest to his affection for the dogs. Carlos "Trio de Trés" Rodriguez, who, like a number of Battle's key associates, made the move to Miami to help facilitate El Padrino's life in Florida, often would be driving with Battle when he would spot a stray dog in the street, looking emaciated and weak. "Stop the car!" Battle would command. He would swing open the door and call for the dog. The animal would be taken back to his property, where it would be bathed and fed and become part of El Padrino's herd of lost canines.

At El Zapotal, Battle had much of what he wanted—his favorite fruit, his roosters, and his dogs. Most of all, he had peace of mind. A primary reason for moving to El Zapotal was that he needed to separate himself from the violence that was being perpetrated in his name far away in New York. This was especially true as the arson wars raged in the boroughs. The Corporation's organizational structure—and geography—insulated El Padrino. Those unfortunate killings in Brooklyn and Manhattan were far away, out of sight and out of mind; they did not reflect his daily life. As the arsons gave rise to a ghastly body count, Battle and the other bolita bankers told themselves that it had nothing to do with them. Ask them who was behind these killings and they would tell you that they didn't know, that it must be some sort of street-level dispute between the various owners and operators of the bolita holes themselves. No one in the Corporation or in La Compañía would take responsibility for the arsons, much less the killings that were a consequence of them.

Even José Miguel, who was not shy about owning up to his violent acts, denied that he had anything to do with the arsons in New York. Especially after the killing of Jannin Toribio, a four-year-old child, no one would admit that the arsons were part of a strategy of payback against the Mafia. Only one man among them had the audacity to underwrite such a scheme. When asked who or what was behind the arson campaign, the boliteros would change the subject, but they knew. It was José Miguel Battle Sr.

In the criminal underworld, violence was often a self-fulfilling prophecy. Sometimes people used violence because they believed it was a solution to a problem. Other times, it was a reflective impulse, the equivalent for some men of thinking with their penis. Anyone who functioned as a criminal boss—and particularly someone who had been doing so for some time—had to know that violence begat violence. Choosing it as a course of action was like lifting the lid off the collective id; you never knew exactly how your enemies were going to respond, but you had to know that it might possibly be with a commensurate level of mayhem.

Battle was impulsive, but he was also a strategist. He chose violence knowing that there would be consequences, knowing that there would be collateral damage. War is hell. Battle knew this because he had lived it. He may have moved far away from the battlefield, which allowed him the illusion of blamelessness, but he never separated himself from the use of violence as a legitimate strategy. He might be innocent today, but he reserved the right to be guilty tomorrow.

The problem with violence was that its demands were often retroactive. You could kill to get ahead in the world, but just as often you might kill as a way of settling old scores. This was something to which El Padrino could attest. Revenge was sometimes impetuous, but sometimes it was merely a necessity, the response to a set of irrefutable facts in which for professional killers and criminals it seemed like the only logical course of action.

Such was the case in March 1984, when El Padrino learned that his old bodyguard and accessory in the murder of Ernestico Torres had been apprehended in Miami. Though there had been an active warrant out for Chino Acuna for eight years, for the last four of those years he had been circulating openly in Miami, albeit under a number of assumed names, including José A. Canales and José A. Chacon. For the last year he had been running a modest bolita office at NE 2nd Avenue and 2nd Street in downtown Miami. It was a seamy area, just east of the Overtown slums, with a large homeless population and street sex workers of the bargain-basement variety.

At 11 A.M. on Wednesday, March 28, Acuna was walking along NE 2nd Avenue when he was surrounded by an armed team of FBI agents from the Apprehension Squad. Acuna surrendered without incident. He was charged on the federal warrant of unlawful flight to avoid prosecution.

With Acuna in custody, the FBI notified the Metro-Dade Police Department (formerly the Dade County Public Safety Department). Sergeant David Rivers of Metro-Dade, knowing Acuna's status as a wanted murderer, arranged to have him transferred to Dade County jail. Sergeant Rivers then contacted the prosecutor's office. Everyone was excited. The Ernestico Torres murder case was going to be reopened. Chino Acuna, who they believed was one of the primary culprits, would be charged with the murder of Ernestico and also the attempted murder of Idalia Fernandez.

The cops and prosecutors may have been excited, but the likely witnesses in the case—Idalia and Charley Hernandez—were not. The trial had been excruciating for all involved. Charley had been separated from his family, with his daughters Kelly and Carol having had their childhoods irreparably altered. Idalia Fernandez, if anything, had an even more difficult time. Her testimony had proven vital in the conviction of Battle. Though she had held back on the crucial detail that Battle was one of the gunmen that day, she had detailed how she and Ernestico had been on the run because Battle, along with others, wanted to kill them. On the witness stand, Idalia made it clear that Chino Acuna was the man who had shot her in the face. If Acuna was going on trial, Idalia would be the star witness.

Furthermore, what if she had decided to tell the *full* truth this time, that Battle was one of the gunmen that day? Battle had done time for conspiracy to commit murder, but now, in light of new evidence, he could possibly be retried for murder.

With the arrest of Chino and the prospect of a new murder trial, the Corporation had a big problem on its hands.

SINCE THE ERNESTICO MURDER TRIAL HAD ENDED IN NOVEMBER 1977, SEVEN YEARS earlier, Idalia Fernandez had been living a transitional existence. For a while, she stayed in Miami with her youngest daughter. Having testified at the trial, she was a marked woman. She lived under an assumed name and had a hard time holding a steady job. Though she had never been officially diagnosed, she suffered from post-traumatic stress from having been brutalized, having her boyfriend murdered, and from the anxiety of the trial, which, as it turned out, continued well after it was over.

She needed to get away from Miami, where these events had taken place. The only people who mattered to her were her mother and her three children. Since the trial, her oldest child had been living with her grandmother in New York City. Idalia needed to be closer to the ones she loved, and so in 1980 she moved back to Manhattan and found an apartment just two blocks away from her grandmother in upper Manhattan.

For Idalia, life had never been easy. Throughout her adulthood, most of her male companions were troubled men, much like Ernesto Torres had been. She had turned to men for protection, for financial support, and for sex. It usually ended badly, though never as badly as with Ernestico.

In New York, Idalia lived off welfare payments from the government, and also she sold weed on the side. Her one-bedroom apartment was in a tenement building at 133 West 90th Street, just a few blocks from Riverside Park, where she used to take her youngest child, Erika, in a stroller when he was still a baby. Erika was now five, and Idalia's boy was eleven.

Idalia learned of the arrest of Chino Acuna through a prosecutor in Miami, who called to tell her there was going to be another trial. The news hit Idalia with a force similar to the pummeling she had taken from Chino. She thought about gathering up her kids and going on the run before she could be served with a subpoena, but she was too tired to do that. Recently, on March 20, she had turned forty years old. In some ways, she was amazed to have made it to that age. She no longer had the energy to outrun the law.

In April, not long after she first learned about Chino Acuna's arrest, Idalia was called on by an unexpected visitor—the former detective Julio Ojeda.

In 1982, at a dramatic trial in Miami, Ojeda had been convicted on racketeering charges and booted from the police department. His relationship with drug kingpin Mario Escandar had ruined his career. Ojeda had appealed his conviction and was out on bail, pending a decision from the Third District Court of Appeal.

At the trial, it did come up that Ojeda had had an "improper" sexual relationship with Idalia, though in light of the multiple sensational charges against the detective, people hardly seemed to notice. Since his conviction, while out on appeal, Ojeda had been working as a private investigator for, of all people, Jack Blumenfeld. Battle's attorney had known Ojeda since the days when Blumenfeld was an A-line prosecutor and Ojeda had just been transferred to the homicide section of the Public Safety Department. Blumenfeld was well aware of Ojeda's legal baggage, so he kept the former detective's name out of the official paperwork, and hence out of the court records.

Idalia was not thrilled to see Ojeda at her door in Manhattan. Since hearing of Acuna'a arrest, she had been living in fear, knowing that she was being dragged back into the realm of José Miguel Battle and everything he represented. Seeing Ojeda was like a visit from the ghost of Christmas past. She had followed his criminal case in the newspapers and knew that he'd been convicted on serious charges. He likely would be going away to prison. Ojeda had the aura of a desperate man.

Ojeda told Idalia that he was there to warn her about the potential dangers ahead if she were to testify.

"You could have told me that over the phone," said Idalia.

Ojeda said that he did not want there to be any record of their having communicated.

After Ojeda departed, Idalia was not reassured. The visit from the convicted ex-detective was unnerving. He was a dirty cop. She didn't know that Ojeda was now working for Battle's attorney. If she had known, it would have made his appearance even more ominous.

A couple of weeks later, Idalia was visited by another cop—Detective Richard Kalafus of the NYPD. She knew Kalafus from Ernestico's murder case. She told him about Ojeda's visit. Kalafus seemed concerned; he told Idalia to contact him immediately if Ojeda tried to contact her again.

In September, Idalia heard that Charley Hernandez had been deposed for the upcoming trial in Miami. The deposition had taken place at the 19th Precinct station house in Manhattan, and was conducted by prosecutors from Miami. Idalia was told that she would likely be deposed the following month.

Idalia wondered whether Battle would let her live long enough to testify against Chino Acuna.

At times, the anxiety was crippling. She tried to live a normal life. Each day, she sent her two children off to school. Then she spent the rest of the day selling and smoking weed.

One day, she was at a supermarket on West 97th Street near her apartment when she saw a man she thought was José Miguel Battle.

How could that be? She followed the man, sneaking between the aisles of the market. Yes, it was Battle. She was certain.

Even though she was terrified, Idalia kept up appearances. She had a boyfriend, a forty-three-year-old Cuban named Armando who worked at an auto garage farther uptown. Armando was not the father of either of her children, but he helped her out financially in exchange for sex.

For Idalia, sex was something of a survival mechanism. Her children were all from different men. She used sex because she could, in the hope that it would improve her situation in life, but her relationships usually made things worse.

In her building, many of her neighbors knew that she was occasionally sleeping with a tenant named Roberto. She had met him through Angie, her babysitter. At first, Roberto was a customer; he bought weed from her. They got high together and had sex a few times, but it was only casual.

There was another guy in the building who was sweet on Idalia. His name was Ramon. He had moved into the building earlier that year after being released from Sing Sing prison and lived in an apartment next door to Idalia (she was in 11D and he was in 11C).

Ramon often saw Idalia in the hallway, and he liked what he saw. He once encountered her in the building stairwell. They talked, and he leaned over to give her a kiss. She did not resist. Ramon took this as a sign, and he began following her. Eventually, Idalia had to tell him, "Look, I'm not interested in having a relationship with you. Stay away from me, stay away from my kids." She told him she was already having an affair with Roberto, whom Ramon knew from having seen him around the building.

This did not go down well with Ramon, who was the jealous type. He cursed at Idalia and threatened her. Idalia was frightened enough to tell a neighbor, Brenda, in 14A, that she believed the guy who lived next to her, Ramon, was going to try to get her and stab her.

"Why?" asked the neighbor.

"Because he wants to have an affair, but I have no interest in that man."

Unbeknownst to Idalia, Ramon began following Roberto around the neighborhood. He did not like that Roberto was sleeping with Idalia, while he had been rejected.

On the night of November 24, Ramon and Roberto had it out on the sidewalk in front of their building. Roberto, who was young and bigger than Ramon, kicked his ass. He gave him two black eyes and a bloody nose.

Ramon was humiliated, and he was irate. On his way back to his room, he stopped outside Idalia's apartment and spread blood from his battered nose all over her front door.

Idalia was not flattered to hear that the two men had had a fight over her. She was more frightened than ever about Ramon.

The day after the fight, an older tenant named Juan, who was part of a tenant patrol group, ran into Idalia in the lobby of the building. She was coming from the laundry room in the basement, carrying a bag of laundry. She asked Juan if he would escort her to her apartment.

"Is there a problem?" Juan asked.

She explained that she had a neighbor, Ramon in apartment 11C, who had been bothering her and banging on her door. Juan walked Idalia to her apartment.

In times of stress, Idalia lit up a joint. She had men all around her—lovers, wannabe lovers, gangsters, cops, ex-cops, and prosecutors. Few of them had her best interests in mind. Some wanted to use her, and some wanted to do her harm.

THE ARSON WARS HAD BEEN GOING WELL, AS FAR AS THE CORPORATION WAS CON-cerned. Yes, there had been some bad publicity, but the feeling was that it would all blow over eventually. Meanwhile, the death of Jannin Toribio brought about a cessation of arsons for the time being.

Willie Diaz stayed busy. He did some goon work for Lalo Pons, roughing up deadbeats who owed money to the Corporation, or doing some vandalism to deliver a message on behalf of the organization. He felt as though his stature was rising, especially after he was introduced one day to Nene Marquez, who was basically the New York boss of the Corporation. "I hear you been doing good work," Nene told Willie.

For a street hood like Willie Diaz, a Puerto Rican, to be recognized by the Cuban Mafia was flattering. He felt as though he was being groomed for something special. That "something" arrived on a day in mid-November when Lalo Pons approached him in Brooklyn and asked, "There's a very important contract I want to ask you about. It involves shooting someone, finishing them off. Do you think you can do it?"

Willie said that he could.

"Good," said Lalo. "El Gordo himself will want to talk to you about this. Meet me here tomorrow. I'll take you to see the guy you'll be working with."

The next day, Pons and Willie drove to a small park on the Upper West Side of Manhattan. Willie met a guy named Angel. Later, Willie would remember, "I thought he was a faggot. He had makeup all over his neck and some on his face. It was weird."

There was a pay phone in the park. Pons dialed a number and spoke to someone, then he handed the phone to Willie. "He wants to talk to you."

Willie took the phone and said, "Hello."

It was El Padrino on the line. "He told me what a great job I had been doing for the organization, first as a bolitero and then for the arsons. He asked me, 'If I need you to do something special for me, you would do it?'"

Willie said yes, he would. He was proud to be doing a hit for the Corporation, but then he was startled when Battle explained that his first job would involve the killing of a woman. "He told me he wanted me to kill a woman going by the name of Maria Castro. He said that she had testified against him years ago and she'd been in hiding using this name. I later found out her real name was Idalia Fernandez."

Battle was very clear about how he wanted the hit done. "I want no mistakes," he said. "Deliver a coup de grâce . . . shoot her directly between the eyes. And you're going to have to get rid of the body. Burn it or bury it, I don't care how you do it. But I don't want the police to find that body, much less be able to identify it . . . Listen to me: we found this woman because she's a marijuanera, a pothead. We have a plan. Lalo will tell you all about it. He'll give you anything you need money, guns, cars."

"Okay," said Willie, "sounds good." He hung up the phone.

Willie, Pons, and Angel discussed the plan. Pons explained, "The reason we're in this park is because the target lives right over there."

He pointed out Idalia's building, which was across West 90th Street and half a block away. He pulled out a manila envelope and produced some pictures. One of them was an old Polaroid photo of "Maria Castro" that appeared to be a police mug shot. Then Pons showed Willie some more recent photos that were of the woman entering and exiting her apartment building.

Pons told Willie, "You're gonna pose as a weed dealer, to gain her confidence. You'll meet her here in this park. She comes here with her kids almost every day. Be friendly, offer her a hit off your joint. Tell her there's plenty more where that came from. You just bought a pound of Colombian Gold. You wanna give her a free sample, but you don't want to pull it out in a public place. Ask her if she lives in the neighborhood. What you want to do is drop it by her place."

Willie listened carefully. He was picturing the hit in his mind.

Angel spoke up, with self-assurance, like someone who had done this kind of thing before. "Once you get to her apartment, there's two ways we can handle this. You can kill her yourself, and I'll come in behind you to help get rid of the body. Or you can get her to open the door, let you in, then I'll burst in and kill her. Either way."

Pons interrupted, saying to Willie, "You do the shooting yourself and you get the larger share. That's how it goes."

Willie said, "Let me think about it."

They went to a nearby coffee shop to have something to eat. As they were sitting there talking, it came out that Angel supposedly knew the target from a time when she lived down in Miami.

"Oh, so she knows you from Miami?" asked Willie.

"Yeah, she knows me," said Angel.

Willie thought about it and said, "Well, in that case, you do the shooting. I'll take the smaller share."

Two days later, Willie met with Pons to get the money to buy the pound of weed to trick Idalia. Again, Pons put Willie on the phone with the boss down in Miami. As Willie remembered later, "[Battle] told me that he changed his mind . . . that he wanted the woman's body left in the apartment afterwards as a message to the feds."

After Willie and Battle were off the phone, Pons gave Willie some money for the weed. "I'll have a car for you tomorrow. And clean guns.

Listen to me: it's important that you don't use any gun I may have given you before. And the one I give you tomorrow, if you use it for any reason, bring it back here to me." Pons explained that guns, if used, would have to be destroyed. He told Willie that the Corporation had their own "armorers" whose job it was to line up guns—.45s, .38s, and 9mm automatics. It was also their job to make the murder weapons disappear by melting them down after they were used.

The next day, the getaway car and guns never arrived. Willie checked with Pons, who told him, "Stand by. I'll get you those items when the time is right." Then another day went by, and then another.

Willie was ready to take part in the hit. At first he had misgivings about being involved in the killing of a female, which was frowned upon in some circles, like on the streets or in prison. But in the interest of getting ahead in life, he was willing to do it. He would be acting on direct orders from the boss, El Gordo, the man in Miami. What could be more prestigious than that?

ON THE AFTERNOON OF NOVEMBER 30, IDALIA WAS HOME WITH A SLIGHT HEADACHE. After getting the kids off to school that morning, she had gone back to bed and slept in late. Rising around noon, she did what she often did after rolling out of bed: she lit up a joint.

Idalia needed to do some shopping, but she was hesitant to leave her apartment alone. Ever since she had seen the man she thought was José Miguel Battle in her neighborhood, she was afraid to go out. Also, there was Ramon next door, who had splattered her door with blood. You could say she was paranoid—but with good reason. If someone knocked at her door, she looked through the peephole to make sure it was someone she knew.

That morning there was a knock at Idalia's door. A neighbor down the hall from her would later say that she saw two men, well dressed in suits and ties, at the door of apartment 11D.

Idalia answered the door and let the two men into her apartment. It was unlikely that she would have done that if she did not know them. She knew them well enough that she let them in and turned her back on them. She did not notice that they were wearing gloves.

With her back to the two men, Idalia heard a click. She turned around to see one of the men fiddling with the chamber of a gun. The click had been the sound of the man pulling the trigger, but the weapon—a .22-caliber automatic with a silencer attached—had jammed. This required that the shooter eject the bad round and manually feed a new round into the chamber.

Idalia ran frantically for the kitchen, toward the phone.

The shooter raised his gun and fired two quick shots, hitting Idalia in the back of the neck and the back of the head. As she fell, he fired two more times, hitting her on the right side of the head and on top of the head.

Idalia slumped to the floor, her blood and brain matter smearing the wall.

The gunman reracked his gun, stepped forward, and pressed the cold barrel of the silencer to Idalia's face. He pulled the trigger, splattering more flesh and bone matter.

There were five shots in all to Idalia's neck, head, and face, with immediate traumatic injury to the brain and spinal cord. She was likely dead before the two hit men quietly exited the building.

That afternoon, Idalia's children, Erika and Freddy, arrived home from school around 3:30 P.M. Mommy had told them that she would be there when they got home. When they arrived at the apartment, they thought it was strange that the door was slightly ajar. The two kids opened the door and entered the apartment. Immediately they saw their mother's body lying on the floor, faceup. At first they thought she might be playing some kind of joke. But as they approached, they saw the blood.

The two children stood over their mother's bullet-riddled body. Blood was flowing from her mouth.

The kids screamed and ran out of the apartment. They knew better than to bang on the door of 11C; that's where the man who had been hassling their mother lived. They ran to door on the other side, 11B, and banged with all their might. "Please, help us! There's something wrong with Mommy! Help!"

One of the first detectives to receive a call that day was Kalafus. His heart sank. Since the arrest of Chino Acuna earlier that year, he had been the point man in touch with Idalia on a regular basis. After she had seen someone she thought was José Miguel Battle in her neighborhood, Kalafus had suggested she have a round-the-clock police guard stationed at her apartment. She had not wanted that, feeling it would only terrify her children. She wanted to hold on to the illusion that she was living a normal life. Kalafus understood that, but he realized now that, at the very least, they should have stationed a police car on guard duty outside the building, whether Idalia wanted it or not.

In the days following the murder, Kalafus showed up at the building in his usual attire of cowboy hat and leather boots, looking like Mc-Cloud. He interviewed five or six of Idalia's neighbors, and others in the building. He heard about the fight over Idalia that Ramon and Roberto had just six days before the murder, how Ramon had smeared blood on Idalia's door. In other circumstances, Ramon might have been suspect number one in Idalia's murder, but Kalafus knew better. One neighbor he interviewed told the detective that he had seen two men knock on Idalia's apartment door. They were well dressed and did not appear to be tenants in the building. When Kalafus began showing to the neighbor photos of possible suspects from his Cuban gangster file, the person became nervous and uncooperative. "I don't want to end up like Idalia," said the neighbor.

The next day, Kalafus received a call from Charley Hernandez. "I heard a rumor that Idalia was murdered. Is that true?"

"It is," admitted the detective.

"That's it. I'm out. There's no way I will testify."

"Now, Charley, you're still under subpoena."

"I've got a family to protect. Do you hear me? I don't want to be the next one to have my brains blown out. Goodbye."

The next day, Kalafus tried to call Charley, but his phone had been disconnected. "He's disappeared," said Kalafus to the prosecutor in Miami.

In truth, Charley had only moved his family eighty-five miles south to Toms River, New Jersey, but if the cops and prosecutors wanted to believe that he had gone into hiding far away in California, or Canada, or Mexico, that was fine with him.

A FEW DAYS AFTER THE MURDER OF IDALIA, WILLIE DIAZ RECEIVED A PHONE CALL FROM Lalo Pons. He was told, "Never mind about that hit. It's been taken care of." Lalo never came right out and named Angel as the killer, but he did say, "That guy you met killed her."

Sensing Willie's disappointment at losing out on a big score, Lalo added, "Don't worry. We'll find another good-paying job for you in the future."

Willie nursed his disappointment with cocaine and hookers. It was true that he had missed out on a nice payday, but now he was in tight with Pons and the Godfather himself. He had no doubt there would be other opportunities to rise up in the organization.

WITH THEIR MAIN WITNESS DEAD AND CHARLEY HERNANDEZ IN HIDING, AUTHORITIES in Florida had no case against Chino Acuna. The prosecutor, Michael Cornely, told a District Court judge in Miami that he could not produce Idalia Fernandez for deposition because she was deceased. He then told the judge something oddly discordant with the facts: "There is no evidence the murder of Fernandez was an attempt to eliminate a witness in this case."

The murder of Idalia sent ripples of fear throughout the Latin underworld in the United States. The killing was reported in the Spanish-language press, and it even made headlines in the *New York Times* and the *Miami Herald* ("Only Witness to '76 Murder Slain in New York"). As with the murder of Palulu, given the number of years that had passed, it was a revenge killing of epic proportions. This killing had the added purpose of obliterating the government's case against Chino Acuna. Coupled with the arson killings of the previous eighteen months, the concept of a violent Latin American criminal underworld was beginning to take shape in the public consciousness.

Cops and federal agents were increasingly aware that some form of Cuban-centric organized crime was under way in the United States, but to most non-Latino citizens it was a foreign concept. Ever since the *Godfather* movies captured the public imagination a decade earlier, the only version of organized crime that registered for most people was Italian. This had consequences for more than just popular culture.

Within law enforcement, at both local and federal levels, it was difficult if not impossible for agents to generate interest or enthusiasm among their superiors for cases involving any crime groups other than the Mafia. Arrests and indictments of Mafia figures made headlines and advanced careers; the others did not.

The lethal arsons at known gambling spots throughout New York, and the killing of a prospective witness in a murder trial, signaled the beginnings of a shift. Cops and investigators were hearing more and more about the Corporation. Those in the know were aware that Cuban American gangsters had a controlling interest in bolita, but what they were hearing now was that the organizational structure, and the profits, were vaster than anything they had imagined.

Throughout 1984 and into 1985, law enforcement intelligence about the Corporation began to work its way upstream from the streets to the hallowed halls of the federal government.

The President's Commission on Organized Crime was an investigative body created on July 28, 1983, when President Ronald Reagan signed Executive Order 12435. The purpose of the commission was "to make a full national and regional analysis of organized crime; define the nature of traditional organized crime as well as emerging organized crime groups, the sources and amounts of organized crime's income; develop in-depth information on the participants in organized crime networks; and evaluate federal laws pertinent to the effort to combat organized crime."

Though the commission would not have the power to arrest or indict people (it was not a law enforcement entity), it did have the power to issue federal subpoenas, compelling witnesses to testify under rule of law.

The commission was governed by a panel of nineteen dignitaries and crime experts appointed by President Reagan. In November 1983, it began hearing public testimony on the changing nature of organized crime, and by October 1984 an interim report was issued, with the title *The Cash Connection: Organized Crime, Financial Institutions, and Money Laundering.*

By early 1985, the commission had turned its attention to the subject of illegal gambling as a long-standing, persistent criminal racket. The intention was to focus on the activities of the Mafia, but then the arsons in New York began to happen, and the idea to focus specifically on the illegal lottery, and the Cubans, gained critical mass.

The hearings were held at Federal Hall in lower Manhattan, in the financial district and near federal and state courthouse buildings. The room was laid out for maximum dramatic effect, with the twenty commissioners seated as a panel, nameplates in front of each commissioner. Behind the panel were the flag of the United States and the insignia of the president. Witnesses giving testimony would sit at a table facing the panel. The rest of the room was set up for spectators, and there was a large area for the media.

The chairman of the commission was Irving R. Kaufman, circuit judge for the U.S. Court of Appeals for the Second Circuit, and a former judge on the U.S. District Court for the Southern District of New York. In a prologue to the first day of testimony, on June 24, Judge Kaufman noted, "Gambling is as old as our nation's history, and the incestuous relationship between illegal activities and gambling has existed for almost as long. Periodically every form of commercial gambling has been infected by organized crime groups . . . Horse racing, casino operations, professional sports, state-run lotteries—legal gambling of all kinds has been infiltrated in some form, at some time or other, by organized crime. Not only the traditional organized crime groups but also numerous emerging groups participate in the lucrative illegal gambling market."

One of the first witnesses to testify was a commission investigator named Anthony Lombardi, a former agent of the Internal Revenue Service. Lombardi was on hand to talk specifically about the Corporation, which would emerge as the most newsworthy angle at the hearings.

Lombardi started by saying, "Mr. Chairman, commissioners, members of the commission, I am about to present a profile of José Miguel Battle Sr. A comprehensive review of the files of various federal, international, state, and local law enforcement agencies, and independent investigation by the staff of the commission, clearly reveals the existence of a tightly knit, well-financed, armed, and powerful group of Cuban racketeers known as the Corporation. These individuals are sometimes CIA trained and anti-Castro sympathizers that had taken part in the Bay of Pigs invasion . . . The evidence you are about to hear represents the first effort to develop a national picture of the Cuban organized crime group known as the Corporation."

To give the commissioners an idea of the scope of what he was talking about, Lombardi estimated that the illegal lottery profits of the organization, based on seized records, reflected a weekly gross of over $2 million. "From this information," said Lombardi, "we extrapolate that the Corporation earns a minimum annual net profit of $45 million from New York City gambling operations alone. This net profit has been estimated as high as $100 million."

Lombardi's presentation took close to an hour. It was startling in its details. The investigator gave an overview of the life of José Miguel Battle Sr. He presented an organizational chart that named all the key players. Along with Battle Sr. were Abraham Rydz, Battle Jr., Nene Marquez, Lalo Pons, and others. Lombardi described recent events that had been in the newspapers, such as the arson deaths and the murder of Idalia, but he also broke new ground by detailing methods of the Corporation that were not commonly known. One of those revelations had to do with the Corporation's use of the Puerto Rican lottery to launder criminal proceeds.

Through an IRS investigation known as Operation Greenback, the feds had uncovered the scheme. Working with corrupt banking officials in Puerto Rico, the Corporation would determine who had won the Puerto Rican lottery. The organization would then purchase the winning ticket from that person who won for a price considerably more than he or she was to receive. If a bettor had a winning ticket for, say, a prize of $125,000, the Corporation would contact that person and offer to buy the ticket for $150,000. Explained Lombardi, "The winner is told that if he travels to Puerto Rico to collect the $125,000, then reports will have to be made to the IRS and the individual will only get a small portion of the winning ticket. The winners always take the $150,000 offer. The Corporation then takes the ticket to Puerto Rico, cashes the ticket, and pays the IRS the full amount of tax due. Our source advised that this is the way the Corporation launders its money. The Corporation has so much money that its members are willing to pay twice as much in illegal money in order to obtain legitimate money."

In an effort to illustrate how expendable large sums of cash were to the Corporation, Lombardi introduced the customs agent who had encountered Abraham Rydz and Battle Jr. at Kennedy Airport. The agent described how Rydz and Battle Jr. were transporting nearly half a million dollars in cash, wrapped up as Christmas gifts. The two travelers claimed the money was not theirs, and furthermore, though they claimed to have been delivering that money to a person in Miami, they had no idea who the man was they were delivering it to. Of special interest was Battle Jr.'s effort to destroy a piece of paper he had been carrying. The commission produced that paper, which had been salvaged by the customs agent and pieced back together. Investigator Lombardi explained that this paper, which he described as a weekly "tally sheet" for the Corporation's New York numbers operation, would be explained in detail by an upcoming witness.

That witness was of particular interest; in fact, this unnamed witness, touted as a high-ranking member of the Corporation, was the main reason the hearing room was filled with media and with spectators. Among those spectators was none other than Battle himself.

A month earlier, while tending to his mamey grove in Miami, Battle had been served with a federal subpoena to appear before the commission. He immediately contacted his lawyers, Raymond Brown and Jack Blumenfeld. Legally speaking, it was a no-brainer: Battle would refuse to testify, citing his Fifth Amendment privilege on the grounds that any testimony he gave would be self-incriminating. For that reason, the commission decided not to call Battle. Instead, he came as a spectator, tanned, well dressed in a dark blue suit, and sat in the spectators' gallery.

He was there to see for himself the witness to whom Lombardi had referred. The identity of this witness was a secret, and it had been learned that the person's face would not be shown. Already to those in the Corporation, the witness was being referred to as "El Enmascarado," the Masked One.

Battle wanted to hear for himself what this turncoat had to say, and also he would thumb his nose at this presidential commission that, he believed, could quote all the numbers and statistics they wanted about illegal lottery profits in New York, but couldn't do a damn thing about putting him in prison and keeping him there.

THE PERSON RESPONSIBLE FOR FINDING EL ENMASCARADO AND DELIVERING HIM TO the commission was Detective Kalafus. For nearly a decade, Kalafus had been working Cuban organized crime cases in the New York area, and he had developed some impressive sources. Some he had coerced into cooperation when they were facing criminal charges; others were people

THE PERSON RESPONSIBLE FOR FINDING EL ENMASCARADO AND DELIVERING HIM TO the commission was Detective Kalafus. For nearly a decade, Kalafus had been working Cuban organized crime cases in the New York area, and he had developed some impressive sources. Some he had coerced into cooperation when they were facing criminal charges; others were people who had run afoul of the Corporation and came to him. In the case of El Enmascarado, Kalafus didn't have to do much. The man reached out on his own, motivated by a fear of El Padrino.

Among the small group of super-bankers who kept the Corporation afloat, the man met regularly with Battle and the other bankers. He believed that he had their trust and they had his. They didn't prick their fingers to extract blood and pledge allegiance to the group, as the Mafia did, but without a doubt, loyalty to the organization was believed to be the highest value.

One evening about six weeks before the commission hearings, the man was kidnapped off the street by three young hoodlums. At gunpoint, he was taken to an abandoned building. He was tied and bound to a chair and then doused with a can of gasoline. The man's eyes felt as if they were on fire, and the stench of the gasoline made him feel as if he was going to vomit. One of the thugs stood over him with a lighter and said, "We know you are a snitch. We know you talked to the cops. Tell us the truth or you will be set on fire."

At that point, the man had never snitched, so it was easy for him to proclaim, "That's a lie. I never snitched in my life."

"El Gordo knows you are the snitch. If you confess, you can save your life. Tell us the truth."

The man was terrified, but he knew that if he "admitted" he was a snitch, he would be killed immediately. "It's not true," he said. "Whoever told you I'm a snitch, that's the man you want."

It went back and forth for half an hour, with the kidnappers threatening to light the man on fire, and him holding firm that they had the wrong man.

Eventually, out of the shadows walked Battle himself. He told his men to untie the man. To the man, he said, "*Mira* (look), I'm sorry. But this had to be done. I'm afraid we have a rat amongst us. I had to be sure that it wasn't you."

The man left that abandoned warehouse that night still shaking from the experience. If Battle didn't trust him now, he would always be under suspicion. He was happy to be alive, but the sense of relief was tempered by the realization that he would never be safe as a banker with the Corporation.

The man found a pay phone and called Detective Kalafus, whom he had never met, but who everyone knew was the cop covering the Cuban gangster beat. "Let's meet," the man said. He and the detective met at a secret location. The man said, "I am a marked man. I want to get out of the Corporation. But it's not that simple. If I leave, given what I know, I will be hunted down and killed. If you can give me a new identity, relocate me somewhere, I will tell you all I know about the organization."

"Well," said Kalafus, "how much do you know?"

"I know a lot. Since 1980, I've been in on every meeting, part of every major decision. I can tell you who the players are—El Gordo, Battle Jr., El Polaco, Nene Marquez, their hired assassin, Lalo Pons. I know everybody."

Kalafus thought about what the man was offering. It took him a while to figure out how best to utilize this golden opportunity that had fallen into his lap. The man had not been directly involved in murders. He alone was not enough to make a racketeering case against Battle, but what he knew and was willing to divulge was unprecedented. Kalafus was still mulling it over when he learned about the upcoming presidential commission hearings. He met with investigators from the commission and was told, "Are you kidding? Having this guy as a witness would be tremendous."

Kalafus said, "I don't know if he'll do it. The guy is living in fear. We have to be able to guarantee that his identity will not be divulged."

The investigators explained that they would have a hood over his head while he was testifying. They would use an interpreter, so that when a question was posed by one of the commissioners, the man would whisper the answer to the interpreter, who would answer for him. "No one will see his face or hear his voice," promised the investigator.

It took Kalafus a while to convince the man to testify. *A presidential commission? Public hearings covered by the news media? Are you trying to get me killed?* Kalafus explained that here it was, his chance to escape the Corporation. After his testimony, he would be relocated—not immediately, because they did not want Battle to know that he was the witness. But eventually they would lay the groundwork so that he could make a complete break from the Corporation without El Padrino ever knowing

get me killed? Kalafus explained that here it was, his chance to escape the Corporation. After his testimony, he would be relocated—not immediately, because they did not want Battle to know that he was the witness. But eventually they would lay the groundwork so that he could make a complete break from the Corporation without El Padrino ever knowing that he was El Enmascarado.

On the day of the hearings, the witness was brought through a basement garage into Federal Hall. Not only was he fitted with a black hood, but he was dressed in a loose-fitting black gown that looked like a cross between a judge's robe and a prison jumpsuit.

The room was packed with spectators and media personnel as the witness was led into the room and seated at the witness table. A female, Spanish-speaking interpreter sat down next to him.

After a few preliminary questions to establish the witness's bona fides as a member of the Corporation, the questioner asked, "Does the Corporation have a leader?"

"Yes," said the witness.

"What is his name?"

"José Miguel Battle."

"Is he also known by the name Padrino?"

"Godfather. Yes."

It was probably to the witness's advantage that he did not know Battle was in the room that day watching from the spectators' gallery. Having to testify was unnerving enough, much less knowing that the man you had just fingered for the first time ever in a public forum as the boss of the Cuban Mafia was in the room, staring you down.

Battle was shocked by what he saw and heard. Not only did the witness identify by name the primary bankers in the organization, but there were organizational charts, with photos of Battle Sr., Battle Jr., Abraham Rydz, and others displayed in the room for all to see. This was, to put it mildly, a potential disaster for the Corporation. For a criminal conspiracy that had been functioning mostly in the shadows, benefiting greatly from the culture and law enforcement's singular obsession with the Italian Mafia, they were now being "outed" in a big way.

Battle was apoplectic, but he knew there were news cameras on him that day. He had to appear as if he had nothing to hide. Afterward, when a photographer from the *Daily News* asked to take his picture, Battle did not object. On the surface, he was placid, but anyone who knew him would have known that below the surface was a smoldering volcano.

Battle had called for an emergency meeting of the super-bankers, to take place immediately following the testimony of the commission's star witness. The meeting was to take place at their old standby, the Colonial restaurant on St. Nicholas Avenue in Washington Heights.

As a reigning banker in the Corporation, the Hooded Witness, as he was now referred to by the media, was expected to be an attendee at the meeting called by Battle. After his testimony, Hoodie, as Kalafus and the investigators preferred to call him, was rushed to the basement garage. Inside a van, he removed his hood and black robe. He was driven to a location where he had parked his own car, in which he drove to the Colonial restaurant. He was seated inside the restaurant with a couple of the other bankers before Battle had even arrived.

When he did arrive, Battle was spilling over with rage. "I knew it," he said. "I knew we had a rat in our midst. We must determine who is this son of a bitch. We must find him and have him killed, otherwise, who are we? Men, or weaklings?"

Battle proposed that a contract of $50,000 be extended to anyone who could find and kill the Hooded Witness. It was agreed that they would all pay an equal share of $10,000 to bankroll the contract.

Hoodie, as one of the boliteros, voted with the others to kick in his share. He contributed ten grand to what was essentially his own death warrant.

IT DIDN'T TAKE LONG FOR THE CONSEQUENCES OF THE COMMISSION HEARINGS TO BE felt. First, there was a flurry of media attention. The *New York Times* ran an article that focused on the Corporation's gambling empire, quoting the Hooded Witness, who claimed that the organization had twenty-five hundred people working at seven hundred bolita sites. The most lavish coverage of the hearings was in the *Miami Herald*. "Crime Boss Rules with a Deadly Fist" was the above-the-fold headline of a front-page story that focused almost exclusively on Battle. Though José Miguel declined to comment for the article, the reporters asked lawyer Jack Blumenfeld if his client had a response. "Bullshit, that's his response," Blumenfeld was quoted as saying. "If he's guilty of all these things, then arrest him . . . He's being accused by dead men and confidential sources . . . It's hard to fight shadows." Blumenfeld added, "He's a Cuban patriot."

The media reporting was so detrimental that Battle did something he had never done before: he devised a public relations counterstrategy. He allowed two reporters from the *Miami News,* a rival of the *Herald,* into his home. "Everything the commission said isn't true," he told the reporters. "None of it is true." Battle gave the reporters a tour of El Zapotal. He even let them look in his refrigerator. "This is the refrigerator of a millionaire? I eat yogurt." The newspaper provided Battle with the press he desired, a portrait of a contented retiree far removed from the hustle and bustle of life in New York and New Jersey. The article was even accompanied by a photo of Battle playing with his pet monkey.

Back in New York, the fallout from the hearings was worse than just bad press. In September, Lalo Pons and ten others were arrested and charged with arson and multiple counts of murder. The prosecutor's star witness would be Willie Diaz, who, after being investigated by cops and threatened with arrest, quickly agreed to become a cooperating witness. Throughout the summer, shortly after the federal commission hearings concluded, Willie had worn a wire and helped gather evidence against Lalo.

At a press conference to announce the indictment, Benjamin Ward, the city's first black police commissioner, noted that all of these men were members of the Corporation, a group headed by Battle.

For years, El Padrino and his gambling syndicate had mostly operated with little attention from the mainstream press and not much more from law enforcement. Now that had changed.

Among those who saw the writing on the wall was Isleño Dávila, whose name had also been highlighted at the commission hearings. In August, a unit of the NYPD's Public Morals division hit dozens of bolita holes belonging to La Compañía. Isleño came to New York to figure out what was happening. He was picked up for questioning by two detectives and driven around Harlem. They showed him where many of his spots had been padlocked and put out of business. "It's over," the detectives told him.

First the arsons, then the commission hearing had brought an unprecedented level of unwanted attention for the boliteros. Now, with the arrest and subsequent trial of Lalo Pons, the inner workings of the bolita empire would be further exposed.

Isleño returned to his home in Fort Lauderdale and immediately began a process of moving his millions out of the country. He made no public announcement that he was out of the bolita business, but those who knew him well—his family, friends, and associates—could see what was happening. Isleño was finished with bolita. Within the year, he had quietly moved out of the United States to Spain and eventually on to Panama. He was rarely seen again in New York, New Jersey, or South Florida, the locations where he had once held sway as a legendary bolita boss.

COCKFIGHTER

MIGUELITO BATTLE HAD STOPPED TALKING WITH HIS FATHER. THE REASONS FOR THIS were cumulative—a lifetime of emotional baggage and strained relations—but there had been a last straw. Sometime in early 1985, Maria Josefa Battle—Miguelito's mother and José Miguel's long-suffering wife—came home to El Zapotal one day to find her husband in bed with two young women. It was a final insult after years of José Miguel's philandering. Maria Battle moved out of El Zapotal to a home at 350 Island Drive in Key Biscayne near her son. There was no talk of divorce, but from then on, she and her husband lived separate lives. She never again set foot on her husband's estate, with the mamay trees and crowing roosters and women so young and nubile they could have been José Miguel's granddaughters.

José Miguel's treatment of Maria had been a sore spot with Miguelito for some time. Years before, he had been brought along by his father to a jewelry store in Manhattan to purchase a diamond ring for someone special. Miguelito assumed the ring was for his mother, but was disgusted to learn that José Miguel was buying it for his mistress. Which raised the question: what kind of man brings his son along to purchase an expensive gift for his mistress? To Miguelito, it was a personal insult; his father was rubbing it in his face that he was cheating on his mother. In a sense, Miguelito never forgave José Miguel for this transgression. He talked about it often with Abraham Rydz, the man who became his surrogate father.

And yet the two men, Battle Sr. and Jr., were still financially entangled in ways that made it impossible for them to simply ignore one another. Junior and Rydz had created a business empire that was at its core dependent on the stature and reputation of El Padrino. It was true that the Corporation was now a multitentacled operation, and that the bolita business in New York more or less ran itself. But contrary to the belief of Miguelito and Rydz that Union Financial Research and the other corporate subsidiaries comprised a self-sustaining business, in the mind of El Padrino, without his reputation—his legend—they were nothing.

In the Cuban American underworld, Battle was still the man. This could be either a good or a bad thing, depending on the motives of those who were banking on the boss's stature. Bosses were feared, but they also became targets. And sometimes their sons became targets by association.

In 1985, not long after the Presidential Crime Commission wrapped up its hearings in New York and José Miguel Battle returned to Miami, his son was kidnapped. This was not an event that would make the newspapers or television news. The entire event was kept quiet by all involved, including the cops and federal agents who responded to the call.

Oscar Vigoa was at the time a sergeant in the Metro-Dade Police Department working a general investigations unit in the Midwest District. One afternoon, his unit received a call of a kidnapping and was told to report to a home at an address on SW 7th Street just off SW 87th Avenue.

Sergeant Vigoa had been on the job for seven years. In that time, Miami had become an international crime center, with cocaine flowing into the city from major Latin American hubs such as Medellín and Cali, and cash flowing out of the city to places like Panama City and offshore banks in the Caribbean. Vigoa was accustomed to arriving at crime scenes where there were layers of law enforcement, from local police squads to federal agencies—DEA, FBI, and ATF, all the way up to CIA. But what the sergeant encountered when he arrived at the house on SW 7th Street was surprising even to him.

"It was a beautiful home," remembered Vigoa. "I thought, 'Whoa, somebody big lives here.' Right away, we were told, the victim is José Miguel Battle Jr. He'd been kidnapped by somebody, we didn't know who. I'd heard the name of Battle Sr., but at the time I didn't know much. Then the organized crime guys showed up. And then the feds. We were told, 'Look, we got this. But we want you guys to stay. Take your unit and guard the perimeter. This guy Battle is a major player.'"

For the next three days, Vigoa and his unit of five detectives nearly lived at what they learned was the home of Battle Jr. Though Junior had purchased a lot and was having a home built in Key Biscayne, next to Abraham Rydz, he was still living at the home on SW 7th Street. His wife and two kids were on the premises, and they were terrified that their father was in serious trouble. A couple times during those three days, Battle Sr. showed up and took control of the situation.

"He seemed to be very calm," said Vigoa. "The others, Battle Jr.'s family, were totally frightened, but El Gordo had the typical square face, cool, collected, like everything was under control."

Over time, Vigoa learned from the organized crime detectives what was going on. It was believed that Battle Jr. had been kidnapped by some "major players," quite possibly the team of Augusto "Willy" Falcon and Salvador "Sal" Magluta, the biggest cocaine traffickers in Miami. The rumor was that Battle had been getting involved in cocaine deals and stepped on some toes. Junior had been snatched off the street and was being held for ransom, though it was believed the act was more a warning to Battle Sr. than an actual moneymaking proposition.

The investigators were worried. Under their breath, they speculated that Junior was already dead, or that he would be "cut up" or marked in some way before being turned over to his family.

All of this made sense to Sergeant Vigoa, who was tuned into the local crime scene in Miami. An old-school gangster like Battle had possibly overestimated his standing among the new-school narcotraffickers. Vigoa could see a kidnapping take place for those exact reasons. But what seemed strange was that at Junior's house, while all the cops and agents and family members took part in some sort of ongoing negotiation for the release of Miguelito, leading the investigation were a handful of mysterious "feds" in suits and ties. Sergeant Vigoa couldn't tell who they were. They weren't FBI or DEA or any of the other federal agencies that he knew well. They may have been CIA or some other intelligence agency.

Also, it seemed odd that the entire negotiation was being run out of the victim's house. The agents and cops never left that location, which to Vigoa created an air of secrecy that made the investigation seem unusual, to say the least.

"On the third day," he remembered, "this guy walks in the door. The family members jump up and start hugging him. It's Battle Jr. He's been released."

Battle Sr. showed up at the scene and shook the hands of the various federal agents who had been there for days. He told them they could go.

The entire matter was calmly resolved. Even so, for Vigoa, suspicions lingered that there was something not right about the entire incident. "Was a ransom paid? I don't know. All I know is that our department received no paperwork from any federal agency, though a few were involved. It was as if this event never took place. The entire thing was swept under the rug."

In the months that followed, Battle's name kept popping up in various investigations that Vigoa was involved in. There was the judicial corruption case in which Alfonso Sepe, the judge who had ruled in Battle's favor back in 1978, was removed from the bench. There were two significant narcotics cases. There was a gun smuggling case out of Miami International Airport that involved local Cuban exiles and the Contras, anticommunist rebels who were fighting against a leftist government in Nicaragua. Battle's name was linked to all of these cases, but he was never charged with anything.

THE PUBLIC HEARINGS HELD BY THE PRESIDENT'S COMMISSION ON ORGANIZED CRIME showed a willingness on the part of law enforcement to shine a light on bolita. A few months later, in January 1987, Lalo Pons and his fellow arsonists were convicted at trial and sentenced to long prison terms. The primary witness against Pons was Willie Diaz. It was the most significant prosecution to date of Corporation operatives. At the same time, La Compañía, with Isleño Dávila having left the country, went into remission. These developments were significant, but they did not bring an end to bolita in New York. People still wanted to bet the number, and the idea of doing so with a well-established organization was still appealing. In that sense, the commission hearings and prosecutions did little to tarnish the reputation of the Corporation.

The broader context that gave rise to the Corporation was hardly touched upon during the hearings. There were references to Battle's history as a member of the 2506 Brigade, and how the Corporation had initially been comprised of numerous veterans from the Bay of Pigs invasion. But the commission was mandated to explore and expose criminal activity, not political context. This context would receive increased scrutiny during an entirely different series of hearings held in the nation's capital.

The Iran-Contra hearings, convened by order of the House Select Committee to Investigate Covert Arms Transactions with Iran and the Senate Select Committee on Secret Military Assistance to Iran and the Nicaraguan Opposition, began in May 1987. The scandal that led to the hearings had been unfolding like a toxic spill for at least three years. For anti-Castro Cubans in the United States, support for the Contras, a group of anticommunist rebel fighters in Nicaragua, was an initiative rooted in the same smoldering cauldron of revenge politics that had served as an impetus—and justification—for the Corporation.

With the reelection of Ronald Reagan to a second term, the anti-Castro movement had been reinvigorated. Though underground terror squads like Alpha 66 and Omega 7 had been put out of business, and organized attempts to assassinate Fidel were now sporadic affairs, efforts to counter the spread of Castroism continued unabated. Covert operators, international mercenaries, spooks, and other soldiers of fortune had, in an effort to circumvent official government policies, became players in a secret history. In the 1980s, the new frontier was Central and South America.

The Sandinista National Liberation Front had shocked the world in 1979 when they overthrew Anastasio Somoza Debayle, whose family had ruled Nicaragua since 1936. The Somozas were products of American culture. Anastasio had been educated at St. Leo College Prep in Florida and attended the La Salle Military Academy on Long Island. He was also a graduate of West Point. Steeped in U.S. military philosophy, Somoza was a proxy of the right wing. The Sandinistas, on the other hand, were a leftist political movement that openly aligned themselves with Fidel Castro, whom they viewed as their spiritual godfather. The Reagan administration saw the Sandinista government as a Marxist-Leninist threat in the Western Hemisphere.

Nicaragua had always held a special place in the heart of Cuban militants. It was from the coast of Nicaragua, at Puerto Cabeza, that the Bay of Pigs invasion had been launched. When Battle and his fellow brigadistas were lined up and ready to board ships that would take them to Cuba, Anastasio Somoza's older brother, Luis, who was president at the time, had made a personal appearance. Wearing a white suit, his face powdered with a layer of white theatrical makeup, he gave his blessing to the departing brigade and told the men, "Bring me a couple hairs from Castro's beard."

Somoza's blessing did little to stave off disaster during the invasion, nor was the president able to alter the course of history in his own country, where a popular uprising would bring about dramatic changes similar to what had happened in Cuba.

The CIA was not about to stand by passively as Nicaragua fell to the communists. A confidential plan to topple the Sandinistas was put into effect as early as 1981. This involved supplying financial, logistical, and tactical aid to various anti-Sandinista groups that had sprung up in the wake of the coup. These groups were referred to as "the Contras," meaning that they were against the prevailing powers in Nicaragua. Eventually, liberal members in Congress who felt that U.S. policy in Nicaragua was immoral and possibly against international law passed the Boland Amendment, which "prohibited the use of funds for the purpose of overthrowing the government of Nicaragua."

The Boland Amendment did not end the Reagan administration's support for the Contras. The CIA and National Security Council (NSC) began a secret campaign of soliciting funds from other nations, including Israel and Saudi Arabia, while arms and other supplies continued to be smuggled to Contra rebels in the jungles of Central America.

Cuban American militants in general—and particularly those who had become actively involved in the anti-Castro movement in the United States—were natural sympathizers with the Contras. In Miami, it was like the mid-1960s all over again. It was estimated that between twenty thousand and sixty thousand Nicaraguans flooded into Miami in the wake of the Sandinista coup. Many were former Somoza government partisans, but some were men and women who had fought alongside the Sandinistas but became disenchanted once the rebels assumed power. Once again, the city of Miami became the host to a subculture of politically disaffected exiles. It also became fertile ground for the CIA, which was actively looking for recruits to serve as soldiers in a guerrilla-style military campaign against the Sandinista government.

Contra training camps were established in South Florida, primarily in the Everglades. The camps were clandestine, though many in the Cuban community were aware of their existence. It was similar to the days and months leading up to the Bay of Pigs invasion. CIA case agents and Cuban militants reunited in a common cause.

AMONG THOSE WHO TOOK PART IN SETTING UP THE CAMPS AND RECRUITING SUPPORT for the Contras were the Fuentes brothers, Ramon and Fidel. It had been more than two decades since the brothers joined José Miguel Battle to ride a truck into enemy territory to save their fellow members of the 2506 Brigade at the Bay of Pigs. Following their release from the Isle of Pines prison and return to Miami, the brothers went on with their lives but remained active in the anti-Castro movement. For many, the rebel war in Nicaragua was a call to arms. The Fuentes brothers became part of a campaign to raise money to purchase weapons for the Contras.

Among those to whom they reached out was Battle, their brigade brother.

As members of the 2506 Brigade Veterans Association, most everyone who took part in the invasion stayed in contact over the years. Every year on April 17, association members came from far and near to lay a wreath at the base of the Bay of Pigs Monument, a sculpture in Little Havana, on Calle Ocho, adorned with an eternal flame and the names of those who had died in combat or in captivity. In 1986, these gatherings became more formalized as the association purchased a house in Little Havana that was turned into a Bay of Pigs Museum. Artifacts such as weapons, uniforms, photographs, and other paraphernalia from the invasion were stored at the facility, which, in addition to being a museum open to the public, contained a small meeting hall where members regularly met to conduct business.

Many brigade veterans had gone on to distinguished careers as doctors, lawyers, and in positions of authority in various branches of the U.S. military. Some remained dedicated to the legacy of the brigade but played little or no role in the anti-Castro movement other than their status as veterans of the invasion. Others had made it their life's work, and they came to the annual gatherings at the Bay of Pigs Museum to reestablish alliances and perhaps further commit themselves to the dream of a free Cuba. In the 1980s, much of the discussion was about the Contras, which had become the latest cause célèbre.

According to Carlos "Trio de Trés" Rodriguez, Battle's longtime *socio* (associate), El Padrino made numerous cash contributions to the Contra effort. On one occasion, Trio de Trés himself delivered $10,000 from Battle to the Fuentes brothers. These payments were to help with operational costs, and also, according to Sergeant Oscar Vigoa, to purchase guns and ammunition. Battle was philosophically predisposed to align himself with the Contras, as were the majority of 2506 Brigade veterans. But El Padrino's reputation as a gangster, and the negative publicity from his having been so prominently mentioned at the Presidential Crime Commission hearings in New York, mitigated against his being more directly associated with the cause.

FULL-THROTTLE GOVERNMENTAL HEARINGS WERE ALL THE RAGE IN THE 1980S. THE Iran-Contra hearings—much like the Watergate hearings in the mid-1970s—proved to be of great local interest in Miami. The long-standing clandestine relationship between the CIA and anti-Castro militants reached its apotheosis in the Reagan administration's efforts to crush the Sandinistas.

For the president's people, it became a problem when the public first learned that the NSC, with Lieutenant Colonel Oliver North acting as point man, had diverted money from an arms deal with Iran to underwrite the Contras. This had been done as a means to skirt the Boland Amendment. Congress, which up until now had exerted little oversight of Reagan administration activities in Central America, called for hearings into what would become known as the Iran-Contra affair.

One of the star witnesses at the hearings was a legendary ex-CIA man who operated under the name "Max Gomez"; his real name was Felix Rodriguez.

Rodriguez was born in Havana but raised in the small city of Sancti Spíritus. His uncle was a minister of public works in the Batista government. At the age of twelve, he was sent to the United States to attend a private school in Pennsylvania. He was there in 1959 when the Batista government collapsed and Castro took over. Just twenty years old, Rodriguez became active in the Anti-Communist Legion, which engaged in military training in the Dominican Republic. In early 1961, before the Bay of Pigs invasion, Rodriguez, as a member of Operation 40, undertook at least three CIA-sponsored missions to assassinate Castro. None of the missions panned out, but Rodriguez began a relationship with the CIA that would lead him on many adventures over the following decades.

For the Bay of Pigs invasion, Rodriguez had been infiltrated into Cuba, where he attempted to organize Cuban resistance in anticipation of the invasion. It was a dangerous assignment that necessitated operating under a false identity and living a clandestine lifestyle. Rodriguez was able to escape Cuba in the wake of the invasion, but like so many others who took part, he was haunted by the disaster.

Following the invasion, Rodriguez, like José Miguel Battle and others, joined the U.S. Army and was stationed at Fort Benning. The Cubans at Fort Benning thought of themselves as an elite squad, and they all knew one another. Rodriguez met and got to know Battle. In personality and temperament, they were different. Rodriguez was a political zealot determined to become a soldier in combating communism around the globe. Battle paid lip service to the cause, but he was a gambler by nature, engaged in poker games that continued late into the night.

And yet they were metaphorical brothers, Cuban exiles who remained devoted to the same goal: the assassination of Fidel Castro and reclaiming the island as their homeland.

The event for which Felix Rodriguez would enter the history books was the execution of Che Guevara. Rodriguez was there as a CIA special agent assigned to liaison with the Bolivian military, which had been hunting for Guevara in the jungle during the rebel leader's attempt to stage a political uprising in Bolivia. In 1967, Guevara was captured and interrogated by Rodriguez and others. Representing the CIA, Rodriguez was the last man to speak with Guevara before he was taken out and shot dead by a Bolivian soldier.

Rodriguez remained an active agent in the CIA until 1976, when he retired. Afterward, he never gave up on his commitment to fight communism wherever it reared its head. By the early 1980s, this meant providing support to the Contras. In his memoir, *Shadow Warrior,* published in 1989, Rodriguez wrote, "I had a commitment to the Contras—getting them some supplies that I had accumulated in Miami . . . Like many of my friends in Miami, I'd been actively helping the Contras since the early eighties . . . I'd acquired equipment to help them make supply drops at night (with infrared lights that a friend of mine built from Radio Shack parts), that I'd advised them on radio-telegraphy equipment, bought them a photocopy machine and other office supplies—and had even sent them several sets of domino so the fighters could entertain themselves at their camps."

By 1985, Rodriguez was in El Salvador, where he had set up a secret camp to conduct bombing raids against communist rebels in that country's civil war. It was there that he was reunited with another Cuban cold warrior, Luis Posada Carriles.

Following the in-flight bombing of the Cuban airliner on October 6, 1976, in which seventy-three people were killed, Posada was charged in Venezuela with having planned the attack. He remained incarcerated until 1985, when he escaped by bribing a prison official and walking out of Venezuela's San Juan de los Morros prison disguised as a priest. Using forged documents, he escaped to the island of Aruba in the Netherlands Antilles and then Central America under the nom de guerre Ramón Medina.

According to Rodriguez, "He was there when I was contacted by an individual who explained Posada's predicament and asked if I would help. My reply was to ask Posada to make his way to San Salvador. When he arrived, I gave him a job . . . I never told the Salvadorans with whom I worked, or the American supply crews, or Oliver North, about Ramón Medina's real identity. I put him to work as the day-to-day manager of the supply operation."

Later in 1985, Rodriguez was contacted by Lieutenenat Colonel North, and his efforts to bolster the military junta in El Salvador against a rebel insurgency were shifted to supporting the Contras, a rebel insurgency attempting to overthrow a military junta. A massive warehouse was constructed and an assortment of mercenaries descended to take part in what was essentially an elaborate resupply operation sponsored by the Reagan administration.

When the Iran-Contra debacle was exposed and congressional hearings began, Rodriguez, who had spent most of his adult life in the shadows as a covert operator, was dragged into the light of day. His nationally televised testimony was riveting. Before a rapt panel of Senate investigators and a television audience in the millions, he detailed how he had, since his involvement in the Bay of Pigs invasion, been involved in perhaps hundreds of covert political operations. Many of these undertakings were dangerous, and in some cases people had been killed (most notably Che Guevara). Most of the operations had been initiated by the CIA and the U.S. government.

LIKE MOST EVERYONE IN MIAMI, JOSÉ MIGUEL BATTLE WATCHED THE IRAN-CONTRA hearings with rapt attention. The Contras had begun at training camps in the Everglades, just miles from where Battle lived in South Miami. Once again, as with the Watergate burglary and hearings that followed, people whom Battle had known since the invasion, or from his time at Fort Benning, were now reluctant players on the national stage. It was as if Cuban exile politics, intertwined with the anticommunist agenda of the Republican Party, were on a loop, replaying every decade or so through covert actions that were never supposed to be known by the public at large.

Over the years, many Cubans whom Battle knew from *la lucha* became embroiled in controversies. These were men who had survived the invasion and met at Fort Benning as young recruits for the U.S. Army. Afterward, they had chosen different paths, but they remained a brotherhood of sorts. Now it was Felix Rodriguez on the hot seat, as Rolando Martinez and other Cuban members of the Watergate crew had been a decade earlier.

These men—Posada, Martinez, Rodriguez, Battle, and others—were part of a generation that saw themselves as combatants in the Cold War.

They felt compelled to embark on a journey that some might have interpreted as morally ambiguous at best, or downright criminal at worst. But their efforts had a built-in self-justification. Whether it was Rodriguez the freedom fighter, Posada the terrorist, or Battle the gangster, they all had something in common. They had convinced themselves they were engaged in an epic struggle not only for their own personal liberty, but also for the liberty of the Cuban people.

IN JANUARY 1988, MIAMI POLICE OFFICER DAVID SHANKS WAS TRANSFERRED FROM the city's South District, where he had worked as a uniformed officer for four years, to the Vice Investigations Section. Vice was a division of the Organized Crime Bureau (OCB). It was a prestigious assignment for Shanks, who was now a fourteen-year veteran of the department.

It had been nine years since Shanks stumbled upon one of the worst shootings in the history of the Miami police department, which had resulted in the death of his friend and fellow officer Billy Cook and the permanent disabling of another officer. The tragedy had a strange effect on Shanks, making him more dedicated than ever to the job but also something of a loner. He was hesitant to become overly attached to his fellow cops, for fear that at any moment they could be lost in an outburst of violence.

In his new assignment at Vice, Shanks would be working under Sergeant James "Jimmy" Boyd, a legendary figure in the Metro-Dade PD. Boyd was a Florida good ol' boy, built like a bull terrier, with a pronounced southern accent. He had married a local Cubana, and he spoke fluent Spanish, but with a Florida drawl. Few cops knew greater Miami better than Boyd. As chief of the Vice Squad, he was on a first-name basis with all of the prosecutors in town, most of the criminal defense lawyers, and a fair number of tier one criminals such as Santo Trafficante and others.

Shanks was enthused by the prospect of joining Boyd's squad, especially when he learned he would be partnered with James "Jed" Leggett. Shanks had known Leggett since their days patrolling the tough Liberty City neighborhood back in the 1970s. They had gone on to other assignments, and now they were being reunited at Vice.

Leggett had already established himself as something of an expert on the subject of bolita. In fact, three years earlier he had been the lone representative from the Metro-Dade PD summoned to testify before the President's Commission on Organized Crime in Manhattan. At the time, Leggett was assigned to OCB's Lottery Investigation Squad. He was the one who uncovered the Corporation's use of the Puerto Rican lottery to launder bolita proceeds from the United States.

From their time together in Liberty City, Shanks admired Leggett, though they had different personality types. Shanks was laconic and introspective by nature, whereas Leggett was another southern good ol' boy, a proud Florida "cracker" with blond hair and blue eyes, whose family had roots in the state going back to before the Civil War. Leggett liked bass fishing, NASCAR, and Busch beer. Shanks knew him to be one of the sharpest cops he had ever met.

Jimmy Boyd ran an aggressive squad. He liked to have his cops execute at least one or two search warrants every week. This meant assigning different teams to different investigations, and then calling them all together when it was time to do a search. Boyd liked to maintain a strong camaraderie within his squad, but he also fostered a kind of internal competition between teams that was sometimes combustible.

On a morning in April, Boyd assigned Shanks and Leggett to investigate an anonymous tip that had come over the department's Crime-Stoppers hotline. The caller had identified a coin laundry that they said was being used as a bolita writing location. The first thing Shanks and Leggett did was set up a surveillance of the location. They quickly determined that the place was indeed a front of some kind. There were many people coming and going, none of them carrying laundry.

"We need to penetrate, get somebody in there," Shanks said to his partner.

"Right," said Leggett. "This is a job for Miss One Hundred."

Miss One Hundred was a large, grandmotherly black female who sometimes worked for Boyd's Vice Squad as a paid informant. Her real name was Mildred. She had been given the code name because that was her informant documentation number: OCB-100.

The goal of the cops was to get enough information about the place, and evidence that something illegal was going on, that they could obtain a search warrant. They met with Mildred, who, for a modest weekly retainer, seemed willing to do almost anything. The idea was for her to enter the fake laundry. Not only would she play a number, but she was also supposed to strike up a conversation with the bolita writer and find out when the place closed for the day. That way the cops could get an idea of when the pickup man came by to retrieve the lottery stubs and cash.

Shanks and Leggett picked up Mildred at her house and dropped her off a block from the location. They told her what number to play so that in court, should it come to that, the cops could explain there was no way the informant could have "rigged the buy." From a surveillance van, they watched Mildred go into the location. She was there for about fifteen minutes. She came out and walked down the street. A couple blocks away, the cops picked her up

"Here's my ticket," said Mildred, handing to the cops the record of her bet. "They said no more bets after six o'clock in the evening."

The cops paid the sweet old lady her informant fee, and she went on her way.

Two nights later, Shanks and Leggett were again at the bolita location. This time, Mildred entered shortly before the 10 P.M. deadline. She stayed inside for a while, engaged in conversation, and then, as planned, exited the location right behind the pickup man. This way the cops would know which customer he was. On this occasion, two surveillance teams were required. Shanks scooped up Mildred a few blocks away from the fake laundromat, while the other team followed the pickup man to a maroon truck. They ran a check on the license plate and determined that the truck was registered to a man named Henry Lee.

The cops followed Lee and watched as he made pickups at other locations—a bar, a mom-and-pop store, an auto garage. They knew that the accumulated cash and betting slips were destined for a counting house. But the Cubans did not normally want the bagman to know the location of the counting house, for fear he might set up the location to be ripped off. For safety reasons, the "pass," or transfer of cash and betting stubs, was set up to take place on a street corner, the location of which was unknown to the bagman until the last minute. The pass usually happened quickly, with a Latino worker from the counting house showing up to retrieve the bag that contained various bundles of cash and lottery tickets collected from the bolita locations.

The cops positioned themselves to be able to see the transfer of the package, a necessity for them to fill out an affidavit in furtherance of a search warrant. They watched Lee hand off what he had to another bagman. Shanks and Leggett stayed with the bagman. They followed him to a duplex located at 2140 NW 34th Street. They saw the man enter a particular unit.

The cops followed this same routine over the course of a few nights. Eventually, a Latino male in his early fifties exited the duplex unit and entered a late-model gold Cadillac. Shanks ran a check on the Cadillac.

Bingo.

The owner of the vehicle was José Pulido, who, they learned after running a check through criminal records, had been arrested by the City of Miami Police Department a few years earlier, in 1985. The charge was operating a bolita enterprise.

Shanks and Leggett began to prepare for a raid. Through the county building and zoning department, they obtained a floor plan of the duplex. They were able to determine all entryways and exits. The cops knew that their entry and seizure of documents at the location had to be sudden and immediate. The moment they entered the counting house, bolita employees would attempt to destroy documents. There was usually a shredder at the location. The success of the raid would depend in part on how quickly they were able shut the place down without evidence being destroyed.

Shanks wrote up the affidavit. It had become one of his strengths as an officer. Not all cops have this skill. It requires that the criminal information that had been gathered so far be condensed into a concise narrative; otherwise a judge might cast the affidavit aside, and the chances of securing his or her signature on the warrant might take days. In high-intensity cases, the passing of days is sometimes the difference between the element of surprise and a compromised investigation.

For this case, Shanks created a solid document, which was immediately signed by a judge. The affidavit was good for ten days. The squad went over their plans: the raid would require three search teams. Shanks and Leggett would be part of the entry team, with Shanks wielding a sledgehammer and Leggett a Remington 870 shotgun.

Standing at the front door to the duplex, Shanks announced, "Open up! This is the police! We have a warrant!"

The sound of rustling came from inside. Shanks saw a woman peek out the front curtain, then turn and run.

"I'm taking down the door," Shanks yelled to the rest of his crew. He drew back the sledgehammer and pounded the lock on the door. The lock disintegrated and the door swung open. Shanks withdrew his weapon; he and a half dozen other cops flooded into the apartment. More cops rushed into the location from a rear door.

It was a successful raid. José Pulido and a couple of employees at the location were placed under arrest. There were tons of documents. Apparently, not only was the location a counting house, but it was some kind of central office for a sizable bolita operation. For Shanks and his squad, it was a dream come true.

As is often the case with a raid that netted a significant amount of evidence, it took days and weeks for the investigators to figure out exactly what they had. Cash totaling in the hundreds of thousands had been seized, but also computer hard drives, disks, and financial documents. A retired agent from the Internal Revenue Service was hired by Metro-Dade police to examine records and financial documents that had been seized. It was often a case of looking for a needle in a haystack to find that one incriminating document amid boxes and boxes of paperwork.

About a week after the raid, Shanks was in the office one day when the former IRS agent said, "David, can you come over here a minute? I need to show you something."

Shanks walked over to the ex-agent, who was surrounded by stacks of documents and opened file boxes. The ex-agent, who was holding what looked like a spreadsheet, said to Shanks, "This guy Pulido works for José Miguel Battle. Everything points that way. I'm connecting the dots, and it's all pointing in the same direction. Battle." The ex-agent showed Shanks a document that indicated large payouts being made to El Zapotal, Inc., Battle's company.

Shanks had heard the name. He knew who Battle was, but he'd only recently begun working organized crime. He knew his partner Jed

Leggett had been up in New York a few years earlier testifying about Battle, so he immediately took the information to Jed.

"Hey, partner, the IRS guy says these records come from José Miguel Battle's organization."

Leggett looked up from his desk in the squad room. In his Florida drawl, he said, "Well, I kind of figured that already."

"Okay," said Shanks. "So what are we going to do about it?"

"You can talk to Boyd. But I don't think you'll get much satisfaction. Boyd thinks that Oscar Alvarez, not Battle, is the ultimate bolitero in Miami. Boyd thinks Battle came down here to retire."

Shanks was dumbfounded. He didn't know much about Battle, but he knew he was a major player. If the evidence suggested that Battle's organization was involved, why would they sit on their hands?

Shanks approached Boyd. For a subordinate to seek out his boss on a matter of investigative priorities was touchy, to say the least, but with Boyd's reputation as a legendary Miami cop, Shanks could not believe he would pass up the opportunity to catch a big fish.

After Shanks explained what had emerged from the investigation, Boyd responded by saying, "Listen, Battle may be big-time in New York and New Jersey, but down here the bolita king is Oscar Alvarez."

Alvarez was indeed a big-time Cuban bolita operator with roots in South Florida. Boyd had a personal stake in catching him. Four years earlier, the sergeant had been part of squad that had arrested Alvarez in his home. But the bolitero slipped through their fingers when he was given a sentence of probation—no jail time—and Boyd had been on his tail ever since.

"Yeah," said Shanks, "but according to Jed's testimony up in New York—" He wasn't even able to finish his sentence; Boyd cut him off.

"I don't want to hear any more about Leggett. You understand? Ever since he testified in front of that damn commission he thinks he's a big shot. He doesn't make the decisions around here. I do. And I'm telling you the guy to go after is Alvarez, not Battle."

Shanks stood in the sergeant's doorway for a beat or two. He didn't know what to say. They had just discovered evidence linking their investigation to a guy who was believed to be the biggest bolitero in America, and his supervisor was blowing it off.

Shanks had a few things he would like to have said. Instead, he said, "Okay, boss," and returned to the squad room.

BY THE LATE 1980S, ABRAHAM RYDZ HAD BEGUN TO SOUR ON THE BOLITA BUSINESS. One of the main reasons was Nene Marquez, Battle's brother-in-law, who Rydz felt had no business being in charge of the Corporation's operations in New York. Though Rydz was living comfortably in Miami, tending to the daily operations of Union Financial Research and other companies owned by himself and Battle Jr., he had to deal with Marquez on a near daily basis. The entire financial structure of Rydz and Battle Jr.'s operation in Miami was like a house of cards dependent on the bolita proceeds flowing from New York. Even after the bad publicity of the arson wars and the Presidential Crime Commission hearings and the prosecution of Conrad Pons, bolita still flourished. The Corporation was still clearing tens of millions on an annual basis, funneling that money to offshore accounts.

The arson wars, in particular, had sickened Rydz. Around the time of the Jannin Toribio killing, he had a baby of his own. Susan Rydz was born on April 5, 1986; she was El Polaco's first and only child with his second wife, whom he had married in 1981. He had an older daughter, Vivian, from a previous marriage, but she was long since grown and gone.

From the time Susan was born, Rydz—who was fifty-two years old—doted on her as though she represented a new lease on life. As a child, and even into young adulthood, she was ignorant of his life as a gambling impresario. She would know him only as a successful businessman. It was Rydz's intention that she remain innocent of his long criminal career.

The killing of Jannin Toribio—a child, burned to death in an arson fire—struck a chord with Rydz. He read about the death in the newspaper and couldn't believe that any organization he was a part of could have committed such a heinous act. Then came the crime commission hearings, at which his name was mentioned as a high-ranking official in the Corporation. Rydz began to lie awake at night with ominous premonitions that it was all going to end badly; they were going to wind up in jail, or dead. His biggest fear was that his own daughter, Susan, would grow up without a father.

Rydz felt powerless. At one time, he had felt as if he could control the financial fortunes of the organization, but those days were over. At the core of his dissatisfaction was the belief that the bolita business had gone from being a financial venture to a gangster enterprise. That side of the business—revenge and punishment killings, turf wars with the Italians, having to maintain a reputation for brutality—was, to Rydz, in the process of destroying it. Many times he said to Battle Jr. and to Nene, "We are in the business of making money. That's what a gambling business is supposed to be about, not getting our names in the newspapers or on the six o'clock news. That is bad for business."

When Rydz talked this way, Nene's eyes glazed over. It was as if he wasn't listening. Nene took orders from one person—Battle Sr., the Bay of Pigs hero, not Abraham Rydz, the Polack.

On flights to and from New York, Rydz complained to Junior, who agreed with him. But there was nothing either of them could do about it. Decisions were being made at the street level in New York. In fact, Rydz got the impression that the more he complained, the more Nene Marquez deliberately went against his wishes. If he complained about the arsons bringing bad publicity and heat from the police, Nene sent a crew out to torch another bolita hole. If Rydz complained about gangland-style murders perpetrated by the Corporation as something that could have a negative impact on their business, three dead bodies from a rival bolita organization would be found dumped on the side of the New Jersey Turnpike. For a while now, Rydz had begun to feel that when it came to crucial decisions about the daily running of the bolita business, he had become expendable.

And so he did something that startled even his best friend Miguelito Battle. He retired from the bolita business. Not from the financial side of things—he would still run an operating office and be paid half a million dollars a year by Union Financial Research. He would still oversee the various shell companies that were being used to launder the organization's profits. But he would no longer be a part of the bolita business, which meant he was relinquishing his 17 percent cut. He was giving up millions of dollars in annual proceeds to be done with the headache of dealing with Nene Marquez.

Miguelito tried to talk Rydz out of it. "What about your family, your daughter?" he said. Miguelito also had young children. Every decision he and Rydz had made, they told themselves, was to provide a legitimate future for their kids.

"What good am I to my daughter if I go to jail?" Rydz answered. Perhaps he was engaging in magical thinking. The fact that he was leaving the bolita business in 1988 was not going to exonerate him from having already been involved with the Corporation for decades. Nevertheless, he set a date for when he would no longer be involved. On that date, he would stop receiving his cut and also would no longer have responsibilities as a bolita banker.

The decision by Rydz sent a ripple through the organization. Not long after it was announced, there was a funeral attended by many members of the Corporation. Sergio "Richie" Battle, the second-youngest Battle brother, had died from a drug overdose. It wasn't exactly a shock. Richard had been struggling with a cocaine and heroin addiction for years.

The memorial service was held at the same funeral parlor in Union City where, sixteen years earlier, Pedro Battle had been laid to rest. José Miguel, Miguelito, Rydz, and most of the members of the organization had flown up from Miami for the service.

Also among the attendees was a young bolitero named Luis Perez, an up-and-coming banker who would eventually be put in charge of the Corporation's main office in Manhattan. Perez was there as a guest of Willie Pozo, his boss and the current *jefe* of the Corporation in Manhattan.

Perez had met Miguelito and Abraham Rydz before. At one point during the service, he stood off to the side as Rydz spoke with Willie Pozo. Rydz had taken a calendar out of his wallet and was showing Pozo the exact date he was leaving the business. "This is the day I'm leaving," he said, circling a date on the calendar. "Have my totals ready on that date."

"Well," said Pozo, "that's when we give out the holiday bonuses. You want your totals before or after we distribute the bonuses?"

The business was based on percentages. Rydz's piece of the pie would be much bigger if he took his payment before the bonuses were paid.

"No," said Rydz. "Make sure everyone gets their bonus first, then give me my totals."

Eavesdropping on the conversation, Perez thought, *Wow, this is a fair guy. He's going to give bonuses first and then leave.*

The date that Rydz set to leave fell on a Sunday. On that day, the Corporation took a major hit. A number that had been wagered on by an unusually high number of customers came in. The organization had to pay out $2 million that day, the single largest daily payout in the history of Cuban bolita in the United States. On that day, Abraham Rydz cashed out of the business. He took it as a good omen that he was getting out at just the right time.

For the Corporation, the $2 million hit was not insurmountable. It was perhaps a testament to the business that Rydz was leaving behind that it could absorb a payout of unprecedented proportions and hardly miss a beat.

DAVE SHANKS AND HIS PARTNER, JED LEGGETT, WERE FRUSTRATED THAT THEIR supervisor seemed to have little interest in going after José Miguel Battle Sr. But they were not about to give up. Leggett suspected that Battle was involved locally in bolita and who knew what else. Maybe he was even involved in narcotics. By the late 1980s, it was pretty much impossible for a major gangster to be operating in Miami and not be involved in the narcotics business to one degree or another.

Leggett contacted an old informant named Angelo who had known the Battle brothers since the 1960s. Angelo was on the outs with the Battles. He didn't have much to offer regarding bolita, but he did tell the investigators that since relocating to South Miami, Jose Miguel had become a major impresario of cockfights throughout Dade County. In fact, Angelo had seen Battle recently at some of the major *vallas,* or arenas, in Key Largo, and also at Club Campestre, a cockfighting venue in suburban Miami.

Shanks was intrigued by the idea of using cockfighting as a means to, at the very least, arrest Battle and use what was a misdemeanor crime to create an opening for a more serious prosecution.

It was only in 1986 that the state of Florida had banned cockfighting outright, meaning that it became a misdemeanor crime even to attend an event. Facilitating the operation by supplying the roosters or managing the venue was, however, a felony, as was the charge of "cruelty to animals."

To raid a cockfight was a massive undertaking. The fights were generally held in the western part of Dade County, where the residential areas thinned out and gave way to agricultural land and horse farms. A cockfighting event might be attended by over two hundred people and usually lasted hours, with dozens of fights. The venues were set up like a poor man's dog or horse track, with makeshift cantinas and Cuban food for sale. Sometimes prostitutes worked these events, and all manner of illegal transactions were known to take place. Some men came armed and ready for anything. The volume of betting was sometimes huge, depending on who was supplying the roosters and who was doing the betting. Sometimes the cockfights went on for days at a time, twenty-four hours a day, like a casino that never closed.

With a big-time bettor such as Battle in attendance, whom Luis Posada Carriles claimed to have seen place a $1 million wager on a single match, the collective purse for a night of cockfighting could be substantial.

Shanks and his Vice Squad determined that there were a series of upcoming cockfights to be staged at an arena in Hialeah Gardens, off of NW 122nd Street. The first order of business was to send a couple of undercover cops into the venue to case the location. This required Latino officers, as the cockfights were attended almost exclusively by Hispanics, mostly Cubans, and a gringo would stand out.

A male-female duo of cops was sent into the venue. It was their job to visually establish that it was indeed a cockfighting venue and that illegal betting was taking place. Equally important, they were to take in the physical characteristics of the venue—entrances and exits, where the animals were stored in relation to the main arena, a description of the organizers and main gamblers, and any other illegal activity that might be taking place on the premises.

After a couple visits, the undercover cops were able to draw up a detailed schematic of the cockfighting venue. Shanks and his Vice Squad—led by Sergeant Jimmy Boyd—teamed up with detectives from a Tactical Squad and also a SWAT team to organize a raid. It was going to be a sizable operation, with over sixty cops. With nearly two hundred participants at the cockfight—some of them intoxicated and armed and revved up from a night of high-stakes gambling—the potential for disaster was significant.

In late 1988 and into early 1989, Miami police conducted numerous raids. Each one netted considerable gambling proceeds and resulted in hundreds of misdemeanor and felony citations. But at none of them was Battle in attendance. The cops were about to give up. Then, on February 3, 1989, at Club Campestre, a commercial warehouse in the suburb of Perrine, they hit pay dirt.

As with the previous raids, the cops hit the location clad in black camouflage gear and carrying shotguns, handguns, and automatic weapons. Some of the attendees thought of making a run for it, but cops had secured the perimeter so that no one could escape.

Shanks and his team arrived with processing equipment to charge and fine attendees right there at the site. In the process of rounding everyone up, the detectives came upon El Padrino himself.

Police officer Willy Vigoa was a part of the team that raided Club Campestre. The younger brother of Sergeant Oscar Vigoa, who earlier had worked the case involving the kidnapping of Battle Jr., he had heard a lot about El Padrino. Vigoa had monitored a couple of wiretaps involving Corporation bookmakers and boliteros and was part of the extended team of cops working the Battle investigation. But he had been beginning to wonder if the legendary El Padrino really existed. Remembered Vigoa, "Far as we were concerned, this was just another cockfight raid. We weren't expecting the main target of our investigation to be there. It was a surprise. . . . Battle was upset that he was going to lose his birds. He had two *gallos* (roosters) there, and those birds can be worth twenty thousand dollars or more. So it was a big loss for him."

As one of the supervisory investigators, Dave Shanks was one of the first cops to enter Club Campestre. What he remembered vividly was that one of Battle's bodyguards, a fifty-year-old cockfight attendee named Adalberto Irizarry, pulled out a .357 Magnum revolver as the SWAT team entered the location. A few tense moments passed before Irizarry lowered his weapon. He was taken into custody and charged with aggravated assault and carrying a concealed weapon.

The birds kept fighting. Oblivious to what was going on around them, in the arena they flapped their wings, squawked, and slashed one another in a battle to the death.

Once Shanks saw that Battle was in attendance, he moved to the shadows. This was the first occasion where he saw the man in the flesh and heard his voice. Fascinated, he watched Battle carefully. "I wanted to try and get a feel for the man. He was built like a middleweight fighter whose muscle had softened to fat. I repositioned myself so I could see and hear him as he was going through the routine. I was appalled to see that about ten of our detectives sat with him individually, just to have their picture taken with him."

Battle was a celebrity. He did not object to having his picture taken with the cops, who afforded him the respect of an OG, original gangster.

Noted Shanks, "I was struck by the similarity of Battle's voice to the gravelly rasp of Marlon Brando's 'Don Corleone' in *The Godfather*. The resemblance was almost eerie. I began to wonder if this was his real voice or if it was something he had practiced.

"In later years, I heard his voice on many more occasions, and I noticed that when he got excited, the raspy Corleone quality disappeared."

Shanks did not speak directly with Battle or call attention to his own presence. He did not want Battle to know that he was being studied like a lab rat.

At Club Campestre, Battle assumed the identity of the Don, and everyone played along. He was served with a PTA, a promise to appear. He would have to appear on a designated date and pay a nominal fine. The whole thing was a minor inconvenience.

For Shanks, it felt like the beginning of a larger-than-life adventure. He was Captain Ahab, and he had just laid eyes on his Great White Whale. The hunt was on.

14

DEAD BUT NOT DEAD

DAVID SHANKS WAS NOT THE FIRST COP TO SET HIS SIGHTS ON JOSÉ MIGUEL BATTLE. Throughout his career, Battle had handled the police. He had been a cop himself, after all. Not that he was immune. He had been indicted and done a cumulative total of three years in prison. Cops like Detective Kalafus in New York had linked him—in theory—to many crimes.

Cops and prosecutors had targeted Battle and made him pay, and yet no one had looked at the totality of his career and stopped to consider the ultimate punishment—a racketeering case under the RICO statutes, otherwise known as the Racketeer Influenced and Corrupt Organizations Act.

RICO had revolutionized the way prosecutors went after criminal organizations. The concept of a racketeering conspiracy was not new; what was new about RICO was that it afforded the opportunity to establish many little conspiracies within the larger conspiracy of the enterprise. These were known as predicate acts, and they had to be prosecuted as if they were mini-prosecutions unto themselves, with enough evidence—including witnesses—to be proven on their own merits and also contribute to a guilty verdict on the overriding charge of racketeering.

Shanks began amassing a dossier on Battle, not just files from local law enforcement, but also his federal files and, most important, criminal files from New York and New Jersey that memorialized his long and active career. Through his partner, Jed Leggett, Shanks made contact with Kalafus, who probably had more knowledge about Battle and the Corporation than any one cop.

"The only reason I'm talking to you," said Kalafus to Shanks on the phone, "is because Jed says you're okay." Kalafus and Leggett had met during the Presidential Crime Commission hearings a few years earlier, Kalafus was of the opinion that many Miami cops and political figures were on Battle's payroll, just as they had been in New Jersey.

Through Kalafus, Shanks began to get a sense of the full narrative sweep of Battle's activities. He listened to the stories of revenge killings, empire building, firebombings, and extortions, related by Kalafus in his modified Texas drawl, as if he was hearing a tall tale. But he wasn't; all of these crimes were in the files, a saga of Cuban American gangsterism that spanned two decades.

For all the crimes perpetrated by the Corporation in New York and New Jersey, Shanks and Leggett were convinced that much of the action had now shifted to Miami. Those suspicions were confirmed in early 1989 when they learned of the killing of a local bolitero named Juan Paez. According to street sources, Battle was behind the murder.

Paez had been gunned down while making a money pickup at a counting house in Liberty City. He worked for two of Miami's biggest bolita bankers, Oscar Alvarez and his partner Gerardo Zayas. Word was that Battle was offended that Alvarez and Zayas had not automatically offered him a percentage of their bolita revenues. So now he was muscling in on their territory.

When Paez was murdered, he was carrying with him more than $5,000 in cash. The hit men did not bother with the money. That was the message: *We don't want your money, we want to take over your business.*

The Paez hit was still an open case, and though there was plenty of speculation and gossip, it was not likely to be closed anytime soon. The paperwork on the case had barely begun to circulate throughout the Organized Crime Bureau when yet another murder lit up the police frequencies, this one involving one of Battle's biggest competitors in Miami.

For decades, Oscar Alvarez had been king bolitero in Miami. Sergeant Boyd believed that he still was. Alvarez's partner, Gerardo Zayas, was his equal. A ubiquitous figure in Miami gambling circles, especially at the ever-popular dog racing tracks, Zayas had the job of placing bets in an effort to alter the odds for a particular race. It was called "bumping the numbers," a tried-and-true method to minimize large losses by a particular organization

ing the numbers," a tried-and-true method to minimize large losses by a particular organization.

On an evening in February, Zayas and his bodyguard, Luis Ramos, were at Hollywood Race Track, the area's premier greyhound racing track. Since 1934, when it was first opened as the Hollywood Kennel Club, the track had become a fixture in the life of local gamblers. Shortly after it opened, a modest casino was added, with legal slot machines and poker games. As in most of South Florida, the clientele at the Hollywood racetrack had transformed over the years from primarily Anglo to Latino, with racing forms printed in Spanish as well as English.

Outside the track, Gerardo Zayas gave the valet his customary heavy tip for keeping his Cadillac parked close to the entrance. Zayas's bodyguard, Ramos, got in behind the wheel, while Zayas took the front passenger seat. They drove away from the racetrack onto I-95, toward the shiny new skyscrapers of downtown Miami.

Zayas was enjoying the latest technology—a cellular phone, which had drastically altered the day-to-day operations of bookies, bolita bankers, and other foot soldiers in the gambling business. It used to be that someone like Zayas drove around with a pocket full of quarters looking for a pay phone every time he needed to make a call. But not now. A bookie could place bets and relay information on the fly.

Zayas was yakking away. He didn't see the dark, SUV-style vehicle pull up alongside the Cadillac.

Suddenly, the passenger window exploded, and Zayas's body lurched toward Ramos, the driver. The right side of Zaya's face was shredded from particles of glass and pellets from a shotgun blast. Ramos weaved away from the SUV, which he saw recede in the rearview mirror. He caught a glimpse of the barrel of a shotgun being pulled inside the rear window.

Thinking fast, Ramos raced to nearby Parkway Regional Medical Center. His quick response likely saved his boss's life. Zayas survived the attack, though he would remain in a coma for a month.

At ten o'clock on the morning after the shooting, Sergeant Jimmy Boyd of the Vice Squad received a phone call from a prominent criminal defense attorney named George Nicholas, who represented some of the biggest boliteros in Miami. It was unusual for a defense lawyer to call a cop unless he wanted to cut a deal for a recently arrested client. But Nicholas had something else he wanted to talk about. He made arrangements to come to the Organized Crime Bureau and meet Boyd.

Nicholas was tall and cadaverous, like Basil Rathbone or John Carradine, one of those old Hollywood actors who routinely appeared on late-night television in black-and-white horror movies. He came into Boyd's office, and the sergeant invited Dave Shanks and a couple of other investigators into the room, then closed the door. Boyd nodded for Nicholas to proceed.

"I'm here on behalf of my client, Oscar Alvarez," said Nicholas. The lawyer explained that late last night Alvarez had received a phone call from "the large, fat man from the Corporation." Everyone understood that Nicholas was referring to José Miguel Battle Sr. "The Fat Man says the Zayas shooting was a warning to Alvarez, that if he doesn't start paying up, he will be next on the hit list."

First Paez, and now Zayas. Alvarez had reason to be concerned.

Shanks asked the lawyer, "Why are you here? Why are you telling us this?"

Nicholas sighed. "My client wants you to know that for the next two years or so, you don't have to bother investigating him. For personal health reasons, he and his family will be leaving the area to go on an extended world tour vacation."

"Wait a minute," said Boyd. "Would Alvarez be willing to come in and testify about the death threat? With that information we could put El Gordo out of business."

"No way," said the lawyer. "He's not going to jeopardize himself or his family by offering information that might end up in a courtroom. I am here today as a professional courtesy, that's all. And to relay a message. As of today, Oscar Alvarez has gone into retirement."

The lawyer departed, and the cops discussed their options. The information from Nicholas came under the heading of hearsay; it wasn't something that could be used at trial. Plus, the lawyer's revelation was protected under attorney-client privilege. But it was actionable information, in the sense that Boyd and Shanks could use the tip in affidavits to secure wiretap authorization and search warrants.

What followed was a flurry of activity, with the Vice Squad, often in consort with a tactical unit, conducting surveillances and planting bugs on anybody and everybody they believed had even a modest connection to the Corporation. The effort was even given a name—Operation Tabletop.

The Metro-Dade PD's Organized Crime Bureau was finally putting in some real effort to determine the full scope of Battle's criminal dealings in Miami. The hope was that painstaking surveillance and daily observation might bear some fruit. As was often the case, however, the next break in the case was not the result of hard work and diligence. It was the result of luck, as a potential homicide case involving Battle fell right into their lap.

ON DECEMBER 9, 1989, SERGEANT ED HINMAN, WHO WAS ASSIGNED TO THE OCB'S Tactical Section, came into the Vice office to speak with Dave Shanks. Hinman was lean, bald-headed, and fastidious, a hoarder of information. It was rare for him to walk in the door and share a case unless he was completely stumped and needed assistance.

It turned out that he had been contacted by prison officials at Dade Correctional Institution, which was located thirty miles south of Miami in a town called Florida City. An administrator at the prison had reported to the sergeant his knowledge of a murder plot that was brewing at the facility. An inmate had approached the authorities to tell them that his cellmate, Frank Suarez, was planning to kill another inmate by slipping poison into his food.

Suarez was a Cuban American in his twenties serving a fifteen-year sentence for drug trafficking. The man to be poisoned was a forty-four-year-old inmate named Roque Torres.

Shanks listened to Hinman. It was all very interesting, but Shanks was wondering what this had to do with Vice, which was currently focused on bolita and bookmaking. Then Hinman told him, "The hit is being done on behalf of José Miguel Battle. The man who ordered the hit is a bookmaker in the Corporation."

As it turned out, Roque Torres, the target, was in the second year of a fifteen-year sentence for the attempted murder of two Corporation figures, Carlos Capdavilla and Aurelio "Cache" Jimenez. These two were familiar to Shanks. Capdavilla was the bookmaker. Jimenez had popped up during occasional surveillances of Battle and his associates. As far as they could tell, Jimenez was Battle's official chauffeur, driving him around Miami in a new white Cadillac, among other vehicles.

Two years earlier, Jimenez and his partner, Capdavilla, had gone over to the house of Roque Torres, who owed a $50,000 gambling debt to the Corporation. The house was at 451 W 33rd Street in Hialeah, not far from the famous Hialeah Park racetrack. Torres made good money as a car salesman in Miami, but as a gambler, he was a serial loser. To Jimenez and Capdavilla, Torres claimed that he needed more time to pay off his debt. As representatives of the Corporation, the two men let him know that they were not running a charity. They needed to be paid.

Torres had suspected the conversation might go this way, and so he had a .45-caliber revolver hidden between the cushions of the sofa where he was sitting.

Torres thought he saw Jimenez reach for a gun, and so he grabbed his first. He fired multiple shots, hitting both Jimenez and Capdavilla. Bleeding profusely, they stumbled out the front door of Torres's house and collapsed, Jimenez on the lawn and Capdavilla in the driveway.

A neighbor heard the shooting and called 911. Fire/rescue and Hialeah police arrived on the scene. The paramedics did their job, saving both men. The police did theirs, taking Roque Torres and his gun into custody.

There was a trial. Torres claimed self-defense, that he was afraid that Jimenez and Capdavilla were there to kill him. The jury didn't buy it; they found Torres guilty on two counts of attempted murder. He was sent to Dade Correctional to serve his fifteen-year sentence.

Out on the street, Carlos Capdavilla wanted revenge, and José Miguel Battle was in accordance. You don't shoot two prominent members of the Corporation—especially El Padrino's personal valet—and get away with it. Torres would be used as an example; he would pay with his life.

From what Sergeant Hinman had been told, the Corporation reached out to inmate Frank Suarez because his mother, Rosa Suarez, worked as a bookmaker for Capdavilla. In fact, Rosa Suarez was also part of the murder conspiracy. She and her son had agreed to kill Roque Torres for a fee of $10,000.

At the age of fifty, Rosa Suarez, in her middle age, had a lady friend named Esperanza Arroz. They had known each other since their childhoods in Cuba. These two women became partners on the hit. They visited Rosa's son Frank in prison and began to sketch out a plan. The first order of business was for Rosa and Esperanza to purchase some poison. After some initial difficulties trying to determine what to buy and where to get it, Frank Suarez turned to his cellmate for help. The cellmate, seeing this as opportunity to endear himself to authorities and maybe get a sentence reduction, snitched on Suarez to the warden, who in turn reached out to Metro-Dade PD and Ed Hinman.

Said Shanks to Hinman, "That's an amazing story, Ed. Let's see what we can do with that."

Shanks arranged for a meeting later that day with him and Hinman, along with Sergeant Jimmy Boyd of Vice and Kennedy "Kenny" Rosario, a cop with the Tactical Section, as well as two other supervisors and Larry LaVecchio, a prosecutor from the State Attorney's Office.

Already, the Tactical cops had put a plan in motion. They arranged for their informant—Suarez's cellmate—to tell Suarez that he knew someone who could purchase the poison for them. That person would be Detective Kenny Rosario, working undercover. Rosario was a street-smart Puerto Rican, originally from the Bronx, and a Vietnam vet who had already distinguished himself on various undercover assignments. Years later, remembering the technique for which he would become greatly admired by his police colleagues, he would say, "Working undercover is more of a mind-set than any costume you might wear. [The targets of the investigation] believe it because you believe it."

Rosario and Rosa Suarez had already spoken by phone and set up a meeting. Tactical was in the process of securing a wiretap on Rosa Suarez's home phone.

Sergeant Boyd spoke up. "That's outstanding. You people seem to have this all under control. My question is, what do you need us for?"

Hinman and the Tactical cops admitted that they weren't sure where to take the investigation. They could nail Frank Suarez and his co-conspirators, his mom, her lady friend, and probably Capdavilla. But the main culprit was Battle. Wasn't there a way they could lure Battle into the picture, maybe get him on a wire talking with Capdavilla, implicating himself in his own words?

Boyd and Shanks loved that idea. The cops discussed their various options and came up with a scheme that was so outrageous, they became giddy as they ironed out the details.

The plan was that they would go through with a fake version of the murder. Kenny Rosario, acting undercover, would sell some fake cyanide to Rosa and Esperanza. When the two women visited Frank Suarez at the penitentiary, guards in the visiting room—who would also be in on the plot—would pretend not to notice the poison being passed to Suarez.

Once he had the cyanide, Suarez and his cellmate would set out to poison Roque Torres. Here's where the plan got tricky: Roque Torres would also be in on his murder by poisoning. After Suarez planted the "poison" in Torres's food, Torres would fake going into convulsions. Prison authorities would play their part. Medical personnel would rush him to the emergency room of the nearest hospital. There, hospital personnel would also be in on the scheme. They would admit Torres into emergency, where, according to plan, he would be reported to have died from cyanide poisoning. If necessary, the city of Miami would issue a death certificate making it official that Roque Torres was dead.

If all of this went according to plan, Rosa Sanchez and her accomplice, Esperanza Arroz, would have the proof they needed that Torres was dead. Ostensibly, they would then contact Capdavilla, the paymaster. The cops would do surveillance and record the payment being made. If they were lucky, somewhere along the line Capdavilla would contact Battle to report that the hit had been successful. The cops would have surveillance records, photos, and wiretap conversations going all the way up the Corporation chain of command.

It was an audacious plot, the cops all agreed. There were a number of ways it could go wrong. For it to work, they had to let a high number of non-cops in on the scheme—Suarez's cellmate, prison authorities and guards, paramedics, hospital personnel, people in city administration, and Roque Torres, the target of the murder. There were a lot of opportunities for someone to leak information about the scheme, which would alert Suarez and also the co-conspirators that something was not right. Even if the cops were able to keep the entire plan secret, they still had to pull it off. There were many moving parts, some of them involving skilled acting and deception on the part of the participants. As the planning for the simulated murder got under way, the cops felt as if they were staging an elaborate Broadway show, with a cast of dozens and a cliffhanger of an ending.

ON THE MORNING OF DECEMBER 10, ROSA SUAREZ AND ESPERANZA ARROZ MET WITH Kenny Rosario, the undercover detective, whom they knew only as "the Puerto Rican." They had been informed by the cellmate of Frank Suarez, whom they knew only as El Perro (the Dog), that the Puerto Rican was his brother-in-law. It had been agreed that he would be paid $5,000 for the poison, which would be delivered in a small vial.

They met at a small bar on Coral Way, in the neighborhood of Westchester. Rosario was wearing a wire. He handed over the vial, which was in a plastic bag marked *Caution: Hazardous Material.* The vial contained a harmless liquid that had been prepared by the Metro-Dade PD crime lab.

In the parking lot outside the bar, Arroz gave Rosario $1,500 in cash, with the promise that the rest would be paid after it was proven that the poison had done its job.

Nearby, a team of detectives from Technical recorded the entire transaction on video, from a white van parked fifty yards away. An hour later, that same crew recorded Esperanza Arroz calling Carlos Capdavilla to report that they had received the poison from the Puerto Rican, whom she described as having "the coldest, deadliest eyes I have ever seen."

A few days later, Rosa Suarez and Esperanza Arroz visited Frank Suarez at the Dade Correctional Institution. Rosa had hidden the vial of poison in her bra. When she believed the guard was not looking, she passed it to her son. After about twenty minutes, the two visitors departed and Suarez was led back to his cell.

On December 19, the following day, everything was in place. Roque Torres, who had been anticipating this day, arrived in the facility's communal dining hall at 5 P.M. The plan, according to the co-conspirators, was for El Perro, Suarez's cellmate, to get into an argument with Torres just as he was sitting down to eat. While he was distracted, Suarez would discreetly put the poison into Torres's food.

It all went according to plan: El Perro hurled an insult at Torres. The two inmates stood up as if to face off in a fight. During this tense exchange, Suarez dumped the poison into Torres's food. Within seconds, guards quelled the disturbance between El Perro and Torres. They were separated and allowed to finish their meals.

Less than thirty minutes after all the inmates had finished dinner and been escorted back to their cells, an inmate yelled loudly from his cell, "Guards! Guards! We got a medical emergency!"

The guards responded to the cell of Roque Torres, who was spread out on the floor, having convulsions. He was foaming at the mouth and writhing in pain. Later, the responding guards and cops who were in on the ruse would say that Torres deserved an Academy Award for his performance that day.

Shanks and the other investigators had set up a command center at Dade County Fire Station in the town of Homestead. A medical response team was set to go. The paramedic team included two undercover Miami police officers, just in case Torres tried to use the occasion to attempt an escape. Siren wailing, the fire/rescue vehicle rushed to the prison; paramedics spilled out and entered the facility. They administered emergency first aid to Torres. Inmates in the area gathered around as he seemingly fell into unconsciousness. The paramedics loaded him on a gurney. Judging by the response from the paramedics, Torres was dead already. He was wheeled out of the prison and loaded into the waiting ambulance.

Once the vehicle left the prison grounds, Torres opened his eyes wide and smiled. The paramedics gave each other a high five. The mood was jubilant. The fake homicide had gone off without a hitch.

The ambulance drove past James Archer Smith Hospital and continued to the fire station command center. Detectives took Torres, handcuffed, and loaded him into an unmarked police car. He was driven a half block away to the adjacent Homestead police station, where he gave a lengthy statement about the events of the last few weeks, including a blow-by-blow account of his "murder" by poisoning. He was then turned over to a team of U.S. marshals, who escorted him to the Federal Detention

Center in downtown Miami, where he was admitted under a new identify. The next day he would be transferred to a federal prison located far away in the Florida panhandle.

Roque Torres's work was over, but for Shanks and the other cops who had hatched this elaborate scheme, the post-homicide part of the investigation was crucial. The response on the part of the various co-conspirators would be scrupulously recorded through surveillance and wiretaps. Their hope was that the aftermath would lead them to José Miguel Battle. Among other things, OCB had planted a pen register device, or trap-and-trace, on the phone box down the street from El Zapotal. Battle had five separate phone lines in his house, which he felt made it next to impossible for the feds to record all of his conversations. But a pen register device recorded the phone numbers of any and all calls made to a specific address, and a catch-and-trace made it possible to overhear certain conversations.

Approximately an hour after the fake murder, Rosa Suarez received a call from her son in prison. "It's done," he said.

"What do you mean, done?"

"It's done. They took him away on a stretcher."

Rosa was astounded. She hadn't been expecting it to happen so quickly. "But was he already dead?" she asked.

"Well, no one knows yet. They took him to the hospital outside. He was wearing an oxygen mask, and his stomach was being pumped."

Suarez put El Perro on the line. He explained that with the amount of poison they used, the prospects for Roque Torres's survival were mini-mal. "That was a deadly dose. That's what they kill animals with."

"So," said Rosa, "he was taken away? To the hospital?"

El Perro said yes and gave the phone receiver back to the son. "Hey, gotta go," said Frank. "I'm going to church now."

Rosa laughed. "Okay."

"To the feast."

"Yes," said the mother. "Go to church and ask God for forgiveness."

"What?" asked Frank.

"Go to church and ask for forgiveness from God."

Annoyed, Frank said, "Ah, let it go!"

"Okay," said Rosa.

"Bye," said the son.

Within minutes, Rosa was on the phone again, with a team of detectives listening in and recording every word. First, she called James Archer Smith Hospital. "Happy holidays," said the female operator. "How can I help you?"

Rosa asked if they had a patient named Roque Torres. She spelled out the name.

"I'll check, sir."

Rosa had a raspy voice that sounded more male than female. On the phone, she was often mistaken for a man.

"Sir? Yeah. I believe that was the patient but he was transferred to the Medical Examiner's Office. Do you want the number?"

Asked Rosa, "Oh, so he passed?"

"I don't know, sir. Would you like me to give you the number?"

Rosa said yes and wrote down the number.

The next day, Rosa called the Medical Examiner's Office. "Is this Jackson Memorial?" she asked.

"No," answered an operator.

"What place is this?"

"This is the office of the Medical Examiner at Dade County Morgue."

"Oh, it's the morgue?"

"Yes."

"Oh my God. So if somebody tells you that they released over there, it's because the person is dead?"

"Yes."

"Oh! Okay, thank you." Rosa hung up.

Now she immediately called Carlos Capdavilla, who had been dragging his feet about making the $10,000 payment until there was verifiable proof that Torres was dead. Capdavilla still objected until the following day, when a brief death notice appeared for Roque Torres in *El Herald,* the Spanish-language version of the *Miami Herald.* The notice, which listed Torres's death as a possible suicide, had been submitted for publication by an undercover detective from the police department's Technical division.

The cops were there in a surveillance van when Rosa and Esperanza Arroz received a payment of $10,000 in cash from Carlos Capdavilla.

For Shanks and the cops at Vice, this was where the good part began. It was their hope that Capdavilla would call the Battle residence and report the hit. They had in place their pen registers and trap-and-traces, which would print out and itemize all calls to and from the five phone lines at Battle's home.

The morning after Capdavilla paid the two women, Shanks walked into the office of the bolita squad and was met by a number of solemn faces. Something was not right.

"Big problem," one of the detectives told Shanks.

"What is it?"

"All our pen registers on Battle—they went dead yesterday."

"What do you mean they went dead? All of them?"

"Yeah, all of them."

"What the hell caused it?

"I don't know," said the detective.

Later that day, a technician from Technical Services conducted an investigation and reported back to Shanks. "Somebody opened the lock on the telephone company switch box down the street from Battle's residence. It wasn't forced. They had a key."

"Okay," said Shanks. "Tell me more."

"Whoever did it, they knew to remove the slaves." The "slaves" were small devices that boosted the signal emanating from Battle's phone lines, so that the police could identify incoming and outgoing calls back at police headquarters and at the main office of the phone company, fifteen miles away.

Shanks knew this meant that their ability to trap and trace calls into Battle's home had been disabled. "So we lost everything," he said.

The technician nodded.

Shanks and the other investigators were in a state of shock. Yes, they would still be able to make an attempted murder case against Frank Suarez, his mother, Esperanza Arroz, and possibly Carlos Capdavilla, but the main goal of their elaborate sting—to entrap Battle—had, after months of preparation and hard work, just gone down the drain.

And that wasn't even the worst of it. Now Shanks and his colleagues had to ponder the very real possibility that José Miguel Battle had an informant, or informants, inside the police department.

EL PADRINO HAD A BAD KNEE. IT WAS AN OLD INJURY FROM HIS DAYS IN THE ARMY, but now, at the age of sixty-one, and because he was normally somewhere between twenty to fifty pounds overweight, the old ailments were catching up with him. A date had been set for surgery to take place, and despite a limp and considerable pain, Battle had increased his visibility. He made the rounds at a number of locations where he liked to meet people and do business—restaurants, bars, and Cuban diners. Usually at his side was his bodyguard and valet, Cache Jimenez.

It was not always an easy job being Battle's valet. One of Jimenez's responsibilities was to start Battle's car in the morning. It was an occupational hazard for Mob bosses that they were frequently the targets of assassination attempts. In the Cuban underworld, especially among those with military or espionage training, the likely method for a gangland hit was explosives. C-4 was good, because it could be affixed to the undercarriage of a car and triggered by a remote-controlled device. But as history had shown with the bombing of Ernestico Torres's car, or the murder of Loco Alvarez in Union City, or the more sophisticated and high-level assassination of former ambassador Letelier, any number of jerry-rigged devices could be used to blow up a car.

The most common method was to plant a bomb that could be ignited through the car's ignition. Turning a key to start the car created a spark that could be used to automatically set off an explosive device. For the average Mob underling, it was a startling realization that being the driver for a boss put him in a vulnerable position. Gangland history was littered with instances of drivers being killed along with or in place of their infamous employers.

On certain occasions, Battle stood in the distance, behind a concrete pillar or across the street, and watched as Jimenez stood alongside the car and reached through the driver's side window. With his arm outstretched, standing as far away from the car as he could, Jimenez reached in and turned the key in the ignition. Often there was sweat on his brow when he did this. Later, in a state of relief, he would sometimes joke about the absurdity of this routine. If there was a bomb, and it was to be triggered by the turning of the ignition, it's not likely that his standing outside the car was going to save his life.

Jimenez liked his job. He revered José Miguel Battle and was proud to be at his side, most of the time. But there were petty grievances that had to do mostly with being taken for granted. Once, in a phone conversation, Jimenez tried to explain his situation to a Corporation bookmaker named Gilberto Borges Sr.

Jimenez and Borges spoke nearly every day. They liked to complain back and forth about their duties as sycophants and errand runners for El Padrino. Jimenez noted that, unlike Borges, he had no set salary for what he did, including serving as driver and bodyguard. He did receive tips, which were alternately extravagant and nonexistent. "But you," said Jimenez, "you make a regular living."

Jimenez also complained that "I do things for [Battle] that I wouldn't do for my own family," like pick up his dry cleaning and deliver flowers to his girlfriends.

Along with the bitching back and forth, the detectives picked up some valuable information off the wire. It was through the Borges wire that they learned the details about Battle's knee surgery, which was to take place at Mt. Sinai Hospital in Miami Beach.

Knowing the date ahead of time gave Shanks and other detectives in his squad the opportunity to set up a multilayered surveillance of the location. They learned that following his operation, Battle would stay in a private room on the fourth floor.

The cops held an impromptu summit meeting at the listening post for the Borges wire, a sparsely furnished apartment in Westchester. It was decided that the half dozen detectives would rotate shifts and divide their time between the listening post, where the wire was being monitored, and the hospital, where they would conduct surveillance starting at 7 A.M.

Luckily for the cops, Battle's room was adjacent to the fourth-floor visiting area. Since none of the cops were known to Battle's people by face, they were able to pose as worried family members of a patient. "It was almost too good to be true," Shanks remembered. "We took turns playing roles and were able to sit amongst Battle's visitors as they came and went. They hardly noticed we were there. They spoke freely between themselves."

Among many valuable details that the cops were able to glean was who exactly constituted Battle's inner circle of advisers and friends. Trio de Trés was a constant presence at the hospital, as was Cache Jimenez. Also there was Luis DeVilliers Sr., a longtime Battle associate from his earliest days in New York, former owner of the Colonial restaurant in Washington Heights, who had recently moved to Miami. From the Borges wire the cops had learned that DeVilliers and Battle's brother Gustavo had formed a company that distributed illegal gambling machines in South Florida and the New York area. The machines created yet another lucrative revenue stream for the Corporation.

On the second day of the surveillance, Battle Jr. and Abraham Rydz showed up at the hospital. Junior seemed agitated, and when he discovered that Borges was the only member of his father's entourage at the hospital, he was outraged. "Where are my father's friends?" he said to Borges. "Where are all the guys who depend on him for their lives? They need to be here. I'm here. Where are they?"

Borges got on the pay phone in the visiting room and started making calls. Shanks and the other undercover detectives listened in. "Get over here now," Borges barked into the receiver. "Migue is here, the son. He's angry. Pick up Beto and Nuñez and Carlos and get your ass over here."

Discreetly, Shanks kept his eyes on Battle Jr. This was the first time he'd seen the son, and, again, the detective felt as though he'd walked into a real-life version of *The Godfather*. Battle was Don Corleone in the hospital bed, and Mike Battle Jr. was Mike Corleone, as played by Al Pacino. The similarities were surreal, and as he had when he first heard El Padrino doing a veritable Marlon Brando imitation at the cockfight they raided, Shanks found himself wondering to what extent Battle Jr. was consciously playing a role.

Among others things, the surveillance confirmed for the detectives that they weren't chasing their tails. The scene at the hospital was like a casting call for the inner circle of the Corporation, many of whom were people the cops had heard about but never seen in the flesh. In the visiting area and fourth-floor hallway, they were able to overhear conversations, mostly personal discussions or family gossip. They heard some of these people refer to Battle as "Padrino," and they witnessed much ass kissing and kowtowing to the Battle family. Shanks, in particular, noticed the close relationship between Battle Jr. and Rydz, which seemed far more like a father-son connection than what Miguelito had with his own father.

Said Shanks, "It was exhilarating to be sitting there listening to people I had been investigating for two years. It was a rare chance to watch and listen. We didn't learn much about criminal activity, but we got to see how everyone interacted. José Miguel Battle was treated as if he were a king."

Back at the listening post, El Padrino's stint in the hospital had "tickled the wire." When he was home, Borges was on the phone constantly making sure that everything was being attended to in the Battle universe. Mostly, Borges and Cache Jimenez continued their ongoing dialogue about who was being asked to do more for the boss. Said Borges, "Last night I had to take the grandchildren, Miguelito's kids, to the movies for two hours while Miguelito was at the hospital."

"That's nothing," said Jimenez. "El Gordo called me late, after ten. Said he had an unquenchable desire for a *media noche* [a Cuban sandwich]. I had to drive from my house in South Dade to find a sandwich—do you know how hard it is to find a *media noche* at that hour?—and then deliver it to the boss at the hospital."

I can top that, said Borges. "Today he had me looking all over Miami for silk boxer shorts, extra-extra large, because the hospital gown was making has balls itch."

Jimenez listened in awe.

"I called him an hour ago. I said, 'How do they feel?' 'Excellent,' he said. I said, 'Do you need any more [silk boxers]?' He said he was okay for now, but it depended how much longer he was going to be there."

Listening on the wire, the detectives cracked up laughing, partly because it was hilarious, and partly to break the tedium of long, incessant hours wearing a set of headphones, listening to mostly meaningless chatter.

Even after Battle left Mt. Sinai, the Vice Squad kept the wire in place. Borges's phone seemed to serve as command central, at least in terms of the personal relationships that constituted the Corporation's "kitchen cabinet."

Everything was going fine until one day the detectives, having just sat down at their monitoring station, heard the phone ring. Borges was not home, so the call kicked over to his answering machine. The voice of a male caller came on the line. He sounded young and spoke in Spanish, clearly and concisely, as if he were reading from a script. "Mr. Borges, you don't know me," he said. "But the police are listening to your telephone conversations, and your cellular phone conversations, too." Then he hung up.

The cops were stunned.

Sergeant Boyd was supervising the listening post at the time. He immediately called in Shanks to discuss the situation. Everyone was slack-jawed by the larger implications, once again, of there being a mole in their midst, but the more immediate issue was, how would they salvage the wire?

Boyd, Shanks, and the assistant state attorney, LaVecchio, discussed their options. One possibility was to obtain a verbal court order from a judge, to be followed up with a written one after the fact, allowing the cops to break into Borges's home and erase the message on his answering machine. They needed to do it immediately. LaVecchio was on the phone making the call to a judge when the surveillance team reported that Borges had already returned home.

It took Borges about an hour to listen to his messages. At the listening posts, the cops picked up the bolitero calling his son in an agitated state. "I need you to come over here right away," he said.

"What's up?" asked the son.

"I can't speak further on this phone. Just get over here."

Shortly thereafter, the surveillance team saw Borges's son arrive at the house and enter. After that, the wire fell silent.

The cops were angry. Clearly, somebody was tracking and sabotaging their investigation from the inside.

The Internal Affairs (IA) Section was called in. Both Boyd and Shanks were interviewed by IA detectives about the situation. Who did they think was the culprit?

Approximately twenty Vice and Tactical detectives had been separated from OCB to conduct the Battle investigations. The logical deduction was that the leaker was one of those detectives.

Boyd and Shanks came up with a plan. They would compartmentalize the various detectives into smaller groups and release information on a need-to-know basis. That way, only certain groups would know certain facts about the investigation, so that if there was a breach, it would be easier to track down the likely source. The second part of the plan was to spread the word among selected detectives that the Borges investigation had been so compromised that the wire was being closed down. In reality, Boyd and Shanks secretly continued to monitor the wire.

IA was never able to establish definitively who the mole was, but a few days after Boyd and Shanks spread the false directive that the wire had been shut down, something interesting occurred. Like a faucet that had been turned back on, Borges started using his phone again. Not tentatively, as if he wasn't sure, but without hesitation, as if he had received an "all clear" signal. One of the first calls was Borges talking openly with his daughter, speculating about who it was that had given them the anonymous warning that they were being recorded.

Boyd and Shanks had established that there was indeed a rat in their midst, but they still didn't know who it was.

The possibility that there were people in the police department on Battle's payroll was disturbing but not shocking. Corruption of the criminal justice system in South Florida had become alarmingly commonplace. The commodity that made it possible was cocaine.

DETECTIVE KENNY ROSARIO HAD AN INFORMANT HE CALLED "PEPSI COLA." FOR months, Pepsi Cola had been telling Rosario that Battle and a few of his closest partners had made the jump from bolita to drug dealing. Pepsi Cola would know. He was himself a former high-end narco dealer whom Rosario had first indicted and then turned into an informant.

Pepsi Cola was normally a reliable source, or at least a very interesting one. He had a habit of dropping bombshells on the Special Investigations Section with his tidbits of information. Years earlier, he had related an anecdote to Rosario that, when passed along to Shanks and others in his squad, blew everybody's mind. Apparently, three Miami hoods— likely Marielitos who didn't know any better—had stormed a cockfight that Battle was attending and robbed the place at gunpoint. "*Tumbe*" was the word Pepsi Cola used, Cuban slang for ripoff. The robbers made everyone get on the ground, including Battle. They individually fleeced everyone in the place. Pepsi Cola estimated that they must have made off with $300,000 to $400,000 from the twenty to twenty-five attendees at the cockfight.

Afterward, everyone was angry—the spectators, the managers of the event, and probably the roosters. Who would be idiotic enough to rob an event that was being patronized by El Padrino?

Battle put out the word that he wanted to know who had done the robbery. A few weeks later, a person was delivered to him at El Zapotal. He was alleged to be one of the robbers. Battle interrogated and tortured the man until he confessed and gave up the names of the other robbers. Then Battle killed the man and went after the other two.

One week later, Battle had killed them all. Their bodies were dumped far out into the Everglades.

It was one of those wild José Miguel Battle stories. The detectives were unable to determine if there had ever been a robbery at the cock-fighting arena because, of course, the crime was never reported. There was no record of the three men being murdered, but, again, it was no surprise that nothing was ever reported. As far as anyone knew, they might have simply disappeared. If they were Marielitos—in this case criminals—it's likely they were undocumented or living under assumed names. No one knew who they were.

The cops were able to verify one thing: three dead bodies, badly decomposed, their lives terminated by violent means and under highly suspicious circumstances, were found dumped on the banks of an Everglades canal. Three Latino males, bound and gagged, shot execution-style, directly between their eyes. The bodies were wrapped in black plastic garbage bags, and in the steamy heat and humid conditions, they had marinated in their own spilled blood and other bodily fluids. It was not possible to establish their identities.

Early on, Pepsi Cola had been convinced that Battle was not dealing cocaine. He once related a statement that Battle had made to him, a comparison of the financial benefits of drug dealing versus bolita. "The way you people make money," said Battle, referring to *narcotraficantes*, "it's like a big faucet. Every once in a while a big rush of water comes pouring out, but then it shuts off for months or even a year. Me, I have a smaller faucet that runs all the time. In the end, my money is consistent and I make more of it. And sometimes I get a big rush like you do."

Apparently, Battle's philosophy had changed. According to Pepsi Cola, El Padrino was now up to his nose in white powder.

Pepsi Cola gave Detective Rosario the names of some prominent dope dealers who had been dealing with Battle. A number of them had recently been convicted on cocaine conspiracy charges and received sentences ranging from fifteen to seventeen years. Maybe some of them would be willing to talk in exchange for a reduced sentence.

The Battle investigators set up a number of clandestine meetings at the federal Miami Federal Detention Center to speak with the imprisoned coke dealers. One of the inmates they spoke with was a smuggler named Roberto Garcia, who told them about his dealings with Battle:

> Garcia stated that he met Jose Miguel Battle around the year 1982. He met Battle in Key Largo at a cockfighting ring called "La Valla del Gallo." Garcia said that he placed several bets against Battle ranging from $1,000 to $10,000. Garcia then stated that Juan Cortez and himself were partners in the drug business and owned approximately four powerboats. The boats were kept at Juan Cortez's farm, located at 168th Street off of Krome Avenue.

Sometime in late 1987 or early 1988, while visiting the Cortez farm to buy and sell roosters, Battle saw the powerboats. He told Garcia and Cortez that he would like to hire them to import a shipment of cocaine into South Florida. Said Garcia:

> The amount of drugs that was to be imported was approximately eight hundred to one thousand kilos of cocaine.

Battle made a down payment of $3,000 to cover preliminary expenses on the shipment, which was later canceled for unknown reasons.

The detectives separately interviewed Garcia's partner, Juan Cortez, and the details checked out. Cortez added that after the cocaine shipment was canceled, Battle came to him again a few months later:

Battle once again contacted Cortez and stated that he needed 25 kilos immediately. At this time Cortez introduced Battle to Ramon Sancerni, who had the 25 kilos for Battle. All three parties met at the farm so that this drug transaction could be executed. Cortez states that Battle paid Sancerni in his presence $400,000 for the 25 kilos of cocaine, at which time Sancerni gave Battle the narcotics. Cortez further states that he made $12,500 for being the middleman in this transaction.

Garcia and Cortez also noted that they had seen Battle use cocaine, with Garcia relating an anecdote about a time El Padrino had a cocaine overdose at La Valla del Gallo. Luckily for Battle, there was a doctor among the spectators who administered CPR on José Miguel and saved his life.

Garcia and Cortez were fascinating, but the detectives scored an even more substantial source when they interviewed Juan Pablo Alonso, a high-ranking cocaine trafficker who worked for the Medellín Cartel, led by Pablo Escobar. Alonso had expertise at arranging transshipment routes via the Bahamas, Jamaica, and other Caribbean locations for cocaine shipments coming from Colombia. Alonso was a major player: he met face-to-face with Escobar, but he dealt mostly with an Escobar lieutenant named Maximiliano Garces.

In late 1989 or 1990, Alonso received a phone call from Garces saying that José Miguel Battle, whom he described as "a very serious man," was in need of Alonso's expertise. Battle, said Garces, was a semiregular customer. Normally he took delivery of his product in South America and made his own arrangements to have the product smuggled in to South Florida. Currently, he had a shipment of a thousand kilos on a mother ship headed for Cayo Arellano, in the Bahamas. Because of mechanical problems, he needed someone who could complete the delivery to Miami, and he needed the exchange to take place within the week.

Alonso agreed to meet with Battle that afternoon. They met at a restaurant on Tamiami Trail and SW 64th Avenue. The name of the restaurant—the Covadonga—had a special meaning to Battle. Cova-

donga was the village in Mantanzas, near the Bay of Pigs, where Battle
engaged in his heroic action that saved nearly two dozen men during the
invasion.

Battle arrived with a partner whom he introduced to Alonso as Pepe
Moranga. The man's birth name was José Gonzalez, but he had used
the name Pepe Moranga ever since he first became involved in the bo-

donga was the village in Mantanzas, near the Bay of Pigs, where Battle
engaged in his heroic action that saved nearly two dozen men during the
invasion.

Battle arrived with a partner whom he introduced to Alonso as Pepe
Moranga. The man's birth name was José Gonzalez, but he had used
the name Pepe Moranga ever since he first became involved in the bolita business back in the early 1970s. In New York, Pepe had operated
mostly as an independent bolitero. Often, he was a pain in the ass to
the Corporation. In Brooklyn, where the two-block rule had become an
issue, he tested the limits by sometimes literally using a tape measure to
determine the point at which he could open his own bolita hole. Like
many independent operators, he frequently used the Corporation to lay
off bets. When the time came to reimburse the Corporation, he stalled,
hoping that he would win a subsequent layoff bet and not have to pay up
at all. If he won a bet, he would demand immediate payment from his
contact at the Corporation counting house.

All in all, Pepe Moranga was an annoyance, but here he was in Miami,
sitting with his old friend and associate, José Miguel Battle, with whom he
was cofinancing a major cocaine deal.

Juan Alonso already knew Battle's problem; he'd been prepped by his
people in Medellín. Alonso had contacts in the Bahamian government.
Over a series of meetings with Battle and Pepe Moranga, Alonso delivered to José Miguel his entire cocaine shipment.

For Shanks and the other detectives, the information from Alonso
was a window into what appeared to be a phase of intensive cocaine
trafficking by El Padrino. Many of these people had been arrested and
convicted in the late 1980s, and, like Garcia, Cortez, and Alonso, they
were willing to talk about Battle if it helped them with a sentence reduction.

One of the men was even higher on the food chain than Alonso.
Edith José Cabrera was serving a sentence of fifteen and a half years for
his role as the Medellín Cartel's main man in Miami. Cabrera related a
story of being contacted by Pablo Escobar himself to handle a dispute
with Battle, whom Escobar referred to as a "serious customer." Apparently, a cocaine load from Colombia, on order by Battle, had been lost

in the Bahamas, and Battle was alleging that he'd been ripped off. He'd never received the shipment and was refusing to pay. The Medellín people insisted that the product was Battle's responsibility as soon as it left Colombia. He owed them $700,000.

A special meeting was set up at El Zapotal. Cabrera arrived to find three officials from the Bahamian government already present. They had helped facilitate the shipment from Colombia. Cabrera worked out a compromise arrangement. Battle would pay the $700,000, but he would be given preferential treatment on future deals.

The detectives were astounded. Here was information that linked Battle not only to a series of substantial cocaine deals, but also to Pablo Escobar, the biggest and most notorious cocaine dealer on the planet.

The cops took the information to Larry LaVecchio, their prosecutorial liaison. LaVecchio informed them that if Cabrera, Alonso, and the others were willing to testify, what the cops had was strong—with one major caveat. Most of the cocaine deals they were receiving information about could not be prosecuted as individual crimes because of statute-of-limitations constraints. They could, however, be used as part of a RICO prosecution, where the rules of law on past criminal offenses were different.

For Shanks, the very mention of a RICO case was exciting. He'd been dreaming of such a strategy ever since becoming involved in the Battle investigation.

Sergeant Jimmy Boyd was less excited. A RICO prosecution meant sharing the case with federal agents. Boyd, a good ol' boy Miami cop, had a natural aversion to working with federal agents, who tended to utilize the hard work of local cops without sharing the glory or credit.

Nonetheless, Boyd could see where all this was headed. If ever there was a criminal career and organization that lent itself to a RICO prosecution, it was Battle and the Corporation. Boyd wanted to make sure that if there were to be a RICO case, Metro-Dade PD would be well represented. What this required was that the Miami cops finally undertake something they had been meaning to do for months—they needed to send a representative to New York to interface with cops in the New York–New Jersey area who understood the full scope of Battle's operations before he ever came to Miami.

There was never any doubt who that representative would be. David Shanks had proven himself to be unusually devoted to the Battle investigation. His knowledge of the Corporation in Miami was substantial, but he needed to extend his education to the Northeast.

Sergeant Boyd, sensitive to the ethnic considerations of having Anglo detectives who did not speak fluent Spanish as lead investigators on a case involving Cuban Americans, assigned to Shanks a new partner. Humberto "Bert" Perez was a young, gung-ho Cuban American cop who had come on the job looking for action, specifically undercover work that would take him into dangerous situations. Shanks was concerned that the Corporation case—and particularly their fact-finding mission to New York—was more in the nature of an intelligence-gathering operation than an undercover sting, but Perez was certainly enthusiastic.

The two cops packed their luggage and booked a flight. In the development of the case against Battle, it was a crucial step. Metro-Dade PD was going to the Big Apple.

Part III

"Lo Hecho, Hecho Está"/"What Is Done, Is Done"

OLD FRIENDS

15

LIKE MANY GANGSTERS, PEPE MORANGA LIVED A LIFE OF CONSIDERABLE PARANOIA—with good reason. It is a fact that everyone dies eventually, but for a gangster the possibility of death is a constant presence.

Moranga had partnered with José Miguel Battle on some major cocaine deals in Miami. At the time, it seemed like a great opportunity. The two men had a relationship that went back decades. It started with bolita, and then later, on a trip to Miami in 1987, Moranga met with Battle and learned that he was looking to get into the cocaine business. At first, Moranga was surprised. Battle had always been against the narcotics business. He more or less made his boliteros pledge that they would not deal drugs. But that was in New Jersey, back in the 1970s. In Miami, El Padrino had apparently succumbed to the temptation of the coke biz, where huge profits had transformed the city into an underworld mecca.

At the age of forty-nine, born in Havana, Moranga was part of a generation of Cuban Americans who were living a life stretched between the frigid Northeast of New Jersey and New York and the urban tropicalia of Miami. Though he and his wife moved from the Bronx to Miami in 1988, Moranga traveled back and forth four times a month. He claimed to be a jewelry broker; he and his wife had opened a jewelry store in Miami in 1988, but it failed and went out of business one year later. Mostly, Moranga was a high-flying coke dealer. He had a cocaine trafficking charge hanging over his head that he'd been fighting in court since 1985. But that hadn't slowed him down.

In late 1990, Moranga had a falling-out with Battle. On the surface, it was over money stemming from their cocaine deal in Miami, but really it went back to Moranga's having been a pain in the ass to the Corporation since the 1970s. Battle didn't like Pepe Moranga. He had been willing to use his expertise to facilitate his branching out into a business he didn't know very well, but that was where the relationship ended.

In the winter many people, for health considerations, leave the frigid climes of the Northeast for sunny South Florida. In January 1991, Moranga did the opposite. He knew that Battle was upset with him. And so for health considerations—that is, to avoid getting whacked—he got out of Miami and traveled to New York, where he hoped to generate some gambling profits for himself.

In the early afternoon of January 27, Moranga met a friend for a bite to eat at Villa Alegre restaurant, located at 178th Street and St. Nicholas Avenue in Washington Heights. Moranga felt comfortable in *el barrio,* where he had thrived as a bolita banker and hustler. Miami was great: you could close your eyes, breathe in the air, and believe you were back in Cuba. But the real money was made in New York, where the streets pulsated with energy and the nights were filled with an alluring kind of menace.

Moranga sat with his friend at a table near the back of the restaurant. He was old school; he did not yet have the newfangled technology of a cell phone. He received a message on his beeper, checked it out, and then excused himself to go make a call at the pay phone, which was located just inside the front door.

As Moranga dialed a number, a man slipped in the door. He was tall and gaunt, a ghostly figure in his late fifties. As Moranga stood facing the pay phone, the man pulled out a .32 automatic, put it to Moranga's head behind his right ear, and pulled the trigger.

The loud *pop!* startled the handful of patrons in the restaurant. Moranga slumped to the floor. The gunman bent down and put the gun to Moranga's forehead, pulling the trigger and shooting him between the eyes.

Moranga's body had fallen in such a way that it blocked the front door of the restaurant. Calmly, the gunman whacked the butt of his gun against the glass of the door. The glass shattered into shards, which the man cleared away. He stepped through the frame of the door and, walking briskly but not running, crossed the sidewalk to a car that was waiting for him in front of the restaurant. He was gone in a matter of seconds.

It was a clean, professional hit. Among the relevant details was the likelihood that whoever had paged Moranga on his beeper was in on the hit. The number on the pager was one he recognized and felt the need to respond to immediately. The gunman had been waiting on the sidewalk in front of the restaurant for the exact moment when the victim stepped up to the phone. The killer, or killers, knew where the pay phone was located within the restaurant and in relation to the front door. They knew that once Moranga stepped up to the phone, they could shoot him dead and make a quick getaway.

NYPD homicide detectives handling the case weren't able to make much headway. They determined that Pepe Moranga's real name was José Gonzalez, and that he was a professional gambler and a coke dealer. Since Moranga had been carrying a Florida state driver's license, with his address listed as 102-51 SW 66th Street in Miami, they contacted cops in Dade County. What they learned was that Pepe Moranga fit the profile of a Cuban gangster affiliated with the Corporation, but that only made the possibility of solving his murder more of a long shot.

There had been a couple of witnesses, but the shooting had transpired so quickly that the descriptions of the gunman were sketchy. One physical description of the shooter that was consistent, however, was that he had deep-set eyes with dark rings around them, and that his complexion was unusually cadaverlike.

That description was very much on the minds of local detectives when, months later, another shooting occurred just a few blocks away, at West 180th Street and Broadway, again in the middle of the afternoon. This time, the reasons for the killing were easier to establish, though the likelihood of closing out a successful murder investigation was equally slim.

Few people over the years had been closer to José Miguel Battle than Angel Mujica. Back when he was in his twenties, he was a gangly cop with big ears who revered José Miguel Battle. His devotion to the man was absolute. Later, they were side by side during the Bay of Pigs invasion and at the Isle of Pines prison. El Gordo y El Flaco, Laurel and Hardy: they guarded the door to the prison patio together. Later, they reunited in New Jersey to launch what would eventually become the biggest bolita business ever seen in the United States.

From the beginning of their criminal ventures together, there was a problem, a structural flaw. Battle was an outsized personality, and Mujica was not. Battle insisted on dominating every situation. He became El Padrino, and Mujica became an afterthought. Few people knew that Mujica was the one had who laid the foundation for the Corporation.

It was when they were all hiding out in Madrid in 1970 that Mujica first recognized that Battle would always be the center of attention. It was one of the reasons why Mujica stayed behind in Spain. He did not want to be Battle's partner anymore, but economic necessity had brought him back to the United States, back into the realm of El Padrino.

Mujica had cashed out of the bolita business in 1979 when Abraham Rydz and Battle Jr. took over the Corporation. It was not the first time he felt as though he was finished with bolita, and it would not be the last. Mujica's legitimate business ventures in Spain all followed a similar pattern: they started out great, with adequate investment from his bolita savings, and then they crashed.

In 1989, Mujica had returned to New York once again. He was back into bolita. He started out small, with a dozen bolita holes, mostly in the Bronx, where he had first begun his numbers business two decades earlier. When José Miguel was told what his old friend was up to, he was not pleased. Mujica had been paid $300,000 to cash out of the business. He sold his entire operation to Rydz and Miguelito. He was not authorized to be opening up competing bolita holes in New York.

Over the phone from El Zapotal, Battle told Nene Marquez, "I don't want to have to come up there. Talk to my old friend. Tell him he needs to shut down his operation, or we will shut it down for him."

Marquez talked to Mujica. "If El Gordo says you are out, then you're out."

Mujica wasn't buying it. In view of his long history with Battle, he couldn't believe that he wasn't deserving of special consideration. And so he did something he had never done before, something he told himself that he never would do—he went to El Padrino, hat in hand, and begged for the right to continue his career as a bolitero.

The meeting took place in Miami. Mujica flew down from New

York. Arrangements had been made for Mujica to speak with Battle at a cockfight somewhere not far from El Zapotal, in Redland. The cockfights had become Battle's favored location for conducting business. In an area separate from the *valla,* the fighting arena, people from the community waited their turn to meet with El Padrino. It was the Cuban version of *The Godfather,* people asking for favors from the Man, with the sound of roosters squawking and gamblers throwing their money around in the background.

"We go back a long way," Mujica said to Battle. "We started this business together. Times are tough for me right now, and I need to make some money. I'm asking you: let me have my little piece of the pie."

It could not have been easy for Mujica. He was the one who initiated the business, and now here he was begging for his right to exist.

Battle was nothing if not sentimental. He said to Mujica, "You're right. We go back a long way."

"Then you agree," said Mujica. "I'm free to have my bolita holes and stay in business."

Battle nodded his head.

It was a great relief to everyone. The boliteros cracked open some Dom Pérignon and placed more bets on the cockfights. It seemed as though everything was good, except that Mujica noticed his old friend was being unusually quiet, staring at him out of the corner of his eye. Needing reassurance, Mujica asked Battle, "El Gordo, we're good, right? Everything is understood between us?"

Again, as he had before, Battle nodded and assured his old friend that everything was okay. As Mujica left the cockfight arena that day, he and Battle embraced, just like old times.

As Mujica left, Battle turned to a couple of associates standing nearby and said, "There goes a dead man. He just doesn't know it yet."

THE HIT ON MUJICA WAS CONDUCTED WITH EXTREME PREJUDICE. THIS WASN'T LIKE the attempts on Palulu, which had been the result of an open contract, where everyone and his mother was looking to do the job and collect the money. This hit would be organized within a tight-knit group of co-conspirators.

On the afternoon of May 8, 1992, Mujica was in Reynold's Bar in Washington Heights having a drink with a friend. His pager was going off incessantly. He used the pay phone in the bar, but at a certain point he told his friend he was going to use the phone across the street, at Broadway and 180th Street. He crossed the street, slipped a coin in the phone, and began dialing. That's when a man approached him from behind and fired one shot.

It was a magic bullet of sorts, penetrating his back and hitting two ribs, fracturing them both, then ricocheting upward, penetrating the chest cavity, perforating the left lung, severing the pulmonary vein and artery. The bullet continued upward to perforate the esophagus and eventually lodged in the right ventricle, causing extensive hemorrhaging. Mujica groaned, a kind of elongated death rattle, and collapsed to the pavement.

There were some witnesses on the street who saw the shooting. They chased after the gunman, who was later described as a Hispanic or Arab male, twenty-five to thirty years old. The man ran to a waiting car, a black Cadillac, and jumped in on the passenger side. Two witnesses caught a glimpse of the getaway driver—a man in his fifties, salt-and-pepper hair, gaunt, with a pale complexion and dark, deep-set eyes.

As soon as it was discovered that the victim was a person with deep-rooted connections to the Corporation, Detective Richie Kalafus was called in.

Kalafus looked over the file for the Mujica shooting and also the shooting of Pepe Moranga. He was struck by the similarities. Killings carried out, it appeared, by two men, one young, one older. They had possibly switched roles for the two shootings. The older man—gaunt, dark rings around the eyes, salt-and-pepper hair—had been the gunman for Moranga and the driver for Mujica. These appeared to be professional hits carried out by a team of skilled assassins.

Kalafus knew enough about the Cuban Mafia to suspect that these hits had been ordered by José Miguel Battle. The victims were veteran boliteros, partners and rivals of El Padrino. Through street sources, Kalafus learned all about Mujica's having had a falling-out with his former best friend. Though no one was willing to come forward and testify in court, the common belief was that Battle was behind the killing. The problem was that he had insulated himself from these acts. Battle was down on his farm in South Florida, feeding his roosters, while the bodies were dropping in New York. The possibility of holding Battle responsible for these hired killings seemed remote.

DAVE SHANKS ARRIVED IN THE BIG APPLE WITH HIS PARTNER, BERT PEREZ, IN JUNE 1992. Kalafus met them at LaGuardia Airport. Shanks had been speaking with the NYPD detective by phone on a regular basis. Kalafus had informed them about the Moranga and Mujica hits, which they both surmised were cases of Battle settling old scores.

The death of Mujica, in particular, had touched off plenty of chatter on the wiretap in Miami. Many in the Cuban bolitero universe were shocked that Battle might have arranged for the murder of his fellow brigadista. Battle and Mujica had been like brothers. The idea that El Gordo might have killed Mujica meant that nothing was sacred. Word spread of Battle's comment at the cockfight—"There goes a dead man"— but many chose simply not to believe it. The cops believed it, but they were a long way from being able to prove anything.

Shanks and Perez were taken straight from the airport to the 6th Precinct in Greenwich Village, where Kalafus had based a number of his homicide investigations. For the cops from Miami, the urban cowboy detective pulled out his massive Cuban Mafia Task Force file, which he had been compiling over the course of nearly two decades. Kalafus had a trove of background information on various key players in the Corporation, and he had a photo album with nearly two hundred mug shots and other photos. For a veteran investigator like Shanks, this was a gift from the heavens, a veritable gold mine of intelligence on Cuban American gangsterism going all the way back to Battle's first gambling indictment in the late 1960s.

In the midst of perusing the files, Bert Perez became bored. The young detective stood up and began pacing, which appeared to annoy Kalafus.

Afterward, Shanks said to Perez, "Didn't you say you have family in Connecticut?" Shanks and Perez were staying at a Holiday Inn in Yonkers, a suburb north of New York City, not far from the Connecticut border.

"Yes," said Perez. "I was hoping I might have a chance to see them."

"Go ahead," said Shanks. "Spend some time with your family. Tomorrow, Kalafus and I will do what we need to do and I'll fill you in later."

Truth was, Shanks was embarrassed by the young detective, though he was not surprised. Perez still had that gung-ho attitude from his days on patrol. Detective work required patience and attention to detail. If his partner could not sit still during debriefings and important exchanges of information, Shanks did not want him in the room.

The next day, Shanks met Kalafus—without Perez. Together, they made a trip to the Manhattan District Attorney's Office and spoke with the chief of their Organized Crime Section. Prosecutors there had convicted Lalo Pons on arson and murder charges. Later, Shanks and Perez met with detectives in the 34th Precinct, in the heart of Washington Heights. They were shown the locations of the Pepe Moranga and Mujica murders, and taken around to various restaurants and bars known to be meeting places for Cuban boliteros. The following day, the Miami cops rented a car and drove out to Newark to meet an investigator with the New Jersey Commission of Investigation. They had compiled a thirty-four-page booklet they called "The Corporation Profile," which contained biographical information and criminal histories for all known members and associates. Later, Shanks and Kalafus drove around Union City, once the home base for Battle and others who had created the largest illegal numbers operation in America.

The cop from Miami found the experience to be amazing. For nearly four years now Shanks had been studying Battle. But these locations had existed only as names and addresses in a police report or newspaper article; seeing them up close and personal was a revelation. It was like having spent years studying the Civil War, reading all the history books, and then for the first time visiting the actual battle sites. You could almost see and feel the ghosts from the past.

ON THEIR FOURTH AND FINAL DAY IN THE NEW YORK AREA, SHANKS AND PEREZ checked out of the Holiday Inn and headed north toward the town of Beekman, in Dutchess County. The brick-and-mortar congestion of

White Plains gave way to maple trees and rolling farmland of the agriculturally rich Hudson Valley.

After eighty minutes or so, they arrived at their destination—Green Haven State Prison. It was an incongruous sight. Spread out like a medieval estate on forty-eight acres, with thirty-foot-high stone walls and circular guard towers, the prison evoked the literary metaphor of "the machine in the garden." Built in 1939, at a time when American prisons were designed to look like industrialized fortresses, Green Haven held nearly two thousand inmates, most of the hard-core variety who had been locked up for murder, rape, robbery, arson, and other serious crimes.

Shanks and Perez were there to see Lalo Pons, who five years earlier had been convicted on arson and murder charges stemming from the Corporation's infamous arson wars. It was Shanks who had come up with the idea of trying to "turn" Pons. They would offer him an opportunity to provide them with information against Battle in exchange for the possibility of reduced prison time. It was a common tactic that sometimes bore fruit, though in the case of Pons they were warned by the assistant district attorney in Manhattan that he was a hard case and not likely to snitch.

Prison authorities were cooperative with the cops, who, they were impressed to hear, had come all the way from Miami. They allowed Shanks and Perez to look over Pons's prison records, which included a visitors' log and a record of deposits to the inmate's prison commissary account. Shanks had heard that Pons was still receiving monthly payments from the Corporation, standard practice for high-ranking members of the organization. Among other things, the money was designed to keep the incarcerated gang member fat and happy and therefore less likely to cooperate with authorities. Judging from Pons's list of regular visitors—which included some known boliteros—and the fact that his commissary account was every month replenished to the maximum limit, it appeared that he was being taken care of.

Pons did not know the detectives were coming. He was told that he had two visitors but had no idea who they were. He was escorted from his cell through a series of metal security doors to the massive visiting area, which included a row of enclosed interview rooms reserved for prisoners to meet privately with lawyers or policeman.

Shanks and Perez were already there when Pons, wearing a brown prison jumpsuit, was brought into the interview room. Shanks had seen mug shots of Pons from the time of his arrest; he was struck by how much Pons had aged in the five years he'd been inside. He was only forty-two years old, but his hair was gray and thinning, and he was smaller than the detective expected.

Shanks was already seated; he motioned for Pons to take a seat across the table. Pons chose not to sit.

The detective began to speak. "My name is Detective David Shanks—"

Upon hearing that Shanks was a police officer, Pons began shouting. "Cops! These are detectives in here! Police in here! I'm not cooperating with them! I'm no rat! You hear me? Take me back to my cell! I wanna go back to my cell!" Pons was shouting to the guards, but he also wanted to make sure everyone in the visiting area could hear him. He was not a rat.

Shanks and Perez were not exactly surprised. They had hoped Pons might listen to what they had to offer, but they knew it was a long shot.

The guards arrived to escort the prisoner back to his cell. As he was being led out of the room, Shanks delivered a parting shot. "Enjoy spending the next twenty years of your life locked up in here."

Shanks and Perez watched Pons being taken down the hall, back to his cell deep within the bowels of the penitentiary.

AFTER FOUR DAYS IN THE BIG CITY, THE DETECTIVES WERE EXHAUSTED. THEY ARRIVED back in Miami at midnight. The next day, they came into the office and were barely able to have their first cup of coffee before a call came from detectives at the 34th Precinct in Washington Heights. "We got another dead body," said one of the New York cops.

"You're kidding," said Shanks.

"Same deal. Shot in a restaurant in the Heights. Gunman described by an employee as in his fifties, tall and gaunt. He fled to a large black American-made sedan. Driver was waiting."

The victim was Omar Broche, another of the founding members of bolita in New York, just like Pepe Moranga and Angel Mujica. These murders all pointed in one direction—Battle.

Omar Broche had been engaged in a dispute with El Padrino. Broche was the person who, back in 1979, had vouched for Isleño Dávila with Robert Hopkins, the Irishman, who was inquiring on behalf of the Lucchese crime family. That made Broche one of the founding members of La Compañía, which put him on shaky ground with Battle.

Around the time of the arson wars, Broche moved to Spain. He stayed there for close to six years, until the bad publicity from the Presidential Crime Commission hearings and the Lalo Pons prosecution had blown over. Upon his return to the United States, Broche opened a number of bolita spots in northern Manhattan and the Bronx. He adhered to the two-block rule, but only by a few inches. One of the spots he opened was exactly two blocks from a Corporation spot. And this spot was more than just a place to make bolita bets. The location had several video slots and joker poker machines, making it what they called on the street a "ghetto casino." The place became so popular that it was taking business away from the nearby Corporation spot.

Battle, at his home in Miami, received regular reports about Omar Broche. On one of his many phone lines at El Zapotal, he listened as Nene Marquez filled his head with stories of ungratefulness and betrayal. When it came to the veteran boliteros with whom Battle had begun the business back in the day, it didn't take much to get him wound up. El Padrino seemed to carry a lingering resentment toward many of these men. His list of grievances was long; it included their unwillingness to help him avenge the murder of his brother Pedro. Broche and the others had started La Compañía while Battle was away in prison. A different kind of man might have let bygones be bygones, but for someone who seemed driven by a deep-rooted need for revenge, the grievance built to a breaking point, and then somebody had to die.

In May, Omar Broche was called to a meeting with Nene Marquez and told in no uncertain terms that he was being offered a choice. Either his place would be burned to the ground, or he could switch spots with the Corporation. They would take over his profitable ghetto casino, and he could take control of their less-profitable bolita hole exactly two blocks away.

It was more of a "fuck you" than a legitimate choice. In a state of humiliation, Broche accepted the offer, but he also began bad-mouthing

Battle and the Corporation all over town. Specifically, he was overheard by a Corporation soldier saying that José Miguel Battle was "a despicable piece of shit," and he referred to Nene Marquez as Battle's "faggot brother-in-law."

The Cuban rumor mill was like a tropical tornado; it went around and around. Battle heard what Broche had said, and then Broche heard that Battle had heard. He had reason to be concerned. And so, like Angel Mujica before him, Broche decided he would go and make a personal plea to this man he had known for thirty years. With all that they shared as exiles and boliteros, surely they could reach an understanding.

The roosters were especially feisty on the day Broche arrived in Miami to speak with El Padrino. It was a good day for a cockfight. Broche waited his turn, which was in itself a bit of an insult, but he kept his cool and swallowed his pride, so that he might cut a deal with Battle.

It was a replay of the meeting between Mujica and Battle, which occurred at the same cockfight *valla* only months earlier. Broche apologized for having disparaged Battle in public. He asked for forgiveness. The two men embraced. Battle told Broche not to worry, that everything was okay.

As Broche was leaving, one of Battle's underlings said, "Well, at least he had the cojones to come to you and apologize."

Said Battle, "Too late. The decision has been made. He has to die."

Broche returned to New York. On June 27, he was at his small storefront restaurant on Lenox Avenue, in upper Manhattan. He was there to meet with Luis DeVilliers Sr., a fellow bolitero who had helped him finance his bolita shops in New York. DeVilliers was worried. He knew Battle; he knew what he was capable of. DeVilliers had heard that Battle had a contract out on Broche and likely on him, too, since he was the one who had financed Broche's recent ventures in New York.

"Luis," said Broche. "You worry too much. I spoke with El Gordo. Everything is good."

DeVilliers left, and within minutes Broche was shot dead, two bullets in the back. He died on the floor of his own establishment.

The Broche murder made it three executions of old-school Cuban boliteros in a span of fifteen months. Though it seemed probable that they had all been killed by the same team of gunmen, there wasn't much

evidence on which to make a case. There were eyewitnesses and forensic evidence that suggested a link, but the gunmen were like ghosts
who appeared and then disappeared. Nobody seemed to know who they
were. Likely, they were hired killers from out of town.

BEFORE LUIS DEVILLIERS EVER MET JOSÉ MIGUEL BATTLE, HE HAD HEARD A LOT ABOUT
him. He first heard about him in Spain, where the DeVilliers family
moved in 1972 after fleeing Castro's Cuba. They arrived with only the
clothes on their backs and very little money. With the help of some
friends, DeVilliers opened a meat and produce shop in Madrid. One of
his regular customers was a fellow Cuban exile named Angel Mujica.

This was shortly after José Miguel and Pedro Battle, Isleño Dávila,
Joaquin Deleon Sr., and the other New Jersey boliteros had left Madrid
and headed back to the United States. Angel Mujica had stayed behind
in Spain to begin an irrigation business. DeVilliers and Mujica became
good friends.

DeVilliers had dreams of moving to New York City. Mujica told
him, "I have lots of good connections there. If you go, stay away from
José Miguel Battle. The person you want to do business with is Isleño
Dávila."

DeVilliers was surprised to hear Mujica talk badly about Battle; he
knew they had been fellow brigadistas during the Bay of Pigs invasion.
He heard from others that Mujica and Battle had been like brothers.
Mujica spoke of Battle as a brother; he told DeVilliers stories of Battle's
heroism during the invasion. But he also seemed to have some sort of
resentment toward Battle that went unexplained.

In 1974, DeVilliers moved with his wife and young son to New York.
He took Mujica up on his offer and reached out to Isleño Dávila, who
offered him a job taking bets by telephone in various residential apartments, all of which were known collectively as La Oficina, the Office.
At first, the money was not spectacular. DeVilliers and his wife made
extra money by running a sewing business out of their apartment in
upper Manhattan. Eventually, with Isleño's blessing, DeVilliers began to
network the street, creating his own clientele. He took bets acting as a
middleman for Isleño, who took 5 percent profit for each bet.

DeVilliers did well for himself. Like Isleño and Battle and the other boliteros, he liked to eat. He was short, fat, and personable, with sandy blond hair and blue eyes, which was unusual for a Cuban. He did so well with his bolita clientele that he eventually broke off from Isleño and became independent.

In 1975, DeVilliers and his son, Luis Jr., opened El Colonial, the restaurant that would become a special meeting place for bolita bankers. It was there that DeVilliers met José Miguel Battle for the first time. DeVilliers mentioned that he knew Angel Mujica from Spain. Battle was impressed. At the Colonial, DeVilliers also met Omar Broche.

Throughout the late 1970s and into the 1980s, DeVilliers continued to operate as an independent bolitero; he used the Corporation as his bank for layoffs. In the mid-1980s, in the wake of the unseemly arson wars, he decided to move to Miami. He left the Colonial restaurant under the management of his son. Like Battle and the other boliteros, he maintained his bolita business in New York while living in South Florida. Once or twice every month, he came to New York to monitor his business. Most of the gambling profits—bales of cash—were stored in an apartment located at 750 Kappock Street in Riverdale. DeVilliers often brought shipments of cash back to Miami on planes and trains.

In 1990, DeVilliers ran into Omar Broche, whom he hadn't seen in years, at a store in Miami where DeVilliers was buying equipment for a barbecue. Broche had recently returned from Spain and was shuttling back and forth between Miami and New York, looking for opportunities.

The next day, Broche came by DeVilliers's home. They chatted about old times, and Broche expressed a desire to return to New York and open a storefront, or *tienda*. He asked DeVilliers if he'd be willing to extend him a loan so he could start his business. He promised the bolita banker a high-percentage return on his investment. DeVilliers had mixed feelings about it; he suspected that Battle might react badly. But he went ahead and invested in Broche's return to New York.

It didn't take long for trouble to surface. Both DeVilliers and Broche began hearing rumors of Battle's dissatisfaction and had been told that a contract was out on their lives. That's when DeVilliers traveled to New York to talk with Broche. He met him at his *tienda* and said, "Omar, he's going to come after us. You need to close down your business or you'll wind up dead."

After being told by Broche that everything was okay with Battle, DeVilliers left the *tienda* to go on about his business. About one hour later, he was paged by a friend. He found a pay phone and called his friend, who said, "Luis, Omar Broche is dead."

"What!" said DeVilliers. "That can't be. I just left him an hour ago."

"He was shot dead in his *tienda* on Lenox. The gunman ran away. Luis, believe me when I tell you, your friend is dead."

DeVilliers immediately returned to Miami. He hid out in his house, wondering if gunmen sent by Battle would be coming to kill him. But the more he thought about it, the better he felt. If Battle wanted him dead, that gunman in Manhattan would simply have entered the restaurant a few minutes earlier, while he was still there. The hit man could easily have killed them both. He had chosen to wait until DeVilliers departed.

DeVilliers stopped hiding; he circulated openly. In fact, he ran into Battle a couple times at the cockfights. In his spare time, DeVilliers was a breeder of gamecocks, just like Battle. Whenever he saw Battle, they greeted one another. The subject of Omar Broche was not mentioned. Like so much other bloodshed, court cases, and trauma, it was water under the bridge. For the founding boliteros who started in business together long ago and had somehow managed to survive, it was always an occasion for nostalgia and reminiscing when they ran into each other.

A few months later, DeVilliers expanded his ventures into the video game machine business, which was the latest craze in illicit gambling. He started a business called Challenger Games Inc., which purchased the machines and placed them in bars and at bolita shops all around South Florida.

In the course of developing his business, he was approached one day by three businessmen from Peru who claimed to have high-ranking contacts in the Peruvian government. These men were looking to open a casino in Lima, Peru's capital city. They claimed to have the ability to secure a casino license from the government. They were looking for U.S. investors and also personnel with casino-related experience.

DeVilliers knew an opportunity when he saw one. He told the men that he had casino management experience, which wasn't true, and he had someone in mind he thought might be interested in making a large-scale investment.

"That is tremendous," they said. "But before we can proceed, we need to see some proof of your experience in the casino business."

DeVilliers had a friend who worked in a casino in Las Vegas. Within a couple days of meeting the Peruvians, he was able to secure a forged letter from a casino in Las Vegas that vouched for his "years of experience" in casino management.

The Peruvians were thrilled. They began the process of obtaining a casino license while DeVilliers went hunting for an investor. Luis had only one man in mind—José Miguel Battle.

DeVilliers remembered that over the years, Battle had mentioned how he dreamed of having a casino one day. El Padrino associated the casino business with his years as a cop in Havana, when Meyer Lansky, Santo Trafficante, and other mobsters presided over the most prestigious casinos in town. To Battle, being a casino boss was the ultimate status symbol for a Mob boss. For one thing, it was legal. Casinos were the perfect business for laundering money in a way that was nearly impossible to verify or trace. A casino boss reigned over his domain like a feudal lord. When he walked out onto the gambling floor, amid the card tables, roulette wheels, and slot machines, he was a celebrity, a man of power and stature.

It was at a cockfight in Redland that DeVilliers told Battle that he had been approached by the three well-connected Peruvians. Everything was in place, said DeVilliers. All that was needed were investors.

Battle's eyes lit up. He wanted in. "I hold the key to your dreams," he told DeVilliers.

DeVilliers said he would relay the message immediately to the Peruvians, though he knew better than to mention Battle by name. With Battle's criminal record and notorious reputation, this would all have to be handled with discretion.

DeVilliers smiled to himself. Only weeks earlier, he had been in hiding, convinced that Battle wanted to have him killed. Now he was going into business with El Padrino on the grandest business venture either one of them had ever undertaken. If they could pull this off, it would change their lives forever. This wasn't just a dream come true. It was a godsend.

SHANKS AND HIS SQUAD STILL HAD WIRETAPS IN PLACE, BUT THERE WAS AN ABSENCE of chatter about the most recent bolita murder in New York. The secrecy surrounding the Broche hit was strange. Normally, cops in New York and Miami had street contacts, people who filled them in on the latest *bola en la calle* (street gossip). There were often rumors about why a murder took place, who was behind it, and who pulled the trigger. In a sense, the Corporation encouraged gossip, because it helped spread the message that there were consequences to being on the wrong side of the organization. But after the Broche hit: silence.

Sometimes, criminal investigations were like the changing of the seasons; if you let nature take its course, a seed became a bud, and a bud became a flower.

In August, just two months after the Broche hit, the cops got a major break in the case. One of the officers on the Miami OC squad had a female informant who came to him with a startling tale. She had recently been in a relationship with an older Cuban who, over many months, related stories to her from his mind-boggling career. The man's name was Roberto Parsons. He claimed to have been a veteran of the Bay of Pigs invasion and also a former operative for the CIA. Parsons told the girlfriend, in considerable detail, about his involvement with Operation 40. This unit of trained assassins, Parsons said, included Watergate burglars Frank Sturgis and Bernard Barker, as well as Cuban "freedom fighters" such as Luis Posada Carriles and Felix Rodriguez, former activists on behalf of the Contras in Nicaragua.

Following the assassination of President Kennedy, after Operation Mongoose was discontinued, some members of Operation 40—including Parsons—remained active within the CIA as a covert crew of hired assassins. Parsons claimed to have done off-the-record hits for the CIA, primarily in Latin America. In the early 1970s, he was cut loose by the Agency.

When José Miguel Battle first made the transfer to Miami in the early 1980s, Parsons was serving as the bolita boss's bodyguard. It was a smart move for Battle to be seen with a personage as storied and feared as Roberto Parsons. It enhanced Battle's own reputation as a former CIA-trained fighter at the Bay of Pigs who had been stationed at Fort Benning with men who had been prominent members of Operation 40.

By the late 1980s, Parsons was an independent operator who hired himself out as a professional killer. According to the girlfriend, Parsons described to her the murder of Pepe Moranga. He claimed that Moranga had been killed because he had cheated José Miguel Battle on a shipment of Mexican brown heroin. Battle ordered the hit, and Parsons brought two partners into the scheme—his nephew, Juan Carlos Parsons, and a fellow hit man named Jorge Gonzalez.

Roberto Parsons was sixty-one years old, but, as his girlfriend put it, "don't be fooled by his age. He's a very dangerous man." She described how, according to Parsons, he had been the gunman in the Pepe Moranga hit, with Gonzalez serving as a spotter and the nephew, Juan Carlos, acting as the getaway driver.

Shanks and his crew ran a NCIC search on Roberto Parsons. The most recent photo on file showed a man with salt-and-pepper hair, gaunt, with a pale complexion and deep-set eyes. He fit the description of the Moranga and Broche shooter and the Mujica getaway driver to a tee.

There were only vague references in Parsons's file to his CIA activities, but his criminal jacket was telling. In Miami he had been arrested twice, once in 1973 when he ran a stop sign and was pulled over and then held for not having a valid driver's license. The officers found a 9mm automatic pistol in his car and three stolen credit cards, all under different names. In 1988, he was arrested by the Organized Crime Bureau's Tactical Section and charged with extortion and kidnapping. He had allegedly kidnapped the girlfriend of a drug dealer who had refused to pay him $9,000 he owed from a narcotics transaction. By the time Parsons was to go on trial, all of the state's witnesses had disappeared. The defendant pleaded nolo contendere and was sentenced to four months in prison, which he had already served while awaiting trial.

According to Parsons's ex-girlfriend, the former spook trained his nephew to serve as his partner. Juan Carlos was tall, thirty years younger than Roberto, and, according to the girlfriend, "some say he looks like an Arab."

One way of assessing an informant is if they are able to provide information that was not publicly known. In this regard, the ex-girlfriend received a high rating. She told Shanks and the investigators a detail that had never been reported in the press or anywhere else, that after the Moranga shooting, the body of the victim blocked the shooter's escape route. Parsons had to shatter the glass door and climb out through the frame of the door.

"How do you know that?" Shanks asked.

"Roberto told me," said the ex-girlfriend.

Over the next few days, the cops sought corroboration; some of it trickled in, and some they created on their own. A bolita informant from New York notified a Miami detective he knew that "the Corporation is killing off competitors." The informant said that they were using an ex-CIA killer named Parsons and his nephew to do the murders. Shanks immediately sent a mug shot of Parsons to the New York detectives investigating the Moranga and Mujica killings. The detectives put together what's called a "six-pack," a display of six photos that included one of Roberto Parsons. A six-pack is the photo equivalent of a lineup. The detectives showed it to four separate witnesses of the murders. Two of the witnesses said they could not make a positive ID; two picked out the photo of Roberto Parsons.

Over the following weeks, the entire Battle investigation zeroed in on the mysterious Roberto Parsons and his nephew. Detectives in Miami and New York became energized, believing that if they could build a case against Parsons for the hired killings, they could use him to get to Battle. Then, in late summer, came a major break.

The man identified as the third wheel in the team of assassins—Jorge Gonzalez—was arrested on a major cocaine importation case in Anaheim, California. Gonzalez's alleged co-conspirators in this case were Roberto and Juan Carlos Parsons. Not only that, but Gonzalez had begun to cooperate with the DEA. Though he made no admission about his role in the Moranga or Mujica murders, he did admit to being present during another murder by Roberto Parsons that took place in Miami.

A task force of agents and officers from three different jurisdictions—New York, Miami, and Los Angeles—took part in the interrogation of Gonzalez. What they learned was mind-boggling. Gonzalez told them that Parsons liked to brag about his days in the CIA; he claimed to have assassinated officials in the government of Fidel Castro both before and after the Bay of Pigs invasion. He also admitted to having been a covert operative doing political killings for the CIA in Latin America in the 1960s.

The murder Gonzalez claimed to have witnessed took place in Miami. A dope dealer named Francisco "Paco" Felipe had received delivery of a cocaine shipment from Parsons but failed to pay for it. Consequently, Parsons lured Felipe to the upscale town of Miramar, 55 miles north of Miami, under the guise of discussing terms of payment. Gonzalez was Parsons's driver that day. He drove his partner to a deserted park, where they met Felipe, who was driving a black Chevy Suburban. Parsons got out of Gonzalez's car and walked up to the driver's side window of the Black Suburban. From inside, Felipe lowered the window. Parsons calmly pulled out a .25-caliber automatic pistol and shot Felipe twice in the head. He opened the door and pushed the body over to the passenger side of the front seat, then he climbed into the driver's seat and put the car in drive. On his way out of the parking area, he pulled up to Gonzalez's car and said, "Follow me. We're going for a ride."

Gonzalez followed Parsons south through Miami along Tamiami Trail until, after ninety minutes or so, they stopped at a rest stop out in the Everglades. It was a classic sweltering South Florida day, with high humidity and swarms of mosquitoes and flies. Parsons stripped the body of Felipe of all valuables—cash, wallet, a Rolex watch, even an expensive pair of sunglasses. Then he wiped down the black Suburban, eliminating all fingerprints or other telltale evidence. Leaving the body to rot in the stifling afternoon heat, Parsons hopped into Gonzalez's car. They drove back to Miami, to Calle Ocho in Little Havana, where Parsons went to a pawnshop and hocked the Rolex watch of his victim for $1,000.

In his detailing of the Felipe murder and other criminal acts by Parsons, Gonzalez never mentioned his own involvement in the Pepe Moranga murder in New York. A witness to the Moranga murder had identified a photo of Gonzalez from a six-pack as having been the get-away driver. The investigators kept this fact quiet. They allowed Gonzalez to believe he was helping them make a case against Parsons. The fact that Gonzalez was withholding evidence about his own culpability in a murder, or murders—clearly a violation of any cooperation deal he might reach with the authorities—was something that would come back to cause him major problems in the future.

In the meantime, an arrest warrant was issued for Roberto Parsons and his nephew. Grand jury hearings began in Manhattan on the Pepe Moranga murder, and in Miami a case was opened on the murder of Paco Felipe.

SHANKS AND THE MIAMI COPS HAD REASON TO BE OPTIMISTIC. ALONG WITH THE PAR-sons investigation, a recent wiretap at the home of a Corporation book-maker named Mario Arcacha brought about a stellar result. On the phone wiretap they came across the voice of Abraham Rydz, who frequently called Arcacha to place large personal wagers.

Rydz, the investigators knew, was a degenerate gambler. He took part in high-stakes card games, regularly went to the track, and was a frequent visitor to the Miccosukee casino, operated by the Indian tribe of the same name in West Miami.

It was exciting enough to hear Rydz on the wire, but then one day they heard him make a statement that, to the investigators, was like an early Christmas gift. Rydz and Arcacha were having a conversation about a $10,000 debt that Arcacha was alleged to owe a fellow Corporation bookie. Arcacha disputed the claim and was refusing to make the payment. Said Rydz over the phone, "Listen, many years ago, when I was sitting in your seat and I was taking a beating, Battle used to say to me, 'Don't get upset about a bad loss or a day here and there. We make our money from the long run. It's the balance sheet at the end of the year that counts, not what you lose one day that matters. So don't worry and never panic or take unnecessary risks.' So, what José Miguel told me back then, I've repeated to you now."

Arcacha continued to argue the point. Finally, Rydz sternly advised, "Listen to me. This relatively small amount of money isn't worth your life. Los Batlles (the Battles) are dangerous people, and you could get killed over this. José Miguel has had people hit for less. If needed, I'll pay the money, just to keep the peace."

Shanks and the other cops were astounded. Professional criminals rarely spoke so openly over the phone.

On a separate surveillance, detectives followed Arcacha making a money drop to Rydz at the office of YMR Fashions, where both Rydz and Battle Jr. showed up every day for work. Immediately, Shanks went to work writing an affidavit request for a wiretap to be installed at YMR Fashions. The affidavit was submitted to Dade County State's Attorney Janet Reno.

By now, every active cop in the state was familiar with Reno, the tough-as-nails prosecutor who had since 1978 been state's attorney, the first female to hold the job. She was a local legend, born near the Everglades and raised by a father who had been a police reporter for forty years. At six foot one, with a gruff, no-nonsense manner, Reno could be intimidating. Shanks would never forget one time when he and a Florida state prosecutor submitted an affidavit to Reno in her office. She looked it over, and then literally threw the forty-page document at the investigators, telling them it wasn't worth the paper it was written on.

This time, Shanks labored over the issue of probable cause, laying out the connection between Arcacha, Rydz, and YMR Fashions to the larger network of boliteros and bookmakers in Miami.

It was late on Friday, August 21, when Shanks delivered his affidavit directly to Reno's home in Kendall. She answered the door herself. "She was very gracious," remembered Shanks. "She promised to read it over the weekend and get back to me."

Shanks didn't hear back from Reno. Over the weekend, a storm hit South Florida that literally altered the landscape.

METEOROLOGICALLY, LATE SUMMER IS A TREACHEROUS TIME IN THE TROPICS. EUPHE-mistically, it is referred to as "the rainy season." In reality, it is a time of heavy storm patterns that frequently intensify to the level of hurricane conditions.

A tropical weather pattern designated as Hurricane Andrew had been brewing out over the mid-Atlantic for days. By the time it came ashore, it was a Category 5 storm, with winds in excess of 165 miles per hour. Andrew hit South Florida with the impact of an atom bomb. The winds were devastating to property, and torrential rains caused flooding from Key Largo to Miami. Sixty-five people were killed. It was the most destructive storm ever to hit the United States.

Much of the area was immobilized. More than twenty-five thousand homes were destroyed in Dade County alone. Many localities were without electricity for days. Government services came to a standstill, as people took account of what was lost and tried to put their lives back together.

For Dave Shanks, the personal toll was immense. He'd been living in a house on stilts in Key Largo, sixteen feet above sea level, that he had built with his own hands. His marriage had not been going well, due in part to the tremendous man-hours and attention that he had been devoting to the Battle case. As a native of South Florida, Shanks knew to take the storm warnings seriously. He drove to his uncle's house nearby. In recent years, he and his mother's brother had become like father and son. The uncle was an irascible Floridian who refused to evacuate. "I'm going to ride it out," he said.

Shanks returned to his house. He and his wife boarded up the place, loaded their parrots and other valuables into two cars, and headed for the mainland. Shanks's wife was a registered nurse. They drove to the home of a fellow nurse and stayed with her. The woman had one small child and was seven months pregnant.

It turned out that the storm hit the Dade County mainland harder than it did the Keys. Shanks and his wife were sleeping in a guest room at the house when he heard part of the roof being blown off. He rose and attempted to investigate, but the howling winds and flying debris forced him back into the bedroom. He noticed that the window in the bedroom seemed as though it was about to buckle. Just as Shanks removed the mattress from the bed and positioned it as a shield, the window exploded, with shards of glass blowing inward.

Shanks gathered up his wife, then the lady of the house and her child, and led them to the master bathroom on the ground floor. Everyone climbed into the Jacuzzi, with a mattress on top of them for protection. There they remained for the next four hours, until the winds began to die down.

There was so much destruction and scattered debris, with downed telephone poles scattered like twigs across roads, and flooding that had turned entire neighborhoods into swampland, that Shanks was not able to get back to Key Largo for days. By then, the National Guard had been called in. Roads were blocked off. Shanks was only able to get through the roadblocks established by the National Guard because of his police identification.

His own house was in decent shape, but his uncle's house and been badly damaged, with part of the roof caved in. The uncle was nowhere to be seen. After hours of searching local shelters and hospitals, he found him in a hospital in Key West. The uncle was in bad shape. He had chain-smoked unfiltered cigarettes for his entire adult life. Shanks didn't know it, but weeks earlier he'd been diagnosed with stage four lung cancer. The stress from his roof caving in on him had pushed him over the edge. He died within the week.

The losses in South Florida were catastrophic, both personal and financial. When Shanks tried to return to work, he was met with chaos. Phone lines were dead. Many cops and detectives were unaccounted for, mostly because they had become absorbed in trying to put their lives back together. It would be weeks before many of them reported for duty. Court dates went unmet. Criminal affidavits went unfiled and unread. For the time being, nearly all police and fire department man-hours were spent dealing with the crisis at hand.

One day, while working with a rescue and cleanup crew in South Miami, Shanks, out of curiosity, decided to drive by El Zapotal. The eye of the storm had passed right over Battle's hacienda in Redland. Shanks heard reports that the house had been hit hard, with the roof having been ripped off. But by the time Shanks arrived to check it out—two weeks after the storm—a construction crew of what looked like fifty Latino immigrants were hard at work. Huge stacks of plywood, drywall, roofing materials, and floor tiles were piled around the property. A generator was being used to pump rainwater from the grounds. The roof of the main house had mostly been restored.

In the effort to salvage his property, Battle was far ahead of the average citizen, though it was a job undertaken solely by his minions. On the two or three occasions Shanks drove by to check out the goings-on at El Zapotal, El Padrino was nowhere to be seen.

16

STORMY WEATHER

ABRAHAM RYDZ WAS NO LONGER RECEIVING HIS 17 PERCENT FROM THE CORPORA-
tion's bolita profits. It had been his choice to opt out of the tens of
millions of dollars the organization generated on an annual basis. On
the other hand, the business structure that Rydz and Battle Jr. had
created, the network of legitimate businesses and shell companies and
secret overseas accounts, was generating as much as or more than the
bolita business. Conservatively, Rydz was taking in $3 million a year
and paying taxes on only a small percentage of the total. He was doing
well for himself.

In early November 1992, Rydz was at Hialeah Park racetrack one
afternoon betting on the ponies. There were a number of friends and
associates in his box, and eventually the conversation turned to the
subject of a casino that Jose Miguel Battle Sr. and some partners were
inaugurating in Lima, Peru. Rydz listened to the conversation, though
he pretended like he was not. When one of the friends asked him, "Polaco, you know anything about this casino?" Rydz simply said, "No, I
do not."

He was not surprised. Over the years, Rydz had heard Battle express
his admiration for Lansky and Trafficante and the other mobsters who
owned and ran the casinos in Havana back in the day. It was a smart
business move, Battle would say. A casino was a legal business, licensed
by the government, ideal for laundering money. Given the amount of
money that streamed through a casino on a daily basis, it was impossible
for the Internal Revenue Service or anyone else to establish what was
legitimate and what was not.

Rydz knew Battle well enough to surmise that his interest in being a
casino boss was less about money laundering and more about ego. Battle

believed that by becoming a casino impresario he would be acquiring the stature of a true Mob boss. He would be putting himself in the same league as Meyer and Santo.

Right away, alarm bells went off for Rydz. His major concern was that Battle might be using partners in this new casino venture that could somehow be linked to the web of companies that he and Miguelito had created. Rydz did not doubt for a minute that this casino venture was a disaster in the making. José Miguel may have loved the *idea* of owning a casino, but he knew nothing about the business. And given that Battle put a high premium on loyalty over knowledge or experience, he was likely to use as his advisers and partners others who were equally ignorant. Nene Marquez, for one. And others whose main qualification was that they played poker with Battle or bet money at the cockfights.

As soon as Rydz left the racetrack, he called Miguelito. "You know anything about this casino?" he asked.

Miguelito was hardly speaking with his father anymore. The latest indignity was that his father had a new mistress, a Guatemalan immigrant named Effugenia Reyes who was younger than Junior. His father squired her around Miami, much to the embarrassment of his wife, Miguelito's mother. "I heard some rumors," said Miguelito.

"Here's what worries me," said Rydz. He explained that it was likely that Battle would bring Nene Marquez, his brother-in-law, in on the venture. If Nene was being brought in, then it was also possible they would want to use Nene's brother Maurilio, the Venezuelan.

Rydz did not have to explain to Miguelito what a potential disaster it would be if the casino partners used Maurilio Marquez in any way. Maurilio was the person Rydz and Miguelito had used as the front man for their many offshore companies. Their entire business operation, including many of their Swiss bank accounts, were in his name. If Battle Sr. used Maurilio as an investor or in any other way, and the casino operation became entangled in legal improprieties or financial complications, as it very well might, then Rydz and Miguelito were fucked. All that they had patiently worked for over the last decade—a seamless, nearly legal financial empire—could come crashing down.

Said Rydz, "I don't want our financial future tied into this cockamamie casino. I don't want a situation where if it goes down, we go down."

"I hear you," said Miguelito.

Rydz suggested that Junior contact Nene Marquez himself and tell him that under no circumstances could they use his brother's name in their casino venture.

Miguelito called Nene Marquez and got right back to Rydz. "He assured me they would not use Maurilio. I made him promise, and he assured me on his mother's grave."

"Good," said Rydz. He should have felt reassured. A potential calamity had been averted. But he knew José Miguel well enough to have his doubts. A sense of unease stayed with El Polaco, like a grumbling stomach, gaseous and unsettled after a big, greasy meal.

BY OCTOBER, THE METRO-DADE POLICE DEPARTMENT HAD, AFTER NEARLY EIGHT weeks of disruption and recovery from Hurricane Andrew, finally returned to regular duties. Shanks and the Organized Crime Bureau under Sergeant Jimmy Boyd resumed the Battle investigation with a renewed sense of focus.

They had reason to be optimistic. In November, Detective Kenny Rosario received a tip from an informant that a close associate of Battle's—Oracio Altuve—had been arrested in Miami on cocaine importation charges. Altuve was one of the original boliteros from Cuba and a high-ranking banker with the Corporation. His roots in the Battle organization went back to its earliest beginnings in Union City.

Altuve first came to the United States in 1950, but was deported in 1954 after being convicted of assault with a knife. In the early 1960s, with Castro's communist gulag in full force, he made his way back to the New York area and went to work for what was then the Battle/Mujica organization.

Altuve had an extensive rap sheet. He was arrested eleven times by the NYPD from August 1963 to January 1991 on virtually every possible charge related to bolita—possession of policy slips; operating a policy business; policy pickup man; promoting gambling; felony gambling banker; and a charge known as "keeping a policy location." Many of these charges were dismissed, and on those occasions when the charges stuck he paid fines ranging from $200 to $2,000. Altuve was Battle's age, sixty-three years old. He had no desire to spend the rest of his life in jail.

Detective Rosario met Altuve at the downtown Miami correctional facility. Theirs was the usual tête-à-tête between cop and criminal facing charges. Rosario dangled a carrot, and Altuve dangled one right back. The bolitero said he might be willing to cooperate. He assured Rosario that he had enough information to sink José Miguel Battle.

"Like what?" said Rosario. "Give me a taste."

"Well," said Altuve, "like the time I helped him get away after a murder." Altuve was referring to having driven Battle to the airport following the Ernestico Torres murder—but he would say no more. Before he would agree to cooperate, he wanted to see how his cocaine case unfolded.

Rosario reported back to Shanks and the other cops. They salivated at the idea of having a cooperating informant like Altuve.

Meanwhile, Shanks was having problems with his partner, Bert Perez. Since their trip together to New York City, Perez had become increasingly disenchanted with his duties at the Organized Crime Bureau. To Shanks, it seemed as though the young cop had come to OCB thinking he would become a deep undercover officer, like he had seen in the movies. Real-life investigative work was more circumscribed and involved patience more than anything else. Perez had not been gifted with patience, and his restless energy was causing problems. One day he used the office fire extinguisher to spray a veteran detective with a chemical retardant. It was meant as a joke, but the detective on the receiving end did not see it that way.

Three days after this incident, Shanks was looking for his junior partner, who owed him a written surveillance report. Perez was nowhere to be found. Shanks was having a bad day to begin with. He and his wife had separated that week, and he was still grieving the death of his uncle.

Shanks walked over to Perez's desk to see if there was any sign of the report. As usual, on his partner's desk was an assortment of notes scribbled on pieces of paper, but no report. It was then that Perez walked into the squad room. Shanks let him have it. "I'm tired of your half-assed paperwork. You have a report due and what do I find? Pieces of paper. Lack of organization. And no accountability."

The other detectives in the squad and their supervisor, Sergeant Boyd, sat quietly.

Shanks crumpled up a handful of notes on Perez's desk and said, "See this? This is how easily important intel can be lost." As he dropped the papers in a wastebasket, he saw Perez coming at him, but it was too late to react.

Perez hit Shanks with a roundhouse right hook. Shanks staggered, then fired back. It wasn't exactly a fair fight. Perez was ten years younger than Shanks and a dedicated weight lifter with a sturdy build. Shanks was someone who liked the occasional beer and rarely spent time in the gym, but he had a barrel chest and a strong jaw. For a few seconds they traded blows until Sergeant Boyd and others jumped in between them and broke it up.

Perez was sent home. Boyd pulled Shanks aside and said, "Look, I know I have to do something about Bert. He's become a problem. I just want to warn you, I'll have to report this incident upstairs. I'll tell them exactly how it went down, but you know how it is."

Shanks nodded. He knew that once Boyd reported the incident to his superiors, it was out of his hands.

Sure enough, a few hours later, Boyd returned to the squad room. He told Shanks to meet him out in the hallway, away from the other detectives.

"They're going to transfer you both," said Boyd.

Shanks was not happy. "And can you tell me why, when I didn't start it and was only defending myself?"

Boyd frowned. "I think the boss is afraid of being branded anti-Hispanic."

Shanks said nothing. He knew that in a police department whose majority and upper management was increasingly Hispanic, any mid- to upper-level manager being branded as antiblack, antifemale, or especially anti-Hispanic would see his career hit a dead end. Boyd was talking about the bosses, but Shanks knew that the sergeant was also a creature of the system. He was not going to put his neck on the line for David Shanks.

"I don't like being chased off my own case," said Shanks. "You'll regret this. You've got a squad full of followers and sprinters, not long-distance runners. You're going to need me again somewhere down the line."

"I don't disagree, Dave," said Boyd. "But for now, you're off the case."

It took a few days for it to sink in. Shanks had been working the Battle case for five years. Because of his dedication to the case, he had devoted countless extra hours, which contributed to the dissolution of his marriage. His life was in a downward spiral, not unlike the entire region of South Florida following its unprecedented hurricane. And now this.

To top it all off, he was assigned to uniformed patrol. He was put in a squad car, driving around the Kendall Division, where his career as a cop had begun. After twenty years on the force, it was like he was a rookie all over again.

BY NOVEMBER, PLANS FOR THE CASINO IN PERU WERE UNDER WAY. BATTLE, LUIS DeVilliers, and Nene Marquez made the five-and-a-half-hour flight from Miami to Lima and inaugurated a corporate entity they called Empresa de Inversiones Orientales. Notably, José Miguel did not use his real name when forming the company, which would oversee financing and management of the casino. It had been determined that, given Battle's criminal record, using his name was simply not possible. It would have sunk the entire undertaking before it ever got off the ground. Rather than bow out, he determined that he would simply use a false name. From now on, in Peru he would be known as Alfredo Walled.

Already, the team of owners had scouted out the location. The casino would be located on the first floor of a hotel known as the Crillón. Located in a part of downtown Lima that was less than savory, the Crillón Hotel was nonetheless a popular spot. Originally built in 1947 and architecturally based on the famous Hôtel de Crillon in Paris, the establishment had become a destination for celebrities and politicos. Movie stars such as Greta Garbo, John Wayne, and Debbie Reynolds had stayed there, as had the Rolling Stones, who allegedly wrote the song "Let It Bleed" while staying at the Crillón in Lima.

In 1960, the hotel expanded from its original eight floors to twenty-two floors, with an impressive top-floor restaurant known as the Sky

Room, which offered panoramic views of the city. By the late 1970s, the hotel had fallen on hard times and filed for bankruptcy. Consequently, the ownership was open to business opportunities such as a casino. It was thought that the casino could generate profits in its own right (the owners would lease space for the casino) and increase the occupancy rate of the hotel. It was the kind of proposition that businessmen, in a rush of capitalistic optimism, often refer to as "win-win."

Located on the Pacific coast of South America, Peru was a Spanish-speaking country coming out from under decades of economic stagnation. Lima, the capital city, was a crossroads for South American commerce, with international banking, a currency that was traded on the New York Stock Exchange, and a new president, Alberto Fujimori, who had been elected in 1990 with a mandate to implement financial reforms.

There had never been a casino in Peru. Only recently, in 1991, had a law been passed making it legal for the government to bestow a gaming license to whoever was able to muster the financial backing for such a venture. Many felt that it was only appropriate that the first ever casino in Lima be at a location as renowned as the Hotel Crillón.

Three men made the venture possible—Felix Fefer, Wilfredo Chau, and Ricardo Chiang. These were the men who had first approached Luis DeVilliers in Miami. Ferer was a Peruvian-born businessman. Chau was an attorney who had in 1989 been appointed to the position of labor secretary in Peru, a job he held until July 1990, when his political party was voted out of power. Chiang was an engineer who currently held the post of general superintendent of immigration in the Peruvian government. All three of these men were politically well connected and, it was believed, in a strong position to handle any bureaucratic complications that might ensue in the launching and management of the business.

There was a meeting in Lima. Luis DeVilliers and his wife, along with Nene Marquez and his wife, traveled to Lima to strategize with the Peruvians. At a lavish dinner, they drank and discussed the possibilities; everyone was excited. Opening the first casino in Peru was historic. Their excitement was tempered somewhat by the fact that there was much work to do. There was no gaming equipment in Lima, so it would have to be shipped into the country from other locations. And recruiting and staffing the casino was another priority. Nene Marquez would be overseeing that; he would travel to Aruba, the Caribbean island where casino gambling had been in place since the 1950s. There he would recruit dealers, pit bosses, security personnel, midlevel managers, and more.

Now that the government license had been secured and the enterprise was under way, the Peruvians felt there was nothing much left for them to do. They could just sit back and collect their percentage of the profits. To their knowledge, DeVilliers and Nene Marquez were the sole investors on the American side. They had not been told anything about a man named Alfredo Walled.

IN LATE 1992, NENE MARQUEZ TRAVELED TO ARUBA. HE SPREAD THE WORD AMONG casino workers there that an exciting opportunity was opening up in Lima. A new casino. The word was that Marquez was offering something that the workers would not receive in Aruba—a percentage of the casino's profits. It was a chance to get in on the ground floor.

The first and most important person that Marquez would meet was Harold Marchena, a manager at the Americana casino inside the hotel of the same name. Marchena had years of experience; he had worked his way up from dealer to supervisor to a manager of surveillance, pit boss, and casino operations manager. His knowledge of the daily operations of a casino was vast.

Marquez knew that if he could land a big fish like Harold Marchena, who was well known in Aruba, it might launch a stampede of other casino workers eager to come on board for this exciting new opportunity in Lima. There were eleven casinos in Aruba, with more experienced workers than anywhere outside of Las Vegas—the difference being that in Aruba a good number of the workers spoke Spanish.

Marquez and Marchena met at the Holiday Inn, where Marquez was staying. They discussed the plans for the casino. Marquez told Marchena that if he came in at this early stage, he would be a shareholder in the casino. Marchena was interested. Said Marquez, "I'm departing this afternoon at two, flying direct to Lima. Why don't you come with me?"

Marchena laughed. "That's impossible. I have a job here. Responsibilities. If I do accept your offer, I have to first notify my employers."

Marquez told Marchena that he was going to send him two airplane tickets to Peru, for him and his wife. "You can visit for the weekend. Just to see the place, see if you like it or not."

Marchena made the trip to Lima. He was impressed with the Crillón, which was a historic location in the city. He was introduced to the Peruvian shareholders and to Luis DeVilliers. After the weekend was over, he told the team of investors he was in.

The name of Alfred Walled or José Miguel Battle was never mentioned. Marchena had no idea that any such man was one of the shareholders.

One investor whom Marchena did meet was the brother of Nene Marquez. His name was Maurilio Marquez, though Marchena would come to know him mostly as "the Venezuelan."

HIALEAH PARK WAS A GORGEOUS RACETRACK. WITH SWAYING PALM TREES, A BEAUTIfully landscaped track, and live flamingos that were allowed to lounge in a man-made lagoon and flutter around the grounds, it was evocative of a tropical paradise. Abraham Rydz often thought that even if he weren't a committed gambler, he would still come to this track as often as possible for the sheer beauty of the place. He was there with his usual coterie of friends and hangers-on when one of them mentioned, "Hey, did you hear the latest about that casino in Peru?"

Rydz's ear pricked up.

"What?" asked one of the others.

"Nene Marquez's brother, Maurilio Marquez, he's one of the owners."

Rydz felt his heart stop. "What!?" he said. "You're crazy."

"I read it in the newspaper. They listed the owners. Luis DeVilliers, some Peruvians with connections in the government, and the Marquez brothers."

Rydz began to sweat. How was such a thing possible? Battle Jr. had been told by Nene, in no uncertain terms, that his brother was not involved in any way.

Rydz left the track. He spoke to no one. He knew that the following day there was to be a birthday party at El Zapotal. Rydz had been invited. He didn't even remember who the birthday party was for. But he would go to José Miguel's house for the party and he would ask him and the others to tell him exactly what was going on.

The following day, he arrived at El Zapotal. He buzzed the outer gate of the property and was allowed to drive in and park. He knocked on the front door and was greeted by Effugenia Reyes, Battle's mistress, who was now living with him at El Zapotal. Rydz entered. As soon as he saw Nene Marquez, he said, "I need to speak with José Miguel, you, and Luis. Somewhere private."

They all went into a small room that Battle used as his office. "Is it true?" asked Rydz.

"Is what true?" said Battle.

"Is it true that you're using Maurilio Marquez in the Crillón casino in Peru?"

Nene, Luis, and José Miguel were silent for a few seconds. Then Battle said, "Yes."

Rydz felt as if he'd been hit over the head with a baseball bat. He looked at Nene Marquez. "You told Migue and me that you would not use your brother. You swore on your mother's grave."

Then Nene shrugged and said the words, in Spanish, that would ring in El Polaco's ears for generations to come: "*Lo hecho, hecho está* (What is done, is done)."

Rydz took a few seconds to gather his thoughts, then he said, "For ten years now, Migue and me, we been working on this foundation of ours. We worked eighteen-hour days. You all know this. It was Migue's dream, and mine, that one day we would have created a business that was legitimate. Using Maurilio was a big part of it, because he was a Venezuelan citizen and could make deposits without triggering an investigation by the IRS. Maurilio was a part of everything we did. His name is on all our documents. And now you've put us in tremendous jeopardy. For what? So you can play cards and roll the dice?"

Rydz was having a hard time understanding how this could have happened. To José Miguel, he said, "Your son devoted his whole life to this. To create something he could leave for his family, his kids, to see to it that everyone would be taken care of for years to come."

Said Battle, "Listen, Polaco, there's no reason Miguelito needs to know anything about this. We would rather you didn't tell him."

Rydz shook his head. "Listen, don't let me out of this room. You're going to have to kidnap me. Because the minute I leave this room, I'm going to tell Migue."

They let Rydz go. From a pay phone, he called Battle Jr. and said, "We need to talk. It's urgent."

On the drive north to Key Biscayne, Rydz lit up one cigarette after another. When he was stressed, he chain-smoked. It crossed his mind that Battle had allowed this to happen out of jealousy. Even though it was José Miguel who had put Rydz together with Junior—saying to him in the prison visiting room, "Take care of my son while I'm away"— Battle was resentful that he and Junior had become so close. Rydz had become the father that Junior never had, and Battle couldn't stand it. So now he was attempting to destroy it.

There was much that went unspoken between Rydz and Battle and, for that matter, all of the boliteros, who were old-school Cubans bound by codes of machismo. They did not talk about their feelings. But they did act on them. That was Battle, a man who would shoot himself in the foot out of pride.

When Rydz told Junior the news, his friend and partner was devastated. He didn't say much, but Rydz could see it had rocked him to his core. They walked around their neighborhood in Key Biscayne, mulling over the implications of having their entire business structure linked to what they suspected was a doomed enterprise far off in Peru.

"Listen," said Battle Jr., "you need to go to Curaçao and to Europe right away. You need to close out all the accounts with Maurilio's name attached. Liquidate everything. Then you create a new foundation using only your name."

Rydz said, "You realize this will be costly. You're talking about selling and buying stocks under the least desirable terms. We could lose as much as half a million dollars on each transaction."

Battle's voice became sad. "What choice do we have, my friend? Do it now, or maybe we lose everything."

The very next day, Rydz got on a flight to Curaçao, to close out some of the offshore accounts, and then on to Switzerland. He stayed at a nice hotel in Zurich and spent the week with brokers and lawyers, selling off stock and closing out accounts, expunging the name of Maurilio Marquez from all of their documents. It was a brutal process that would shrink their overall holdings by 25 percent, but it had to be done.

On the way back to Miami, Rydz did something he rarely did—he drank on the airplane. He was trying to do something that people in the criminal life often have to do—forget the past.

IN JANUARY 1993, ROBERTO PARSONS WAS ARRESTED IN FRONT OF A FRIEND'S HOUSE in Hialeah. It was a relatively undramatic arrest. Even though the search for Parsons had reached from coast to coast and involved the FBI, DEA, and many local police departments, Parsons was, like so many criminals, a creature of habit. He was sitting in a pickup truck with his friend when he was surrounded by a SWAT team of lawmen that included agents from the FBI's Violent Criminal Fugitive Apprehension Unit and detectives from the Metro-Dade Police Department. Parsons was handcuffed and taken into custody.

The Federal Detention Center in downtown Miami had held its share of notorious criminals in recent years. Throughout the 1980s and into the 1990s, the burgeoning drug trade had turned Miami into the hottest crime beat in America. The jails and prisons were filled to capacity with international criminals from South America and the Caribbean, as well as homegrown narcos. Into this mix came Roberto Parsons, a Bay of Pigs veteran, former CIA covert operator, and professional hit man for the criminal underworld.

Even in federal detention, Parsons remained active. Within a month of his incarceration, it was discovered that he had concocted a plot to kill three people who were cooperating against him, including Jorge Gonzalez, who had participated in the murder of Pepe Moranga in New York City. Gonzalez had also witnessed the murder of Paco Felipe in Miramar and driven with Parsons to dispose of the body in the Everglades.

The prison murder plot was exposed when one of Parsons's co-conspirators turned out to be a snitch. Parsons was charged with conspiracy to commit murder. He pleaded guilty and was facing significant time. At this point, his lawyer hinted that his client might be willing to cooperate with authorities if it worked to his advantage.

Parsons agreed to be interviewed by NYPD detectives who were investigating the Moranga, Mujica, and Broche murders. In his statement, Parsons threw out many false leads designed to cloud the investigation. Pepe Moranga, he said, was killed by drug dealers. Angel Mujica was murdered when he returned to New York City and began operating policy spots. "I hear he was killed by the Italian Mafia," said Parsons. He talked a lot but admitted nothing except that, yes, he had at one time been a bodyguard for José Miguel Battle, whom he considered a war hero from the Bay of Pigs.

Parsons did admit to the detectives that he had once been a member of Operation 40 and had conducted covert ops for the CIA in Cuba and Latin America in the 1970s. He viewed himself as a dedicated soldier in the Cold War. Motivating most of what he did, he claimed, was the overarching dream of killing Castro and taking back Cuba. He hinted that his work for the Agency continued into the 1980s, but he would not go into detail. "That's all classified," he told the cops.

Since Parsons remained unwilling or unable to tell authorities the truth about anything that implicated him in a crime, there was no deal to be made. He remained in jail. Months later, he would be indicted for the murder of Pepe Moranga. But he never made it to trial. Parsons's gauntness, and the deep-set eyes with dark rings—physical features that had been noticed by witnesses to the murders of Moranga, Mujica, and Broche—were the consequence of early-stage pancreatic cancer.

After less than two years in prison, he died of cancer at the age of sixty-four.

His nephew, Juan Carlos Parsons, was convicted on cocaine smuggling charges and sentenced to twelve years in prison. He was never charged for his alleged role in the murder of Pepe Moranga.

THE STRUGGLE TO LIBERATE CUBA WAS NEVER-ENDING.

On January 20, 1993, Bill Clinton, a Democrat, was sworn in as the forty-second president of the United States. After twelve years of Reagan and George H. W. Bush, a former director of the CIA, Cuban exiles could no longer count on unquestioning support from the administration in power. The legacy of the Iran-Contra scandal, even more detrimental for the exiles than the Watergate fiasco, had set back the cause of covert operations in general and, once again, cast a troublesome light on the Cuban

of Reagan and George H. W. Bush, a former director of the CIA, Cuban exiles could no longer count on unquestioning support from the administration in power. The legacy of the Iran-Contra scandal, even more detrimental for the exiles than the Watergate fiasco, had set back the cause of covert operations in general and, once again, cast a troublesome light on the Cuban connection. From the Bay of Pigs invasion through Operation Mongoose, the Watergate burglary, undertakings in Latin America, culminating most recently with the Nicaraguan Contras, Cuban exile involvement in the country's secret Cold War history was like an unprotected hot wire, dangerous to the touch. There was no circuit breaker. The dream of a destabilized Cuba was the energizing factor. That dream had not died, but it was unlikely that the post–Iran-Contra CIA or the new Democratic Party administration of President Clinton would be a reliable underwriter of the ongoing narrative.

Old warriors never die. Luis Posada Carriles had been at it for thirty years. He had traveled to and lived in multiple countries, conducted numerous violent operations in consort with intelligence agencies and gangsters from many governments, been incarcerated in and escaped from foreign prisons, and he was not ready to retire. Not as long as Fidel Castro was still alive.

In February 1992, Posada was interviewed by two FBI agents at the U.S. embassy in Tegucigalpa, Honduras. The agents advised Posada, who was one week away from his sixty-fourth birthday, that they were there on behalf of the Office of the Independent Counsel (OIC), who was investigating the "Iran/Contra matter." They wanted to know about events that occurred in El Salvador in 1985 and 1986. Posada agreed to be interviewed.

Special Agents Michael Foster and George Kiszynski spoke with Posada for six and a half hours. The report they filed was extraordinary in its detail. Posada described how in 1985 he was able to escape from a Venezuelan prison thanks in part to $50,000 in bribe money smuggled to him by Jorge Mas Canosa, president of the Cuban American National Foundation (CANF). Jorge Mas was perhaps the most politically powerful Cuban American in the United States, the friend of Republican presidents, most notably George H. W. Bush. In 1992, in the waning days of his presidency, Bush attended a $1,000-a-plate fund-raising dinner in Miami for CANF and declared, "I salute Jorge Mas."

Posada described to the agents how he wound up in El Salvador working with his old Bay of Pigs cohort Felix Rodriguez. He noted that though the Contra resupply operation in Ilopango was a joint covert op directed by Ollie North's NSC and retired CIA agents, the Cubans formed a separate clique within the unit. The entire Contra support operation crashed and burned when an American mercenary named Gene Hasenfus was captured behind enemy lines. The story exploded in the U.S. media, leading eventually to the televised Iran-Contra hearings.

Posada was hiding out in a tiny house on the beach in Xanadu, on the Pacific Coast in El Salvador, at the time of the hearings on television. He waited until much of the media attention died down, then he moved to Guatemala.

Meanwhile, in Cuba, Posada was tried in absentia for his role in the bombing of Cubana de Aviación Flight 455. Even the CIA suspected that he was guilty, as revealed in internal memos that would eventually be made public. Among human rights activists, he was a notorious figure, a terrorist who was quite possibly being protected by people in the U.S intelligence community. In Miami and Union City, he was a freedom fighter. Jorge Mas Canosa and CANF were, through back channels, secretly negotiating with President Clinton for Posada's return to the United States.

In Guatemala, Posada reinvented himself as a special consultant to President Vincio Cerezo. Cuban American cold warriors, trained by the CIA at Fort Benning, were now highly valued anticommunist operatives throughout Latin America. He was hired to set up a special squad to help investigate a number of political assassinations that had taken place in the country. But his privileged position with President Cerezo caused jealousy among some of the other ministers in the government.

In 1990, Posada was walking on a street in Guatemala City when he was ambushed by gunmen. He was shot multiple times in the torso and also the jaw. He was rushed to a private clinic, where he received expert medical care under the arrangement of the president.

It was a long and painful convalescence. Posada lost part of his jaw and a portion of his tongue. He let it be known to aides of the president that he did not have the money to pay for his medical bills, which came out to $16,000 for the doctors and $4,000 for the hospital. The aides told him not to worry; the president would cover his bills.

Posada had a close friend who was acting as his assistant, handling all financial matters. The friend told him that the president had only come up with $4,000 owed to the hospital and not the $16,000 owed to the doctors. Posada was stunned. Eventually, to avoid government bill collectors, he was forced to leave Guatemala and relocate to Honduras.

Months later, purely by chance, Posada ran into then ex-president Cerezo on an airplane flight. He confronted the man: "You lied. Your aides told me you would cover all my bills, and you only came across with four thousand."

Cerezo was startled. "What do you mean?" he said. "We gave to your assistant a total of twenty thousand dollars."

Later, Posada did some investigating and determined that, yes, his close friend had stolen the other $16,000.

A few years had passed, but Posada's feelings were still hurt. To the FBI agents who had come all the way to Tegucigalpa to interview him he said, "It upsets me very much to think that a friend could steal from me while I was laying in a hospital bed, but that's what happened."

As for the attempt on his life, Posada believed that it had to be hit men sent by Cuban intelligence, on orders from Castro himself. Posada had become Public Enemy Number One in Cuba. No one wanted him dead more than Fidel, though the aging cold warrior had to admit that the list of his enemies was substantial, and it was getting longer with each passing year.

BY EARLY 1993, THE MIGRATION OF EXPERIENCED CASINO WORKERS FROM ARUBA TO Lima was well under way. Once Harold Marchena was hired to serve as general manager, he began recruiting experienced casino people from Aruba. His first hire was Manuel Zambrano, a slot machine technician. Zambrano was sent to Miami to retrofit the slot machines owned by Luis DeVilliers. Humberto Salazar was brought from Aruba to train blackjack dealers and also dealers for the craps tables. A Dutch national,

Jacobo Van Der Linden, was brought from Aruba to help train the dealers, with the understanding that he would become an assistant manager once the casino opened. Francisco "Chito" Quandas came from Aruba to serve as another assistant manager. George Croes, also from Aruba, became head cashier. A Peruvian native, Mario Masaveu, was hired to serve as an assistant security director under General Guillermo Castillo, an active officer in the Peruvian army, who was the casino's director of security.

Dozens of others were hired. The Crillón was nowhere near as big as the average casino in Las Vegas or Atlantic City, but it was the only casino in town, and it would be open twenty hours a day. In total, there would be a staff of 125 people, including dealers, cashiers, greeters, pit bosses, floor managers, bartenders, waitresses, and security personnel. And that was just out on the floor. Behind the scenes were personnel managers, money managers, accountants, lawyers, and assorted bosses and investors.

From the beginning, there were complications due to the fact that the original investors knew little or nothing about the business. Nene Marquez and DeVilliers thought that they could ship gaming tables from the United States, but it turned out to be cheaper to have them made in Lima. Also, in the opinion of those arriving from Aruba, there were some serious budgetary problems. The casino owners were planning on paying their dealers between $100 and $150 a month. Chito Quandas objected, saying that if you paid the dealers so little, you were practically encouraging them to steal. After considerable negotiation, it was agreed that the dealers would be paid $400 to $450 a month.

The new employees noticed that everything was being paid in cash, which was unusual. Not only that, but the currency was U.S. dollars, which was even more unusual.

Maurilio Marquez, the Venezuelan, was the casino's financial manager. He was the one making payments for equipment and to the various managers and trainers, who were on salary even though the casino was not scheduled to open for three months. Quandas remembered seeing Maurilio carrying cash around in a brown paper bag, which seemed highly unprofessional. But since this was a new operation being organized and underwritten by people with no experience in the business, irregularities were to be expected. Or at least that's what Quandas and the other experienced casino people from Aruba told themselves.

Getting any large-scale business ready for opening day can be intense; the Casino Crillón was no different. But Harold Marchena was alarmed. A veteran casino operator, he was having a hard time figuring out what could be chalked up to inexperience or ineptitude, and what might be the result of something more sinister.

Marchena once heard Maurilio on the phone with Luis DeVilliers telling him they needed hundreds of thousands of dollars. After he finished the phone call, Maurilio told Marchena, "Okay, the money is going to be here. It's being wired from a Swiss bank account and will arrive in Peru shortly." Later in the day, Maurilio learned that the money had not arrived, and would not be arriving by wire. He also became aware that his name had been removed from the accounts associated with the holdings of Rydz and Battle Jr.

Still, the owners seemed to have the money, but it now required various employees—Marchena included—to make semiregular cash runs to Miami. The employees would load cash in their bags and in their pockets and concealed on their bodies. Marchena and other shareholders made these money runs two or three times a week.

After learning he was no longer associated with the Swiss accounts, Maurilio Marquez, in the eyes of Marchena, seemed to lose faith in the enterprise. Marchena suspected that Maurilio had begun to skim money by inflating construction costs and then keeping the overage for himself. Labor costs in Peru were cheap, but the installation costs for doors, moldings, floorboards, and other expenses, Marchena noticed, were coming in unusually high. He once mentioned it to Maurilio, who winked and said, "Don't worry. I'll take care of you."

This concerned Marchena even more. He had been lured away from a comfortable job in Aruba on the premise that he would have a percentage of the overall business in Lima. If Maurilio Marquez was skimming from the Casino Crillón, he was stealing from him too.

The final straw for Marchena was when the shareholders began interfering with his hiring of casino personnel. Marchena had been given two months to work through 240 people who were trained to work as dealers, pit bosses, cashiers, and so on. It was a grueling process. After a month or so, Marchena noticed that the casino was in some cases hiring people who had not passed the training course. He confronted the Cuban American owners and was told that one of the shareholders was Effugenia Reyes. He was not told that Effugenia was the mistress of José Miguel Battle. Effugenia was a front person for Battle, but nonetheless she was insisting that, as a "shareholder," she be allowed to make sure a certain number of jobs went to relatives and friends of hers.

Marchena was outraged. He told the Marquez brothers and DeVilliers, "Listen, if you want me to run the casino as a professional operation, then we hire only professionals, not friends. Don't make me look like a fool."

Marchena knew that a casino's reputation for professionalism was sacrosanct. If you wanted to attract high rollers—international gamblers who might be given a credit line of $25,000 to $50,000—they had to know that the establishment adhered to the highest standards. It wasn't just a matter of professional pride. As a shareholder with a stake in the company, Marchena knew that prospects for making any real money from his efforts at the Casino Crillón depended on its reputation.

All in all, Marchena was getting bad vibrations from what he was seeing and experiencing in Lima. He lay awake at night with the terrible feeling that he'd made a big mistake. But it was not too late. His employers in Aruba had extended to him a grace period in which if things didn't work out with his new job, he could return. This was standard practice in the highly volatile casino gambling business, where new ventures were known to be high-risk and frequently crashed and burned.

Just weeks before the Casino Crillón was scheduled to open in May, Marchena resigned. Nene Marquez and Luis DeVilliers tried to talk him out of it, but he had already made up his mind. Feeling rattled and bruised, he returned to Aruba.

FELIX FERER, ONE OF THE ORIGINAL THREE PERUVIAN SHAREHOLDERS IN THE CRILLÓN, was also having his eyes opened to certain "irregularities" that were taking place as, in a state of panic and under great pressure, the casino approached its opening date. Ferer, more than the other two Peruvians, was integral to the financial operations of the venture. He and Maurilio were the financial managers, the only ones with the authority to cash checks and make deposits or withdrawals.

Truth be told, there were no withdrawals. Money to pay for construction and management expenses was not coming from the bank, it was arriving as cash shipments from Miami.

Much to his chagrin, Ferer, like Marchena and other shareholders, found himself functioning as a money courier from the United States. On trips to Miami, Ferer, sometimes with partner Ricardo Chiang, was given blocks of cash to transport. The cash was rubber-banded together in denominations of fifty- and one-hundred-dollar bills. The blocks were packaged in stacks just thick enough to fit in pockets or to be secured on the body without being detected. On seven different trips, Ferer transported a total of $800,000 in cash.

Among Ferer's responsibilities, as comptroller for the casino, was to oversee the bank account associated with the business. Two months into the construction of the casino, Empresa de Inversiones Orientales, the controlling business entity, had run out of money. The company bank account was in bad need of an infusion of cash. So far, Maurilio Marquez and other owners had gotten away with paying their bills with cash smuggled into the country. But there were larger expenses that needed to be covered, such as the cost of a backup generator for the casino, which would be $60,000.

The owners turned to their bank for a loan. Banco Continental had underwritten the casino venture with considerable hesitation. There was no casino business infrastructure in Peru. It seemed like a risky venture. But they went ahead with the relationship based on the belief that the casino's corporate entity would be kept flush with U.S. investment.

Felix Ferer was the person responsible for applying and advocating for the loan. Banco Continental looked at the numbers and turned down the application.

This created a mini-crisis for Inversiones Orientales, one that was averted by implementation of an ingenious scheme. Using a local Peruvian business, cash from Miami was laundered. The owner of this business, a prominent man with connections to the Fujimori government, deposited the cash from Miami in his account, claiming it was profits from his business. Then he wrote checks to the Casino Crillón, which were deposited in the account of Inversiones Orientales. On the surface, it appeared to be a legitimate transaction.

Ferer presided over these financial maneuverings, knowing full well that they constituted a criminal act. As far as he was concerned, the horse had left the barn. The Casino Crillón had been announced in the local media in Lima, and many prominent personages in government, the business community, and entertainment had taken an interest. The casino's grand opening would be a huge social event, one of the biggest soirées in Lima in a long time. There was simply no room for failure.

At the same time, Ferer was no dummy. He could see that the financial underpinnings of the venture were not only shaky, they were steeped in corruption.

As bad as it looked, Ferer did not yet know the half of it.

17

BEGINNER'S LUCK

ONE THING THAT COULD BE SAID—AND OFTEN WAS—ABOUT JOSÉ MIGUEL BATTLE WAS that he had big balls. Cojones. In Latin culture, as in most patriarchal societies, being noted for having big balls was a metaphor for courage and the highest form of praise. Machismo is the logical manifestation of this philosophy, the belief that all life originates with the male organ and the precious seed that is, after all, conjured from within the testicles. Big balls connote power, because a person with big balls is a person without fear.

There are at least two sides to every story. If you were a soldier on the battlefield, say, a brigadista pinned down behind enemy lines at the Bay of Pigs, having a platoon mate with cojones could be the difference between life and death. Instinctively, that platoon mate attempts to come to your rescue, because a person with big balls does not wither in the face of risk. He does not care about the odds. He acts. Duty calls. He takes that chance because he has big balls. In any given situation, there is normally a fifty-fifty chance that a person will have made the wrong choice. Having big balls has little to do with intelligence. Sometimes the guy with an excess of moxie is the dumbest guy on the block.

José Miguel Battle invested a lot of money in opening the Casino Crillón. He paid off customs officials in Peru so that the shipping costs of large items like slot machines, air-conditioning units, and electric generators—and smaller items such as chips, dice, and thousands of tokens for the slots—were grossly undervalued. Thus his import tax liability was minimal. Even so, when all was said and done, he shelled out $4.5 million to launch what most people around him, including some of his partners and employees, thought was at best a high-risk venture.

It would be easy to say that Battle followed this course because he was a man with big balls but no brains. That does not tell the full story. He was also a romantic. To him, a casino represented the impossible dream. If this made him seem like Don Quixote tilting at windmills, he did not see this as a liability. Life was meant to be lived. He did not invest only his money in the Casino Crillón—he invested his hopes and dreams.

On May 29, 1993, the casino opened with a lavish party in the Sky Room, attended by the shareholders, the casino management, and many Peruvian dignitaries, including people from the Fujimori government.

The Peruvian shareholders, casino management, staff, and bankers with an interest in the casino met Battle for the first time. He was introduced to them individually as Alfredo Walled. Some were told that he was a shareholder, but some were not. Battle simply showed up on the scene; it was up to the hired help to determine whether or not he held an important role in the management of the casino.

It was not hard to figure out. From the start, Battle conducted himself as if he were the *capo di tutti capi,* boss of all bosses. He moved into one of three hotel suites that were reserved for casino upper management, a spacious apartment on the sixteenth floor. The suite next door was occupied by his three bodyguards. He shared his suite with Effugenia Reyes, who had already made her presence felt by casino employees for her insistence on the hiring of her friends and family members.

If anyone doubted Battle's role in the operation, he told them. "I am the Godfather," he said to Felix Ferer the first time they met. Ferer thought the man was joking. His amused expression was met with a chilling glare from El Padrino.

The other two Peruvian investors, Chiang and Chau, were with Ferer at the time. Years later, Ferer remembered, "When we met this man, we did not like him. He was a very unpleasant person. And he would say he's the owner of the business. And not only that, but it bothered him that we had anything to say there. We didn't like the way he spoke. We didn't like the way he acted. He walked around with a revolver stuck in the back of his trousers, under his coat."

Chito Quandas, who had been elevated from a trainer of dealers and pit bosses to one of the casino's three managers, was having a hard time figuring out the pecking order between the Marques brothers, Luis DeVilliers, and Battle. So Battle told him, "If I tell those men to lick the bottom of my shoes, they have to do it."

Within the first month of Battle's arrival, it was clear that he was there to do whatever he wanted. He spent a lot of time cultivating men in the political establishment, most notably military and police authorities. He established a standing rule at the Crillón that when a high-ranking general or police captain came onto the floor, he was automatically given $1,000 to $5,000 worth of chips with which to gamble. Some of them played blackjack for a few minutes and then cashed out, keeping the rest of the money for themselves.

Battle did not care. It was clear from the start that this brash Cuban from the United States had an agenda for the casino that was quite different from that of the rest of the investors and staff. Battle was there to exert his power, and to allow his ego free rein.

He was also there for a good time. From the day he arrived, he started drinking; he appeared to be intoxicated much of the time. It was difficult to tell whether he was there to make money or to party. Actually, it wasn't hard to tell: he was there to party.

Casino management hired a public relations man, a venerable sixty-year-old Peruvian actor named Luis "Lucho" Cabrera. In movies, telenovelas, and, most notably, in a popular Peruvian television ad for Honda, Lucho Cabrera was a comic presence. He was also popular with the ladies. Though he was past his prime as a performer, he was still a star of sorts, who was employed as a meeter and greeter. This was a casino tradition that Battle remembered from Havana. In the 1950s, the Casino Capri, owned by Santo Trafficante, had hired George Raft, the American movie star, who earlier in his life had made a career out of playing suave tough guys. Raft was known to have grown up on the wrong side of the tracks, in the Manhattan neighborhood of Hell's Kitchen. He was on a first-name basis with many mobsters. He became something of a house mascot for the Mob in Havana.

Cabrera was hired for his popularity, but primarily his duties involved rounding up women and cocaine for Battle and his friends.

Sometimes, the debauchery was for fun, and sometimes it was done for a specific purpose. Once, a special party was arranged at the Crillón for a deputy minister who was allowed to gamble for free and then retire to a room on the eleventh floor. A bevy of women known as the Chin Chin Girls, who performed a popular strip show in Lima, were hired to give the deputy minister a private show. The highly intoxicated deputy minister lay on the floor while the women stood over him and stripped. Battle arranged for the entire encounter to be secretly videotaped, for blackmail purposes, should he ever need the aid of a deputy minister in future criminal endeavors.

Battle's use of a fictitious name in Lima seemed to be merely pro forma. With his co-shareholders and casino staff, he did not try to hide who he was. In fact, he bragged about it often. To Ferer, Quandas, and many others, he related his personal history as the Godfather of the Cuban Mafia in the United States. He explained that he made his money from bolita, and that he personally cleared $3 million per year. He told them he had ordered the killing of many men on his rise to the top, and he would be willing to do it again if it proved to be necessary.

Though he insisted that everyone refer to him as Señor Walled, it was with a wink and a smile. Whenever he reached into the breast pocket of one of his tailored silk or linen suits, he held open the coat long enough so that they could see embroidered in the lining *Made Exclusively for José Miguel Battle,* and also the initials *J.M.B.*

In its first few months of operation, the casino ran surprisingly smoothly, and patronage was brisk. The city of Lima had never seen anything quite like it, a Las Vegas–style casino in one of its most venerable old hotels. Everybody wanted to be seen at the Crillón; it was the place to be. And at the center of the action was the swaggering, slightly mysterious Señor Walled.

EFFUGENIA REYES HAD BEEN A PRESENCE AROUND THE CASINO EVEN BEFORE BATTLE, so most of the staff knew who she was. Once Battle arrived, it became apparent that she was either his special lady friend or his wife. She referred to Battle as "my husband," which was interesting to the staff because they knew Battle as a skirt chaser whose tastes tended toward the young end of the spectrum. He had begun a none-too-secret dalliance with a recently hired cashier named Evelyn Runciman. She was nineteen going on twenty.

In a workplace that contained within its walls over two hundred hotel rooms at your service, it wasn't difficult for Battle and his new mistress to find ways to consummate their affair. For a while, he was able to keep it secret. He was sleeping around with Evelyn while still sharing a bed at night with Effugenia. Their combined ages were equal to that of his son.

Effugenia had spies and snitches among the casino staff, and before long she found out what was going on. She did not immediately confront Battle. Instead, she began an affair of her own with Juan Solano Loo, an accountant at the casino.

The problem with spies and snitches was that everyone had them. Battle certainly did.

Velario Cerron was the stepfather of Evelyn Runciman. He worked at the casino as a slot machine mechanic. Cerron learned that Effugenia was having an affair. He approached Battle and said, "Señor Walled, I think there's something you should know." He told Battle about Effugenia's affair with Solano.

A ripple of tension passed through the entire casino; everyone could feel it.

Solano, learning that Battle knew of the affair, quit his job and disappeared from the premises. On top of what he had learned about Battle from the man's behavior at the casino, and the stories circulating about his long life of crime, Effugenia had likely filled his head with stories of El Padrino's murderous lust for revenge. The rumor was that he fled into the hills outside Lima, where the altitude was high and small towns were not easily accessible. Apparently his life was more important to him than whatever amorous entanglements he had with Battle's "wife."

Effugenia and Battle had it out, right on the floor of the casino for all to see. No one knew who initiated the confrontation—Battle or Effugenia—but it escalated into a shouting match, with profane accusations of infidelity on both sides, and Effugenia eventually being reduced to tears.

Within days, Effugenia announced that she was leaving El Padrino. She intended to make a trip to Miami to retrieve all of her belongings at El Zapotal, and then she would be flying back to Guatemala to live with her family.

One person who derived great pleasure from this development was Velario Cerron. He had been angling for his stepdaughter to win the undivided affection of El Padrino, and now the coast was clear. Cerron's own agenda involved the rise of Evelyn, and, by extension, his own fortunes within the world of Alfredo Walled. Everything was on the right track.

DAVE SHANKS HAD BEEN OFF THE BATTLE INVESTIGATION FOR NINE MONTHS WHEN HE received word that his services were requested back at the offices of OCB. The news was delivered without fanfare. There was no departmental announcement or welcome wagon. Whatever bureaucratic fault lines that had opened up leading to his banishment to Siberia had miraculously been spackled over and forgotten. The detective was brought back into Jimmy Boyd's bolita squad as if he had never left.

The first thing Shanks learned was that the crew who had assumed leadership of his investigation had completely lost track of Battle. He had not been sighted in Miami in months, and no one knew where he was. With El Padrino off the grid, the investigation had come to a standstill. Shanks was chagrined that the trail had gone cold, but he was most annoyed that the investigators had used the disappearance of Battle as an excuse to stall the investigation.

Shanks had always seen the investigation as being more about the Corporation than about Battle. Yes, El Padrino was *el jefe,* the big rooster, but the most important thing Shanks had learned in his many years on the case was that the Battle operation was like a private social club, with members and fellow travelers in every nook and cranny of the underworld. The Corporation seemed to encompass every bolitero and bookmaker in Miami, not to mention *narcotraficantes* and corrupt lawmen. If Battle was not around, there were always others in the Corporation network of hoodlums, some of them key players, who could be pursued.

The Battle investigation team had changed since Shanks was away, but luckily he still had Kenny Rosario, who had the best street sources Shanks had ever seen.

For some time, the squad had been aware of an old-time bolita banker named Raul Fernandez. Now seventy years old, Fernandez had followed the tried-and-true bolita trail from Cuba to New Jersey to Miami. For a number of years he had been in retirement, but the detectives heard from one of Kenny Rosario's informants that he was back on the scene. Working together with his wife and three sons, he had what the informant described as the largest illegal gambling business currently operating in Miami.

With Fernandez's long criminal history, it was not difficult to write up an affidavit for a sixty-day wiretap, with tracers being put on a number of phone lines at the bolita banker's home in the Dadeland area.

Janet Reno was no longer Dade County state's attorney, a job she had held for fifteen years. In March 1993, she was appointed U.S. attorney general by President Clinton. With Reno gone, the standard for securing approval from the State Attorney's Office had been lowered, but the process had become less personal and more chaotic. Eventually, the investigators were able to get authorization and install tracers. What they discovered was surprising.

The Fernandez operation was indeed massive. Raul and his wife, Rita, kept two phone lines singing sixteen hours a day. They also had an additional fax line that cranked out over thirty pages of bets twice a week. Between husband and wife and three sons, all of whom were active in the operation, Shanks figured the Fernandez family had over 120 numbers writers circulating in Miami on any given day, taking down bets and submitting them to the organization.

It was so busy that one of the sons, Mayito, brought in his daughter Esperanza to take over some of the numbers writers, to ease the burden. She was set up in an apartment on Bird Road, on the west side of 67th Avenue. The cops were also able to place a tracer on her phone.

All in all, with the Fernandez family also taking layoff bets from some forty other boliteros outside their own thriving policy operation, it was clear that this multigenerational Cuban family had become the central bank of all bolita in Miami.

One afternoon, investigators monitoring the Fernandez wire overheard a conversation between Raul, the patriarch, and an old friend named Luis Adel Bordon. On the phone, Bordon complained that Mayito, Raul's son, had not showed up for a scheduled appointment to make a money drop at "the store," which the cops learned was a reference to Gulf Liquors, a convenience store owned by Bordon in Hialeah. The two men talked back and forth, bad-mouthing Mayito, with Raul finally saying, "Let me look into it, find out what happened."

Raul called Mayito's wife and learned that he had left the house on time that morning to go to the meeting at Gulf Liquors. She had not heard from him since, which was unusual. After a series of frantic calls between Raul, Rita, and others in the Fernandez universe, they became genuinely concerned. It was not like Mayito to disappear with a briefcase full of money and no explanation.

About three hours later, Raul Fernandez received a call from his son. "I was kidnapped and robbed," he said. He told his father to come pick him up at the apartment of a friend just north of Bird Road.

With wiretap operations, in addition to the human monitors stationed in a nearby apartment or in a van, there was always a surveillance crew on call. Dave Shanks happened to be part of the surveillance crew that day. He and two other cops immediately drove to the apartment building that Mayito had mentioned. From a distance, Shanks watched through binoculars as Raul arrived and picked up his son, who, the detective noted, looked disheveled and shaken up.

According to Mayito, that morning on the way to Gulf Liquors, he stopped at an Office Depot on Ives Dairy Road to pick up some supplies. In the parking lot, he was grabbed at gunpoint by two men and forced into a white van with two additional men. They blindfolded him and tied him up. Using his car keys, they retrieved his car, where they found in his briefcase more than $22,000 in bolita customer checks and $7,000 in cash.

The kidnappers wanted more. They drove Mayito around in the van for hours, berating and pistol-whipping him, trying to get him to reveal where his father kept his bolita cash reserves. Mayito said he didn't know. Eventually, they dumped him on a deserted street. Once Mayito figured out where he was, he made his way to a friend's apartment and called Raul.

At the listening post, the police monitors listened to a wave of phone calls within the Fernandez family, with Mayito, now safe, describing to everyone what had happened. To his wife, he said, "[Those kidnappers] could search for years and never find the safe with the cash and records. And it's big, the kind of safe you can walk into."

Over the next few days, the investigators heard many phone conversations between Raul Fernandez and people in his organization. Raul told a fellow bolitero that if one of the kidnappers was found, he would likely have to be tortured to reveal the identities of the other three.

Whenever something like this happened, the cops were required to write up an Amended Wiretap (Shanks was given the task) detailing a possible conspiracy to commit murder. The revised affidavit was submitted to the same judge who approved the original application. The legal time frame to keep the wiretap up and running was automatically extended.

Eventually, Raul Fernandez asked around among his associates for a "friendly" private investigator who might help them track down the kidnappers without revealing anything about their criminal enterprise. The person recommended was Raul Diaz, a notorious former Metro-Dade cop.

Back in 1981, Detective Raul Diaz had been appointed boss of Centac-26, a prestigious narcotics unit comprised exclusively of homicide detectives that worked cases jointly with DEA. Diaz was given the authority to handpick his own team of detectives. Among those he selected was Julio Ojeda. At the time, Ojeda was riding high from having served as lead detective on the Ernestico Torres murder case, which resulted in the conviction of José Miguel Battle. Within months of Ojeda's selection for Centac-26, he became enmeshed in the criminal case that would result in his conviction on narcotics and racketeering charges. Not long afterward, the high-flying Diaz became entangled in a controversy of his own. Eventually, under a cloud of corruption charges and at the peak of his notoriety, he was forced to resign from the police department. He went on to become a private detective.

Raul Fernandez hired the disgraced ex-cop to find the people who had kidnapped and robbed his son. Shanks and his detective partners now found themselves surveilling Diaz, a former police colleague, and his PI associates. This lasted for a few weeks until Fernandez felt that the investigation wasn't leading anywhere and grew weary of paying Diaz's exorbitant fees—a fact he complained about on the phone with anyone who would listen.

The kidnapping and robbery of Mayito had raised an interesting question. Since most of the stolen money was in the form of checks, wouldn't the robbers reveal themselves if and when they sought to cash or deposit those checks? Shanks and his supervisor, Sergeant Boyd, had discussed the likelihood that Fernandez and his organization must have some mechanism for tracking checks, in the event that one bounced or, in this case, was stolen.

This quandary revealed itself one afternoon following the robbery when Fernandez called Luis Bordon at Gulf Liquors and asked him to be on the lookout for any checks that came in with a circled number 14 written on the front.

For Shanks and the cops, this answered the question of how the organization was tracking their checks, but even more important, it suggested that Bordon and Gulf Liquors were being used as a way for the Fernandez organization to launder their bolita proceeds.

"This is a big deal," Shanks said to Sergeant Boyd. It meant that the investigation would now expand to take in Gulf Liquors and Luis Bordon. A bolita investigation was now also a money-laundering investigation. To Shanks, these were isolated bricks in a big wall, potential predicate acts in what he still dreamed about on an almost daily basis—a multicount racketeering case against the man he believed was the Godfather of everything, José Miguel Battle.

SO FAR, THE INVESTIGATORS HAD NOT ESTABLISHED THAT THE FERNANDEZ OPERAtion, as active as it was, was in any way connected to the Corporation. That would all change with the introduction of Luis Bordon. The connection was criminal, but it was also personal and historical, rooted, as were many things related to the Corporation, in the legacy of the Bay of Pigs invasion.

Thirty-two years earlier, at the age of twenty-one, Luis Bordon arrived at the Bay of Pigs as a paratrooper in the 2506 Brigade. Dropping from a World War II–vintage C-47 airplane, he landed near the town of San Blas. From the beginning, it was an immersion into hell, as the brigade was hit from all sides. For three days, Bordon fought alongside his men, until it was clear that defeat was certain. Unlike the majority of the men, who were either killed or captured, Bordon was able to escape and make his way on foot into the Escambray Mountains, forty miles east of where he landed. He lived in the wild for a month, scavenging for food and shriveling up from dehydration.

Finally, on the verge of starvation, he was discovered by a campesino. Unlike most of the country people in the Escambray area, this campesino was anti-Castro. He took Bordon into his home, gave him food to eat and water to drink, and nursed him back to health. He also hid and protected him from squads of Fidelista soldiers who were patrolling the area looking for stray brigadistas. That campesino's name was Raul Fernandez.

Bordon owed Fernandez his life. It was an act of charity he would never forget.

He was able to secure a raft. Along with six others, he made the perilous journey that so many others would attempt in the decades to come. He crossed the Florida Strait and six months after the invasion arrived in Miami as one of the few brigade veterans to escape the island.

In the mid-1960s, Bordon married and made the move to Union City, the land of opportunity for many Cuban émigrés, though the streets were mean and the winters were brutal. Luis and his wife had two sons, Luis Jr. and Adel. Bordon worked in the produce business, but he also began running numbers as a *listero* for the bolita operation of two fellow brigadistas, José Miguel Battle and Angel Mujica.

What Bordon did not know was that his savior, Raul Fernandez, had also left Cuba and settled across the river from him in New York City. Fernandez, who had been a bolitero back in Cuba, also made his living through the illegal lottery, working with Spanish Raymond Marquez, the Puerto Rican bolita boss of East Harlem.

These two men—Bordon and Fernandez—lived and worked on opposite sides of the Hudson River without knowing the other was there.

In the early 1970s, Fernandez made the move to Miami and expanded from bolita into bookmaking. In the mid-1970s, Bordon made the same move. Finally, the two men met and traded stories about their similar paths.

Bordon managed a number of Miami supermarkets in the 1970s, and in 1979 he had the opportunity to purchase partial ownership of his own location, a medium-sized market in the neighborhood of Little Havana. He went to his friend and savior Raul Fernandez for financial backing. Fernandez said yes, but as part of the agreement he requested that Bordon allow him to use the market as a means to launder checks from his bolita business. Bordon agreed.

For ten years, the men maintained their mutual arrangement, which was highly profitable for both of them. Then Bordon sold the store. Later, he opened Gulf Liquors in Hialeah. Before long, he was in financial trouble. He sought out his old friend, Raul, and suggested that they could operate the same sort of money-laundering operation as they had before. Fernandez, whose operation had grown considerably, thought that was a splendid idea.

By the 1980s, Bordon's money-laundering business included not only Fernandez but also many satellite boliteros and bookies who worked with Fernandez. Many of these men, including Gilberto Borges, were also affiliated with the Corporation.

To all of them—Bordon, Fernandez, and now José Miguel Battle—it seemed like a strange kind of fate: Cuba, the Bay of Pigs invasion, bolita, New Jersey, New York, Miami. And now here they all were as *viejos* still treading the same path, feeding at the same trough.

David Shanks and his investigators set up surveillance of Gulf Liquors, including wiretaps of various phone lines at the location.

Right away, the cops learned that Bordon's two closest associates were his sons, Luis Jr. and Adel. Luis Jr. was an ex–U.S. Marine who still looked like one, with a flattop haircut and bulging muscles. Adel was the taller of the two, heavyset and soft around the middle. The cops surmised that if they were able to flip one of the sons, it would likely be Adel.

The surveillance at Gulf Liquors turned out to provide a major bounty of information for the cops. The location was a hub for boliteros picking up and dropping off cash. A who's who of the Miami faction of the Corporation, including Borges and others, passed through on a daily basis. Bordon and Fernandez spoke on the phone numerous times every day, with Mayito Fernandez, the son, making daily money drops on those occasions when he wasn't dodging kidnappers.

The surveillance continued for two months, with cops compiling phone records of gambling transactions, wiretaps of conversations, and photos of key players meeting at the location. All they needed now was actual physical evidence—cash proceeds, betting slips, business ledgers, and whatever else they might find. David Shanks felt it was time for a major raid, and Sergeant Boyd agreed.

On June 24, 1994—a Friday—the cops were ready. They had acquired two dozen search warrants to be executed at various locations, starting with Gulf Liquors but also including the homes and businesses of many of the boliteros they targeted. In total, there were twenty-four different locations spread out around the city. It would require a coordinated effort, with over one hundred detectives, including sergeants, lieutenants, and other supervisors.

At 6:30 P.M., rush hour, the entire team of officers fanned out and executed their warrants. After Gulf Liquors, the most important locale was the Fernandez home. Raul, Rita, and the sons basically ran their entire operation out of the house, so the cops knew there had to be business records on the premises.

The house was a veritable fortress. Two dozen cops were used to search the location, and still nobody was finding anything useful until a lieutenant found a garage door opener in the master bedroom. Why would there be a garage door opener in the bedroom? The lieutenant pushed the button and—voilà—a six-foot section of the wall opened up to reveal a secret walk-in safe. Inside, stacked on shelves, was the mother lode: business ledgers going back years, canceled checks, plus a stockpile of cash, gold jewelry, and other valuables.

At Gulf Liquors, the cops discovered two sets of books—one that the Bordons kept for the benefit of the IRS, and a second to keep track of everything that was left out of the first.

It took seven hours for the cops to execute all the warrants, secure the locations, gather evidence, and bring it all back to the police station property room. Dave Shanks went to bed around 6 A.M. the next morning. But he could hardly wait to get up and go into work later that afternoon. In the bounty of evidence, there had to be some gems.

It was actually three days later that the gem was uncovered, and it had nothing to do with any criminal evidence, per se. At one of the locations where a stack of papers and ledgers had been confiscated, there was a Spanish-language newspaper called *El Comercio*. The paper was from Lima, Peru. On the paper's society page were a number of items involving notables from around the city of Lima. At the bottom was a photo of a Latin male, in his midsixties, dressed in a tuxedo, sitting at a table with a young woman.

The cop who found the paper said to Shanks, "Doesn't that look like Battle?"

Shanks looked at the photo. "It sure does." He examined the caption for the photo. "It says Alfredo Walled and his new bride. What the hell?"

Shanks called for Sergeant Boyd, who was standing nearby. Fluent in Spanish, Boyd read the caption out loud, translating it into English: "The wedding of the year. Mr. Alfredo Walled, a New York businessman and owner of the Casino Crillón, is no longer single. He has been snagged by the beautiful Evelyn Runciman, twenty years of age. To celebrate the event, the husband had a big party at the elegant five-star hotel. Walled arrived in Lima one year ago to inaugurate the Casino Crillón. Months later he met the young Runciman, with whom he initiated a torrid romance, culminating at the altar."

The cops stood dumbfounded.

"That's Battle," said Shanks. "That's our man. That's why we haven't been able to find him all this time."

TO THE SURPRISE OF NEARLY EVERYONE, THE CASINO CRILLÓN IN ITS FIRST SIX months of operation was a smashing success. Considering that many of the key managers were new to the game, it may have been a case of beginner's luck. People crowded around the roulette wheel and the baccarat tables. The blackjack tables were full, as were the poker tables. The slot machines were occupied round the clock, and they still had more slots coming in future shipments from Miami. In the opening weeks, on

average, the casino took in $350,000 per week, and during the initial six
months the casino reaped $3.5 million.

All of this could have been cause for celebration, but Battle was upset
about one thing. There was a sizable discrepancy between the amount of
money that was coming into the casino and the amount that was showing up as profit and being paid out to the shareholders. "Somebody," said
Battle, "is stealing."

From Miami, Battle brought in Orestas Vidan, the Cook, accountant extraordinaire. The casino's books were opened for Vidan to study;
he would track the proceeds from the gambling tables all the way to the
bank and determine where things didn't add up.

After a week, Vidan came to Battle and said, "Your financial manager is skimming off the top."

"Maurilio?" said Battle.

Vidan nodded.

Battle was not surprised. He'd heard that Maurilio Marquez had
been inflating various costs and keeping money for himself. Battle had
even heard that Maurilio had a safe in his room where he kept stolen
cash.

Before confronting Maurilio, Battle had hotel security let him into
his room. He brought a locksmith along to crack open the safe. Inside,
he found $75,000 in cash.

On the floor of the casino, with other management people listening,
he told Maurilio, "You're fired. I want you out of the hotel by the end of
the day."

Maurilio tried to raise an objection, but Battle told him, "Listen, just
because your brother is married to my sister doesn't mean I won't have
you killed."

Maurilio gathered his things and was not to be seen at the Crillón—or
in Lima—any longer.

Nene Marquez did not get in the way of his brother's firing. Many
had seen it coming. Maurilio's pilfering had been suspected by others.
Battle did not hold it against Nene, though Marquez did take it upon
himself to find a replacement. He had an idea—he traveled to Aruba and
begged Harold Marchena to return.

The situation was now different: the casino was up and running, and it was turning a profit. Whatever operational matters had bothered Marchena enough to make him resign had obviously been fixed or at least were not damaging the profitability of the venture. Plus, Nene offered Marchena a hefty percentage of the casino take. This was no small thing since it had already been established that the venture was generating substantial revenue. Basically, the Battle organization was making Harold Marchena an offer he could not refuse.

Marchena returned to Lima to take over for Maurilio Marquez as the financial manager of the casino. A potential crisis had been averted.

Running a casino was like any other corporate enterprise. There were challenges from within, involving personnel and operational procedure, and there were environmental challenges. Casinos generate money, so there is the perception that on a daily basis the cash is flowing, which makes the business attractive to thieves and extortionists. Since the people of Peru did not know the Crillón was owned and run by a gangster, there was no reason to surmise that the owners could not be intimidated. The Crillón was as susceptible to the vagaries of Peruvian crime and politics as any other business in Lima.

In December 1993, an envelope was delivered to the management of the casino. Inside was a message from the Peruvian terrorist group Sendero Luminoso (Shining Path) stating that the Casino Crillón was an affront to the Marxist principles of the organization, and also an exploitation of the Peruvian people. Sendero Luminoso demanded a large cash payment from the casino, or, the message stated, there would be consequences. If anyone did not understand what those consequences might be, the senders of the message provided a visual aid. Inside the envelope, accompanying the message, was a single bullet.

The envelope and message were brought to Battle, who read it over and held the bullet in his fingers. "*Hijo de puta,*" he exclaimed.

As a former brigadista, a fellow traveler of the Cold War, and a one-time cop, Battle would have known about Sendero Luminoso. The organization had recently come to dominate newspaper headlines in the Latin American press through its occasional bombings and political assassinations. In the ongoing worldwide war between radical leftists and right-wing authoritarianism (in which Battle was an adherent of the latter), Sendero Luminoso was the latest flowering of what some saw as the bitter fruit of Castroism.

The tactics of Sendero Luminoso were brutal. They set off bombs in commercial districts, leading to the deaths of innocent victims. Founded in 1980, the organization took its name from a statement by the founder

latter), Sendero Luminoso was the latest flowering of what some saw as the bitter fruit of Castroism.

The tactics of Sendero Luminoso were brutal. They set off bombs in commercial districts, leading to the deaths of innocent victims. Founded in 1980, the organization took its name from a statement by the founder of the Communist Party in Peru: "Marxism-Leninism will open the shining path to revolution." The group's leader, Abimael Guzmán, stated that "the triumph of the revolution will cost a million lives." He was only slightly exaggerating. Throughout the 1980s, a guerrilla-style war between the group and the country's repressive military regime created a vicious climate of terror. In an effort to enforce loyalty among the peasantry in rural Peru, Sendero Luminoso engaged in numerous mass slaughters, in which fifty and sixty people at a time were killed. Sometimes their throats were slit and their bodies left out in the open.

"Human rights are contradictory to the rights of the people," stated Sendero Luminoso in a message to the world. "We reject and condemn human rights because they are bourgeois, reactionary, counterrevolutionary rights, and are today a weapon of revisionists and imperialists, principally Yankee imperialists."

The government responded with its own reign of terror. Death squads known as *rondas* were armed by the military and sent out to round up and kill anyone believed to be sympathetic to Sendero Luminoso. Often this approach had the opposite effect of what the government wanted: it created the sense that in a war between two equally horrific options, it might be best to side with the "people."

Alberto Fujimori had been elected president on a strong antiterrorism platform. One of his first acts was to issue a law giving legal status to the *rondas,* which were now officially known as Comités de Autodefensa (Committees of Self-Defense). Peruvian police scored a major success in September 1991 with the capture of Guzmán. President Fujimori touted the arrest as the end of Sendero Luminoso.

And it seemed that way, for a while, until car bombs started being detonated all over Lima. The most horrific had been bombs planted in two vans in a popular section of Miraflores, the city's most fashionable neighborhood. In July 1992, just as the Casino Crillón was beginning to formulate as a gleam in the eyes of its investors, the bombs, each packed with 1,000 kilograms of explosives, detonated at 9:15 P.M. The target was a bank on Tarata Street, but the collateral damage was immense. Twenty-five people were killed and 155 injured by the blast.

Two days later, the government responded with the La Cantuta massacre, in which nine students and a teacher from the National University of Education, believed to be Shining Path operatives, were kidnapped and disappeared during the night by members of the Grupo Colina death squad. In the press, they were accused of having perpetrated the Miraflores bombing.

If all of this wasn't enough to send a chill up the spine of a capitalist businessman in Lima, it was also a fact that the Hotel Crillón held a special place in the dark heart of Sendero Luminoso. In 1986, when a group of government ministers were meeting at the Crillón to discuss terrorism, a Shining Path guerrilla accidentally blew herself up attempting to fire a mortar round into the lobby of the hotel.

In being forced to absorb the recent history of the Shining Path, José Miguel Battle may have been experiencing a sense of déjà vu. He had been a cop in Havana in 1958, during the Night of One Hundred Bombs. Cuban rebels set off a series of bombs all around the city, and there wasn't much local authorities could do about it. Afterward, the government responded with a commensurate level of violent repression, the inevitable result being more rebel activity. In Havana, as in Lima, the citizenry were caught in between.

Now, to the management of the Casino Crillón, it appeared as though Sendero Luminoso had delivered a threat. Battle knew enough to take it seriously; the question was, how seriously? It was Battle's belief— informed by attitudes commonly expressed by followers of the Fujimori government—that Sendero Luminoso, despite the occasional car bombing, had been defeated. According to the government, the group simply didn't have the audacity or power they once had. Thus perhaps this written threat was a bluff, a toothless missive from a once terrifying terror group that now didn't have the collective cojones to stage a terror campaign against the Crillón.

Not being Peruvian, Battle called in his security director, General Guillermo Castillo, to discuss the situation. Along with being in the employ of Battle, Castillo was still an active officer in the Peruvian military.

Castillo read the letter and looked at the bullet. Battle was expecting the general to adopt the position of the Fujimori government, that these pesky Marxist hoodlums had been stamped out and were no longer a threat. But Castillo expressed the opposite. "Look," he said. "What this is is a threat from Sendero Luminoso. You have to take this seriously. I suggest that you pay the money. Give them what they want, or they could start setting off bombs and bring your business to a standstill."

It was not the answer Battle had been hoping for, but he was inclined to listen to the general. He was ready to make the payment, but then, out of the blue, he was quietly approached by a member of his security staff who had some information about the letter that he felt might be useful.

Mario Masaveu was a black belt in karate who had been hired by General Castillo himself. Once Battle got a look at Masaveu, who was musclebound and solid, he made him one of his three bodyguards—or, as Battle liked to call them, deputy security directors. It was an attorney for the casino who told Masaveu, "Listen, you need to be on the lookout for anything suspicious. We've received an extortion letter from the Shining Path. It came with a bullet."

Masaveu was startled. "Wait a minute," he said. "I know about this letter."

"What are you talking about?" asked the lawyer.

Masaveu explained that a few days earlier, he had overheard two staff members of the hotel talking about a letter from the Shining Path accompanied by a bullet. It was in a basement hallway in the hotel. Masaveu wasn't clear whether they were talking about sending or having received the letter. He hadn't thought much about the conversation until now.

The lawyer immediately brought Masaveu to Battle, in the casino office, to relay his story. The bodyguard told Battle the story, and then added, "Boss, I think these are the guys who sent you this letter. This smells like a scam. They're not Sendero Luminoso."

Battle sent Masaveu and his two other private guards to find the two hotel employees and bring them to him, which they did. The two young hotel workers, terrified, stood in front of Battle, who said, "I know what you did. I want you to admit it. Your lives depend on it."

The two hotel workers admitted their guilt. They were not Peruvian terrorists, merely hustlers who had come up with a plan to extort money from the casino. Battle asked them if General Castillo had been in on the scam. They said no, but Battle wasn't sure he believed them.

The two workers were fired. General Castillo was also fired. Mario Masaveu took over his job as director of security for the Casino Crillón.

It was a big promotion for the young black belt. He basked in the glory of his elevated status in the universe of El Padrino. He was the guy who had exposed the bogus extortion plot, which, it seemed, had nothing to do with the dreaded Shining Path.

A couple of weeks later, on Jirón Ocoña, a narrow street behind the Hotel Crillón, a car bomb exploded with a thunderous sound that rattled through the lobby and lower floors of the building. In the casino, the blast cracked plaster and shattered glass. George Croes, the head cashier, remembered that "everyone stopped what they were doing. We had to evacuate the casino." Outside, three passersby were killed, and thirty people were wounded. The lobby of the hotel was used as a makeshift triage center to deal with the injured, one of whom had had a leg blown off.

The bombing had all the earmarks of Sendero Luminoso.

EFFUGENIA REYES HAD HUNG AROUND THE CRILLÓN FOR A FEW WEEKS AFTER HER public argument with Battle. She was in no hurry to leave. She insisted that she be put up in her own room, and there she stayed, running up her tab at the hotel until finally leaving in a huff. She flew to Miami to collect her belongings from El Zapotal.

She was there on a night in July 1994, packing her clothes and other belongings into suitcases and, with the help of a friend, moving them out to a car in the driveway. She had a flight leaving later that night for Guatemala, where she would be met by her family. She was finished with her life as the mistress of El Padrino.

As she loaded her belongings into the car, a couple of police cars pulled up. Out stepped four Metro-Dade cops, one of them with a police dog on a leash.

The cops were from the department's Narcotics Bureau. An informant of theirs, who was jammed up on a narcotics charge and looking to better his situation, had given them a tip that José Miguel Battle was known to store large amounts of illegally obtained cash in the walls of his house. Everyone in law enforcement knew that many bills in Miami, by that time having been used to snort cocaine by a sizable portion of the population, were known to have traces of cocaine on them. The cops figured they would see if they could gain entry to the house. They brought along a dog from the canine unit. The dog wasn't trained to smell money, but it was trained to smell cocaine. If there was cocaine on those bills, the hound would sniff it out.

The cops weren't expecting much. They didn't even have a search warrant. They arrived to find Effugenia and her friend busily packing. The lead detective asked if they could do a "consent search" of the home.

"What's that?" asked Effugenia.

"Well, pretty much just like it sounds. We ask to search the premises, and you give us your consent. It'll only take a few minutes. We promise not to damage anything. Just wanna run the police dog through the house."

Effugenia had been through the wringer with Battle, who had humiliated her in front of everyone at the Crillón and treated her like a *puta*. Whether she was driven by a desire to get revenge or was simply busy packing and not fully focused on what the cop was suggesting, she gave her consent. She even signed a document that allowed the officers to search the premises.

The cops couldn't believe their luck. They did a run-through with the dog but found nothing.

A few hours later, Effugenia was on a plane to Guatemala, where she hoped to find refuge in the loving embrace of her family.

In Lima, Battle received the news about Effugenia's signing a piece of paper letting the cops search his house. He was livid. How could she do that? Okay, the cops hadn't found anything incriminating, but still, it was the principle. On top of everything else, she had violated his trust. Again.

Maybe it was also residual anger at the public way in which the relationship with Effugenia had ended, which was embarrassing to Battle. His anger at his former "wife," as she was known around the Crillón, was teetering in the danger zone. People like Nene Marquez and Luis DeVilliers in Lima, and Abraham Rydz in Miami, knew that when Battle became this angry, it was not beyond the realm of possibility that somebody was going to die.

18

DOWN AND OUT IN LIMA

THERE WERE NO SUBSEQUENT BOMBINGS BY SENDERO LUMINOSO IN THE AREA ADJAcent to the Hotel Crillón, though there were other explosions around the city. For Battle, that was somebody else's problem. The war between Marxist-Leninism and capitalism was no longer the primary focus of his life. He had more immediate issues to contend with, namely the survival of his casino.

In the casino gambling business, as with all gambling enterprises, there is always risk. As Abraham Rydz would say, "That's why they call it gambling." The Casino Crillón had gone up like a balloon filled with helium, but by the seventh or eighth month of operation it began to deflate just as quickly. This was not entirely unexpected. The bombing had not helped, though over the years Peruvians had become hardened to overt acts of terrorism. More pertinent to the Crillón's downward financial turn was the opening in 1994 of two additional casinos in Lima. The Crillón was no longer the only game in town.

A gambling venture will ebb and flow; that is the nature of the beast. The important thing is that during the fallow period there be sufficient cash flow, a salve to stem the bleeding until fortunes shift and the enterprise is again taking in more money than it is dispensing. The problem with the Crillón was that it was being financed entirely with dirty money. Getting cash into the casino on a daily basis to cover operational costs was not as simple as a wire transfer between banks. Loading up human money couriers on flights from Miami may have been enough to get the operation off the ground. But keeping up with the daily expenses required more than a bunch of fifty- and sixty-year-old Cuban émigrés with shipments of U.S. currency stuffed in their underwear.

The government entity that served as the regulatory commission over-seeing casino gambling in Peru was called CONACA (Confederación Nacional de Agencias Comerciantes). CONACA had a rule that each morning a casino had to have at least $250,000 in its coffers in order to operate. An inspector from CONACA came to the casino every morning and counted the money in the "cage," the central location for cash on the casino floor. If the minimum money requirement was met, the inspector gave authorization for the casino to begin business for the day.

More and more, the Casino Crillón did not have the money in its coffers. What they did then was lean on their bank.

Banco Continental was no longer associated with the Crillón; they had pulled out. The new bank was Banco Banex, which was located just blocks away from the casino. Banex had opened a teller exchange window in the casino, making it easy for customers to access their accounts while gambling and also change currency from U.S. dollars to soles, the Peruvian currency.

Knowing that the inspector from CONACA was arriving every morning at a certain time, casino management simply borrowed money from the Banex teller and put it in the cage. Once the inspector had finished with his duties and left the premises, the money was moved back to the bank teller's vault.

When the management at Banco Banex learned what was happening, they were concerned. This practice constituted bank fraud, and, if discovered, would cost the bank its license. Plus, Banex had already extended to the Casino Crillón a number of overdraft loans that were past due. The financial situation at the casino was headed in a bad direction. Executives at Banex felt that it was time that bank management had a talk with the owners of the Crillón to put an end to the practice. As their emissary, they sent Salvador Ramirez, a managing director.

Ramirez had become familiar with the Crillón and particularly familiar with Battle. Perhaps unbeknownst to his employers, Ramirez had fallen under the thrall of the American Mob boss. He became part of Battle's posse, drinking, snorting, and partying late into the night. He began to dress like Battle and started carrying a loaded .45-caliber handgun stuffed in the back of his pants, under his jacket, just like El Padrino.

Now Ramirez was being given the unpleasant task of informing José Miguel and the other owners that certain things needed to change at the Casino Crillón.

The meeting took place in the lobby of the hotel, which had been remodeled expressly for these kinds of important meetings. There was a reserved area with a glass door, for privacy.

There to meet with Ramirez, along with Battle, were Luis De-Villiers and Nene Marquez. Ramirez brought up the overall financial condition of the business, which had become alarming, but first he delivered the message that bank executives were insisting that whoever was responsible for using his teller outlet to commit bank fraud be fired and replaced.

At the start, the meeting went well. DeVilliers and Marquez listened quietly as Ramirez spoke. But when he got to the part about firing the casino manager, Battle went ballistic. He stood up and shouted, "Who do you think you are to come in here and talk like that to me!? You think you can tell me how to run my casino?" Nene stood and tried to calm Battle, but he wasn't having it. "Salvador, do you realize what you have done here? I can even order to have you killed, and nothing is going to happen if I do."

The room went quiet. Ramirez turned pale. DeVilliers stood to escort him out of the room.

Even though he was clearly rattled, Ramirez had the presence of mind to say, "Gentlemen, the bottom line is that for the casino to remain solvent, you need an infusion of capital of two million dollars."

"Get him out of here," said Battle.

Later that day, Ramirez spoke with the Peruvian investors, Ferer, Chiang, and Chau.

"What happened?" asked Ferer.

"He threatened to kill me."

Chiang and Chau were exasperated. Ferer put a hand on Ramirez's shoulder and said, "That's the way it is, I'm afraid. He believes he is El Padrino, the Godfather."

"What can we do about it?" said Chiang.

"I know what we can do," answered Ferer. "Get out of this business before we all wind up in jail, or dead."

That day, the three Peruvians divested themselves from the Casino Crillón. They agreed to a buyout of $100,000 each, money they would possibly never see unless the casino was able to get back on a winning streak.

Another person who was worried about how things were going with the casino was Harold Marchena. When he returned to work at the casino, Marchena had at first been impressed that it was able to function at all given the inexperience of the owners. He had his concerns; he knew about the efforts to fool the inspectors from CONOCA. In his entire career, he had never seen anything like that being done. But he chose to overlook a number of warning signs, believing, perhaps wishfully, that the kinks would be ironed out and the casino would soon be run as a legitimate operation.

A major sign that things were not right was when Nene Marquez announced that casino management and employees would temporarily not be paid; the payroll expenses had not been met. Whatever money they had would be used to pay bills—electrical, water, maintenance, and so on. Management employees would have to forgo salary for a few weeks.

This made Marchena nervous, and it also reminded him that he had not yet received any profit share, as he had been promised. He demanded to see the books. Reluctantly, Nene Marquez allowed Marchena to look at the ledgers. There were many fraudulent line items and obviously fake invoices. Said Marchena, "These books are nonsense. We need to have an independent auditor come in here and do an evaluation. This is not right."

Nene closed the books and told Marchena he'd bring it up at the next shareholders' meeting.

Before then, Nene told Battle, "I think we have a problem." He relayed the news that Marchena was demanding that an independent auditor be brought in to examine the books. Battle made the decision to fire Marchena.

Nene Marquez told Marchena to pack up his things and leave. Marchena thought to himself, *I'm not going to take this lying down.* A few days later, he went to see a lawyer and filed a lawsuit against the Casino Crillón for unfair termination. He was asking for $160,000 in damages.

When Battle and the other owners were informed about the lawsuit, they became concerned. A lawsuit of this type could force the casino to open its books in a courtroom, which would be disastrous for the owners. At first, casino management tried to intimidate Marchena. At his apartment in Lima, he received phone calls from Evelyn Runciman, Battle's new bride, who was now listed as a shareholder of the casino. Using vile language, Runciman cursed out Marchena, telling him that if he persisted with his lawsuit he would never again work in the casino business.

When the harassing phone calls didn't work, the casino bosses tried to buy him out. Nene Marques contacted Marchena and told him they wanted to pay him off. "We'll give you twenty-five thousand dollars to drop your lawsuit," said Nene.

Marchena answered, "No way."

"Okay. Thirty-five thousand."

Marchena thought about it. Recently, he had learned that Battle had attempted to pay a bribe to the judge in the case, forcing Marchena's lawyer to demand a change of judges. The lawyer was successful, but clearly Battle was going to play dirty. His legal fees were going to be substantial. Thirty-five thousand dollars sounded better than nothing.

Nene explained the deal. "We'll send you an airplane ticket. You fly from Lima to Miami. In Miami, we're going to give you your money."

Marchena could think of no reason he needed to fly from Lima to Miami to receive his money, unless, of course, the Battle people intended to make him disappear. "You know what?" he said to Nene. "Forget about it. We go through with the case."

For Marchena, it was a matter of principle. But he had to admit, he was scared. He was taking on the Godfather.

ANOTHER HIGH-LEVEL CASINO EMPLOYEE WHO WAS HAVING PROBLEMS WITH THE management was Chito Quandas, whose title was director of operations. Unlike Marchena, the Peruvian investors, and some of the others, Quandas had actually started out liking José Miguel Battle. Quandas lived in an apartment on the same floor as Battle, and he sometimes stopped by to meet with his boss. Once he got past the bodyguards into Battle's inner sanctum, what he often encountered was Battle sitting in his underwear, or in a bathrobe, with a shotgun on his lap as he watched videotapes of one of the *Godfather* movies on the television.

Everyone at the casino knew that Battle was obsessed with the *Godfather* movies. It was a running joke among the employees. *Señor Walled thinks he is Don Corleone.* Sometimes after watching scenes from these movies all morning or afternoon, Battle would come down to the casino floor talking as if he were doing an imitation of Brando as the Don.

Not knowing the full extent of Battle's criminal career, Quandas found it all charming in a certain way. Battle was playing a role. The problem was that in the movie the Don was a man of principle who eschewed narcotics and placed family values above business. For Battle, as his dream of a casino seemed to be heading down the drain of financial ruin, he became less like the Don and more like Sonny, the hotheaded son whose temper tantrums drove him to make intemperate miscalculations.

Quandas knew that Battle was drinking a lot and using cocaine. Sometimes he witnessed Battle snorting coke while watching *The Godfather,* mouthing dialogue from the movie from memory. The director of operations was not about to tell Battle what he could or couldn't do in his personal life, but when El Padrino started doing the white powder out in the open, Quandas realized he needed to say something about it.

It was all on videotape. One day, a member of the security staff showed Quandas a tape, taken from one of the hotel's security cameras, of Battle snorting coke with his bodyguards in a hotel hallway. Quandas called Battle into his suite and showed him the tape. Battle became enraged. He pulled the tape out of the video player and tried to destroy the machine. "You record me secretly without my permission!? I could have you killed."

The relationship between Battle and Quandas was never the same after that. Having your boss threatening to kill you tended to sour employer-employee relations. Plus, Quandas was aware of all the same improprieties as Marchena and the others—bank fraud, false invoices, pilferage by the owners, and, most notably, an inability to meet payroll.

The casino owed Quandas over $100,000 in back salary. He brought it up at one of the shareholders' weekly meetings and knew right away it was a mistake. From then on, he was on the receiving end of a campaign of intimidation that he believed was designed to either drive him crazy or force him to resign—probably both.

One morning at 5 A.M., Quandas came back to his room after a long night on the casino floor to find in his bathroom the severed head of an animal—a lamb or a goat—and blood from the animal splattered around the bathroom. On another occasion he noticed a terrible smell in his room. He looked around to find out where it was coming from. In the ceiling he noticed that a small hole had been drilled and a clear liquid was dripping through the hole and onto the floor. He had no idea what the liquid was, but the odor was so bad that he had to move to a different room.

The campaign of intimidation achieved its goal; Quandas wanted out. One afternoon, he summoned his courage and confronted Battle in his room. *The Godfather* was on the television, and Battle was high on cocaine and scotch whiskey.

"Let's settle our disagreement once and for all," said Quandas to El Padrino. "Let's reach a fair financial settlement, come to an agreement."

Battle was not in a reasonable state of mind. "No. I'm not agreeing to anything. I want you out of here."

"Yes," said Quandas, "I'm going out of here. That's what we both want. Now let's agree to a settlement. I'm asking for twenty thousand dollars."

Battle became quiet and said, "I could probably have you killed for less than that." Then he continued rattling on about how people were trying to take advantage of him. "I built this casino. Me. I'm the one who supplied the capital. And now everyone is trying to destroy it, to bleed it dry."

Quandas gave up. He approached the other owners and quietly reached a settlement. He would resign and agree not to sue the casino. In exchange, he received the $20,000 he asked for and was given a one-way ticket back to Aruba.

HAROLD MARCHENA WAS STILL PURSUING HIS LAWSUIT. IT WAS CAUSING BATTLE AND his partners considerable consternation. One morning, Marchena received a call from Evelyn Runciman. He was ready to hang up, thinking she was about to launch into one of her profane tirades, but her voice was calm. She asked if Marchena could come by the office at the casino. She and her husband wanted to speak with him.

Marchena agreed. As he prepared to go to the casino, he was feeling relieved. Maybe Battle had finally come to his senses. The lawsuit was costing them both time and money. Maybe Battle was finally ready to reach some sort of agreeable settlement.

Marchena went to the office at the Casino Crillón. Battle was not there. In attendance were Evelyn and her stepfather, Valerio Cerron, who, after Chito Quandas had quit, was promoted from slot machine technician to managing director of the casino.

Evelyn was seated at the desk. To Marchena, it was somewhat comical because she was hardly big enough to see over it. Cerron stood at her side like a diligent turkey vulture.

Evelyn called Battle on the phone and handed the receiver to Marchena: "Here. Señor Walled wants to talk with you."

Marchena put the phone to his ear. "Yes," he said. He was half expecting an apology, or at least some sensible conversation from Battle; instead what he got was this: "You listen to me, you fucking *maricón*. You think you're smart? If Evelyn wanted to, she could open the desk drawer, take out a gun, and shoot you right now."

Marchena tried to speak, but he realized he was only stammering.

"If you don't leave Peru within the week, I'm going to have you eliminated. Do you understand? This is nothing for me. I'll have you know that I already eliminated my first wife, Effugenia. That's right. You remember her? She got on my bad side and now she's gone. I will do the same with you. Drop your lawsuit. Get out of Peru. Otherwise I'm going to have you killed."

Marchena gathered his wits enough to say, "You know what? I'm going to go straight to the embassy, the Dutch embassy, and notify them. And I'm going to notify my lawyer. You can't go around threatening people."

Battle had begun to respond—"You do that, you fucking . . .—but Marchena didn't wait for him to finish; he handed the phone over to Evelyn. Then he left the office.

In his car, Marchena couldn't stop shaking. He was disturbed by the threat, obviously, but right away he wondered about the reference to Effugenia Reyes having been killed. He had not heard anything about that. When he got to his lawyer's office, he immediately called Juan Solano Loo, the former accountant at the casino who had had an affair with Effugenia. Solano was now living in hiding somewhere outside of Lima.

Solano had not spoken with Effugenia in a while; he didn't know anything about any murder. He gave Marchena her home phone number in Guatemala City.

Marchena dialed the number. A man answered the phone and said, "Yes?"

Marchena cleared his throat. "I would like to talk with Effugenia."

After a pause, the man said, "Who's calling?"

"A friend of hers from Lima, Peru. Why do you need to know?"

The man said, "Because Effugenia is dead. She was killed earlier today."

Marchena was stunned. "Who is this?" he asked.

"I'm with the police. I'm here investigating the crime." Then the man asked, "Do you know José Miguel Battle?"

He did not say Alfredo Walled. He said Battle. José Miguel Battle, Marchena knew, was Walled's real name, though no one in Peru used that name for El Padrino.

Marchena was dumbstruck. He held the phone for a few seconds, then he hung up.

His attorney had been listening. He looked at his client, who had turned pale. "What is it?" he said.

"That man said he was a policeman. He said that Effugenia is dead. She was murdered in her home in Guatemala earlier today."

The lawyer took Marchena straight to the Dutch embassy in downtown Lima. As a Dutch citizen, Marchena wanted to lodge a complaint that his life had been threatened by a man who called himself Alfredo Walled, though his real name was José Miguel Battle Sr. It was the first time that Battle's actual name had been entered into any official document since he had arrived in Peru.

EVER SINCE LEARNING THAT BATTLE WAS IN PERU, SHANKS AND HIS SQUAD HAD BEEN sniffing around for information. First, they had to verify what they read in the Spanish-language newspaper, that Battle owned a casino in Lima under the name of Alfredo Walled. They did so by contacting the Diplomatic Security Service (DSS), a division of the State Department that, among other things, enforces passport laws. An agent from DSS contacted the U.S. embassy in Lima. They were able to establish that, yes, Alfredo Walled had entered the country on a U.S. passport that, under the circumstances, was likely forged. In their investigation, they also learned something interesting about Battle. Though he had become eligible for citizenship back in the early 1960s when President Kennedy made a special allowance for Brigade 2506 veterans, Battle had never applied for it. Technically, he was not even a U.S. citizen.

At the very least, the cops might have a case to make against Battle for passport fraud, which would be a federal charge. But to make that case, they had to have him in the United States. They had no jurisdiction in Peru. Some thought was given to devising a plot to lure Battle back to Miami.

Meanwhile, Shanks got a call from an officer he had worked with years earlier. The officer had a friend he had known since grade school. The woman had over the years become friendly with certain people within the Battle family circle of influence. She was in a position to know and have heard certain things about Battle that others might not know. She was willing to talk.

Shanks met the woman one day, at a café far away from the police station. The woman was nervous, but after a while she settled down and began to open up. She described some of the interpersonal dynamics of the Battle family, how Junior and Senior hardly spoke with one another; how the matriarch of the Battle family lived separate from El Zapotal.

After a while, Shanks asked, "Why are you here? Why are you willing to talk to me like this?"

"Effugenia Reyes," said the woman.

Shanks was familiar with the name. "Battle's mistress, right? She lived with him at El Zapotal."

The woman nodded. "She was my best friend."

Shanks cocked his head. "Wait a minute, you said 'was.' What happened?"

"You don't know? She was brutally murdered."

This was the first time Shanks was hearing this information.

The woman explained how Effugenia learned that Battle was having an affair in Lima. She felt betrayed and left Battle, returning first to Miami to gather her belongings before continuing on to Guatemala. She was living there when two men broke into her house and murdered her. The woman was certain José Miguel Battle was behind the murder. "That's the kind of man he is," she said. She was talking to Shanks because she hoped it might one day lead to some form of justice for Battle.

Shanks told her that he would look into it. He asked the woman if they might meet again and on a semiregular basis. Since she was still in contact with people close to the Battle family, she could be his confidential informant.

"You mean like Deep Throat?" she said, referencing the Watergate source that famously fed information to journalists Bob Woodward and Carl Bernstein.

"Right," said Shanks

"So what's my code name?"

Shanks gave it some thought, but before he could say anything, she offered, "How about 'Sexy Cubana'?"

"Okay," said Shanks. The common initials for a confidential informant was C.I. For her, he would use C.S., which was "Sexy Cubana" in reverse.

Back at the office, Shanks told the other investigators. By now, he was working on loan to the U.S. Attorney's Office and serving under Larry LaVecchio, who was now an assistant U.S. attorney (AUSA). LaVecchio was intrigued by what he heard. He had Shanks call the U.S. embassy in Guatemala City; they called the Guatemalan National Police and learned that Effugenia Reyes had indeed been killed. The crime had taken place supposedly during what was ruled a home invasion robbery, though no money or valuables were taken from the residence. Effugenia was killed with a knife, her throat cut so violently that her head was almost completely severed from her body.

LaVecchio called together the entire team of investigators, a group that included Shanks, Kenny Rosario, and four other detectives. They discussed their options. If Battle had indeed ordered this murder, it was going to be difficult to even investigate. They couldn't charge Battle solely on what they had learned from Sexy Cubana. They didn't know if the hit men were local killers, assassins from Peru, or from the United States. If they were from the United States, that would put the conspiracy within the jurisdiction of American law enforcement, but they were a long way away from knowing those details.

"The fraudulent passport," said LaVecchio. "That's still our best bet for getting him kicked out of Peru and brought back here to face the music."

After the meeting was over, LaVecchio said to Shanks, "That's a helluva source you got there. Mind telling me who she is?"

"No can do," said Shanks. "This woman is putting herself at great risk talking with me. I promised her no one would know her identity, not even my supervisor."

LaVecchio was annoyed; Shanks could see that. But Shanks knew he was within his rights. It was an unwritten rule about street informants. If they offered information under a cloak of secrecy, a promise from their cop overseer that their identity would not be divulged, that promise had to be honored. If it wasn't, that was a betrayal, and then what difference was there between the criminals and the cops?

SEPTEMBER 14, 1994, WAS BATTLE'S BIRTHDAY. HE WAS SIXTY-FIVE YEARS OLD. IN honor of this momentous occasion, he threw a birthday party for himself in the Sky Room on the top floor of the Crillón. But first he had a mariachi band come into the casino and serenade him in front of the entire staff. He had people open bottles of champagne and make sure all casino personnel had a glass. Battle announced, "I want everyone to know, you can go ahead and steal today. I stole the money myself. And it's my birthday. So you can go ahead and do what you want."

He hoisted his glass and gave his signature salutation: "Let's drink champagne and raise a toast to our enemies."

Everyone drank, but the atmosphere was not exactly convivial. Morale among the casino employees was not great, as paydays were often missed and managers were being fired on a regular basis. Attendance at the casino was down.

The night of Battle's birthday party, Hubert Dominico Salazar, a cashier at the casino, was told by a regular customer, "Your boss, I hear, is a very dangerous man. They say he had his former wife killed in Guatemala."

Salazar was one of the employees who had come from Aruba, a friend of both Harold Marchena and Chito Quandas. Already he was disturbed by the turmoil and firings; this was the final straw. He approached a manager and asked, "Is it true what they say about Walled?"

"What's that?"

"He had his ex-wife killed?"

The manager shrugged. "I hear she was found with her head cut off."

The manager could see that Dominico was shaken. "Listen," he said. "My advice is that you keep your mouth shut about these things. Don't ask too many questions."

Dominico did ask more questions, and then he was fired. Not only that, he was told that he would not be paid the remaining money he was owed under the terms of his contract.

Dominico requested a meeting with Battle. Years later, he remembered the incident: "I asked if I could meet him, and he came down. At first, he was very nice. He asked if I wanted something to eat. Then I asked him why I was being fired, that I did a good job training [the other cashiers]. And he said, 'Well, I paid you for the training and I don't want you there anymore.' We got into an argument, and he said, 'You can go to five, six, seven lawyers, I will not pay you to the end of the contract. And I advise you that you better leave or something bad might happen to you.'"

As with others who had come from Aruba to work at the Crillón, Dominico made a hasty and unceremonious exit.

For Battle, the road to fulfilling his dream of being a casino boss like Lansky and Trafficante had become a downward spiral. Left and right, he was threatening floor workers, managers, and bankers—nearly everyone with whom he was doing business. Even for someone who had frequently used thuggery in his life and business dealings, he had never been so out of control.

The possibility that he had ordered the murder of Effugenia Reyes, a young woman whom most everyone at the casino had known while she was there, was a new level of depravity. Killing a woman is normally beyond the pale, even for a gangster. You don't kill women and children. If it was true, not only was Battle acting in bad faith, but he had lost his soul.

Mario Masaveu, onetime bodyguard and now director of security for the casino, was one person who stayed with Battle through thick and thin. In Battle's suite, on those occasions when the boss wasn't occupied watching *The Godfather I, II,* or *III,* Masaveu would chat with the man he always referred to as Padrino.

In late 1994, an article about Battle appeared in a major newspaper in Lima. For the first time Alfredo Walled was identified publicly as José Miguel Battle, a notorious crime figure from New York and Miami. Battle had finally been outed, and Masaveu, meeting with Battle in his suite, expected that El Padrino would be upset. But he was not. Battle was in a sanguine mood. He told his security director details about his life that were not in the article, from his time with Brigade 2506 to his involvement in certain gangland-style killings in New York City. He told Masaveu that the reason he had come to Peru and opened the casino was that he had to get out of the United States. He was certain he would soon be arrested there and was living a kind of glorified life on the run.

For the first time, Masaveu saw Battle as a tragic figure, a perennial exile whose reputation as a Mob boss was not something he was ashamed of but instead cherished. Because at this point in his life, it was all he had.

BACK IN MIAMI, SHANKS AND HIS SQUAD WERE ATTEMPTING TO APPLY PRESSURE IN certain diplomatic circles to get Battle deported from Peru. They were aware of the article that had appeared in the Peruvian newspaper and sensed that this perhaps represented a shift in attitude toward this larger-than-life Cuban American who had made such a big splash with his Casino Crillón.

Two agents from the Diplomatic Security Service in Miami were assigned to the case. One of them, Robert O'Bannon, had worked in the embassy in Peru for many years. He had connections in the Peruvian

National Police, who began looking into the case of Alfredo Walled. Once it was established that a false passport had been used, getting Battle deported should have been a mere formality. But Battle had his own connections among the military and governmental people he had lavished with complimentary chips and money at his casino.

It took five months, but in April 1995 it was announced that José Miguel Battle was being deported as an "undesirable alien." But he was not put on a plane to the United States. Instead, he was able to fly to Buenos Aires, Argentina, where he hunkered down and began plotting a way to get back into Peru.

In exile, Battle came to the conclusion that many of his enemies were behind the deportation. First on this list was Juan Solano Loo, Effugenia's former boyfriend, who had returned to the casino as soon as Battle was banished from Peru. Reinstated as the casino's accountant, Solano made the argument to the shareholders that Battle had become a major liability to the casino's prospects of ever recouping its losses. He proposed that Battle's shares be sold off to the highest bidder. Through his internal spies, Battle learned about this meeting and about Solano's proposal. He was irate. Mostly, he blamed Luis DeViliers and Nene Marquez, his two closest associates at the Crillón, for even taking part in such a discussion.

From his hotel room in Buenos Aires, Battle stewed in his own toxic brew of bitterness and resentment. Every day he was on the phone with various contacts in Lima, plotting his return. Evelyn, his wife, and her stepfather, Velario Cerron, were sent as emissaries to see the deputy minister whom the casino had once treated to a private sex show featuring the Chin Chin Girls. It was time for the deputy minister to return the favor.

The man told Evelyn and her stepfather that it would be difficult. Battle's case had now garnered international attention, with much pressure being applied at the highest levels of government. The implication was that not only would the deputy minister need to be compensated for his efforts, but he also would likely have to spread the money around. He required a payment of $250,000.

"No," said Battle. It was a special level of ingratitude when an old man, a deputy minister, who has been given a sex show with strippers dancing over him while he lay on the floor, tried to take advantage of a friend in need. The price was too high. Battle would find his own way back into Peru.

Among the calls Battle made to Lima on a daily basis were those to Nene Marquez. His brother-in-law, for better or for worse, had become his first line of defense, both his confidant and whipping boy.

Over the previous year, Nene had had to do more than his share of cleaning up after José Miguel. Nene had watched Battle become more and more unhinged, drinking every day and using cocaine as if it were a condiment. Nene never stood up to him, neither publicly nor privately, but he had begun to have his doubts about El Padrino's fitness to continue as an owner of the hotel. Now that Battle was in exile in Argentina, Nene expressed these doubts. Battle heard about this and had now added Nene to the list of betrayers who were out to screw him over.

Battle called Marquez. What he didn't know was that Nene had recently begun taping his conversations with José Miguel. By now it was almost standard practice within the universe of the Corporation for people to be taping one another. Battle taped Ernestico; Ernestico taped Battle. Charley Hernandez taped Chino Acuna. A recording device was placed on all phones at the bolita offices, to record the bets. The cops had placed dozens of wiretaps on Corporation phone lines all over South Florida. Voices on top of voices were being recorded in the midst of various levels of collusion and betrayal.

As soon as Nene heard that it was Battle, he clicked on the recorder. Battle was in fine form, inebriated and possibly high on coke. He began speaking as if the conversation had already been under way for hours. "Why?" he said. "Why do they want what's mine? Tell me why."

"Who wants what's yours?" said Nene. "Nobody wants what's yours."

Whenever they were on the phone, the boliteros spoke obliquely. There was always the possibility that cops could be listening. Marquez explained to his brother-in-law that he was guilty of nothing. It had not been his idea that Battle's stake in the casino be divested. He had merely attended a meeting to hear what was being suggested.

Battle wasn't having it. He boasted that at every turn, when money was needed to keep the venture afloat, he was the one who provided the cash. "Nene, when you guys haven't had the money to bring, that's when I sent it, Nene."

"Okay, okay, I agree with that. I agree."

"Listen to me, Nene. Because I haven't stolen a penny. I'm not a thief."

Now Marquez became emotional. Battle was accusing him of stealing from the casino. "I would never in my life say something like that to you. But now you've said that to me."

"I've said that to you because you want to take what's mine. My share."

Marquez was being accused; he struggled to maintain his composure. "Listen, listen, let me tell you one thing. You've been handling everything for one year or whatever, I haven't involved myself in anything. What you've wanted has always been done."

Battle turned his anger to the subject of Luis DeVilliers. "But Nene, Luisito was negotiating, which I knew, with Fefer and the others. Luisito was negotiating while he was telling us stories."

"Well, that's possible. Look, I don't care what Luis does. Luis can do whatever he wants."

"But you back him up, Nene. I'm telling you, if you guys don't take care of that problem, kill me. Kill me, because if you don't I'm the one who's going to kill."

Marquez was startled to hear Battle speaking so openly on the phone. "All right, all right," he said, trying to pacify his boss.

Said Battle, "I do things straightforward, Nene . . . I'm afraid of you guys now, of an attack from you guys."

This annoyed Marquez. "Look, listen to me for a minute. I'm definitely not afraid of being killed. You can have it at your disposal whenever you want, you know?"

"Your life is not at my disposal, Nene . . . I'm not a traitor like you guys."

"I'm not afraid. I'm not afraid at all."

Battle finally got to the point of his call. "Call that faggot Solano, that sodomite . . ." He could barely contain his anger.

Nene interrupted. "I'm asking you a favor, listen to me. You're not listening to me."

Battle got quiet. "Tell me."

"Okay, look, I'll be there tomorrow. I'm going to make a decision for Luis, for me and for you, for the three of us . . . Now, you tell me what you want me to do, who's going to be the boss, who's going to conduct the orchestra, who's going to do what you want. Just tell me that."

"Remove Solano from there," said Battle. "Valerio is director for me until I arrive." He explained, "They've been able to get me out of there, but it's not going to be forever. I'll get in with another passport through somewhere else. And once inside I'm going to raise hell . . . So call Solano. I don't want to call him because I don't want him to record the threat that I can make to him. I won't hold back . . . Damn. I'll kill them and I'll kill myself first. I'm willing to give my life for that, Nene. I'm not going to let you guys make fun of me, Nene."

Nene groaned. This was the part where José Miguel started to feel sorry for himself. "Nobody wants to make fun of you or ruin your reputation. Nobody."

Battle wasn't listening. "Because unfortunately my heart breaks apart for saying this, Nene, but I'm an honest man. I'm going to die like that, Nene. What more could I want than to trust my very own brother, my brother for twenty years. What a bitter thing to swallow right now, Nene. The only thing that makes me happy is my wife. This woman I have who's worth gold, Nene. Because, look, a young girl leaves her school behind, she leaves everything behind to follow her husband, huh? She said to me, 'I'll go with you, married or not married. I'll die with you.' She told me, 'My sweet old man, I'll die for you.'"

"All right," said Nene. "Well, never in my life did I expect to hear this."

"And, fuck, it breaks my heart that my very own brother, my best friend, to see him betray me, dammit. I'd rather die before having to see this, Nene. I'd rather die, Nene."

Nene could hear Battle weeping over the phone. "All right, all right," he said, trying to calm him down.

The conversation continued, with many emotional highs and lows. The crux was that Battle wanted Solano fired immediately, but there was a deeper context. Was Battle drunk, or was he losing his mind? Certainly he was wallowing in a deep funk. The only thing that snapped him out of it was when he chose to remind himself that he had the power. "I have friends, Nene. Don't think because I'm here now in exile that I'm not going to have friends anymore . . . Because our family with problems or without problems is always a family."

Nene almost smiled. This was Battle doing his Don Corleone imitation. "Well," he said, "let me tell you something. You have a man here, you know, and no one has ever been able to prove to me otherwise."

"I'm also a man, Nene. And let's see if we're ready to die. Let's see if we're both ready to die for the same cause."

"Exactly."

"If fate puts us against one another, may God have mercy on us."

"Well, it's not going to be because of me."

"Because of me neither . . . Because I have the balls to impose my rights, I don't want a war between you and me. I don't want it, Nene. You're the father of my grandchildren, my sister's husband, Nene. And I love you a lot, Nene. Take care of things for me, brother."

"I always take care of things."

"Brother, take care of it."

"Always, always."

"Take care of it, my dear brother, take care of it."

"Okay."

It was like soothing a baby to sleep, Battle repeating "Take care of it, brother" like a mantra, and Nene saying, "I got it, everything's fine."

The conversation lasted forty minutes before the two men said goodbye.

BATTLE SNEAKED BACK INTO PERU. IT WASN'T DIFFICULT. HE FLEW FROM BUENOS Aires to La Paz, Bolivia, where he was met by Mario Masaveu and his other two personal bodyguards. Using a newly created false passport, he was driven across the border into Peru. He arrived in Lima early on a morning in late April. One of the first things he did was go to the Casino Crillón—early—before any of the managers or directors had arrived for the day. These men, he believed, were engaged in a campaign to screw him over and likely had played a role in his being exiled. They never thought he would get back into Lima. Well, he had a surprise for them.

Standing on the floor of the casino, cell phone in hand, he first called Luis DeVilliers. When DeVilliers answered, Battle said, "Luisito, good morning. You'll never guess where I am." He held the cell phone next to one of the slot machines, slipped in a token, and pulled the lever. The machine made its usual rattling, clanging, cacophonous sound—the unmistakable sound of a casino in operation. The massage was clear: *Take that,* maricónes. *El Padrino is back!*

Battle's time of gloating was short-lived. As soon as the Peruvian government learned that he was back in the country, a court order was issued to have him apprehended and expelled. He hired a local attorney and fought the order in court. The lawyer put forth the claim that Battle, because he had married a Peruvian citizen, should be given the rights of a citizen. Lawyers for the government countered that since Battle had married Evelyn Runciman under a false name, that argument was not valid. So Battle quickly ran out and married Evelyn again, this time using his actual name, José Miguel Battle.

The government wasn't swayed. Battle's lawyer informed him that he was certainly going to receive an unfavorable ruling on his petition. In all likelihood, he would be deported, this time back to the United States.

Battle didn't wait around. He and Evelyn Runciman, using false passports, hopped on a flight to the Caribbean island of Curaçao. He believed they could hide out there until he came up with a new strategy.

Battle was traveling under the name Franklin Pena Jr., and Evelyn under the name Elsa Montes. Immigration officials at Hato International Airport in Curaçao recognized that the two travelers were using fake passports. They were held in custody and their baggage searched. Inside Battle's bag were various false identifications and his recent marriage license to Runciman. The immigration agents asked themselves, *Who are these people?* They contacted the local U.S. consulate, which was able to determine that it was Battle and Runciman. The two forged passports were seized, and the two offenders were put on a plane and sent back to Lima.

Police officials were waiting. Battle was immediately taken into custody. Evelyn, a Peruvian citizen, was released under her own recognizance.

The date was May 21, 1995. Battle was escorted onto a plane and flown back to the United States. Half thinking he might be arrested as soon as he arrived at Miami International Airport, he had arranged for his attorney to meet him there. He was not arrested, though he had reason to believe that the long arm of the law would be reaching out to embrace him sometime soon.

19

PRESIDENT IN EXILE

DAVID SHANKS AND HIS SQUAD WERE BUSY. THE ILLEGAL GAMBLING AND MONEY-laundering cases against the organizations of Raul Fernandez and Luis Bordon seemed to be never-ending. Gulf Liquors was still under surveillance. Shanks had compiled a dossier on both organizations that included close to one hundred names. What they needed now were potential witnesses. What followed was a scrupulous fishing expedition. Shanks and Boyd separated out the players who had criminal records or criminal matters currently pending in court. Those people were served with subpoenas. Shanks himself did the honors, with Boyd there to translate, if necessary.

They were usually brought in to the U.S. Attorney's Office to be interviewed. Almost always, they would start by invoking their Fifth Amendment rights. Shanks explained, "Look, we are investigating your bosses for various crimes. You have not been charged—yet. In other words, we are offering you this opportunity as a witness. Fifth Amendment doesn't apply." Shanks would then show them what is called a queen-for-a-day letter. The letter specified that under the agreement, the witness could not be charged with anything he revealed during the interview. He was free to tell the truth. If he lied, however, that was a different story.

Even with such a strong motive to be truthful, in Shanks's experience, they always lied. That's when the cops applied pressure.

"Okay," Shanks would tell the potential witness, "all that you just told me is bullshit." He would explain to the person how he knew it was a lie. "So now you've violated our agreement. What do you want me to do? Throw you in a cell with your boss on a racketeering charge? I'm not playing with you. I'll give you one last chance. Let's start all over from the beginning."

It was through this process of cajoling and manipulating that the cops acquired useful information and began to assemble potential witnesses in their case against Fernandez and Bordon. Shanks was careful not to mention Battle's name, because he noticed that when he did, people clammed up. It wasn't loyalty that made them quiet; it was fear.

Even so, the investigators never lost sight of Battle. The gambling and money-laundering cases were seen as stepping-stones to their dream of a RICO case against the Corporation. That dream seemed to have taken a big step toward reality with the news that El Padrino was back in Miami.

Four days after Battle's return, the cops set up two surveillances in South Miami, one at a cockfighting arena where they thought Battle might show up, and another at El Zapotal. Kenny Rosario and another detective were watching the house. In the early evening, they saw Battle pull up to El Zapotal in a car driven by José Aluart. The cops knew Aluart to be one of Battle's drivers, bodyguards, and gofers in Miami. Aluart was five foot seven, with black hair, and he had a permanent kink in his neck that caused his head to be crooked to the right. His nickname among associates in the Corporation was "Cinco a las Seis," Five Minutes to Six, a reference to the angle of his head.

Aluart walked with Battle into the house, then a short while later, he reappeared, got in his car, and pulled away from the property. He was gone for ten minutes or so and then returned.

"Let's see what we can get from this guy," Kenny Rosario said to his partner.

They got out of their car and approached Aluart. They showed their IDs and identified themselves as Metro-Dade officers. Aluart said to Rosario, "Yes, I recognize you from one of the cockfighting raids at Club Campestre."

Rosario asked Aluart if Battle was home. "Sure," said Aluart.

"We would like to speak with Mr. Battle," said Rosario. "Would you go back into the house and tell him there are a couple detectives who'd like to have a word with him?"

"Okay," said Aluart.

The cops looked at one another. Rosario had been half joking, not expecting Aluart to concede without so much as a discussion.

While Aluart went inside, the cops waited. Within a few minutes, Battle emerged. He buzzed the front gate so that Rosario and his partner could enter. The cops walked up to him and introduced themselves, and he welcomed them into his home.

The cops could hardly believe it; they were now inside the lair of El Padrino.

They had been inside for five mintues when Rosario received a cell phone call from his supervisor, Sergeant Boyd. He was at the front door with two other detectives, and he wanted in.

"Hey," said Rosario to Battle, "it's my supervisor on the line, Sergeant Boyd. He's at the front door with two other detectives and would like to come in."

"I know Sergeant Boyd," said Battle. "Let him in." He gestured for Aluart to let the detectives in.

Boyd and the others were brought into the front room. There were now five detectives in the house. As the ranking officer, Boyd took charge. He explained to Battle that he was not under arrest. "We won't be reading your rights or anything like that. We're just here to ask you a few questions."

For the next hour, they chatted. Battle readily admitted much of what had been established about his time in Peru. He was able to purchase false documents by bribing a governmental official in Peru, he said. They asked him about Effugenia Reyes, and he said, yes, she had been a girlfriend of his. He had heard she was killed in Guatemala, and this made him very sad. He didn't know anything else about her death.

They asked Battle about the Corporation. *Are you president of the organization?*

"Look," said Battle. "I was the president, okay? But that was years ago. I'm retired now."

Said Boyd, "Well, does that make you the president in exile?"

"Yeah," said Battle. "That would be a good way to put it."

The cops mentioned that a lot of people associated with the Corporation had been charged with and found guilty of crimes. Battle said,

"I don't know anything about that. And even if it's true, what does that have to do with me? It's like the president of General Motors—if some employees of his are guilty of crimes, does that mean the president is responsible? No. You can't blame me for something other people have done."

Throughout their chat, Battle was respectful and polite. The cops left the house knowing that was one of the most open and unusual conversations they would ever have with a Mob boss.

SHANKS HAD BEEN ON A RARE VACATION WHEN BOYD AND THE OTHERS INTERVIEWED Battle. He was trying to salvage his marriage. He and his wife had driven up the coast along with his stepson, age fourteen, and the stepson's best friend. Their destination was Myrtle Beach, South Carolina. The point of the trip was for Shanks to separate himself from work, to unplug and show his wife that he could do it, that he could be a devoted husband separate from his job as a cop. But the whole time he was there, he'd been wondering about the case. When he called in to Kenny Rosario and learned that he and Boyd and a few others had met directly with Battle, it was as if Christmas had happened without him.

The vacation was going well. One morning, Shanks came back to the condo after a round of golf, and at the motel front desk there was a message for him. There was an envelope, left by two FBI agents, with a plane ticket with his name on it. The message said: "Call Larry." It was LeVecchio from the U.S. Attorney's Office. When Shanks called LeVecchio, he was told that they needed him in the office immediately. There had been a sudden opening on the judge's calendar in the Fernandez/Bordon case, and they had much prep work to do.

Shanks told his wife, "You're not going to believe this."

She knew what it was, and she was not happy. She dropped Shanks off at the nearest airport.

Forever after, when Shanks thought about the exact moment when his marriage ended, he thought of this moment.

Back at the office, the investigators had been hit with a tidal wave of work, and it came in the form of canceled checks from Gulf Liquors.

The Republic National Bank of Miami had been served with a court order to produce canceled checks that had been deposited into the account of Gulf Liquors. This was a staggering request that required they produce literally thousands of checks. When the bank protested, the investigators agreed to narrow down their request to a crucial three-month period where checks from bolita bankers coincided with physical surveillance of the location. Cops witnessed the boliteros cashing checks at the liquor store, which was a rare case of investigators actually seeing the act of money laundering in real time.

The boliteros used a coded system to mark their checks for identification purposes. The cops had learned that the Fernandez organization used the number 14 written on the check; other boliteros had their own designations. What the cops now had to do was go over each and every check cashed at Gulf Liquors during the three-month period, separate those that had special markings, and determine which checks came from which boliteros. For the cops, it was going to be a mind-numbingly laborious process.

There was a collective groan from the entire squad when the checks arrived. They were delivered stacked on two wooden pallets, six feet high and four feet wide. A team of seven people would be putting in full workdays going over the checks and devising an indexing system to identify and categorize the bolita markings and codes on each check. It was a painstaking job that took many months to complete. Eventually, Shanks and the investigators would determine that over an eighteen-month period Gulf Liquors cashed $17,659,323.58 in checks, and of that $2,252,474.55 was in checks with bolitero markings.

At the same time, the cops continued working toward their ultimate goal, the arrest of El Padrino.

Through the U.S. consul general in Curaçao, the cops had sworn statements from the two Dutch immigration official who had encountered Battle and Evelyn Runciman using false passports when seeking to enter that island. The "Alfredo Walled" passport used by Battle had not yet been recovered. That fact was used as probable cause to apply for and receive a search warrant for the premises of El Zapotal.

Shanks and his team debated what to do about Evelyn, who was still back in Lima. They were trying to decide whether they should, at the same time they searched El Zapotal and executed the arrest of El

Padrino, coordinate Runciman's arrest in Peru, which would be a tricky international maneuver.

At the very time they were pondering this decision, as sometimes happens, the cops received a gift from the heavens. Their office was notified that Evelyn Runciman had applied for a U.S. visa to enter the country to visit her "husband." Normally, the fact that Evelyn's marriage was bigamous in nature (Battle was still married to his original wife, Maria Josefa) and the allegation that she had already used a forged U.S. passport, her request would have been denied. But upon hearing of the application, Robert O'Bannon, the DSS agent working the Battle case, sent a request to the visa section at the U.S. embassy in Lima to approve the request.

Evelyn Runciman would be free to waltz through customs into the United States, whereupon she would immediately be placed under surveillance.

It would take weeks to prepare for the raid on El Zapotal. A huge team of cops would be simultaneously executing a search warrant and arrest warrants. The arrest warrant on Battle was for passport fraud, but this was in many ways a pretense for an equally important aspect of the operation: a comprehensive search of the premises. In the ongoing dream of bringing a RICO case against Battle and the Corporation, the raid on El Zapotal would be the cops' own mini-version of the Bay of Pigs invasion, only they were hoping theirs might be more successful.

IF AMERICAN LAW ENFORCEMENT WERE TO EVER BRING A COMPREHENSIVE CASE against the Corporation, it would not be made solely in Miami. A unique aspect of the criminal organization that had grown up around Battle over thirty years was that it was spread across a number of jurisdictions. The financial engine of the Corporation was not located in South Florida; it was in New York City, which still—even after Battle disappeared to Peru for a couple of years—continued to generate bolita proceeds for Battle Sr., Battle Jr., Nene Marquez, Luis DeVilliers, and other aging lions of the Cuban bolita generation.

Up until then, no prosecutorial entity in New York City had ever attempted a major case against a bolita enterprise. The case against Lalo

Pons, which involved arson and second-degree murder charges, had focused on street soldiers, not on the bankers.

For a long time, the NYPD did not view policy or numbers gambling as a serious crime. Beginning in the 1970s, throughout the 1980s, and into the 1990s, New York City had seen one of the most sustained periods of violent crime of any American city in recent history. In 1990, there were 2,245 murders recorded in the five boroughs of New York. Many of these killings were related to the crack cocaine business. Armed robberies and other violent crimes were also at all-time highs. Bolita, viewed mostly as a victimless crime, was small potatoes.

In 1994, police officer Thomas Farley was assigned to a squad within the Public Morals division that dealt with street gambling. At first, when Farley heard he would be busting local numbers spots, he felt guilty about it. As a kid growing up in the neighborhood of Bayside, Queens, he had heard about people betting on the number. Usually it was little old ladies or unemployed people trying to get lucky at minimal cost. Even off-duty cops sometimes made a wager with the local numbers runner. Said Farley, "Back when I first came on the job, in 1986, if you came in with an arrest for gambling—rackets or promoting—you would get laughed out of the precinct."

What changed all that for Farley was when in 1994 he began doing regular "bet and bust" operations at bolita holes in a section of the city referred to as Brooklyn North. Dressed up in the uniform of a bus driver, an auto mechanic, or some other identifiably working-class profession, Farley would enter a spot, place a bet, and leave with his receipt. Sometimes he would hang around the location to see what else was going on. Two or three times a month his squad would make a bust (once on a day when Farley actually held the winning number).

Through it all, the cop began to get a sense of the amount of money that was passing through the average bolita hole in New York. It wasn't as much as in a crack house, or from powder cocaine or even marijuana sales, but it was a steadier stream. Using the comparison of the tortoise and the hare, bolita was the tortoise, a slower financial trickle but in the end a steadier flow and nearly as lucrative.

On a daily basis, making bets and busts, Farley never saw the upper echelon of the organization. Names like Spanish Raymond, Isleño

Dávila, and José Miguel Battle did not come up. But Farley could tell that cash left these locations on a daily basis and was transported to a counting house, or "bank." Money from all over the city was flowing into these bolita banks. Somebody was getting that money. Somebody was controlling the organization from the top, making sure everyone in the hierarchy got his little piece of the pie.

The case against Lalo Pons had brought home the fact that the stakes were high. Two dozen people burned to death. To Brooklyn prosecutors, it was hoped that the conviction of Pons and others would have inflicted damage on the bolita structure in New York. What Farley and his Public Morals squad learned was that by the mid-1990s, bolita was stronger than ever. And it was still controlled by the Cubans.

In 1995, around the same time that Battle returned from Peru, an organized crime squad from the Brooklyn District Attorney's Office had under investigation a faction of the Lucchese crime family. The targets of the investigation were two brothers, Victor and Benito Iadarola, who ran an illegal betting operation that involved sports betting and numbers. On a wiretap of the Iadarolas' social club in the Brooklyn neighborhood of Fort Greene, the investigators overheard a call from a bolitero who identified himself as "Alex from the Corporation."

Over a series of phone calls, it was established that Victor Iadarola was having a territorial dispute with the Corporation. "Everyone knows that's been our turf since the fifties," said Iadarola. He told Alex to shut down his spots or "we'll send some people down there to close it for you."

Alex did not back down. He said to the mafioso, "You know and I know, if you send ten guys, I'll send twenty. If you send fifty, I'll send one hundred. If you send a hundred, I'll send two hundred and fifty. We have you outnumbered." And then, in a not-so-veiled reference to the arson wars, Alex said to Iadarola, "We beat you before and we'll beat you again."

The Mafia wasn't what it used to be. Over the previous ten years there had been a steady stream of major prosecutions, including a conviction of Fat Tony Salerno on racketeering charges that put him away for life. More recently, in 1992, the *capo di tutti capi,* John Gotti, had been convicted. Fewer and fewer Italian American males viewed the Honored Society as a viable career option.

Victor Iadarola felt the heat, and he backed down. The Cubans overruled the Lucchese crime family, and the Corporation kept their bolita spots right where they were.

This conversation indicated to the team of investigators listening in that as far as the numbers racket was concerned, the Corporation in New York had overtaken whatever was left of La Cosa Nostra.

About the same time that Tom Farley and his squad were making bolita busts at the street level, the Rackets Division of the Brooklyn DA's Office was beginning to see the bigger picture. It was estimated, conservatively, that the Corporation during the mid-1990s was bringing in half a million dollars on a weekly basis—not as much as the heyday of the 1980s, but still substantial. There were more than four hundred active bolita holes throughout the five boroughs. The concept of bolita money accumulated in New York City making its way to Miami, where it was laundered through Gulf Liquors and other outlets, was not yet on anyone's radar, but it was only a matter of time.

Discussions began in New York law enforcement circles about mounting a major racketeering case against the Corporation. Local cops and prosecutors had no idea that there were similar plans afoot in Miami. If prosecutors in these two jurisdictions could get their acts together, it would be the mother of all RICO cases.

NOW THAT BATTLE WAS BACK IN MIAMI, ABRAHAM RYDZ KEPT HIS DISTANCE. NEITHER he nor Miguel Jr. had much interaction with El Padrino. They were not surprised to hear that the casino in Lima was going down the tubes. At one point, Rydz stepped in and tried to help Nene Marquez, on behalf of José Miguel, negotiate the sale of the casino to a group of investors. Rydz told Nene, "If you're smart, you'll take your shares and give them away to those investors, then maybe you get rid of your problems."

Rydz and Miguelito had created a life for themselves that was completely separate from the old Cuban bolita culture. They were living the American dream, with luxurious homes in Key Biscayne, half a block away from one another, with Maria Josefa—Miguelito's mother—also in a home nearby. Their families were close; they had many family gatherings together. José Miguel Sr. and his new paramour, Evelyn, were persona non grata at these gatherings.

Rydz's daughter, Susan, was eleven years old at the time Battle Sr. returned from Peru. Though José Miguel Jr. was like an uncle to her, she never met his father. She frequently heard his name mentioned. Her own mother once said of Battle Sr., "That man is crazy," but young Susan had no way of knowing what that meant. Was it just a figure of speech? Or was he literally a person with mental problems?

One time when the family dog developed a bad allergy and it became clear that the animal would have to be removed, her father said, "We'll take him to the ranch. He'll be in good hands there." She later learned that "the ranch" was the home of José Miguel Jr.'s father. Susan thought to herself, *How crazy can the man be if he's kind enough to take in sick animals?*

Sometimes Susan found it unusual that her father and Miguelito were so close, like father and son. How did Battle Jr.'s own father feel about this? It wasn't something she thought about often, because Battle Sr. was not a presence in her life. Her father treated Miguelito like the son he never had.

It was clear to anyone who knew Abraham Rydz that he also adored his daughter. He was attentive to Susan's needs. He ate dinner at home every night and was there to help his daughter with her homework.

Susan knew that her father liked gambling. He took her to the racetrack, which she loved, and he also placed bets. At home he had regular poker nights with his friends; Miguelito was often in attendance. When he wasn't at the track or playing poker, he watched sporting events on television. He usually seemed more interested in the result of the game than the game itself, because he had money riding on the outcome. It was the daughter's impression that he won far more often than he lost.

For Rydz and his business partner, Miguelito, life was sweet. The fact that the old man's casino dream was fading out was of no big concern to them. In fact, it was probably a good thing for them. From what they heard, Maurilio Marquez had gone back to Venezuela. Nene Marquez, hearing rumors that he was the target of a murder conspiracy investigation, soon left the United States to live in Spain. It seemed that many of the people who had been in a position to cause problems for Rydz and Miguelito were no longer around. From everything they could tell, they were in the clear from any criminal entanglements that might endanger their highly successful business ventures. They were living the good life, and it appeared it was going to stay that way for the foreseeable future.

IN SEPTEMBER 1995, SERGEANT JIMMY BOYD ANNOUNCED HIS RETIREMENT FROM THE Metro-Dade Police Department. After thirty-five years of service, it was a long time coming. Boyd was a local legend, revered by many for his knowledge of the city, which predated the infusion of Cuban exiles, the arrival of the Marielitos, the Cocaine Cowboy era of the 1980s, and the reign of José Miguel Battle.

The relationship between Boyd and Dave Shanks had always been uneasy. Shanks had the impression that Boyd respected his acumen as a detective, but when it came to investigative matters Boyd had a hard time sharing credit. Years earlier, the sergeant had resisted Shanks's contention that Battle was becoming a major player in Miami gambling circles. And Shanks would always harbor a degree of resentment that Boyd had not backed him up when he had his office scuffle with Bert Perez, his former partner.

Both, however, were team players who were willing to let bygones be bygones. Shanks respected Boyd for his years of service, and the sergeant had come to value Shanks for his intelligence and dedication. It was enough that they were both professional cops; they didn't have to be best friends.

The retirement party for Boyd was a major event. It was held at Miami International Airport, inside the 94th Aero Squadron, a restaurant with plate-glass windows overlooking the airport's west runway, in view of modern jetliners taking off and landing. The restaurant was decorated to look like a World War I French chateau that had been turned into a wartime headquarters for a flying squadron.

The party followed the pattern of most retirement events, only on a more grandiose scale. Over the years, Boyd had himself served as a master of ceremonies for many events of this type, so it was especially enjoyable for many veteran cops to roast the retiree and regale the audience with stories from the epic career of Jimmy Boyd. In a show of Boyd's stature in the culture of the Metro-Dade Police Department, the director of the department was on hand to present a special plaque and declare the day as "Jimmy Boyd Day."

Later that night, as the party wound down, Boyd and Shanks sat off to the side and made peace with each another. Not that there had been a major rift, but Boyd wanted Shanks to know that his contribution to the Battle case had been stellar, and that his continued involvement was essential. Said Boyd, "If the investigation ever does make it to the RICO level, you will be the man who gets it there."

In fact, the reason Boyd pulled Shanks aside was to let him know that he would be hearing from the new state prosecutor, Tony Gonzalez. Now that Boyd was retiring, the State Attorney's Office was going to need a new "expert witness" from the Organized Crime Bureau. Boyd had recommended Shanks for the role.

A few days later, Shanks had a meeting with Gonzalez. A first-generation Cuban American who had grown up in the Hialeah area, Gonzalez was something of a department wunderkind. Having graduated from high school at the age of sixteen and completed undergraduate studies at the University of Miami, he finished law school at the top of his class. He passed the bar exam on the first try and, in 1991, at the age of twenty-two, was hired by the Dade County State Attorney's Office as an entry-level prosecutor. He rose through various departments— Misdemeanor, Juvenile, Public Corruption—until he had tried cases in many jurisdictions, including federal court. He was ambitious and driven, with a reputation for putting in long hours on a case.

Shanks and Gonzalez hit it off immediately. They had a similar approach to their work, and it helped that they both had a sharp wit and appreciated a good glass of red wine.

They talked about what it would take to build a federal case against Battle. One problem was that most of what would make up the "predicate acts" in an indictment against Battle would be largely historical in nature. They needed to come up with more recent criminal charges as well. Both agreed that El Padrino's recent foray in Peru might prove to be the key. No doubt, Battle had set up and used the casino as a money-laundering scheme, which would be crucial to a superseding indictment. This meant that the investigators had much work ahead of them building a fresh evidentiary base for taking down Battle. It was agreed that a search of Battle's home would be essential. If they could uncover documents relating to the financing and mismanagement of the Casino Crillón, they would be on their way.

Shanks was not the first person to notice that Gonzalez reminded him of a Miami version of Rudolf Giuliani, the New York prosecutor who made a name for himself taking down a number of major Mafia bosses, including Anthony Salerno. Giuliani was an Italian American and could therefore not be accused of being anti-Italian in his prosecutions. Miami was ripe for a bold, crusading Cuban American prosecutor to take on the same role in Magic City.

EL PADRINO SPENT MONTHS UPON HIS RETURN TO MIAMI TRYING TO GET HIS HOUSE IN order. Now that his true love, Evelyn Runciman, was living with him at El Zapotal, he did not want to lose her. Evelyn applied for a Florida driver's license, took the exam, and passed. She received a license in her name on August 23. The following month, she and José Miguel devised a scheme so that she could become a U.S. citizen. They arranged for her to marry Battle's thirty-seven-year-old nephew, José Angel Battle. Once they were wed and she became a citizen, Evelyn and José Angel were divorced.

There were still some loose ends with Casino Crillón. Technically, Battle was still one of the shareholders. A new managing director was hired, a man named José Mendez whom Battle interviewed for the position at El Zapotal. Mendez took over and was informed by Banco Banex in Lima that the casino needed $2.7 million to continue operating. The money was smuggled into Peru by all the usual suspects, including Luis DeVilliers and Nene Marquez, in ten different "body shipments" over four weeks. The casino had developed such a bad reputation that even with the infusion of capital, it continued to lose money.

In August 1996, Battle made the decision to suspend operations. "Why should I pay more money into a casino I can't even walk around in anymore?" he said to a gathering of shareholders at El Zapotal. For a time, they tried to negotiate the sale of the casino for $4.8 million to

Allied Gaming, a small company based in Reno, Nevada. The sale fell through, and on December 31 the casino officially closed its doors and went out of business. Estimates put Battle's loses on the venture at more than $12 million.

THE TIME HAD COME FOR THE RAID ON EL ZAPOTAL. IT WOULD BE THE RESULT OF meticulous planning. The raid would include four Metro-Dade Special Response Teams (SRT), or SWAT teams, accompanied by fifty Metro-Dade detectives, three IRS agents, six immigration officials, and a representative of the Humane Society to deal with the various dogs and roosters. The fact that Battle's primary residence was surrounded by a secondary residence, a barn, hundreds of rooster coops, dozens of dog-houses, and acres of mamey groves made carrying out the raid a potentially dangerous undertaking. There were many areas where the SRT teams and detectives could theoretically encounter resistance. The cops weren't anticipating armed confrontation with Battle and his staff, but any raid had to be planned as if that were a possibility.

On the morning of December 18, 1996, the entire team of agents and cops gathered at a staging area, the parking lot of a convenience store on Krome Avenue at SW 200th Street. The Op Plan, prepared by Sergeant Ed Hinman, was twenty pages in length, with pictures and diagrams of the property. It was distributed to various supervisors, including Shanks.

A reconnaissance team was sent to Battle's home to scout it out before the order was given to commence the raid. The detectives arrived at the house at 8 A.M. Everything was in order, except for one problem. Battle was not home. His Cadillac was not in the driveway.

Everyone waited. After about an hour, the decision was made to proceed whether Battle was there or not.

The first to arrive at the front gate of the property was an SRT team in a specially equipped wrecker truck with sideboards, so that a crew of six cops, riding on both sides of the vehicle, could hop off and deploy quickly. Behind that was a van with more SRT cops. Then came a green-and-white Metro-Dade police car containing Shanks and other detectives. Behind that was a bevy of vehicles filled with agents and cops. Other law enforcement personnel were stationed at the back gate and other points of egress, to prevent the possibility that anyone might try to escape from the property.

Once everyone was in position, the lead SRT team quickly wrapped chain cables around the wrought-iron gate of El Zapotal. The cables were securely affixed to the rear of the wrecker truck. As the truck pulled away, there was a loud boom as the gate was pulled off its hinges and torn away from the concrete columns to which it was bolted.

The raid teams flooded onto the property. As a supervisor, Shanks hung back, communicating with the various team leaders via walkie-talkie.

The first order of business was to secure the two homes, both the main residence and the back residence, where the farm workers and hired help lived. Once that was done, Shanks radioed to make sure the perimeter of the property was secure. Once everything was on lockdown, the search teams could begin to execute the warrants.

Evelyn Runciman was in the house; she was placed under arrest. Others among the workers and house staff were rounded up and interviewed by INS agents. Some of the workers were undocumented; this was their unlucky day. A half dozen were taken away to a detention facility, to later be deported.

The house was a beehive of activity. Shanks had stepped out to his squad car to retrieve a notebook when he noticed Battle's white Cadillac coming down SW 192nd Street toward the house. The Cadillac suddenly stopped, and the driver began to navigate a U-turn on the narrow street. Shanks jumped into the cruiser, turned the ignition, and floored it. He came up alongside the Cadillac while it was in the process of turning around.

Jumping out of the police car with a Remington 870 pump-action shotgun in his hand, Shanks blocked the Cadillac with his body. He pointed the shotgun directly at the front windshield. He could see José Aluart, the driver, and in the passenger seat, José Miguel Battle.

"Out of the car! Hands above your head! Now!" shouted the detective.

Both Battle and Aluart complied.

Shanks lined them spread-eagled against the hood of the Cadillac. He switched from the shotgun to his service handgun and searched them both for weapons, at the same time calling for a backup unit.

Shanks handcuffed Battle and put him in the back of his squad car. Backup cops arrived, and they took away the handcuffed Aluart.

Shanks drove Battle back toward the original staging area for the raid, the parking lot on Krome. He looked in the rearview mirror: there was the man he had been hunting for nearly nine years now. El Padrino. It was hard to believe he finally had him sitting in his car.

After the initial shock of being arrested, Battle seemed resigned to his fate. Ever since he'd been deported from Peru and brought back to Miami, he had to have known this day was coming. The arrest represented a new stage in his struggle to remain free.

In the parking lot, Shanks had Battle get out of the car so he could be more thoroughly searched. Shanks and another cop took everything out of Battle's pockets, including a wad of $3,000 in cash. In the light, Shanks noticed how much Battle had aged since the last time he'd seen him, at the hospital in Miami Beach having knee surgery five years earlier. El Padrino appeared sallow. His skin color was off—not the rich suntan he usually had but yellowish, as if he were having liver or kidney issues.

They put Battle back in the squad car and drove back to the house. Shanks left Battle under the watchful eye of two armed officers and went into the house to help with the search.

The interior of the house was impressive, but not lavish. The walls were light gray, with matching Italian tile floors. There were many fine furnishings, including artwork from South America. There were surveillance cameras inside the house, and also, in Battle's office, surveillance monitors showing different angles from around the outer property. The master bedroom suite was spacious, with sliding glass doors that opened onto a back patio and pool.

The investigators were not there to look at furnishings or take in the surroundings; they were there in search of criminal evidence. Narco-sniffing dogs were brought in. Unlike the previous time, when Effugenia Reyes had let them in to the house and they'd found nothing, these dogs immediately sniffed out a spot near the headboard to the bed. A cop from Technical Support removed the top of the headboard and discovered $87,400 neatly stacked in tight packets.

Shanks and a team of detectives searched a large walk-in closet—so large that, along with more than fifty expensive Italian suits of different styles and colors, it accommodated an antique mahogany desk. The desk was stuffed with paperwork. The investigators loaded up boxes with the contents of the desk. This material, which included bank statements, tax returns, business records relating to El Zapotal, Inc., and other documents, would be examined back at the police station.

It was like perusing the hidden caverns of an ancient pharaoh. Shanks felt as if there might be a jewel around every corner. On a shelf in the closet he found a file entitled "2506/66," which contained newspaper and magazine articles pertaining to Brigade 2506 and also regarding Alpha 66, the Miami-based anti-Castro militant organization. There were letters from representatives of Alpha 66 and other anti-Castro groups, thanking Battle for his financial contributions, a testament to his support for the never-ending struggle to kill Castro and take back Cuba.

Nearby were two framed photos, one of President John F. Kennedy and his wife, Jackie, at the Orange Bowl, paying tribute to the brigade members who had just been released from prison.

The other photo was even more startling: Battle, in a formal setting, at a dinner or award banquet or fund-raiser of some type, seated next to Jimmy Carter, the forty-second president of the United States. It turned out that the photo was from a political fund-raiser in New Jersey in 1975, when Carter was a presidential candidate. Shanks and the other cops gathered around the photo. It was Battle's testament to his stature as a player at the highest levels.

Ledgers, phone and address books, audiotapes, personal correspondence, and more were boxed up and carted away, but one legal file of documents immediately caught Shanks's attention. It was labeled "Crillón."

Inside were documents detailing expenditures and payouts. There were minutes from shareholders' meetings. On one document, a spreadsheet of the casino's weekly expenses, Battle had handwritten in the margins words like "liars" and "thieves." Numbers were circled, with an arrow pointing to where Battle had written, "This is the point where they started to steal from me."

Reading these notations, Shanks realized for the first time that Battle must have had a falling-out with his partners, DeVilliers and Marquez. If that wasn't startling enough, the file also contained faxes of receipts from the casino to Battle for money that had been brought into the country via cash couriers. Here was perhaps explicit documentation that the casino was being used to launder bolita proceeds from the United States.

Finally, the pièce de résistance was a loaded rifle and handgun the cops found in Battle's bedroom. As a convicted felon, it was against the law for Battle to be in possession of a firearm. The guns alone were going to be enough to hold El Padrino in jail without bail.

IT TURNED OUT THAT SHANKS WAS RIGHT ABOUT BATTLE. HE WAS NOT HEALTHY. HE was suffering from kidney failure and had begun dialysis treatment the week before the raid on El Zapotal. Now that he was in federal custody, the government was responsible for his medical care.

As a convicted felon who had once been charged with unlawful flight to avoid prosecution, Battle fit the definition of a flight risk; he was held without bail at the federal holding cell in downtown Miami. Evelyn Runciman, charged with passport fraud, was released on bond.

David Shanks and the investigators set out to devise a legal strategy that would neutralize Battle's ability to operate while they continued to build toward what they hoped would be a RICO case against the Corporation. Battle was charged with passport fraud as well as possession of a firearm by a convicted felon.

Since these were federal charges, and Shanks would be working these and other Battle-related prosecutions, the decision was made that the detective would be moved to the main U.S. Attorney's Office in Fort Lauderdale, forty miles up the coast from downtown Miami. Shanks was deputized as an agent of the Immigration and Naturalization Service and also as a special deputy U.S. marshal. If there was any doubt that his law enforcement career had become swallowed up by his pursuit of the Corporation, it was now official.

During the search at El Zapotal, many significant documents had been uncovered, some with handwritten notations. Shanks suspected that the notations had been written by Battle, but in order to establish this as fact, they needed a court-authorized handwriting sample. A documents examiner told Shanks, "You need to get samples from José Miguel Battle. Have him write until his hand falls off."

Shanks brought Detective Kenny Rosario to Jackson Memorial Hospital Ward D, the prisoner ward for the Dade County Department of Corrections. Though Battle was being held in federal custody, he was temporarily housed in the county facility so that he could get his dialysis treatments with fewer logistical difficulties.

When Shanks and Rosario arrived at the hospital, Battle was sitting in a chair in his room, watching television. He looked slightly better than on the night of his arrest, but not much. His complexion was yellowish, and he looked worn and depleted. He was dressed in a baggy green hospital shirt with matching drawstring pants. The feared Mob boss was now just another patient in a jail ward.

The cops first spoke with Battle's doctor, who told them that the patient's kidney function hadn't really improved much, but his weight, blood pressure, and blood work all showed significant improvement since he had been at the hospital. Apparently, removing Battle from his regimen of food, drink, and perhaps cocaine on the outside was beneficial to his overall health.

The cops entered Battle's room and shut off the television. El Padrino recognized them both. His English was fine, but he preferred to speak Spanish, so Rosario took the lead in explaining why they were there. As usual, Battle was polite. Often when he was around cops, he tried to give off the attitude that he was one of them.

They handed Battle a piece of paper with a phrase printed on it. They asked him to write out the phrase in his own penmanship. El Padrino was cooperative, but around the fourth page he stopped and looked sternly at Shanks and Rosario. "You two aren't going to stop until I die in jail. That's what you want, isn't it? For me to die in jail."

"Look," said Rosario, "we're just doing our job. It's what we're paid to do. I'm sure you understand that."

Battle grunted in response and continued writing.

All the while, Shanks was thinking of Jannin Toribio, the little girl who had been burned to death in the arson fire in New York. He was thinking of Idalia Fernandez, a government witness who was executed in her apartment, left there for her children to come home from school and find. He was thinking of Effugenia Reyes, the ex-girlfriend, who had been brutally murdered in Guatemala, possibly on orders from Battle.

Looking at the Godfather, Shanks was thinking, *Do I want you to die in jail? You bet your ass I do. You deserve to die in there, broke and powerless.*

On their way out, Shanks and Rosario stopped at the desk to examine the visitors' log and also a log that documented the patient's movements. They saw that Battle had been visited on numerous occasions by Jack Blumenfeld, his attorney, and also occasionally by Evelyn Runciman.

It was Shanks who noticed a discrepancy. The transport times showed that it was taking Battle a good forty-five minutes longer to be transferred from Ward D to the dialysis clinic than it was for him to be returned. "Something's not right here," said Shanks. He thought about it and said, "I don't know what's going on, but I'll bet he's getting some kind of special favor, paying somebody off."

When Shanks returned to the office of the U.S. attorney, he made a point of bringing it up. An assistant U.S. attorney put in a call to the Dade County Corrections Internal Affairs (IA) Unit and lodged a formal complaint. IA assigned an investigator who began tracking Battle's movements within the facilities. The investigator soon had his answer.

The investigator discovered that, once a week, Battle was being wheeled into a vacant room while one of the corrections officers stood guard outside the door. The IA investigator arrived as this was happening and removed the guard. He pulled open the door: there was Evelyn Runciman, on her knees, giving Battle a blowjob.

Battle had been paying off the guards to arrange his private rendezvous with Evelyn. At the age of sixty-eight, El Padrino was still being serviced. And he was still gaming the system.

The corrections officer was fired, and the patient was no longer afforded the privilege of receiving his dialysis treatment at Jackson Memorial's Ward D. Battle was transferred back to federal custody.

20

PERSEVERANCE

IT WAS A SULTRY SATURDAY MORNING IN HAVANA ON JULY 12, 1997, WHEN A LOUD *BOOOOOM!* rocked the lobby of the Hotel Capri, shattering glass and kicking up a cloud of dust that spread out into the street. Police cars arrived at the scene. Apparently someone had planted a bomb in the lobby of the hotel. A number of people were shaken, some with cuts and bruises from having fallen to the ground, but, miraculously, no one was seriously injured.

The Capri was one of the city's famous hotels from the era of the 1950s. Back then it was owned by Trafficante, and the Casino de Capri, located just off the lobby, was where actor George Raft presided as a meeter and greeter. In its glory days, the Capri had been a meeting place for cops, criminals, and government officials. It is likely that José Miguel Battle, the young vice cop, would have met Trafficante there to pick up a briefcase filled with cash destined for the presidential palace.

While the police were still surveying the damage at the Capri, two blocks away at the Hotel Nacional, there was an even louder blast— another bomb, timed to go off within minutes of the one at the Capri. This one had been planted in the lobby of the hotel near a bank of pay phones. Again, the damage to the lobby of the hotel was substantial, but no one was seriously hurt.

The Nacional was, if anything, even more famous than the Capri. The hotel had been the site of a legendary Mob conference in November 1946, when Meyer Lansky, Santo Trafficante, and twenty other high-ranking U.S. mobsters met to discuss their plans for setting up Havana as a base of operations. More recently, the Hotel Nacional had been transformed into a showcase for the Castro government. Whenever a political conference or film festival or cultural gathering took place in

Havana, dignitaries inevitably stayed there, on a bluff overlooking the famous Malecón seafront promenade.

No one claimed responsibility for the bombings at the two prestigious hotels, but the Cuban government had no doubt who was behind them. Said the Castro government's minister of tourism, "Obviously, this was done by our enemies."

Seven weeks later, more bombs rocked Havana. The Copacabana, Chateau, and Triton hotels in the Playa district were all hit within a period of sixty minutes. The first and worst of the three blasts took place at the Copacabana at 11:30 A.M. The bomb had been planted in the lobby, and the explosion led to the death of Fabio Di Celmo, a native of Genoa, Italy, who was a resident of Montreal. Additional tourists were injured in the blasts.

This time, the Cuban government was unequivocal in its contention that the bombings were the act of "anti-Cuban terrorist groups" in the United States. Said the interior minister of Cuba, "These terrorist acts are encouraged, organized and supplied—both in terms of material and personnel—from within the United States territory."

It had been thirty-six years since the Bay of Pigs invasion, when anti-Castro forces in the United States secretly launched its campaign to overthrow the Cuban government and take back the island. Since then, the effort had become a clandestine subtheme of the Cold War. Many lives had been lost in countries throughout the world. Average citizens in the United States had grown weary of this struggle. In public opinion polls, it was clear that the majority of Americans wanted to end the U.S. embargo against Cuba and restore diplomatic relations. Many could not understand why the embargo persisted and the strained relations continued. In 1997, the idea that American citizens, of Cuban extraction or otherwise, were still engaged in violent anti-Castro activities seemed like a strange relic from another time.

But for those whose lives were devoted to the overthrow of Castro, the struggle never ended.

The person who had masterminded the most recent spate of bombings in Havana was no stranger to the Cuban government: Luis Posada Carriles, who was described by Castro himself as a "monstrous criminal."

For decades, Posada had perpetrated his counterrevolutionary war against Fidel mostly in the shadows, but after the hotel bombings he was ready to step into the light. Frustrated that the bombings had not received more attention in the international press, Posada agreed to be interviewed by a reporter from the *New York Times*. From an undisclosed location in the Caribbean, he sat down with journalist Ann Louise Bardach. Now seventy years old, he was no longer the spry young Army lieutenant who played poker late into the night with José Miguel Battle and others at Fort Benning back in the early 1960s.

Posada proudly confessed to having organized the bombings in Havana, which he described as acts of war intended to cripple a totalitarian regime by depriving it of foreign tourism and investment. "We didn't want to hurt anybody," he told the reporter. "We just wanted to make a big scandal so the tourists don't come anymore. We don't want any more foreign investment."

Not only did Posada admit his role in the bombings, but also he claimed that financing for the operation came in part from the Cuban American National Foundation. This claim was denied by a spokesperson for CANF.

Since its inception in 1981, CANF had emerged as the most powerful Cuban exile lobby group in the United States. Not only had the foundation become closely aligned with numerous U.S. presidents, but the group's founder, Jorge Mas Canosa, had become a powerful figure in his own right.

Mas passed away in November 1997, at the age of fifty-eight. His death perhaps led his longtime compatriot Luis Posada to believe that the time had come to be more open about the involvement of CANF in the anti-Castro struggle. Posada spelled it out: "Jorge controlled everything. Whenever I needed money, he said to give me five thousand dollars, give me ten thousand, give me fifteen. And they sent it." Posada estimated that over the years Mas had sent him more than $200,000. Mas knew that when he sent money to Posada it was for violent activities—bombings and assassinations—though, Posada said with a chuckle, the money usually arrived with the message, "This is for the church."

To exiled militants, the effort to destabilize Cuba was a holy war.

For José Miguel Battle, the holy war had shifted. In spite of the efforts to overthrow Castro, the secret plots to assassinate him, the efforts to intimidate and punish people and nations that did business with Cuba, the Bearded One was alive and well. Battle, on the other hand, was hampered by deteriorating kidneys and a persistent officer of the law who was determined to make him pay for what he had done.

In April 1997, Battle pleaded guilty on the charge of passport fraud. By doing so, he could likely avoid jail time on this charge. But the following month, he was indicted on the more serious charge of possession of a firearm by a convicted felon. This charge carried with it a potential sentence of three years, but for Battle, at his age and with his health beginning to wane, a few years could quite possibly be a death sentence. He would fight the charge at trial.

His lawyer, Jack Blumenfeld, was ready to get into the ring. Unlike twenty years earlier, when the lawyer first met Battle at the time of the Ernestico Torres murder trial, this time Blumenfeld would not have Raymond Brown at his side. The legendary New Jersey trial lawyer was now eighty years old. Incredibly, Brown was still practicing law, but he hadn't tried a case in court in years, and it would have been a burden to have him travel to Florida for what was a comparatively minor case. Blumenfeld, on the other hand, had been Battle's Miami lawyer for years.

To Blumenfeld, the various charges against Battle smacked of a vendetta. The idea of the Metro-Dade bolita squad bringing a passport fraud case was unusual, to say the least. Then the government had added another charge alleging that Battle had lied on his nationalization forms when reentering the United States. One of the questions was "Have you ever advocated polygamy?" Battle's answer was no. The government was claiming that because Battle was still married to his first wife while married to Evelyn, he was guilty of polygamy.

Blumenfeld contacted the U.S. attorney and said, "I'm sorry, but you people need to look up 'polygamy' in the dictionary. Polygamy is more than two. My client may be a bigamist, but that has nothing to do with polygamy."

The prosecutors threw out the charge.

Blumenfeld felt that on the gun charge they had a solid defense. He was told by his client that the shotgun belonged to Cache Jimenez, his bodyguard and driver. Jimenez had gone hunting earlier that day and left the gun leaning against the wall in a closet in Battle's bedroom. Jimenez would take the stand and testify that the gun was his.

A trial date was set for late September. In the meantime, Battle was held in custody without bail.

ONE THING BLUMENFELD NOTICED WAS THAT, IN THE MONTHS LEADING UP TO THE trial, when he met with Battle to discuss legal matters, José Miguel Jr. was often in attendance. This was something new. Blumenfeld knew that the father and son had a fractured relationship. He had been told the stories about how Senior's philandering had alienated him from Junior, who felt that his mother had been disrespected. Blumenfeld was used to Battle's having difficult relationships with family members. He was once in the same room with José Miguel and his brother Gustavo when the two men argued over everything from the weather to the price of a newspaper.

With Battle Sr. incarcerated and in need of regular medical attention, power of attorney had been signed over to Miguelito, who was now in charge of El Zapotal, Inc., and other family assets. Evelyn Runciman was still living at the house, with a staff and grounds crew. But the time had come to consider selling off the house. Battle needed money to pay his mounting legal fees.

The idea was to divide up the property into various parcels and sell them off for maximum profit. Battle Jr. posted a sign on the property that read *For sale by the owner,* with a phone number.

Miguel Cruz, age fifty, was in the market for a house in the South Miami area. In the fall of 1997 he and his son, Ian, were driving around the area when he saw the sign at El Zapotal. He liked the location, the house alongside the grove of mamey trees so redolent of his native Cuba. From what he could see of the house behind the gate, it was a lovely place. He wrote down the number and called the next day.

It was a Sunday afternoon when Cruz and his son met Battle Jr., who arrived with José Aluart, otherwise known as Five Minutes to Six because of his crooked neck. Junior showed them around the property. Cruz and his son immediately fell in love with the place.

Battle Jr. liked that Cruz was a Cuban émigré and that he was with his son. Cruz got the impression that for the Battles, selling the house was more than just an economic proposition. The property had sentimental value, and they wanted to make sure it wound up in the right hands.

When Junior heard Cruz's personal story, he liked what he heard. Not only was Cruz a fellow Cuban, but his life involved the kind of historical drama that was so common for those of the Bay of Pigs generation.

Cruz had been born in Camagüey, in the town of Sancti Spíritus, in 1945. He was only fourteen years old when the revolution occurred. Initially, his family remained in Cuba, but it soon became apparent that the Castro government was to be a totalitarian regime. In 1961, Miguel Cruz was on the last official Delta Airlines flight out of Cuba before the U.S. government severed diplomatic relations with the island and imposed an economic embargo.

After a brief time in Miami, Cruz moved with his family to New Orleans. In August of 1963, he was seventeen years old, with a summer job working in a convenience store managed by Carlos Bringuier. Bringuier was a Cuban exile active in the local anti-Castro movement. He was a delegate for Directorio Revolucionario Estudiantil, and he lived with Celso Hernandez, another anti-Castro activist.

On the afternoon of August 5, a young man who identified himself as Lee Harvey Oswald came into the store and offered his services in the struggle against Castro. He told Bringuier that he had been a U.S. Marine and was trained in guerrilla warfare, and that he was willing not only to train Cubans to fight Castro but also to join the fight himself. The next day Oswald returned to the store and left for Bringuier a paperback entitled *Guidebook for Marines,* a book published by the U.S. military.

Bringuier didn't know quite what to make of Oswald. He told young Miguel Cruz, who worked for him at the store, that he thought Oswald might be some sort of spy or double agent.

Two days later, on August 8, Bringuier's roommate, Celso Hernandez, came into the store. He said he had just come across Oswald nearby on Canal Street. Oswald was handing out pro-Castro flyers on behalf of a group called Fair Play for Cuba. It was as Bringuier had suspected. Oswald had been presenting himself as anti-Castro when in fact he was an operative for the other side.

Said Hernandez, "Let's go over there and stop him right now."

Miguel Cruz tagged along with the two older men. Certainly, he shared their anti-Castro sentiments, but he was hardly an active member of the movement. At the time, he was looking forward to his senior year at Francis T. Nicholls High School, with the new school year beginning in one month.

The three Cubans arrived on Canal Street and immediately came upon Oswald, who was wearing a placard around his neck proclaiming *Fair Play for Cuba* and was handing out flyers.

They angrily confronted Oswald, calling him a communist and attempting to grab the flyers out of his hands. A tussle ensued, with a small crowd gathering around. Neither the Cubans nor Oswald were backing down.

After a couple of minutes, a police squad car pulled up. Two cops separated the combatants. Everyone was placed under arrest for disturbing the peace. They were all cuffed and put into a paddy wagon together.

Miguel Cruz looked directly at Oswald, who, at age twenty-three, was not much older than him. The young man had piercing blue eyes that seemed vacant and devoid of humanity.

Later that day, the charges against Cruz and the other two Cubans were dismissed. Oswald spent the night in jail and was interviewed the next day by a lieutenant in the New Orleans Police Department. At Oswald's request, he was also interviewed by a local FBI agent. The arrestee claimed to be a member of the New Orleans branch of the Fair Play for Cuba Committee, which he said had thirty-five members. He was in fact the only member of the "New Orleans branch," which had never been chartered by the national Fair Play for Cuba Committee.

Later that day, Oswald was released on bail. Two days later he pleaded guilty to the charges against him and paid a ten-dollar fine.

Three months later, on November 22, Miguel Cruz was sitting in his physics class at Nicholls High School when the principal entered and turned on the television. There was a dramatic news report under way describing the assassination of President John F. Kennedy. A picture came on the television of the man who was suspected of having done the shooting. It was Lee Harvey Oswald.

Cruz felt as if he'd been kicked in the stomach; the air was sucked from his body, and he felt as if he couldn't breathe. He was in a state of shock. He gathered himself and said to the school principal, "I know this man."

After describing his encounter with Oswald to the principal, Miguel was sent home from school. Within a half hour of his having arrived home, he was visited by two FBI agents.

On the grounds at El Zapotal, thirty-four years later, as Cruz related this vivid memory, Miguelito Battle was enraptured. It was, after all, an amazing piece of history, not only for its significance as to the assassination of a president, but also as yet another tributary of the Cuban diaspora.

It would take time for the sale of the house to transpire. Cruz could not afford the asking price. Battle Jr. broke up the property into smaller parcels until the price of the house was within Cruz's range. It took two years for the deal to be finalized, even though everyone involved felt that it was right that the house should wind up in the hands of Miguel Cruz.

Eventually, the man who had tussled with Lee Harvey Oswald moved into the house of José Miguel Battle Sr. He remains there to this day.

THE TRIAL OF BATTLE ON THE CHARGE OF POSSESSION OF A SHOTGUN BY A CONVICTED felon began on September 29, in the courtroom of Judge Alan Gold. It was not expected to be a lengthy proceeding. The government had one major witness: Ruby De Los Santos Torres, the cleaning lady at El Zapotal who, upon being interviewed back when the raid took place and the gun was seized—and later in front of a grand jury—said that she had seen the shotgun in the closet three months before the raid.

The problem for the prosecution, which included Assistant State's Attorney Tony Gonzalez and Shanks, was that in the weeks leading up to the trial, Ruby Torres went into hiding. It took numerous court-ordered wiretaps and late-night surveillances for the cops to find out where she was. Most of her time was spent at her mother's house. She was taken into custody on a material witness warrant and held until the trial. But the prosecutors had no idea if when she took the stand she would stick to her grand jury testimony or say something contradictory.

Before the testimony phase of the trial, the prosecutors and defense lawyer Blumenfeld needed to select a jury. As with many Miami jury pools, there was always the possibility that the prospective jurors would include Cuban exiles or their children. Normally this would be irrelevant, but in the case of Battle, having a juror who was sympathetic to the anti-Castro cause might be a problem for the government.

Prosecutor Gonzalez encountered just such a problem during the phase of jury selection in which the prosecutors and defense lawyer are allowed to question each prospective juror to determine if he or she is able to hear the facts of the case without bias or prejudice. Voir dire is crucial for both sides to lay the groundwork for a fair process. During voir dire, each side is allowed a certain number of "peremptory challenges," an opportunity to disqualify a juror based on some issue or conflict, such as the person knowing someone related to the defendant, or a familiarity with either of the attorneys or with the victim. There are myriad reasons why a person could be disqualified, but a lawyer is only allowed to use a limited number of peremptory challenges, so they are employed sparingly.

During jury selection, the lawyers came upon a young woman whose father was a veteran of Brigade 2506. During her voir dire, Gonzalez asked a series of questions in open court that were designed to reveal bias on the woman's part in favor of anyone associated with the brigade. The idea was to make her bias so apparent that the judge would automatically disqualify the woman, in which case Gonzalez would not have to use one of his peremptory challenges.

Judge Gold queried the woman himself. To Gonzalez and Shanks, it appeared obvious that she would respond in an emotional way to the Bay of Pigs history should it come up during the trial. But the judge would not disqualify her, and defense lawyer Blumenfeld was all too happy to have her on the jury. Gonzalez chose not to use one of his peremptory challenges. The young woman wound up on the jury, a development that the prosecutors would eventually regret.

Once the trial began, the first witness on the stand was Shanks, who described the circumstances of the raid on El Zapotal and the discovery of the rifle. Robert O'Bannon testified as the original affiant on the federal search warrant and also described Battle's use of a false passport. Then Ruby Torres took the stand.

A Honduran immigrant who did not speak English, Torres had been working at El Zapotal for nineteen months at the time of the raid. It had been six months since her grand jury testimony, in which she innocently stated that she had seen the shotgun in the closet. Now, speaking through a courtroom translator, she changed her story, saying it had been less than a week before the raid that she first saw the shotgun, not three months. She also added that she had seen Cache Jimenez, Battle's driver, bodyguard, and cook, out on the grounds of the ranch using the gun to hunt pigeons—a new wrinkle she had not mentioned in front of the grand jury.

Prosecutor Gonzalez, faced with his primary witness's having changed her story, was confronted with a delicate proposition. He wanted to show that Torres had changed her story, possibly out of fear or because she had been coerced, but he did not want to destroy her credibility entirely. She was his witness, after all.

Gonzalez confronted Torres with a transcript reading of her previous testimony. She buckled slightly, conceding that it might have been two months before the raid that she saw the gun.

The star witness for the defense was Cache Jimenez, described as Battle's valet and cook. For years, Jimenez had shown a willingness to do many unpleasant tasks for El Padrino, including starting his car in the morning—the least popular assignment for a Mob underling.

From the stand, Jimenez told a story of meeting Battle for the first time only six months before the raid, when he was at the ranch looking to buy some mamey. He and Battle became friendly. Battle let Jimenez shoot birds on his property, and it was there, a week before the raid, that he was shooting pigeons and doves. Afterward, he retired to a nearby bar on Krome Avenue, where some friends invited him to accompany them on an overnight fishing trip. Jimenez accepted the invitation. He was concerned about keeping the rifle in his car, since he would be leaving the car in the parking lot of the bar. He drove back to El Zapotal and asked Evelyn Runciman (Battle was not home) if he could leave his gun in the house. After the fishing trip, he forgot to retrieve the gun, and there it was on the morning Shanks and the other cops raided the place.

Unchallenged, it might have seemed like a reasonable story. But on cross-examination by Gonzalez, the story quickly unraveled. Gonzalez asked Jimenez, "Why didn't you just park your car at El Zapotal?"

Jimenez stumbled with his answer. Apparently he had not anticipated this simple question. "I don't know," he answered. "I just, uh, well, decided not to."

Gonzalez then went in for the kill. What Cache Jimenez did not know was that the investigators had surveillance photos and wiretap conversations of Jimenez going back five years, to when the cops first planted a court-authorized tap on the phone of Gilberto Borges.

Gonzalez asked the witness, "Mr. Jimenez, isn't it true that you would do anything that Mr. Battle asked of you, including lying here today?"

"No, definitely not."

"Isn't it true that you have said, 'I did things for Battle I would not do even for my family'? Did you say that?'

Jimenez answered confidently, "No. I don't even know him that well."

Gonzalez asked Judge Gold for permission to play the tape of a conversation from the Borges wire. On it, Jimenez complained about having to get up in the middle of the night to get Battle a Cuban sandwich and deliver it to his hospital room at Mt. Sinai in Miami Beach. The jury listened to Jimenez, in his own words, say on the tape, "I do things for Battle that I wouldn't even do for my own family."

Jimenez was stunned. "That's not my voice," he said, and then quickly changed direction by adding, "That's not what I meant when I said that."

Gonzalez then put Shanks back on the stand to introduce four-year-old surveillance photos of Jimenez and Battle at a restaurant called the Bahamas Fish Market, where they met with a number of boliteros and bookmakers. Not only were the photos shown to the jury, but Shanks and the prosecutors were now able to introduce evidence they hadn't been able to before, including a recollection by the detective of the time they watched Jimenez lean in the driver's side window of Battle's car and turn on the ignition, as if he were anticipating—and dreading—a car bomb explosion. While Jimenez did this, Battle was hiding behind a concrete pillar.

The defense rested on a Friday. The judge gave the jury instructions first thing on Monday, and they were off to deliberate. Gonzalez and Shanks were expecting a quick verdict. It was not a complicated case. Either you believed it was Battle's gun or you didn't. Either way, there was not much to deliberate about.

Surprisingly—at least to the prosecutors—the deliberation dragged on all through the first day and into a second day. "This is not good," Gonzalez told Shanks. Perhaps the jury was deadlocked and could not reach a verdict.

At the end of the second day, the jury foreman notified the court that they were ready to deliver their verdict. Gonzalez and Shanks were tense, until they saw the jurors stream back into the jury box. The young woman with the Bay of Pigs history in her family was in tears. The body language of the other jurors seemed to suggest that they were relieved to have reached a conclusion.

The judge read the verdict: "Guilty."

Afterward, Shanks ran into one of the jurors outside the courthouse. The juror explained that as soon as they entered the jury room and took their first vote, everyone voted guilty except for the young Cuban woman. She kept saying, "I can't believe that sweet old man, a Bay of Pigs hero, would be so devious." It took the rest of the jury sixteen hours to wear her down with the facts of the case until she finally gave in.

A few months later, in February 1998, Battle, Shanks, and the other investigators and lawyers were back in court for a hearing on the issue of sentencing. Assistant U.S. Attorney Bob Lehner had designated the sentencing as an opportunity to go for an "upward departure," which involved an unusual quirk of federal law. By legal statute, it was permissible at sentencing to introduce new evidence against a convicted party in an effort to show that he or she was a more serious criminal and therefore worthy of a sentence that exceeded the guidelines for the crime of which he was convicted.

The prosecutors went to great lengths to make their case. Lehner had prepared a thirty-page motion about the upward departure, and he had Shanks prepare a two-hundred-plus-page exhibit packet, tabbed and broken down into various components, all of which were referenced in Lehner's motion. In addition, the prosecutors were allowed to put witnesses on the stand. At the hearing, they paraded a number of jailhouse witnesses into the courtroom to testify specifically about Battle's involvement in cocaine trafficking.

Drug dealing had always been a sore subject with Battle. He protested loudly to those around him that he was against dealing cocaine. His public position was perhaps founded on his love of *The Godfather,* in which the character of Don Corleone contends, "This drug business will be the downfall of all of us." In reality, Battle's forays into cocaine dealing, though not extensive by the standards of Miami in the 1980s, were no secret to people in the underworld.

And yet it was also possible that the various jailhouse witnesses being brought into court to make Battle look bad were in fact gilding the lily. These witnesses were not being held to the standard of a criminal trial. The burden of proof was low, and it was impossible to fully verify the facts of their various accusations.

After listening to this testimony for the better part of an afternoon, Battle had had enough. To one of the witnesses in the midst of telling cocaine tales about him, El Padrino shouted, *"Mentiroso* (liar)!" Then he cursed at the prosecutors and said with a scowl, "Dirty, dirty . . . Drug traffickers."

Jack Blumenfeld immediately moved to quiet his client. He was surprised. Battle had never lost his cool in court before. He had always been calm and controlled.

The outburst led Blumenfled to do something he'd never done before—put Battle on the stand. He figured he had nothing to lose. He wanted Battle to express his disgust at being called a drug trafficker.

Battle was wearing his best suit, a teal blue linen/cotton combination. On the stand, he was gentlemanly. "I did not address the witness," he said, in regard to his outburst. "I just said it was dirty to bring him in here . . . Let them sentence me to one hundred years. This kind of thing is just not done."

Blumenfeld said to the judge, "I can't defend against a drug case where my client was not indicted, about something that happened nine years ago . . . This is very unfair."

Judge Gold listened to all the testimony and various legal arguments, and on March 19 he emphatically ruled against the upward departure. In a statement, the judge ridiculed the government's position, questioning why all that evidence was brought into a sentencing hearing in the absence of a RICO indictment.

Five days later, Judge Gold sentenced Battle to eighteen months in prison—the low end of the guidelines. He cited Battle's poor health as one reason for not sentencing him to more time.

Once again, the judicial system had smiled on Battle. With time off for good behavior, he could be out in a year.

DAVE SHANKS WAS PISSED OFF BY THE JUDGE'S LIGHT SENTENCE. PART OF THIS WAS the usual cop's annoyance at "liberal" judges working against the better interests of the public. In Shanks's mind, José Miguel Battle was a gangster, a murderer of women and children, and a serious menace to society. The fact that he had a good lawyer who was adept at working the system to the advantage of his client only made Shanks angrier. The ability of Battle to commit heinous crimes—murders—and receive only a modest punitive response from the system was to the veteran cop a travesty of justice and a cruel joke.

On top of that, Shanks was especially peeved by the judge's belittling reference to a RICO indictment. Mostly because he knew the judge was right. If the government wanted to use RICO-type evidence against El Padrino, then they needed to mount an actual RICO case against the Corporation. Shanks had always dreamed of such a reality, but he was one local cop—albeit a pesky cop—without the institutional authority to undertake the kind of massive and expensive investigation required to take down the Corporation.

On March 26, one day after the Battle sentencing, Shanks's dream moved closer to reality when Tony Gonzalez, perhaps his strongest advocate on the prosecutorial side, left the State Attorney's Office to become an AUSA for the Southern District of Florida.

Shanks and Gonzalez were now possibly in a position to make things happen, but the truth was, they didn't yet have the witnesses. They knew that the Corporation's criminal history stretched back decades, but if they were to establish those early crimes as predicate acts in a RICO conspiracy, they needed to be able to put people on the stand who had firsthand knowledge of these crimes.

There were some likely prospects, among them Willie Diaz, the arsonist who played a key role in the arson wars of the 1980s. Diaz had already taken the stand in the 1987 trial of Lalo Pons. He could be compelled to do so again in a RICO trial.

Also, there was Vincent "Fish" Cafaro. To the astonishment of many, Cafaro in 1986 secretly became an informant for federal authorities. For five months, from October 1986 to March 1987, he was wired up with a recording device, which he wore while attending high-level Mafia meetings. On March 20, 1987, the government revealed in court that Cafaro had been working for them. Many mafiosi were indicted, including Cafaro's own son, Thomas.

In the late 1980s and in 1990, Cafaro testified at a number of major Mob trials in New York, including two trials involving John Gotti, the *capo di tutti capi*. Afterward, Cafaro disappeared into the federal witness protection program.

Already, at a Lucchese crime family trial in the early 1990s, Cafaro had testified about how the Cubans—and specifically José Miguel Battle Sr.—were partners with the Mafia in the city's highly lucrative numbers racket. Cafaro could be a valuable witness against the Corporation—if Shanks was able to track him down.

Finally, there was Robert Hopkins, another organized crime figure who could link the activities of the Corporation to the Mafia. In 1987, Hopkins was put on trial for the murder of a Cuban bolitero, Pedro Acosta, at the summit meeting of the members of the Corporation, La Compañía, and the Mafia. Hopkins was there and, along with everyone else, ducked for cover when a drive-by shooter gunned down the bolitero on the sidewalk in front of the restaurant where the meeting took place. Prosecutors later claimed that Hopkins had arranged the murder, but they had no real case. He was acquitted.

As often happens when a criminal defendant beats the government in court, to "save face," Hopkins was soon indicted on follow-up charges. Currently under indictment on gambling charges, and out on bail, he might be willing to talk if it would help him out with his legal complications.

Shanks and Gonzalez discussed the prospects of being able to round up these and other crucial witnesses. To begin the process, it was necessary to officially transfer Shanks to the U.S. Attorney's Office and have him deputized as a special investigator, making him technically an employee of the federal government. The next order of business was to send him to New York to reconnect with Detective Richard Kalafus of the NYPD.

In his thirty-third year on the job, Kalafus had announced his pending retirement. Once he was gone, he would take with him the most encyclopedic knowledge of the Cuban bolita culture in the New York–New Jersey area of any cop who had ever walked the streets. Though Shanks had met with Kalafus before, he needed to do it again, this time with a focus on who throughout the bolita universe—either in prison or still out on the street—could be squeezed into a position where he might take the stand against Battle and the Corporation.

On the flight from Miami to New York, Shanks thought about how far he had come, and how far he still had to go, in his pursuit of the Corporation. To go after a RICO indictment required the approval of the Justice Department in Washington, D.C. Shanks and perhaps Gonzalez would have to make their pitch to U.S. Attorney General Janet Reno. From experience, Shanks knew how tough Reno could be. She had been the nemesis of every lazy cop in South Florida during her tenure there, and now she was the top law enforcement official in the federal government. To Shanks, it seemed only right that he would have to pass muster with Reno to make his case against the Corporation. He had a lot of work to do.

KALAFUS HAD A TENDENCY TO FREE ASSOCIATE, THROWING OUT CUBAN SURNAMES and nicknames of people Shanks had never heard of. He also had a tendency to mix in gossip with his cold, hard facts. There was, for instance, the rumor that Battle had been given a pardon by President Jimmy

Carter. The rumor was intriguing. Shanks recalled the photo they had confiscated during the raid on El Zapotal of Battle together with Carter at some sort of formal campaign event, but there was no evidence of a pardon or even that the men knew each other beyond the single photograph of them at a public event.

The interviews with Kalafus took place at the U.S. Attorney's Office in downtown Manhattan. For Shanks, the first order of business was to play for the detective two audiotapes that were confiscated at El Zapotal during the raid. The tapes were not from phone calls. They seemed to be of two separate police interrogations done by Kalafus.

The tapes were lengthy. Kalafus listened to portions of both and confirmed that these were taped interviews that he and Steven Mc-Cabe, deputy chief of investigations for the Hudson County Prosecutor's Office in New Jersey, had done with Charley Hernandez back in December 1976. At the time, Charley was cooperating with the authorities, and his revelations on these tapes would lead to the indictment of Battle and Chino Acuna for the murder of Ernestico Torres.

The question was, how on earth had these tapes fallen into the possession of José Miguel Battle?

McCabe had passed away in February 1997, so there was no way of knowing his role. As for Kalafus, he claimed to have no idea how the tapes got into the Battle's hands.

For ninety minutes that morning, and then again in the afternoon for ninety minutes, Kalafus regaled Shanks with tales of the Corporation.

Shanks was mesmerized; he could have listened to Kalafus all day long, but he had other important interviews to conduct while in the New York area. One he had hoped to do was with Fish Cafaro. Though Cafaro had been relocated somewhere in the United States under a new identity, Shanks assumed he could arrange for the U.S. Marshals to fly him to New York City for an interview. But Cafaro, it turned out, had a phobia about flying. To interview the former mafioso, Shanks had to fly to Charlotte, North Carolina, where Cafaro now lived. Shanks arranged to be met there by Kenny Rosario, his Miami police partner. They interviewed Cafaro at the Holiday Inn in Charlotte, where the detectives had booked a room.

Once Cafaro started talking, he couldn't be stopped. He had spent nearly a lifetime in the Mafia and had many stories to tell. Though the detectives were fascinated by his many anecdotes, they tried to restrict him to his experiences with the Cubans, and particularly Battle.

After finishing with Cafaro, Shanks headed back to New York to meet with Robert Hopkins.

The Hopkins interviews was fascinating to Shanks. For one thing, they met at Hopkins's apartment at Trump Tower, which had only recently opened as a luxury condominium in midtown Manhattan. Shanks didn't know it at the time, but Hopkins co-owned the pad with Petey DiPalermo, a member of the Lucchese crime family and Hopkins's longtime friend and associate.

Hopkins had recently been arrested on gambling and drug charges. He was interested in cooperating with the government under a "queen for a day" letter, which would give him immunity for whatever he might reveal.

Hopkins did not look or sound like a gangster. To Shanks, he looked a little like Elvis Presley, which was even more interesting after Hopkins explained that when he wasn't being a criminal, he was a nightclub singer who had some Elvis songs in his repertoire.

Like Cafaro, Hopkins had an amazing story to tell. Among the many details that caught Shanks's undivided attention was that Hopkins said he was among the initial prospective investors in the Casino Crillón in Lima. In 1993, Luis DeVilliers had approached Hopkins to become an investor. Hopkins even flew down to Lima to check out the location at the Hotel Crillón. He had traveled to Lima with none other than Roberto Parsons.

Hopkins suspected that Parsons had played a role in the murder of Omar Broche, among others, but he didn't know the details. He had been friendly with Broche and even staked him some money to restart his bolita operation in New York. This angered Battle, who ordered Broche's murder, a job that was undertaken by Parsons.

As was sometimes the case in the underworld, the man who eliminates your partner becomes your new partner, whether you like it or not. DeVilliers, who was thankful that he had not been murdered along with

Broche, introduced Parsons, the assassin, to Hopkins, the Irishman. At some point, DeVilliers made the decision to go with Battle as sole investor in the Crillón and cut Hopkins and Parsons out of the deal.

Shanks listened to all this, and recorded it, with a sense of wonder. The various strands of the Corporation story—the seemingly endless cast of characters—were beginning to come together in his mind. Details were beginning to fit together like pieces in a gigantic jigsaw puzzle.

On the flight back to Miami, Shanks tried to bend his mind around all that he had learned. From years of investigating Battle and the Corporation, he thought he knew a lot. Clearly, he had a lot more to learn.

BEFORE SHANKS AND TONY GONZALEZ COULD DEAL WITH THE CORPORATION, THEY had to deal with the criminal prosecution of Raul Fernandez and Luis Bordon. Both had been indicted, separately, along with multiple co-defendants, on illegal gambling and money-laundering charges. These were massive cases involving years of investigation, and the two trials were likely to last many months.

Some thought had been given to folding these prosecutions into a RICO case against Battle, but it was quickly determined that that would not work. These cases were too large in their own right and needed to be tried separately. It was a daunting task that was simplified somewhat in May 1998, when Raul Fernandez died as a result of complications from diabetes before going to trial. The other defendants accepted plea deals. That left only the Bordon trial for the prosecutors.

It was a massive undertaking that stretched on for seven months. Though many defendants chose to plead out (between the Fernandez and Bordon indictments, forty-four of forty-six defendants accepted plea deals), the trial involved a staggering accumulation of evidence. Luis Borden and his two sons stood accused of laundering more than $41 million in checks through Gulf Liquors over a four-year period.

At the trial, two pallets stacked six feet high with 250,000 individual checks were wheeled into the courtroom. Both Shanks and Kenny Rosario testified at length about surveillances and wiretaps.

Like Battle, Luis Bordon was a Bay of Pigs veteran, a member of

Brigade 2506, and there was some concern among the prosecutors that jurors could be swayed or influenced by his personal history. In the end, that was not the case. Bordon and his two sons were found guilty on illegal gambling and money-laundering charges. Later, at a separate forfeiture hearing, the government seized $5.25 million in assets from the Bordons. Luis Bordon was sentenced to ten years in prison, and the sons received sentences of nine years each.

A money-laundering conviction may not have been as "sexy" as a case with multiple homicides or stacks of brick cocaine seized by agents, but because of the amount of money that was recovered, the Bordon case was a major feather in the caps of Shanks and Gonzalez. Their bargaining position within the institutional hierarchy of the system was greatly enhanced. It was the perfect time for them to make their pitch to the DOJ regarding a RICO case against the Corporation.

Shanks would be the lead man to make the pitch. He had become the inheritor of all institutional knowledge accumulated over the years about Battle, and he would be the one responsible for accumulating the evidence and helping to craft a theory of prosecution.

Battle himself may have suspected as much. Though he had been transferred to a federal prison in Springfield, Missouri, where he was receiving dialysis treatments on a weekly basis, he must have known that there were further indictments waiting for him on the other side of his sentence for gun possession. Though he was not healthy, he was not the kind of man to take matters lying down.

IN NOVEMBER 1998, WITH BATTLE FOUR MONTHS AWAY FROM AN EARLY RELEASE (based on time off for good behavior) Dave Shanks arrived home one afternoon at his house in Key Largo. Though Shanks was currently renting out the house and living in a separate home three blocks away, he still came by to pick up his mail at an old-style roadside mailbox. On this afternoon, as he approached the mailbox and prepared to open it, he heard the unmistakable rattle of an eastern diamondback rattlesnake.

Shanks pulled his hand away from the box, then stepped back, looking around the base of the wooden mailbox post and in the nearby crabgrass for the source of the rattling sound. Nothing. Again, he reached cautiously toward the lid of the mailbox. Again, loud rattling. Then he heard something moving inside the box.

Shanks went back to his police vehicle and retrieved a flashlight. He came back to the mailbox and tapped on the side of it with his flashlight. The hissing became more vehement and pronounced. Gingerly, Shanks reached over and opened the box less than an inch. He flashed the light inside. What he saw was a coiled rattlesnake, ready to strike, its tongue flicking in and out.

Shanks closed the box. He unholstered his department-issue 9mm, took aim at the mailbox, and unloaded his weapon. The sound of rapid gunfire hitting metal resonated loudly and echoed down the street. When the weapon was empty, Shanks put a fresh clip into the gun. He listened carefully and heard rumbling and thumping inside the box, probably the sound of the snake going through its death throes. But the detective was taking no chances. He raised his weapon and fired seven more rounds into the now tattered mailbox.

With his ears still ringing from the gunshots, Shanks opened the box and saw the dead snake.

He went back to his car and sat for a while, thinking. Someone had planted a killer rattlesnake in his mailbox. Was it the Bordons? Was it Battle? Or was it someone else among the dozens of other boliteros he had played a role in putting away in recent years?

And how did they get his address? In the state of Florida, police officers are allowed to have unlisted addresses, with their actual residence not even listed on their driver's license. The only way someone could know his address was if they had access to his police file. Who was savvy enough to gain access to that sort of information? There was only one answer: Battle.

There were rules for discharging a firearm. Shanks was supposed to call the local police department and file a report. His supervisor would be notified, and someone from Internal Affairs would investigate.

Over the years, Shanks had lost faith in the ability of the system to safeguard information. If Battle was behind this, bringing in other cops was not wise.

He got out of the car and carefully picked up fourteen spent bullet casings from around the mailbox. Then he went home, got some tools, an empty shoebox, and returned to the mailbox. Carefully, he put the carcass of the dead snake into the shoebox. Then, using the tools, he removed the bullet-riddled mailbox and post and threw them into the trunk of his car.

Later, at home, he cut the rattle off the snake and discarded the dead reptile. He thought for a while about what might be the best way to handle the situation. Eventually, he decided to put the snake's rattle into an envelope and mail it to El Zapotal. Shanks knew that Battle was away in prison, and he wasn't even sure if new owners had moved into the house or not. But he was reasonably certain that if he addressed the envelope to José Miguel Battle, he would at least hear about it.

Shanks wanted to let the old man know that he could not be intimidated.

Go ahead, put a lethal poisonous snake in my mailbox. Resort to cheap gangster tactics.

It would only strengthen his resolve.

21

CÓMO FUE/HOW IT WAS

IN THE NEW YORK METROPOLITAN AREA AT THE DAWN OF THE NEW CENTURY, the bolita business was alive and well. Though there were maybe half as many bolita holes as there had been fifteen years earlier, there were also fewer boliteros, so the percentage taken in by each banker was larger, making it a viable enterprise.

Miguelito Battle had followed in the footsteps of Abraham Rydz and divested himself from the business. He no longer collected a percentage. That left El Padrino, Battle Sr., whose percentage had remained at 17 percent. While Battle was away in Peru, he had accepted things the way they were. Now that he was back and facing legal expenses, he wanted more. He put the word out that he was now demanding 30 percent of the cut.

It was only right. The reputation of the Corporation, which was still the preeminent brand in the bolita business, rested on his shoulders. "I want what I deserve," was how Battle phrased it.

Willie Pozo, the current operational manager of the Corporation, heard all about this on a trip to Miami. Pozo met with Rydz, who was still a friend from the old days even though Rydz was out of the business. Rydz told Pozo, "Willie, be careful. I hear José Miguel wants to reclaim the business. He wants to force you out."

"What do you mean, force me out?" asked Pozo.

Said Rydz, "There's a contract out on your life."

Pozo returned to New York. He called for a meeting with Luis Perez, his number two man. "I gotta go into hiding for while," he told Perez. "The Old Man is trying to have me killed. I want you to take over."

To Perez, this was not the greatest of developments. For one thing, the business had not been going well lately. The Corporation had shrunk from three central offices to one. Regional offices had gone from ten to four or five. On paper, the cut was the same among the various bankers, but the totals were getting smaller and smaller every day.

Willie Pozo went into hiding, and Luis Perez took over, but it seemed to him that everyone was fighting over a diminishing pie.

The irony was that out on the street the name of the Corporation was bigger than ever. Wherever bolita was happening, the Corporation dominated the business.

Investigators in New York had been aware of this for years, at least since Detective Tom Farley first began doing bet-and-bust raids in the mid-1990s. More recently, the Brooklyn DA's Office had become involved in an investigation that suggested there was a new bolita hierarchy in New York.

In 1997, out of the blue, La Compañía reemerged as a rival to the Corporation. That particular organization had been dormant for nearly a decade, but they were back, especially in Brooklyn. The leaders of this new version of La Compañía were Manny Alvarez Sr. and his son Manny Jr., who had been around since the original formation of La Compañía.

In July 1999, Alvarez Sr. and Jr. were arrested, along with thirty-seven others, in a joint FBI-NYPD case aimed at the hierarchy of La Compañía. The investigation resulted in the seizure of $5.8 million, including $982,000 in cash from the New Jersey home of Alvarez Sr. and $262,000 from the home of Alvarez Jr. Both men posted bond and were back out on the street, but the arrests had weakened La Compañía. As in the old days, the Corporation, in apparent violation of the two-block rule, began opening bolita holes near locations where La Compañía once operated. This ignited a war between the two Cuban-controlled organizations. It wasn't quite as violent as the arson wars of the 1980s, but in recent months there had been at least three homicides in New York that were believed to be connected to this new outbreak of the bolita wars.

These killings caught the attention of a young assistant DA in Brooklyn named Dennis Ring. Born and raised in Queens, the son of an electrical worker for Con Edison, Ring had only recently become a member of the Rackets Division under supervisor Trish McNeill. They became interested in the murders and also the very real possibility that the Cubans were working in partnership with the Lucchese crime family, most notably with the Iadarola brothers, Victor and Benito. On a wiretap of the brothers, they intercepted phone calls with a bolita banker referred to as Cuban Tony. Eventually, the investigators determined that Cuban Tony was Tony Dávila.

The name Dávila represented bolita royalty in New York. Isleño Dávila had been a legend before his disappearance back in the 1980s. His brother Tony had remained and was now functioning as a co-boss of the Corporation with Luis Perez.

With the introduction of Dávila on the wiretaps, Ring and McNeill targeted the Corporation. As a lead investigator on the case, they brought in Tom Farley, who from his years with the Public Morals gambling squad had acquired knowledge about the inner workings of the bolita business at the street level.

The prosecutors were not yet thinking of their case as a federal RICO prosecution. At the time, Farley, Ring, and McNeill didn't know much about Battle or the historic roots of the Corporation. Battle may have been a legendary figure in Cuban bolita circles, and the name the Corporation had been around for decades, but as of yet the historical context of the operation didn't have much bearing on the specific gambling crimes that the Rackets division was investigating.

That all changed when Dave Shanks came to town. While making the rounds, the Miami cop had learned that the Brooklyn DA's Office was mounting a bolita case that involved the Corporation. When Shanks returned to Miami, he said to AUSA Tony Gonzalez, "Hey, why don't we see what Brooklyn is up to? Maybe there's some way we could incorporate their case into ours."

Gonzalez immediately recognized the value of having New York prosecutors involved. Tracking down potential witnesses for, say, the arson crimes of the 1980s would be much cheaper and more practical for a team of investigators from New York than from Miami. In fact, a co-prosecution would make it possible for the two jurisdictions to split the workload down the middle, with Brooklyn prosecutors handling the New York and New Jersey crimes, including those involving the more recent configuration of the Corporation. Miami would handle the financial crimes related to the businesses of Battle Jr. and Rydz, and also, most significant, the casino in Peru, which constituted one big money-laundering conspiracy.

On behalf of the U.S. Attorney's Office in Miami, Gonzalez contacted Trish McNeill and Dennis Ring in Brooklyn. Then he flew up to New York to meet them face-to-face. The three prosecutors went out for pizza together and discussed the case.

Said Gonzalez to McNeill and Ring, "If your office comes on board, you're not here just to back us up. I want you to have skin in the game."

Speaking for the Brooklyn DA's Office, McNeill and Ring were all for it. This was a chance to finally take down the Corporation and make it pay for decades' worth of crimes. Their boss was pledging total cooperation.

To make it official, Ring and McNeill were deputized as U.S. attorneys, so they could co-prosecute the case in court, if need be.

The very next day, the Brooklyn's DA's Office brought on NYPD detective Tom Farley as lead investigator. Farley would be in New York what Shanks was in Miami, their ace in the bullpen. His first job was to find and interview all of the various witnesses to the arson firebombings fifteen years earlier, including Willie Diaz, who had long ago disappeared into WITSEC, the U.S. Marshals' witness protection program.

JOSÉ MIGUEL BATTLE WAS RELEASED FROM PRISON IN SPRINGFIELD, MISSOURI, ON March 5, 1999. While he'd been away, the sale of El Zapotal had been finalized. The place was no longer his. Battle moved into a condominium in The Hammocks, a bland, affluent suburb west of Miami.

He remained a dichotomy: on the one hand, still engaged enough in the business to be ordering hits from prison, and on the other, a sick old man.

He still required dialysis twice a week, and in Missouri he'd been diagnosed with COPD (chronic obstructive pulmonary disease). His daily regimen of medications and physical therapy required a full-time caretaker. By mutual consent, Evelyn Runciman had moved on. She remained loyal to Battle, but she had gotten her green card and was living on her own and seeing other men.

People wanted to believe that Battle was a sickly old man, but from what Dave Shanks was hearing, El Padrino was still in the game. According to Sexy Cubana, Battle took pleasure in the fact that his ultimatum of "pay up or die" to Willie Pozo and others had created a frenzy in New York, just like the old days, when the mere mention of his name evoked fear. With Luis Perez and Tony Dávila now calling the shots in New York, Battle was having to deal with a new cast of characters, and it was wasn't always clear how the new Corporation made its payouts.

Shanks was relieved that the Brooklyn DA's Office was now involved. They could handle the current investigative work, which included surveillance and wiretaps on Perez, Dávila, and the ongoing activities of the Corporation. Shanks's job was to delve into the past, especially as it related to the Casino Crillón, which, it appeared, was going to be a major component of any indictment of Battle.

In December 1998, Shanks went to Lima for the first time. There would be many more trips after that. The bankruptcy of a venture on the magnitude of the Crillón created a kind of sinkhole, with financial institutions, government officials, and international financiers all with a vested interest in making the casino's shady financial history disappear.

Operating as a cop in a foreign country was complicated. Shanks had to go through the U.S. State Department, which connected him with the Regional Security Office (RSO) of the U.S. embassy in Lima. All overtures to government people in Lima or financial institutions were made by agents of the RSO known as Foreign Service Nationals, or FSNs. Two FSNs were assigned to the case and would be working with Shanks as partners throughout his time in the country.

Shanks took along Kenny Rosario, who would serve as a translator, if needed. The first potential witness they interviewed was General Guillermo Castillo, who had served as the casino's first director of security, until he was fired by Battle. Castillo lived at a sprawling estate outside of Lima; he met with Shanks, Rosario, and the two FSNs in full military dress, dripping with medals and armed with handguns.

A formal man in his late seventies, Castillo described how Battle, once it emerged that he was the casino's primary shareholder, liked to throw his weight around. He fired many people in his first few months on the scene. Castillo took pride in the fact that he had been right about

Sendero Luminoso. The car bombing near the hotel, he believed, was what began the venture's downward spiral into financial oblivion.

On subsequent visits to Lima in 2000 and again in 2001, Shanks tracked down many other significant players, including Ferer, Chau, and Chiang, the three Peruvians who had secured the government license that first made the casino possible. They spoke only under threat of subpoena, which would have seen them extradited to the United States. They told terrifying stories of Battle threatening their lives and the lives of others. Eventually, they felt lucky to have divested themselves of the venture before it went under.

Throughout 2001 and into 2002, Shanks tracked down many other witnesses. Many of them had left Peru, which necessitated Shanks making trips to Aruba, Rio de Janeiro, Amsterdam, and Paris. He logged hundreds of frequent flyer miles in pursuit of interviews with, among others, Harold Marchena and Chito Quandas, former managers of the Crillón; Juan Solano Loo, the accountant who had had an affair with Effugenia Reyes; Mario Masaveu, Battle's loyal head bodyguard; and Salvador Ramirez, the account manager from Banco Banex who had worshipped Battle, dressed like him, and adopted his gangster demeanor, until he gave El Padrino an honest picture of the casino's prospects for survival and Battle threatened to kill him.

Shanks took down notes and recorded statements from all of these people. He listened to tales of cash shipments being flown by body courier from Miami to Lima, and Battle threatening his partners and employees with death if they didn't submit to his will. It was a staggering story that took the prosecution of Battle above and beyond anything Shanks had imagined before. Most of all, the cop in Shanks was excited, because he felt as though they were getting the goods. These were witnesses for the prosecution who would testify in court. The case against the Corporation—as it would play out in court—was beginning to take shape, and it was a beast.

BACK IN MIAMI THERE HAD ALSO BEEN SOME BREAKTHROUGHS. THE INVESTIGATIVE team had grown in size, and a key piece of the puzzle fell into place when a connection was made between Maurilio Marquez, the casino, and the business operations of Battle Jr. and Rydz. From what Shanks had been hearing in Lima and from his source, Sexy Cubana, he knew that Maurilio was one of the original shareholders at the Casino Crillón. Other than that, the investigators knew little about the older Marquez brother, who up until then had lived mostly in Venezuela.

The investigators uncovered a Suspicious Activity Report from 1985 that had been filed against Maurilio and Orestes Vidan. The two men had been detained on April 2 of that year while attempting to body carry $700,000 in cash through Charles de Gaulle Airport in Paris on their way to Zurich, Switzerland. They had arrived in Paris on the Air France Concorde from JFK Airport in New York the previous evening. Maurilio was eventually charged in federal court for failing to report the cash incident.

While investigating this incident, investigators discovered that Maurilio was listed as the president and sole corporate officer of two Florida-based corporations, Stanara Company Corp. and Aztec Financial. The primary shareholders of both these companies were Battle Jr. and Rydz.

This was the discovery that Abraham Rydz had always feared. Now that Maurilio Marquez was financially linked on paper to Battle Jr. and Rydz, the jig was up. The connection had now been made that linked Maurilio to the casino and to many of the shell companies that were at the root of the Battle Jr.–Rydz partnership. This led the investigators to subpoena the financial records of YMR Fashion Corp., Ambar Industries, Tyma Inc., and many other subsidiaries that Battle Jr. and Rydz had been using to launder money for more than a decade.

The Corporation's entire house of cards was about to fall. Shanks and Tony Gonzalez were now ready to make their pitch to the DOJ.

Back at the Fort Lauderdale office of the U.S. attorney (and at nearby Il Molina restaurant), Shanks, Gonzalez, and the rest of their team spent countless hours going over their strategy. One of the key decisions was deciding exactly who would be included in the indictment. Most of the names were obvious. Shanks's wish list included El Padrino, Battle Jr., Abraham Rydz (consigliere), Nene Marquez (financial manager), Maurilio Marquez (financier), Gustavo Battle (in charge of illegal gambling machine business in Miami), Julio Acuna (hit man), Conrado Pons (hit man), Luis DeVilliers Sr. (financier, money launderer, and also operator of joker poker machines in Florida and New Jersey), Orestes Vidan (accountant), Cache Jimenez (bodyguard who perjured himself during Battle's shotgun possession trial), Luis Perez and Tony Dávila (having taken over leadership of the Corporation in New York), Rolly Gonzalez and Orlando Cordeves (New Jersey bosses of the Corporation), and José Aluart (bodyguard and money courier to Lima). Also on the list were Evelyn Runciman and her stepfather, Valerio Cerron, for their money-laundering roles with the casino, and Vivian Rydz, the elder daughter of Abraham Rydz, who back in 1977 had once been arrested by the NYPD for running one of her father's bolita spots.

There were another ten names on the list of people who had been in-volved over the years to varying degrees. Tony Gonzalez ruled out four of them, including Conrado Pons, who was already in prison for the arsons and would be for at least another ten years.

In early October 2003, Tony Gonzalez crafted a five-hundred-page prosecution memo, which was approximately four hundred pages longer than most prosecution memos. Included were the various counts of the indictment, including all the predicate acts, and the list of twenty-five potential indictees. The memo was sent to the hierarchy of the South Florida U.S. Attorney's Office, and also to DOJ headquarters in Wash-ington, where it would be reviewed by the Organized Crime Section and also U.S. Attorney General John Ashcroft, who had been appointed by President George W. Bush.

Now it was a waiting game. The investigators allowed for the time it would take for the bosses to absorb the complexity of the case. This was a joint prosecution involving jurisdictions in two separate states, Miami and New York. It was not your usual case. Though Gonzalez had not been in the game as long as Shanks, his career had been remarkably far-reaching for a man of his age. They both knew that when you threw something new at the bureaucracy, it didn't always respond well, and certainly not quickly. They surmised that it might take days or even weeks before they heard back from the powers that be.

Two weeks went by, and then three weeks, and then a month. Gon-zalez and Shanks were trying to determine if the delay was the result of bureaucratic inefficiency or cowardice. There wasn't much they could do. But then an incident occurred that startled anyone from within the system who had been following the Corporation case. It seemed to evoke the worst, most violent impulses of the Corporation since the organization was first formulated in the mid-1960s, almost forty years earlier.

MANNY ALVAREZ SR., AGE SIXTY-FIVE, AND HIS SON MANNY JR., AGE THIRTY-SEVEN, were among the last of the old-school boliteros. They weren't as old as Battle and his generation, but they were among the generation that had inherited much of what had been created in the 1970s and 1980s. After a series of New York–area bolita indictments in the late 1990s, the Alvarezes had sought to consolidate their power under the umbrella of La Compañía.

On the morning of November 23, Alvarez Sr. and Jr. were driving in their Cadillac, the de rigueur vehicle for boliteros since at least the early 1970s. They were on the Harlem River Drive in Manhattan, Junior at the wheel and Senior in the backseat on his cell phone. Near 145th Street, the Alvarezes found themselves boxed in by a truck in front of them, another vehicle behind them, and the railing on their right side. A white van abruptly pulled up on their left side. The side door of the van flew open and two gunmen brandishing MAC-10 submachine guns cut loose with a barrage of gunfire. The bullets riddled the side of the Cadillac and lacerated the car's occupants. Alvarez Jr. was hit in the head, and his father was hit more than twenty times. The Cadillac veered out of control and crashed into a barricade at 146th Street.

The three cars that had taken part in the hit sped away.

The Alvarezes survived the hit, though the injuries were catastrophic. Junior got the worst of it; he suffered brain damage from which he would never recover. The father spent a week in a coma. When he came out of it and learned what happened, he vowed vengeance against the Corporation.

Craven acts of violence have a trajectory all their own, with residual consequences that often reverberate well beyond the intended target. In Miami, Tony Gonzalez heard about the shooting, and he was livid. From his partners in the Brooklyn DA's Office he'd heard that La Compañía and the Corporation were at odds. Gonzalez suspected there were likely to be casualties; he indicated as much in his voluminous prosecution memo.

Gonzalez and AUSA Jack Blakey got on the phone with the higher-ups at DOJ and let them have it. Said Gonzalez, "We have to hit the Corporation now! Or there's going to be an old-fashioned street war. And it won't just be boliteros getting killed. There's going to be collateral damage. Innocent people are going to die!"

Gonzalez's harangue was effective. DOJ's Organized Crime Section gave their approval. The time to execute search and arrest warrants had finally arrived.

SUSAN RYDZ LOVED HER FATHER. IN HER YEARS GROWING UP IN KEY BISCAYNE, DOWN the street from Battle Jr. and his family, she was blissfully unaware of any criminal activity on the part of her dad or his best friend, Miguelito Battle. She knew they were well off, which she assumed was a result of her father's success as a businessman. He often took her to the textile plant—once in the Dominican Republic—where his company made clothes sold at Arnold Stores, among other well-known retail outlets.

By late November 2003, Abraham Rydz seemed to be home more than usual. Susan, who was in her senior year of high school, had the impression that perhaps her dad had retired from the clothing business. His ability to spend more time at home turned out to be a godsend, because in March 2003, tragedy entered the Rydz home when El Polaco's wife, Margaret, was diagnosed with stage four cervical cancer.

On the day that her mother received the news, Susan saw a side of her father she had never seen before. He asked his daughter to join him out on the balcony at their house, and he told her the news. "Your mother only has, at most, a few years to live." He was on the verge of tears.

Susan was stunned. Her mother was twenty-two years younger than her father. None of them could ever have suspected that she would die first.

Four months later, in late November, Susan was in her bedroom, home from school, when she heard a loud ruckus from the front room of the house. She went out to see what was going on and was met by a phalanx of more than twenty federal agents and cops, with guns drawn.

Before she could even process what was happening, her father was brought down the stairs by four agents who had him surrounded. Rydz was cuffed, with his head hanging low. Susan's mother, who had begun chemotherapy treatment for her cancer, was distraught and yelling hysterically at the lawmen.

Taking a cue from her mother, Susan also became combative with the cops, who were being aggressive.

A local Key Biscayne cop took Susan aside and explained, "Look, your father is being arrested. The way these things go, he'll be taken in for processing and he'll probably be back home in a few hours. I know this is stressful, but you have to remain calm."

Back in the house, some of the agents were engaged in a search, going though closets and drawers. Others had taken Rydz and his wife to the dining room and sat them at a table. One of the agents said to Rydz, "Have you eaten anything?"

Rydz shook his head.

The agent said to Susan, "Why don't you make your dad some breakfast. He might not get a chance to eat for a while."

Susan made her father some eggs and toast and placed it on the table in front of him. He said, "Thank you," but was distracted, trying to take in the full dimensions of this nightmare that had descended upon his peaceful home.

The agents and cops took Rydz away. Susan was stunned. To see her father so vulnerable, to think that he was going to be scared and in distress, was more than she could handle. "What's going on?" she demanded of her mother. "What is this all about?"

Her mother said, "It's not anything you need to know about."

Susan felt the frustration choking at her throat. Her mother had cancer and was dying; she seemed to be overwhelmed by everything that was happening. Susan's father was the rock in her life, and now he was gone.

Still, Susan's mother would tell her nothing. Susan insisted on going with her to her father's arraignment in court. Maybe there she would learn some things.

At the federal courthouse in Miami, Susan and her mother waited. Rydz was brought into the room. They had a chance to speak briefly with him as he waited for the judge to appear. He did not say, "Don't worry, everything will be okay." He was nervous and worried.

The prosecutors came into the room, and then the judge. To Susan, it was like a dream. She didn't hear any of the names mentioned nor notice the faces. She looked only at her father. In a strange, disembodied voice, she heard the prosecutor say that Abraham Rydz, also known as El Polaco, was being charged with racketeering and conspiracy for his role in an ongoing criminal enterprise.

Susan had no idea what any of those words meant. When she got home, she looked them up on the Internet.

OTHER ARRESTS AND SEARCHES WERE COORDINATED TO TAKE PLACE SIMULTANE-ously with that of Rydz. Given the name "Operation Corporate Raider," the undertaking was massive: various arrest teams involved 170 detectives and sergeants and 66 federal agents.

Nene Marquez was taken into custody by the Policía Nacional at his home in Spain.

Luis DeVilliers was arrested at his home in Miami. His son, Luis Jr., was arrested at Challenger Video, their warehouse filled with illegal joker poker machines.

Hit man Chino Acuna was taken, without incident, on a Miami street where he was being followed by undercover cops.

Orestes Vidan, the accountant, was arrested at his office, which was filled with ledgers and documents related to the operation of the Corporation going back decades.

Evelyn Runciman was arrested at Gables by the Sea, an exclusive gated community where she lived with her new husband, one of the richest men in Miami. Runciman had recently given birth to a child. She was allowed to change clothes and then taken into custody.

In New York, Tony Dávila was arrested at his home in Queens. Luis Perez was served with an arrest warrant at Rikers Island correctional facility, where he was already being held on other criminal charges. The detectives who served Perez then drove by El Baturo, a bar and book-making spot in the Bronx that was popular with Cuban boliteros. They entered the bar and announced, "All of your Corporation buddies just got arrested all over the world. The government also took every penny they have and every piece of property they own. So unless you want to cooperate with us, you'll be next."

In the suburb of The Hammocks, west of Miami, José Miguel Battle woke up and prepared to have his live-in nurse drive him to the local Publix supermarket to buy groceries. Battle had been feeling better, but his condition was problematic. Aging was a bitch. Going to the supermarket was his biggest adventure of the day.

As he left his condominium, he first stopped by a series of kennels on the property where he kept his dogs. Two dozens dogs had been preserved from El Zapotal, a small number compared to what he used to own. El Padrino fed the dogs. He watched them jump around and slobber all over one another. It was one of the last remaining pleasures he had in his life.

Battle got into in the front passenger seat of his Cadillac. The nurse got in behind the wheel and drove them both to the market. Neither Battle nor the nurse realized that they were being followed by a surveillance team of detectives.

At the market, in the produce section, Detective Doug Mew walked up to Battle and informed him of his rights. He was placed under arrest.

They drove back to Battle's condo, where he was allowed to change his clothes and retrieve his identification and some other incidentals. As he walked out the front door of his condo surrounded by detectives, he turned to his nurse and said, "Please take care of my dogs. I don't think I'll ever see them again."

ONE FINAL ARREST NEEDED TO TAKE PLACE, AND THAT WAS OF MIGUELITO BATTLE. When the team of cops arrived at his home on the morning of Operation Corporate Raider, they discovered that Junior and his wife were not there. They were on a cruise ship currently out on the Caribbean. At his home, the search team found their itinerary. The couple were in the Presidential Suite aboard the *Celebrity Summit*. According to their itinerary, the ship's next port of call was Costa Rica the following morning.

Shanks, Gonzalez, and other lead investigators met at the mobile hcadquarters in downtown Miami. It was around noon, and a press conference was scheduled to announce the arrests at 3 P.M. They needed to make a decision about Battle Jr.

It was determined that the *Summit* had Internet access. Shanks figured that Miguelito would hear about the arrests of his father and everyone else before they reached Costa Rica and was therefore a flight risk. They would have to arrest him at sea before the ship arrived in port.

On a day filled with complicated maneuvers and an unprecedented use of manpower, the investigators now set out to arrest Battle Jr. on the high seas.

The U.S. Coast Guard had no cutters in that area of the Caribbean. Shanks contacted the Pentagon and spoke with a captain from the U.S. Navy. He was told that naval warships on cruises in the southern and western Caribbean usually carried a Coast Guard law enforcement contingent on board. The captain told Shanks, "We have two ships in the area. But unfortunately they are not positioned between your cruise ship and the port. Even at full speed, I'm not sure we could catch them before they arrive in Costa Rica."

Shanks told the Pentagon Navy captain that he would get back to him. When he did, it was on a conference call with the chairman of the board of Celebrity Cruise Lines.

Shanks explained the predicament to the chairman, placing an emphasis on Battle Jr.'s role in the Cuban Mafia and that he was likely facing a life sentence, meaning that when faced with arrest he might resort to desperate means. Initially, the cruise line chairman was not impressed. "My vessel can't just heave to in the middle of the ocean and come to a halt. We have thousands of passengers to consider."

Said Shanks, "Sir, if we can't do this at sea, I will arrange for armed guards from the U.S. embassy in Costa Rica to be on the pier. They, along with naval personnel, will obstruct your vessel from disembarking until after we have boarded what we now consider a hostile vessel to arrest Mr. Battle. We would rather not subject your passengers to that, but unless you order the *Summit* to slow down so that we can intercept at sea, you give us no other choice."

The cruise line chairman was quiet, and then he said, "Is there a way to arrest this Mr. Battle while it's still dark out?"

"Affirmative," said the Navy captain. He gave the chairman a course and speed for the *Summit,* plus a longitude and latitude so that the cruise liner would rendezvous with the USS *Thomas S. Gates,* a guided missile cruiser of the *Ticonderoga* class. The *Gates* would maintain a distance of one mile and send out a Coast Guard law enforcement detachment to make the arrest of Battle at 2:30 A.M., under cover of darkness. If all went according to plan, the operation would be conducted without most passengers on the vessel even knowing that it had taken place.

Everyone agreed. Shanks went to a nearby hotel and took a nap (he hadn't slept in nearly two days). He awoke, showered, and went back to headquarters. It was an astounding experience. Shanks and the other lead investigators of Operation Corporate Raider were piped into all radio transmission between the Navy and Coast Guard vessels, as well as being in on an open mic on one of the arresting officers. They listened to the sound of the Coast Guard ship's engine and the splashing of waves as the officers approached the cruise ship, where they were met by security personnel who allowed them on board and led them to the Presidential Suite. Using a passkey to enter the cabin, the officers surprised Battle in bed and placed him under arrest.

From their post in downtown Miami, it was, for Shanks and his fellow investigators, as if they were there. They could even hear Battle's wife, Grace, crying as her husband was informed of his rights and taken into custody.

THE FIRST TO FLIP WAS LUIS DEVILLIERS, WHO FEARED THAT IF HE REMAINED IN lockup, Battle would find a way to have him killed. Oracio Altuve, who had been flirting with becoming an informant for fifteen years, also agreed to testify. Luis Perez cut a deal and agreed to testify. A woman named Consuela Alvarez, who had been a bookkeeper and secretary for the Corporation in New York and in Miami, was in jail at the time of the arrests. She reached out to the U.S. Attorney's Office and offered her services as a witness.

The biggest fish of all was Abraham Rydz, whom Shanks and Gonzalez had set their sights on from the very beginning. Rydz's older daughter, Vivian, had been arrested and charged with being a member of the Corporation on what even the prosecutors, if they were being honest with themselves, would admit was a bogus charge. Her involvement in one of her father's bolita spots back in the late 1970s was ancient history, but the investigators had acted on the expectation of using her arrest as a bargaining chip with Rydz. And they had another bargaining chip. On the day after El Polaco's arrest, they set up surveillance cameras at the safe deposit boxes of DeVilliers, Battle, Rydz, and others. On camera, they caught Margaret Rydz stuffing a carrying bag with cash. After she emptied out the account, she left behind a newspaper article in the safe deposit box about the arrest of her husband.

Shanks and Gonzalez met with Rydz in an isolated room at the federal lockup. They told him that not only were they charging his daughter, but they were also going to charge his wife with money laundering for removing ill-gotten proceeds from their safe deposit box. What the two men did not know, until Rydz told them, was that she had been diagnosed with inoperable cancer and didn't have long to live. Getting Rydz to flip was not difficult. In exchange for his cooperation, the charges against his daughter and wife would be dropped, and he would be released pending his testimony at trial, so that he could spend her remaining months with his dying wife.

As the trial date approached, it sometimes seemed as though the case might become ungainly and get out of hand. Coordinating the efforts of so many different jurisdictions was difficult, with investigators in New York not always aware of what the Miami investigators were doing, and vice versa.

In New York, ADA Dennis Ring and Detective Tom Farley were responsible for tracking down Willie Diaz, who would be an essential witness on the subject of the arsons. The only problem was that nobody knew where Diaz was. For a time, he had been relocated into the witness protection program, but in the 1990s he had voluntarily left the program and disappeared from the radar. The New York investigators had been looking, but they were stumped. Then one day Ring was at a family party speaking with a postal inspector he knew who was involved in a criminal investigation in Brooklyn. The investigator asked him, "Hey, you're working a big Cuban Mafia case, right?"

Ring said, "Yes, I am."

"Well, I got this guy we've been using on one of our investigations. This probably won't mean anything to you, because everything he's telling us is old news from the 1980s, but he's loaded with stories about an arson war between the Cubans and the Italians back in the day."

Ring listened to the postal inspector, not saying anything until he was sure. "You're talking about Willie Diaz."

"That's not the name he uses."

"Brown-skinned Puerto Rican, about three hundred pounds, surly disposition?"

"Well, yeah, that does describe him pretty well."

Willie Diaz had returned to Brooklyn under a different name, had gotten himself into trouble with the law, and was now cooperating with postal investigators as a way to avoid criminal charges.

Detective Tom Farley and an NYPD apprehension team picked up Willie Diaz and brought him into the office of Dennis Ring, on Jay Street, near the entrance to the Brooklyn Bridge.

"Guess what?" said Ring. "There's a big racketeering case about to take place down in Florida and you are going to be one of the star witnesses."

Willie Diaz wasn't happy to hear it; he cursed and said, "No."

Ring explained that he would either be a witness or a codefendant. "Your state cooperation agreement from the 1980s isn't binding with the federal government. You could now be charged with everything you admitted to on the stand at the Lalo Pons trial."

Diaz was livid, but he had no choice.

Willie was immediately taken into the custody of the Brooklyn DA's Office; he was put up in a hotel and kept under twenty-four-hour guard. But he still had a phone, and on a number of occasions he called the office phone of Dennis Ring and left messages saying "I will fuck you up," among other threats. Diaz blamed Ring for all his problems.

Certainly, when a man who has admitted to playing a role in the killing of eight people threatens your life, you take it seriously. But the prosecutors needed Willie Diaz. And since they had him under lock and key, they felt they could monitor his every move. Still, it was unnerving for Ring and the other investigators.

THE TRIAL GOT UNDER WAY IN FEBRUARY 2006, TWENTY-THREE MONTHS AFTER THE arrests of the defendants. By the time jury selection began, many of those indicted had become cooperators or copped pleas and been dropped from the case. Left standing were nine defendants, and two of those—Evelyn Runciman and her stepfather, Valerio Cerron—had been severed from the case. They would be prosecuted at a separate money-laundering trial.

On the day opening statements were scheduled to begin, Battle Jr., surprisingly, tried to negotiate a plea deal. The prosecutors, including Tony Gonzalez and co-prosecutor David Haimes, were for the deal. Miguelito would plead guilty to most of the charges against him. Some of the charges would be dropped. In exchange, he would receive a two-year sentence, which meant, if he were given credit for time served, he could be out of prison in months. Plus, the deal specified that the government could not go after his share of a $100 million real estate deal in the Canary Islands that the investigators had learned about after his arrest.

Shanks was against the deal. In fact, he was outraged that the government would even consider it.

A few months before trial prepartions began in earnest, Shanks had retired from the Miami-Dade Police Department. More than thirty years had been devoted to the department, with the last half of those years working cases related to Battle and the Corporation. Upon his retirement, Shanks was immediately employed as a special investigator with the U.S. Attorney's Office, so that he could see the trial through to the end. Though he was not a supervisor on the case, merely a hired gun, Gonzalez and the other prosecutors recognized Shanks's singular devotion to the case. He had been given veto power, which meant that his insistence that Battle Jr. be prosecuted to the full extent of the law be given deference.

Said Gonzalez to Shanks, "Okay. We'll do it your way. But if we lose on the Battle Jr. counts at trial, it's on you."

On March 2, the presentation of evidence finally commenced in the courtroom of Judge Alan Gold—the same judge who had scolded Shanks and Gonzalez for having tried to use RICO-type evidence against Battle at his gun possession trial. Now the tables had been turned and they were all involved in one of the biggest RICO trials ever presented in the Southern District of Florida.

Tony Gonzalez gave the opening statement for the prosecution. From his first words to the jury, Gonzalez went for the jugular, the emotional main vein of the case. Before even mentioning bolita or Battle or the Corporation, he told the story of Jannin Toribio, burned to death in an arson fire on her fourth birthday. It was a startling opening, unsettling, some might say a cheap stunt, but it certainly worked by establishing the horrific image of that child's death as a motif that would haunt the trial for the six months of its duration.

To say that the government's case was ambitious was like saying an astronaut hopes to get off the ground. The investigators had succeeded in putting together the case that Dave Shanks had always dreamed about—a sprawling assemblage of racketeering acts and conspiracies spanning forty years. The danger was that the size of the case—the sheer number of witnesses and predicate acts and criminal charges involving multiple defendants—would overwhelm the jury, making the trial narrative too dense or complicated for anyone to follow. Another issue was the ages of the defendants and many of the witnesses. Battle Jr. was the only defendant under the age of seventy. Looking at the defendants, so clearly in their final years, begged the question: why not just let these old codgers die of old age and save the government the massive cost of prosecution?

The answer to that question was Jannin Toribio, a child whose death cried out for justice.

If the trial had a star witness, it was Abraham Rydz, El Polaco. From the stand, Rydz talked with a wistful nostalgia about the vagaries of the gambling business, what a crapshoot it was, how you could be up one minute and down the next. "It was a Sunday morning about nine-thirty, ten o'clock, and we were bragging with each other about how much money we had. And he told me, 'I have something like one hundred fifty or two hundred thousand dollars,' and I said I had about the same.

That same day, Sunday, at three o'clock in the afternoon, we had to go looking for people to borrow money from to pay the hits. So, that's the kind of business we're talking about. We're talking about even when you made money, it wasn't a sure thing, you were gambling. The word is 'gambling.' You could get hit very big, and you could lose everything."

Most of all, Rydz talked of the highly personal nature of the relationships between the generation of Cubans who had come from the island, in the wake of revolution and displacement, and formed a tight cultural bond around the concept of bolita, a game of chance and business partnership based on each banker's willingness to cover for the other in times of need.

To Rydz, it was about business, making money, and it was on this account that he eventually parted ways with José Miguel Battle.

During cross-examination, Jack Blumenfeld asked Rydz, "Let's talk about when the three of you would discuss business or policy issues or have to make decisions."

"What do you mean, the three of us?"

"You, José Miguel, and Migue."

"The truth is, sir, José Miguel was out of it. José Miguel was not interested in making money. José Miguel was interested in his name, in his pride, in the way he dressed, and other things. But he was not interested in the business at all."

Rydz, during his cross-examination by the attorney for Battle Jr., seemed to pull his punches, hedging his testimony to give the impression that Junior was not involved in many of the crimes for which he had been indicted, especially as it related to the murders of Ernestico Torres and Palulu Enriques, and also the many arson deaths. This angered the prosecution team, especially Shanks, who whispered under his breath to Tony Gonzalez things like "this is bullshit," and "this is a violation of the terms of his cooperation agreement."

As annoyed as Shanks was by Rydz's covering for Battle Jr., the defense lawyers in the case became disgusted by Shanks. At numerous times during the trial, when the prosecution, due to scheduling conflicts, was unable to have one of their many witnesses at the courtroom when they were scheduled to testify, Shanks was put on the stand. Having been designated as the prosecution's primary "expert witness," he was used to stall until the original witness was able to arrive. The defense lawyers got sick of hearing from Shanks, and his longtime involvement in the investigation became an issue at the trial. One lawyer suggested that Shanks's "vested interest" in a guilty verdict was what the case was all about, the need of one cop, on behalf of the entire criminal justice system, to justify a career devoted to virtually only one case.

Through it all, José Miguel Battle Sr. watched with a wary detachment. At times it seemed as though he was enjoying having his life laid out in such a comprehensive and dramatic fashion. A life lived in fragments, or stages, is often hard to comprehend. To have it dramatized, complete with witnesses and accumulated evidence, might seem like the Greatest Story Ever Told, particularly for someone with such a grandiose ego and personal sense of drama as El Padrino. It was, undeniably, a larger-than-life story, but even so, Battle's health deteriorated noticeably as the trial wore on. At one point the trial shut down as he was rushed to the hospital for emergency dialysis treatment. One week later, when he returned to the courtroom, it was in a court-designated Barcalounge chair, almost like a bed with an electronic headrest. Now heavily medicated, Battle sometimes dozed off during the proceedings and began to snore in court.

On April 27, almost two months into the trial, Blumenfeld stood before Judge Gold and said, "You Honor, my client is ready to plead guilty to certain charges." Blumenfeld had worked out a deal with Tony Gonzalez and the prosecutors. If they agreed to drop the charges against Evelyn Runciman and Valerio Cerron, and knowing that evidence presented against him might bring down his son, he was ready to plead guilty on the RICO counts in the indictment. He did so with the full knowledge that it would bring about a sentence that guaranteed he would die in federal custody.

Without El Padrino, the remainder of the trial was anticlimactic, though it dragged on for another four months. In the end, like most RICO cases, it resulted in guilty verdicts on many of the counts and not guiltys on some of the others. On most of the major racketeering counts, the defendants were found guilty across the board.

At sentencing, Battle Jr. faced time ranging from five years to fifteen. Since Jr. had not been found guilty on the murder counts, he and his family were expecting a light sentence. But at the sentencing hearing, Shanks once again engendered the enmity of the Battle defense team by taking the stand and arguing strenuously for the stiffest sentence to be imposed against the man who, he said, had more than any other used the criminal actions of the Corporation to make himself rich.

Judge Gold agreed with the prosecution. He gave Battle Jr. the maximum sentence of fifteen years in prison.

As for Senior, given his age and declining health, it hardly mattered. But the dictates of the state concede favor to no man, and so José Miguel Battle Sr. was also, on the charges for which he had pleaded guilty, given the maximum sentence—twenty years in prison, which for him was the same as a life sentence.

FOR SUSAN RYDZ, THE TIME OF THE CORPORATION TRIAL WAS A PERSONAL HELL NOT of her making. For one thing, ten months before the trial began, on June 5, 2005, her mother died from a brain tumor caused by the spreading of her cancer. Her mother's death had come sooner than either she or her father had anticipated, and it threw Susan into a state of deep concern about her father. For a time, he seemed to have a lot of anger. Eventually the anger turned into concern for Susan, who, he noticed, was becoming withdrawn and perhaps overburdened by the distressing turn of events in her young life.

Susan was stressed, but she soldiered on. In September, she began her first year at college in Boston. Occasionally she flew back to Miami to be with her father. He had moved out of their house in Key Biscayne (which had been seized by the government) into a small apartment. For a while, he was required to wear an ankle bracelet, until the trial got under way and he was moved to a separate location and kept under guard.

One day, Susan was in court when he testified. He acknowledged her presence with a slight nod. On the one hand, Susan found it difficult to see her father on the stand being grilled by lawyers. But she also felt pride that he was doing what he had needed to do to be with his wife and daughter at the time. All they had now was each other.

Seeing the defendants, Battle and the others, Susan felt no resentment or judgment toward these men. Now that she was learning for the first time what her father had done with them, she half admired their ingenuity and moxie, though it clearly had not ended well. Her father, Battle Sr., the others—they were exiles who had done what they needed to do to provide for their families. Susan didn't pretend to know the ins and outs of everything that had taken place, but she knew her father was a good man, and she believed him when he told her that he had not been involved in any of the killings.

Susan returned to school in Boston. She spoke with her dad on the phone almost every day. As the trial neared an end, Rydz often talked of his plans for the future. From the beginning, in exchange for his testimony, he'd been told he would likely be receiving a sentence of three years, and with a friendly ruling from a judge, that was likely to be house arrest with three years' probation. "Maybe I can get them to relocate me somewhere near Boston," he told her, "so we can be together."

By the time of sentencing, Susan was home from college on summer break. The day before her father was scheduled to appear in court to learn his fate, she met with him, along with her grandmother, at the small house where he now lived. Her father seemed oddly despondent, which she thought was strange given that tomorrow he'd be receiving his expected sentence of three years, with likely probation. Rydz gave his daughter a diamond ring that he always wore, and a gold chain, and told her to put it in a safe deposit box. He told Susan to take her grandmother and go to the bank.

On her way to the bank, Susan called her father on a cell phone. "I'm coming back there, you know. Is there anything you need from the grocery store? Something I can cook for dinner?"

"No," he said sadly.

Susan hung up. *What's wrong with this picture?* she thought.

What Susan didn't know was that the sadness in her father's voice was because he had been told the day before that the government was not going to give him the light sentence they had promised. They felt that he had reneged on his obligation to testify fully and truthfully, that he had deliberately shaded his testimony to benefit Battle Jr. Rydz's lawyers had told him to expect the worst: fifteen years, with no probation.

Coming back from the bank with her grandmother, Susan received an urgent call from her aunt. "Something bad happened at the house, something happened at the house." The aunt didn't know what it was, but the maid had called, and she was hysterical.

Susan and the grandmother arrived back at the house just as the aunt was arriving. They entered the house. The maid, who seemed to be in shock, pointed toward the bathroom.

On the kitchen table, Susan found a note, which she recognized as being in her father's handwriting. It read:

> *Dear Susan:*
> *I am sorry I am*
> *ending this way, but I*
> *am tired of living like this.*
> *Thank you for being my*
> *baby and giving me all*
> *the pleasures that you did*
> *for me and my wife.*
> *Thanks to my family*
> *for all the support they gave*
> *me. Have a healthy and happy life.*
> *(Papi)*

Still carrying the note, Susan went into the bathroom. There she found her father's body slumped in the tub.

Abraham Rydz had knelt down and put his head over the tub, so he wouldn't make a mess. Then he put a gun in his mouth, pulled the trigger, and blew his brains out.

DAVE SHANKS WAS UNMOVED BY THE DEATH OF ABRAHAM RYDZ. IT WAS UNFORTU-nate, even tragic, certainly for his daughter. But as a seasoned detective, he had seen the game played a million different ways. Rydz, along with his attorney, had negotiated a cooperation deal for himself that involved actually cooperating, and Shanks felt that he had reneged on that deal.

There had to be consequences. That was how the system worked. The suicide was horrible, but that was a decision that Rydz had made, and as far as Shanks was concerned, it had no bearing on him. A few days after the verdicts had been announced at the trial, the investigator stepped down from his job with the U.S. Attorney's Office. After three and a half decades in law enforcement, he was now a civilian. He moved out of the Miami area and became merely an occasional visitor to the city of his birth, but memories of the Corporation case remained permanently embedded in his psyche.

For El Padrino, life had also been reduced to a series of distant memories. Havana, Brigade 2506 and the invasion, the murders, the women—it was all gone now. He was a slave to his declining health. Initially, after pleading guilty, he had been free on a signature bond of $1 million. Given his various ailments, his mobility was severely limited. Along with kidney failure and COPD, he had developed hepatic sclerosis due to hepatitis B, which diminished his eyesight. He was permanently restricted to a wheelchair.

Battle was awaiting an available bed at the prison medical facility at Fort Devens, Massachusetts, where he was scheduled to be incarcerated. Meanwhile, there was among the medical professionals tending to Battle the belief that his COPD and breathing problems required immediate specialized care. There was some discussion as to whether he could be transferred to a specialized unit at an overseas hospital. This would require some sort of "compassionate release," where a foreign government would agree to take him in even though he was a convict.

Jack Blumenfeld became Battle's de facto executor. José Miguel's brother Gustavo and son Miguelito were now behind bars, and his long-time, estranged wife, Maria, refused to deal with him directly. Blumenfeld was the only person he had left.

By mid-2007, Battle's health had reached a critical stage. Being transferred to an overseas hospital would be arduous, but it might be the only thing that would save his life. With his client's consent, Blumenfeld explored options. At first, Costa Rica agreed to take in Battle, but then they changed their position, Blumenfeld was told, after objections from the U.S. State Department. Then Honduras agreed to take Battle, but they also reneged on the offer after pressure from the U.S. government.

Finally, the Dominican Republic agreed to take in Battle, on the stipulation that he would be entering the D.R. by way of a third country. This way, the D.R. would not be in violation of U.S. visa requirements. Given the state of his health, it was not likely Battle would survive a long flight to a third country unless it was somewhere near the D.R.

Asked Blumenfeld, "How about Cuba?" Given that the United States had no diplomatic relations with Cuba, Battle could be flown to and from that island nation without a visa. But would Cuba, under the guise of a compassionate release, allow José Miguel Battle Sr. to spend a night at a hospital in Havana while on his way to the D.R.?

Blumenfeld had been representing a notorious client who was accused of being a spy for Cuba and had developed some contacts in their government. Through diplomatic circles, he checked and was told the Cuban government, in the interest of humane considerations, would allow the patient to spend a night in a Havana hospital.

For anyone who knew Battle and his Bay of Pigs history, it was an astounding proposition. Battle had not set foot on the island of his birth since he was released from the Isle of Pines prison in 1963. For much of his life, resentment toward the government of Fidel Castro had fueled his will to live. Spending time in Cuba, even one night, was a tacit acknowledgment of the legitimacy of the Castro government.

When Blumenfeld told Battle that the Cuban government had agreed to take him in, he did so knowing the immensity of what was being proposed. These two men—lawyer and client—had had many discussions over the years about Battle's feelings toward Castro. Blumenfeld had suspicions about José Miguel's financial and maybe even tactical support for the anti-Castro movement in New Jersey and Miami. He knew Battle to be a hard man—resolute and stubborn on matters of principle. To his client, Blumenfeld put it bluntly: "Would you be willing to stay over in Cuba on your way to a facility in the D.R.?"

Wheelchair-bound, partly blind, his breathing labored and sporadic, Battle said, "Better Fidel Castro than George Bush."

During the years of his recent incarceration and prosecution, Battle had developed a special animus toward the Bush family. The father, George H. W. Bush, had as director of the CIA relied on Cuban exiles to do many "dirty tricks" in South America and elsewhere. Many exiles believed that later, as vice president, Bush sold them out during the Iran-Contra scandal. Now, in the new century, the son had become president, and, as far as Battle was concerned, had undertaken a prosecutorial vendetta against him and everyone in his orbit. By so doing, he was a betrayer of the Cuban cause.

Betrayal was a concept that Battle understood. At every turn, he and his generation had been subjected to cycles of betrayal by politicians, community leaders, business associates, lovers—by the very country that had taken them in as exiles. Sometimes the slights and indignities inflicted by one nemesis became overshadowed by newer and more immediate betrayers.

Better Fidel Castro than George Bush.

Battle agreed to the unthinkable—spending a night in Castro's Cuba.

As it turned out, it was not to be. U.S. authorities would not allow such a transfer to take place. Battle was moved to a private medical facility in Columbia, South Carolina, with a state-of-the-art pulmonary care center. It was there, on August 4, 2007, that he died from what was officially attributed to liver failure.

The final indignity came when the U.S. government refused to pay for the transfer of Battle's body from South Carolina to Florida for a burial. Blumenfeld paid the expenses out of his own pocket. The lawyer told a newspaper reporter, "He was a good friend to me, and he was a tough, fearless guy. He was a great friend to his friends and a better enemy to his enemies. He was one of a kind."

Battle was buried in a small plot at the Caballero Rivero Woodlawn Cemetery on SW 8th Street—Calle Ocho—in Miami's Little Havana.

Down the street from the cemetery, in a small park, is a monument to Brigade 2506. At the top of a stone monolith is an eternal flame that burns day and night, in honor of the men who died during the invasion.

EPILOGUE

IN NOVEMBER 2000, WHILE THE U.S. ATTORNEY'S OFFICE IN MIAMI WAS JUST BEGIN-
ning to formulate the possibility of a RICO case against Battle and the
Corporation, Luis Posada Carriles, age seventy-four, was once again
plotting to assassinate Fidel Castro. His three partners in this scheme,
who, like himself, were aging veterans of the movement, included his
longtime compatriot Guillermo Novo.

The plot involved bombing the Cuban dictator's motorcade as he
made his first appearance since 1959 at the semiannual Ibero-American
Summit in Panama. But the three anti-Castro collaborators must have
been slipping. Their plot was infiltrated by Cuban intelligence agents.
Posada and the others were arrested in Panama City in possession of two
hundred pounds of explosives. Castro held a press conference announc-
ing the sting arrest, at which he described Posada as "a cowardly man
entirely without scruples."

In 2004, as the arrests of Battle and other Corporation members
were being conceived and executed, Posada and his cohorts were tried
and convicted in a Panamanian court. At the same time that the Corporation case was making headlines in Miami, Posada's case was also in
the news. Sometimes the two stories ran alongside one another in the
local press, as if they were parallel narratives of a final denouement for
members of the Bay of Pigs generation.

The difference was that Posada was seen by some in Miami as a freedom fighter. Powerful Cuban American members of Congress rallied to
his cause. They wrote letters on official U.S. Congress stationery to the
Panamanian president seeking the release of Posada and the others on
humanitarian grounds.

In August 2004, Posada and his fellow conspirators received a last-minute pardon by the outgoing president of Panama. The president had been lobbied hard by the Cuban American anti-Castro lobby.

Posada triumphantly returned to Miami. To some, he was a hero. But to the Bush administration he was a thorn in the side. In the wake of 9/11, and the 2002 Patriot Act, it seemed to some as if the United States was being hypocritical. As the U.S. government put pressure on countries around the globe to turn over suspected jihadi terrorists, to play an active role in the war on terrorism, here was a man who had admitted in the *New York Times* to, among other things, playing a role in the bombing of an airplane that killed seventy-two innocent people.

One man's terrorist is another man's freedom fighter, as the saying goes. In what was viewed by people like José Miguel Battle Sr. and other supporters of *la lucha* as a blatant act of betrayal, on May 17, 2005, Posada was arrested in Miami by U.S. immigration officials. He was whisked off to an immigration facility in El Paso, Texas, and charged with violations of U.S. immigration law for having entered the country illegally by using a false passport and lying on immigration forms. Supporters in the anti-Castro movement viewed Posada as a political prisoner of the Bush administration. Others saw him as a terrorist who was being protected by elements of the American right wing that had cultivated and exploited Cuban militants since the earliest days of Operation Mongoose.

Fidel Castro called for Posada's deportation, so that the "scoundrel" could be tried for his crimes in a Cuban court. But there was never much danger that the Bush administration would allow that to happen—though they were actively looking for ways to make their "Posada problem" go away. It was later revealed that the U.S. ambassador to Honduras had asked the president of that country to grant political asylum to Posada. The president turned down the request, he later said in a newspaper interview, because he believed that Posada was a terrorist.

In May 2007, the immigration charges against Posada were thrown out of court by a judge. Posada was released from detention and returned to Miami.

Some in the international human rights community were outraged. Said Fabián Escalante, Cuba's former chief of intelligence, "Posada is a hired assassin, a paid terrorist. He is a killer, an assassin like those in U.S.

movies, who would murder anyone without a trace of emotion, just for money, out of self-interest . . . But he is a very, very dangerous witness [against the United States] . . . He knows too much and constitutes a real danger for those who used him for more than forty years."

In August 2008, a federal judge in the Fifth Circuit Court of Appeals ruled against Posada, reversing the previous judge's ruling that had freed the man. Once again, he was arrested and held in detention in El Paso.

In April 2011, Posada was found not guilty of the charges against him. He returned to Miami and lives as a local hero. When interviewed for this book in 2016, though his physical health was not good, he remained chipper and upbeat. His memories of José Miguel Battle Sr. were sharp and remained fond. When asked if he knew that Battle was a gangster, he answered, "Later, I learned that, yes. It was in the newspapers. And I heard the stories from people who knew him better than I did."

To Posada, it did not matter if Battle was a criminal or a killer. "To me, he was a patriot above all else. He supported any cause that was anticommunist. He made financial contributions to many of our causes, including the Contras. He supported *la lucha* wholeheartedly. Any time we ran into each other, the topic of conversation was the same—the need to kill Castro by any means necessary."

Asked whether he would be hesitant to accept the support of someone who was a notorious gangster, Posada said, "I did not care whatever they say he did. We were united by a common cause, and to me, he was a stand-up guy. For the cause, I would take money or resources from wherever we could get them in order to keep the mission moving forward. I never kept a penny for myself. I'm old now, without any money of my own. I get by with help from my remaining friends.

"For me, there are no lines. I would cross any and all lines if it got me to the ultimate prize—the elimination of Castro."

Not everyone from the movement was as hard-line as Posada. Felix Rodriguez, revered by many for his lifelong commitment in the war against communism and his role as a supporter of the Contras, does not accept that the struggle involves suspending any and all moral perogatives. Of Battle, Rodriquez said, "He turned bad. He became a bad man. No, I would not knowingly collaborate with such a man." At the core of Rodriguez's feelings about Battle is the fact that he is alleged to have killed, among others, Angel Mujica, his closest compatriot from the days of Brigade 2506. To Rodriguez, a man who would kill his onetime best friend and fellow brigadista was not a man who could be trusted.

ON MARCH 20, 2016, THE WHEELS OF AIR FORCE ONE TOUCHED DOWN AT JOSÉ MARTÍ International Airport in Havana for the first time ever. The same airport the CIA bombed in 1961 was now the point of entry for President Barack Obama, who was the first U.S. president to visit Cuba since Calvin Coolidge in 1928. For one week, at least, the tortured relationship between the governments of Cuba and the United States was front and center in the eyes of the world.

Obama and his diplomatic entourage were there to meet with, among others, President Raúl Castro, who had taken over as leader from his more famous brother in 2006, after Fidel suffered a debilitating gastrointestinal illness that almost killed him. Obama had initiated the extraordinary détente with Cuba in the interest of opening up diplomatic and financial relations, but that could not happen without at least an acknowledgment of the past.

In an unprecedented speech to the Cuban people at the Gran Teatro de la Habana, Obama noted, "Havana is only ninety miles from Florida, but to get here we had to travel a great distance—over barriers of history and ideology; barriers of pain and separation. The blue waters beneath Air Force One once carried American battleships to this island—to liberate, but also to exert control over Cuba. Those waters also carried generations of Cuban revolutionaries to the United States, where they built support for their cause. And that short distance has been crossed by hundreds of thousands of Cuban exiles—on planes and makeshift rafts—who came to America in pursuit of freedom and opportunity, sometimes leaving behind everything they owned and every person that they loved."

Obama, age fifty-six, noted that "the Bay of Pigs [invasion] took place the year that I was born," but he wanted the people to know that "I have come here to bury the last remnant of the Cold War in the Americas . . . Because in many ways, the United States and Cuba are like two brothers who've been estranged for many years, even as we share the same blood."

It was a speech many Cuban Americans thought they would never hear. Even though there were still cold warriors and hard-liners who advocated for a continuation of hostilities with Cuba—and political figures who still curried favor with once-powerful lobby groups like the Cuban American National Foundation—polls showed that a younger generation of Cuban Americans wanted to move on. Obama's visit to Cuba seemed to encapsulate this spirit. It was as if a cloud had lifted, and those old warriors who had devoted a lifetime to the covert, violent dictates of *la lucha* could now lay down their arms.

Before the year was over, another seismic event took place that shook the universe of Cuban-U.S. politics. On November 25, Fidel Castro, at the age of ninety, died in his sleep. The passing of Fidel was, if anything, even more monumental than the Obama visit had been in terms of what it represented for the anti-Castro movement in the United States. It was not the resounding repudiation of Cuban communism that so many had hoped for, with the overthrow of Fidel and the fantasy harbored by people like Luis Posada and others that they might one day strangle Castro to death with their bare hands. Castro had not been killed, but he was dead, and this was cause for celebration.

In Little Havana, people danced in the streets. Posada, who could barely walk on his own, was brought into the street by his caretakers and allowed to revel in the passing of a man whose death had been the focus of his entire adult life.

One week before Castro expired, in an event that garnered no attention in the local press, José Miguel Battle Jr. was released from prison after having served twelve years of his fifteen-year sentence. Battle was now sixty-two years old, young enough to still have some good years ahead of him. He reunited with his two boys, who were now grown men, and his mother, Maria Josefa, who was still alive at the age of eighty-two.

Throughout his prosecution in court and his time in prison, Battle Jr. kept his mouth shut. It was with great sadness and consternation that his family observed the testimony of Abraham Rydz, whom Miguelito had considered his surrogate father and closest friend. The fact that Rydz became a snitch, testifying against the Corporation, severed the close ties between the Battle and Rydz families. It did not matter that the government came to believe that Rydz had altered his testimony to protect

Miguelito. It did not even matter that Rydz had ultimately taken his own life. It was one of the great disappointments of Battle Jr.'s life that Rydz had agreed to testify against the organization. Even in late 2016, flush with his newfound freedom, the sense of betrayal lingered.

Still, a lot had changed. Battle Jr. was willing to acknowledge that much. After all, only a few months before his release and before Fidel Castro disappeared from the earth, there was the president of the United States, an African American, no less, standing on a stage in Havana, the city of his birth, saying to the world, "It is time, now, for us to leave the past behind. It is time for us to look forward to the future together—*un futuro de esperanza.*"

As the new year dawned, Miguelito was living at a federal halfway house, with weekends off to live with his family, until the terms of his release had been fulfilled.

The road ahead was paved with uncertainty, but it was good to be free.

ACKNOWLEDGMENTS

THIS BOOK CAME TOGETHER UNLIKE ANY BOOK I HAVE PUBLISHED BEFORE. IN THE spring of 2015, I was approached by two Miami-based movie producers— Jaydee Freixas and Tony Gonzalez (no relation to AUSA Tony Gonzalez)— who were developing a project on the story of José Miguel Battle Sr. and the Corporation. They had come to the conclusion that before they could pitch the subject matter as a film project, it should first be published as a book. Based on my having written *Havana Nocturne,* a *New York Times* bestselling book on the subject of the Mob in Cuba in the 1950s, they concluded that I might be the right person to tackle the story. They contacted my literary agent and asked: Has T. J. English ever heard of José Miguel Battle and the Corporation? And, if so, would he be interested in writing a book on the subject?

I had been following the story at least since the late 1990s, when Battle was arrested in South Florida and held on RICO charges. In 2007, when Battle died, I was deep into the research and writing of *Havana Nocturne* and had become well aware of the Corporation. I had begun to see the criminal activities of this organization in the larger context of the Cuban exile experience, especially the Cuban American underworld, which traced its roots to the era of the Mob in Havana in the 1950s. I knew enough to know that it was an incredible story, but at the time I felt that I didn't have the sources or contacts in the Cuban crime world or law enforcement to seriously entertain the idea of writing a book on the subject.

Which is what made the offer from Jaydee and Tony so intriguing. They had secured as a source David Shanks, the ex-Miami cop who had played an integral role in eventually taking down the Corporation in a court of law. With a contact like that, I felt it was possible to explore the idea of embarking on this project. My answer to Jaydee and Tony was, "Hell yes, I am aware of the Battle story. I am interested."

Both Jaydee and Tony were born and raised in Miami. Through family and other personal connections, they had links to many key interview subjects and other sources of information. They helped set up interviews. Tony, in particular, sometimes acted as a translator, and some interviews took place at his beautiful home in the neighborhood of Coconut Grove, Miami. Both Tony and Jaydee traveled with me on a research trip to Havana. They were cohorts on this project in many ways, and I am grateful for their hard work and friendship.

Dave Shanks was also an invaluable contributor. Having lived this story from a law enforcement perspective, he had much to offer. His original manuscript helped lay the groundwork for this book, and his perspective added depth and insight to the story of the Corporation. I owe a debt of gratitude to Mr. Shanks for his cooperation.

In doing my research, it soon became apparent that the story of the Corporation was more than a crime story: it was the story of an entire generation of Cuban exiles in the United States. This tale involved those whose personal and cultural trajectory in America was shaped by the revolution and everything that came afterward. Exile and dislocation were aspects of this story for the majority of post-revolution Cuban Americans. For those who became participants and fellow travelers in the story of the Corporation, it involved violence, secrecy, paranoia, and fear.

Though the Corporation was a criminal organization, it had within its structure an emphasis on family—brothers, fathers, cousins, and in-laws made the best co-conspirators, on the theory that they could be trusted. The younger children—too young to be involved in the criminal activity—were in many cases witnesses to "the life." They experienced firsthand the paranoia and fear of their elders' lives outside the law as exiles, gangsters, and, in some cases, as enablers who simply got in over their heads. The children were there when their parents hid the money, or had to go on the run, or became witnesses for the government. In some cases, their parents were murdered while they were still young.

I was startled by the degree to which the inheritors of this legacy came forward to be interviewed. Enough time had passed; most of the major players were now deceased. As kids, and into adulthood, the sons and daughters had adhered to a strict code of secrecy that is at the core of many criminal conspiracies. With the Mafia, it's called *omertà,* having to do with manhood. In the case of the Corporation, this code of secrecy was absorbed deep into the family ethos. You kept your mouth shut. You talked to no one. Only now, many decades after the events of this story had taken place, did they feel they could tell their side of the story. Not only were they willing to speak, they *needed* to speak as a process of letting go and moving beyond the dark memories of the past. In doing so, they contributed mightily to the telling of this tale and the creation of this book.

For their role in helping to make this book possible, I would like to thank the following people:

In Miami and South Florida: Natalee Fernandez, for her tremendous work helping to organize the research material; Alina Gonzalez, for her unerring and gracious hospitality; Maria "Edi" Gonzalez and Joaquin "Pipo" Gonzalez; Jack Blumenfeld; Bruce Fleischer; Tomas "Tito El Conejo" Guerra; Pedro Marquez; Pepe "Chamby" Campos; Frank "Sergio" Gonzalez; Raul J. Garcia; Chris Sotolongo; Freddy Castro; Raul Martinez Urioste; Art Hernandez; Adam Arnholt; Francisco "Pepe" Hernandez; Luis Cristobal; George Dávila; Humberto Dávila Jr.; Joaquin Deleon Jr.; Miguel Cruz; Ian Cruz; Elpido Guzman; AUSA Tony Gonzalez; Christian Fong; Alex and Adrian Battle; José Miguel Battle Jr.; Koki Freixas; Sophia Marie Banda.

In New Jersey and New York: Susan Rydz; Carol Ann Daly and Kelly Noguerol; Wayne Chesler; Tom Farley; Dennis Ring; Scott Deitche; Michael Dávila; Joey "Coco" Diaz; Henry, Daniel, and David Raymont; Stuart Deutsch; Jack Brown; Teresita Levy; Ben Lapidus.

In Havana: Geo Darder; Mario Villa; Ciro Bianchi; Osmani Garcia; the lovely Loreta.

In Lima, Peru: Christina Lorenzato, who served as my personal assistant in Lima; Modesto Julia Jara; Justi Polanco; Gilberto Diaz del Castillo; George Croes.

In Madrid, Spain: Ernesto Torres Izquierdo, son of the late Ernestico Torres (El hijo pródigo), and Antonia "Monica" Izquierdo, his mother.

David Shanks would like to thank the following people for their contributions to the investigation and prosecution of the Corporation:

Sexy Cubana, the secret source who provided information on the Battle family; Assistant Director of Miami-Dade Police Department (MDPD) Steve Rothlein (ret.); MDPD Lt. Victor McEachin; FBI special agent Brian O'Rourke; criminal IRS agent Santiago Aquino; Florida Dept. of Law Enforcement analyst Vonnie Aimes (ret.); New Jersey Commission of Investigations agent Judi Gore (ret.); State Dept. FSN investigator Manuel Ramirez from the Lima Embassy; Broward County Sherriff's Det. Al Lopez; MDPD Det. Dick "Crash" Krtausch (ret.); MDPD Maj. Bobby Munecas (ret.); MDPD Lt. Joe Lopez (ret.); MDPD Sgt. Joe Aja (ret.); MDPD Tech Supports Dets. Jay Huff, Kevin Verstraten, Joe Iteralde, and Ron Cooksley; AUSA administrative assistants Wanda Hubbard, Milly Perez, and Kerri Isern.

As always, special thanks to my agents Nat Sobel and Judith Weber at Sobel Weber Associates; and at William Morrow/HarperCollins Publishing, my editor David Highfill and his stellar assistant Chloe Moffett.

The work is sometimes stressful, and on the many research trips from my home base in Manhattan to Miami, I sought refuge in the local music scene. For providing stress relief and inspiration, I would like to thank the great band Spam Allstars for those late nights at Hoy Como Ayer, and especially Tomás Diaz, their percussionist; Locos Por Juana, most notably lead singer Itawe Correa, for the beautiful music filled with joy; and the hip-hop legend El B of Los Aldeanos, for his flow, his integrity, and the ways in which his work embodies an indomitable Cuban spirit.

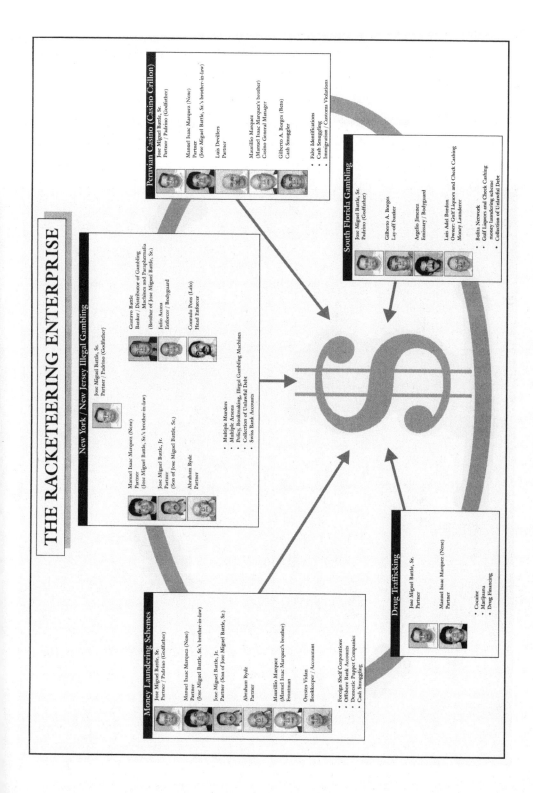

THE RACKETEERING ENTERPRISE

New York / New Jersey Illegal Gambling

Jose Miguel Battle, Sr.
Partner / Padrino (Godfather)

Manuel Isaac Marquez (Nene)
Partner
(Jose Miguel Battle, Sr.'s brother-in-law)

Jose Miguel Battle, Jr.
Partner
(Son of Jose Miguel Battle, Sr.)

Abraham Rydz
Partner

Gustavo Battle
Banker / Distributor of Gambling
Machines and Paraphernalia
(Brother of Jose Miguel Battle, Sr.)

Julio Acuna
Enforcer / Bodyguard

Conrado Pons (Lalo)
Head Enforcer

- Multiple Murders
- Multiple Arsons
- Policy, Bookmaking, Illegal Gambling Machines
- Collection of Unlawful Debt
- Swiss Bank Accounts

Peruvian Casino (Casino Crillon)

Jose Miguel Battle, Sr.
Partner / Padrino (Godfather)

Manuel Isaac Marquez (Nene)
Partner
(Jose Miguel Battle, Sr.'s brother-in-law)

Luis Devillers
Partner

Maurillio Marquez
(Manuel Isaac Marquez's brother)
Casino General Manager

Gilberto A. Borges (Beto)
Cash Smuggler

- False Identifications
- Cash Smuggling
- Immigration / Customs Violations

South Florida Gambling

Jose Miguel Battle, Sr.
Padrino (Godfather)

Gilberto A. Borges
Lay-off banker

Argelio Jimenez
Emissary / Bodyguard

Luis Adel Bordon
Owner: Gulf Liquors and Check Cashing
Money Launderer

- Bolita Network
- Gulf Liquors and Check Cashing
  money laundering scheme
- Collection of Unlawful Debt

Money Laundering Schemes

Jose Miguel Battle, Sr.
Partner / Padrino (Godfather)

Manuel Isaac Marquez (Nene)
Partner
(Jose Miguel Battle, Sr.'s brother-in-law)

Jose Miguel Battle, Jr.
Partner (Son of Jose Miguel Battle, Sr.)

Abraham Rydz
Partner

Maurillio Marquez
(Manuel Isaac Marquez's brother)
Frontman

Orestes Vidan
Bookkeeper / Accountant

- Foreign Shelf Corporations
- Offshore Bank Accounts
- Domestic Puppet Companies
- Cash Smuggling

Drug Trafficking

Jose Miguel Battle, Sr.
Partner

Manuel Isaac Marquez (Nene)
Partner

- Cocaine
- Marijuana
- Drug Financing

NOTES

INTRODUCTION

Post-revolutionary Cuba (political executions): The legacy and historical veracity of the executions is still a controversial subject. The Castro government acknowledged that some executions took place but have never specified an exact number. *Cuba: The Pursuit of Freedom,* revised ed. (New York: Picador, 2001), by Hugh Thomas, considered by some to be the definite history on Cuba, estimates as many as five hundred political executions.

Cuban diaspora in the United States: Luis A. Perez Jr., *On Becoming Cuban: Identity, Nationality and Culture* (New York: Ecco, 1999).

Atmosphere of corruption in Havana: T. J. English, *Havana Nocturne: How the Mob Owned Cuba, and Then Lost It to the Revolution* (New York: William Morrow, 2008).

The Mob in Havana: Ibid.

Martín Fox and the Tropicana: Rosa Lowinger, *Tropicana Nights: The Life and Times of the Legendary Cuban Nightclub* (New York: Harcourt, 2005; Coralstone reprint edition, 2016).

José Miguel Battle-Vargas Sr.'s background: Certificación de Nacimiento, Registro del Estado Civil, República de Cuba [Cuban birth certificate]; Battle's military file, U.S. Army, including education and employment records from Cuba; criminal file, State of New Jersey, accessed by U.S. Attorney for the Southern District of Florida; President's Commission on Organized Crime, Record of Hearing, June 1985.

Incident with "Jesús": Interview with Jesús, May 10, 2016.

Santo Trafficante Jr.: Scott Deitche, *The Silent Don: The Criminal Underworld of Santo Trafficante Jr.* (Fort Lee, NJ: Barricade, 2007); Scott Deitche, *Cigar City Mafia: The Complete History of the Tampa Underworld* (Fort Lee, NJ: Barricade, 2004).

Battle's arrival in United States: Battle military file, U.S. Army.

"At the time he had nothing": Testimony of Abraham Rydz, *U.S.A. v. Battle et al.,* 2006.

Earliest formations of the Bay of Pigs invasion: Interview with Francisco "Pepe" Hernandez, October 15, 2015; interview with Raul Martinez, February 4, 2016;

interview with Luis Posada Carriles, October 23, 2015; interview with Felix Rodriguez, February 17, 2017; Victor Andres Triay, *Bay of Pigs: An Oral History of Brigade 2506* (Gainesville: University of Florida Press, 2001).

PROLOGUE

Account of Ernesto "Ernestico" Torres and Idalia Fernandez on the run: Testimony of Idalia Fernandez, *Florida v. Jose Miguel Battle Sr.,* November 8, 1977; statement of Carlos "Charley" Hernandez, Renaissance Hotel, Newark, NJ, December 23, 1976; other statements and deposition of Charley Hernandez, October 19, 1977; testimony of Charley Hernandez, *Florida v. Battle,* 1977; interview with Jack Blumenfeld, October 21, 2015.

Attempted murder of Idalia Fernandez and murder of Ernestico Torres: Testimony of Idalia Fernandez, *Florida v. Battle,* November 8, 1977; statements, depositions, and testimony of Charley Hernandez.

"You don't have to be scared anymore": Police interview with Idalia Fernandez, translated by the State of Florida, exhibit 458-00625, *Florida v. Battle,* 1977.

1. BRIGADE 2506

The invasion: Triay, *Bay of Pigs;* Jim Rasenberger, *The Brilliant Disaster: JFK, Castro, and America's Doomed Invasion of Cuba's Bay of Pigs* (New York: Scribner, 2011); Haynes Johnson, *The Bay of Pigs: The Leaders' Story of Brigade 2506* (New York: Dell, 1964); Peter Kornbluh, *Bay of Pigs: Declassified* (New York: New Press, 1998); interview with Raul Martinez; interview with Ramon and Fidel Fuentes, February 6, 2016; interview with Pepe Hernandez; interview with Felix Rodriguez.

The Fuentes brothers: Interview with Ramon and Fidel Fuentes.

Raul Martinez Urioste: Interview with Raul Martinez.

Account of Battle's heroic act: Interview with Ramon and Fidel Fuentes; interview with Raul Martinez.

In June 2016, the author visited the site of the invasion at the Bay of Pigs, including the various locations traversed by Battle and the men who were interviewed for this account.

Dispatches of Pepe San Román: Rasenberger, *The Brilliant Disaster,* pp. 271, 281–83.

Capture of Martinez: Interview with Raul Martinez.

Capture of Battle and the Fuentes brothers: Interview with Ramon and Fidel Fuentes.

"If I'd known it was you": Interview with Jack Blumenfeld.

Asphyxiation of prisoners: Rasenberger, *The Brilliant Disaster,* p. 324; Johnson, *The Bay of Pigs,* p. 181.

Treatment of prisoners: Interview with Raul Martinez; interview with Ramon and Fidel Fuentes; Rasenberger, *The Brilliant Disaster,* pp. 313–81; Johnson, *The Bay of Pigs,* pp. 197–76; Triay, *Bay of Pigs,* pp. 131–79.

"We talked about whorehouses": Interview with Raul Martinez.

Battle and Mujica together: Ibid.

"Albert, I want to tell you something": Ibid.

Release of the prisoners: Interview with Raul Martinez; interview with Ramon and Fidel Fuentes; Rasenberger, *The Brilliant Disaster,* pp. 363–75; Johnson, *The Bay of Pigs,* pp. 291–325; Triay, *Bay of Pigs,* pp. 136–55.

"It wasn't until we were transported": Interview with Raul Martinez.

2. BIRDS OF A FEATHER

"I hated the United States": Johnson, *The Bay of Pigs,* pp. 210–11; Rasenberger, *The Brilliant Disaster,* p. 342.

Pepe San Román's speech at the Orange Bowl: Johnson, *The Bay of Pigs,* pp. 330–31; Rasenburger, *The Brilliant Disaster,* p. 380.

JFK at the Orange Bowl: Text of President Kennedy's speech, Presidential Papers, John F. Kennedy Library and Museum, viewed via official website; Johnson, *The Bay of Pigs,* pp. 329–32; Triay, *Bay of Pigs,* pp. 82, 179.

"Most of my attention that day": Interview with Raul Martinez.

"It was the first time it ever snowed at the Orange Bowl": Triay, *Bay of Pigs,* p. 137.

Brigade members' feelings toward JFK: Triay, *Bay of Pigs,* p. 82; Johnson, *The Bay of Pigs,* pp. 332–33, 336–37; interview with Raul Martinez; interview with Felix Rodriguez.

Brigade veterans given opportunity by Kennedy to join U.S. armed forces: Triay, *Bay of Pigs,* pp. 179–80.

Battle enlists in the U.S. Army: Battle military records, U.S. Army.

Brigade veterans stationed at Fort Benning: Fabián Escalante, *JFK: The Cuba Files* (New York: Ocean Press, 2006); Lamar Waldron with Thom Hartmann, *Ultimate Sacrifice: John and Robert Kennedy, the Plan for a Coup in Cuba, and the Murder of JFK* (New York: Carroll & Graf, 2005).

CIA-Mafia attempts to assassinate Castro: Fabián Escalante, *Executive Action: 634 Ways to Kill Fidel Castro* (New York: Ocean Press, 2016); Fabián Escalante, *CIA Targets Fidel: The Secret Assassination Report Inspector General's Report* (New York: Ocean Press, 1996); Don Bohning, *The Castro Obsession: U.S. Covert Operations Against Cuba* (Washington, DC: Potomac Books, 2005); Jon Ellison, *Psywar on Cuba: The Declassified History of U.S. Anti-Castro Propaganda* (New York: Ocean Press, 1999); Hernando Calvo, *The Cuban Exile Movement: Dissidents or Mercenaries?* (New York: Ocean Press, 2000).

CIA files: In 2008, the CIA declassified all files related to their partnership with certain Mafia figures to assassinate Fidel Castro. These documents, part of what the Agency refers to as "the family jewels," were made public on the CIA website and are also archived with the National Security Archive at George Washington University.

The Cuba Project: Ellison, *Psywar on Cuba,* pp. 65–126.

Rescate and Tony Varona: Escalante, *Executive Action,* pp. 145, 149–50.

Meeting with RFK: Interview with Francisco "Pepe" Hernandez.

Hernandez's experiences during the invasion: Ibid.

"I got the impression": Ibid.

Poker games at Fort Benning: Interview with Luis Posada Carriles.

Brigade veterans at Fort Benning: Ibid.

"I liked him": Ibid.

Operation 40: W. Thomas Smith Jr., *The Encyclopedia of the CIA* (New York: Facts on File, 2003), includes an entry that reads, "Operation 40 was the code name for a CIA-sponsored counterintelligence group composed of Cuban exiles. The group was organized during the planning stages of the ill-fated invasion of Cuba at the Bay of Pigs in 1961 and continued to operate unofficially for nearly a decade after the invasion. The group was disbanded in 1970 after allegations surfaced that a cargo plane flying in support of Operation 40 that had crashed in California had been transporting a large cache of cocaine and heroin."

Over the decades, among conspiracy theorists who believe that Cuban exiles were behind the assassination of JFK, the history and lore of Operation 40 loom large. Though there is a body of evidence showing that individuals associated with Operation 40 have been involved in innumerable covert actions, both independently and on behalf of the CIA, there is no convincing evidence of Operation 40 involvement in political assassinations.

Frank Sturgis: Testimony of Frank Sturgis, President's Commission on CIA Activities (also known as the Rockefeller Commission), April 3, 1975; Steve Dunleavy, "Sturgis Exclusive Story: Marita Pressured by Reds," *New York Post,* November 3, 1977.

The testimony of Sturgis at the Rockefeller Commission hearings, probably more than any other single event, gave rise to the concept of Operation 40 as a secret assassination squad responsible for many political murders, including perhaps the JFK assassination. That Sturgis was sometimes linked to the assassination did not bother him: in fact, he seemed to revel in the notoriety, appearing on television talk shows where he liked to give the impression that he knew more than he could say publicly.

Carlos Marcello's feelings about JFK: John H. Davis, *Mafia Kingfish: Carlos Marcello and the Assassination of John F. Kennedy* (New York: Signet, 1989), pp. 88–101, 154–56, 301–9.

"If you want to kill a dog": Ibid., p. 154.

Marita Lorenz: Deposition of Marita Lorenz, case of *E. Howard Hunt v. Joseph Okpaku Publications et al.,* Southern District of Florida, January 25, 1978; testimony of Marita Lorenz, House Select Committee on Assassinations (HSCA), May 31, 1978.

Paul Meskill, "Ex-Spy Says She Drove to Dallas with Oswald & Kennedy 'Assassin Squad,'" *New York Daily News,* September 5, 1973; Ann Louise Bardach, "The Story of Marita Lorenz: Mistress, Mother, CIA Informant, and Center of Swirling Conspiracy Theories," *Vanity Fair,* November 1, 1993.

House Select Committee on Assassinations (HSCA): The committee was formulated in 1976 and issued a final report in 1978. An investigator for the committee, Gaeton Fonzi, later published a book entitled *The Last Investigation* (New York: Basic Books, 1993), considered to be one of the essential texts in the JFK assassination canon.

The Secret War by Fabián Escalante: The series is comprised of three books: *The Cuba Project: CIA Covert Operations Against Cuba 1959–1962; JFK: The Cuba Files;* and *Executive Action: 634 Ways to Kill Fidel Castro.* Escalante's work has provided landmark information and intelligence on the many plots to kill Castro, the anti-Castro movement in general, and the assassination of JFK, but it should also be noted that since he was a former director of Cuban intelligence, his investigative work is driven by a very specific agenda. Escalante is unambiguous in his belief that anti-Castro Cuban exiles were key players in the Kennedy assassination.

Battle military records: Battle's complete military file was entered into evidence at *U.S. v. Battle et al.,* 2006. The file totals more than one hundred pages.

Battle Sr. settles in New York City and Union City: Battle's military records show that upon discharge from the service he listed his address on West 83rd Street in Manhattan. Within months his official address had switched to Union City, New Jersey.

For a valuable historical and sociological portrait of Union City, see Yolanda Prieto, *The Cubans of Union City: Immigrants and Exiles in a New Jersey Community* (Philadelphia: Temple University Press, 2009).

3. SANTO

Trafficante's background: Deitche, *The Silent Don;* Andy Rosenblatt, "Triumphs and Trials of a Mob Boss as Rivals Eye His Turf, an Ailing Santo Trafficante May Face His First Term in an American Jail," *Miami Herald,* July 17, 1983; interview with Julio Ojeda, February 6, 2016.

José Miguel and Gustavo Battle meet with Trafficante: FBI intelligence report, from Lieutenant Charles Black, Supervisor Criminal Intelligence Section, to George E. Leppig, Acting Director. Subject: Santo Trafficante. December 6, 1966.

The Trafficantes and narcotics: Ibid. Among other things, the memo states: "Concerning TRAFFICANTE'S recent trip to Madrid, Spain, on November 22, 1966, it has been learned that the purpose of this trip was to meet with VICENTE IGLESIAS ARMADA, who is reputed to be a major figure in international narcotics traffic. On his return to the United States through New York, TRAFFICANTE was strip-searched by U.S. Immigration Inspectors, and a new address book was obtained and copied."

Tampa/Ybor City crime history: Deitche, *Cigar City Mafia,* pp. 6–9, 19–21.

Alejandro "Alex" Pompez: Adrian Burgos Jr., *Cuban Star: How One Negro-League Owner Changed the Face of Baseball* (New York: Hill and Wang, 2011).

Racism toward "the Spanish Menace": "The Spanish Menace in Harlem," *New York Age,* January 28, 1929.

Battle meets Mafia bosses in New Jersey and New York City: Testimony of David Shanks, *U.S. v. Battle et al.*, 2006; Shanks/Rosario interview with Vincent Cafaro, January 31, 1998.

Mujica's role in the early formation of bolita syndicate in New York City–New Jersey area: Testimony of Abraham Rydz, *U.S. v. Battle et al.*, 2006.

The Cuban Mafia: The origin of the term seems to come specifically from this era when the bolita bosses and Mafia numbers bosses formed their alliance. The term refers to "old school" Cuban organized crime, not to be confused with the *narcotraficantes* of the 1980s and 1990s, who generally operated as an entity separate from the Italian Mafia.

Incident at Tony's Barbershop: Interview with Jesús.

Assault charges against Battle dropped: Battle's criminal record shows that he was arrested by the Union City Police Department on December 12, 1968, and charged with aggravated assault with a firearm, with the outcome listed as "No Disposition."

Trafficante Jr. setting up tryst for Senator Kennedy in Havana: This incident is depicted in English, *Havana Nocturne,* pp. 210–11.

Hector Duarte and the attack on the presidential palace: R. Hart Phillips, "Cuba Suppresses Youths' Uprising, Forty Are Killed: Students Storm Batista's Palace Routed as Tanks and Troops Attack," *New York Times,* March 14, 1957. This seminal event is depicted in all the major books on the Cuban Revolution, including Thomas, *Cuba,* pp. 614–17; Carlos Franqui, *Diary of the Cuban Revolution* (New York: Viking, 1980), pp. 147–61; and many others.

Duarte as a "dangerous hoodlum": At the same time Duarte was designated as a dangerous hoodlum, he was being recruited by both the Cuban Intelligence Service (CIS) and the CIA. The Americans knew Duarte was working for CIS and sought to use him as a double agent. CIA DISPATCH; from Chief of Station JMWAVE to Chief of Special Affairs. Title: Operational Report on personalities known to Hector Duarte Hernandez. File No. 201-147801. January 27, 1964.

Battle-Duarte shootout in Little Havana: Miami PD Crime Scene Search Report, case #664094, Records and Identification Unit, December 26, 1969; Miami PD Field Report, December 26, 1969; Miami PD interview reports with Gustavo Battle, Pedro Battle, Manuel Chacon, and assorted witnesses; Miami PD Supplementary Report, January 5, 1970.

Duarte killing ruled justifiable homicide: Miami PD, Supplementary Report, February 5, 1970.

Gustavo Battle narco conviction: Gustavo's criminal record shows arrest on June 21, 1970, in Miami for Federal Conspiracy to Sell/Import Cocaine. He was found guilty on October 12, 1970, and sentenced to ninety-eight months in prison at Atlanta Federal Penitentiary.

Bernardo de Torres: FBI memo, Newark office, Organized Crime Division, July 8, 1966. Filed office File No. 165-619. Report made by S.A. Anthony P. Rezza.

INS **"not conducting investigation":** Ibid. The memo states: "On 6/17/66, investigator ED WHALEN, INS, furnished information that his office would not be conducting an active investigation with regard to the subject since it is their belief that the subject is anti-Castro and anti-communist in his beliefs."

The Kelly brothers: FBI memo, Newark office, Organized Crime Division, July 8, 1966. Report made by S.A. Anthony P. Rezza.

Battle and Pete Kelly: Ibid. The memo includes log of surveillance conducted by Special Agents Kenneth F. Hackmann and Anthony P. Rezza.

FBI surveillance of Battle: Ibid.

4. THE RAIN IN SPAIN

Carlos Rodriguez meets Battle: Interview with Carlos Rodriguez, October 20, 2015.

Rodriguez biography: Ibid.

Incident at El Brinque: Ibid.

"Why is he a friend of yours?": Ibid.

Indictment of Battle et al.: *U.S. v. Jose Battle, Angel Mujica, William Alter, Rolando Mirabente, Orestes Destrade, Gerardo Martinez, Juan Diaz, Erdio Gomez, Lazaro Delgado, Mario Lopez, Francisco Menesses, Raomon Enriquez, Aldo Battle, and Hiram Battle.* U.S. District Court of New Jersey, Criminal Docket No. 350-70, AUSA Frederick B. Lacey. July 22, 1970.

Incident with Alejandro Lagos: Lagos interviewed by David Shanks, who drafted a report stating, "Between October 16, 1997 and October 21, 1997 a series of interviews were conducted by [Detective David L. Shanks] with ALEJANDRO N. LAGOS regarding his knowledge of the illegal activities of JOSE MIGUEL BATTLE." Case No. 331829-J.

"Listen, the man that hit you is El Padrino": Ibid.

Battle flees to Madrid: *U.S. v. Battle et al.,* 1970.

Los Cubanos in Madrid: Interview with Joaquin Deleon Jr., May 12, 2016; interview with George Dávila, May 10, 2016; interview with Ernesto Torres Izquierdo, September 15, 2016; interview with Antonia Izquierdo, February 18, 2017.

    In May 2017, the author traveled to Madrid and visited many of the locations where Battle, Ernestico Torres, and the others lived and socialized.

Background on Joaquin Deleon Sr.: Interview with Joaquin Deleon Jr.

"He could be loud": Ibid.

"He wasn't like his father": Ibid.

Isleño Dávila background: Interview with Michael Dávila, April 18, 2016; interview with George Dávila; interview with Humberto Dávila Jr., September 15, 2016.

    In telling the story of the Corporation, the Dávilas were especially concerned that the role of their family be accurately portrayed. Both Michael and George, who were nephews of Isleño Dávila, and Humberto Jr., his son, were generous with their time and memories. Humberto Jr. even traveled from Panama City to Miami to be interviewed for this book.

Ernesto Torres in Spain: Interview with Ernesto Torres Izquierdo; interview with Antonia Izquierdo; Certificación de Nacimiento, Ministerio de Justicia, La Habana [birth certificate for Ernesto Heriberto Torres y Alsina] states that he was born on May 22, 1953, to Ernesto Ramon Torres y del Valle (father) and Librada Ada Alsina y Acanda (mother).

Ernesto Torres Sr. and Battle: Interview with Ernesto Torres Izquierdo.

Antonia meets Ernestico: Interview with Antonia Izquierdo.

Confrontation between Ernestico and Isleño Dávila: Ibid.

Pedro Battle serves as godfather: Interview with Ernesto Torres Izquierdo; interview with Antonia Izquierdo.

Killing by Ernestico in Spain: Interview with Joaquin Deleon Jr.

Cubans vacationing together at Costa del Sol: Ibid.

Battle apprehended upon return to the United States: *U.S. v. Battle et al.,* 1970. Battle was arrested by FBI special agent Wendell W. Hall and delivered to court in Newark by Deputy U.S. Marshal Jack Drazen on September 22, 1972; FBI Memo, Subject: Case #590-48-7001. From SA Jose A. Valdes and CIA agent Vonnie Ames to Bureau Chief Rolando D. Bolanos. A chronological criminal history and intelligence summary on Jose Miguel Battle Sr. and his organization. June 27, 1984.

Battle at Danbury prison, meets Eugenio Rolando Martinez: Interview with Eugenio Rolando Martinez, August 10, 2016.

Battle presents watch to Martinez: Ibid.

Posada, the Alejos conspiracy, and other early CIA efforts: FBI memo, May 17, 1965. "It is noted that ROBERT ALEJOS ARZU, 180 Palm Drive, Palm Island, Miami Beach, Florida, is a wealthy Guatemalan national and has been conspiring to overthrow the government of Guatemala." Among the items confiscated by U.S. Customs were: portable flame thrower, fifty-one M-21 hand grenades (fragmentation), sixteen Bazooka rockets, forty-four sticks of dynamite (military), and ten thousand rounds of ammunition for everything from a Thompson submachine gun to a .45-caliber M-3 Grease gun.

Various other FBI and CIA memos detail Posada's extensive counterespionage career. These documents are online at the National Security Archive website in a special section entitled *The CIA File on Luis Posada Carriles, Electronic Briefing Book No. 334,* by Peter Koenbluh and Erin Maskell.

Posada and Jorge Mas Canosa: CIA Field Report No. UFG-7310. Subject: Plan of the Cuban representation in exile (RECE) to blow up a Cuban or Soviet vessel in Veracruz, Mexico. July 1, 1965.

CIA assessment of Posada: CIA DISPATCH from Chief of Station, JMWAVE to Chief, White House. September 22, 1965. Posada's initial CIA contact was Grover T. Lythcott, whom he knew as "Walt Albein."

Posada in Venezuela: CIA INTELLIGENCE INFORMATION REPORT. In 2003, as per request from the U.S. Department of Justice, the CIA released a sixteen-page report on its dealings with Luis Clemente Posada Carriles, including much of his activity in Venezuela. The report's summary reads in part: "The [CIA]'s first contact with [Posada] was in 1961, in connection with planning for the Bay of Pigs invasion. Posada was a paid asset of the CIA from 1965 to 1967 and again from 1968 to 1974. From 1974 to 1976, CIA had intermittent contact with Posada . . . During that same period, Posada occasionally provided unsolicited threat reporting."

Posada sees Battle bet $1 million at cockfight: Interview with Luis Posada Carriles.

Novo brothers attempt to assassinate Che Guevara: Homer Bigart, "Bazooka Fired at U.N. as Cuban Speaks," *New York Times,* December 12, 1964; Saul Landau, "Guillermo Novo and Me," *Counterpunch,* September 19, 2003.

José Elías de la Torriente: FBI Intelligence Report, File No. 4C-82, May 2, 1984. Subject: Guillermo Novo-Sampol. The source that provided information about Battle's involvement in the murder was evaluated as "highly reliable."

Zero Group claims credit for Torriente murder: Dick Russell, "Little Havana's Reign of Terror," *Miami New Times,* October 29, 1976.

Palulu and Pedro Battle cocaine rivalry: Shanks manuscript; statements, depositions, and testimony of Charley Hernandez.

Murder of Pedro Battle: Extensive NYPD file on Pedro Battle homicide, including follow-up reports by investigating officer Detective Thomas E. Henry. December 23 and 24, 1974.

5. BRING ME THE HEAD OF PALULU

"They killed Pedro, my little brother": Interview with Carlos Rodriguez.

At the county morgue: Ibid.

Battle and *The Godfather:* Interview with Carlos Rodriguez; interview with Joaquin Deleon Jr.; interview with David Shanks. Virtually anyone who ever met Battle commented on his similarities to the fictional Vito Corleone. Those who knew him attested to his fascination with the movies, which eventually included the original and two sequels—but Battle's preference was always for the original, the only one where the Don is the central character.

Memorial service for Pedro Battle: Statements, depositions, and testimony of Charley Hernandez; testimony of Abraham Rydz, *U.S. v. Battle,* 2006.

Recollections of Carlos "Charley" Hernandez: The public narrative of Ernesto Torres, José Miguel Battle, Chino Acuna, and others, both criminal and personal, in relation to the Corporation is dependent in large part on the recollections of Charley Hernandez. Eventually, Charley would submit to numerous law enforcement interviews, give statements on the record in sworn affidavits, be deposed twice, submit to a lie detector test (he passed), and testify under oath. The accumulated result of these statements and testimony is a massive public record, especially on matters regarding Ernestico and Battle. The relevant documents are as follows: (A) Interview with Charley Hernandez, Renaissance Restaurant, in the presence of Detective Richard Kalafus, NYPD, December 23, 1976. (B) Interview with Charley Hernandez, Hudson County Prosecutor's Office, Office of Deputy Chief Charles Rossiter, in the presence of Detective Stephen McCabe, Detective Charles Kehoe, and Detective Raul Cox, December 27 and December 28, 1976. (C) Statement of Charley Hernandez, Metro-Dade Police Department, Dade County Public Safety Department Building, in the presence of Detective Julio Ojeda and Detective Ralph Hernandez, June 16, 1976. (D) Deposition of Charley Hernandez, *Florida v. Battle,* September 21 and October 19, 1977. (E) Testimony of Charley Hernandez, *Florida v. Battle,* October 1977. (F) Deposition of Carlos Hernandez, *Florida v. Acuna,* 19th Precinct Station, Manhattan, September 15, 1984.

"Pedro was your blood": Statements, depositions, and testimony of Charley Hernandez.

Ernestico and Acuna take on Palulu murder contract: Ibid.

Account of Battle brothers' gun possession arrest: Extensive Union City PD file on the incident, with interviews of all the participants, lab reports on the weapons, etc.; statement of Patrolman Diego Mella, Hudson County Prosecutor's Office, April 14, 1975; Grand Jury testimony of Patrolman Robert N. Shelton, Union City Municipal court; testimony of Special Officer Andrew Pisano, Hudson County Court, April 10, 1976; testimony of Sergeant John Messina, Hudson County Courthouse, May 7, 1976.

Herman Bolte background: Agustin C. Torres, "The Chief Who Cracked Down on Castro," *Jersey Journal,* February 20, 2010.

Scarafile, Musto, and gambling in Union City: Robert Hanley, "Senator Musto Indicted on Charge of Conspiring to Protect Gambling," *New York Times,* November 18, 1977; Agustin C. Torres, "Scarafile, Defendant in Infamous Musto Federal Corruption Trial, Dies," *Jersey Journal,* August 27, 2009.

Ernestico and Acuna on killing rampage: Statements, depositions, and testimony of Charley Hernandez; deposition of Detective Richard Kalafus, *Florida v. Acuna,* September 14, 1982.

Shootout between Ernestico and Palulu in Central Park: NYPD incident and investigation reports, including interviews with witnesses to the shooting.

Palulu in hospital: Deposition of Detective Richard Kalafus, *Florida v. Acuna,* 1984.

Attempted hit on Ismael "Loco" Alvarez: Statements, depositions, and testimony of Charley Hernandez; Union City PD investigation, arrest, continuation, and property and evidence reports, file #33551.

Idalia Fernandez meets Battle: Depostion and testimony of Idalia Fernandez, *Florida v. Battle,* 1977.

Car bomb murder of Alvarez: "Murder Witness Killed as Bomb Destroys Car," *Hudson Dispatch,* January 28, 1976

Malagamba, Tati, and Monchi: Statements, depositions, and testimony of Charley Hernandez.

6. THE PRODIGAL SON

Dream books: For a cultural history on dream books see Ann Fabian, "Dream Reading: Interpreting Dreams for Fun and Profit," *Lapham's Quarterly,* https://www .laphamsquarterly.org/luck/dream-reading.

la charada: Kathy Glasgow, "Bolita in Havana," *Miami New Times,* December 19, 2002; Vanessa Bauza, "Illegal but Beloved Bolita Endures," *South Florida Sun-Sentinal,* January 30, 2005; Nick Sortal, "Give Me a Ballerina on a Bicycle," *South Florida Sun-Sentinel,* May 27, 2012.

Isleño Dávila and the Corporation: Interview with Michael Dávila, April 18, 2016; interview with George Dávila; interview with Humberto Dávila Jr.

Battle complaining to Ernestico about Isleño: Statement, depositions, and testimony of Charley Hernandez.

Meetings at Colonial restaurant: Proffer of Luis DeVilliers (undated); testimony of Luis DeVilliers, *U.S. v. Battle et al.,* 2006.

Nickname "the Prodigal Son": Statements, depositions, and testimony of Charley Hernandez.

"Is that how you would treat your own child?": Interview with Carlos Rodriguez.

Ernestico wants to be a banker: Statements, depositions, and testimony of Charley Hernandez.

Battle proposes Ernestico as banker: Testimony of Abraham Rydz; statements, depositions, and testimony of Charley Hernandez; proffer and testimony of Luis DeVilliers, *U.S. v. Battle et al.,* 2006.

Ernestico as banker: Deposition and testimony of Idalia Fernandez, *Florida v. Battle,* 1977; Statements, depositions, and testimony of Charley Hernandez.

Battle tries to help Ernestico: Deposition and testimony of Idalia Fernandez, *Florida v. Battle,* 1977.

"Are you taking baseball bets?": Ibid.

"It's true you are no banker": Ibid.

Home life of Charley Hernandez: Interview with Kelly Noguerol and Carol Daley, June 10, 2016; statements, depositions, and testimony of Charley Hernandez.

Charley's attitudes about Castro: Interview with Kelly Noguerol and Carol Daley.

Charley first meets Ernestico: Statements, depositions, and testimony of Charley Hernandez.

Contract to kill El Morro: Ibid.

Phone conversation between Chino and Ernestico: Transcript of phone conversation, entered as evidence, *Florida v. Battle,* 1977.

Ernestico proposes kidnapping of bankers: Statements, depositions, and testimony of Charley Hernandez.

Extortion of Mallin: Ibid.

Botched kidnapping of Morrero: Statements, depositions, and testimony of Charley Hernandez; police report; testimony of Idalia Fernandez, *Florida v. Battle,* 1977.

Ernestico with wives of Tati and Monchi: Statements, depositions, and testimony of Charley Hernandez.

"Hey, look, there's El Gordo": Ibid.

"Hello, brother, how are you?": Transcript of phone conversation between Battle and Ernestico (undated).

Bombing of Ernestico's car: "Cliffside Man Survives Auto's Grenade Blast," *Union City Reporter,* December 17, 1975. Ernestico and Idalia were identified as "Ricardo and Idalia Maldonado." The article further noted, "The Spanish-speaking couple apparently kept to themselves and did not even have a phone at the apartment"; police reports, Cliffside Park Police Department, from Patrolman Thomas A. Reuther to Chief Filipowicz; deposition and testimony of Idalia Fernandez, *Florida v. Battle,* 1977.

Shooting of José Morín Rodriguez: Statements, depositions, and testimony of Charley Hernandez; deposition and testimony of Idalia Fernandez. *Florida v. Battle,* 1977.

"Ernesto, we need to get out of New York": Deposition and testimony of Idalia Fernandez, *Florida v. Battle,* 1977.

David Shanks joins police department: Interview with David Shanks, October 19, 2015; Shanks manuscript.

Shooting of officers Hodges, Curlette, and D'Azevedo: Ibid.

7. RASPUTIN IN MEXICO

Rene Avila delivers bail money: In his deposition for *Florida v. Battle,* 1977, Avila admitted paying bail for Chino Acuna on at least two occasions, though he claimed he did so on behalf of Acuna's girlfriend, not José Miguel Battle. Further references to Avila paying bail are found in the depositions and testimony of Charley Hernandez, as well as police reports from detectives Kalafus and Shanks.

Avila's income: In his deposition for *Florida v. Battle,* 1977, Avila claimed that his income was "around ten thousand dollars" a year. In the article "Grand Jury Report Raises Questions About Editor, Law" by Marilee Loboda Braue, *Asbury Park Press,* December 14, 1986, his income is listed as "$60,000 a year."

Avila involvement with Battle organization: Avila's role in the organization's nexus of power was a focal point of the Presentment of the Special Hudson County Grand Jury—Panel A, In the Matter of an Investigation into Corrupt Activities and Influence in the Union City Police Department and City Government, February 6, 1986. Also, Braue, "Grand Jury Report Raises Questions About Editor, Law," *Asbury Park Press,* December 14, 1986; statements, depositions, and testimony of Charley Hernandez; Det. David Shanks interview with Alejandro Lagos, Investigation into the Illegal Activities of Jose Miguel Battle, et al. (Case No. 331829-J), October 16, 1997.

In the eyes of detectives like Kalafus and Shanks, who worked the Battle investigation over the years, Avila got off easy. Despite the damning conclusions of the Hudson

Country Grand Jury report in 1986, Avila escaped indictment until September 2003. In the run-up to the RICO case against Battle and the Corporation, Avila was charged with three counts of felony tax fraud, covering the years 1997 to 1999. He was unable to account for the luxurious properties and automobiles he owned based on the minimal salary he claimed on his tax returns. He wound up pleading guilty to a charge of Attempt to Evade or Defeat Tax and was sentenced to twelve months and one day in prison, with two years of supervised release. *USA v. Avila*, Case No. 03-672-01, U.S. District Court, District of New Jersey; "A Felony with that *Croqueta?*" by Isaiah Thompson, *Miami New Times,* April 10, 2008.

Chi Chi Rodriguez: Presentment of the Special Hudson County Grand Jury—Panel A, In the Matter of an Investigation into Corrupt Activities and Influence in the Union City Police Department and City Government, February 6, 1986.

"If you want a job, call Chi Chi": Ibid.

Ernestico and Idalia on the run: Deposition and testimony of Idalia Fernandez, *Florida v. Battle*, 1977; statements, depositions, and testimony of Charley Hernandez.

Planned kidnapping of Isleño: Statements, depositions, and testimony of Charley Hernandez.

Burglary of ex-cop's home: Ibid.

"This guy has become a big problem for us": Testimony of Abraham Rydz, *U.S. v. Battle et al.*, 2006; testimony of Luis DeVilliers, *U.S. v. Battle et al.*, 2006.

"Charley, my friend, you're in a lot of trouble": Statements, depositions, and testimony of Charley Hernandez.

Chino gives ultimatum to Charley: Ibid.

Charley meets at home of Battle: Ibid.

Presence of Battle Jr. at meeting: Ibid.; Battle Jr. testified for the defense in *Florida v. Battle,* 1977, and denied that he was present at this meeting.

Manolo Lucier: The kidnapping of Fangio is another of the events that has become part of the lore of the Cuban Revolution. The leader of the kidnappers, Oscar Lucero Moya, was captured by Batista intelligence police, then tortured and murdered. Thomas, *Cuba,* p. 651.

Charley and Ernestico's phone conversation: Transcript of phone conversation, entered into evidence, *Florida v. Battle,* 1977; statements, depositions, and testimony of Charley Hernandez.

Charley meets with Battle and Chino again: Statements, depositions, and testimony of Charley Hernandez.

"Miguelito, what do you think?": In his testimony, Battle Jr. denied that this conversation took place.

"You know, that Ernestico Torres is going to take you down": Statements, depositions, and testimony of Charley Hernandez.

Battle said, "I hear you have a nice family": Ibid.

Box seats at Yankee Stadium, 1976: Interview with Joaquin Deleon Jr.; interview with Jack Blumenfeld.

Upbringing of Battle Jr.: Statements, depositions, and testimony of José Miguel Battle Jr., *Florida v. Battle*, 1977; deposition and testimony of Battle Jr., *Florida v. Battle,* 1977; Hudson County Pretrial Intervention Project, Superintendent of New Jersey, File No. 76-1924. Report by Court Liaison Cynthia Land. April 4, 1979.

"They used to have their wives iron their money": Interview with Joaquin Deleon Jr.

Joking with Lieutenant Mona: Ibid.

Battle Jr. arrested for gun possession: Hudson County Pretrial Intervention Project, Superintendent of New Jersey, File No. 76-1924. Report by Court Liaison Cynthia Land. April 4, 1979.

"Arriving promptly for his appointments": Ibid.

Idalia observations re: Ernestico and Charley relationship: Deposition and testimony of Idalia Fernandez, *Florida v. Battle*, 1977.

"My friend, what have you been drinking?": Statements, depositions, and testimony of Charley Hernandez; deposition and testimony of Idalia Fernandez, *Florida v. Battle,* 1977.

Battle's reaction to Charley's "cockamamie story": Statements, depositions, and testimony of Charley Hernandez.

Shooting of Ernestico by Gustavo Battle and Monolo Lucier: Deposition and testimony of Idalia Fernandez, *Florida v. Battle*, 1977.

Battle and Acuna devise plan to kill Ernestico: Statements, depositions, and testimony of Charley Hernandez; testimony of Abraham Rydz, *U.S. v. Battle et al,* 2006.

Shooting of Idalia Fernandez and murder of Ernestico Torres: Public Safety Department, Dade County, multiple homicide reports, including interviews with people in the area and a schematic of the apartment, case No. 146689-V; Report of the Office of the Medical Examiner, Dade County, Case No. 76-1459, including autopsy of Ernesto Torres; police interview with Idalia Fernandez, translated by the State of Florida, exhibit 458-00625, *Florida v. Battle*, 1977; Louise Montgomery, "One Killed, One Hurt in Gunfire," *Miami Herald*, June 17, 1976; Deane E. Bostick, "Death of a Hit Man," *Master Detective,* June 1976.

In the police reports, the witness who saw three men fleeing the scene provided physical descriptions that were remarkably accurate: the injured man (Gustavo) was described as a Latin male, approximately forty years old, five foot seven or eight, approximately 160 pounds, with brown to graying hair and a distinctive bald spot. The man helping him (José Miguel) was described a Latin male, forty-five to fifty years old, 200 to 250 pounds, five foot ten or eleven, with "a large beer gut." The driver (Chino Acuna) was described as mulatto, twenty-five to twenty-eight years of age, five foot eight, 150 to 160 pounds, slim, with "black kinky hair."

"I need you to come over to the place where I'm staying": Testimony of Oracio Altuve, *U.S. v. Battle et al.,* 2006.

"You won't have problems with Ernestico Torres no more": Testimony of Abraham Rydz, *U.S. v. Battle et al.,* 2006.

8. COUNTERREVOLUTION

Palulu on trial for Pedro Battle killing: Shanks manuscript.

Palulu at Dannemora prison: Ibid.

CIA file on Eugenio Rolando Martinez: Glenn Garvin, "Miami's Watergate Mystery Man at the Heart of Newly Revealed CIA Report," *Miami Herald,* August 30, 2016; CIA Official Watergate History—Working Draft. Obtained by Judicial Watch via FOIA. http://www.judicialwatch.org; James Rosen, "Watergate: CIA Withheld Data on Double Agent," FoxNews.com, August 30, 2016.

Car bombing of Orlando Letelier: Timothy S. Robinson and Stephen J. Lynton, "Evidence Links Letelier Death to Anti-Castro Unit," *Washington Post,* February 1, 1977.

"Are you the wife of Orlando Letelier?": Jeff Stein, "An Army in Exile," *New York Magazine,* September 10, 1979.

Bombing of Cubana de Aviación Flight 455: The National Security Archive maintains an entire section devoted to CIA documents obtained via FOIA on the bombing of Cubana de Aviación Flight 455, under the heading *NSA Archive Briefing Book No. 202.*

Formation of CORU: Ann Louise Bardach, *Without Fidel: A Death Foretold in Miami, Havana and Washington* (New York: Scribner, 2009), pp. 117–19; CIA report on Luis Clement Posada Carriles re: Anti-Fidel Castro Activities, declassified 2003, accessed via NSA.

Car bombing of Emilio Milián: Dade County Public Safety Department, Organized Crime Bureau Report. Meeting with WQBA Director E. Milian. Submitted by D. Benitez, Terrorist & Security Unit. January 25, 1977.

Killing of Juan José Peruyero: Dick Russell, "Little Havana's Reign of Terror," *Miami New Times,* October 29, 1976; Dan Christiansen, "The Coast Guard Memorandum: Miami Police Have Some New Leads in Their Hunt for Exile Assassins. Too Bad They Couldn't Get the Information from Official Sources," *Miami Magazine,* April 1978.

"Cuban exile terrorists have blown up ship": Report: Metro-Dade Police Department, Organized Crime Bureau (OCB), File on Cuban Exile Terrorism. June 18, 1979; Metro-Dade Police Department, OCB, list of all Cuban terrorist bombings 1975 to 1983, June 29, 1983.

Anthony "Fat Tony" Salerno: James Dao, "Anthony (Fat Tony) Salerno, 80, Dies in Prison," *New York Times,* July 29, 1992.

Salerno 1976 tax indictment: Arnold H. Lubasch, "Salerno, 67, Given 6 Months in Prison in Gambling Case," *New York Times,* April 20, 1978.

Cuban bolita bankers cultivate Salerno: Testimony of Abraham Rydz, *U.S. v. Battle,* 2006; interview with David Shanks; interview with Humberto Dávila Jr.; Shanks interview of Robert Hopkins.

Isleño-Battle rivalry: Interview with George Dávila; testimony of Abraham Rydz, *U.S. v. Battle,* 2006; Shanks interview with Hopkins.

"Hombre, did you hear?": Statements, depositions, and testimony of Charley Hernandez.

Charley's arrest by Lieutenant Mona: Ibid.

"Carlos Hernandez, we need to speak with you for a minute": Ibid.

Kalafus interviews Charley: Transcript of interview, December 23, 1976; deposition and testimony of Detective Richard Kalafus; statements, depositions, and testimony of Charley Hernandez.

Kalafus's background: Interview with David Shanks; Shanks manuscript; deposition and testimony of Richard Kalafus.

Charley gives statement to Hudson County prosecutors: Transcript of interview, December 27 and 28, 1976.

Detective Julio Ojeda: Interview with Julio Ojeda, February 6, 2016.

Ernesto's phone conversation with his mother: Transcript of conversation (undated), recording made by Ernesto Torres, entered into evidence, *Florida v. Battle,* 1977; deposition and testimony of Julio Ojeda, *Florida v. Battle,* 1977.

Miami detectives interview Charley: Transcript of interview, May 5, 1977; deposition and testimony of Julio Ojeda, *Florida v. Battle,* 1977.

Charley relocated to Miami: Deposition and testimony of Julio Ojeda; statements, depositions, and testimony of Charley Hernandez.

Masferrer killing: Interview with Julio Ojeda.

Johnny Roselli murder: Nicholas Gage, "Mafia Said to Have Slain Roselli Because of His Senate Testimony," *New York Times,* February 25, 1977; interview with Julio Ojeda.

"Santo was very cordial": Interview with Julio Ojeda.

"Your family is in danger": Interview with Carol Daley and Kelly Noguerol.

Adventures of Carol and Kelly: Ibid.

Battle arrest: Deposition and testimony of Detective Richard Kalafus; Louis Salome, "Opa-Locka Murder Suspect Arrested," *Miami News,* July 7, 1977.

9. THE COUNSELOR

Raymond A. Brown: Michael Y. Park, "Raymond Brown Believes No One Is Beyond Redemption," *New Jersey Super Lawyers,* April 2009; Joseph Berger, "Raymond A. Brown, Civil Rights Lawyer, Dies at 94," *New York Times,* October 11, 2009; David Gianbusso, "Prominent N.J. Attorney, Civil-Rights Leader Ray Brown Dies at Age 94," *Newark Star-Ledger,* October 10, 2009; Richard J. H. Johnston, "Butenko and Ivanov Guilty in Spy Case," *New York Times,* December 3, 1964; Walter H. Waggoner, "Joanne Chesimard Convicted in Killing of Jersey Trooper," *New York Times,* March 26, 1977; interview with Jack Blumenfeld.

Alfredo Duran suggests Jack Blumenfeld: Interview with Jack Blumenfeld.

Brown and Blumenfeld meet Battle: Ibid.

"Listen, I'm not afraid of death": Ibid.

Charley goes to work for DEA: A letter from Detective Ojeda to the Miami office of the DEA was a crucial reason Charley was hired. Wrote Ojeda, "This is to verify that informant Charles Hernandez was a paid informant for the Hudson County Prosecutor's Office from December 26, 1976, through April 23, 1977. During this period of time, he was instrumental in solving eleven murders which occurred in New York and Union City, New Jersey."

In order to be hired, Charley had to first take and pass a polygraph test, which he did in Miami on April 27, 1977.

Mario Escandar: Marjorie Hunter, "130 Seized in Drug Raids Here and in 9 Cities," *New York Times,* June 22, 1970; *Escandar v. Ferguson,* U.S. District Court of South Florida, October 5, 1977; Arnold Markowitz, "Valachi to Genovese, Mario Knew Them All," *Miami Herald,* June 16, 1982; Jeff Leen, "Escandar Dies in Prison; His Drug Tales Sent 4 to Jail," *Miami Herald,* August 20, 1986; Carl Hiaasen, "Dade's Scarface Played System Adroitly and Lost," *Miami Herald,* August 22, 1986.

Centac-26 relationship with narcos: Paul Eddy, Hugo Sabogal, and Sara Walden, *The Cocaine Wars* (New York: Norton, 1988), pp. 26, 70–71, 82–83, 90–96, 200, 268–72, 347–53.

"We want to put you in the home of Mario Escandar": Statements, depositions, and testimony of Charley Hernandez.

"Mario couldn't live without cocaine": Ibid.

"It was unbelievable": Ibid.

"Ojeda was getting laid by Idalia": Deposition of Charley Hernandez, *Florida v. Acuna,* 1984. Charley was not questioned about his relationship with Escandar or Ojeda's relationship with Idalia until he was deposed for the Acuna trial in 1984.

Escandar on Ojeda-Idalia relationship: Testimony of Mario Escandar, *U.S. v. Ojeda et al.,* June 1982.

Ojeda's relationship with Idalia Fernandez: Interview with Julio Ojeda. When asked point-blank by this author about allegations that he had an improper sexual relationship with Idalia, Ojeda answered, "That's bullshit."

Blumenfeld goes to Yankee Stadium: Interview with Jack Blumenfeld.

Florida v. Battle, **1977:** Entire trial transcript, including opening statements, testimony of Ojeda, Kalafus, Idalia Fernandez, Monino Herrera, and Charley Hernandez; interview with Jack Blumenfeld; interview with Julio Ojeda.

Battle admits being shooter to Blumenfeld's secretary: Interview with Jack Blumenfeld. Julie, Blumenfeld's former secretary, declined to be interviewed for this book.

Victory party at Escandar's house: Testimony of Mario Escandar, *U.S. v. Ojeda et al.,* 1982; testimony of George Pontigo, *U.S. v. Ojeda et al.,* June 1982; Arnold Markowitz, "3 Officers, Former Magistrate Sniffed Cocaine, Witness Says," *Miami Herald,* June 3, 1982; Arnold Markowitz, "Witness Says He Gave Cocaine to Policeman," *Miami Herald,* June 9, 1982; Arnold Markowitz, "Ex-Detective's Words Come Back on Tape to Haunt," *Miami Herald,* June 11, 1982.

"You'll have to be patient": Interview with Jack Blumenfeld.

Old gun possession charge against Battle: Ibid.

Battle's prison meeting with Abraham Rydz: Testimony of Abraham Rydz, *U.S. v. Battle et al.,* 2006.

"I want you to look out for my boy": Ibid.

Battle's prison meeting with Salerno and Cafaro: Shanks interview with Vincent Cafaro.

Murder attempt on Palulu and Gerardo Juan: NYPD police report, Cuban Task Force, Detective Richard Kalafus, April 26, 1984.

Another stabbing of Palulu at Dannemora prison: Criminal History, Disposition and Corrections Data, Jose P. Enriquez, State of New York, Division of Criminal Justice Services, October 12, 1983; Shanks manuscript.

10. CORRUPTION

Search warrant executed at Escandar's house: *U.S. v. Ojeda et al.,* 1982.

"jeopardizing the department's credibility": Paul Kaplan and Bob Murphy, "Cops Probe Witness Had Homicide Files in Home," *Miami News,* December 24, 1979.

Indictment and trial of Ojeda et al.: The trial of the corrupt police officers, with Mario Escandar as the star witness, took place in 1982 and was one of the most lurid such proceedings in the city's history—though it could be argued that it would be surpassed by even more outrageous police narco corruption cases in subsequent years.

The following articles are all by Arnold Markowitz, *Miami Herald:* "Eight Policemen Sold Out to Racketeer, Jury Told," May 28, 1982; "2 Officers, Former Magistrate Sniffed Cocaine," June 3, 1982; "Ex-Officer's Testimony Similar to Racketeer's," June 17, 1982; "He Took Cash, Whiskey and Drugs as Gifts, Not Bribes, Ex-Officer Says," June 18, 1982; "Ex-Policeman Denies More Crimes Than He's Accused Of," August 18, 1982; "4 Ex-Detectives Convicted," September 24, 1982.

The trial of the officers lasted sixty-three days. Two officers—Charley Zatrepalek and George Pontigo—made deals with the government and testified against the other officers. In the end, the verdict was mixed. Fabio Alonso was found guilty of five charges and not guilty of one; Pedro Izaguirre was found guilty of five and not guilty of eight charges; Robert Derringer was found guilty of two and not guilty of eight; Julio Ojeda was found guilty of eleven charges and not guilty of eight. One officer, Raymond Eggler, was charged with six crimes and acquitted on all counts.

After the trial, Mario Escandar received a sentence of fifteen years for his crimes. He died from a heart attack on August 15, 1986, at the age of fifty-one, while serving his sentence. Jeff Leen, "Escandar Dies in Prison; His Tales Sent 4 to Jail," *Miami Herald,* August 20, 1986; Carl Hiaasen, "Dade's Scarface Played System Adroitly and Lost," *Miami Herald,* August 22, 1986.

Police shooting of May 16, 1979: Interview with David Shanks; Shanks manuscript.

Court of Appeal vacates Battle's conviction: Interview with Jack Blumenfeld.

Blumenfeld negotiates plea deal: Ibid.

Murder of Eulalio José Negrin: Karen Yaremko, "Negrin Shot in Union City: Pro-Castro Leader Murdered," *Hudson Dispatch,* November 26, 1979; Karen Yaremko, "Union City Cops Can't Protect Cuban '75,'" *Hudson Dispatch,* November 27, 1979; Associated Press, "Police Quiz Cubans Regarding Enemies of Murdered Man," *Asbury Park Press,* November 27, 1979.

At the 1984 trial of Eduardo Arocena, leader of Omega 7, FBI special agent Larry Wack testified that Arocena told him the names of the two gunmen, and that he, Arocena, had contracted the hit on Negrin. At the time, Arocena was supplying information to Wack on the possibility that he would become an informant. Arocena admitted that Omega 7 had been created partly to take credit for certain criminal acts and serve as a smokescreen for the Cuban Nationalist Movement led by Guillermo Novo. Testimony of FBI special agent Larry Wack, *U.S. v. Arocena,* August 28, 1984.

Cuban anti-Castro activity in New York–New Jersey area: Daniel Hays, "Organized Crime Now Has a Latin Flavor," *New York Daily News,* January 30, 1978; Daniel Hays, "Cuban Gangsters Are Using Military Tactics," *New York Daily News,* January 31, 1978; Jeff Stein, "An Army in Exile," *New York Magazine,* September 10, 1979; Richard T. Pienciak, "Slain Cuban Called Top-Level Castro Spy," *Weekend Dispatch,* September 13, 1980.

FBI and Omega 7: Testimony of FBI special agent Larry Wack, *U.S. v. Arocena,* August 28, 1984. Wack testified that the task force was first formulated in 1975.

Battle pleads in court of Judge Sepe: Interview with Jack Blumenfeld.

"That judge and his wife had a nice vacation in Vegas": Interview with Joaquin Deleon Jr.

Operation Court Broom: Mike Clary, "Miami Court Scandals Reveal Tarnish on the Scales of Justice," *Los Angeles Times,* May 18, 1992; Warren Richey, "'Court Broom' Judge Gets 15 Years in Corruption Case," *Florida Sun-Sentinel,* July 16, 1993; Staff report, "Ex-Judge Admits Taking Bribes," *Florida Sun-Sentinel,* March 3, 2000.

Rydz and Battle Jr. take over the bolita business: Testimony of Abraham Rydz, *U.S. v. Battle et al.,* 2006; interview with Jack Blumenfeld.

Derivation of "the Corporation": Testimony of Abraham Rydz, *U.S. v. Battle et al.,* 2006.

Harlem as fertile ground for the numbers racket: Charles Grutner, "Dimes Make Millions for Numbers Racket," *New York Times,* June 28, 1964; Fred Powledge, "Pick a Number from 1 to 999," *New York Times,* December 6, 1964; Thomas A. Johnson, "Numbers Called Harlem's Balm," *New York Times,* March 1, 1971.

"Who's behind these new bolita stores?": Shanks interview with Robert Hopkins (undated); testimony of Abraham Rydz, *U.S. v. Battle et al.,* 2006.

Isleño-Hopkins relationship: Shanks interview with Hopkins; interview with Humberto Dávila Jr.; interview with George Dávila.

Hopkins, Petey Beck DiPalermo, and the Lucchese crime family: Shanks interview with Hopkins; Don Gentile, "Life in the Fast Lane and a Collision with the Law," *New York Daily News*, September 2, 1988.

Birth of La Compañía: Shanks interview with Hopkins; testimony of Abraham Rydz, *U.S. v. Battle et al.,* 2006; testimony of Luis DeVilliers; interview with Humberto Dávila Jr.; interview with George Dávila.

Conrado "Lalo" Pons: Testimony of Abraham Rydz, *U.S. v. Battle et al.,* 2006.

Nene Marquez endorese Pons: Ibid.

UNESCO fund: Testimony of Abraham Rydz, *U.S. v. Battle et al.,* 2006.

Entries from NYPD Task Force intelligence files: In the early 1980s, the Detective Bureau Manhattan (DBM) Task Force kept extensive intelligence files on the subject of Cuban organized crime. The head of this task force was Detective Richard Kalafus.

La Compañía doing well: Interview with Humberto Dávila Jr.; interview with George Dávila; Shanks interview with Hopkins.

Origins of the two-block rule: Testimony of Vincent Cafaro, *U.S. v. Manna et al.,* March 10, 1989; Shanks/Rosario interview with Vincent Cafaro, January 31, 1998; Shanks interview with Robert Hopkins.

"I'm here to see if we can't settle this": Shanks interview with Robert Hopkins.

Meeting between Isleño, Battle, and Hopkins in Fort Lauderdale: Interview with George Dávila; Shanks interview with Robert Hopkins.

"It's going to get ugly in New York": Interview with George Dávila.

11. SMOKE AND FIRE

Palulu released from Dannemora prison: Criminal History, Disposition and Corrections Data, Jose P. Enriquez, State of New York, Division of Criminal Justice Services, October 12, 1983; Shanks manuscript.

Attack on Palulu and Argelio Cuesta on street: NYPD Confidential Report, Intelligence Received from Informant, Det. R. Kalafus, April 26, 1984.

Marielitos: Refugees from Mariel were not predominantly criminals nor mental patients, but they were all economically destitute. See Joan Didion, *Miami* (New York: Random House: 1987), pp. 17–18, 41–42.

Attack on Palulu and Cuesta at Riverdale condo: NYPD Confidential Report, Intelligence Received from Informant, Det. R. Kalafus, November 11, 1983.

Battle and Santería: Interview with Jack Blumenfeld; interview with Joaquin Deleon Jr.

Hit attempt on Palulu in Belmont: NYPD Confidential Report, Intelligence Received from Informant, Det. R. Kalafus, April 26, 1984.

Battle standing over Palulu: Deposition of Detective Richard Kalafus, *Florida v. Acuna,* 1984; Shanks interview with Kalafus.

Rydz, Battle Jr., and Union Financial Research: Testimony of Abraham Rydz, *U.S. v. Battle et al.;* copious financial records for Union Financial Research and other companies cofounded by Rydz and Battle were obtained via subpoena for *U.S. v. Battle et al.,* 2006.

Planning the hospital hit on Palulu: Testimony of Abraham Rydz, *U.S. v. Battle et al.;* Shanks interview with Detective Kalafus.

The hit on Palulu: The murder of Palulu generated dozens of NYPD reports, starting with crime scene reports from the first investigators on the scene, the Bronx Detectives Area Nightwatch, to the 48th Precinct Homicide Detectives unit that interviewed everyone from Leroy Middleton, Palulu's roommate, to Deloris Edwards and Ramona Baptista, the night nurses on duty, to each and every patient interned on the seventh floor.

Police efforts to solve the homicide ranged far and wide. Through various informants, Detective Kalafus learned that Conrad Pons was the paymaster for the hit. Initial tips suggested that the gunman was a person named "Pepito," but later Kalafus was told that Matanzas was the gunman. In the days and weeks following the murder, all of these men were arrested, held for questioning, and then released for lack of evidence.

Dominguez was never arrested, and only later, after he was murdered in the Bronx, did interviews with street informants reveal that he was killed at the behest of Battle, who heard that he had been talking publicly about his role as the gunman in the Palulu hit.

An unusual addendum to the Palulu murder emerged in October 1997, when Detective David Shanks interviewed Alejandro Lagos regarding criminal activities of the Corporation. The Lagos interview, as described below, is captured in Detective Shanks's investigative report from October 16, 1997, Investigation into the Illegal Activities of Jose Miguel Battle, et al. (Case No. 331829-J.) Lagos was the person whom Battle had assaulted in 1975, believing that he had been in a fistfight in the street with Miguel Jr. Lagos later went to work for the organization. Lagos told Shanks that in 1984 El Padrino had asked him if he wanted to kill Palulu for $50,000. Lagos turned down the contract but offered to play a subsidiary role in the conspiracy. Battle paid Lagos $5,000 to steal a car to be used as a getaway vehicle and also to procure a male nurse's uniform. Battle told Lagos to get rid of the car and all of the items inside.

As Lagos would tell Detective Shanks, weeks later, Lagos was escorted to the getaway car by Rene Avila, the newspaper publisher and alleged Battle associate. Avila told Lagos to get rid of the car and all items inside.

Inside the car Lagos found a male nurse's uniform consisting of white pants, a shirt, and a lab coat. He noticed that there was blood on parts of the uniform. Attached to the lab coat was a plastic clip-on hospital ID card. In a small bag were a stethoscope and a handgun—the Palulu murder weapon.

When he got home, Lagos rolled up the gun in the nurse's uniform and stuffed them into an empty five-gallon metal paint can. He put a twenty-five-pound dumbbell inside the can with the items, then sealed the can as tight as possible. He put the can in the car and drove to a nearby river in Edgewater, New Jersey. He dumped the can into the river and watched it sink. Then he drove to an abandoned lot, doused the car in gasoline, and set it on fire.

A few years later, Lagos was in New Jersey's Northern State Prison on a narcotics possession charge. He was housed there with a fellow inmate he knew from the

Corporation named Oscar Rodriguez. They had numerous conversations about their days with the Battle organization: Rodriguez told Lagos that he was the one who had killed Palulu.

He described the hit in detail: how Battle wanted to use a gunman from the New Jersey side of the organization because there had already been too much police heat in New York. Rodriguez dressed in a male nurse's uniform and went to Palulu's room unchallenged. He shot Palulu in the forehead, right between the eyes. Rodriguez noted that he got some blood on his nurse's uniform while committing the murder. Then he fled the hospital. He told Lagos that he did the hit because he needed the money.

Rodriguez was never charged with the crime. Avila was never questioned about Lagos's account and was not charged with wrongdoing. To this day, the Palulu murder case remains unsolved.

"It's done. Palulu is dead": Testimony of Abraham Rydz, *U.S. v. Battle et al.,* 2006.

"Let's drink champagne and raise a toast to our enemies": Many people noted that this was a phrase Battle often used; interview with Joaquin Deleon Jr.; testimony of Abraham Rydz, *U.S. v. Battle, et al.,* 2006; interview with Jack Blumenfeld.

Rydz and Battle Jr. create financial structure of the Corporation: Testimony of Abraham Rydz, *U.S. v. Battle et al.,* 2006.

Use of Maurilio Marquez: Ibid.

Orestas Vidan as "the Cook": Ibid.

"We had a saying about this era": Interview with George Dávila.

Distribution of profits: Testimony of Abraham Rydz, *U.S. v. Battle et al.,* 2006.

Transportation of cash: Ibid.

Rydz and Battle caught with cash at airport: Ibid.

Meetings between Hopkins, the Italians, and the Cubans: Testimony of Abraham Rydz, *U.S. v. Battle et al.,* 2006; Shanks interview with Hopkins.

"Isleño. He's sneaky": Testimony of Abraham Rydz, *U.S. v. Battle et al.,* 2006.

Gandhi **on the marquee:** Ibid.

"Tony, I'm never the one to throw the first stone": Ibid.

The shooting of Pedro Acosta: William G. Blair, "Trump Tower Resident Held in 72nd St. Killing," *New York Times,* March 14, 1986; Kirk Johnson, "Crime Group Feud on Gambling Seen," *New York Times,* March 15, 1986; Shanks interview with Hopkins.

Willie Diaz: The details of Diaz's upbringing in Brooklyn, his criminal background, and his involvement with the Corporation are revealed in numerous sources, including police and prosecutor interviews of Willie Diaz; statements, deposition, and testimony of Willie Diaz, *New York v. Pons et al.,* 1987; tape recording of Kalafus phone interview of Willie Diaz; Shanks interview of Willie Diaz, August 22, 1997.

"Our organization is like a Mafia family of Cubans": Statements, deposition, and testimony of Willie Diaz, *New York v. Pons et al.,* 1987.

The various arsons: John Randazzo and Paul Meskill, "Cuba Mafia 11 Held in 8 Deaths," *New York Daily News,* October 8, 1985; Leonard Buder, "11 Are Accused in

Fatal Blazes at Betting Sites," *New York Times,* October 8, 1985. Documents for *New York v. Pons et al.,* 1987, and *U.S. v. Battle et al.,* 2006, list all of the arson deaths in great detail.

12. A PRAYER FOR IDALIA

Battle estate (El Zapotal): Financial record for El Zapotal, Inc., entered into evidence for *U.S. v. Battle et al.,* 2006.

Mamey sapote: Kenneth F. Kiple, *The Cambridge World History of Food* (Cambridge: Cambridge University Press, 2001), p. 1808.

"Stop the car!": Interview with Carlos Rodriguez.

Arrest of Chino Acuna: "FBI Agents Nab Alleged Hit Man," *Miami Herald,* March 29, 1984; "FBI Arrests Suspect in '76 Murder," *Miami News,* March 29, 1984.

Idalia in New York: Shanks interview with Detective Richard Kalafus, Case No. 331829-J, January 23, 1998. By this time Shanks was working with U.S. Attorney's Office under AUSA Lawrence D. LaVecchio.

Ojeda visits Idalia: Ibid. NYPD Report, Housing PD/Major Case Squad, January 11, 1985. Dade Co. prosecutor Michael Corneley interviewed via phone by NYPD Detective H. Sanchez: "Mr. Corneley stated that he has knowledge that a Det. in the Miami P.D. who is no longer working for the dept. had also visited Ms Fernandez in New York, and said Det. is Julio Ojeda."

Ojeda conviction on racketeering charges: Arnold Markowitz, "4 Detectives Convicted," *Miami Herald,* September 24, 1982; Mike Boehm, "Ex-Police Get Terms in Prison; Dade Officers 'Led Double Lives,'" *Miami Herald,* December 21, 1982.

Blumenfeld uses Ojeda as private investigator: Interview with Jack Blumenfeld.

Kalafus visits Idalia: Shanks interview with Detective Richard Kalafus.

Charley Hernandez 1984 deposition: *Florida v. Acuna,* 1984.

Idalia's life at West 90th Street building: NYPD homicide file, Case No. 1200. Interviews of tenants at 133 W. 90th Street and others who knew Idalia Fernandez, conducted by Homicide Major Case Squad, Housing police and Det. Richard Kalafus.

"El Gordo himself will want to talk to you about this": Shanks/Kalafus/McCabe interviews with Willie Diaz, July 23 through July 25, 1997. A series of interviews were conducted with Diaz by Shanks, Kalafus, and Detective Kenneth McCabe, Manhattan office of the U.S. Attorney. Report filed by Shanks on August 22, 1997, Case No. 221829-J.

Murder of Idalia: NYPD Forensic Report, Crime Scene Unit, complaint No. 12069, December 13, 1984; Autopsy of Idalia Fernandez, Case No. M849224. Findings: Five penetrating gunshot wounds of head and neck with injury to brain and spinal cord. Cause of death: Multiple gunshot wounds to head and neck with internal injury and hemorrhage.

"There is no evidence the murder of Fernandez": Al Messerschmidt and Larry Bevins, "Only Witness to '76 Murder Slain in New York," *Miami Herald,* December 5, 1984.

The reasons for Idalia's murder were not hard to fathom; it had everything to do with her role as a potential witness. Four months before the murder, at a pretrial hearing before Judge Sidney Shapiro, it became clear that the issue of Idalia and Charley Hernandez using cocaine and marijuana at the house of Mario Escandar was going to be a major issue at the upcoming trial. The lawyer for Chino Acuna made it clear that all evidence of wrongdoing by police detectives handling Idalia and Charley should be obtained under subpoena and presented to the defense as legitimate discovery material. Said the lawyer, "While in Mario Escandar's home, various homicide detectives visited her and engaged in drug usage . . . Also, during the same time frame, these Metro homicide detectives were involved in a racketeering enterprise with Mario Escandar." The lawyer made it clear that the detectives' relationship with Idalia would be a major component of his defense.

None of the detectives were mentioned by name, but it was clear that *Florida v. Acuna*—if defense counsel had his way—was going to be a reexamination of the sleaze and corruption surrounding the detectives' handling of Idalia Fernandez as a witness. It was possible that the names of Julio Ojeda and others would once again be dragged through the mud, and further criminal charges against the detectives were a possibility.

Origins of the President's Commission on Organized Crime: David G. Schwartz, "The Significance of the President's Commission on Organized Crime (1984–1986) Gambling Hearings," *Gaming Law Review and Economics* 17 (November 8, 2013).

Manhattan hearings of the commission: *Organized Crime and Gambling,* Record of Hearings VII, President's Commission on Organized Crime, June 24–25, 1985.

Lombardi's statement: *Organized Crime and Gambling,* Record of Hearings VII, President's Commission on Organized Crime, June 24–25, 1985, pp. 101–11.

Operation Greenback: Ibid. " 'Operation Greenback P.R.' Probes $14 Million-a-Week 'Laundry' Scam," *San Juan Star,* June 25, 1985.

Battle subpoena: Eric Schmitt, "U.S. Panel Says Cuban Emigres Run a Bet Ring," *New York Times,* June 25, 1985.

El Enmascarado: Shanks interview with Detective Richard Kalafus; Sherry Conohan, "Operations of 'Cuban Mafia' Outlined by Mystery Witness," *Asbury Park Press,* June 25, 1985; Eric Schmitt, "U.S. Panel Says Cuban Emigres Run a Bet Ring," *New York Times,* June 25, 1985; Gary Langer, "Crime Commission Says Organized Crime Profits from Gambling," Associated Press, June 27, 1985.

Battle at the hearings: Eric Schmitt, "U.S. Panel Says Cuban Emigres Run a Bet Ring," *New York Times,* June 25, 1985.

Identity of El Enmascarado: Some of the investigators involved now know the identity of El Enmascarado. It is believed that even though decades have passed, if the identity of this person were revealed it could be a danger to the person's family and/or associates, and so the name will not be disclosed.

"Bullshit, that's his response": Jim McGee and Jose de Cordoba, "Crime Boss Rules with a Deadly Fist," *Miami Herald,* August 26, 1985.

"Everything the commission said isn't true": Ellen Hampton and Steve Konicki, "Alleged 'Godfather' Lives Quiet Life on Ranch Here," *Miami News,* June 27, 1985.

Indictment of Lalo Pons: Leonard Bruder, "11 Are Accused in Fatal Blazes at Betting Sites," *New York Times,* October 8, 1985; John Randazzo and Paul Meskill, " 'Cuba Mafia' 11 Held in 8 Deaths," *New York Daily News,* October 8, 1985.

Isleño Dávila leaves the United States: Interview with Humberto Dávila Jr.; interview with Michael Dávila; interview with George Dávila.

13. COCKFIGHTER

Battle caught by Maria Josefa: Memo Florida Department of Law Enforcement, Case No. 590-48-7001, report filed jointly from SA Jose A. Valdes and CIA agent Vonnie Ames to Bureau Chief Rolando D. Bolanos. Subject: "The following is a chronological criminal history and intelligence summary on Jose Miguel Battle Sr. and his Organization." June 27, 1984.

Battle Sr.–Battle Jr. relationship: Testimony of Abraham Rydz, *U.S. v. Battle et al.,* 2006; interview with Joel Kaplan, February 6, 2016; interview with Jack Blumenfeld; interview with Joaquin Deleon Jr.; interview with Carlos Rodriguez.

Kidnapping of Battle Jr.: Interview with Sergeant Oscar Vigoa, May 9, 2016.

"It was a beautiful home": Ibid.

"He seemed to be very calm": Ibid.

Conviction of Lalo Pons: "Man Is Convicted in Betting Parlor Fires," *New York Times,* October 12, 1986.

Luis Samoza and the 2506 Brigade: Interview with Raul Martinez; Rasenbeger, *The Brilliant Disaster,* pp. 6, 97.

Formation of the Contras: Glenn Garvin, *Everybody Had His Own Gringo: The CIA and the Contras* (Washington, DC: Brassey's, 1992); Peter Kornbluh and Malcolm Byrne, *The Iran-Contra Scandal: The Declassified History* (New York: New Press, 1993); *Report of the Congressional Committees Investigating the Irish-Contra Affair* (New York: Times Books, 1988).

Contra connection in South Florida: Buddy Nevins, "Exiles Remember Bay of Pigs by Vowing to Support Contras," *Florida Sun-Sentinel,* April 18, 1986; Marshall Ingwerson, "Miami a Rebel Base Again; First Anti-Castro Cubans, Now Nicaraguan 'Contra' Forces Operate Out of Florida City," *Christian Science Monitor,* May 30, 1986; "Bay of Pigs Survivors Find Common Cause with Contras," *Washington Post,* October 26, 1986; James LeMoyne, "First Group of the Contras Completes Florida Training," *New York Times,* January 9, 1987; "Cuban-American Indicted: Six Accused of Training Contras in Florida Camps," Associated Press, August 23, 1988.

Fuentes brothers and the Contras: Interview with the Fuentes brothers.

2506 Brigade Museum: David Smiley, "Miami's Bay of Pigs Museum Won't Be Declared Historic," *Miami Herald,* November 3, 2016.

The museum is run by the 2506 Brigade Association, which selects a new president every few years. Felix Rodriguez has served as president on a number of occasions. He remembers one year, in the late 1980s, when José Miguel Battle showed up for the annual April 17 commemoration of the invasion. By then, after copious media coverage of the Presidential Crime Commission hearings, he was a notorious crime figure. Said Rodriguez, "He wouldn't come inside. He said he didn't want to tarnish the reputation of the event." Rodriguez added, "I don't approve of what he became, but I believe that was an honorable thing to do." Interview with Felix Rodriguez.

Battle donates to the Contras: Interview with the Fuentes brothers.

Felix Rodriguez and the Iran-Contra hearings: Interview with Felix Rodriguez; Jay Nordlinger, "The Anti-Che: Felix Rodriguez, Freedom Fighter and Patriot," *National Review,* August 7, 2013.

"I had a commitment to the Contras": Felix I. Rodriguez with John Weisman, *Shadow Warrior: The CIA Hero of a Hundred Unknown Battles* (New York: Pocket Books, 1990), pp. 271–72.

Rodriguez-Posada relationship: Ibid., pp. 290–92; FBI interview with Posada in Tegucigalpa, Honduras, February 7, 1992; interview with Posada.

Shanks transferred to Vice: Shanks manuscript.

Sergeant James "Jimmy" Boyd: Interview with Kenny Rosario, February 15, 2017; Shanks manuscript.

Miss One Hundred: Shanks manuscript.

Henry Lee leads to José Pulido: Ibid

"I don't want to hear any more about Leggett": Ibid.

Rydz's reaction to the arson wars: Testimony of Abraham Rydz, *U.S. v. Battle et al.,* 2006.

Birth of Susan Rydz: Interview with Susan Rydz, September 2, 2016.

Rydz's attitudes toward Nene Marquez: Testimony of Abraham Rydz, *U.S. v. Battle et al.,* 2006.

Rydz leaves the bolita business: Ibid.

Memorial service for Richard Battle: Testimony of Luis Perez, *U.S. v. Battle et al.,* 2006.

"This is the day I'm leaving": Ibid.

$2 million payout on the day Rydz leaves the business: Testimony of Abraham Rydz, *U.S. v. Battle et al.,* 2006; testimony of Luis Perez, *U.S. v. Battle et al.,* 2006.

Raid on cockfight near Hialeah Gardens: Interview with Willy Vigoa, June 15, 2016; Shanks manuscript.

Raid on Club Campestre: Metro-Dade Police Department Offense-Incident Report, Fighting or baiting animals, statute 828.122(4)(b), Club Campestre Rincon Criolla, 18689 SW 105 Place. Officer reporting: W. Vigoa. February 3, 1989.

Upon questioning, Battle gave his occupation as "farmer."

"I wanted to try and get a feel for the man": Shanks manuscript.

14. DEAD BUT NOT DEAD

"The only reason I'm talking to you": Interview with Shanks; Shanks manuscript.

Killing of Juan Paez: Ibid.

Sergeant Boyd's obsession with Oscar Alvarez: Ibid.

Killing of Gerardo Zayas: Ibid.

"I'm here on behalf of my client, Oscar Alvarez": Ibid.

Sergeant Hinman approaches Vice: Ibid.

Shootout between Roque Torres and Carlos Capdavilla and Cache Jimenez: Metro-Dade Police Department, Incident Report, Attempted Murder, Case No. G-1402, Patrolman I. Torres. January 4, 1987.

Plot to kill Roque Torres: The conspiracy to murder Roque Torres was unusual on many levels, one being that law enforcement was secretly involved in the conspiracy from the very beginning. Consequently, documentation of the sequence of events through memos, reports, and transcripts is extensive. These include reports from Metro-Dade police, affidavits from various officers involved, internal reports from the Dade County correctional facility and James Archer Smith Hospital, as well as transcripts of secretly recorded conversations among the various parties involved in the conspiracy.

Rosa and Arroz meet with undercover agent Rosario: Interview with Kennedy "Kenny" Rosario, February 15, 2017.

"It's done": Transcript of phone conversation between Rosa Suarez and her son. Case No. 594624-J/156, solicitation to commit murder, December 19, 1989.

"Happy holidays. How can I help you?": Transcript of conversation between Rosa Suarez and hospital operator. Case No. 594624-J/156, solicitation to commit murder, December 20, 1989.

"Is this Jackson Memorial?": Transcript of conversation between Rosa Suarez and Medical Examiner's Office. Case No. 594624-J/156, solicitation to commit murder, December 21, 1989.

"Big problem": Shanks manuscript.

Cache Jimenez starting Battle's car: Testimony of David Shanks, *U.S. v. Battle,* 1997; testimony of David Shanks, *U.S. v. Battle et al.,* 2006.

"I do things for Battle": Transcript of conversation between Jimenez and Borges.

Police surveillance of hospital: Shanks manuscript.

"It was exhilarating to be sitting there": Ibid.

"El Gordo called me late": Transcript of conversation between Jimenez and Borges.

"Mr. Borges, you don't know me": Shanks manuscript.

Internal Affairs investigates leak: Ibid.

Rumors of triple homicide by Battle: Interview with Joaquin Deleon Jr.; Shanks manuscript.

"The way you people make money": Shanks manuscript.

"Garcia stated that he met Jose Miguel Battle": Report of interview, Metro-Dade Police Department. Interview conducted by Sgt. James Boyd and Det. I. Martinez of the Metro-Dade PD, Special Investigations Unit, at the Federal Court House via the U.S. Marshal's Office. April 2, 1993.

Involvement of Juan Cortes: Ibid.

Juan Pablo Alonso: Internal Revenue Service, Memorandum of interview, Juan Carlos Alonso interviewed by Det. Kenny Rosario and Det. Nick Pimentel, MDPD, and IRS SA Santiago T. Aquino. July 9, 2003.

Alonso meets Battle at Covadonga restaurant: Ibid.

Pepe Moranga facilitates coke deal: Shanks manuscript.

Battle dealings with Medellín Cartel: Ibid.

Prospects for a RICO case: Ibid.

Shanks assigned new partner (Bert Perez): Ibid.

15. OLD FRIENDS

Pepe Moranga murder: NYPD intelligence, crime scene, homicide, and medical examiner reports.

Angel Mujica murder: NYPD intelligence, crime scene, homicide, and medical examiner reports. Detective Muldoon from the 34th Precinct interviewed, among others, Ernesto Mujica, son of the deceased, who reported that "his father had been involved in the numbers business years ago and had left the United States to put the business in the past . . . The deceased started a successful irrigation parts company in Madrid, Spain and did not return to the United States until 1989 after his wife became ill with cancer and had gone to Sloane Kettering Hospital for treatment."

"There goes a dead man": Shanks manuscript.

Trajectory of bullet in Mujica hit: Report of Autopsy, Case No: M92-3536, Yvonne I. Milewski, M.D., City Medical Examiner. May 10, 1992.

Shanks and Perez in New York City: Shanks manuscript.

Shanks and Perez visit Lalo Pons in prison: Shanks manuscript.

Omar Broche murder: NYPD intelligence, crime scene, homicide, and medical examiner reports.

Luis DeVilliers Sr.: Proffer, Luis DeVillers Sr. (undated); testimony of DeVilliers Sr., *U.S. v. Battle et al.,* 2006.

DeVilliers approached by the Peruvians: Ibid.

DeVilliers approaches Battle with casino deal: Ibid.

Shanks squad learns about Roberto Parsons: Shanks manuscript.

Background on Roberto Parsons: Metro-Dade Police Department file, Investigation into the arrest of Roberto Parsons, Det. A. Moore, January 2, 1993.

Jorge Gonzalez as snitch: Interview report, U.S. Attorney's Office, Los Angeles, CA. Interview of Gonzalez conducted by AUSA Jackie Chooljian, Investigator Don Klein, Anaheim Police Dept., and Michael Brennan, attorney for Gonzalez. December 11, 1991.

Murder of Pepe Felipe: Metro-Dade Police Department, Case No. 17933-L, Det, Nicholas Fabregas, January 2, 1993.

"Listen, many years ago, when I was sitting in your seat": Transcript of Rydz conversation with Arcacha.

Hurricane Andrew: Mark Silva, Charles Strouse, and John Donnelly, "Destruction at Dawn," *Miami Herald,* August 25, 1992; "Path of Terror: Andrew Wreaks Havoc in S. Florida," *Florida Sun-Sentinel,* August, 25, 1992; Peter Slevin and Dexter Filkins, "WE NEED HELP: Bush Sends 2, Troops: 'More Destruction Than Any Disaster' Ever in America," *Miami Herald,* August 26, 1992.

Shanks's experience with Hurricane Andrew: Interview with David Shanks; Shanks manuscript.

16. STORMY WEATHER

"Polaco, you know anything about this casino?": Testimony of Abraham Rydz, *U.S. v. Battle et al.,* 2006.

"Here's what worries me": Ibid.

"He assured me they would not use Maurilio": Ibid.

Oracio Altuve: Interview with Kenny Rosario; Shanks manuscript.

Altuve account of post–Ernestico murder meeting with Battle: Testimony of Oracio Altuve, *U.S. v. Battle et al.,* 2006.

Shanks fight with Bert Perez: Interview with David Shanks; interview with Kenny Rosario; Shanks manuscript.

Shanks transferred to Kendall Division: Shanks manuscript.

Creation of Empresa de Inversiones Orientales: Testimony of DeVilliers, *U.S. v. Battle et al.,* 2006.

Casino Crillón history: The rise and fall of the casino in Lima, Peru, would ultimately become one of the major criminal narratives in *U.S. v. Battle et al.,* and as such was thoroughly investigated. Financial documents were amassed, and many of the key players involved in the creation and daily operation of the casino were tracked down and interviewed by Detective David Shanks and others. Later, most of these people were deposed by prosecutors, and many testified at trial. The documentation of this testimony was essential to the research for this book. The author has added to the public record, where possible, through additional interviews and also via travel to Lima to the site of the former Casino Crillón.

DeVilliers and Marquez meet with the Peruvians: Testimony of DeVilliers, *U.S. v. Battle et al.,* 2006; Federal Grand Jury testimony of Felix Fefer, Miami, FL, July 2, 2002.

Marquez travels to Aruba, meets Harold Marchena: Federal Grand Jury testimony of Harold Marchena, Miami, FL, June 25, 2002.

Rydz at racetrack, learns of Maurilio Marquez's involvement in casino: Testimony of Abraham Rydz, *U.S. v. Battle et al.,* 2006.

"Is it true?": Ibid.

"Lo hecho, hecho está": Ibid.

Rydz meets with Battle Jr.: Ibid.

Rydz travels to Switzerland: Ibid.

Parsons apprehension: Metro-Dade Police Department file, Investigation into the arrest of Roberto Parsons, Det. A. Moore, January 2, 1993.

Police interview of Parsons: Ibid.

Parsons dies in prison: Shanks manuscript.

Posada interviewed by FBI agents: Record of interview, File No. IC-600-1. Office of the Independent Counsel, Washington D.C., SA Michael S. Foster and SA George R. Kiszynski. Interview conducted at Tegucigalpa, Honduras, February 6, 1992.

Posada in Guatemala: Ibid.

Hirings at Casino Crillón: Federal Grand Jury testimony of Felix Fefer; interview with George Croes, February 11, 2017.

Harold Marchena resigns: Federal Grand Jury testimony of Harold Marchena.

Felix Fefer financial dealings: Federal Grand Jury testimony of Felix Fefer.

17. BEGINNER'S LUCK

Battle pays off customs officials in Peru: Federal Grand Jury testimony of Hans Bunte, Miami, FL, June 4, 2002; Federal Grand Jury testimony of Felix Fefer.

Opening night for Casino Crillón: Federal Grand Jury testimony of Francisco "Chito" Quandas, Miami, FL, December 3, 2002; interview with George Croes.

Battle moves into special suite: Federal Grand Jury testimony of Chito Quandas; Federal Grand Jury testimony of Mario Masaveu.

"I am the Godfather": Federal Grand Jury testimony of Felix Fefer; Federal Grand Jury testimony of Chito Quandas; Federal Grand Jury testimony of Mario Masaveu; Shanks interview with Wilfredo Chau, October 16, 2001; Shanks interview with Jacobo Van Der Linden, November 15, 2001.

"If I tell those men to lick the bottom of my shoes": Federal Grand Jury testimony of Chito Quandas.

Battle extends free chips to police and military: Federal Grand Jury testimony of Harold Marchena; interview with George Croes.

Luis "Lucho" Cabrera: Federal Grand Jury testimony of Mario Masaveu.

Private party for deputy minister: Ibid.

Battle with name embroidered in lining of his jacket: Ibid.

Effugenia Reyes at the Casino Crillón: Federal Grand Jury testimony of Harold Marchena; Federal Grand Jury testimony of Hubert Dominico Salazar, August 6, 2002.

Battle's affair with Evelyn Runciman: Federal Grand jury testimony of Chito Quandas; Federal Grand Jury testimony of Mario Masaveu.

Effugenia affair with Juan Solano Loo: During interviews with David Shanks, Kenny Rosario and federal investigators, Solano would neither confirm nor deny his affair with Effugenia Reyes, but aspects of the relationship were witnessed by and testified about by four separate workers at the casino, including Mario Masaveu and Harold Marchena, both of whom mentioned the affair in their Federal Grand Jury testimony, and also a woman who worked as an assistant to Solano in his capacity as accountant.

Investigation of Raul Fernandez: Shanks manuscript.

Kidnapping of Mayito Fernandez: Ibid.

Ex-detective Raul Diaz: Along with his checkered history as a cop, Diaz, as a PI, had many criminal clients. In a Metro-Dade Police Department OCB Intelligence report dated October 30, 1986, a confidential informant told Detective J. Leggett, Lottery Squad, that "RAUL DIAZ, [address redacted], is a Battle associate. The CI says this Diaz was formerly a ranking supervisor in this department." The CI was ranked as "usually reliable." The rise and fall of Diaz's storied police career is detailed in *The Cocaine Wars* by Paul Eddy with Hugo Sabogal and Sara Walden (W.W. Norton, 1988.)

Luis Adel Bordon: Shanks manuscript.

Gulf Liquors investigation: *U.S. v. Bordon et al.,* June 1998; Prosecutorial document, U.S. Attorney's Office, undated. Prepared by David Shanks. "The following is a summary of the potential witnesses already interviewed by this writer, along with other pertinent information; including the subjects which the witness can testify against; the type of testimony; and the availability of the witness to testify." The document is forty-eight pages long.

Luis Jr. and Adel Bordon: Shanks manuscript.

Raid on Gulf Liquors (June 24, 1994): Shanks manuscript.

Article on "Walled" in *El Comercio*: "La Boda del Año: Dueño del Casino Crillón perdrá soltería en Lima," *El Comercio*, date unknown.

"Doesn't that look like Battle?": Shanks manuscript.

Casino Crillón opening months: Shanks interview with Manuel Luis Zambrano, November 20, 2001; Shanks interview with Wildredo Chau; Federal Grand Jury testimony of Felix Fefer.

Maurilio Marquez fired from casino: Federal Grand Jury testimony of Felix Fefer.

Harold Marchena rehired as manager: Federal Grand Jury testimony of Harold Marchena.

Extortion threat from Sendero Luminoso: Federal Grand Jury testimony of Mario Masaveu; Shanks/Rosario interview with General Guillermo Castillo.

History of Sendero Luminoso: David Scott Palmer, ed., *Shining Path of Peru* (New York: St. Martin's Press, 1992). Steve Stern, "Family, Culture and Revolution: Everyday Life with Sendero Luminoso," in *Shining and Other Paths: War and Society in Peru, 1980–1995* (Durham, NC: Duke University Press, 1998).

Miraflores bombing 1992: "At Least 18 Die in Lima Bomb Blast, 140 Are Injured in Attack by Sendero Luminoso Rebels," Associated Press, July 18, 1992.

Sendero Luminoso guerrilla accidentally blows herself up at Hotel Crillón: Shirley Christian, "Inmates Shot After Giving Up, Peru Senator Says," *New York Times,* June 22, 1986.

General Castillo gives advice on extortion threat: Federal Grand Jury testimony of Mario Masaveu; Shanks interview with Mario Masaveu; Shanks/Rosario interview with General Guillermo Castillo.

"Wait a minute, I know about this letter": Federal Grand Jury testimony of Mario Masaveu; Shanks interview with Mario Masaveu.

Car bombing on Calle Jirón Ocoña: "Car Bomb Near Tourist Hotel Kills 2 and Injures 30 in Peru," *New York Times,* October 22, 1993; "Guerrillas' Car Bomb Kills 3, Hurts Nearly 50 in Lima," *Orlando Sentinel,* October 23, 1992; interview with George Croes; testimony of George Croes.

Metro-Dade police search of El Zapotal: Shanks manuscript.

18. DOWN AND OUT IN LIMA

Using bank money to fool CONACA: Interview with George Croes; Federal Grand Jury testimony of Felix Ferer.

Salvador Ramirez: Federal Grand Jury testimony of Salvador Ramirez, Miami, FL, July 9, 2002.

Battle threatens Ramirez: Ibid.

Three Peruvians divest from Casino Crillón: Federal Grand jury testimony of Felix Ferer; Shanks interview with Wilfredo Chau.

Harold Marchena demands audit: Federal Grand jury testimony of Harold Marchena.

Marchena lawsuit: Ibid.

Marchena receives threatening calls from Evelyn Runciman: Ibid.

Chito Quandas views Battle watching *Godfather* movies: Federal Grand Jury testimony of Chito Quandas; Federal Grand Jury testimony of Mario Masaveu.

Battle on security camera using cocaine: Federal Grand Jury testimony of Chito Quandas.

Attempts to force Quandas out of the Crillón: Ibid.

"I could probably have you killed for less than that": Ibid.

Harold Marchena meets with Evelyn Runciman and Valerio Cerron: Federal Grand Jury testimony of Harold Marchena.

"If you don't leave Peru within the week, I'm going to have you eliminated": Ibid.

Marchena learns of Effugenia murder: Ibid.

Shanks meets "Sexy Cubana": Interview with David Shanks; Shanks manuscript.

Effugenia Reyes murder in Guatemala: Shanks manuscript.

Battle birthday party: Federal Grand Jury testimony of Hubert Dominico Salazar.

"I hear she was fond with her head cut off": Ibid.

"And I advise that you better leave": Ibid.

Masaveu and Battle: Federal Grand Jury testimony of Mario Masaveu.

Battle's use of fraudulent passport: Affidavit of Robert A. O'Bannon, Special Agent, Diplomatic Security Service, U.S. Department of State. April 1996.

Battle deported from Peru, settles in Buenos Aires: Ibid.

Attempt to bribe deputy minister: Ibid.

Battle's phone conversation with Nene Marquez: Transcript of phone conversation between Battle and Nene Marquez (undated).

Battle sneaks back into Peru: Federal Grand Jury testimony of Mario Masaveu.

Battle calls Luis DeVilliers from inside the casino: Ibid.

Battle and Evelyn Runciman flee Peru: Affidavit of Robert A. O'Bannon, U.S. Department of State.

Battle and Evelyn apprehended in Curaçao, returned to Peru: Ibid.

Battle deported from Peru to United States (May 21, 1995): Ibid.

19. PRESIDENT IN EXILE

Cultivating informants and cutting deals: Shanks manuscript.

Encounter of José Aluart and Battle by Rosario, Boyd et al.: Metro-Dade Police Department report, Case No. 331829J.013, SYNOPSIS: Interview of JOSE MIGUEL BATTLE on May 23, 1995 at his farm residence "El Zapotal." Prepared by Det. K. Rosario; interview with Kenny Rosario.

Shanks on vacation with wife: Interview with David Shanks; Shanks manuscript.

Checks from Republic National Bank of Miami: Testimony of David Shanks, *Florida v. Bordon,* 1998.

Evelyn Runciman applies for visa: Affidavit of Robert O'Bannon, U.S. Department of State.

NYPD's Tom Farley and Morals Squad: Interview with Detective Tom Farley, June 7, 2016.

"Back when I first came on the job": Ibid.

Bets and bust: Ibid.

Incident with Iadarola brothers: Interview with Tom Farley; interview with Dennis Ring, January 7, 2017.

"If you're smart, you'll take your shares and give them away": Testimony of Abraham Rydz, *U.S. v. Battle et al.,* 2006.

"That man is crazy": Interview with Susan Rydz.

Susan and her father: Ibid.

Sergeant Boyd's retirement party: Shanks manuscript; interview with Tony Gonzalez.

Shanks and Boyd make peace: Shanks manuscript.

Shanks meets Gonzalez: Interview with David Shanks; interview with Tony Gonzalez.

Evelyn Runciman receives Florida driver's license: Affidavit of Robert O'Bannon, INS.

José Mendez hired as managing director: Federal Grand Jury testimony of José Mendez.

"Why should I pay more money": Shanks manuscript.

Raid on El Zapotal (December 18, 1996): Affidavit for Search Warrant, Jacob W. Wohlman, Supervisory Special Agent, Diplomatic Security Service, U.S. Department of State, December 16, 1996; Shanks manuscript; interview with David Shanks.

Arrest of Battle: Interview with David Shanks; Shanks manuscript.

Discovery of evidence at El Zapotal: Ibid.

Shanks, Rosario, and Battle at Jackson Memorial Hospital: Shanks manuscript; interview with David Shanks; interview with Kenny Rosario.

"You two aren't going to stop until I die in jail": Interview with Kenny Rosario; interview with David Shanks.

Battle getting "special favors" at the hospital: Shanks manuscript.

20. PERSEVERANCE

Bombings in Havana, 1997: "Explosions at 2 Havana Hotels Cause Minor Damage: Interior Ministry Blames Americans," CNN World News, July 23, 1997; "Cuba Edgy After Bombings," CNN World News, July 23, 1997; "Explosions Hit 4 Hotels in Havana, Killing 1," CNN World News, September 4, 1997; "Accused Cuban Bomber Calmly Confesses on TV," CNN World News, September 16, 1997; Anita Snow, "U.S. Probes 1997 Cuba Hotel Bombings," *Washington Post,* May 10, 2007.

Mob pedigree of Capri and Nacional hotels: T. J. English, *Havana Nocturne,* pp. 26–38, 44–45, 127–29, 240–42, 303–4, 312, 319.

"Obviously, this was done by our enemies": "Explosions at 2 Havana Hotels Cause Minor Damage: Interior Ministry Blames Americans," CNN World News, July 23, 2007.

"These terrorist acts are encouraged": "Explosions Hit 3 Hotels in Havana, Killing 1," CNN World News, July 23, 1997.

Posada interview with *New York Times:* Ann Louise Bardach and Larry Rohter, "A Bomber's Tale: Taking Aim at Castro, Key Cuba Foe Claims Exiles' Backing," *New York Times,* July 12, 1998.

Battle's legal travails: Interview with Jack Blumenfeld; Frances Robles, "Alleged Crime Boss Held in Jail; Attorney Presses for Release," *Miami Herald,* December 20, 1966.

"I'm sorry, but you people need to look up polygamy": Ibid.

Battle Jr. assumes power of attorney for his father: Ibid.

Background on Miguel Cruz: Interview with Miguel and Ian Cruz, May 15, 2016.

Incident with Lee Harvey Oswald: This incident became known to investigators from the Warren Commission, and was included in the Warren Commission Report. Over the years, the incident has been reinterpreted by some (including filmmaker Oliver Stone in *J.F.K.*) to suggest that Cuban exiles recruited Oswald, a known Castro sympathizer, to make it appear as if Cuba were complicit in the assassination of JFK. To which Miguel Cruz says, "That's just stupid."

Trial of Battle on gun possession charge: Shanks manuscript; Frank Davies, "Surprise Witness Complicates Gun Case," *Miami Herald,* October 6, 1997.

Jury selection process involving daughter of brigade veteran: Interview with Tony Gonzalez.

Testimony of Ruby Torres: Testimony of Ruby Torres, *U.S. v. Battle,* 1997.

Testimony of Cache Jimenez: Testimony of Cache Jimenez, *U.S. v. Battle,* 1997; Frank Davies, "Alleged Kingpin's Luck Finally Runs Out," *Miami Herald,* November 11, 1997.

Shanks speaks with juror post-verdict: Shanks manuscript.

Hearing on "upward departure" on Battle sentence: Interview with Jack Blumenfeld; Frank Davies, "Accused Gambling Kingpin Lashes Out at Witness," *Miami Herald,* February 6, 1998.

"I did not address the witness": Ibid.

Shanks meets with Kalafus: Report from Shanks on interview with Det. Richard Kalafus, Case No, 331829-J, January 23, 1998.

Playing of Charley Hernandez tapes for Kalafus: For a time, the investigators believed that Battle must have acquired these tapes through corrupt means, that is, paying somebody off. Eventually the mystery was solved when it was learned that the tapes had been presented as "discovery material" to the Battle defense team prior to the 1977 Ernesto Torres murder trial, which is why Battle had them in his possession.

There is a possibility that Battle may have solicited the involvement of Kalafus on another matter. According to Jack Blumenfeld, around the time of the gun possession trial in 1997–98, Battle told Blumenfeld that he once made a payment of $5,000 to Kalafus. Blumenfeld remembers that Battle told him the payment was somehow connected to the Palulu murder. One detail of the Palulu murder that always remained a mystery was why Palulu's security detail of police officers was pulled from outside his hospital room that night. Who gave that order? In testimony before the President's Commission on Organized Crime in 1985, Kalafus said that the security detail was removed at the request of Palulu's family. But Palulu did not have children or siblings in the area. Blumenfeld believes that it's possible that Kalafus was paid $5,000 (the equivalent of $12,300 in 2017) to remove the security detail at Palulu's hospital room, making it possible for the assassin to enter the room, do the deed, and escape.

Shanks/Rosario interview with Cafaro: Transcript of the interview, January 31, 1998.

Shanks interview with Hopkins: Report on the interview by Shanks (undated).

Trial of Luis Bordon and sons: Arnold Markowitz, "Store Owners' Arrest Tied to Gambling," *Miami Herald,* June 11, 1998; Ana Acle, "Merchant, Sons to Forfeit Millions: Men Convicted of Money Laundering, Running Gambling Ring," *Miami Herald,* August 29, 1998; transcript of *U.S v. Bordon,* 1998.

Battle transferred to Springfield, Missouri: Interview with Jack Blumenfeld.

Shanks discovers snake in his mailbox: Interview with David Shanks; Shanks manuscript.

21. CÓMO FUE/HOW IT WAS

"I want what I deserve": Shanks interview with Sexy Cubana, from Shanks manuscript.

Contract on Willie Pozo: Testimony of Luis Perez, *U.S. v. Battle et al.,* 2006.

"I gotta go into hiding for a while": Ibid.

1999 arrest of Alvarez and thirty-seven others: Jayson Blair, "39 Face Gambling Charges in New York Area and Miami," *New York Times,* July 30, 1999; *The Changing Face of Organized Crime*, A Status Report, State of New Jersey Commission of Investigations. Cuban/Latino Organized Crime, 2004.

Dennis Ring and Trish McNeill involvement: Interview with Dennis Ring.

Name of "Cuban Tony" (Dávila) emerges: Ibid.

Brooklyn DA's Office targets the Corporation: Ibid.

"Hey, why don't we see what Brooklyn is up to?": Interview with David Shanks.

Tony Gonzalez meets Ring and McNeill in Brooklyn: Interview with Tony Gonzalez; interview with Dennis Ring.

Battle's health: Interview with Jack Blumenfeld; Frank Davies, "Reputed Gambling Boss Off to Court over Health," *Miami Herald,* January 12, 1998.

Shanks/Rosario interview of General Castillo in Lima: Shanks manuscript.

Shanks travels in pursuit of witnesses: Ibid.

Suspicious Activity Report involving Maurilio Marquez: Ibid.

Deciding who will be indicted: Interview with Tony Gonzalez; interview with David Shanks.

Gonzalez's five-hundred-page prosecution memo: Interview with Tony Gonzalez.

Shooting of Manny Alvarez Sr. and Jr.: Kati Cornell Smith, "Bet War Eyed in Highway Shooting," *New York Post,* December 1, 2003.

AUSA Jack Blakey: Regarding implementation of the RICO law, Blakey's pedigree was strong. He is the son of G. Robert Blakey, the man credited with having drafted the 1970 Organized Crime Control Act, Title IX of which created RICO.

Arrest of Abraham Rydz: Interview with Susan Rydz.

Operation Corporate Raider arrests: Kati Cornell Smith, "Cuban Heels; Cops, Feds Nab Brutal Head of 'Havana Mafia,'" *New York Post,* June 1, 2005.

Arrest of Battle: Interview with Jack Blumenfeld; Shanks manuscript.

Arrest of Battle Jr. on the high seas: Shanks manuscript; Larry Lebowitz, "Accused Godfather of Cuban Gambling Organization Arrested on Cruise Ship," *Miami Herald,* May 19, 2004.

Getting Rydz to become a witness: Interview with Tony Gonzalez; interview with Davis Shanks; Shanks manuscript.

Dennis Ring finds Willie Diaz: Interview with Dennis Ring.

Willie Diaz threatens Ring: Interview with Dennis Ring; interview with Tom Farley.

Battle Jr.'s plea deal nixed by Shanks: Interview with David Shanks; Shanks manuscript.

Tony Gonzalez's opening statement: Trial transcript, *U.S. v. Battle et al.;* Casey Woods, "Trial Begins for Alleged 'Corporation' Members," *Miami Herald,* March 3, 2006.

Testimony of Abraham Rydz: Transcript of Rydz testimony, *U.S. v. Battle et al.,* 2006.

Defense lawyers' feelings about Shanks: Interview with Kaplan; interview with Jack Blumenfeld.

Battle dozes off during testimony: Interview with Jack Blumenfeld.

Battle pleads guilty: Interview with Jack Blumenfeld; Akilah Johnson, " 'Cuban Mafia' Tale Comes to an End with Leaders' Conviction," *Miami Herald,* July 27, 2006.

Final ruling on the Corporation: The verdict resulted in the criminal forfeiture of $1.42 billion in property and financial assets from the various guilty parties, the largest such criminal forfeiture until the Bernard Madoff verdict in 2008.

Suicide of Abraham Rydz: Interview with Susan Rydz.

Rydz's farewell note to Susan: Provided courtesy of Susan Rydz.

"Better Fidel Castro than George Bush": Interview with Jack Blumenfled.

Death of Battle: Evan S. Benn, "Former Crime Lord Battle Dies," *Miami Herald,* August 6, 2007; Madeline Diaz, "Jose Miguel Battle Sr., Reputed Mobster, Dies," *South Florida Sun-Sentinel,* August 7, 2007; Jessica Rosero, "Death of a Legend; North Hudson's Cuban Godfather Dead at 77," *Hudson Reporter,* August 19, 2007.

Battles's burial site: Viewed by the author.

EPILOGUE

Posada plot to kill Castro in 2000: Interview with Luis Posada Carriles; Bardach, *Without Fidel,* p. 149.

Posada trial in Panama 2004: Bardach, *Without Fidel,* p. 149.

Posada pardoned by Panamanian president: Ibid., p. 150.

Legal travails of Posada: Ibid., pp. 156–62, 164–75, 177–79.

"Posada is a hired assassin": Jean-Guy Allard, "Fabian Escalante on Posada and Operation 40," *Granma International,* January 11, 2011.

"To me, he was a patriot above all": Interview with Luis Posada Carriles.

"For me, there are no lines": Ibid.

"He turned bad. He became a bad man": Interview with Felix Rodriguez.

President Obama in Cuba: Carol E. Lee, "Obama Arrives in Havana, Looking to Engage; First Visit by U.S. President to Cuba Since 1928," *Wall Street Journal,* March 21, 2016; Dan Roberts, "Obama Lands in Cuba as First US President to Visit in Nearly a Century," *Guardian,* March 21, 2016.

"Havana is only ninety miles from Florida" (Obama speech): Transcript of remarks by President Obama to the people of Cuba, Gran Teatro de la Habana, Havana Cuba, March 22, 2016, https://www.whitehouse.gov.

"The Bay of Pigs took place the year that I was born": Ibid.

Death of Fidel Castro: Anthony DePalma, "Fidel Castro, Cuban Revolutionary Who Defied U.S., Dies at 90," *New York Times,* November 26, 2016.

Battle Jr. released from prison: Battle Jr. was released in November 2016. The author met with him, his two sons, and his attorney in February 2017.

SOURCES

WRITING THIS BOOK WAS A JOURNEY INTO THE SUBCULTURE OF BOLITA AND ALSO THE anti-Castro Cuban exile underground. It has required uncovering documentation that has been buried for decades, discovering archival sources that few knew existed, and of course finding and securing the cooperation of interview subjects, people with firsthand or even secondhand knowledge of the events that are portrayed in this book. As always with projects of this magnitude, it was a daunting undertaking, with information derived from various types of source material.

Interviews

Whenever possible, this book is based on interviews with people who lived the events. However, since many of the key characters in the story are no longer alive, interviews sometimes took place with people who were a step or two removed.

One person who did not agree to be interviewed was José Miguel Battle Jr. During most of the research and writing stage of the book, Battle Jr. was incarcerated in federal prison. Subsequent to his release in November 2016, I met with him to discuss the possibility of interviewing him for the book. After considering the offer, he declined to cooperate.

Listed below are the people who were interviewed and the dates on which the interviews took place:

David Shanks (10/19/16); Carlos Rodriguez (10/20/15 and 5/10/16); Jack Blumenfeld (10/21/15 and 5/11/16); Francisco "Pepe" Hernandez (10/22/15); Luis Posada Carriles (10/23/15); Raul Martinez (2/4/16);

Ramon and Fidel Fuentes (2/6/16); rooster breeding interviews: Pedro Marquez and Tomas "Tito" Guerra (2/5/16); Ramon Milian Rodriguez (2/7/16); Julio Ojeda (2/6/16); Joel Kaplan (2/6/16); Henry Raymont (5/7/16); Oscar Vigoa (5/9/16); "Jesús" (5/10/16); Michael Dávila (4/18/16); George Dávila (5/10/16); Joaquin Deleon (5/12/16); El Zapotal interviews: Miguel Cruz and Ian Cruz (5/15/16 and 9/13/16); Tom Farley (6/7/16 and 1/7/17); Kelly Noguerol and Carol Ann Daley (6/10/16 and 9/21/16); Willy Vigoa (6/15/16); Ciro Bianchi (6/18/16); Rolando Eugenio Martinez (8/10/16); Susan Rydz (9/2/16); Humberto Dávila Jr. (9/15/16); Elpidio Guzman (9/13/16); Ernesto Torres Izquierdo (9/15/16 and 2/19/17); Dennis Ring (1/7/17); George Croes (2/11/17); Kenny Rosario (2/15/17); Tony Gonzalez (2/17/17); Felix Rodriguez (2/17/17); Antonia Izquierdo (2/18/17); Joey "Coco" Diaz (9/14/17).

Law Enforcement Documents

Over the years, through legal proceedings involving José Miguel Battle Sr. and many other individuals associated with the Corporation, a substantial public record was amassed. Some of this material was entered into evidence at the 2006 RICO trial; it comprises a treasure trove of information on most of the key events and characters in this story going back nearly half a century. Generally, the information from these files can be divided into the following categories:

I. Police, FBI, and CIA records

This includes surveillance logs, and arrest and crime scene reports from the NYPD, Miami-Dade police, and other relevant police organizations. Also, numerous wiretap tapes and transcripts, as well as transcripts of consensual phone conversations and law enforcement interrogations and interviews. In addition, intelligence reports from various police departments and the FBI Cuban Terrorism Task Force and the CIA that were acquired through court order as evidence for the numerous trials.

II. Military, immigration, and psychiatric records

Records on Battle Sr., Angel Mujica, Luis Posada Carriles, Felix Rodriguez, and others were amassed as evidence for the various trials, or, in some cases, obtained by the author through official and non-official channels. The psychiatric report on José Miguel Battle Jr. is from the Hudson County Pretrial Intervention Project, office of the Superintendent of New Jersey.

III. Governmental reports

The hearings of the President's Commission on Organized Crime were published in their entirety in June 1985. Also relevant to this book was a report by the State of New Jersey Commission of Investigation entitled *Profiles of Jose Battle Corporation Members and Affiliated Businesses*, compiled in March 1988 for internal law enforcement purposes. Also, a Presentment of the Special Hudson County Grand Jury, Panel A, on the subject: In the Matter of an Investigation into Corrupt Activities and Influence in the Union City Police Department and City Government, February 1986.

Other reports are cited in the notes section of this book.

IV. Newspaper articles, magazine articles, and books

The Corporation file amassed by Detective Dave Shanks and various prosecutors over the years includes media reports on Battle and the Corporation going back decades. Still more articles were accessed by the author for this book. Relevant publications include the *New York Times, Miami Herald, Florida Sun-Sentinel, Miami Magazine, New York Daily News, New York Post, Washington Post, New York Magazine, Miami New Times, New Jersey Dispatch, Newark Star-Ledger, Jersey Journal, Camden Courier-Post, New York Law Journal, Asbury Park Press, Christian Science Monitor, Village Voice, San Francisco Chronicle, Guardian, Counterpunch,* and *Master Detective.*

Numerous literary sources informed this book, including tomes on a variety of subjects, including Cuban history; the history of the revolution; the Cuban American experience, particularly in Union City and Miami; aspects of organized crime; Watergate; the Iran-Contra scandal, and so on. These books are cited in the notes section where relevant.

V. The Shanks manuscript

In the years 2010 to 2015, David Shanks wrote a manuscript about the investigation of the Corporation, drawing on the above-mentioned documents and also on his own experiences as an investigator with the Metro-Dade PD and federal government for thirty-five years. The manuscript is neither sourced nor indexed, but it contains within its pages one of the most complete narrative descriptions ever written of a police investigation. It is not meant to be an objective account. Shanks expends much ink settling scores with cops, judges, and prosecutors who annoyed him over the years, and his depiction of José Miguel Battle Sr., Battle Jr., and others in the Corporation is unsparing.

The Shanks manuscript was essential to the writing of this book, though I deviate from its narrative, and thesis, in many crucial ways. In nearly all cases where the manuscript is cited as a source for this book, I have attempted to uncover the original documentation used by Shanks and cited those sources in the notes section.

VI. Institutions

The National Security Archive, at the George Washington University, is an important repository for files and information gathered through the Freedom of Information Act, especially CIA and other documents relating to the anti-Castro Cuban exile underground and other clandestine activities of U.S. intelligence agencies. The Cuban Information Archives are also a tremendous source of declassified documents on subjects relating to Mafia activity in pre-Castro Cuba and also the activities of anti-Castro exiles. The Mary Ferrell Foundation is another online source for files, reports, and documents on subjects ranging from the Kennedy assassination to U.S. government efforts to assassinate Castro, information obtained through FOIA and made available online to the public.

Grand Jury and Trial Transcripts

There were many trials over the years, and thousands of pages of witness testimony, opening and closing statements, sidebar conferences between lawyers and judges, and legal proffers were an essential ingredient of this book. Some of these legal proceedings involved primary characters in the story, while others were incidental though important for their informational value to the overall story of the Corporation. The essential proceedings involved the FBI gambling case against Battle et al. in 1970; the Ernestico Torres murder trial in 1977; the Conrado Pons arson/homicide trial of 1987; José Miguel Battle Sr.'s gun possession trial of 1997; and the Miami RICO trial in 2006.

Hundreds of witnesses testified at these proceedings, and their testimony is reflected in this book. Among the key witnesses who testified at grand jury and/or trial proceedings, sometimes at great length, are: David Shanks, Charley Hernandez, Idalia Fernandez, Julio Ojeda, Richard Kalafus, José Miguel Battle Jr., Rene Avila, Willie Diaz, Consuela Alvarez, Oracio Altuve, Luis DeVilliers, Luis Perez, and Abraham Rydz.

Freedom of Information Act (FOIA)

The FBI's Cuban Terrorism Task Force existed from the early 1960s into the twenty-first century, and its files contain hundreds of pages of documents relating to José Miguel Battle Sr., much of the information never before publicly revealed. The Battle file was accessed through a FOIA request.

In 2016, I made a similar request to the CIA for information on Battle, Alpha 66, and/or Omega 7. A year after my request, I received a letter from the CIA stating that "we can neither confirm nor deny the existence or nonexistence of records responsive to your request. The fact of the existence or nonexistence of such records is itself currently and properly classified and is intelligence sources and methods information protected from disclosure by Section 6 of the CIA Act of 1949 . . . Therefore, your request is denied."

In intelligence work, sometimes one hand does not know what the other is doing. Many documents relevant to Battle and the anti-Castro underground have previously been accessed, through FOIA requests by the National Security Archive and others, and long ago posted online. In instances where I have used information from those records, they are cited in the notes section where appropriate.

INDEX